THE EDUCATION OF DESIRE:
PLATO AND THE PHILOSOPHY OF RELIGION

Religion is a word that Plato never used. Yet throughout his life he raised questions about religious matters and offered solutions to religious problems. From those ancient roots is drawn this wide-ranging, erudite, and highly readable introduction to the philosophy of religion that links classical approaches with those of modern Christianity.

Plato believed that well-being comes to those who have weaned themselves from appetites that hinder the life of the mind and the pursuit of justice. Therefore he saw religion as a way of educating the desires of ordinary people, to encourage friendship among them and to facilitate the practice of virtue.

Despland demonstrates how Plato thus came up against the reality of eros and its potential for both destruction and construction, individual and social. The philosophical therapy, or therapy of words, educates desires and opens the door to the good life. In this task the philosophy of religion plays an important part: layers of individual and social desire find expression in religious practice and thought.

Despland points out a number of aspects of Plato's heritage that are relevant today, as well as one fundamental difference between the Greek and Christian religions: the former educated desire; the latter seeks to educate the will. Such connections enable the reader to grasp more fully the role of religion and philosophy in today's society.

MICHEL DESPLAND teaches in the Liberal Arts College of Concordia University, Montreal.

MICHEL DESPLAND

The Education of Desire: Plato and the Philosophy of Religion

UNIVERSITY OF TORONTO PRESS
Toronto Buffalo London

© University of Toronto Press 1985
Toronto Buffalo London
Printed in Canada
ISBN 0-8020-2502-1 (cloth)
ISBN 0-8020-6524-4 (paper)

Canadian Cataloguing in Publication Data

Despland, Michel, 1936–
    The education of desire: Plato and the philosophy of religion

    Bibliography: p.
    Includes index.
    ISBN 0-8020-2502-1 (bound). – ISBN 0-8020-6524-4 (pbk.).

    1. Plato. 2. Plato – Religion. 3. Religion – Philosophy. I. Title.

B398.R4D47 1985   20'.1   C84-099529-6

This book has been published with the help of grants from the Canadian Federation for the Humanities, using funds provided by the Social Sciences and Humanities Research Council of Canada, from Concordia University, and from the Publications Fund of the University of Toronto Press.

Contents

Preface

This book contains a fresh discussion of some aspects of Plato's philosophy. I should like to offer it also as an introduction to the art of doing philosophy of religion. (It can be read by those who are not familiar with Plato.)

As commonly seen, philosophy of religion is a specialized philosophical activity that takes religion as its subject-matter. But what is religion? Here views differ. Plato, looking at the realities of his day, believed it had to do with the arousal of socially beneficial desires and with the curbing of socially (and personally) harmful impulses. He also thought that philosophy brings about a therapy of individual desire, a lenient therapy, the only one in fact that uses words to bring the self to the reverent contemplation of all that which truly is. Thus, as far as Plato was concerned, the business of philosophy of religion was, simply put, the education of desire. According to this view philosophy of religion is a necessary part of the search for wisdom. This is my view too.

The manner of doing philosophy of religion that will be found here differs from other contemporary approaches. Until quite recently most philosophers in the English-speaking world have assumed that the aspect of religion that is of interest to them consists in doctrinal propositions which they label *beliefs*. The task of philosophy is to examine, to test the meaning of, these propositions. The beliefs considered are nearly always traditional Christian ones: does God exist? is the soul immortal? what are the origin and goal of life? Some studies have concluded on the rational tenability – or untenability – of all or some of these beliefs; others have shown that the basis for holding them is non-rational, and then either legitimate or illegitimate.[1]

This sort of philosophy of religion has now come under increasing attack. One can easily point out that the list of topics is rather arbitrary; it comes from the Christian world and then from only one strain of it, that which has elaborated a

Christian metaphysics or philosophical theology. Richard R. Niebuhr has sought to shift our attention to 'the energy of believing' that we expend when we strive to take hold of our daily life; in his account beliefs (what is believed) become secondary sedimentation of interpersonal living ('beliefs come from believing').[2] W.C. Smith has discredited attention to beliefs in another way: in religion we find living faith, which has only a tenuous connection with believing. Smith argues that only Westerners in the modern period hold that religious people are primarily people who have beliefs.[3] Both Niebuhr and Smith might agree with what the anthropologist Rodney Needham has shown most conclusively: one cannot probe into – or discuss meaningfully – what are ordinarily called 'the beliefs' of other people; the term should no longer be used in ethnography.[4]

Not surprisingly, a move is then commonly made away from the examination of 'sentential meaning' towards that of 'living meaningfulness.'[5] The object of study ceases to be propositions and becomes people. Note that fresh skills and a new quality of attention are henceforth expected of the philosopher. (This should be stressed because not all philosophers are aware of the demands peculiar to humane learning.) In this second, now widely shared, approach religious people are viewed as people who have certain attitudes and cultivate certain types of behaviour. T. Patrick Burke's *The Reluctant Vision: An Essay in the Philosophy of Religion* is a good example of this new style. The scope is not restricted to one particular religion. The author is not committed to any simple view of the essence of religion: 'The phenomenon of religion is a bundle of diverse historical activities that we have tied together into a package and put a common label on.'[6] We are thus given to see how religion, in general, works.

Unfortunately the truth question evaporates in the course of such inquiries. We are given a 'theory' of religion which is broad and presents a credible picture of the commonality underlying all religious casts of mind. The account offered is often phenomenologically insightful, sociologically shrewd, and morally sound. But can such philosophy claim to accept the full range of traditional concerns if it does not face squarely the epistemological question? What does the religious man *know*? The twenty pages weighing the traditional proofs of the existence of God in Ninian Smart's *The Philosophy of Religion* make welcome reading: they seek to settle an important question.[7] Far from being a concession to an older approach that is content with proving – or disproving – beliefs, Smart's discussion invites to the honest facing of a permanent issue. It enables the reader to ponder his choices: where is the truth? what must I be critical of in religion? what must I keep of my religious heritage and what must I discard?

We can already see that the very notion of philosophy of religion is symptomatic of an intellectual quandary. If we were fully religious, knew what our religion was and what was its worth, we would have no need of a philosophy to look at it. Our possession of the truth would presumably be full and we would be entirely satisfied with it. Some religious people – or some people who pass for religious – may have had a religion in that sense and some perhaps still do. Likewise, if we had a philosophy and rested content in it, there would be no call for embarking upon complex detours examining the various ways of viewing the world and of handling ourselves in it. If our philosophy were philosophy pure and simple, it would not need to be a 'philosophy of...,' an expression which intimates a discursive nature or a need to pay attention to something outside itself. We might do well to recall here that in any case philo-sophy is not wisdom, but the love of it: by definition, it seems, it cannot aim at being secure in any possession, not even in the possession of itself.

This quandary means we have to think hard. Our examples have also shown that our thinking has to decide where to start. We can begin with problems of great conceptual definiteness and linguistic precision, for example, 'Was the world created by God?' In this case we run the risk of remaining trapped within the confines of historical, Christian doctrinal problems. Or, we can start with something very general and evoke experiences which are hard to put into words, for example, 'the religious man sees something differently.' The risk then is remaining lost in the indefinite. 'Philosophy finds religion, and modifies it,' writes A.N. Whitehead, who adds: 'conversely, religion is among the data of experience which philosophy must weave into its own scheme.'[8] But where do we start? With the religion lying closest at hand, there for all to see in its definiteness, its doctrines, and its rituals? Or with the more elusive 'data of experience' which the philosopher has already woven or deems he must weave in?

I, for one, want to start with something definite. But I want it to be clear that by definite I do not mean the conceptually definite. I merely refer to what is out there, in the open, for all to see. There is no religiosity without some concrete, specific believing and doing. And faith and observance are lived, historical, visible realities. As Susan Sontag puts it in an eloquent article: 'My own view is that one cannot be religious in general any more than one can speak language in general; at any given moment one speaks French or English or Swahili or Japanese, but not "language".'[9]

Of course it takes longer to become familiar with a religion as a historical reality (and what it has meant to the people who were or are touched by it) than it takes to assimilate some more or less acceptable generalizations about religion; just as it takes longer to learn a language than to acquire some generalizations on language. (It takes even longer to learn to know the people who use any given language one has learned.) Smart and Burke both stress that philosophy of religion 'must not be pursued in the abstract' and must break loose of its usual 'deplorable constriction of interest'.[10] But this is easier said than done. The items of religious life they briefly include in their account are inevitably few and out of their full historical context.[11] The religious life of mankind is enormously vast and varied; to enter into it both sympathetically and critically is a huge task.[12]

This, then, is the problem today: can philosophy of religion break out of the limitations set to it by the history of peculiarly Christian issues and by the traditional philosophical intellectualism that weighs only propositions and beliefs? and can it do so while keeping in touch both with full human historical definiteness and with the desire common to all alert people to know the truth?

At this juncture, the reader may see the point of a book on Plato's philosophy of religion. Such a study starts at the beginning. It has been said that philosophy can be learned only by returning to its origin, to the point where it got started.[13] I shall accordingly show how a specific set of topics arose in fifth-century Athens and how philosophy of religion then took shape. The set of topics may perhaps appear to be arbitrary. Be that as it may, the set was formative. Secondly, since we see the issues being born, we can place them in their full context – including the non-verbal one – and clearly see the logic of their rise. And, thirdly, Plato strove mightily to put truth into words; as we shall stress, he found this to be no small task.

We shall start in the midst of the realities lived by a group of human beings at a point in time.[14] The study of the history of Athens is very rewarding. It is not ours and yet it is connected with ours. And – this may be of some comfort – there is not too much of it. Many words were written between the battle of Marathon (490 BC) and the death of Plato (347 BC) and undoubtedly much more was said, but all that remains can now be read in a year. This includes the works of Aeschylus and Thucydides; the scope of issues found in that manageable corpus is unmatched.

This, I have said, is also a book on Plato, a much practised author. The contribution of this book to Plato scholarship lies in its attempts to discern his philosophy of religion rather than his religious philosophy or his philosophical theology. The latter two have been common subjects of investigation, with unequal success. Attempts to present his religious philosophy can rest on centuries of religious Platonism but they suffer from the fact that Plato as a religious man is inaccessible to us now. Considerations of his thought-out theology rest on firmer ground and first-rate studies on this subject are available. But they do not look at what I would like to focus on: namely the demands for attention that the religious life of Greece presses upon Plato's mind and the sort of attention Plato pays to it. The Athenians of his age have begun to sense that there is something in their midst which can be called their religion and which they should ponder.[15] My argument is that we find in Plato the perplexity about this something called religion that is crucial to the endeavours of a philosophy of religion. Plato is not in the full light (or total darkness) that comes from being religious without ambivalence (or from having a religion so unambiguously that one does not even know one has one). Neither is Plato living in the full light (or total darkness) of the one who has no religion at all and feels such an absence of religion that he has no interest for it – and in it – and no wish to philosophize about it. The soft, even grey hues inherent in this twofold predicament give to Plato's work a very intriguing quality. His deep sense of uncertainties is to me a requirement essential to any philosopher of religion.

This book starts with an examination of the beginnings in Socrates: what questions did Socrates come to raise about religion? We find the answer to this question in an early dialogue, *Euthyphro*. We then ask how Plato handled these questions. The book thus goes on to examine the dialogues of the mature and later periods to show the range of issues Plato dealt with and the set of answers he provided. At this stage my aim is to understand what Plato says.[16] His philosophy of religion, I also venture to think, gives us a good idea of the overall task he saw philosophy as taking on, and of the wisdom he attained.

The conclusion, however, is un-Platonic, as it ought to be. We Westerners have witnessed the collapse of Greek piety, the spread of the Christian church, the development of Christian views of the world and of man – and related new developments in philosophy proper. I nevertheless believe that Plato's writings have an enduring significance. They can still teach us philosophy of religion as an art, an art of discerning meanings and of making meaning truly available to contemporary minds desirous of knowing the truth. I know that philosophy of religion has been viewed as offering true utterances, either defending the truth of religion or stating the truth that religion misses or hides. Both views, obvious heirs of western religious and intellectual history, overestimate our actual grasp of truth. We do not find it once and for all in any religion; neither can we find it securely apart from religion. Philosophy of religion thus cannot be the sort of gnosis that claims to do nothing except explain or make manifest the truth already inherent, albeit in a somewhat veiled manner, in the Christian or any religion.[17] Neither can it be a doctrine that enables human beings to know the truth without the work of creating and interpreting cultural forms, including religious ones. Truth for us is always mixed. We always produce it in a mixed form and always have resources to work on the ore and purify it somewhat. We always have a religion structuring our desire and we can – and should – philosophize about it.

Completion of this work offers an opportunity to ponder gifts received and debts incurred. The period stretches over more than a decade and the list of colleagues, students, and friends I should like to acknowledge would be long. Some gave formal support; let these be formally thanked and stand for all others. The chairmen of the Department of Religion, Professors J. Lightstone and M. Oppenheim, the dean, Dr J. Chaikelson, the vice-rector, Dr R. Breen, were helpful in many ways. Susan Slater, Aida Melkonian, and Elizabeth Maclean did good work with the notes and the typing. I am very grateful to the two readers of the manuscript, especially Professor J. Moline. At the Press Joan A. Bulger was very patient, ever helpful, and competent.

MD
June 1984

THE EDUCATION OF DESIRE:
PLATO AND THE PHILOSOPHY OF RELIGION

1

Euthyphro

I The story of a homicide in Naxos

Around 404 BC a homicide occurred on a vast estate in Naxos. The estate was owned and run by an elderly Athenian but his son Euthyphro shared in the administration and even hired in his own name some of the day labourers. During a drinking bout one of these workers picked a quarrel with a slave belonging to the estate and cut his throat. The witnesses agreed that the homicide was unprovoked. The father of Euthyphro, as owner of the slave and master of the estate, took control of the situation, had the killer bound hand and foot, and left him in a ditch while he sent a messenger to Athens to inquire from the religious advisers as to what should be done. Such advisers expounded Athenian traditional religious law and gave guidance on all cases where a religiously proper course of action was not clear. Homicide, which involved pollution, frequently called for such consultation.[1] The owner of the estate thus proved scrupulous: under Athenian law he had, as owner of the slave, full right to execute the murderer on the spot unless he obtained from him the price of the slave. We cannot surmise what aspect of this particular case led Euthyphro's father to seek advice.

The story of the homicide became really complex when it was found that the day labourer, bound and neglected, died in his ditch, of hunger and cold, before the return of the messenger from Athens. At this point Euthyphro began to be disturbed by the notion that the responsibility for this second death might rest with his father. This notion of responsibility, however, is our modern way of formulating the problem: the Greeks were particularly remote from us on this point. Euthyphro's fear was that his father might have incurred pollution from the deed and that the whole family – including himself – might be risking contagion from it. So he undertook to bring a suit against his father, for murder. This was also a conscientious step. It is in everyone's interest that pollution, if any, be removed.

The swift unfolding of the story was, however, interrupted. In 404 the course of the Peloponnesian War forced the Athenians to leave their holdings in Naxos. They then suffered a decisive defeat at the hands of Sparta and its allies. In a change of regime an aristocratic group, the Thirty, took over the government of Athens. In 403 another political change restored democracy and a constitutional revision was undertaken. At this point the laws of Solon and Dracon were adopted, but, as John Burnet puts it, 'there was great uncertainty about their application.'[2] The revisions of the laws were completed in 401 and the courts, which had been practically inactive until then, resumed their work. One can imagine what a backlog of cases they had and what contentions could arise from the fact that the current laws perhaps differed from those in force at the time of the offences. Furthermore, there was a policy of amnesty: part of the political settlement of 403 was an agreement not to bring up certain old issues born out of political strife. To these public juridical tangles domestic ones must have been added to Euthyphro's case. We can surmise that the father and the relatives put obstacles in the way of Euthyphro's prosecution. Euthyphro tells us they were indignant.[3] They must have attempted to make representations to court officials to defend the view that Euthyphro's suit could not be received.[4]

Finally in 399 Euthyphro stood on the steps of the king's tribunal waiting for an opportunity to appear before the official and put his case. The 'king' was one of the nine archons of Athens. He was appointed by lot and succeeded to the religious functions of the ancient kings (and so inherited the title as well). He performed the most important sacrifices and had judicial competence in all cases where both state and religion were involved. His task was to secure a preliminary instruction: he received depositions from the witnesses who would subsequently testify at the trial; after this he would send the case to trial or dismiss it. Euthyphro's case before him was based on the Greek conception common at the time: homicide is a religiously polluting act that can be cleansed only by due process. Such process unfolded without having recourse to a state prosecutor. The system worked but always depended on the prosecution of the murderer by one interested citizen. Euthyphro saw himself precisely as such a citizen. He knew how his father treated the killer. He shared roof and table with his father and was constantly exposed to the probable pollution.[5] One does not and cannot know whether Euthyphro expected to win his suit. Some argue that he did and add that he expected to see his father exiled. Others believe that Euthyphro was merely an overscrupulous person who expected his suit to be dismissed, but in the process he would gain clear conscience and the assurance that no shadow of pollution was hanging over his family.

We have every reason to believe that the story of the homicide in Naxos occurred exactly as Plato described it in the *Euthyphro*.[6] The story is too good not to be true and the character of Euthyphro has the marks of a portrait drawn from life. The complexities of the case are beautifully confusing. Euthyphro takes his stand on doing the *hosion* thing, that is the pious, or the religiously proper, thing.[7] But he is caught in a tangled web of conflicting claims. Not only is it not clear what body of law applies to the case of the death at Naxos, but Euthyphro's initiative is bound to arouse controversy. This pious scrupulous man acts in a way very offensive to pious minds: a son brings hiw own father to court. What should be our governing moral perceptions? Should his concern for purity be labelled pious (*hosion*), or should his lack of filial piety be called impious (*anosion*)? Euthyphro in his own small way reflects the conflicts of a Greek era immortalized by such figures as Orestes, Antigone, and Socrates. They all experienced conflicting claims, each endorsed by the most sacred authorities Greece knew at the time. A son must avenge his own father, a sister must bury her brothers, a philosophic man must tend his own soul above all, and a religious man must honour the requirements of a complex body of pollution legislation. But, must one perform all these duties even if it means killing one's mother, disobeying a king, breaking the laws of the city, or bringing one's own father to trial? Note that the dilemma is not the old-fashioned conflict between selfish interest and the demands of common morality. What is occurring here is that diverging bodies of usages or laws, conflicting moral demands, are pressing their claims upon an easily baffled individual. In *Euthyphro* Plato gave us good drama. Euthyphro's case is legally interesting, his dilemma is morally live; the whole story vibrates with an appeal for clarification of standards.[8]

2 Note on Athenian homicide law

Having heard Euthyphro's story, Socrates proceeds to question him and ask him to substantiate his claim to know the religiously proper course of action. The two thus embark on a discussion that amounts to the beginnings of a philosophizing on religion.

Euthyphro's story touches upon practically every aspect of Greek city life: institutional realities are involved as well as individual decisions. This case of homicide touches upon traditional religious, moral, and legal conceptions as well as upon queries that intellectuals had come to be exercised about. The events in Naxos therefore provide a very rich context for the discussion of 'the religiously proper thing to do.'

First of all, Athenian homicide law has features that come from the depths of the religious past common to Greek cities. Two stages of culture are reflected in the law as it stood at the end of the fifth century. First, there is the inheritance from the old kinship system (of which we find evidence in Homer). At that time a champion arose from the family of the slain man and undertook to pursue the murderer and exact vengeance upon him, that is kill him.

These old aristocratic practices were slowly displaced largely thanks to the growing influence of a novel notion of pollution. A post-Homeric religious movement taught that all people who shed human blood, whether in self-defence, in anger, or with premeditation, were polluted, impure, and contagiously so, and thus a threat to all those – individuals and cities – who came in contact with them. This second attitude was spread by a new Apollinian religion. The Delphi sanctuary, in particular, did much to foster it. New religious authorities offered the path to purification as well as enforced the notion of pollution. Homicide then ceased to be simply tort made to a family, that is simply a private wrong; it also came to be perceived as an affront to the city and to the gods; as such, killing was *anosion* and a threat to the entire society. A sharp change had been brought about. In Homer murderers, although pursued by relatives, were not marked with any stain and commonly received hospitality. After the seventh century aristocratic killers might have a high reputation with their peers, but, being polluted, they were cursed and their reputation could not save them.[9]

From our point of view we can readily see that the new homicide-is-pollution school of thought has two advantages. First it demands justice for all. Under the old system it was obvious that, if the slain man belonged to a poor peasant family while the killer belonged to the rich aristocratic warrior class, any champion might be intimidated before even starting on his errand. Hesiod is the decisive new voice on this point. He protests against the injustices committed by a noble class guilty of a harsh misuse of its power and enlists the gods in the struggle for an ideal of public justice which upholds the claims of the weak: 'the deathless gods are among men and mark all those who oppress their fellows with crooked judgements, and reck not the anger of the gods.'[10] Hesiod links the presence of justice in society to the just functioning of judicial institutions. Secondly, the new system strives to put an end to the pattern of a champion seeking vengeance and opening a chain of vendettas. We find in Aeschylus a dramatic account of events breaking the fatal series of killings avenging killings. The *Oresteia* climaxes in the creation by the goddess of a court that takes the trial (if not the prosecution) forever out of the hands of the family.

The city-state thus manages to create public courts with judges and jurors, similar to ours. The notion of pollution, however, remains central. (We hear in the Platonic corpus of tables, houses, temples, and cities being soiled by the presence of murderers.) In the fifth century Athenian courts always deal with homicide within a framework of pollution fears; their procedures restore all-around purity either by purifying through punishment and ritual a murderer found guilty, or by purifying through ritual alone the man charged with homicide but found innocent.

But they keep features of the older, aristocratic private-tort conceptualization: the dead man still has to be championed by a relative who starts a suit before the courts.

This of course leaves a problem since in some cases no champion would arise, either because the slain man had no relative, or because the potential champion did not dare, or because the murder having occurred within the family, any possible champion was also a blood relative of the murderer as well as of the victim. (Athens, unlike Rome, had no law actually forbidding a suit by a relative, but no example of prosecution for murder by a blood kin is documented in Greek legal history.) The legal system, however, found ways to cope with such cases.[11] In these circumstances any member of the public could start a suit for impiety, which would charge that something was amiss in a city where those guilty of homicide shared in sacred rites and where the necessary process was not initiated after human blood had been shed. These suits would set the public machinery in motion. We know of cases where the suit for impiety was technically lodged against a relative who failed to pursue the murderer in his own family even though he had killed someone of the same kin; these cases were handled by the court, however, as suits asking for punishment of the murderer and not of the delinquent relatives who had remained silent.

The history of homicide law thus enables us to observe a crucial development in the history of Greek religion from its tribal beginnings to its flowering in the city. The evolution of the law is also woven with important features of Greek social and institutional history. Simultaneously with the spread of the pollution concept, it also became clear that the power to deal with homicide and restore the order threatened by the shedding of blood is vested exclusively in the public institutions of the city. The gods themselves are believed to want it that way.

The homicide laws of the Athenian city-state result therefore from a blend of 'irrational' as well as 'rational' factors. The religious turmoil of the seventh century and its 'dark' concern with pollution lie at the origin of the laws. But the operation of these laws is equally unthinkable without the courts as public institutions of the city. A *dike*, namely a sentence that closes a case, states what is right (or renders justice), and allows normal life to go on, is by the fifth century something which only the city through its courts and their open, public procedures can render. The gods uphold the right but entrust its working out to the orderly gatherings of deliberating citizens. The archaic kingly dispenser of justice is not replaced by ordeals or other signs presumed to manifest the divine will. The *Oresteia* offers a particularly telling message: to ensure justice and ascertain degrees of guilt Athena gives the Areopagus to her city, namely a system of courts and jurors.

We should not, however, visualize the Greek legal revolution as a radical one giving the city a completely coherent system. Cumbersome features of the tort system survived. The history of fifth-century Athens witnessed also a shift of power between the older Areopagus and the newer, yet more democratic, citizens' courts, the former keeping only the right to hear cases of homicide. J.P. Vernant quite rightly emphasizes that Greece did not have a legal system but rather a superposition of *dikai*, namely of bodies of law.[12] Older customs survived and so did conflicting moral and religious representations. No common theoretical base undergirded the various practices. Legislators and legal reformers in Greece seem to have done their work always piecemeal. Euthyphro's position caught between the rival claims of filial piety and pollution legalisms is thus quite typical.

But in spite of the variety of *dikai*, there was also a clear search for that single thing, *dike*, namely justice. *Dikaios*, the adjective coming from the same root, has come to mean 'just' in the most general sense. It also comes to designate the virtue that is felt by the ordinary man to be most essential to all social life. From Hesiod on, justice is the value dear to all those who speak in the name of the common man and Zeus is made into the fountain and guarantor of justice. (Justice is a dear daughter, and sits beside her Father, we hear in the *Works and Days*.) Righteousness, sings Aeschyles, is shining in the smoke of mean houses. She spurns the strength of gold. Her blessing is on the just man.[13]

The dominance exercised in the fifth century by this quest for justice is readily apparent in the meeting between Euthyphro and Socrates. In the course of their discussion they quickly agree that piety is a part of justice and hint that a knowledge of justice would provide us with a knowledge of piety. Euthyphro grants that the point is really whether his father was *en dike*, namely, had just grounds to cause the death of the murderous day labourer.[14] The conversation between Euthyphro and Socrates therefore belongs right in the mainstream of what was perhaps the quest most steadily sustained by the Greek minds in their age: what is justice? (The *Republic*, we may point out, attempts to deal with this problem; the work is commonly seen as the apex of Plato's philosophy.)

Measured against our system, Athenian courts lack an official public prosecutor and clearly defined fundamental rights. No distinction is made between a juridical and a political process. When the ostensible concern of the court is to rid the city of pollution, it becomes easy for the argument before it to abandon discussion of what would be just treatment of the accused to move into a debate on the decision most expedient to the city. Democratic courts especially often shift from discussions of law to political debate. One also finds constant incoherence on the issue of legal responsibility: Solon's laws gravely insist on bringing to court dogs that have caused a homicide. Aristophanes knew how to make fun of that; see *The Wasps*. Plato recognizes that the behaviour of children is not actionable but he does insist – gravely, again – on sentencing (one year in exile) those who cause a death.[15]

Characteristics of voluntary and therefore responsible action are progressively adumbrated but never lead to a decisive principle.

Political subversion of court procedures and absence of clearly defined notions of voluntary behaviour, all this was bound to cause strains in the courts and give food for thought. Euthyphro believes that the demands of piety will resolve these tensions. He stands by his view of what is *hosion* in spite of the fact that his relatives keep arguing that his father was in his right.[16] The fact is that no clear principle is available to adjudicate either the father's responsibility in the death of the bound man or the son's obligations after that death.

The absence of such a clear principle is confirmed by a study of the legal reforms which the mature Plato proposes in the *Laws*. On many points he has a solid grasp of new and decisive principles of reform, especially on procedural matters, as we shall see later. But on pollution and on responsibility Plato remains entirely within the tradition, its weaknesses and its insoluble deadlocks.[17] Under Plato's laws Euthyphro's father would probably be let free, with at most purifying rites for pollution incurred. The right of any murderer to trial, the sufferings of the day labourer in the ditch, the notion of criminal negligence, these points so important to us moderns, if perceived at all by Plato, do not outweigh the right of the owner of a slave to kill the murderer when that murderer is not a free man who can pay for the damage done.[18] The mature Plato sees no need to correct the 'superstitious' fear of pollution. As a matter of fact, most of his reforms of the homicide law in the *Laws* reinforce the notion of pollution and require strict purifying rites in cases of involuntary homicide.[19]

To sum up, homicide law drew upon ancient strains, ninth-century kinship law, seventh-century religion, and fifth-century civic institutions. The notion also arose that justice was a single simple thing (*dike*) that often failed to be embodied in the decisions of the courts (*dikai*). Such insight led to efforts in reform. But the problem raised was obviously a complex one. The moral demands implicit in the single notion of justice taxed the minds of Euthyphro, but also those of Aeschylus, Sophocles, and Plato. Each in his own way tried to set straight Greek thought and practice in these matters.

3 The man Euthyphro

Let us return to the concrete drama portrayed in Plato's dialogue. After the narration of the homicide a second story unfolds, the exchange between Euthyphro and Socrates. There we learn that Euthyphro, like Socrates, has come to believe that the Athenian people are in a state of unwisdom. He offers his sympathy to Socrates when he hears about the prosecution he faces; he acts like one member of a morally upright minority meeting another. He has heard that Socrates had 'a divine sign' that came to him on unexpected occasions; well, he too is a prophet or diviner, the recipient of divine communications. (Prophet-diviners cultivated a variety of skills or arts that enabled them to discern the will of the gods.) Readers will quickly notice the difference between the prophetic soul of Socrates and the prophetic claims advanced by Euthyphro, but at this stage Euthyphro takes similarity for granted.

If Al Ghazali is right, the mark of a holder of a traditional faith is that he does not know he is a traditionalist.[20] Euthyphro is clearly beyond this innocence. He is aware of the debate in his society. He knows that some have departed from the tradition and have debunked religion. He also knows that many, confused by the presence of conflicting teachings, lead an unthinking and unsettled life. For his part he attempts, in the crisis of his age, to be an articulate religious conservative. He remains loyal, and consciously so, to the old religious customs, as he understands them.

Teiresias, in the *Bacchae*, also saw himself as a conservative but this pious man added: 'we entertain no theories or speculations in divine matters. The beliefs we have received from our ancestors – beliefs as old as time – cannot be destroyed by any argument, nor by any ingenuity the mind can invent.'[21] Euthyphro does not make such simple affirmation. His beliefs and practices are not those of the many traditionalists who have remained unaffected by the criticisms of the intellectuals. He wishes to add expertise to his faith. He believes he is able to refute the irreligious, articulate progressives: he claims to have exact knowledge of some divine things and sets forth a precise doctrine. (M. Nilsson points out that in the fifth century seers and interpreters of oracles learned to defend their art: naturally 'the defense of the old religion also fell to their lot.'[22]) Of course this claim of Euthyphro's to know makes him a perfect candidate for Socratic interrogation.

Among other characters found in Plato, Euthyphro is best compared to Polemarchus, the host of the discussions recorded in the *Republic*. Polemarchus occupies the centre of the stage in book I, shortly after the testimony given by his aged father, Cephalus. While Cephalus, a pious man, merely gives a short testimony before he goes to attend some sacred rites, Polemarchus offers to explain what justice consists in. Cephalus is a pious and wise old man whose wisdom is self-authenticating; he is not put under scrutiny. We might say that he embodies the tradition and speaks out of an experience shaped by it. But as R.L. Nettleship has pointed out, his son belongs to a new generation which 'has inherited the experiences of the old, but in a partial way.' The younger man's views are the traditional ones but he has accepted these by acquiring doctrinal opinions and without fully assimilating them. He answers the question about justice 'not with the result of his own experience, but with the borrowed principle of which he is the master.'[23] He quotes as authoritative a maxim taken from a poet,

Simonides – 'Justice consists in helping one's friends and harming one's enemies' – and seeks to defend the wisdom of this piece of traditional baggage. Polemarchus, however, is not up to this task. His doctrines do not survive cross-examination by Socrates, and he is exposed as intellectually helpless. Most significantly, his deficiencies launch the inquiry in the *Republic*; he triggers the anger of the Sophist Thrasymachus, who cannot hold his tongue at hearing affirmations which to him are pure nonsense.

Let us, however, give both Polemarchus and Euthyphro their due. They cling, rigidly, to a few, selected beliefs, but both care about justice and piety. And Euthyphro has firmness in his intellectual commitment. Having set his hand to plow the furrow of piety and strict observance of pollution laws, he consistently discards rival claims. His confession that he is prepared to sue any impious person, be he his father, his mother, or anyone else, is not without greatness because of the implied universalization of his principle.[24]

Furthermore, Euthyphro pays the price of his commitment. He does dare the opprobrium of being laughed at in the assembly when he addresses it on divine things and foretells the future.[25] And it must have taken some strength to resist the barrage of reproaches that came from his family when he started the suit and pursued the project for five years through the legal semi-chaos prevailing in Athens from 404 to 399. When discussing piety with Socrates, he fully knows that his life is under scrutiny; he does not play at having an idle intellectual conversation on curious and intriguing subjects. His seriousness and even stubbornness compare rather favourably with the empty head of the brilliant Alcibiades, who must confess to Socrates that 'when you put questions to me I am of different minds in successive instants.'[26] Unlike Meno, Euthyphro does not come to a confession of utter perplexity and intellectual numbness prompted by the Socratic interrogation.[27] Rather, he admits he does not know how to tell Socrates what he means, since Socrates seems to succeed in turning everything he says into something different from what he meant.[28] But he is sure he means something. He is rattled, but not thrown off course. In his apparent discomfiture he remains confident he has views and could expound them if he were free to express himself in his way. He does hold a doctrine and he is not easily blown hither and thither.

4 Euthyphro's doctrine

Asked by Socrates to state what he believes to be the pious and the impious, Euthyphro first answers with the good conscience of a fully convinced man: 'I say that the pious is that I am doing now, prosecuting every doer of injustice.'[29] As proof of his statement he advances divine examples. There are divine precedents for filial prosecution of an unjust father: Zeus put Chronos in bonds 'for swallowing his children unjustly.' Euthyphro knows all the stories of the gods and has many other things to tell about them;[30] one guesses that he has a story to settle each dilemma of conscience, as it arises.

Socrates, however, wants the general characteristic of all pious behaviour. Euthyphro's second definition, which rises to this level of abstraction, states that 'what is liked by the gods is pious and what is not liked by them is impious.'[31] From this theology Euthyphro does not really depart. He defends it against Socratic objections by claiming that on important things *all* of the gods are at one on what they like and dislike. (This third definition is the second one modified.[32]) When offered an alternative between a theology that affirms that the pious is pious because the gods love it and one that states that the gods love it because it is pious, he chooses the second alternative and thus refuses to make the pious dependent upon divine will or caprice. But having approached the notion of the pious as an intrinsic quality, he does not see that, in the light of this point, his definition stating that the pious is what the gods like is misleading, or at least unsatisfactory.[33]

Socrates then pushes Euthyphro to relate pious behaviour to the just one. Drawing upon the common Greek notion that justice consists in giving everyone what is owed to him, Euthyphro introduces a division: there is the justice that gives the gods their due and that which give men theirs. He thus advances a fourth definition: the pious is a part of justice and it consists of the art of tending the gods.[34] J.Y. Chateau suggests that the common quest for an understanding of piety takes a bad turn here: piety loses its identity with justice.[35] *To hosion* has ceased to be the appropriate behaviour of the man who treats everything and everyone right and becomes the feature of those who treat the gods right. This point being reached, Socrates can easily make Euthyphro say that the gods hardly need our care. Thus prompted, Euthyphro tries yet a fifth definition: pious behaviour is service to the gods. This brings us back to the notion that knowledge of what pleases the gods is the basis of piety, and thus we are back to a previously rejected doctrine. But Euthyphro does not see that: his current view that piety is service of the gods brings, he claims, benefits, not just to the gods themselves, but to individual families and states as well.[36]

Responding to this view, Socrates volunteers a definition, which makes piety a science of sacrificing and praying, and which Euthyphro declares himself satisfied with. Starting from this basis Socrates brings some damaging statements out of Euthyphro. (This damage was implicit, I think, in the acceptance of the division between justice to the gods and justice to men.) Euthyphro quickly falls from his previous height: piety is no longer loved for its own sake: it now becomes some kind of barter between gods and men, men offering something in order to get something else in return. The gods get praise from us and we get all good things from them.[37] Euthyphro starts to appear in a poor light: not only is his piety now under suspicion of being mercenary, but gaps in his theological articulateness are exposed and Euthyphro must admit he has contradicted himself. The pious cannot be both what pleases the gods (because of its intrinsic value, we might add) and what is beneficial to them. To Socrates' proposal to start all over again Euthyphro answers that he has another engagement and thus brings the conversation to a close. This last move hardly improves the light in which he is now cast. While he has made a brave attempt, he has not held up his end of the conversation and certainly has not made good his claim to give a full account of what piety is.[38]

By basing his knowledge of what is truly pious (and what is not) on the recorded stories of divine behaviour Euthyphro made a move not at all infrequent in Greece, where Homer and mythological stories were the common possession of the people. Rich, powerful, colourful, and telling accounts of divine life were widespread and abundantly commented upon. It was natural that such images of gods should become models for human life to imitate. Often the very plastic value of these gods and their representations called for imitation. But, finding in this lore the basis of his theological knowledge, Euthyphro is also making a move that had come under an increasingly vigorous attack from a moral point of view. Aristophanes, another articulate conservative (who, however, had a good deal more talent), has a character in the *Clouds* trot out the story of Zeus and his father. The character who brings this forward is the Unjust Argument who seeks to refute what the Just Argument said about divine justice. Obviously, to settle a theological point by referring to one instance of divine behaviour recorded in the mythology (and an unseemly instance at that) was to Aristophanes and his audience a poor method of reasoning. (The Unjust Argument is a master at specious and weak argumentation.[39]) Plato himself refers to the stories of Ouranos, Chronos, and his son in the *Republic* and proposes to bury them in silence. He especially fears that immoral young men may find an alibi by drawing upon such divine examples to justify their wrongdoings.[40]

Unsatisfactory though it may be, Euthyphro's way of drawing upon sacred stories remains very typical of a whole category of religious men. R. Guardini calls Euthyphro's religious and theological style mythical. Men like him feel original sacred powers immediately at work in the world and in their destiny. And stories show these sacred powers at work in the past. The pious man understands his existence with the help of received and transmitted 'figures' (we might also say images or representations) that have decisive authority in the telling of the truth about the world and the will of the gods and in pointing the way for the guidance of one's life. As Guardini puts it, these figures have power, and in the mythical attitude 'man has not yet come to dissociate himself by critical judgement and technical skill from those forces,' but is still directly controlled by them.[41] Such 'mythical men' of course do not describe themselves in such terms. We see their lives in a framework established by myths; they see themselves as attuned to realities.

Guardini carefully establishes a contrast between the figures or myths and the concepts of science (which lead to the formulation of laws) and the gratuitous images subsequently produced by poetry in its newly acquired aesthetic independence, that is when poetry has become fiction. To the mythical minds the representations really express what it means to be a human being. A man who draws his knowledge from them, who lives in their atmosphere and is guided by them, receives from them both his identity and a knowledge of his destiny. Piety then consists in the ability to refer to divine example. 'As long as all this holds good, piety means ... a revering gaze, a respectful self-surrender, a constant interpretation of one's own life, as of the surrounding world, in accordance with those figures and legends which have been received from experiences of past years and handed down by religious tradition.'

Plato's mature thought would blame Euthyphro for simple *mimesis*, that is uncritical copying of a model at hand, and an embodied concrete figurative model at that.[42] There is thus a twofold distortion in Euthyphro, or a double remove from the truth. He takes his bearings from the tradition because it is the tradition, and he prefers it to the progressive theories, unlike Cephalus who lives the tradition because it mediates to him the truth of life. Having thus seized upon something that, though noble, is not quite the truth, he becomes ready for a second kind of corruption. Such tradition as he holds onto is a cramped and ungenerous one, a dried and partial version of the whole, the product of polemical defensiveness. Among the wealth of models of divine behaviour which are found in the divided city, some are seized upon because they justify his action. Euthyphro, I would like to add, is not a simple embodiment of the mythical attitude. There is something doctrinaire about him: what happens is that he has recourse to *some* myths; he may be accused of choosing the myths that suit him. The content of the tradition is no longer the rich and coherent source of the shape of life; we see, rather, disjointed fragments of it held on to by rather pitiful, possibly self-serving, traditionalists. Such a critical note is already apparent to the discerning eye in the early dialogue: what we ought to think of Euthyphro's power of prophecy and of his 'science' can be learned from his prediction of the outcome of Socrates trial. Plato's fine hand appears in a similar manner in *Laches*: Socrates there has a discussion with a defeated general and one about to be defeated. Euthyphro and the generals are not enemies of piety or courage. They strive to embody these virtues. They mean well. Nevertheless they fail.

2

Socrates

I The story of a teacher accused

At the beginning of their conversation Euthyphro asks Socrates what *he* is doing at the door of a court-house: how unlikely that a man of his character should have lodged a suit against anyone! Socrates confirms Euthyphro's guess: he is there because a public suit has been lodged against him, one that charges he is doing harm to the city. The accuser is a young man, Meletus, who claims that Socrates corrupts the youth. Socrates speaks of Meletus in an ironic vein: the young man must be quite wise for his age, if he knows how the young are corrupted and who corrupts them! But, at any rate, he is the only one of the politicians who shows some sense, since he is concerned about the interests of the young and seeks to protect them from the false teachers who mislead them. Meletus has made his indictment quite precise: Socrates introduces new gods and does not honour the old ones. Euthyphro immediately sees that this is a trumped-up charge and offers his sympathy to Socrates. He points out that clever men can easily excite the prejudice of the people by formulating accusations of innovations in divine matters. Being ignorant, the people will fail to see the innocent and the wise for what they are. He himself, Euthyphro, is often laughed at when he addresses the assembly on religious topics. To this Socrates answers that he is prosecuted, not laughed at. The matter is serious; the charge is a capital one.[1]

We now know that the statement made by Socrates in *Euthyphro* does not exactly reflect the precise indictment. The actual formulation presented in court is that found in the *Apology*: Socrates was accused of introducing new religious observances (rather than new gods), corrupting the youth, and not accepting the gods of the city (or not giving them the customary worship).[2] The formulation of the charge shows a nice appreciation of the complexities of the trials for impiety: it stops short of accusing Socrates of introducing new gods. Such accusations had been formulated in the past against Ionian philosophers who called the elements divine. The political settlement that emerged with the restoration of democracy in 403 included a kind of amnesty: it invalidated laws antedating the revision of the code and was accompanied by a common desire to refrain from raking up old coals. Meletus's charge, therefore, is formulated in such a way that the trial of Socrates will not be a direct descendant of the older impiety trials. The crowd, however, would not observe this nicety and would quite happily renew their feelings of intolerance for those who hurt the city by not respecting its sacred traditions or by introducing foreign innovations.

The charge of corrupting the youth would also be an emotionally potent one. While there is no evidence that 'corrupting the youth' was a legal offence, the move was politically a clever one. Fifth-century Athens was still enough convinced of the authority of the old to believe that they can corrupt the young, and to blame youthful errors on bad influences from the older generation. (It takes a twentieth-century American professor to suggest seriously that it was rather the fifth-century youth who corrupted their elders.[3]) It was probably the third charge, not accepting the gods of the city, that was legally the most operative. 'The charge is one of nonconformity in religious practice, not of unorthodoxy in religious belief.'[4] On the whole it must be said that, with the legal situation existing in 399 BC, the legal basis for such an indictment was rather frail. But Meletus, who was something of a fanatic concerned to keep the city religiously pure and free from innovation, was not one to be stopped by that. In his view Socrates was a threat to the health of the city and its *mores* and had to be dealt with. One might not be wide off the mark in attributing to Meletus the sentiments expressed in a speech uttered in the same year, 399, charging a certain Andocides with impiety. The speech addresses the assembly in the following manner: 'it is not possible for you to live with our ancestral laws and with Andocides at the same time: it must be one of the two things, – either you must wipe out the laws, or you must get rid of the man.' The people of the city are in a position to give the gods the vengeance they require, and, if they fail to do so, they will be guilty.[5]

We know that Meletus was not the driving force behind the accusation against Socrates. Plato knew it already and everything confirms it. Anytus, a leading Democrat and a rather honourable member of the new political establishment, was the brain in the affair. It seemed that he doubted the loyalty of Socrates to the painfully won political settlement. Socrates had too often said that the crowd was stupid and easily misled to appear a good Democrat. Furthermore, his former association with notorious anti-Democrats like Critias and Alcibiades did not help. But such political *règlement de compte* was precisely what was politically forbidden. An impiety trial, however, which Anytus thought would end with voluntary or imposed exile, was feasible and would undoubtedly bring beneficial results to Anytus and his party. Making use of Meletus, a willing although unperceiving instrument, was the obvious solution. The attack on Socrates was, thus, really political, not religious, and his accusers did not wish to kill him but merely to put an end to such influence as he might have on public life.

When he meets Euthyphro, Socrates does not spend much time telling his story, but gets Euthyphro to narrate his. Expressing pleasure in meeting somebody who knows what he is doing, Socrates quickly suggests that he should become the pupil of Euthyphro and learn from him what piety and impiety consist in. Properly informed, he will be able to refute Meletus and show the court that Meletus does not know what kind of religious observances the city needs, whereas Socrates is the wise one, being the pupil of Euthyphro, an expert in these matters. Euthyphro accepts the challenge; he is confident that, were he in court, he would quickly find the weak spot in Meletus's position.[6] So the dialogue starts with the ostensible purpose of preparing Socrates for his defence before the court. But Socrates' interest is also philosophical: he would genuinely like to know what exactly piety is. Here too Socrates is ironic: he professes to be awed at the certainty – and special knowledge – Euthyphro claims to have. Euthyphro, however, senses nothing of the irony; in good faith he rushes to exhibit his wisdom.

2 The problem of education and the ethics of speech

The accusation of corrupting the youth is formulated in a city that has just suffered defeat and has a keen memory of its grandeur in the past. There is in Athens at this point a widespread feeling that the children are not worthy of the fathers and that some sort of decay or rot is at work in the city. And Socrates turns his meeting with Euthyphro into an opportunity for a long, precise discussion closely involving two people. This is characteristic of Socrates. These two facts must be correctly appreciated.

Werner Jaeger begins his study *Paideia* on the ideals of Greek culture by formulating the problem of education: 'Men can transmit their social and intellectual nature only by exercising the qualities through which they created it – reason and conscious will ... Education, if practised by man, is inspired by the same creative and directive vital force which enables every natural species to maintain and preserve its own type; but it is raised to a far higher power by the deliberate effort of human knowledge and will to attain a known end.'[7]

The Greeks, argues Jaeger, forged a uniquely valuable ideal of the culture that is to be transmitted and recreated. I should like to add that their history also shows with beautiful clarity a series of successive transformations in the process of transmission. Eric Havelock has gathered very convincing evidence for one stage of the process; for centuries the paradigms for *paideia* were transmitted orally.

Poetry was the basic cultural book: in this 'preserved communication,' easily memorized and transmitted, the Greeks recorded their notion of acceptable usage on a very wide range of matters. Homer is, of course, the best illustration. For generations the Greeks learned from the epics the standard ways of doing things, both *nomoi*, that is social customs, and *ethea*, that is personal attitudes. They also learned tales of aristocratic ancestors that were obvious models. Through the means of poetry, publicly recited, this 'tribal encyclopaedia' became a relatively common possession of the people. It could serve in the education of many of the young. Being largely oral, its ideal of culture could be a possession of the many. All could memorize lines, argue, cite. It is notoriously hard to put one's finger on what is unique about ancient Greece; to point to that widespread oral culture may not be too wide off the mark.[8]

Thus, the Greeks, very early, became highly conscious of the process of speaking. They clearly saw the connection between speech, discourse, and the process of civilization and education. They also noted that their own small society (or societies?) differed from the large neighbouring ones in that the right to speak became the possession of every citizen. This, of course, is the clearest sign of their thrust towards democracy. The world where only a few speak in public (standing before the many) gave way to one where all sit in a circle and each speaks in turn.[9]

From Hesiod on, the Greeks are visibly 'enthralled by the power of speech' and strive both to master this wonderful social instrument and to grasp its nature.[10] Poets, the traditional speech-experts, acquire a new, more self-conscious, more distant rapport to their skills. While in the *Odyssey* one occasionally hears of words – and wiles – being woven, from the time of Simonides on (born in 556) poets openly compare themselves to artisans in general, and sculptors in particular. (Poets claim superiority: my odes travel, says Pindar, unlike statues stuck on their pedestals.[11]) They possess a 'professional' skill, for which they get paid, and the quality of which can be evaluated. Words remain highly valued (the work of a poet is not ever destroyed) but, being crafted (*poien* – from which *poietes* – is 'to make') and being sold, they acquire a sort of visible materiality.

The truth-value of speech is not lost sight of for all that. But it is not so clear who tells the truth. Herodotus, the first historian, contrasts himself with the poets: he does not fabricate his stories; he freely inquires and then writes.[12] Speakers or writers who have seen are deemed more reliable than those who have heard. And through drama the visible behaviour of humans who assemble words to make utterances is reintegrated within an overall meaningful statement that has qualities of truth. What is done is again reappropriated by speech.

To show humans at work, and to make of this display the occasion of a truthful utterance, is the supreme – and most complex – achievement of tragedy. What we can sense of the history of the genre hints at the numerous social dimensions of this uniquely conscious flowering of speech. With the rise of urban festivals the Greeks learn to celebrate and rejoice in a new style. They no longer merely watch or participate in parades with short skits. A new disposition of space, the theatre, enables them to sit as a large group, watching a long performance, following a plot designed by an Aeschylus or his like. These new departures help the citizens understand what is taking place in their new civility. Watching for practically a whole day the complex interaction of strong, heroic, characters (including impressive women), the citizens see models of a wide range of feelings and acquire a vocabulary adequate to the expression of complex actions and passions. But, beside this obvious psychological enhancement, they also watch a story, namely a whole, something which, as Aristotle puts it, has a beginning, a middle, and an end.[13] They appropriate versions of human becoming. They no longer simply respond to deep symbols of fertility, joy, pain, sorrow. They ponder stories that show the making of human disaster and the finding of human release. In Homer the events narrated were ancient and the common man was present only as background or as audience. Tragedy, writes G.F. Else 'for the first time brought the far-away directly into the present and the great man into direct contact with the little man.'[14] Drawn into the circle of heroic action, citizens can now deliberate with fellow-citizens about what situation they are in, what brought it about, what they should do next, and what they may expect in the end. There is pleasure in seeing likeness, writes Aristotle, because thereby we learn, we learn how things are (how they are in human affairs, I might add).[15] Here, above all, we see the Greeks keen to learn the skills and joys that language brings, and uniquely deft at such learning.

The rise of the tragedy may well have been the last achievement of this public, largely oral process of poetic transmission and creation. In the course of the fifth century the process of transmission of paradigms of culture takes a new turn. Literacy increases. Specialized, learned, literate teachers, the Sophists, appear on the scene. They speak well, but they also write, and they want to teach the literate few. And they want to teach them how to speak to the illiterate many. Thereby they foster new attitudes.

The poets, at this point, are no longer the single public source of wisdom and virtue. They appear to be the *traditional* source. Their writings begin to be treated as the nearest approximation the Greeks had of a canon. For instance, there grew up in Athens a sort of halo around Solon, the poet-legislator who had curbed the rapaciousness of the big land-owners and gave prudent written laws to his city (592). Henceforth Athens took pride that the law was written, there for all to see, rather than embodied in custom as interpreted by those in authority. Even literacy – that traditional source of the entrenched power of priests and kings – was seen in Greece as part of the thrust towards democracy. The poets in general came to be seen as the fountainhead of a virtuous ethos that was believed to account for the great deeds of the last pre-Sophistic generation, the generation that fought at Marathon (490).

The Sophists were clearly innovators. Appearing in the middle of the fifth century, they had outgrown the city of their birth and offered their skills wherever the asking was (and that was mainly in Athens). Their teaching had assimilated recent results in science (medicine especially) and logic. They were also consciously aiming to prepare young men for the new conditions of life prevailing in the cities now that they had given themselves democratic courts and assemblies. They presented the art of achieving the good life as a new art, adapted to new conditions, destined to eclipse the old. They were the first conscious, enlightened progressives.

The gap between the poets and the Sophists is perhaps best understood by referring to the new requirements of public speaking. Solon's wise laws did not prevent the rise of tyrants who managed to subvert them. These tyrants, however, were overthrown, and Cleisthenes (507) proceeded to 'refound' Athenian democracy by breaking up the old tribal system (and the power of the old families) and by basing the political rights on the fact of residence. Henceforth power is unambiguously in the hands of the people (*demos*) assembled. Now knowing how to speak in public before the common man becomes a skill of paramount importance; and it becomes quite distinct from the art of speaking wisely in the presence of one's elders or prudently with one's peers. The Sophists offer themselves as the expert teachers of the new skill; they claim to understand the nature of the new institutions.[16] Gorgias in particular has a high idea of the possibilities of language and sees the link with democratic processes. He invents a highly literate – that is elevated, poetical, persuasive – prose and stresses that its power, unlike that of 'inspired' poetry, is available to all who bother to learn the rules.[17]

The simultaneous presence of poetic orality and prosaic literacy is enough to add new dimensions to man's perennial problem of transmitting his social and intellectual nature. There are now two statements of the good life proclaimed before the Greek people and each is liable to provoke ire and refutation from the other. There had of course been dissension among Greeks all along. Nevertheless, as we observe older forms of dissension, in Hesiod, for instance, we see the statement of a cultural ideal that claims to be in continuity with the old ways, although in fact it seeks to reform them. The ostensible enemies to such ideals are evil, corrupt, and unjust men living in a dark age. Polemics is against entrenched vice, not against false teachers and their doctrines.[18] In the fifth century 'old' ways and 'new' ways manifestly move apart, and strife arises between good men who claim to have the key to the good life and denounce each other. The conflict is between divergent paradigms of culture. Two forms of life are in opposition and each claims the polish of civilization. One of the parties to the debate is an organized class of itinerant teachers, who take pay for the teachings they have to impart to youth and offer themselves as professional improvers of the ways of the city. From now on, there is a new level of deliberateness, conscious will and choice, in any citizen's participation in his society's educational task: either one puts one's son in the care of one of these new teachers, or one does not.

The position of Socrates in this ideological conflict is far from clear. That he is a teacher is beyond doubt, but what kind remains obscure. He does not miss an opportunity to show weaknesses in the traditional teachings conveyed by the poets – witness the treatment received by Simonides in Book I of the *Republic*. He spends his time in the public places of the city with élite young men, discussing and questioning apparently accepted premises. All this seems to put him in the camp of the Sophists. But he stays in the city of his birth, has served in its army, does not write, founds no school, and occasionally hits the Sophists where they hurt. He accepts no pay, unlike the Sophists, and hints that selling one's mind is no better than selling one's body.[19] He questions the value of their attempt to train young men to speak persuasively before assemblies of citizens. He argues that before a multitude, which is not informed, an able rhetorician can speak more persuasively than an expert.[20] Knowledge of the art of persuasive speech he considers to be dangerous, because it can become a surrogate for knowledge of the realities of the case at hand. The Sophists call the opinion of any assembled multitude wisdom, but an assembled multitude is like a great dumb beast; it is easily misled. The Sophists flatter it, deferring to it in every way that counts in the eyes of the beast; in fact, they manipulate the beast and exploit it to their own advantage and that of their friends. They give the multitude what it likes but they alone get what they want. Taking a longer view, they always end at an advantage.[21] Clearly Socrates is not at ease either with the traditionalists or with the progressives, and neither group has sympathy for him. Aristophanes, a conservative, attacks Socrates in the *Clouds*, and lumps him along with the progressive, Sophistic crazies. But Callicles (in *Gorgias*) obviously thinks Socrates is as out of date as Homer. Socrates seems to have a standpoint from which he can discern and expose the weakness of both poets and Sophists. But that standpoint is not immediately apparent, far from it.

In what is perhaps one of his most famous passages, Thucydides argues that war, political strife, and heart-felt moral differences lead the city to experience a crisis in its language. 'Words had to change their ordinary meaning and to take that which was now given them.' War, a rough master, changes men's characters and forces them to alter their views of the various social virtues. What used to be called reckless audacity is now considered courage. What used to be labelled prudent hesitation is now felt to be specious cowardice. 'Frantic violence became the attribute of manliness; cautious plotting, a justifiable means of self-defence.'[22] In times of conflict men, restless in their desires, learn to manipulate words. They use the strong language of praise to give moral legitimacy to behaviour that is expedient. And they draw upon all the vocabulary that condemns vice to paint the enemies they fear with the darkest possible colours. (Note that there is here a vicious circle: war and crisis bring about brutal speech and brutal speech hastens the coming of war. The quick recourse to power becomes the common rule.)

Nothing differentiates traditionalists from progressives more than their response to this crisis of language. Faced by this new use of words, each side comes to a different implicit or explicit theory of the nature and use of language. Traditionalists hold on to the view that words mean what they mean. They remain close to the old poets who say the things as they speak of them. 'Sing, goddess, the anger of Achilles.' Such is the beginning of the *Iliad*: the poem is not *about* this anger; it sings it, says it, manifests it. The words of the poem have a sort of divine sanction or absolute authority; the poet, with the goddess, creates or re-creates the reality. He is not a historical reporter, whose words are to be assessed to see whether they tell the story fairly or not. Such a formulation implies too much distance between the words and the things: the anger cannot *be* anything else than what the goddess sings. In 399 Euthyphro still shares in this attitude (which by then had become a happy naïveté) over one of the most contentious words in the language. When he says an action is just or unjust, he is entirely confident he is making a clear non-controversial statement that merely calls a spade a spade and declares the true nature of an obvious fact. He adds that everybody agrees that unjust acts should be punished. He fails to see what problem there might be in such a plain matter. Socrates has to point out to him that people caught in the act of some alleged injustice promptly deny that what they did was unjust.[23] Should Euthyphro learn to see that his words are merely expressions of his own opinions rather than a divinely sanctioned utterance? Can he learn it? Breaking off the discussion, Euthyphro remains something of a literalist, convinced that things are what he calls them, even though he knows that quibblers keep trying to twist things. 'Somehow or other,' he says, the definitions proposed 'seem always to turn around and walk away from us.' He realizes that his words do not stay still but he is confident that they would if the world were not mixed up. Socrates agrees that it would be nice if words were to keep meaning what one thought they meant, but he seems to think that bringing about such a state of affairs would be quite a feat, possibly beyond his powers.[24] Socrates is genuinely perplexed about words whereas Euthyphro is perplexed about people who, so far as he can see, perversely misuse them. Consider the indignation that accompanies his statement that 'people will say anything to avoid a penalty.'[25]

Contrasting with Euthyphro's position on language is that of the conventionalists. About words like 'just' or 'unjust,' 'pious' or 'impious,' 'they are willing to say with confidence that no one of them possesses by nature an existence of its own; on the contrary, that the common opinion becomes true at the time when it is adopted and remains true as long as it is held.'[26] What words mean depends on conventions among men. In time these conventions change. The Athenian progressives took some form of this view for granted. The stage is set for the tyranny of an unthinking multitude which is able to give things their name. It is also set for the tyranny of an articulate minority that knows how to capitalize on the prestige of innovative, enlightened views.

The novel situation characteristic of the second half of the fifth century may be summed up by saying that what people do and what people should do when they speak in public has become a subject of serious and perplexing reflection. The amazing power of speech has become fully conscious of itself in the context of a crisis. One does not know readily to what end people should use this power. There has always been a sort of contention in all speech,[27] but in Socrates' Athens the contention has become a sharp struggle. The 'good opinion' is not simply perpetuated by tradition but is fought over in a city-wide contest: each side has its intellectual leaders; the various sides become also political parties. All speech has become suspect: it may be the tool of partisanship.

Philosophy, I would like to think, was really born when men began to search for an answer to this problem. How men use words had clearly become a social crisis and a moral problem. Somehow words had to be used in a manner that would straighten out words and heal speech. Given this state of affairs, education, which is based on words to a larger extent than any other human activity, becomes very problematic, not to say entirely dubious. Can teachers speak the truth about things, or do they merely express their feelings or seek to gain control over their fellow-men? (While Hebrew literature may be said to seek to fathom the mystery of those who have ears and cannot hear, the Greeks wrestle with the problem of those who have mouths and yet do not speak.) The issue is a large one: can we teach people anything, say a truer conception of justice? If we mean by justice what everybody means, our reforming impact will be minimal or non-existent, and yet, if we give the word 'justice' some new meaning of our own, how will we be understood? Thus the *Republic* points out Thrasymachus's error: his views on justice are interesting; the trouble is that what he calls justice has nothing in common with what most people mean by it. 'Words are ill-treated and need fathers to help them.'[28] This is easier said than done. By taking time for discussion and asking exactly what Euthyphro means, Socrates takes the first step he knows to be in the right direction. As he puts it in his intellectual autobiography (*Phadeo*), he had started by trying to investigate realities, the things which are (*ta onta*); but he really began in earnest when he looked at what people say (*logous*): 'he would (henceforth) look at objects as reflected in reasoned argument.'[29]

3 The man Socrates

There is more to be said about Socrates besides the fact that he talked a lot yet used words warily.[30]

Let us note first of all that in a day when ideological camps are sharply divided Socrates is quite prepared to talk to an articulate religious traditionalist and see what wisdom he has to offer. Socrates may be a little disingenuous in going along with Euthyphro's confident notion that his expertise in religious affairs will easily confound Meletus. There is irony in Socrates from the start, and one senses right away a suspicion in him that Euthyphro could not possibly know as much as he claims to. But this irony is without animus and Socrates is not trying to humiliate Euthyphro as he exposes the confusions in his mind. The same initial openness to the wisdom of religious men is found in the *Republic*, where we see Socrates listening to the wise old man Cephalus. Cicero remarked that it would be inappropriate for Socrates to question Cephalus and put his wisdom and piety to some tests. As R.L. Nettleship puts it: 'philosophy comes to learn from this experience not to criticize it.'[31] Socrates seems predisposed to believe that traditional piety has wisdom to offer.

Many sources confirm this. In religion, says Xenophon in his *Memorabilia*, Socrates followed the advice of the Priestess at Delphi: 'Follow the custom of the city; that is the way to act piously.'[32] He expresses his intimate sense of vocation by using some of the most traditional concepts of Greek religion. The duty to cross-examine people has been signified to him from God by the usual means: 'I have been commanded to do this by the god, through oracles and dreams and in every way in which any man was ever commanded by divine power to do anything whatsoever.'[33] For him, to live quietly, without talking, would be disobedience to the god.[34] A divine sign occasionally holds him from some course of action he has been contemplating.[35] In jail a command to write verse comes to him in a dream and in the end he, like the swans, receives a gift of prophecy from Apollo.[36]

Besides the confessions couched in the most traditional religious language of Athens we also find in Socrates expressions of religious conviction which are to our ears as self-authenticating as any we hear from any figure of the past. Religious feeling and philosophic conviction merge in a strong sense of vocation. His duty is to inquire after what we do not know. Where he differs perhaps most from the Sophists is in his constant sense of knowledge yet unattained. He is sure that a confident pursuit of this task 'will make us better and braver and less helpless than the notion that there is not even a possibility of discovering what we do not know.' For this point he is prepared to do battle.[37] This is a statement of rationalism, but a rationalism that is consciously based on the faith that nothing can forever frustrate the attempt to combat one's ignorance. The same confidence that goodness and reason can prevail is found in the *Apology*, where it is expressed as confidence in God: 'I believe it is not God's will that a better man be injured by a worse.'[38] We are chattels of the gods and they tend us wisely. 'I am going to gods who are good masters,' he says in *Phaedo*.[39] Hence his unyielding commitment to his God-inspired way: 'I care with all my might not to do anything unjust or impious.' He would rather die than act in a way which he considers neither honourable, nor right, nor pious.[40] Phaedo concludes that if a man ever can enjoy the protection of the gods then Socrates surely will; upon his arrival in the abode of the dead, 'it would be well with him, if it ever was well with anyone.[41] 'No evil can come to a good man, either in life or after death, and God does not neglect him.'[42] Socrates has not only taught that but his example has also persuaded Phaedo of the truth of it. As N. Söderblom puts it, Socrates has founded the religion of good conscience and overcome all dread of the gods by a trust in God depending on loyalty to one's vocation.[43]

That is where Socrates stands when the chips are down. His daily manner, however, does not immediately indicate this. What strikes those who meet him is his habit of claiming ignorance. Being so ignorant, he can play with all kinds of ideas, apparently helpless at distinguishing those that are sound from those that are not. Euthyphro finds Socrates' mind too mobile and blames him for the fact that the ideas they exchange cannot stay put but keep being replaced by new ones that modify or discredit the previous ones.[44]

But in this sea of eloquent ignorance some hard truths nevertheless emerge for those who have eyes to see and ears to hear. First, Socrates can tell when somebody is ignorant. He *knows* that Euthyphro does not know what piety is. Socrates does not know what it is either, but he has enough knowledge to know that Euthyphro does *not* know, even though he remains powerless to replace this ignorance by knowledge. As *Charmides* points out, there is one thing Socrates is good at, namely observing the distinction between 'thinking one knows' and 'knowing one knows.'[45] Second, Socrates knows what brings about the errors of those who 'think' they know. Euthyphro is intellectually stiff, wedded to his pseudo-certainties. In *Lysis* the conversation on friendship and love cannot go far with Lysis and Menexenus; they are too young, too passionately involved, too much in love, to discuss the topic with any agility.[46] Third, Socrates fully knows what he wants to know. He demands full and exact knowledge. He, for instance, wishes to know what piety is, itself, by itself; likewise with justice; the answer that it consists in helping one's friends and in harming one's enemies is no help to him because it merely calls for another, more difficult, question: who are my friends?[47] This knowledge of what exactly he wants to know makes him a good deal wiser than those who rest content with a belief that they know perfectly well or vaguely feel they ought to know a bit more.[48]

This condition of knowledgeable ignorance gives to the mind of Socrates a strange and ambivalent wit, which is at the same time both quite threatening and very attractive to those who encounter him. Convinced of his own shortcomings, he is very humble. But he is equally convinced of the ignorance of others and often amused by the pompousness which goes with their pseudo-knowledge. So in front of them, most of the time, he really plays at being humble and his humility is either mistaken for arrogance or passes over into arrogance itself. Socrates professes to love human beings (*philanthropia*), and this makes him eager to spend time with any one, talking things over.[49] But this zeal for dialogue irritates. There is irony in his profession of philanthropy. His love for men causes him to be hated.

Socrates also plays with ideas a great deal, as if they were all equally acceptable, and yet through this playfulness there occasionally shines through the seriousness of the mind which is totally committed to thinking it through. His seriousness is not the plodding one of Euthyphro. Socrates's seriousness is compatible with humour, even requires it, but it is a very hard kind of seriousness nevertheless. In his attempt to sum up Socrates' character John Burnet speaks of an enthusiasm tempered by irony.[50] We might also say that Socrates had an irony buoyed up by faith: his vast ignorance and his meagre knowledge never ceased to reinforce each other and make him confident that yet more knowledge could be obtained. P. Friedländer is perhaps right when he traces Socratic irony to the state of affairs in which a mind cannot say what justice is, while being sure it can tell a just man, or an unjust one, when it sees one: 'Socratic irony, at its centre, expresses the tension between ignorance – that is, the impossibility ultimately to put into words "what justice is" – and the direct experience of the unknown, the existence of the just man, whom justice raises to the level of the divine.'[51] But irony is not just an awareness of the limitations of language; it also entails a certain sensitivity about human beings: Socrates had two gifts, writes Philip Vellacot: 'the knowledge that no mind can receive new truth unless it is looking for it, and the ironic self-restraint to put that knowledge into effect.'[52]

Socratic irony is not very creative in its encounter with Euthyphro: Euthyphro does not learn the salutary lesson about his ignorance. As for ourselves, we learn enough to know that Euthyphro does not know, but we do not learn much about piety. Socrates fails to make clear to Euthyphro, or to us, what he thinks it to be, although he does mysteriously hint that Euthyphro has come very close to saying it, thereby tantalizingly implying not only that there is an answer to the question about piety but that we come very close to knowing it.[53] There is only one obvious result: at the end of the dialogue the reader knows that Socrates and Euthyphro are very different indeed. Euthyphro at the outset has treated Socrates as a fellow-member of a religious élite, and, at first, although quickly, Socrates has only mildly marked the difference. However, it becomes apparent that, if they are both in a minority, they belong to very different minorities. A gap has opened and progressively widened between Euthyphro and Socrates. At least one illusion has been dispelled by the dialogue: for all the sympathy Euthyphro and Socrates have for each other, their minds are not at one; and it seems they cannot become one, unless they go on to wrestle much more closely with each other and with their question.

4 Socrates' doctrines

The religious quality of Socrates' intellectual confidence is obvious and so is the inquisitive and ironic quality of his mind. It is not so easy to see what doctrines he adhered to. Clearly he was a man who doctrinally would travel light. But besides his personal impact he also left something of a teaching. A man with his convictions and his intellectual curiosity was bound to focus on the few crucial doctrines that would express the uneasy balance in his mind between the ignorance that is helpless and the ignorance that is knowledgeable. In his case these few doctrines all have to do with virtue and the conduct of life, as is emphasized by the old saying, originated by Cicero, about his having brought philosophy 'down from the heavens' to focus on human affairs.

First of all, Socrates has a doctrine about the psyche, or soul. We do not refer here to the wider circulation he apparently gave to the Pythagorean doctrines about the immortality of the soul as a substance quite distinct from the body, for that belongs more to the side of the convictions he affirms and in which he sees a noble venture of faith. Philosophers who came after him could leave that aside and still keep something of the Socratic cast of mind. We refer rather to his insistence that the soul, whatever it is, should direct men's lives. Such affirmation receives with him an intellectualist colouring: the soul is the capacity to think; often we should rather call it the mind.[54] It also entails a new activism. (The soul moves itself, Plato has argued with vigour.[55]) The Socratic affirmations are a decisive step towards a grasp of human autonomy: there is in man a principle of self-determination: the soul. As A.E. Taylor points out, in Homer the soul is the ghost, but it is not the self.[56] Knowledge of the truth and living one's life according to it are the supreme business of the soul. Henceforth the soul is seen as the great battle-ground, an eternal battle-ground Plato will emphasize, for the contests between good and evil, health and disease. 'The soul should be our first and greatest care.' This is the common human task which geunine philosophers proffer and in the pursuance of which they may have a unique contribution to make. 'The soul must be tended,' and such care is taken in conversations which encourage moderation and self-control.[57]

The well-tended soul is strong and this strength is manifested by its numerous virtues. This could be called Socrates' second doctrine, but we should hasten to add that about virtues he has more questions than answers. As John Rist puts it, Socrates seems to know *that* there is a good beneficial to the soul but not exactly *what* it is.[58] What exactly are the virtues, these characteristics of the healthy soul? How are they acquired? Can they be taught? Is there a virtue at the top of the hierarchy of virtues? By what common character are all virtues virtue? In spite of these numerous uncertainties Socrates remains with some of the old Greek assumptions; more specifically, for him virtue is a human excellence and it consists in a power to do something. Such virtues were first seen as the aristocratic ability to enjoy the good things of life; heroes can do things and can get them done. In a more democratic age virtue as power to do things takes on the colouring of the skill of the artisan who, in his way, enjoys some achievement in the performance of the activities in which he excels. In the fifth century it is commonly acknowledged that an application of the mind and a cultivation of practical know-how (or of 'knowledge of men') are the way to acquire virtue. Xenophon, for instance, affirms that 'every kind of virtue named among men is increased by study and practice.'[59] But Socrates pays sharper attention to the internal condition of the soul. Virtues, it seems, are to be rooted in some internal health.[60] Hence a crucial question on the role played by justice in the plotting of the soul's way towards the possession of virtue: Must justice be joined to strength? Or is strength alone sufficient?[61]

The third doctrine is that knowledge is a necessary ingredient of virtue. All along 'I know' has meant in Greece: I know how, how to handle, how to fix. Socrates has taken over this assumption even to the point of affirming that vice always results from lack of knowledge and that no one does evil willingly. But he (or if not Socrates, certainly Plato) sees the limits of the analogy between the knowledge held by virtuous men and the knowledge exemplified by the skills of the artisans. In both cases there is cultivation of a rational, dependable, and predictable practice, but the virtuous man is not only a man who *knows how*; he is also a man who *knows that*. For instance, the virtuous man knows that the unexamined life is not worth living, or that a well-tended soul is the only secure source of happiness. Still, what virtue is a knowledge of remains somewhat uncertain. How much one can say about the internal and external economy within which the virtuous man lives is not fully clarified. With the appearance of that second meaning of knowledge it is no longer simple to say *what* it is exactly that virtue is a knowledge of.

Finally, Socrates, who twits experts, teases them, and occasionally tears them apart, does believe in a special authority of experts as the people who 'have' knowledge. He informs Laches that the question about a sound education for a child 'must be decided by knowledge, and not by numbers, if it is to be a right decision.'[62] He has a famous example about a fancy cook and a doctor each of whom has a diet to propose to an assembly of boys. The doctor alone is a scientific dietician; his science, of course, makes his proposal less palatable than that of the cook who knows how to flatter his customers. Outvoted though he may be, or will certainly be, the doctor still is the one who is right.[63] For while both know what will please an audience of boys, the doctor also knows what is healthy. The *Republic* underlines the message: any expertise consists of a set of rules that is objective, tested by experience, and effectively overrules the experts' own immediate interest.[64] A shepherd knows what is good for the sheep, and will pursue that good, even if the pursuit is unpopular with the sheep or inconvenient to the shepherd. We turn to experts because their expertise rests on independent objective realities. The shortage of genuine experts and the popularity of false ones are to Socrates both a great personal trial and a sad comment on the state of the city, but he holds on to his view about the authority of experts. Let us add that the dilemma is of great urgency in the Athens that tries to make democratic institutions work. Are we going to agree with the demagogues who keep telling the assembly that all are experts and know what is best for the city? Shall we agree with Athenagoras in Thucydides that, 'though the rich are the best people for looking after money, the best councillors are the intelligent, it is the many who are best at listening to the different arguments and judging between them'?[65] Or are we going to pursue the aristocratic premise and seek to cultivate specialists who will acquire expertise in the art of just rule?

On virtue and knowledge Socrates at first seems right in the mainstream of the Greek moral tradition. The good life is an art of living, of living happily, of enjoying the good things of life and a good reputation with gods and men alike. And some have argued that for Socrates morality consists in realizing in the overall pursuit of life the kind of success that each technique achieves in its specialized domain.[66] In my mind, however, Socrates decisively undermines this moral tradition. His expert begins to be the one who objectively knows, who has the science, not the one who has the successful knack. We have moved away from the world of Homeric values where human virtue lies in the prowess that gets good things and makes a good name for one's self (and holds in check those who want the good things for themselves or want to tarnish our name). The knowledge of the virtuous becomes modelled less on that of the warrior or that of the artisan and more on that of new characters who have appeared in Greece, the scientists and the philosophers. These two kinds of men do not claim to have a knowledge that is a sort of enhanced or specialized *savoir-faire*. Their knowledge is qualitatively different; it may be useful, but it is above all disinterested, and acquires thereby a peculiar prestige and significance. This new connotation of the word 'knowledge' appears most clearly in Socrates' emphasis upon justice. The virtue of justice is essential to the soul, and justice has the quality of something which is objectively right: it is not simply some skill applauded by the many.

Socrates thus establishes a kind of distance between the soul, or mental part, of man and the rest of the human being (commonly called the appetites). All desire entails some knowledge of the desired object, that is deems it desirable.[67] But appetites, Socrates argues, are greedy and often deceived; striving to give them what they want brings no enduring happiness. The soul must not give in to them and must rule over the whole human being. Since the soul is capable of independent, reliable knowledge, it can presumably offer a service to the whole man,[68] rule him successfully, and chart a path to genuine happiness.

Socrates thereby also sets in motion the process of redefinition of the result or product which virtue assures. He does not want to keep hearing more 'poetry about the happiness of kings or of men with gold in store.' He wants to think about 'the whole question of human happiness and misery.'[69] What is indeed the beautiful work that gods and pious men seek to produce by working together?[70] In Socrates' generation, and especially as a result of his probings, the nature of the happiness that everybody wants ceases to be self-evident. Some begin to guess there might be more pleasure without power and some doubt about the contribution made by sensual self-indulgence to the achievement of happiness. (Can one imagine the revulsion Achilles would have felt for Diogenes?) The new definition of happiness includes satisfaction of cognitive needs. Man henceforth wants to know what he is doing, needs to feel in charge of his own life, and wants to be able to give an account, satisfactory to himself at least, of his own style of life. I am not saying that these cognitive needs become the paramount ones; they become a component, able to cause tension in the functioning either of appetites or of social rewards.

Socrates, therefore, is only apparently in keeping with the Greek moral tradition. In fact, he departs from it or even subverts it in a decisive manner. How clear this was to himself is a moot question. What is certain is that many of his contemporaries thought he was on a different wave length. It is easy to trace the root of his reformulation of morality to his novel conception of the soul: if it is the soul that must rule the body, and if the soul must rule itself first, then obviously whatever the body and society have to offer will become secondary among the blessings to be striven for. Morality will then become an interior thing, a psychic state, something rather like a good conscience, and not exteriorities such as aristocratic glory or the ease of a respectable theatre-going artisan. In this new perspective, 'only one thing creates happiness: a life based on the sole knowledge that has to do with good and evil.'[71] The soul is the proper characteristic of man; its unique function will bring forth a specific achievement that is distinct from all the products of the senses and of the social arts. Only adherence to the truth can bring happiness to the soul. Henceforth a higher art of living becomes distinct from the lower ones, and a higher happiness becomes so distinct from the common happiness as even to become compatible with the worst form of misery the world knows. 'Doing wrong is to be more carefully shunned than suffering it.'[72]

Conservative though he is in religion, in his conception of morality Socrates is thus genuinely innovative and moves far away from the Sophists who, progressive though they are, merely dress up for fifth-century needs and tastes the old Homeric notions about pleasure and power being the source of the good life. With Socrates moral conscience no longer takes the form of a series of teachings about the desirable virtues and personal skills that are socially rewarded. To teach morality is no longer to teach recipes but rather to seek to teach an art of thinking, and there is no telling what a free man in a confused society will do if he begins to think. With him, as Victor Goldschmidt puts it, moral conscience gives up the constitution of a moral science that can be inculcated.[73] We can understand Bruno Snell's statement that 'after Socrates all exhortations to virtue go by the board; they become antiquated.'[74] Exhortations to virtue from the Socratic standpoint are merely recipes that work at a given time in a given society and deliver the happiness that people seem to want. But none of the exhortations tells us what happiness we should want. None teaches us what the good is. From now on, the moral good will no longer be what a cultural tradition says it is. While he seeks to say what it truly is, Socrates will for the time being say that the good is the methodical and conscientious choice of the good. What life is worth living is not as clear as most might wish but it is certain that the unexamined life is not worth living.

The individual will have to rest content with this answer and, like Socrates, stake everything on the, it is hoped, well-scrutinized conscience. Others had said before that justice is virtue, but Socrates is ready to die for this belief. There are an unprecedented firmness and strength of the soul here. From the time of Homer, the Greeks fully knew that life was serious and full of irrevocable and inevitable fates. But with Socrates an individual mind becomes serious, and that on a matter of principle, not of desire or of honour. While all words keep shifting, the statement that it is better to suffer injustice than commit it 'remains unshaken.'[75] Morality for Socrates has become both an autonomous human reality and an absolute.[76]

3

The first steps in philosophy of religion

I A serious encounter with serious consequences

There is in Euthyphro a didacticism that is characteristic of many professors of philosophy and there are in Socrates a clarity and power of conviction that earn him a place among the world's great religious figures. Without denying this, nevertheless, for better or for worse, religion has come to be associated with the Euthyphros and their like and Socrates has become a symbol of philosophy.[1] Thus the encounter on the steps of the court house may stand as an early example of the meeting between religion and philosophy. Such a reading of the situation is perhaps rather loaded in favour of philosophy. In Socrates we find philosophy either at its best or very close to it. Euthyphro is not the lowest of the low among religious characters, but he is hardly near the top. He is rather average, and that Socrates certainly is not. But such a situation may not be untypical. Most of us encounter religion in traditional and unglamorous forms. Prophets and religious geniuses are rare. Furthermore; no philosopher was around to match wits with Moses, Isaiah, Jesus, or Muhammad when they were with us. But all philosophers meet types like Euthyphro. So we shall let the identifications Euthyphro = religion, Socrates = philosophy stand.

But in the encounter between Euthyphro and Socrates we do not yet see philosophy and religion meet (or fail to meet) as hard and fast objectified realities. Euthyphro and Socrates are not personifications but real people. The advantage of catching the dialogue between philosophy and religion at this early stage is that neither partner has yet grown into a fully developed tradition, with its habits and its dogmas; both are still open enough to learn, to notice new possibilities.[2]

Although they are not monumental entities staring down at each other, religion and philosophy each have a distinct identity of their own and thus each have something of their own to bring to the dialogue. Such differentiation of identities is still very recent in the history of the Greek mind. In Homer we do not find either philosophers or people who clearly are more religious than others. The characters in the epics think about life, war, games, women, and gods but none of them thinks about philosophy or religion. They have no word for either. By the fifth century we encounter in Greece people who make subtle differentiations among the realities which are part of the Greek world and in particular see a difference between the religious world and the ordinary world. The reality of the former ceases to be as palpable as that of the latter. The distinction is made between Aphrodite and sex. The stage is set for wondering whether Aphrodite is not less real, or derivative, while sex is more real and fundamental. One can from now on begin to doubt whether the gods exist, or whether their influence amounts to what one was told it was. With such differentiations, and many others, there is the possibility of beginning to think about religion. While the Greeks did not fasten on one name to designate this whole area that we map out by calling it all 'religion,' they did grow into the sense that 'divine matters,' 'holy things,' and other related affairs constituted a whole that deserved specialized investigation.[3]

There is a satisfactory proof of this in the emergence in the fifth century of two complementary intellectual movements. The first one, which actually has roots in the sixth century, offers a series of philosophical theologies that try to teach a more adequate notion of the gods than was available in the tradition as commonly transmitted. They are theologies because they mean to speak the god-inspired truth about God (or about the gods). They are philosophical because they believe that their truth is the one to which reason arrives and is thus rooted in an authority other than that of the tradition or of the private vision. Most famous perhaps among such theologies is that of Xenophanes, who taught that the representations of gods in the human likeness are quite unworthy of the divine.[4]

On the other hand we see also the appearance of a whole set of theories on the nature and origin of religion which have in common the rejection of the idea that the gods were original realities that existed before men existed. They all tend to make religion derivative and a result of some data of human nature, or of some feature of the human situation. Some thinkers explain how clever men invented religion. Others show how men gave the name of gods to some beneficient and natural realities. Others show how religion arose out of fear of overwhelming natural phenomena. One of these theories was put forward by Plato's own uncle, Critias: for him the world of religion was invented in order to set a check upon those crimes that remain hidden and that the city cannot control.[5]

Euthyphro and Socrates, therefore, both have antecedents of sorts. Euthyphro is no Xenophanes but as a religious and thinking man he can turn to great teachers; he derives from them some reassurance and a belief that those who claim to know better about the gods than the tradition or the crowd are not necessarily fools.

Socrates is far from the assurance of Critias, who is sure he has found out the truth about religion, but he does know of great inquirers who preceded him; as a result his wish to leave no stone unturned in his investigation of piety is strengthened, and he feels free to raise any question he sees fit. That there are impious questions one should not ask is a notion he does not need to dispel – at least in the privacy of philosophical circles. (As a matter of fact, as we see in the *Phaedrus*, Socrates came to feel that the liberty of philosophical speech had gone too far and he disowned one of his speeches because it was blasphemous.[6])

Euthyphro and Socrates have thus enough consistency to make their encounter a real one. Furthermore they meet in the shadow of a court-house: Socrates is supposed to figure out what reply to give to this accusers. Speech in court-houses has peculiar features: it is channelled by set procedures and leads to decisions which are momentous and enforced. Talk in the court-house is not like talk in the market-place or the classroom; the rules are simpler and the consequences more immediate. One's life may hang on what one has to say. The need to use words carefully is brought home in a uniquely potent way.

A second point, not so obvious, is equally important. Most interpreters of the history of Greek moral evolution agree that what we call 'moral decisions' were taken in court-houses of brick or marble before they were taken in the inner tribunal of conscience. The classical picture of moral deliberation, as the art of listening to both sides and then deciding, derived from institutional realities. The courts, their procedures, their debates played a crucial role in the moral education of Greece. The sense of selfhood developed, moral growth occurred, because these institutions found out, on the anvil of debate between both sides, that some old notions were inadequate; and because these institutions came up with decisions that called upon new insights. Debates and decisions in the courts led, for instance, to the moralization of the notion of pollution and the setting aside of the notion of inherited guilt. They also brought to the Greeks intimations of the notion of individual responsibility. Aristotle's discussion of the will reflects the terminology of the courts.[7] What happened in the courts thus set the tone of Greek moral life long before Socrates told his Athenian jury that the good name of the whole state was at stake in their decision.[8]

That Socrates and Euthyphro meet on the steps of a court-house dramatizes the seriousness of their encounter. Philosophy of religion makes its first moves in an ominous atmosphere. Socrates and Euthyphro occasionally refer to the city, to 'what people think.'[9] This third, absent partner will soon occupy the centre of the stage: the jurors will shortly examine charges against Socrates and they will have the last word (or will they?). 'The people' will make a decision and thus the philosophers' wisdom will be put to a test of some sort. Both Euthyphro and Socrates acknowledge that the purpose of their whole discussion is to prepare the defence that Socrates will have to speak on his own behalf.

In the circumstances the test that will be made of Socrates' wisdom will be a sweeping one. With our independent judiciary, our modern courts are highly specialized institutions with precise procedures that are finely honed to settle as well as can be very narrow and specific questions. The accused is under the burden of answering only a specific charge and any attempts to discredit him or show him to be innocent by bringing in irrelevancies are ruled out of order by a professional judge who is alert to precisely such waylayings of the issue. Every possible precaution is taken to ensure that the jury will be free to make up its own mind on the question put to it. The jury has the benefit of expert advice from a judge, and this 'objective' expert is constantly watched by two adversaries who are also professionals. Thus questions of fact and questions of law are carefully kept apart. Without prejudging the question of fact, the judge makes clear to the jury what the law is when that is clear, and clarifies what the questions of law are when such exist. A jury then commonly judges only the question of fact, or, if its deliberations involve it in the question of law, it judges of that in full knowledge of what it is doing.

The rules of the Athenian courts in the fifth century are very different. The jury is made up of five hundred people. The case is decided in a day. The jurors' deliberation is non-existent and their vote public. A simple majority carries the issue. Judges preside but can hardly offer advice and correct misrepresentations. The accused speak for themselves without the help of a trained lawyer, although they may get a prepared piece from a professional speech-writer. The accuser is not a professional crown prosecutor but a well-meaning citizen, possibly a personal enemy, an amateur in any case. Witnesses are heard by the court, but the right of cross-examination does not exist, so that it is difficult to expose lies and fallacies. The accused, however, may cross-examine the accuser. In our courts the accused is insulated from the jury and the whole procedure is organized so that the accused can neither appeal to the prejudices of his jury nor anger them. In contrast, Socrates, like all the accused in Athens, will face his jury in the atmosphere of a public meeting, in which he must somehow sway a majority in his favour. All the tricks in the book are necessary to achieve this feat, and all are permitted. The accused usually blurs the question of responsibility by citing his past services to the state and evoking future ones. He will also create confusion by begging for mercy and bringing his weeping family to the stand without however going as far as admitting guilt. He will try to flatter his audience and amuse it. He will have to choose whether it is in his interest to seek to tear apart his accuser and elicit hostility against him or whether it is best not to attack him at all. If found guilty, he still has an opportunity for a second performance, in which he is called to set his own penalty, which the jury may then accept or not. A suitably crestfallen and humble willingness to accept a moderate penalty at that stage may impress the jury and deflect the more serious penalty the accuser proposes. But the gamble may be lost and a penalty too moderate may drive the jury to vote for the penalty proposed by the accuser. Our courts are devised to hold rhetoric in leash; theirs gave it full sway. To prove himself innocent, for such is the issue, an accused needs the talent of a political orator and of a culture critic. For not all five hundred men in the jury are fools. Some are genuinely concerned about the health of the city. Unable to reform the tradition, they are unwilling to abandon it. It will help if the accused appears to them to be in tune with the right values, to be a good man as well as an able speaker.

It is clear that any trial in that system can be politicized and in fact many were. In many cases the accuser emphasizes that the confiscation of the wealth of a rich man will swell the coffers of the city – from which comes the jurors' pay. In others the defendant recounts the services he has rendered to his fellow citizens. In the *Iliad* Achilles gives the second prize to Eumelus even though he finished last in the race, 'because he is the best man.'[10] Who is 'the best man' counts in the courts of the fifth and fourth century. Such administration of justice is obviously in deep trouble: there is 'a hopeless tangle of values.'[11] Those who argue that the law protects those who are innocent yet weak end up having a singularly poor case.

This kind of law, of course, is very poor law, although it is better than such law as a kinsman with his axe or a king in his *megaron* is likely to have. But this poor law has the merit of making clear something that our better, more specialized legal institutions tend to obscure. In a court of law decisions are taken, the making of which draws upon the very substance of a culture, and the enforcing of which reinforces the most deep-seated convictions of a society. Drawing upon our modern distinctions, we have said that Socrates was not tried for religious reasons but that the motive of Anytus was political. But this is misleading if it implies that the Athenians were divided between those who wanted purity of religious doctrine and practice and those who wanted to remain in control of the machinery of the state. Meletus and Anytus have in common the wish to do what is good for the city, and what they appeal to is the jury's notion of what this good is. In our narrow sense of the word the jury's decision will be a legal one. But it will also clearly be a political, moral, and religious one.

The court decision in the trial of Socrates is thus the closest approximation known to that society of a global democratic decision on what is good. A trial for impiety was the only kind of trial that brought to the city a concern about its total health. It was, then, the only public suit. The trial of Socrates is therefore not the type of heresy trial that is fought in the backwaters of a society, nor is it a mere episode in the conflict of political factions. It is an opportunity for testing whether the goodness of Socrates is a goodness acceptable to his city, even a goodness able to educate his city and raise it to a new level. Few philosophers have had such opportunity of putting their person and their teachings to the test. In this circumstance a successful philosopher would not only vindicate his innocence but would also uplift his entire society. His speech, one can imagine, would give such clear expression to the ideals and deep-seated convictions of the best men of Athens that quibblers would not dare discredit it. Such speech would promptly enter among the classics taught to schoolchildren, and be carved on rock so that all citizens can see it. A successful speech would, for instance, replace Pericles' funeral oration as exemplification of all the values that made Athens great.

One can surmise that Socrates is prepared to see his speech to the jurors in these terms and accept the challenge. He has told Euthyphro that what men need (and gods too for that matter) is a method for adjudicating disputes that involve moral issues. Quarrels and wars arise when some call just what others call unjust.[12] In the dialogues he searches for the method that can settle these differences of opinion (which elicit dreadful consequences) and he uses such elements of the method as he has come to master.

Before his jurors his overall ability will be put to the test: can he speak so persuasively that his virtuousness will become apparent and have a self-authenticating quality? Can Socrates lift the city to some new insight into its own welfare? Or has he lived in vain as he tried to enlighten his contemporaries on the true nature of virtue? While waiting to meet his judges, he admits that his whole life had been preparation for this speech.[13]

The sweeping nature of the issues embraced by the philosophizing about religion can also be illustrated by referring to the issues at stake in the law suit initiated by Euthyphro. Let us imagine a speech by Euthyphro before his jurors that manages to reconcile all the different claims present, however dimly, in the tangled case: the claim of the father to conscientious behaviour in seeking advice on what fate should be meted out to the untried murderer, the claim of the untried murderer to some due process without negligent cruelty, the claim of the family to see the spell of pollution cast out, the claim of shed blood if not for vengeance at least for justice. Such a speech would have to *create* a new conception of justice. To resolve all these points Euthyphro would have to rise to a new understanding of justice that somehow embodies the insights of all the more or less well-meaning people who have come to confront each other in this case. Could a Euthyphro, helped by Socrates, manage to do that? A philosophy of religion should do no less.

2 Disease in the city

The encounter between Socrates and the court does not seem to start on the right foot. Socrates has a low opinion of his judges and fears that they habitually lack wisdom. Xenophon states in his *Apology* that, shortly before the trial began, Hermogenes asked Socrates this question: 'do you not observe that the Athenian courts have often been carried away by an eloquent speech and have condemned innocent men to death, and often on the other hand, the guilty have been acquitted either because their plea aroused compassion or because their speech was witty?'[14] Socrates has indeed observed this. The people who make up the assembly, Socrates says, still according to Xenophon, 'think of nothing but buying cheap and selling dear.'[15] And Socrates is not the only one to think so. Aristophanes also is very critical of the behaviour of the courts. His comedies poke biting fun at plaintiffs and judges. Jurors in particular are seen as mere worthless drones who have grown to be dependent on – and greedy for – the modest jurors' fee.[16]

For his part, Plato came to see in the life of the law an illustration of the disease of the social body. There is a revealing aside in the *Phaedrus*: to persuade truly one must know the soul perfectly, and know what has noble and vulgar effects, but 'that is not necessary for persuasion in courts.'[17] In *Theatetus* we hear that those who spend a long time in the study of philosophy appear ridiculous when they enter the law courts as speakers. Law courts display moral decadence: one learns there shrewdness and deceit; souls become small and warped.[18] Plato is also clearly appalled at the speed with which the process of subversion does its work. In *Letter VII*, his one autobiographical comment, he tells us that 'both the written laws and the customs were being corrupted with surprising rapidity.'[19] Traditional law may not be ideal in Plato's eyes, but what men make out of it as they wrangle in their pursuit of their naked self-interest indicates the decay into which the public life of Athens has fallen. Constant recourse to law, adds Plato, is a sign of a fault in society, just as constant recourse to a doctor is a sign of disease in a body.[20] On this count Athens is sick indeed. Their people love litigation, they enjoy the show of wit, ruse, and the subtle play of hypocritical skill that is involved in trying to win the legal game.

That courts of law should function without dignity indicates that a new virus has penetrated into the social body. The place in society where words should most be watched, where they have the most verifiable consequences, has become the place where talking is a game in which the clever try to trick and bluff each other. Speech becomes a skilled hypocrisy and no institutional check remains to encourage people to tell the truth or run the risk of shameful exposure. Athens has become like a theatre.[21] Actors move in a gripping manner, and according to a rich variety of scripts, but none of these motions are true; they are all lies uttered by people who pursue some other, hidden end.

The poor performances of the courts are thus only the tip of an iceberg. The sense of a pervasive moral decay is haunting many minds at the end of the fifth century. It is commonly accepted that the institutions of Athens while sound on the whole do not work well because people, having become corrupt, misuse them. Legal and social crises are thus traced back to a moral failure of the group.

Such sense of moral breakdown is of course frequently echoed by simple, nostalgic, conservative minds. But it is also articulated in the most brilliant piece of social analysis the Greeks ever formulated, namely Thucydides' *History of the Peloponnesian War*, the history which shows how a particular war became a problem far worse than any it was aiming to solve. We have already referred to the famous passage that shows how in times of war and civil conflict people get in the habit of a gross misuse of words. The historian goes on to say that there was 'a general deterioration of character throughout the Greek world.' To fanatical minds revenge became more important than self-preservation. Breaches of faith became common. The verdict is firm: 'Love of power, operating through greed and through personal ambition, was the cause of all these evils.'[22]

Thucydides proceeds to show in painful detail how a spirit of brutal self-assertion became a dominant feature in the behaviour of the citizens. Above all, his analyses show the deterioration of character extending itself to a social reality. His demonstration is both simple and irrefutable: public bodies act (for example, decide whether to start a war and how to pursue it) after deliberation; debate and vote set them in motion. This political dimension of human living has numerous social ramifications that remain mostly in the dark. Subsequent deliberations and decisions interlock with the earlier ones. The momentum of each choice, plus the contingent events that occur in between, provides a framework for the subsequent persuasive attempts to guide the further choices. This chain does not determine the outcome of each new deliberation, but it creates a powerful social-affective context of hopes and fears, which weighs heavily upon individual actors and creates opacities even when human beings openly assemble to deliberate lucidly. What *we* did and how *I* feel about it affect my outlook as *I* listen to arguments about what *we* should do next.[23]

As he shows the social context of public rhetorical efforts in fifth-century Greece, Thucydides tells a progressively darker story: he tells of a war that became a total war. Public character grew more belligerent, more uncompromising. He also formulates generalities. He points out the danger inherent in leaving the decision to a large gathering: in a crowd an imprudent scheme can easily gather an irresistible momentum.[24] Men driven by 'their private ambition and covetousness' can freely control the multitude.[25] The art of persuasion, which had emerged at the end of Aeschyles' great trilogy as the key to peace and justice,[26] is now extremely suspect: there are demagogues around. Private men can move cities to murderous and suicidal wars. Thucydides shows how his own city of Athens practised the brutal affirmations of its interests and did not consider itself bound by treaties to allies or by sacred customs. (The start of the Athenian Empire is commonly dated to a unilateral decision to use the sacred treasure of the Delian League for domestic expenses.) Thucydides lucidly analyses this Athenian descent into the naked use of force. One factor in it is the very habit of greatness of Athens: a city able to build the Parthenon does not get into the habit of watching what others think. But Thucydides also shows cold, shameless violence: the inhabitants of Melos are told not to reason with the Athenians but simply to submit and acknowledge that the Athenians have the greater power. They are warned that nothing will restrain the city at war. It is 'a general and necessary law of nature' that the powerful will rule whenever they can. So speak the envoys of the city that knows no law beyond itself.[27]

Thucydides sees that in the case of collective self-interest the pursuit of one's interest as one sees it declares itself quite openly. He shows us Alcibiades addressing the Assembly and stating that unrestrained imperialism is what Athens really wants. 'It is not possible for us to calculate, like housekeepers, exactly how much empire we want to have.'[28] In the debate on the treatment to be meted out to Mytilene, a city which has just surrendered to Athens, Cleon sets aside all traditional restraints. His words are, of course, again those of Thucydides: to feel pity, to practise the arts of diplomacy, to listen to the claims of decency 'are three things that are entirely against the interests of an imperial power.'[29]

Under conditions of war against external enemies, adds the historian, the spirit of ruthless self-assertion tends to seize more individuals. There are perhaps always people who want to feel free to do anything that their fancy dictates and that they can get away with. In times of great social stress, however, their 'ungovernable passions' become unleashed, argues Thucydides. 'With the ordinary conventions of civilized life thrown into confusion, human nature, always ready to offend even where laws exist, showed itself proudly in its true colours, as something incapable of controlling passion, insubordinate to the idea of justice, the enemy of anything superior to itself.'[30] We must add, however, that brutal self-interest will still not openly declare itself, for this would amount to a declaration of war upon those who hear him rather than upon absent foreigners.

To the testimony of Thucydides we may also add that of Sophocles. The loss of restraint or shame (*aidôs*) is a key theme in his plays. This disease has both a social and a personal dimension. 'Laws will never be kept rightly in a city that knows no fear or reverence,' we hear in *Ajax*.[31] *Oedipus Rex* is the drama of a man who has lost *aidôs* and, in tragic crisis, relearns it. At the beginning of the play the king embodies the Athenian virtues of swift action based on intelligence. He is a man in charge and accustomed to taking charge (he does it with zeal and brilliance when there is need to search for the murderer). His language is not far from that of the fifth-century rationalists. We might attribute to him an ability to cope with everything, the vigour of the man who is never caught off balance. Against this view of the world, that invites man always better to master his skills, the play reaffirms the religious view of a divinely ordered universe. The truth of something as old-fashioned as prophecy is vindicated. The magnificent intelligence of Oedipus is brought face to face with a reality he did not see and which breaks him.[32]

We can now return to the encounter between Euthyphro and Socrates on the steps of the court-house. Philosophy and religion meet in a society that experiences heated discussion in its search for the good life. The cruelties of the war among Greeks are there for all to remember; and there are fears that this literal war is but a manifestation of an underlying moral war of all upon all. We also see in *Euthyphro* that the philosopher and the religious man have identified their common enemy. Both Socrates and Euthyphro see the threat to the city in a new class of ruthless, ambitious public men who speak loudly before the assembled people and look upon the city as a hunting ground for their acquisitive or predatory skills. Among the certainties available to Euthyphro and Socrates, one is that such new men must be stopped. The point is not that there are new, more selfish individuals in the city; it is that the heat of debate provides opportunities for a more blatant, expansive greed. The common sense of man's obligation to his fellow-man or to the gods is openly ridiculed. New men derive pride in a disciplined emancipation from such 'relics,' which are seen as an oppression that the individual must overthrow if he can.

Socrates, of course, is sharper and more lucid in his diagnosis, and his views on the false teachers must have served as a basis of Plato's classical case against them in *Gorgias* and the *Republic*. No order for the person, let alone the city, can be based upon such ruthless individualism, Plato will argue. In the *Protagoras* Socrates refutes the common view of courage upheld by the great Sophist and does not accept that one can lack the other virtues and still have courage: it is not true that the political dimension of existence requires men of courage who are devoid of the other virtues of justice, piety, and moderation. Euthyphro, of course, is more muddled in his diagnosis, but he too rejects the ambition that lets no tradition stand in its way. Thus both could perhaps agree that ruthless individualism dissolves tradition and leads to disorder, since ruthless individuals always voice against tradition arguments that are consistently self-serving in nature. Tradition then, unsound though it may be in fact, suddenly wins the dignity of being at least a moderating influence upon greed and opportunism. Tradition strengthens the resistance of the common man in his struggle against the mellifluous arguments of adventurous sweet-talkers who seek to play upon his desires and encourage him to embark upon new schemes. In a society without tradition confidence men have more scope. Tradition also puts some taboos inside the individual and thus hampers his acquisitive and hypocritical skills.

This prudent sense of the worth of tradition that Euthyphro and Socrates share should not mask the profound differences between them. They differ above all in the therapy they propose. Euthyphro wants to strengthen aspects of the tradition. He is selective and stubborn; yet he has no clear principle for the selection. What Socrates wants is not as clear at first, although he does behave entirely in conformity with the tradition, especially in religious matters. He mainly wants to talk, persistently, patiently, and accurately, about things. He also insists on talking with just a few people at a time. Euthyphro and Socrates clearly stand for two very different kinds of response.

We might add that there is yet a third kind of minority created by the disturbing presence in the city of these new ruthless man. We refer to the two young men in the *Republic*, Glaucon and Adeimantus, the ones who ask Socrates to teach them. They have drunk at the well of the modern enlightenment and have shared the table of the articulate progressives. They have learned to denounce the nonsense found in the traditions and the cruelties that result from an imposition of its ways. They have seen through the pompous ignorance of the traditionalists. They have learned also to act in an emancipated manner, to laugh at religious practice and probably to tease religious conservatives. They certainly get bored in the company of dull sticks like Euthyphro. But Adeimantus and Glaucon are not fully in the enemy camp. They are dissatisfied with the modern enlightenment and yet cannot see its flaw. Both the school of tradition and the school of progress are discredited in their eyes. They believe that the way to the good life lies elsewhere and they come, alone, to Socrates with very tough questions. Socrates is clever and they like him. What is justice? 'Is there a kind of good which we could choose to possess, not from desire for its after effects, but welcoming it for its own sake?'[33] They put Socrates on the spot and test whether his best is good enough for their serious questions.

To sum up, philosophy and religion meet in a city where not all is well in the best of all possible worlds. Both know it and both are equally exercised in their distinctive manner about this unsatisfactory state of affairs. There is broad agreement in their diagnosis: a widespread, ruthless, passionate individualism is found in the city, and checks upon it, cures for it, are either not available or hardly functioning. Social deliberation seems to be mainly an extension of greed, hardly a cure for it. In any case it has become suspect. By individualism we do not mean spiritual independence but an impulsive assertion of self, in contempt of everything else. The assertion is hungry for power and acquisitive: the ruthless individualist wants to get and keep the good things of life and he wants to have more of them than the average citizen. Thus, the society in which philosophy and religion meet experiences a moral decay with personal and social dimensions.

We can now complete our picture of the skills required of Socrates if he is to teach his assembled city. Skills in addressing the Assembly will have to be a synthesis of the skills acquired in encounters with three different kinds of minorities: he must be able to educate Euthyphro, to curb the desires of the ruthless men who get out of hand, and to inspire Glaucon and Adeimantus and their like. These skills, Socrates seems to think, will be acquired in face-to-face conversations. Such dialogues are therefore Socrates' starting-point. They are the kinds of discussion which Socrates is sure are properly philosophical. They are also those in which he has come to excel.

3 The Socratic practice

Socrates' manner as a philosopher is first exhibited in conversation in small groups, frequently in sustained dialogue with a single individual. This may seem quite far from the art of addressing a crowd, but how is he to learn what goes on in the mind of his fellow-citizens except by speaking with all kinds of men? The early Socratic dialogues written by Plato are our best source for seeing Socrates at work. They all show a social drama, Socrates arguing with representatives of a variety of shades of opinions. They also narrate a process of intellectual exchange and growth. Every dialogue, says Victor Goldschmidt, records the struggle of thought to disengage itself from error, confusion, and unthought, and then to 'engage itself' (in a cure, or healing action, we might add).[34] D. Grene puts it this way: 'It is the peculiar value of the dialogues that they constitute the artistic recreation of the moments of illumination – in conversation, in chance happenings, and, as it were, in particular intellectual silhouettes. They are not philosophy, as philosophy has since been understood, but the artistic correlative of the experience that makes philosophy.'[35] We can discern some of the skills Socrates exercises in order to nurture the condition for this experience. They all have to do with the cultivation of sober and accurate prose.[36]

The practice of philosophical conversation must be undertaken with a minimum of seriousness. There is, of course, an element of play. Light banter arouses the minds, and youthful minds are the most nimble. But these two important ingredients should not make philosophical conversation into a game that draws upon competitive instinct. 'Young men, when they first get a taste of disputation, misuse it as a form of sport, always employing it contentiously ... They delight like puppies in pulling about and tearing with words all who approach them.'[37] Such spirit discredits philosophy. Then the interlocutor should not answer questions by referring to commonly accepted opinion. Answers that begin with 'people say ...' or 'it is ordinarily agreed ...' do not bring us nearer the truth. 'Always answer just what you think,' Socrates tells the young slave in *Meno*.[38] Crito is asked to try to reply to Socrates's questions 'to the best of your belief' and not to agree verbally to something he does not really believe.[39] Socrates wants the results of the individual mind's serious wrestling with the truth as it appears to it, so he will not accept a citation of a poet, or even a learned exegesis, as an answer. In *Protagoras* he points out that gentlemen who have had a proper education can have a pleasant party without hiring entertainers: let us therefore think our own thoughts, 'making trial of truth and of ourselves.'[40] In *Phaedrus* Socrates tries to shame his partner by the example of the grasshoppers who do not take a siesta but keep on singing during the heat of the day; when reaching the apparent end of their wits, philosophers should not turn to a consultant and ask a Lysias to prepare a speech; they should rather make the effort to talk on.[41]

Furthermore, an interlocutor who consents to a statement by saying 'you might put it this way, if you want, Socrates' is not staying on the right track. What Socrates wants is a statement that puts it the way his interlocutor wants it. When Euthyphro answers evasively, asking what is there to hinder one from accepting Socrates' latest suggestion, Socrates swiftly replies that nothing hinders him, so far as he is concerned, but he asks Euthyphro carefully to consider his own position.[42] The man with whom he finds himself arguing is the one 'whose vote I know how to take, whilst to the multitude I have not a word to say.'[43] The serious assent of Polus is worth more to Socrates than the consensus of all the crowd. In this light Euthyphro is, on the whole, a good partner for philosophical discussion. He means what he says, even if he does not always know what he means. His being is at one with his affirmations. His affirmations reveal his individual level of existence. He does adhere to the rule given in *Theaetetus*: 'we must do our best with such lights as we have and continue to say what we think.'[44] Euthyphro's statements are not mere words. Out of the clash between his seriousness and the serious requirements of Socrates genuine philosophical results may emerge.[45]

The manner of Protagoras is very different. He makes long speeches, and these, to Socrates, only delay the dawn of the philosophical event; they allow the mind to make a lot of statements without actually running the risk of being pinned down to any single one. Callias tolerantly suggests that Socrates and Protagoras should have the right to talk each in his chosen style. Alcibiades, answering for Socrates, points out that Socrates has already yielded to Protagoras that he himself has no skill for long discourse but would like to make another test, namely, their relative ability in argumentation.[46] Socrates therefore maintains that he would like short answers because he quickly forgets the long ones.[47] The learned Hippias tries to arbitrate the quarrel by advising Socrates that he should let his speeches have their head with a loose rein but warning Protagoras that he must not let out 'with full sail, as you run before the breeze and so escape into the ocean of speech, leaving the land nowhere in sight.'[48] Such compromise, in the eyes of Socrates, we may be sure, allows a dangerous proximity between philosophical inquiry and rhetorical fireworks.

Callicles has another technique to run away from the moment of philosophical seriousness. He keeps changing his mind, or perhaps (it is hard with him to tell the difference) he keeps saying different things and changing his definitions of words. Socrates is frank with him: 'I charge you with never saying the same thing on the same subject; but at one moment you defined the better and superior as the stronger, and at another as the wiser, and now you turn up again with something else: 'the manlier' is what you now tell us is meant by the superior and better. No my good friend, you had best say, and get it over, whom do you mean by the better and superior.'[49]

The road to philosophical discovery is long and rough and most prefer a shorter, smoother one.[50] But, in addition to the need for personal seriousness, Socrates has a few more pointers to show the way. All people do strive for some coherence in their speech and that fact should be used as a starting-point. When Euthyphro testily says that people will say anything to get themselves off the hook, Socrates corrects him: 'not quite anything.' A man charged with murder will not state that his deed was a monstrous injustice and add that he is nevertheless innocent.[51] There are some crude contradictions of oneself that all speakers try to avoid. Most will never depart from an ostensible loyalty to logic; this is verified in the case of Thrasymachus. As Adkins tellingly puts it, Thrasymachus is an intellectual bandit: he believes that force always prevails and always will, that moral suasion is useless, and that it is, in any case, only a disguised application of force. But bandit though Thrasymachus is, he is an intellectual one. He has some standards and accepts logical suasion. He will grant any conclusion that can be shown to follow from his own premises, and will doubt a conclusion if Socrates can show that it does not necessarily follow from his own premises.[52] Others who are not so rationally minded will cultivate at least social if not logical respectability. These individuals, of course, are complete weathervanes, since what it takes to be socially respectable varies with the men in whose company they find themselves. But even these characters may be cajoled into contributing seriously: because they want to appear coherent, they will lend themselves – until they find an excuse to break the exchange and run away – to an effort to make them say what they really believe. They will yield to the social pressure that asks them to speak and they will use their intelligence to prevent the appearance of too gross a contradiction between what they say they believe and what they publicly do. So in either case one can proceed as Socrates did with Euthyphro and start with what the interlocutor claims to know, or with what he says in moments when he is prepared to reveal where he stands. 'The most dialectical way,' says Socrates in a statement that summarizes the first two points of his method, 'is not merely to answer what is true, but also to make use of those points which the questioned person acknowledges he knows.'[53]

The third point of Socrates' method is illustrated in all the early Platonic dialogues. He proceeds to refute his interlocutor and show that his statements do not agree with each other, or do not follow from his accepted premises. Socrates points to hidden difficulties and shows in one way or another that his interlocutor's account is not as rounded, coherent, and complete as he thought it was. In the most severe cases he shows that the interlocutor only thought he knew but did not really know. Euthyphro is made to see at the end of the dialogue that he has returned to a statement that a while ago was commonly agreed to be false.[54]

The real test of the interlocutor comes at this point: he has had to exhibit all along the kind of honest courage that is required by plain and serious speech, tested by cross-examination and compared with the speaker's actual life-style. 'Don't get discouraged,' Euthyphro is told.[55] But there is keen embarrassment in being publicly convicted of ignorance and incoherence. At such a crossroads the interlocutor may turn left along a downhill road, speeding away from the serious process in which he was beginning to be involved. A witticism is the most gracious exit: it usually makes friends and effectively masks the absence of thought. A less elegant way is to attack Socrates and seek to discredit him. Finally one can always argue a previous commitment and excuse oneself. This is Euthyphro's way: he is not a clever man but he is not a snarling one either.

However, the interlocutor may choose to turn right, change mental gears, and take the uphill road, and then he can really start to learn. Not only may this happen, but most want it to happen. Socrates does believe that, on the whole, and in normal circumstances, the human mind wants to rise to more coherent and better, more tested views. In the end people want at least to appear to be in possession of a notion of what is good.[56] The successful turn to the right is usually made when the partner in a dialogue takes seriously a new hypothesis suggested by Socrates. Note that Socrates merely suggests the hypothesis at the appropriate moment. It raises the discussion to a new level only if the interlocutor sees some point in examining it. Socrates guides the thinking of the ignorant, but leaves the actual steps towards progress up to them. Through the new hypothesis Socrates suggests that, in order to answer the first question, another, more fundamental question must be settled. Does he thereby change the subject? No, but he does change the line of investigation. His new hypothesis is always broadly conceived in such a way that, if verified, it would indeed shed genuine light on the subject one started with. This move is not fully illustrated in *Euthyphro*. Euthyphro, as we have said, is too sure of his knowledge to be a willing pupil, open to a new hypothesis. Socrates, we may also suggest, was not at his best on the day of their encounter. We can nevertheless discern a fragment of this move when Socrates suggests that the question of piety is linked to the question of justice. This hypothesis merely opens up a new question: what is justice? which is as large a question as there is. But this new question is more embracing, and an answer to it would enable one to return to the question about pious behaviour with valid and applicable knowledge. Euthyphro, however, who is keen enough to try to walk this new road, actually turns in circles, since he makes piety the part of justice that has to do with service to the gods and returns to a previously contradicted affirmation – he makes the art of being just in relation to the gods the art of giving them what they like.

The turning to the road on the right is illustrated fully in *Phaedrus*, where Socrates changes the debate about whether a boy should yield to a lover or to a non-lover into a debate, not about the prudent managing of bodily pleasures, but about the true nature of love. Does true love, even if based on physical desire, transcend it or not?[57] An answer to that question, should we get one, would undoubtedly settle the dilemmas of adolescents approached by older men. But note that the raising of the discussion to the level of the superior hypothesis (our use of spatial metaphors should be shameless) provides one with an entirely different kind of answer. If one knows what true love is, the advice one gives to boys will no longer be based on pragmatic knowledge of what kind of activities are on the whole both pleasant and acceptable, but will be based on a truth of a different kind: a truth about human life in general, its nature and its purpose; a truth based on knowledge and not on an understanding of what common opinion says one can safely steer one's life by. By taking the road on the left the pupil remains at the level of a pastry cook who knows how to flatter the palate; by taking the one on the right he acquires the knowledge of a physician who knows what food is good for man.[58] The enquiry has started from the point of view of ordinarily accepted notions and the daily conduct of life; it arrives at the knowledge of the truth. Ever since A. Diès used the word 'transposition,' it has been the term employed to describe this art of shifting the question to another, better one.[59]

Phaedrus illustrates another important feature of Socrates' desire to effect the turn to the right. If one makes this turn, one learns about noble love, the love that deserves to be praised, or the one that brings beauty into life. If one turns to the left, not only does one not learn about love but one is tempted by all the vilifications of love. Such vilifications are common. Some people 'brought up among low sailors' have never seen 'a generous love.'[60] There is much vulgarity abroad in our society; more importantly, there is a propaganda that casts aspersion on all apparently noble and generous styles of life, saying that they are really only subtly masked forms of brutal self-interest. Socrates believes philosophy should put an end to such vilifications of virtues and the attending brutalization of life. He therefore wants to know what true piety is, or true justice, or true love. He believes human life can attain these virtues and will be better for it. He also believes his speech can show how to attain them and usher in our passage from the diseased to the good life. Note that Socrates thereby also claims to be able to cure language. His words are not mere sounds; on his lips a speech on love introduces a description of the real thing and un understanding of its nature. Thus Socrates claims to be able to arrive at a genuine 'science' of love that makes love possible and introduces the correct 'division,' showing, on the left, the vulgar love that needs to be censored and is hurtful to man (namely, the greedy behaviour that gets called love but does not deserve the name), and on the right, the noble love that is good and worthy of praise. One can surmise that to the one who knows piety there is both an impious piety that has only the appearance or reputation of piety and a genuine, good one.[61]

We must note, therefore, that in each dialogue Socrates demonstrates a certain firmness. He ferrets out any miscommunication. He sticks to the topic, persistently. He demands coherence. In some cases the flash between him and his interlocutor reveals deep moral and social conflicts behind the polite intellectual exchange: in *Gorgias* Callicles at one point makes a veiled threat. But, here again Socrates does not waver: he still thinks what he thinks; he still resists the vilification of the virtues; he still believes that real light is to be gained if one keeps on talking, and that all will be lost if one yields to the suggestion that the 'real' problem is elsewhere, in a power conflict, for instance. This firmness of Socrates and the quality of his moral resistance to anti-intellectual force have come to symbolize the courage of the philosopher, but they do impair his attractiveness to non-philosophers. He does not adhere to all the rules of polite discourse; he is too stubborn, always striving to bring the conversation back to the point.[62]

On the day of his trial the method that Socrates has developed in small encounters must meet a new challenge and adapt itself to an entirely different genre. Socrates, we have seen, must make a long speech to a crowd of five hundred jurors. Can his speech instruct his listeners on the distinction between the noble and the ignoble? Can he teach what genuine virtue is so that the members of the jury will be able to recognize it when they see it? Can he turn the desires of his listeners towards that which is genuinely good for Athens? One should expect Socrates by now to be familiar enough with his fellow Athenians and enough master of his skills to succeed in this task.

It seems that Socrates did not prepare his speech. Xenophon tells us that he was stopped by his divine sign and that he felt he had prepared his defence by being a good man all his life.[63] The sequence of speeches at the trial transmitted by Plato squares rather well with that. Dealing with the charge against him, Socrates states that he is not accustomed to court oratory and that he will tell the truth without art. He knows that he has a special wisdom; the Delphic oracle has confirmed that it consists in knowing he is ignorant. This special wisdom makes him hated since most people think they are wise. He avails himself of the right to cross-examine Meletus. Meletus comes out rather well; when he is asked what can educate the youth whom Socrates supposedly corrupts, he answers that the laws will, an answer which suits the ears of the jurors better than Socrates' abrupt declaration of his calling. Socrates rather bluntly puts his life before his judges and affirms that, throughout it all, he has remained faithful to the station the gods have assigned to him. He flings a sharp challenge: if he were to be offered acquittal provided he promised silence, his reply would be 'Men of Athens, I respect and love you, but I shall obey the gods rather than you. I shall never give up philosophy.' In the end he flaunts his uncompromising sense of what is right, honourable, and pious: 'I shall not bring any of my children here and put before you a pitiable scene; for the judge is not here to grant favours in matters of justice but to judge justly.'

Found guilty in the first vote, Socrates has the usual opportunity for a second speech in which he may suggest his own penalty. Anytus has requested death. Socrates, half in jest, rather thinks he deserves a pension from the city for the rest of his life since he needs leisure to exhort the Athenians. His friends apparently prevented him from making too ironic or flaunting an expression of his sense of philosophical vocation and, all jesting aside, he suggests a fine of thirty minae.

The second speech loses him some friends, for at the second vote there is a larger majority against him. A third speech is a valedictory. He lacks shamelessness and does not attempt to say what people want to hear. 'I much prefer to die after such a defence than to live after a defence of the other sort.' He adds: 'It is not hard to accept death; it is much harder to escape wickedness.' He has good hope: 'I go to die and you to live; but which of us goes to the better lot, is known to none but God.'

Was there something in Socrates that thought it would be demeaning, possibly dishonest, to try hard to persuade? Is Xenophon reliable when he attributes this saying to Socrates: 'Anyone who applies force merely discovers his rascality, but he who uses persuasion corrupts the soul of the one upon whom he prevails'?[64] Socrates' uncompromising stand has become a classic of ringing integrity. But since there was humility in him, how was it that mainly arrogance was expressed? He knew how to reproach kindly; why did he have to insult as well? and insult his judges as well as his accusers?

The seriousness of the clash between Socrates and his city appears in its full light only when we realize that Anytus was not a hysterical villain. A.E. Taylor has rightly emphasized that Anytus had no unworthy motive but wanted to consolidate the peace under a democracy, and he certainly expected Socrates to trim his sail or, if he was condemned, to run for his life. The jury, Taylor adds, showed, if anything, liberality of mind.[65] Socrates, however, proved cantankerous and must have struck any reasonable man on the jury as behaving rather rudely. In his speech most references to his principles were accompanied by some unyielding comment that was offensive to the public meeting.

On the day of the trial it became clear that the position of the city and that of Socrates were not reconcilable. As long as Socrates was on the streets, he could believe that, however much they might differ, the city would tolerate him. As he spoke before his jurors, it became increasingly clear that he would have to be defiant and that they would have to condemn him. According to some, Socrates was too lucid: he died, says Goldschmidt, because no society can bear people who force it to live according to its ideology.[66] Hegel took another view and spoke on behalf of the city: the individualism of Socrates was not exploitative but it too dissolved the social bonds that existed then. The city had to defend itself against it.[67] Socrates, we must agree, was not like Euthyphro, just a member of a quaint minority. The power of his mind made him more dangerous. He was clearly subversive. His love for the city was too ironic not to hurt that very city. His death merely climaxed this paradox. he was a conformist but a subversive one. His total loyalty to the laws of his city forbade him to attempt to escape the execution. Such attempts were commonly expected, tolerated, and even encouraged. Friends of Socrates worked out a plan for him to escape but he refused to go. So Socrates did not disobey the laws, a disobedience which would have left their majesty untouched. He obeyed the laws, but his obedience broke their back because it exposed their corruption, and the corruption of those who applied them. We may also point out that Socrates, who was unconditionally faithful to all the rites of traditional religion, was also the one who, by the firmness of his stand, shattered the fundamental principle of that religion, namely the sacredness of the city's traditions as the very voice of the gods.

4 What shall the next steps be?

We have almost completed the characterization of the encounter between philosophy and religion that can be drawn from Plato's *Euthyphro* and the life of Socrates. At this point I should like to summarize our findings thus far and indicate what steps are next suggested by the stage that has been reached in the meeting between philosophy and religion.

A summary first. Euthyphro and Socrates inquire about a matter of daily practical interest: what is the pious thing to do? or what is piety? They inquire mostly about a quality in actions and in persons; what it is that causes a course of actions or causes a man to be called genuinely pious. Philosophy of religion starts by being concerned about orthopraxy, that is good life-style, not orthodoxy or sound belief. Religion being what it is today, we should also add that it is not concerned with orthophrony either, that is the soundness of internal attitudes or dispositions. This philosophy is concerned with a problem of the moral agents, not of the moral judge or critic. It asks: 'how is a man to achieve his true moral stature?' not 'how can people who make moral judgments establish the truth of their statements?'[68] Cicero has clearly expressed this quality which classical philosophy has inherited from Socrates: 'Philosophy, to interpret the word, is nothing else but the pursuit of wisdom; and wisdom, as the old philosophers defined it, consists of knowledge of things divine and human, and of the causes by which these things are maintained.'[69] This philosophy is interested in words, but only to the extent to which they enable us to find our bearings among the world of things divine and human.

The secret of how to maintain things divine and human is a matter of urgency because these things are threatened by crisis and decay. When philosophy meets religion, the city is in crisis and a dissension over religion is part of it. Euthyphro is sure he has found an answer to the malaise over religion, but Euthyphro's diagnosis and his cure are not very bright. Religion, with only the likes of him to help it, is clearly in need of further light. Without such a deficiency in the tradition there would hardly be any vacuum for philosophy to grow into. The philosopher, as he arrives on the scene, sees that people need to become more moral and that society needs to be reformed. He thinks he has on these points something to teach the religious spokesman. Therefore he is not a religious philosopher, that is someone who draws upon the wisdom of the tradition and couches it in philosophical language. The young philosopher of religion is nevertheless confident that he can arrive at an understanding with the religious man. The philosopher is pious and wishes to take the turn to the right and learn to praise true piety; the religious man need not be alarmed by his independent pretension. But such a move does mean that philosophy takes the initiative in the dialogue, although it does it with the interests of both religion and philosophy in mind. (We shall have to wait until St Augustine for a theologian who meets the philosophers on their own ground, who knows enough philosophy to take the initiative with them and tend to the interests of religion and of philosophy as a theologian sees them.)

Such are the features of the first encounter between philosophy and religion. It is not clear how much Socrates learned from his encounter with Euthyphro or from similar encounters. What is clear is that he did not learn enough to make a successful speech to his jurors. He was sentenced to death and chose not to take any of the escapes available to him. He decided to obey the laws of the city and drink the hemlock. This turn of events is not irrelevant to our inquiry about piety. Discussing Socrates' own religion, we have quoted texts from his defence before the court and from his conversation in jail: they show Socrates assured enough of his divinely inspired vocation to walk an unwavering line. At this point he had no doubts about what was the pious thing, and he was confident that his behaviour exhibited it. His death was thus also a commentary on Euthyphro and his like: they were friends of Socrates and meant to help him. They were probably part of the large minority in the assembly that voted for his acquittal. But their support, for some reason or other, was not vigorous enough and not effective. *Euthyphro* and the *Apology* thus complement each other. While Meletus came from the party of traditional religion to accuse Socrates (admittedly steered and manipulated by cleverer men), these other religious spokesmen who admired Socrates remained powerless, incapable of rescuing him from his enemies. The intellectual incoherence and bankruptcy of traditional religion are exposed in *Euthyphro*. Euthyphro was not permeable to Socratic influence. The events narrated in the *Apology* demonstrate the moral bankruptcy of the traditional religious ethos, or at least its powerlessness in moral crises. It could not curb evil men.[70]

This at any rate seems to have been the conclusion of Plato. We must now turn to him since it was left to him to take the next steps in the intellectual course we are interested in charting. Plato started by ruminating over Socrates' death and concluded that it put a seal on the diagnosis of a moral decay in Athens. However glorious may be Athens's past and however excellent its institutions, Athens in full daylight committed 'the judicial murder of the man most just.' Socrates was a patriotic honest man who was confident that his city would let him pursue his intellectual interests as a private man, allowing him at least there to be true to himself.[71] Plato knew better: the city killed Socrates.

This Platonic severity appears at many points. Socrates had doubts about the Sophists; Plato clearly sees in them a major source of the disease of the city. Plato has also decided that no class in Athens is exempt from the corruption. We know that, in addition to the articulate or baffled intellectuals (Thrasymachus, Callicles, Euthyphro, Polemarchus, Glaucon, etc), there were in Athens many ordinary men who distrusted all these intellectuals and trusted in the wisdom of menfolk who do not talk much. Anytus, for instance, in *Meno* speaks of the ordinary common sense of the Athenians: 'Any Athenian gentleman he comes across, without exception, will do a boy more good if he will do as he is bid than the Sophists.'[72] This trust in the common sense of the people is shattered by the verdict of the assembly, filled as it is with ordinary people, the very people who in the words of Thucydides are best at deciding after having heard both sides.[73] Socrates had doubted that such deep-seated wisdom existed in the wider classes of society. He actually said so to his jurors: 'The good artisans who also seem to me to have the same failing as the poets (that is lack of wisdom); because of practising his art well, each one thought he was very wise in the other most important matters.'[74]

Plato's verdict is therefore final. The city, and especially Athens, cannot possibly be the measure of all things. Plato agrees that Socrates has demonstrated that 'doing as one pleases' is not the road to full human stature and the attainment of human excellence. Socrates' death has also demonstrated that doing as Athens pleases, or assimilating oneself to Athens and becoming a loyal member of the commonwealth, cannot be the answer either. Note that this conclusion is formulated at a time when already two or three generations have been taught to see in 'the glory of Athens' a political objective that tolerates no opposition. Two forms of obedience to Athens and its ways have to be rejected. The quiet conformists bring themselves down to the level of vulgarity and immorality of the masses and share in their sins of omission. The shrewd, ambitious conformists exploit the masses whose prejudices they flatter and they become guilty of sins of commission. In both cases Athens is the authority that can do no wrong. Thus the disciples of Socrates, after learning that they should suspect their selfish individualistic impulses, have to learn that loyalty to the city of one's fathers is in its way another source of evil. As Plato is to put it, in this world appearances (*to dokein*) are stronger than truth and they determine our worldly fate. To feast our eyes upon the truth, our eyes must turn away from the city: 'the plains of truth' are elsewhere. [75]

We realize that Plato may have overdramatized his analysis of the death of Socrates (and that our account of the whole story may have inherited this flaw from Plato). We must take note of Ian Crombie's conclusion to his discussion of Plato's diagnosis of Athenian democracy: 'Probably Plato was mistaken in this estimate of Athenian democracy; probably the Athenians were more sensible than either he or Socrates realized. The truth may be that neither of them understood the gradual and frustrating pace of progress in public affairs and that both of them were too inclined to treat every setback to common sense as the final triumph of folly.' [76] This indeed may be true. Aristocratic taste and moral indignation make too easy an alliance in Plato not to be suspect. But to such a train of thought we can answer that the Greek city as a political form did die about a century after Socrates was put to death and after Plato and others pronounced it sick. And even if the judicial error of 399 was more a blot on the copybook of the Athenians than a symbol of their moral decadence, it still remains that such blots should be fussed over. I shall therefore let a threefold lesson stand. In the Athens of 399 honest men like Euthyphro are aware of injustices and are confused by conflicting notions of justice or bodies of law (*dikai*); only dogmatism extricates such men from confusion. Socrates rises a step above this and sees that the question to be asked is about justice itself (*dike* in the singular). Plato then, along with Socrates in his last days, sees that this inquiry is a most practical one: the city is so steeped in injustice that it is not worth living in – and literally for some, cannot be lived in – until the question of justice is solved.

Socrates' death thus reinforced in Plato's mind the more pessimistic side of the Socratic lesson about the state of things in Athens. The work of Plato's life was the founding of a school: the creation of a small, protected environment where philosophical practice could go on. [77] Much in Plato was concerned to protect the memory of his great teacher, to maintain the practice of his art, and to continue the resistance offered by this great soul to the disorder in society. We can best understand Plato's distinctive effort if we realize that in 399 he is still a young man with his life before him. He undertakes a second assault on the corruption of Athens in the spirit of his teacher and has the time and the energy to marshall more in the attempt – more weapons, more remedies, more science, more wisdom, more men dedicated to the same task.[78] We shall not be far wrong if we picture Plato as trying to cast a larger net and cast it wider in his search for the cure that Socrates was trying to find. After all, Socrates, who excelled in bringing a few individuals to a sense of what virtue is, had totally failed when he had to address the masses. That he could not educate them was bad enough but could be lived with; that he did not persuade them to tolerate him was worse. One must try to do better than he. Plato has a few advantages Socrates did not have: time first, and the knowledge of hindsight; also money and family connections.

We can add that, while both wanted to teach Athens, Plato was less wedded to the city, more alienated from it. That Socrates chose death in his city rather than escape has always been a puzzle. Xenophon's explanation that Socrates realized that such old age as naturally remained to him would be filled with infirmities and devoid of any pleasure has convinced no one.[79] Aristotle in similar circumstances did not hesitate a moment. He left the intellectual centre of the world, announcing that he would not let Athens sin twice against philosophy. Moses and Muhammad, admittedly young men then, also left the metropolis when they found no hearing in it, and went into a cultural desert, where they did find people who listened. Perhaps Socrates was for all his independence still too caught in the value-system of the city to think of exile as a fresh start. But Plato, I suspect, would have run. The search for a solution would in his case prevail over the desire to apply it right away to the city of his birth. He had grown detached enough from Athens to seize the opportunity to try his solution in Syracuse. This however did not make Plato a rootless Sophist, ready to peddle his merchandise anywhere; he built his school in the city of his birth.

Moreover, Plato made a larger effort than Socrates in the sense that he tried to engage in politics. Socrates spoke in this way to his jurors: 'You know full well gentlemen that if long ago I had tried to engage in politics I should have been executed long ago and of no use either to you or to myself.'[80] The casualty rate among politicians in the generation of Socrates was very high so his abstention from politics when he was young was his way of not counting his life cheap. Plato, like his teacher, knew that politics are difficult in a mad world. What is one to do if one is unwilling to join others while they do wrong, yet is powerless to oppose their savagery alone or with such friends as one has, and unwilling to meet a quick death?[81] But Plato tried harder to learn such shrewdness as is necessary to good men who want to reform their world. He tried to pierce and master the secrets of the art of power. Here Plato was like Thucydides: born in a family accustomed to rule, he felt he must learn to grasp large events. He tried to fathom such rules as there may be in mass behaviour and social evolution. The social critic was therefore also a social observer and even a theorist. One has difficulty imagining Socrates reading the first histories: what good is there in reading about others when one does not even know oneself? Plato clearly read Herodotus and Thucydides and tried to refine the art of passing philosophical and moral judgments on the events that shake cities and empires.

Finally, Plato attempted to bring the resources of the religious tradition more fully to the help of the philosopher reasoning with his city. Plato and Socrates shared the notion that those forces which ruined myths and dissolved the society that got its order from them must be checked and that a norm must be found for these new 'rational' forces. Both agreed also that Euthyphro's reinstatement of some old myths by investing them with absolute value was not the answer. The order of society cannot be based on the facts and precedents of the past, even precedents with mythical authority. Socrates therefore did not share in the dissolving of myths. Although he clearly implied that the destruction of myths should stop, the evidence is that he did not tell myths.[82] Plato frequently did. Socrates discerned many of the flaws of the new enlightenment but he was still wedded to many of its thought forms: questioning, in particular. Plato wielded irony more prudently. In Plato, as K. Jaspers puts it, we see the first great movement of thought against the dangers and falsification of enlightenment.[83] There was in him a fairly conscious return to those things which the enlightenment had discredited; myths are but one example. We have already referred to his sense that truth is elsewhere. Here Plato was unlike Thucydides: he was also looking for the divine truth as well as for the truth which is accessible to intelligent observers of the ways of power among men. He wanted to dig deep into the ways of Athens, but he wanted also to rise above them. Plato, writes U. Wilamowitz-Moellendorf, was the first to realize that a new religion and a new social order were necessary. He also saw that the two go together.[84] I hasten to add that Plato was not a Euthyphro who shies away before Socratic reasoning. As Jaspers puts it, Plato proposed to overcome the weakness of the enlightenment by way of increased enlightenment.

So Plato, like other disciples of Socrates, tries to transcend the limitations of his master. Socrates after all, symbol of philosophy though he was, was also an idle urban Athenian, a son of a stonemason, who had seen active service in the Peloponnesian War and who spent his later life in the streets and the market-place. It was not hard for his disciples to have a broader experience: Xenophon, for instance, soldiered as an officer and he can speak well of marriage and praise rural life. We must not be surprised that Plato goes farther than his teacher. For example, nobody ever imagined Socrates educating a woman, but Plato had two female pupils in the Academy.

Thus we can imagine the mature Plato making a rather different speech to the assembly had he been in Socrates' position. Socrates after all did not reason very much with his accusers and jurors. Plato, a poet, did not share such diffidence, though it is a good antidote to the excesses of rhetoric, and he tried to find the rules of a higher, proper, healthier rhetoric. We can thus picture him using the full range of arguments appealing to all that was best in his audience. He would leave no stone unturned in the attempt to make goodness and virtue win votes in this world as well as being acknowledged the supreme authority in the next. His speech would aim at a reconciliation among all genuine values. Paradoxically, Plato, who thought worse of Athens, would try harder to appeal to it and would attempt to do more than merely proclaim to it – or flaunt before it – his sense of vocation.[85]

We should also imagine Plato preparing himself differently for that speech. His philosophy of religion in particular will be part and parcel of his search for this better-remedying speech that will reconcile all conflicts of values and all divisions among men. For religion nurtures the roots of the deepest choices of values. Socrates spoke to Euthyphro, and conversations with Diotima and Cephalus are also reported. One must picture Plato more busily hunting up such remnants of ancients religious wisdom as may be found. In the *Meno* he has Socrates refer to the doctrine of the immortality of the soul as something he has 'heard from wise men and women who told of things divine.'[86] (*Meno* is the first of the middle dialogues; we can safely hear in it Plato's distinctive voice.) If the *Letters* are right, Plato went to Italy to learn what there was to be learned from the Pythagoreans. One can safely affirm that the Orphic cycle of beliefs held some appeal to him.[87] Whether he ever went to Egypt (or heard about India) is probably forever doubtful, but there is ample documentation that the Academy was at the centre of a very strong interest in the Orient and had access to adequate information about it. Eudoxus, a friend of Plato's and an astronomer, had made inquiries during his sojourn in the East.[88] I do not wish to suggest that these new areas are in any way an important philosophical source for Plato. His basic ontology remains within the framework set by the conflict between Parmenides on the one and Heraclitus on the many. He clearly does not consider Pythagoreanism a philosophy.[89] But he does have a passionate curiosity for – and a desire to penetrate into – non-philosophical realities. Plato's texts themselves show him delving deep into the imagery of various religious traditions. P.M. Schuhl can document religious antecedents for most of the imagery of the parable of the cave – the theatre, the shadows, the light, the dazzlement, the conversion, and of course the cave itself.[90]

As he casts a wider net, Plato nevertheless keeps going in the same direction as Socrates. With the hindsight of one who saw Socrates condemned he tries to fathom the nature of a crisis that is both deep and wide. To call it a crisis in the transmission of the paradigms of culture is to give it a good label; it does not, however, provide a solution. Along with Socrates, Plato keeps on asking for precise definitions. He wants to know what piety, or courage, or justice truly is. But he also wants to understand – and reorient – the process of *paideia* among ordinary Greeks. And this leads him into an investigation of what we would now call their religion. Provisionally I shall take the problem to be this: how can a philosopher strive to maintain – or renew – a widespread sense of piety, that inner sense of restraint or of obligation without which there is no moderation and no health in the human handling of human affairs? The unsolved questions of *Euthyphro* and *Apology* remain on Plato's agenda. These texts come to a conclusion but only as texts. Plato's thinking does not stop there. What is piety? How can we stop impious men? How can we be sure that the city will never again sentence and execute a man most just? What is justice? To give up on the search for piety would be to hand the victory over to the men who killed Socrates.[91]

My point, thus, is that the project in philosophy that Plato pursued after 399 involves what is commonly called philosophizing on religion. He wanted to rethink the opinions Greeks shared, or disputed, about the world or man's place in it. He came to discuss specifically, and at length, the role of poetry in shaping these opinions and the moral impact that these opinions can be shown to have. But underlying these discussions there is a concern about the piety that is characteristic of good human beings who seek to understand the world and the other human beings around them. In other words the inquiry barely begun in *Euthyphro* is not an opening of little subsequent significance. We are left with the inquiry unresolved in this dialogue but we can stay with the questions.

Our task is thus mapped out for chapters 4 and 5. We must first examine the doctrine of forms, which in Plato's eyes is the direct correlate of the philosophical practice as exemplified and understood by Socrates. And we must then examine Plato's relationship to that complex reality, the Greek religious tradition. Chapters 6 to 9 will go on to examine Plato's actual performance as he philosophizes on religion.

4

The question is the existence of forms

I A definition of philosophy

A look at the doctrine of forms or ideas forces us to acknowledge the existence of what is commonly known as the Socratic problem: how can one sort out the statements admiring disciples put into Socrates' mouth from those the historical Socrates actually made? So far in my exposition I have been able to avoid the more difficult aspects of this problem. Every time I have spoken of Socrates, I have been referring to the Athenian who began to talk in the streets of his city around 440 BC and died in 399. The ideas I have attributed to Plato or 'the mature Plato' are those of a pupil of Socrates who began to write around 395 BC and died around 348. One is able to distinguish between the views of the one and those of the other on the basis of what is now a widely shared consensus about the relationship (continuity and differences) between the two thinkers. But as we turn to the doctrine of forms, we move onto shakier ground. We find scholars who with A.E. Taylor and J. Burnet do not hesitate to attribute the full doctrine found in Plato's dialogues to the historical Socrates, but we find others who cannot accept that a patently metaphysical doctrine could possibly have been taught by the man who proclaimed he knew nothing. In this case, too, the boat is probably best handled if rowed from the middle, but where the middle is may not be easy to find. In this chapter I shall continue to speak now of Socrates and now of Plato but the reader should realize that here my attributions are more tentative.

What is known as the question about forms makes its appearance when Socrates asks Euthyphro 'what sort of thing do you say the pious and the impious are?' He clarifies his meaning in this way: 'is not the pious always the same in every action, itself by itself? and is not the impious the opposite of everything pious, always the same with itself; and does not that which is impious possess a certain single characteristic of impiety?'[1] This question, to which Socrates returns whenever necessary, provides the topic for the dialogue. Socrates wants to know what is the form or idea of piety, that is that which makes all pious acts pious. The Greek *to eidos*, which some translate as 'form' and others 'idea,' may in this context also be translated by 'characteristic.' Socrates wants to know 'the very characteristic thanks to which all pious things are pious.'[2] The asking of this question lies at the very core of all Socratic philosophizing. If we understand what kind of inquiry is started by a question like this, we shall understand what philosophy is and know what intellectual activity is proper to it or is the common feature found in all its plural pursuits.

The point may also be made by saying that an understanding of forms will indicate to us what definition of philosophy Plato inherited from Socrates. We strike a new note by raising the matter of the *definition* of philosophy. So far we have presented a portrait of philosophy. Such a portrait can create in us an interest in philosophy. Seeing Socrates at work started Plato on his way. Plato even came to picture Socrates as a symbol or embodiment of philosophy. But one needs more than a taste through symbols to be able to philosophize on one's own. One must arrive at a grasp of the one plain, single thing philosophy is all about. One must see at what point Socrates moves beyond brooding over problems, or turning them over in his head (something human beings had done for a long time), and starts formulating a precise philosophical question. Such a grasp we might have if we were to say that philosophy consists in a search for forms. Such a definition Socrates might well have given if he could ever depart from irony and from teasing his interlocutors on the subjects that are most dear to him. Only some such understanding can at any rate prevent the pupil of Socrates from becoming a mere slavish imitator. To be a philosophical disciple of Socrates one must be able to tell which of the many features of his mind and of the many facets of his life are essential to his vocation and activity as a philosopher, and which are only secondary, however interesting and endearing they remain. One must also be able to tell, among all the things that are obviously important to Socrates, which are properly philosophical and which, while equally worthwhile, are not philosophical in nature but rather, for instance, religious. Such are the issues involved in Plato's and in our own attempt to grasp what Socrates is after when he asks the kind of question that is most typical of him – what is piety itself?[3]

2 What are forms?

Socrates asks about *to hosion*, which we have translated as 'the pious' or 'piety.' This kind of phrase, a neuter adjective with the article, has an interesting history in the Greek language. It is most common in Plato, where we hear also of *to kalon*, 'the beautiful,' and of *to dikaion*, 'the just.' Such phrases were of relatively recent usage. Hesiod, who has a lot to say on justice, never uses the phrase *to dikaion*, 'the just.' He uses the neuter adjective without the article to refer to 'a just act' and frequently uses *ta dikaia* to speak of 'the series of individual just acts.'[4] This last form, the neuter plural with the article, has been frequently used by Greeks groping towards abstract conceptions to denote a group or family of things which share in common some characteristic. *Ta theia*, 'the divine things,' is a common phrase for referring to all matters of concern to gods or to man in his relationship to the gods. It is a Greek antecedent or near-equivalent of our general notion of 'religion.' Euthyphro uses this phrase and claims to be an expert in precisely these matters.[5] The neuter singular represents a further step in the move towards abstract thinking. As R.E. Allen points out, it has three uses. It can refer to some particular pious course of action: it means then the pious thing to be done (or that was done) in this case. It can be used generically to speak of the group of those things that are pious, in which case it is equivalent to *ta hosia* (to which Socrates also refers in *Euthyphro*).[6] Finally, and this is the most interesting usage, it can be used as an abstract noun, 'piety,' or, to use a clumsy phrase, 'the pious.' In this case it is equivalent to the noun *hosiotes* (which Socrates also introduces in *Euthyphro* as an apparent equivalent to the *to hosion* which has been used all along).[7] This abstract noun can take on a very general meaning: it suddenly moves far beyond piety as a quality of pious persons; it can mean 'holiness' as a quality found in sacred objects or 'the holy' as a quality common to temples, divine beings, religious laws and customs, and good, pious people. The same is also true of *ta hosia*, which can mean sacred laws and rituals as well as the kind of acts pious people do. But while an inquiry about *to hosion* would in Greece branch into all these realms of discourse, it still remains that as a religious expert or theologian Euthyphro says he knows all about *ta theia*, divine matters. When he claims specifically to know *to hosion*, he means that he can show what is the religiously appropriate or pious course of action.[8]

Socrates asks Euthyphro 'what is piety?' because he does not wish to start talking with him about it unless he knows what they are to talk about. A measure of agreement on the nature of piety seems to him to be necessary for any intelligent exchange of ideas on pious and related matters. As he puts it at the very end of *Meno* after a discussion bearing on whether virtue is a divine dispensation or not, 'before asking in what way virtue comes to mankind we must set about enquiring what virtue is, in and by itself.'[9] This pedestrian point often needs to be made, since men who are quick to disagree about things are often slow to discover that they are not disagreeing about the same thing at all but rather have entirely different ideas of what topic they are addressing themselves to.[10] Euthyphro is sure he knows what he is talking about. 'Piety is what I am doing just now,'[11] he answers by way of an example. He is just like Hippias who answered the query 'what is the beautiful?' by saying 'a pretty girl.'[12] Both are quick off the mark, having achieved certainty in the matters which interest them most, be it pollution laws or pretty girls. Socrates shows both that an example, or even a long series of examples, is not the answer to his question. He wants to know 'the form' of piety (or of beauty.) It turns out that Socrates wants thereby to know three kinds of things. He wants to know a *universal*; namely he wants to be told the characteristic feature which is the same in every pious action. Such a question moves from asking 'what do all pious things look like?' to 'what is *it* they look like?' – a rather natural transition which, however, introduces a new component, namely the 'it' in the 'what is it?' Socrates also wants to know a *standard*, which would enable him to sort out pious behaviour from impious behaviour. 'Tell me now then what this one characteristic is, so that keeping my eye fixed upon it and using it as a model, I will be able to say whatever is done by you or somebody else and is of this sort is pious, and whatever is not of this sort, is impious.'[13] Finally he wants to known an *essence*, namely the nature of piety when pure, unmixed, by itself, in and of itself. Such essence is to be distinguished from properties which are connected with pious behaviour.[14] By asking to know the form of piety Socrates is seeking to have as perfect, as complete, and as definitive a definition of piety as he can conceive.

That Socrates means all this when he asks about forms can, I think, be assumed. True, his vocabulary does not include technical terms for universals or essences, but since he repeatedly asks questions about them, we can safely conclude that he knows what he is after, and that he does not merely hit unknowingly upon a notion that is named and really grasped only after him. (Let us remember that Socrates and Plato, for all their cultivation of clear speech, do not put their trust in technical language in the way many philosophers have done since Aristotle.) Following R.E. Allen's conclusive study, we can go a little further and affirm that Socrates, even though he does not have the distinction in those terms either, wants a real definition, not a nominal definition, of piety.

A nominal definition states what piety is by referring to how the word 'piety' is ordinarily used. Piety, then, is what people commonly mean by the word. Or a nominal definition can also be a warning about the meaning the author will attach to the word when he uses it, or a prescription stating how he wishes the word to be used. It is, in either case, a definition of a word. A real definition purports to say what piety *really* is. Armed with this knowledge, we should be able to say whether words are correctly used or not by making a reference, not to social custom or personal intention, but to that which is. There is, it is assumed, in the overall order or economy of the world, room for something like piety which is also unlike anything else. The task of the philosopher in this case is to find what this room is and thus to know what piety is like (or to know what is missing from somebody's understanding of the world, if he does not know what piety is). Definition, if real, will do just that. All definitions focus mental activity and 'slice up' reality. A real definition assures us that the world is not like a piece of cheese that can be carved in a variety of appropriate ways but like a fowl that has articulations demanding mental attention from the carver.[15]

The point may also be made that the real definition purports to say what ideal piety is. The use of the adjective 'ideal,' however, is misleading because it may cast doubt in modern minds upon the reality of this 'ideal' piety. The real definition purports to say what real piety is, and real piety is conceived as something existing independently of the human aspirations to piety or human shortcomings in the area of piety. Socrates sets out to know what piety truly is so as to know the differences between piety and impiety, or between piety and the impiety which succeeds in taking the appearance and winning the reputation of piety.

Finally Socrates also plans to reform the use of the word 'piety' so that the term shall be applied only to the genuine thing. We must emphasize that his plan for reform, according to him, is not based either on those usages in our society which best succeed in achieving communication or on his own private vision. To be worth anything – in his terms – his definition of piety must be rooted in something permanent, objective, and universally accessible (like the world, or the human condition, or being itself). This is what it means to say that his definition must be based on the essence of piety. His use of words is to be grounded in the characteristics of things. To him, and to Euthyphro, there is such a thing as piety. There always was and always will be. One's task in pious matters is to conform to it. Piety to them is not an idea, in the sense of something people have in their heads. It is not an ideal, in the sense of a desirable thing people strive after. To say it is an essence rejects these two possibilities. Essences already exist before we think of them. Euthyphro has some sense of this when he allows that the pious is loved by the gods because it is pious, not pious because it is loved.[16] The pious is 'there,' so to speak, before the gods, not to mention human beings, make their affective choices. Jean-Yves Chateau writes that one must be summoned by forms before one can rise to a knowledge of them.[17] R.E. Allen puts it in another way: the forms 'do honest work' or 'affect the career of the world.' Socrates and Euthyphro agree that true piety exists somewhere in the world, although Socrates is not sure where he can find it. If the form of piety did not exist, 'the world would not be what it is.'[18]

We might also add that, if the forms did not exist, there would not be genuinely pious men, or genuinely pious men would not be what we ordinarily think they are. Genuine virtue to Socrates is not a self-ascribed or a socially recognized quality. It is a real quality. The difference between pious and impious has to do with reality or with facts that are not just social facts.[19] What is piety, what is justice, are not matters that can *really* be settled by a court. That one man is wiser or more virtuous than another is not a matter of opinion, but depends on what one might call, for emphasis, an *objective* reality.[20] The virtuous man, or the pious one, is healthier: he alone embodies or realizes something that is present in the economy of the world, in the potential of human beings. When somebody is said to be just, what matters is not who says it, or why, but whether what is said is true.[21] The truth of the statement depends on whether the man in question embodies the form of justice or not. And that is something for philosophy to settle.

This understanding of forms entails, need we say, a pretty sizeable claim about what intellectual activity and philosophical discussion in particular can achieve. It means that the mind can grasp the truth and that words can convey it. 'If we address people scientifically we shall show them the real and true nature of the object we talk about.'[22] And we shall be able to tie down an argument to something secure.[23] Since there are forms, the quibbling can stop.

Such a position, of course, is metaphysical in that it entails a claim *to know what really is*. Knowledge is still seen as a necessary ingredient in virtue; knowledge however is no longer know-how, specialized technical skill that can resolve 'a problem.' Knowledge is now seen as knowledge of the whole. A whole, the whole, all that is, starts being constituted in some philosophical minds as the totality of that which is susceptible of being known. Man is thereby asked always to remember that there is in the matter being considered a reality about which either he knows or fails to know, as the case may be.[24] Potential objects of knowledge are sharply differentiated from the Cyclopes, on the subject of which Thucydides said that we must rest content with what the poets have said and with the opinions of individuals about the matter.[25] Words, then, either are correctly related to such objects or they are not. If correctly related, words hang together to give an enduring account, an account I can defend fully with reference to the actualities of the case and of the whole.[26]

Such a position differs sharply from the teaching of practically all the Sophists, who were, as we have seen, conventionalists and believed that words are properly used when they are made to say what most people use them for. This position, however, also cuts against the unthinking dogmatism of a Euthyphro. It is just not possible to use a myth to nail down, so to speak, a word that, like 'piety,' has an elusive meaning. The negative spirit of the conventionalist is here an ally of the philosopher against the dogmatist: both seek to wrench the self free from such adherence to entrenched myths. Private language is not healthy language. P. Friedländer attributes to Euthyphro a threefold error: he makes a formal mistake in definition and refuses to see the point of a real definition; he exhibits an egocentric arrogance in giving himself as the measure of all piety; and he appeals to a pernicious myth.[27] All the errors are linked: he dogmatically tries to freeze language and rejects the endeavour of reason to establish its proper use through the discovery of forms. Individual firmness of conviction is not a path to the correct use of words. When it comes to guaranteeing truth, psychological mechanisms are no better than social ones.

3 What if forms do not exist?

Such was, we believe, the seeking of forms that Plato learned from Socrates. But Plato begins to see problems just at those points where his teacher arrived at a solution.

First of all Plato sees logical difficulties in a notion of forms that *exist* – or had such difficulties pointed out to him. Where are these forms? In what sense can they be said to be? Is there a form for each Greek word? One for 'Socrates' as well as for 'man'? is there a form for 'cat,' 'justice,' 'evil,' and 'chaos'? What is the relationship among forms that have a family resemblance, such as piety, justice, temperance, wisdom, courage? Are all the forms of the virtues subordinate to the form of virtue? Can we perhaps put *all* the forms in a hierarchy? Furthermore, if a definition is to be universally valid, it must be a definition of a constant reality. Where do we draw the line between those realities which are abiding and thus can be defined properly, and those that are not and thus can be exemplified only in a vague sort of a way by looking at the flux of changing things?

These are real difficulties and Plato seeks to meet them, either by refuting the objections or by making modifications in the doctrine of forms he has developed. This leads him to write the most technical passages in his works. Through it all, however, he keeps returning to talk of two worlds, one the Heraclitean world of flux and appearance (where everything changes) and the other the Parmenidean world of abiding reality where the forms endure. In the end, I think, he has to take it on trust that people will *see* the forms, and see the point of there being forms.[28] This is the time to recall the anecdote narrated by Simplicius: 'he who has no eye for the form,' said Plato, 'could not be made to see it even by a Lynceus.'[29] Jacob Klein, I might add, has managed to translate and discuss Plato using the English word 'look,' never the pseudo-Latin term 'form,' or the English word 'idea' with its seventeenth-century connotation.[30]

The forms in fact met with another kind of attack, a more serious one than any of the logical difficulties mentioned so far or even all of them taken collectively. That attack came from a scepticism that doubted what Socrates and Euthyphro never hesitated to take for granted, namely that there is such a thing as piety. This scepticism moved beyond the common-sense attitude that believed that piety is piety is piety.[31] It doubted as well that any purpose was served by trying to ascertain what virtue really is or by trying to be the kind of philosopher Socrates was. Such sceptics allowed that pleasure is pleasure and money is money but they did not allow that love is love. They also announced that after surveying all the alleged embodiments of piety they found nothing but sick clinging to outdated traditional notions, hypocritical attempts to be respectable, romantic attachments to illusion, quirks of behaviour, priestly greed, and popular superstition. All cases of piety are mere masks for something else: the stupid or intelligent pursuit of one's interest as one sees it, atavistic behaviour, or calculated hypocrisy. And these sceptics held similar views on all alleged exemplifications of justice, or temperance, or courage. Socrates got onto the track of forms because he wanted to know what these virtues are, and because he assumed that they are an abiding reality. But whether virtue exists at all was questioned – and denied – by currish men.

Now Plato's point is, first, that these men make up a party and have a doctrine. They are not just a group of people who like to think critically. Nor are they just a group of people who practise selfish individualism: they believe that selfish individualism is all there is. Their doctrine is quite coherent. They always practise the sort of argument that 'pays no more heed to the noble than the ignoble.'[32] They teach, for instance, that people cultivate virtue because the appearance of it is rewarding, but that of course there is no such thing as virtue by itself, capable of exposing fraudulent virtue and vindicating the genuine one. Forms do not exist. All talk of virtue is merely the strategy of individual desire trying to pass itself off as obedience to a universal norm. Xenophanes had teased anthropomorphic representations of God by saying that Negroes believed in flat-nosed, black-faced gods and Thracians in gods with blue eyes and red hair.[33] This lesson is twisted to teach that *all* talk about virtues is merely propaganda. No aspect of life escapes from the touch of this doctrine. These men develop a 'scientific' explanation for everything. They teach that works of art are an investment, that love is a name for a physical instinct and the pleasure of (fleeting) possession, that piety is 'really' a feeling born of fear, that justice is 'only' successful moral propaganda from the strong, that telling the truth is the 'policy' one should praise in all circumstances and observe only when it is the best policy. These men subscribe to what might be called the ideology of pan-domination: all relationships are power relationships. Their views can draw on the prestige of 'recent scientific findings' and are very quickly grasped. Their speeches are erroneous but have a simplicity that is refreshing.[34]

Plato begins by clearly identifying these men as a party. He puts the giants of the Sophistic era back on the stage – recalling them from the dead – to show clearly the source of this thinking. His major dialogues are repeated assaults on the doctrine of these men. Enjoy the world, they say; get what you want. Use the appearances; concern yourself with the truth only to the extent necessary to your purpose. Their doctrine, Plato argues, negates the very point of philosophy. Such men might accordingly be called nihilists. Many young men are drawn to their message: once they discover that saying what any virtue consists of is difficult, they are tempted to get over their youthful infatuation with philosophy and conclude that virtue does not really exist and that philosophy is a waste of time. They will come to agree with Callicles that philosophers are unmanly types who spend their days whispering in a corner with three or four lads and never utter anything spirited.[35] They will become the kind of mature men who have learned the art of power play and no longer 'look at objects as reflected in reasoned argument.'

Plato, of course, is not about to let philosophy die. The argument of the *Republic* starts with the questions of Glaucon and Adeimantus, two young men who are close to granting that perhaps there is no such thing as justice. They nevertheless come to Socrates: can he tell them about justice in itself and by itself?[36] Of course they are asking about the form of justice. Sure enough, Socrates gives them an answer, but it takes a long time to marshall it, and this time Plato speaks through him – a Plato who sees the far-reaching implication of the challenge to the existence of forms and fully realizes that the discussion about the form of bed is but a rehearsal or a side issue when compared with the question about the forms of the virtues, and of justice in particular. Here again, casting his net as widely as he can, Plato seeks to come to the rescue of what matters about the doctrine of forms.

One set of answers comes from science, from mathematics in particular. We cannot have triangles without having triangularity and the geometer who has a science speaks about illustrations of triangularity not about the particular triangles he perceives with his senses. Or as *Ion* purports to show, a man who knows Homer by heart does not know poetry (that is he ignores the form of poetry), has only a limited sort of knowledge that does not extend to the whole and does not deserve the name of knowledge. The most general form of this argument is that knowledge and science exist; geometers as geometers are not involved in a king-of-the castle social game (although they may, imperfect men that they are, derive petty pleasure from refuting other geometers). Science and knowledge must have enduring simple objects, and these objects must exist. A whole dialogue, the *Theaetetus*, develops the argument that knowledge is impossible without the forms and links epistemology to metaphysics.

The other set of answers has moral and religious sources. A godly group of moralists before Plato hd maintained before the Greek people that a truer justice must be discovered. They had also nurtured the faith that such a justice may be discovered. Both the *Odyssey* and Hesiod had affirmed that Zeus wanted justice to prevail. Aeschylus had put on the stage gods who offer solutions for a better justice. The Orphics, in their turn, had tried to show how the universe and the gods strive to effect justice. These traditions, in spite of their differences, all formally had linked the gods to the existence of justice, and vice versa. In keeping with all of them Plato tries to stake a claim for such higher, better, truer justice, as a possibility for mankind that is already, in a sense, a reality before mankind has come to desire it.

Thus the matter is simple: in Plato's opinion virtue without the forms is but an appearance, and philosophical practice but a game. So he has drawn a dramatic picture: our fate would be worse than that of animals if we were unable to grasp true justice and find true piety in our midst. He explains about triangles, even with full knowledge that talk about triangularity probably never will persuade an unjust man to become just, or an unthinking man to see the point of reasoning things out. Thus all his arguments in the end hang on whether one, with him, wants the good life, and on whether one believes, with him, that it can be found, however enormous the difficulties may be in practice. Plato wants to take common human pursuits beyond the mere struggle for power and the intervention of chance to make them into an art wedded to knowledge and in particular to knowledge of what is true and what is good. Endorsement of this philosophic purpose seems to commit one to the existence of forms.[37] It seems to Plato that anyone, if pressed, wants to see this purpose realized. This is his way of getting to rock bottom where all would agree. Ian Crombie puts it another way: by holding on to the existence of forms Plato intends to reject the proposed notion that mind is a product of matter. The forms have to be independent of the physical world. And, thanks to them, mind or intelligence can rule. Forms are 'those entities that must be independent if the world of intelligence is to be independent.'[38] We might also add that 'independence of intelligence' is something all people prepared to talk should be willing to grant.

In the end Plato's task is cosmological in the most general sense of the word. The world must be such that the human beings in it can approach the truth. The world must be thought of, and clearly thought of, in such a manner that the possibility of science and piety be manifest to all. As we shall see, the thinking of the world leads Plato to draw, inevitably, from the cosmological and cosmogonic language present in the religious tradition.

For now, I must stress that philosophy involves rethinking, reorientation of one's habit of thought. J.N. Findlay speaks of the 'great inversion of the common ontology': people who think that instances are more real than ideas are told just the opposite.[39] The issue is that 'piety' is greater, better, more real, than the known individual embodiments of it. The earnestness of Socrates in pursuing this point is what must be driven home to the reader – this matters more than the value of his arguments.

Plato thus commits philosophy to a course that may properly be called radical and reconstructionist. Philosophy, writes Clémence Ramnoux, is a break from a tradition and a break from a thought (or a heap of thoughts) in which thinking does not recognize itself.[40] There is an autobiographical truth in that: philosophers acquire convictions from childhood about what is just and honourable, but they have since encountered refutations, sceptical arguments which undermine their confidence. They know that such questions must be accepted, even though they believe they should go on being able to honour only that which is truly honourable.[41] There is also a social necessity in the rise of philosophy. In a complex society tradition is no longer enough. The 'upright opinion' or sound tradition is discredited and maintains itself only by chance.[42] A new start is to be made: and this new start is to be thorough and far-reaching; to know virtue we are to know what is the nature of the soul, and to know that we must know the nature of the universe. Our science must have the full soundness of a physician who knows to whom, when, how much of which remedy is to be given.[43] We can say that the philosopher – and he alone – is in search of *transcendence*; he is involved in 'a search for authenticity outside the institutionalized offices and structures of the seeker's society.'[44] He thereby brings rationalism to a new height and an increased scope: everything is open to rational criticism, and everything in human life will be improved if it yields to the persuasive power of reason. The forms are sovereign: the world is amenable to the power of reason and is not merely a stage for the clashes of desire. To believe in forms, to turn to the right, is to make an act of rational faith: the good can be found and will be found by a displacement of impulsive and selfish desire through the use of reason. In contrast to a life made up of dramas of power, Plato invites us to the use of reason as that which is most appropriate in the universe as it is, and is the only key to our fulfilment. That is why we are to stop quoting poetry about the happiness of kings or of men with gold in store and start thinking about the whole question of human happiness and misery.[45]

Socrates' habitual asking for definitions and Plato's serious commitment to the doctrine of forms set philosophy on what was to be its historic course. But such foundational acts, now that we look at them with the wisdom of hindsight, can still be deemed somewhat ambivalent. Were these philosophers seeking a perfect language, a conceptual framework that would establish the conditions of all sound inquiry? Were they trying to rise to a use of words that would be founded not in the schemes of a desirous self but in reality itself? Did they wish to find a vocabulary that would guide us to all there is to know and could discriminate among all utterances making a claim to knowledge? In other words, were they systematic, that is in search of a system that could forever account for all our possible knowledge? Or were they, more modestly, seeking a better manner of speaking, searching for some mental distance, some gift of sight and perspective, some broadening of the customary framework that invites the consideration of richer hypotheses? Were they trying to achieve a conversational art that would make each open to the meanings discerned by the other? Were they trying to find a vocabulary to weigh the relative merits of claims to knowledge and enable one to arrive at more probable views, buttressed by sounder arguments? In other words, were they therapeutic, seeking to liberate speakers from captivity to narrow, confining opinions? Socrates and Plato were clearly convinced of the dignity and seriousness of all hard thinking about the truth. But what did they envisage as arising from such intellectual effort?[46]

4 Philosophy as contemplation

The most visible cleavage in society in Socrates' time was that between the conservatives and the progressives, although Socrates did note the existence of smooth talkers who could exploit everyone's confusion for their own ends. There was ground for hope even in such a serious split because the progressives, while they debunked the virtues of the conservatives, were conscientiously interested in the welfare of a whole, the city, which was greater than their own immediate group or selves. Plato, coming after the drama of Socrates' death, finds that those whose talk misleads are no longer a threatening minority but dominate the city. And he develops a diagnosis of this situation: many people keep taking turns to the left in their intellectual development, that is they keep arriving at nihilistic doctrines where despair is allayed only by the self's ability to cultivate pleasures and exercise power over others. More importantly, these people have become accustomed to the possession of power and are skilled at keeping themselves in charge of the affairs of the city. We can also put it this way: most people no longer fasten their eyes upon noble lovers (who are friends and love each other's souls as well as their bodies), finding in such lovers the norm of love. Rather, they have their eyes glued on more vulgar lovers (in whom love of bodies is paramount), and find the norm there. Note that the meaning of norm has changed: now it means what is average, or the lowest common denominator found among all lovers. And these 'realists,' sure of the role of self-interest in all men, successfully manipulate most.

Plato thus sees his society divided into two groups who do not live in the same world and do not find the same things real. He believes the intellectually and morally deficient ones to be the majority. Even if he were wrong on this point, the nature of the very cleavage he sees in his society is extremely serious. The dissension is about the highest matters. 'Morality and religion as chief interests are signs of an emergency,' Nietzsche has written, presumably because such debates absorb all the energies of the society.[47] There is no longer agreement on what is appearance and what is reality. Plato's diagnosis is thus more pessimistic than that of Socrates. Intelligent communication and convergence of minds will be difficult among people who have taken such different turns at such a fundamental level of the mind's orientation in the world.

Philosophy thus acquires with Plato both a heavier baggage (the cosmological doctrines, for instance) and a different tone. With Socrates philosophy was a conversational art; what exactly was behind the commitment to this art was not easy to discern, and still is not. With Plato a distinct, deep underlying attitude is taking clearer shape. He tends to start with a rejection, rather than a weighing of accepted opinions voiced in conversation. Or, perhaps better, instead of Socrates's habitual, kind ironic rejection, Plato starts with a sterner opposition. The truth is elsewhere. A new way of looking must be found, although it may be painful to part from the old ones.[48] In brief, philosophy for Plato has also become contemplation. Philosophy thereby is rooted in something deeper, older, than urban practice. The practice of civilized conversation is justified on the grounds that it opens the path to the sheer disinterested vision of the truth.[49] For Plato something of that vision has already been achieved by science and by religion. C.H.A. Festugière can quite correctly present Plato's philosophy as a transposition of science and religion. According to this view the Greek scientific tradition and the religious tradition mediate to Plato, in theie different ways, access to that which really is. They achieve – to varying degrees it must be said – contemplation (*theoria*), an attitude in which the self transcends the life of desire and work to see and acknowledge the truth of that which is.[50] Whatever may be the merits of this view, it does seem that the doctrine of forms is intrinsically related to the notion of contemplation. Receptivity to truth is not possible to the human mind without the forms and without the eye of the mind to behold them.[51] The forms thus provide Plato with a base on which to build his own theory and practice of the intellectual and moral life. What is at stake in the existence of forms, therefore, is ultimately the good life based upon the contemplation of the ultimate truth. At stake also, one should not forget, is the possibility of truthful language, namely words that unveil the true being that has been contemplated.

One also finds in Plato something of a sense that error is culpable. Those who ask what forms are like, adding, with seeming innocence, that they have never seen one and wonder whether they are like horses or rather like unicorns, are not perceived as innocent. Plato deems that their very manner of asking indicates that they are not seriously interested in an answer. Those who take a turn to the left, we hear in *Phaedrus*, are sensual and greedy. the philosopher will have to drag such people to the right, along the uphill road, as far as they may consent to go.[52] Plato thus comes to doubt that dialectic alone can achieve a reversal of the world-view of those who keep turning to the left and thus live in a world which they have turned completely upside down. Perhaps only the gods can bring about this conversion, a hypothesis that Socrates was not eager to espouse, if he could ever be said to have leaned towards it at all. Plato's diagnosis, at any rate, leads him to doubt whether political activity alone can redress this unsatisfactory state of affairs; he thereby gains an insight that sharply clashes with his original determination to do better than Socrates and stir the city more deeply and with greater craft in order to obtain its cure. Plato feels more intensely than his teacher the conflict between the determination to act in the city and the need to withdraw from it to think matters over and arrive at the truth which can be the only spring of right and restorative action. He thus comes to see that, paradoxically, political action can be both essential to human self-realization and secondary. With him political action, important though it may be, becomes subservient to something else, namely the cultivation of the ability to know the truth. And what it takes to achieve this ability becomes articulated for its own sake.

We find in Plato, therefore, the classic form of the dilemma that forces man to choose between action and contemplation. The Greeks traditionally favoured men of action. Phoenix reminded Achilles that he was 'to be both a speaker of words and a doer of deeds.'[53] Words in this context are also deeds whereby one's self becomes present to and influential upon one's fellow-men. This art of imposing oneself by the active style of one's presence became the common ideal among Greeks. Only in Socrates, who thus brings together the inheritance from a few philosophers and scientists who have preceded him, do we find a man who departs from this life style. He always wants time to think before acting, and time to talk before deciding what he thinks. The gods send him signs that hold him back rather than empower him to perform the shining and heroic deed the moment seems to call for. With him, at least in the eyes of his successors, classical philosophy begins to commit itself to leisure and to the search for pure knowledge, unadulterated by compromise with what will be acceptable or useful in the everyday world of desire and work. This knowledge will be contemplation of that which really is. The commitment requires taking such time as is necessary, and neglecting such other activities and even obligations as may detract from it.[54] Socrates, who accepted all the duties of a citizen, left politics aside; in the generation that came after Socrates some were to renounce all civil duties.

Plato nevertheless puts together as full a case as one can make for requiring political activity from the philosopher. Our inquiry has begun with a discussion between Socrates and Euthyphro on a practical matter: what is the correct course of action? Socrates, even though he has dropped many activities to seek the answers to such questions, never lost sight of the fact that he planned to find answers to practical questions about the guidance of life and the health of the city. Plato keeps this commitment, even analysing further what it takes to be a good politician in an imperfect or corrupt city as a question intrinsic to the quest of any philosopher. But he also fully knows that the primary and specialized business of the philosopher is contemplation, if that is still something one can have business with.

A philosopher, Plato articulates, must be a man who learns to see the truth, even though it is more practical to manipulate the half-truths which guide the life of most men. Without such contemplative ability, he adds, all the crucial distinctions between good and evil, virtue and vice, lose their meaning, or rather have no other meaning except that which men commonly see in them. And to nurture this contemplative ability, we may add, the philosopher needs to be economically self-sufficient, living modestly on inherited income or polishing lenses. He needs to be a private man, who unlike a doctor, a lawyer, or a poet does not have to sell the product of his intellectual work.[55]

At the end of a day, or of a life, or in the work of one's disciples, the fruits of contemplation are indeed expected to issue forth in action, but action is not the primary purpose of the philosopher. The proper proportion between action and contemplation to be maintained in one's life is an act of wisdom for which there are no rules, except to say that it depends on one's own individual gifts and on the opportunities, and demands, of the time. If these two can be matched, action is wise, but if they cannot, inaction is wise too, provided it is accompanied by contemplation rather than sloth. No imperative to action could possibly blame Socrates for staying out of politics; he may have been entirely right to do so. No imperative to contemplation could blame Plato for having entered the world of action, for his action did not diminish his commitment to contemplation, and one can even discern in him a desire to know how the world of political action really works. Thus it is always right for the philosopher to contemplate while it is not always right for him to act.

5 The speech of a philosopher

Socrates is always talking with people; he examines their statements and aims at securing definitions, 'looking at objects as reflected in reasoned arguments.' Philosophers work with language, examine language, and seek more adequate language. In saying that, for a while, they 'contemplate the truth' Plato puts them, for a while, apparently above language; but, having seen the truth, they are to say what they have seen – in words. We have also seen that the Greeks were fascinated with the power of speech. It is now time to review this historical context, focusing particularly on the promise of truth tantalizingly held forth in language and on Plato's own art of delivering, rather than betraying, this promise.

Marcel Détienne, in *Les Maîtres de vérité*, lays the basis for a history of the function of language among the Greeks by showing that two kinds of speaking contend against each other in the earliest historical period. On the one hand, there is the speaking assumed to be intrinsically efficacious, which Détienne calls magical-religious speech. When a priest, or poet, praises a god, a real thing happens: the god acquires praise. When a king pronounces a sentence, the case is closed; justice, by definition, has been rendered. This speaking is done by a 'legitimate' speaker facing a receptive audience. It is the privilege of a few who have divine authority to speak things as they are or to make things be what they say they are. Their words create reality, renew an order. On the other hand, in different social contexts, probably first of all in warrior fraternities, a second kind of speaking can be observed. Men place themselves in a circle, and each, in his turn, comes to the middle to say his piece. In the *Iliad* Agamemnon tries to reassert his authority by breaking the pattern and speaking seated, from his place. In the *Odyssey* the speaker whose turn it is to step into the middle receives a sceptre which he holds while he speaks.[56]

This second manner of speaking is deliberative and requires a dialogue of sorts. The men discuss what to do next. Human beings meet as agents and share their views. This kind of speaking is also, to use Détienne's word, secularized. What is talked about is what goes on in human time. Men speak to each other to elaborate common plans and, for instance, to urge each other to boldness or restraint. Their speech bears upon highly contingent events, not upon abiding realities. Instead of establishing knowledge, speaking is, in this case, a sort of groping in the dark.

The development of the Greek city-state brings about the flowering of the deliberative, secularized speech. The institutional settings for the unadulterated magical-religious speech become fewer and fewer. The Greeks invent the *agora*, a public, open space with a variety of formal activities and opportunity for a yet greater variety of informal ones. Nothing immune to discussion in the particular atmosphere of this place. There are two verbs related to the root of the word *agora*: *agoreuein* means to talk in public; *agorazein* means to buy and sell. The transactions conducted in that urban space range from the ignoble to the most noble.[57] A king like Cyrus has contempt for the practices prevalent there: I have never yet been afraid, he says, of men who have a special meeting place in the centre of their city where they get together to tell one another lies under oath.[58] Aristotle would like to clean up the place a bit: he urges different locations in it for trade, for religious activities, and for free discussion.[59] We may surmise that this advice was given in vain: nothing lies closer to the root of the intellectual vigour of Greek culture than this environment, so conducive to discussion, argument and counter-argument, plot and counter-plot. Bawdy comedies and sublime tragedies are performed in the same theatre, on the same day, before the same audience. There are few taboos in the exercise of speech; speakers will ordinarily have their say no matter what.

In this atmosphere all Greeks (that is all free adults males) can aspire to be like

Achilles, 'speakers of words' (or tellers of stories; the word in Homer is *mythos*) and 'doers of deeds,' although few may rise to his heroic excellence. Words and deeds are contrasted, but the contrast is relative. Words are perceived as uttered in a social context: they are deeds, of a kind, too. The Dorians in particular claimed to achieve a harmony between their deeds and their words; the former were eloquent, the latter weighty.[60]

Distinctions also quickly emerge among the speakers of words. When the warriors of the *Iliad* want to persuade Achilles to return to the battlefield, they ask Ulysses to head the embassy; he is, notoriously, the most skilful in speech. In his reply Achilles, not too politely, stresses the difference between himself and that kind of orator, who speaks 'softly': 'Resourceful Odysseus, without consideration for you I must make my answer, the way I think ... For as I detest the doorways of Death, I detest that man who hides one thing in the depths of his heart, and speaks forth another.'[61] He of course cannot be persuaded, skilful though Odysseus may be. So some speaking is blunt and straight; some other is something else, harder to label except that it is ordinarily more successful at moving one's fellow-man.

The art of honeyed or mellifluous speaking is of course particularly precious in the eyes of the descendants of the old royal masters of magical-religious speaking who must adapt to new circumstances. Hesiod portrays the situation exactly. (These new circumstances are already visible in Homer: compared to Agamemnon, Ulysses has learned to adapt.) A wise prince, says Hesiod, is loved by the Muses, who pour sweet dew upon his tongue: 'from his lips flow gracious words.' He can persuade with gentle words and put an end to even great quarrels.[62] Princes still have authority but persuade they must.

At this juncture the awe that the Greeks feel before the power of speech reaches its classical form. This awe is highly focused: poets and public speakers are considered 'inspired,' while sculptors, painters, and architects are seen as mechanics. The power of speech is celebrated in a very loaded metaphor: Orpheus, the mythology said, *charmed* wild beasts with music and song.[63] As the Muses convey 'knowledge' to the poet, they enable him to cast a spell upon the listeners. Poetry begins to be compared to wine, to drugged wine even. The magic of powerful speech is thus seen as something that victimizes others. Able speakers are seen as capable of transforming their listeners, whether they want it or not. We all know the beautiful appeal to the power of persuasion made by Athena at the end of the *Oresteia*. We must recognize that 'persuasion' also appears in the mental apparatus of the Greeks as a very suspect type of speech. In the *Agamemnon*, the first play of the same trilogy, persuasion is labelled the 'strong daughter of designing Ruin.'[64] 'There is no remedy,' adds the chorus. The cat that peeked out of the bag in Achilles' speech is now fully out in the open: speech can mislead, words can lie and be like an irresistible drug. Hesiod makes the distinction early in the *Theogony*: one can speak the truth or one can speak truth-resembling words.[65] Simonides wrestles with the accusation that poets are liars. Very early, that is much before the Sophists, the Greeks have become aware of the human power to create illusion.[66]

At this point there is a parting of the ways. On one side we find the philosophers conveniently lumped together under the label 'pre-Socratics.' On the other side we shall find the Sophists. The philosophers seek to recapture the art of speaking the truth and put it on a firm secure base.

Parmenides uses poetry, the traditional medium of authoritative language. He claims to offer a trustworthy speech, *piston logon*, which he contrasts to the 'names' (*onoma*) that mortals laid down believing them to be true. He tries to express what he 'saw' during an ecstatic experience and issues a call to correct mental activity. Parmenides makes one fundamental point: the philosopher says what is the case; there is a link between *logos* and reality. More than that, he affirms the identity of *logos* and being: 'It is the same thing that can be thought and that can be.' Veridical speech, contrasted with opinion (the realm in which men are most at home), can bear only upon being. 'One path only is left for us to speak of, namely, that *It is*.'[67] Speaking the truth is possible, or philosophic speech is possible, because being is one. Note, however, that such speech will be terse: what else can be said of being, after one has said that it is? Henceforth a whole tradition of 'religio-philosophical sects' (Détienne's term) declines to see any genuinely truthful speech in the utterance of opinion and maintains the search for inspired speech, 'the unshaken heart of well-rounded truth,' or for the speech that, unlike the babble that deals with himan trivialities, makes afresh a claim once made by the Muses in Hesiod, namely to unveil the truth.[68]

Heraclitus also believes that the majority of mankind is obtuse: 'they fail to notice what they do after they wake up just as they forget what they do when asleep.' And what they fail to understand, both before they have heard it and once they have heard it, is the *logos*. The *logos* is within the reach of all, but, 'although the *logos* is common, the many live as though they had an understanding peculiar to themselves.' What the *logos* is for Heraclitus is not as clear as some might wish; we are told however that, listening to the *logos*, 'it is wise to agree that all things are one.'[69] Clémence Ramnoux, a most helpful interpreter, stresses that Heraclitus seeks to cope with the mutation of sacred language: divine names have lost their value as signs; they have become sounds. To awake means to have one's mind alert to meaning. To philosophize, then, is to shake off a spell, a hypnotic sleep. A discipline of conversation emerges as the way that will let the true *logos* emerge.[70] This interpretation is probably correct. It remains significant, however, that Heraclitus writes oracular statements or gnomic utterances. (Parmenides wrote terse poetry.) These philosophers have seen that the clear language of mortals who explain everything at length is suspect and has lost touch with truth. The wise thus have to run the risk of obscurity. They even seem to court the risk.

That, however, is not the worst predicament that awaits those who refuse to use debased coinage. Aristotle tellingly describes the peculiar dead-end in which pre-Socratic philosophical minds can land themselves; observing that 'no true predication can be made of that which changes, they supposed that it is impossible to make any true statement about that which is in all ways and entirely changeable. For it was from this supposed view that there blossomed forth the most extreme view ... such as Cratylus held, who ended by thinking that one need not say anything, and only moved his finger.'[71]

But life goes on even when deep thinkers stall. In the fifth century the Greek city sees a vigorous intensification of deliberative speaking, of public speaking, where no word can claim the sort of inspiration that is supposed to silence all other speakers. Prose flowers as a medium. The courts institutionalize the society's trust in the power of the *logos*. The structures and rules for speaking in a trial schematize the activity in such a way that the power of speech stands out in clear outline. An evolution is then completed: the power of speech used to belong in the main to judges; it is now very much an instrument of the litigants. It is clear by now that Parmenides' ontology and his attempt to anchor the *logos* in the world of being were a rearguard action. Speaking is seen as part of human social and conflictual behaviour.

The Sophists are the end product of this evolution. They ponder the power of speech over human beings without feeling uneasy about its potential to spread lies. The pre-Socratic philosophers cannot endure the suspicion that speech creates illusion; they want to overcome the suspicion. The Sophists are prepared to live with it. Let speech be a drug. The point is to find drugs that are pleasant and effective. Protagoras is not interested in speech that would be truthful or straight (*orthos*); he wants speech that is *kreittôn*, stronger, that is able to prevail over the talk of others. The power of speech is defined by exclusion: speech is neither true nor common to all; what matters, then, is that it should work.[72]

Gorgias, in his *Praise of Helen*, argues that 'language is a powerful tyrant.' It can 'stop terror, remove suffering, promote joy and increase compassion.' He does not shy away from medical comparisons. 'One can speak of the power of speech toward the mobilization of soul as one speaks of the mobilization of drugs toward the nature of body.' It is not irrelevant to add that this passage on speeches that drug and charm the soul is part of a plea for the innocence of Helen, or rather for the absence of any responsibility in Helen. Whether the woman was abducted by force or seduced by pretty words is all the same: she was helpless in any case. James Redfield, commenting on this text, correctly notes that 'the doctrine of the absolute power of appearances is a core doctrine' of the Sophists.[73] Sophistry by rallying all powers of persuasion (and allowing that there are no antidotes to this drug) makes tyranny possible. Nothing can resist social power. For our purpose, however, it is more important to note that rhetoric as an emerging tradition seeks to supplant religious and oracular philosophical speaking. The efficacy of rhetoric makes no claim to be an ontological one. It is quite content with a pragmatic, social power. It does not bring truth but is an art of social living among the contingencies of this life. Prose brings about consensus. It is the language of deliberation that ponders the pros and cons. So far so good. But prose is also the language of insinuation. It is prose that spreads suspicions about the certainties of others, that, for instance, doubts the ponderous truths of inspired poets and wise men or the advice of elder statesmen. We may also note with Heraclitus that this sort of speaking, immersed in the flux of things, may at best aim at saying the truth all the time and yet is never able fully to say it. Philosophy if it is to be pursued in the new rhetorical mode takes on the characteristic of an endless discourse that can start at any point but is never completed. It pursues truth (again at best) but never catches it. W.K.C. Guthrie sums up the situation well: 'In such an atmosphere it is not surprising that an epistemology should gain favour according to which "what appears to me *is* for me, and what appears to you *is* for you", and that no man can be in position to contradict another.'[74] Rhetoric is allied to epistemological scepticism.

And also, possibly, to nihilism. In the context of the second half of the fifth century the 'magic' connected with words is no longer the archaic one. Powerful prose, unlike the old poetry, is deemed to be a craft (*technè*) that the speaker can master. There is no sense of a charm coming from the gods through the speaker. But there is still the search for the charm coming from the speaker and exercised upon his audience. Speech is no longer sacred to Gorgias; it is demythologised by him. It is a tool for bending others to one's will. 'Sacred magic was mysterious; Gorgias's magic is technical.'[75] The drug he is talking about is not that of a Circe. It is not approached with awe. It is the drug of new scientific doctors. But whereas the doctors use drugs only for the welfare of the patients, eloquent speakers bent on deception use their magic to pursue exclusively the ends that suit them.[76]

We are now in a position to explain the constant semantic shifts that occur around the words *logos* and *mythos*. Practically every meaning found for *mythos* in some context can be found for *logos* in another, and vice versa. To some *mythos* is sacred language bringing from the past an authoritative message on reality and the order of things; in contrast *logos* is then viewed as mere human talk. To others *mythos* is just tales, with only the appearance of truth – and a shabby appearance at that; in contrast *logos* is the speech to be trusted; confidence is placed in the ability of human minds to reason in order to discover and convey the truth. Those who uphold the way of *mythos* see in it a language which celebrates what is. Truthful speaking is repetition of something received or seen. Those who put their trust in *logos* are aware that the human act of speaking has its own unique potential for the discovery of truth. *Logos* at the outset is seen as a social phenomenon; Gilbert Murray has put it this way: 'it was the word spoken; it was the power of language; it was the word which implies reason, persuasion, interpretation, and which settles differences instead of the armed hand.'[77] Furthermore, *logos* at the outset is also aware of the distance between the things and the words, which are *our* words. Where myth saw or, better, created a unity, *logos* sees a difference. What we say is what *we* say: what things are is something else. *Logos* is aware of the distinction between what it talks about and what it says about it.

Heraclitus puts in a nutshell the predicament proper to language: 'One could not speak of justice, if there was not also injustice.'[78] If the word 'justice' 'naturally' stuck to just acts, there would be no speech. There is speaking because the appearance of justice is somewhat attached to injustice, and vice versa. Speaking is thus necessary to find the proper label for 'realities.' Some speaking manages to utter words that cling to the realities in deep unity. Some speaking merely glues on misleading labels. The unity which *mythos* offers may or may not be genuine. The probings of *logos* seeking to insinuate themselves between the label and the reality may or may not be in the interests of truth. In some circumstances we may have to say that myths are old wives' tales. In other circumstances we may have to say that discursive prose is *agora* babble. Such is the cost of human speaking. Ants communicate effectively but their mental world ignores the difference between words and things. None of their signs is ambiguous. But behind each human speaking, there is a (suspect) speaker. Human speaking nevertheless can be truthful, and not just a gratuitous exercise in diversionary noise-making or skilled manipulation. Let me add that the problem of the speaker's motives is not the only question mark on the truthfulness of human speech. However simple the truth may be, it still takes time to *say* it. How then can the truth, abiding, timeless, ever identical to itself, be expressed in a temporal medium?

Now that we have a picture of the battleground on which Plato enters, we are also in a position to understand why he wrote philosophy as he did. There is in him an equal distrust of the old poetry and of the new prose. Each tells its own kind of lies, stultified and possibly evil dogmas or flattering manipulative schemes. Each of the two dominant modes of speech in the sick city is a cause as well as a symptom of social crisis. The language of the traditionalists and that of the innovators fan the flames of war. None of these can cure the crisis of speech and put an end to the brutal clash of wills that passes for public life. The 'oracular' philosophers try to improve on the poets, but their speaking, when aware of its own limits, is too close to silence for comfort. The 'worldly' philosophers make countless fine points, but their speaking, when aware of its own limits, looks much like the continuation of the clash of opinions merely transferred to another ground. Against both sides Plato tries to reconquer some space for philosophic speaking. After the failure of Socrates, Plato wants to reaffirm the moral dignity and the moral efficacy of language. Reflection on speaking is at the souce of his philosophy and a metaphysical foundation is sought for good speaking. That a new departure was necessary may be stressed by recalling the tradition according to which young Plato burned his poems after meeting Socrates.[79]

The new sort of speech, we can add, will have to be somewhere in between (or above) the ritualized speech of tradition deemed sacred in which the speaker is absent as speaker but is a mere mouthpiece that transmits dead coinage and the speech invented by the strategies of desire in which the thing spoken of is absent since language has become the tool a self uses to wield power over another. What is spoken must be determined not only by what it is spoken about but also by the living mind that speaks it. What counts in philosophy is not just the topic but the way one speaks of it. A. Kojève undertakes to tell us what philosophy is by stating that, whatever it talks about, it always also talks about its own talking about it.[80] Words are no longer simply what 'they' say; they are not either what 'I' say. They are an event, the meeting between speakers who intend to speak the truth, are aware of the attempt, and use the right words.

Plato knows all this. He also experiences a split between the speaker and his audience. He no longer shares in the happy naïveté of those who speak authoritatively, confident that what they say is the truth. He does not share either in the happy naïveté of the *raconteur* who enjoys a sociable feast. As the studies of Eric Havelock have shown, Plato has broken from the cultural patterns of oral society where poet and audience are one. His is a solitary learning, literate, abstract.[81] One does not learn by mixing with others but by withdrawing. And then one writes: alone with one's words, and the readers out there, somewhere. Distinctions come, made between body and soul, appetites and mind; between rational persuasion and emotional persuasion; between rigorous dialectic and easy dialogue. I should stress, however, that such ringing dichotomies are not all that is found in Plato. He writes dialogues.[82] The people argue but they also, for a while, share in a living experience. They claim to be rational and are affected by each other. True, the 'academic affections,' love of truth and willingness to listen, are the only ones sanctioned, but such affections create an atmosphere in which the intellectual and the affective are not split from each other. Reflection of objects in reasoned argument is something that happens as people talk to each other. As Emerson puts it in his essay *Plato*: 'he is intellectual in aim; and therefore, in expression, literary.'

This literary form enables Plato to present arguments within a set realistic framework. The reader observes both the attempt to link or deduce truths and the interaction between at least two minds. He can observe both words and deeds of the participants. In *Euthyphro* we see two men exchange ideas on piety. We also see an ostensibly pious man being tested – and not doing too well – by a man who has been charged and is about to be sentenced for impiety. There is a lesson in that as well as in the affirmations made in the course of the dialogue. Just as there is a lesson in the fact that the encounter breaks off, inconclusive. As the *Laches* embarks upon a discussion of courage, Plato builds his drama on the motif, familiar to every Greek, of word and deed (*logos* and *ergon*). One character, Laches, is a man who excells in action but cannot account very well in words for what courage is. Nicias is better at words, but then he lacked endurance when tested, so there is some doubt about his grasp of courage. What the speakers are is like a counterpoint to the points they are making. In the *Lysis* no communication occurs on the subject of friendship between Socrates and the young man because they have only words on the subject; they do not know it as an *ergon*.[83]

That words do not necessarily reveal the truth, or the whole truth, or nothing but the truth is also at times made fully explicit. The *Hippias Minor* echoes a traditional query: referring to the passage in Book 9 of the *Iliad*, it asks who is the better man, Achilles who is true and simple, or Ulysses who is wily and false? The dialogue cites Achilles' abhorence of those who do not speak their heart. Hippias, a specialist on Homer, argues that Homer made Achilles to be the better man; if he utters falsehoods, it is never by design. Socrates is very argumentative: he who can utter falsehoods at will knows more and has more power than he who utters falsehoods only unwillingly. And furthermore it is possible that Achilles uttered falsehoods by design and was so good at it that nobody discerned his design. The dialogue is inconclusive. Hippias stands his ground but cannot refute the arguments that Socrates has brought forward. Socrates, by the way, does not claim that his arguments are any good; he merely puts them forward in order to be instructed by Hippias.

In *Phaedo* Plato has Socrates show more of his hand. There are lots of worthless arguments (*logoi*). One should not, however, become misologists or haters of reason (*logos*) itself. If there were just one argument that is true and sure and can be learned, what a pity it would be to miss it. 'Let us not admit in our souls the notion that there is no soundness in arguments at all.'[84]

Cratylus shows Plato's fullest attempt to display arguments on language and conquer visibly some space for philosophic speaking. To Hermogenes words mean what a speaker intends them to mean: he is aware of the need for consistency on a speaker's part but fails to account for the communicative power of language. His position does not make clear how speakers come to share conventional meanings. What is clear is that words cannot be objects of knowledge: they are but sounds subject to the vicissitudes of the Heraclitean flux. Cratylus offers an alternate theory. Words are natural signs. They reflect, imitate, or represent that to which they refer. To know the word is to know the reality. But how are we to know that the original giver of names did his job properly? The two doctrines contradict each other sharply. What is not so obvious is that they both deny that there is any point to dialectic or to philosophizing by talking: according to one view words are quite cut off from things; according to the other they are allegedly close copies of them. Dialectic is either pointless or unnecessary.

Socrates makes his point by shifting the topic: instead of words or names, he wants to talk about the activity of naming. Names must enable us 'to distinguish things according to their natures,' it being assumed that things 'have some fixed reality of their own.'[85] The position has a conventionalist aspect: naming is an ongoing human social activity. But the conventions are not good enough if they are only conventions: they must be dialectically refined to convey a knowledge of the truth. The answer is here again found in the familiar recourse to the forms and the search for proper definitions. The dialogue particularly tellingly links our understanding of language with the very possibility of philosophy: 'If everything is in a state of transition and there is nothing abiding,' knowledge cannot be.[86] But the only instrument of knowledge we have is language, an instrument which we receive as an imperfect, conventional one. Language is such that it does not convey knowledge at the outset but it is also such that it can be used to achieve knowledge. There is a distance between words and things but that distance can be bridged in time and through philosophical labour.[87] *Euthyphro* remains inconclusive: the question must be lived with some time more; the dialogue aims at a mental act, not at a veridical proposition.[88]

Plato is no longer naïve, innocent about language. He does not become utopian about some new way. He uses language as he finds it. He is resourceful enough to be able to play with it, and serious enough to work to change it. He wants to educate speakers. He has been brushed by the wit and versatility of the Sophists and knows that behind words there is always a self that uses them (except that Plato would say there is *also* a self which uses them). And he wants to improve selves. His writing has, therefore, the quality proper to a writer who knows perfectly what he is about as he writes. His choice of literary genre is, need I say it, entirely deliberate. The sentences are clearly prose, but the prose is contained within a new but distinctively poetis type of creation: the drama of a philosophical discussion. Through the form of the dialogue Plato both has some things said and also shows some others (and leads us to ponder – if we can – the relationship between the two).

Most of the prose Plato writes is miles away from that of public speeches. Each point can be put promptly to the test of intelligent discussion. (A few intelligent men are a more demanding audience than a theatre full of fools.[89]) Uninterrupted tirades either lose the audience or lull them into hypnotic sleep. Using the same metaphor as Heraclitus, Plato sees unphilosophic minds as 'dreaming,' whether awake or asleep.[90] Just asking men (there are no women in the dialogues) to rephrase their statement helps to wake them up. It 'abruptly disrupts the complacency felt' about one's felicitous formulation.[91]

The dialogue form, being also dramatic, enables Plato to face squarely the socio-cultural conflict. Conflict is shown to go deeper than the power struggles among politicians or the diverging senses of reality among ignorant men. Conflict is taken right into philosophizing. Plato, writes P. Shorey, undertook to show the ethical logomachies of the day.[92] The people in the dialogues both talk and confront each other with their non-negotiable ultimate differences. Some are in the eleatic strain: words have but one meaning and I know it. Others are in the Sophistic strain: words have many meanings and I'll use whatever meaning you – or is it I? – want. But the thrust of the dialogues is to make these intellectual conflicts subject to rules and we can see whether the disputants agree to discuss their differences in honest speech or whether they choose not to. The fundamental rule is that of consistency with a hypothesis: let words – for the time being – mean the same thing all the time. This piece of social common sense plays right into Socrates' search for real definitions and the knowledge of forms. We can then *see* whether human beings are persuaded by each other or whether they are persuaded by the truth. And we can see that talking does help, or helps really. The conventions of polite discussion are thus quite legitimately the privileged context for Socratic philosophizing. Such conventions give a chance to truth. A. Gouldner writes that 'the dialectic is the strategy of forcing an alliance between reason and *thymos* by placing the individual in a social interchange where, in order to avoid shame, he must be reasonable.'[93] It is possible, therefore, if not always easy, for Socrates to guide the exchange towards the discovery of the only truth that matters. Hence Détienne's conclusion: Plato is in the tradition of Parmenides and of the other 'maîtres de vérité'; with him, however, this 'religious' truth dares to submit itself to open, rational discussion. Or, as J.P. Vernant puts it, Plato's philosophy has kinship with the initiation of the mysteries and the controversies of the *agora*.[94]

There is more to be said on the confluence in Plato of two previously incompatible traditions. For the time being, I should stress that Plato as writer can be the heir both of Parmenides and of Protagoras because he holds on to, and probably makes more explicit, the conventions of civil discourse in fact-to-face relationships among educated men. He has found in his society a pattern of discourse in which people are willing to mean what they say and say what they mean. This milieu is reconstructed in his dialogues as the one conducive to philosophy.

We may add that Plato also thereby manages to draw out the lessons to be learned from both Socrates and Thucydides. Socrates focused his inquiries on the virtuous individual. Thucydides gave an account of a civilized group's descent into barbarity. Plato tries to see the roots and the products of the decay both in the individual and in the society. His diagnosis thus includes the portrait of the Sophist who handles words as if they were stuff in his fingers (he twists them this way and that) and who appears to know everything ('knowing all the words they gain the reputation of knowing everything when they know nothing').[95] It includes also an analysis of the moral ethos proper to decadent democracy. Written public law has clearly not solved everything. If there are perversions of the social order when a few aristocrats settle justice in a secret huddle, other sources of chaos are let loose when all issues are brought out in the open to become the subject of a public debate that is dominated by a few clever speakers. Plato's point, of course, is that what people do with their institutions matters (just as it matters what these institutions are). His analysis then of litigiousness and dishonest speeches in courts points to the area where the moral decay is most serious. How can one restore the conventions of honest face-to-face relations if even courts are taken over by the disease? In the corrupt city, argues Plato, all speech has become heated, with heat not from the gods but from that of uncontrolled will. And yet, even then, a few individuals can, privately, submit themselves to the discipline of slow, patient, controlled dialogue.

The philosophic dialogue is thus Plato's way to build on rock, even though he tries to keep up with shifting sands. All speakers, as they speak, express a faith in language and in education, at least ostensibly. No speaker (until some twentieth-century literary movements) is willing to get caught using speech to destroy the point of speech. All do affirm that through truthful exchange 'the truth' or at least 'a truth of some sort' is to emerge. In Plato's eyes this assumption is one that is commonly held in some contexts and is the stronghold of decency among men; it is an implicit existential affirmation and as such is the firm experiential base for the doctrine of forms. Men do want to cultivate the unique power of speech, and for this they must believe in the forms as ultimate ground of truthful speech. The point is quite tellingly made at the crucial moment in *Parmenides*: 'If a man ... should deny that there are forms of the things that are and he should not distinguish a form of each, then he will turn to where he will possess no understanding, since he denies that the nature of each of the things that are is always the same, and thus he will totally destroy the power of discourse.'[96] Plato's fundamental philosophical commitment is to the power proper to discourse. 'The power of speech is a guidance of the soul' (*psychagogia*), we hear in *Phaedrus*;[97] it is a function of speech to lead souls by persuasion; the contrast with the speech-as-drug theory of *Helen* is obvious. Human beings feed and thrive on discourse, but they are not tyrannized by it. People desire to talk and they desire as they talk. The philosopher shows under what circumstances they educate each other while talking. Whereas some Greeks went on uttering presumably solid words, which they felt shielded them from the conflictual realities of human greed, and others talked swiftly in the pursuit of their own appetites, Socrates and Plato became philosophers. They spoke and wrote to educate desire.

5

Philosophy of religion in the making

I What teachings should be transmitted?

Let us imagine Plato gathering all the wisdom available in the accumulated experience of good and pious men in order to find the solution that can bring the Greek city back to a state of good health. But digging into the past is to Plato only a way of grasping the size of the problem and the origin of the present state of affairs. To find the base for a complete solution the philosopher must rise above his day and above past history to contemplate the nature of things. Plato's purpose remains throughout eminently practical. The word of truth should be uttered, the doctrine unfolded, the laws formulated, the paradigms of culture found that will restore good sense and just order among men and make another trial of Socrates impossible. The question of piety raised in *Euthyphro* has given way to a higher, more encompassing question: what is justice? One should not, however, assume too quickly that the philosophy of religion finds thereby a subservient part in the architectonics of the whole. It is true that piety is made part of justice and not the other way round but, as Plato's readers have been quick to see, his conception of justice is pious. The gods are guarantors of justice and the just man is one who has risen to contemplation of and even union with the divine.

Our inquiry however, I must repeat, is not into Plato's religiousness, or what some might call, with U. Wilamowitz-Moellendorf, his 'believing heart,' but into his grasp of the problem of religion. Plato, I maintain, strives to understand the Greek religious tradition; he wants to reform it. In religious matters, as elsewhere, the philosopher wants to bring back to disturbed Athens a sound insight into the true nature of its own welfare. The assumption is that religion plays a crucial role in the transmission of paradigms of culture. The assumption remains that true piety is something that exists. But the way of true piety is to be exhibited by a discriminating look as what has traditionally passed for piety.

Such is, I contend, the nature of Plato's undertaking as philosopher of religion. This hypothesis, however, needs immediate testing because it introduces a modern concept, that of religion, which is nowhere found as such in the Greek texts. Is Plato really aware of a problem in religion? What was Greek religion like in his day anyway? What did Plato think of it? The object of this chapter is to answer these questions, and thus initiate a more precise discussion of Plato's relationship to that complex reality: the Greek religious tradition.

The themes which are part of our horizon of thought when we think about religion unfold themselves in Plato's work primarily as he ponders the problem of cultural transmission. What wisdom a society should seek to maintain in its midst and transmit becomes with him a fully articulated theme.

In Plato's proposed reorganized city the transmission of the paradigms of culture (and the training of men for creative participation in the establishment of a just order) is made into a public undertaking entrusted to an official. It is the highest task and only the wisest of the authorities in the state will be worthy of it. Education for Plato is a process that nurtures the mind, shapes the character, and strengthens the soul. To avoid the narrowing of the imagination that seems to occur when we hear of education. W. Jaeger has refused to translate Plato's word for it and goes on using the Greek word *paideia*. 'Education is not the cultivation of certain abilities; it is not the communication of certain branches of knowledge – at least all that is significant only as a means and a stage in the process of education. The real essence of education is that it enables men to reach the true aim of their life.'[1] The mandate given to the minister of public education is therefore a very sweeping one (the official might perhaps best be called a minister of culture and education). So sweeping in fact that one might wish to instil some suspicion of the office by calling it the ministry of truth. But the problem arising in connection with the mandate should not obscure the basic fact. *Paideia* is a social process, and societies, at times, seek to reorient this process. And the state is the institution societies have invented for this end.

Plato was the first but certainly not the last European to have asked the state to undertake a task of cultural reform. Legal reform especially is indissolubly bound to the state. Any attempt to review the existing laws, to give them greater coherence or more sensible rationality, calls upon a principle of organization and a central authority that can proclaim the new whole. Plato's minister of culture and education is the manifest counterpart of his plan for legal reform. He merely makes explicit what remains often implicit; thought out, state-guided reform undertakes a systematization of beliefs.[2]

The social and even state dimension of the process of *paideia* does not deny that the process, in the end, produces individual human beings. Education is not social conditioning. My *paideia* is unqualifiedly and purely mine; it is that which will remain mine in all circumstances. 'The soul takes with it to the other world nothing but its *paideia* and life style (*trophe*).'³ My *paideia* is the identity, the strength, the character which is unique to me. But I have acquired it in a social context, in a lifetime of acting and being acted upon, of work and of leisure.

Greek religion is thus to be seen as a part of the spiritual inheritance or moral atmosphere into which any living Greek is initiated as he grows up in his city. He sees shrines, in the agora, at street corners, in his home. He learns familiar gestures in connection with them. Socrates, like most, takes all this for granted: 'I have altars and shrines, domestic and ancestral, and everything of the sort that other Athenians have.'⁴ And there are tales. All men know of 'stories which they used to hear, while infants and sucklings, from the lips of their nurses and others – stories chanted to them, as it were, in lullabies, whether in jest or in earnest: and the same stories they heard repeated also in prayers and sacrifices, and they saw spectacles which illustrated them, of the kind which the young delight to see and hear when performed at sacrifices; and their own parents they saw showing the utmost zeal on behalf of themselves and their children in addressing the gods in prayers and supplication ... and at the rising and setting of the sun they heard and saw the prostrations and devotions of all the Greeks and Barbarians, under all conditions of adversity and prosperity.'⁵

The worth of these devotions and stories is usually taken for granted. They are part of a civic atmosphere or cultural ethos. No clerical caste has a monopoly of exposition. Sound doctrine and correct critical practice are known by an implicit knowledge. They are part of the way of the fathers.

The stories in particular (and the sayings associated with them) purport to offer wisdom on problems most burdensome to man. Plato's generation, we must add, could fully appreciate the seriousness of the problems and the precariousness of the answers. Consider, for instance, the words of the nurse in Euripides' *Hippolytus*:

All the life of Man is pain, and there is no rest from trouble. But that Other – whatever it be – that is more precious than life, darkness enshrouding covers it in cloud. A nameless thing that shines across the world: and it is plain that for this we are sick with longing, because we have no knowledge of another life, because we have no revelation of the things under earth, but still drift vainly upon a tide of legend.⁶

This 'drifting upon a tide of legend' is not an incurable condition in Plato's eyes. Such lines nevertheless convey fairly what religion must have been about in his mind. Furthermore, like Euripides and everybody else, Plato knows that the poets as the most important actual transmitters of the stories are commonly accepted as 'experts' of a sort in the matter of prayers and sacrifices, but Plato, again like Euripides, doubts that the poets know what they are talking about. Plato also occasionally lengthens his list of the sources of this religious culture. We hear religious accounts 'from those who are reputed the best of poets, orators, seers, priests and thousand upon thousands of others.'[7] Significantly the list is open.

Beside the stories (*mythoi*) Plato is aware of an existing heritage of sayings (*logoi*). There is an ancient saying (or ancient doctrine or tradition), we hear in *Phaedo*, that claims that the souls of the dead go to a nether world and come from there again.[8] Such an ancient account is presented as something that should not be dismissed lightly. As cautious a historian as W.K.C. Guthrie confirms Plato's respect for these ancient traditions by affirming that Plato's own growth as a philosopher is dependent upon the impact of such teachings. They have set Plato's feet 'on the upward path from the Cave.'[9] In certain contexts these ancient *logoi* are clearly more ways of doing things than doctrines. The legislator, warns Plato, should not touch the ancient traditions 'whether derived from visions or from some reported inspiration from Heaven.'[10]

Aware of a transmitted tradition, Plato is also sensitive to the fact that this lore has an abiding power in any society and can thus be considered the most important common source of wisdom and insight. The religious ways are those of the ways of the fathers that are least quickly displaced. The individual may then come to feel that religious lore, rather than being one set of traditions among others, is the most potent, the most ancient, the one that it is most ill advised for us to neglect and forget, since it claims to maintain access to the divine.

Plato's awareness of such existing religious tradition is confirmed by the presence in the dialogues of at least three characters whose identity is defined primarily by their own attitudes towards these traditions and the questions they pose. We have already met Euthyphro and Cephalus. To these two pious men directly presented on the stage we should now add Adeimantus, whose intellectual restlessness focuses primarily on the spiritually perplexing question: can the gods perhaps be conveyers of injustice? Adeimantus is an example of the serious, well-meaning, but confused youth whom Plato tries to educate out of the crises of the age. His quest is largely religious in nature: is the human quest for justice upheld by the gods and the forces which rule the universe? People like Cephalus, Euthyphro, and Adeimantus make us see the problem about religion: which teachings ought to be transmitted – and are true – and which ones should be 'buried in silence.'[11]

2 Strains in Greek religious life

It will be useful at this stage to open a parenthesis to provide a brief account of the nature and history of Greek religion.

Greek religion is largely a modern invention. Historians, archaeologists, philologists have reconstituted for us a Greek religious world. Today we usually have trouble seeing the religion as a whole. Gilbert Murray has called it an inherited conglomerate: a geological metaphor which suggests that Greek religious data, like a boulder, were assembled out of various materials and sat solidly somewhere in the scenery.[12] Using an organic metaphor which does more justice to the living changes undergone by Greek religion, Martin Nilsson has compared it to a great forest. The great gods are the tall trees, the lower figures of popular belief are the brushwood, and below it all we find the grass which is the undergrowth of belief and custom.[13]

That Greek religion is hard to see as a whole is not just because of the difficulties inherent in finding, gathering, and interpreting meaningful data about a religion which today is no longer alive in the way it once was; rather the Greeks simply did not have a religion in the sense in which people familiar with today's 'higher religions' consider that individuals or societies have a religion. The Greek religious life – some such phrase we must use to signal its peculiarity – was not unified by any of the factors which commonly unify a religion. Homer was not the Bible of the Greeks. While everyone allows that the epic poetry was the storehouse for all the basic attitudes common to Greek society, everyone can also see that the Homeric poems did not become a canonical scripture exercising authority over the development of Greek religious and intellectual life. The religious life of Greece cannot, therefore, be compared with that of the societies where religion is a cumulative tradition, with the same fundamental authority interpreted and reinterpreted as the centuries pass by. Consider also that in Greece priesthoods were tenable only for a year, 'a sure proof of amateur status,' writes E.R. Dodds.[14] No clear authority ever emerged in the Greek religious world. This being said, we should hasten to add that it would be imprudent to compare the Greek religion to the so-called primitive religions that have no scripture.[15] Unlike those rather timeless religious systems, Greek religion had a history and very quickly knew it; the society included highly literate authors. we can see that Greek religion evolved first because of the mixing of populations, then because of the more internal process of change in a society that went through a rather dramatic history.

One can best account for the plastic kind of unity exhibited by Greek religion through its history by showing first the various strains that went into the making of it. Much in Greek religious life can be grasped by focusing on the contrasts in it. Between 2000 and 1600 BC people that are part of an eastern Mediterranean cultural world (we have their art, called Cycladic,[16] and we can trace its development out of earlier neolithic art) see their country invaded by Indo-Europeans coming from the north. As a result, two types of ritual contend and become juxtaposed. The tension between them has become a sort of settled coexistence in Mycenaean times and the two strains will remain distinguishable throughout Greek history. Mycenae seems to have stabilized a language, a mythology, a pantheon that became the heritage of all Greeks. Mycenaean society was destroyed by another group of northern invaders who began to move in around 1200. The search for a cultural equilibrium started again but seems to have arrived at very much the same results. One exception: cremation stopped and inhumation returned. The familiar contention between northern and Mediterranean elements remains.[17]

The Mediterranean gods are worshipped in caves, the northern ones in the open. Amalgams, of course, occur; Zeus, a notorious northern sky-god, is said to have been born in a cave in Crete. Some sacrifices are poured into the ground, some onto altars under the sky. Female figures are in some cases the source of all goodness and all life (early clans were matrilineal); in other cases females are frequently foreign, seen as a dark threat to the civilized order that prevails in the Greek city (succession subsequently became patrilineal).[18] Some rituals are rural and can be seen only as part of village festivals. Other rituals require the assembling of a larger group such as the whole city. The contention between the two elements reappears in *Euthyphro*: the pious man there believes both in archaic pollution and in the modern civil consensual judicial process (note that Euthyphro is not in the least aware of the conflict). Can these heterogeneous elements form a stable amalgam?

This tension between the chthonic and the heavenly, the fertility cults and the Indo-European ones, is not the only one. We should rather see in it the basic tensions, the presence of which allows other dualities, polarities, to come to expression. C.R. Beye has pointed to the Greek taste for contrasts and oppositions: 'It is obvious from the language that the ancient Greeks had a pronounced tendency to pose things in antitheses.'[19] In the fifth century Thucydides develops with relish the antithesis between Athens and Sparta and in the fourth Plato writes dialogues in which Socrates is pitted against an interlocutor and keeps asking him for decisions on logical alternatives. Such art of formulating illuminating clashes, while heightened by political deliberation, may well be rooted in the ongoing viability of the cultural duality. Contemporary authors still enjoy seeing contrasts between two periods and two authors. Consider, for instance, the often cited contrast between Homer and Hesiod. There is a chronological difference between them but the corpus of these authors also reflects, perhaps more significantly, a class or cultural difference.[20] Homer reflects the values of the religion proper to the entourage of warring aristocrats and sea-going élites. Hesiod speaks for the rural world of small landowners. All share the cult of the Olympians but put a very different colouring on Zeus for instance. Louis Gernet points out another contrast between the epic tradition where 'wise men' are barely visible and hardly matter and a tradition, well attested since the seventh century, of deep respect for 'wise men,' 'diviners,' and 'prophets.'[21] There is furthermore a duality in the epics themselves. The *Iliad* wrestles with Achilles' identity problem: the hero is torn between his personal integrity (and dignity) and his social obligations; his own self is put in question by Agamemnon's pretension to being 'better.' In the *Odyssey* the identity of the self is secure; it is the world that is complex. Ulysses never looks into himself but his ingenuity is constantly challenged by problems the world throws at him. A pragmatic Greek tradition thus comes to expression in contrast with a heroic and tragic one.[22] One can also point out that the *Odyssey*, unlike the *Iliad*, has some use for subterranean Hades, is highly aware of women (their awful bewitching power but also their moral strength and loving affection), and is commonly found to have a more civilized sense of moral proprieties.[23]

It is clearly the northern strain that plays the dominant role in the elaboration of the institutions of the classical city-state. The religion of the twelve great Olympians – more or less those found in Homer – occupies the centre of the stage and provides the world with its religious order. The city is built by men and its gods are predominantly masculine. They are led by Zeus. There are two important goddesses. One is temperamental and never fully integrated: Hera's loyalty to the Olympian order is shaky and she is the only one who remains something of a challenge to Zeus. The other seems only too well integrated: Athena is undoubtedly a very good daughter of Zeus – she even has no mother – but this cerebral virgin has neither lovers nor children, deprivations which males in the pantheon would never tolerate. The Olympians' predominance nevertheless does not erase memory of what went before. The victory of the gods over the Titans is part of the remembered lore. And Hesiod gives to the story a near scriptural status. Olympian civilization knows it can be challenged by forces it does not entirely control. Sophocles provides us with a telling example of the two religious worlds clashing: Antigone pays heed to the archaic blood law; against this law of night Creon enforces the law of daylight, the public law of the city. The whole *Oresteia* likewise hinges on the contest between the new institutions of the city and an older cultural stratum. In the end killing one's legal husband is deemed worse than killing one's natural mother. For R. Pettazoni the history of Greek religion is the history of the city. As new populations, rural or lower-class, try to gain access to the life of the city, new themes find their way into the religious life of the city; the centre of gravity shifts as the balance of power does in the population.[24]

The official public religion of the city thus does not occupy the full stage at any point. At the periphery other cults, other beliefs prosper, emerge, or linger. A few miles from Athens stands Eleusis and the sanctuary of Demeter and Persephone. This cult is partly integrated into the life of the city: an annual public procession leads to Eleusis from the Acropolis. But it also has strong continuity with rural fertility themes: a 'mystery' is 'shown' in a room there; it is not open and it makes a special promise to the initiates. Or to take another example, the *manteis* or diviners, a frequent presence in the life of most if not all cities, never become anything like an official clergy in Athens. But such institutionalized divination, frequently associated with Apollo, prospers in pan-Hellenic sanctuaries, such as Delphi and Dodona, and thus finds fertile soil outside the *polis*.[25] The whole tradition of the Seven Wise Men (also Apollinian) is another one of these aspects of the Greek religious life that keeps, and more importantly renews, its vitality outside the life of the city. The same point could be made about the important figure of Dionysus, and his promise of an extraordinary fullness of life.

The religious history of the city from the sixth century on is thus made up of a series of flowerings of 'special' cults that express 'truths' alien to the official worship. These special cults tend to be more 'popular,' since the official worship is largely in the hands of the city's aristocracy. 'Popular' means that they have individual appeal. This appeal, however, cuts across all classes. Orphic religion gathers literate adepts; obviously individuals there acquire a sense of being saved and the conversion to a new life that did not obtain in the larger group. Dionysus gains devotees (he was not one of the twelve in Homer, but he has made it by the time Athens builds the Parthenon.) In his cult too one finds a quality of vibrant piety that seems absent from the ceremonies of the great city. And there is the cult of Adonis that recruits women; it too offers something not available through the public religious channels. Jean-Paul Vernant points out that women, being less integrated into the city, its rites and its political life, are particularly prone to these 'other' cults.[26]

Most commentators find in these other cults a common feature of mysticism and ecstasy. Most do indeed offer either initiation or salvation from an evil which the public religion does not seem even to attack. E. Rohde and, following him, Guthrie find a yearning for heavenly bliss and a faith in immortality in all those cults, while the public religion seems to concern itself mainly with the decorous life, teaching that the gulf between man and the divine is impassable.[27] Dario Sabbatuci argues, correctly, I think, that these pre-Hellenic, pan-Hellenic extraurban sanctuaries provide a springboard, as it were, and a shape to radical mystical challenges of the polytheistic system.[28]

In a recent study Marcel Détienne, basing himself on the Adonis cult, draws a contrast between a public religion that offers sacrifices to the gods, eats cooked consecrated meat, and commends and protects marriage, and unofficial cults that attempt to break down the barriers in which man is enclosed and establish an immediate unity with the gods: these cults speak favourably of sexual licence or of celibacy, of vegetarianism or of homophagia (that is, they reject the prevailing civilized mores).[29] One can point out that Ares and Aphrodite, two gods guilty of adulterous union, are rejected to sanctuaries beyond the confines of the Hellenic world.[30] War and eros undermine civil order.

The presence of these cults is a useful reminder of the stresses which the Greek *polis* knew during the time of its brief flowering. See for instance the judgment of Voegelin: 'The pathos of the *polis* was the pathos of a dynamic participation of the people in a culture that originated in the aristocratic society.' The dynamics were on the side of the 'people.'[31] One should not forget, however, that the religion of the fifth century and its civilizing power are the result of a public sort of piety. Most commendations of Greek religion accordingly speak well of the Olympian gods. They are emblems of high humanity and religious reform, writes Gilbert Murray; they arise above low superstition; their victory against the Titans symbolizes 'the strife, the ultimate victory, of human intelligence, reason and gentleness, against what seems at first the overwhelming power of passion and unguided strength'; they bring intellectual order; and, through them, the Greeks stride towards a notion of one supreme God, Lord of all. Finally the Olympian gods manage to win the fervour of all Greeks and bring a measure of control to the strife among them.[32]

Walter Otto also speaks most favourably of the wisdom and piety these gods elicit. Thanks to them, the Greeks associate 'reverent recognition with acute observation of reality.' Above all, the gods teach measure to man. Differentiation between divine and human is the burden of the doctrine and admonition emanating from the gods. They do not speak to man of mysterious origins and ordinances; they show him no path from the natural form of his being to a superhuman condition of perfection and bliss. On the contrary, they warn him against overweening thoughts and aspirations and sharpen his perception of the order of nature. Dionysiac and Orphic sects believe that revelation has vouchsafed them a higher knowledge and that they know the sacred path that leads to perfection, but they stand apart from mainstream piety. The Olympians, who inform the character of religion from Homer to Socrates and who speak to us still on the lips of an Aeschylus or Pindar, have no thought of initiating man into supernatural mysteries or of revealing to him the secret character of their divinity.

The sacrifices practised in mainstream Greek tradition confirm this sense of settled boundaries between gods and human beings. Prometheus has helped mortals by stealing fire and shown them how to cheat the gods. Only the fat, the bones, and the skin of the sacrifice are burned on the altar; human beings obtain the meat; all that is left for the gods is scented air. but this order is safe, appropriate. Mortals sustain their life with sacrificed, cooked meat and the gods receive their due. The Orphics, who want to be pure, reject the deception and sustain such life as they want with vegetables.[33] Vernant shows that Greek sacrifices establish rules that settle men in an orderly, disciplined middle area, halfway between beasts and gods. They define appropriate, precise roles.[34]

It follows naturally that in the Olympian religious tradition man must study not heaven but himself. This self-scrutiny, however, does not imply examination of conscience or confession of sin. The admonition 'know thyself,' which goes back, if not in the identical words, to the Homeric Apollo, rather means: 'Observe the sacred form of nature, consider the limitations of humanity, realize what man is and how great an interval separates him from the majesty of the eternal gods!'[35] As Vernant puts it, true piety, in the Olympian religion, always acknowledges a distance between god and man; piety is wisdom and 'discipline' (or restraint).[36]

Greek religion thus derives from the Olympians a uniquely humanizing power. Consider the judgment of Cedric Whitman: 'Greek polytheism is the greatest of all religions in the matter of its illimitable responsiveness to knowable experience.' In Homer's case 'the gods were conceived to ratify and enlarge a human scheme in a poetic context, not to define the nature of divinity abstractly, in and of itself.'[37] Bruno Snell puts it this way: 'The more the Greeks begin to understand themselves, the more they adopt of this Olympian world and, so to speak, infuse its laws into the human mind.'[38] Such gods ask no sacrifice of the intellect. Their existence is self-evident, inherent in nature. It is after all absurd to say one does not believe in Aphrodite.

There is some truth in all this. It is enough to read the *Oresteia* to sense something of the genuine pride that could be felt about the civilizing power of Olympian religion. As Aeschylus told the story, Athena and Zeus gave to the city institutions that established its civilized order and put an end to barbaric warfare among the tribes or within families. And it is enough to read the *Bacchae* to sense the emotional pull that comes from the other cults: to many readers, however, that uniquely powerful play drives home the constant destructiveness of these strong 'beautiful' emotions.

One should not, however, give credit too exclusively to the Olympians. We have already emphasized that Greek religion remained an unstable mix in which a variety of elements contended for supremacy. In any case the official Twelve that includes Hera, Demeter, Dionysus, and Apollo had made a compromise with the non-*polis*, chthonic element. Some authors have not hesitated to see throughout the history merely the contention between two religions. Hegel, for instance, has suggested that the older religion went deeper but had more limited powers.[39] And G. Rachel Levy has found in the religious revivals of the sixth century a return to the old order of the Minoan (that is Mediterranean) energies, which were those of the neolithic religion of reciprocity. The Greeks for her could not for long remain severed from their roots in the old order and rest content with the Olympian abstractions. They returned to the religion of communion and of support for everything human in nature and in her power, a return which became abundantly clear in the Hellenistic era.[40] According to this view, then, the *Bacchae* testifies to the bankrupt emptiness of the traditional religion of those who were in charge in the city. Both sets of views are perhaps something of an oversimplification. It is probably more prudent to take a cue from another comment of Hegel: Greek religion he compares to a progressive wet-nurse who never resents the growth of her child.[41] The presence of the basic dualities made for an intellectually fluid situation. There were enough interstices in the system to allow for prompt expression of new forces and new insights. Minds could look for the other side of any question.

This situation certainly prevented Greek religion from providing the direct doctrinal leadership we have come to associate with religion. In the absence of a strongly organized clergy – a fact which probably reflects the strain more than explains it – the conditions simply did not exist for formulating great creeds which would be assented to by nations or for weaving together political groups and classes around a religious dogma. In Greece, I must stress, all that a religious heretic had to do was change cities. No one could possibly perform all the rites; no one was expected to honour all the gods. The Greeks were uniquely free to portray the gods as they chose. The priests in Greece did not burn books, the prophets did not preach crusades, diviners at most delayed battles, if that.[42] This, of course, made for tolerance; in the ancient world it was philosophies that formulated exclusivities based on doctrine. It also made for an incapacity on the part of Greek religious culture to create around its sanctuaries religious reformers who could reorient the whole religious culture, give it a new impulse, and forge a new cultural unity. Delphi came closest to that, and we know that it did not come close enough. Greek religious culture was a rich soil for intellectual growth but it did not formulate an all-inclusive commitment and it did not produce intellectual leaders in its own midst. This, of course, gave many political Greeks the impression that Greek religious culture could easily be manipulated, or reformed, since no major authorities were likely to stand in the way. That much is true, but it is also true that no reformer could gain much authority in a religious culture that was not accustomed to being led by authorities but remained closely wedded to the customs of cities and villages. The Seven Wise Men were an exception of sorts and emerged (retrospectively, in all probability) as some kind of patriarchs. No authoritative record of their sayings and doings, however, emerged. Quickly the personnel of Greek religious culture, diviners, the priests, the prophets of the sanctuaries, became quite distinct from the 'scientists,' the philosophers, and the other articulate public speakers. Greek religious personnel never preached, hardly ever taught. The 'poets' did that, in their way. Greece is a unique case where what we call literature is a public phenomenon. 'The literature is perhaps the greater social institution,' writes Beye. Without scriptures, sanctuaries did not keep libraries. Book-learning was to grow elsewhere.[43] Speculative theology was thus independent of cult to an exceptional degree even though all prospered on the same soil.[44] It acquired at the outset the flavour of an intellectual rather than a religious exercise.

The absence of a clerical orthodoxy and the presence of a literary tradition may also explain why the Greeks so quickly grew aware, and largely all by themselves, of shortcomings in their own religion. The Greeks were probably the first undefeated people to undertake a criticism of the religion that flourished in their midst. The moral shortcomings of the Olympians were the first targets of such denunciation. Nilsson rather flatly says that 'the intellectual development of Greece brought the defects of her gods and of her religion into the open.'[45] Cornford, more usefully, traces that very intellectual development and inquisitive spirit to the tension within the religious culture and the split between the mystic gods and the Olympians.[46] The rise of scepticism, the attack on the gods, the sarcasm over their immorality, all this can largely be accounted for by referring to the variety of strains in the religious life and its impact upon an intellectually lively people.

Our account has emphasized the dramas of change, rooted in a fundamental tension and worked out for centuries in a largely non-literate culture. No books were burned, but how many myths were lost in the shift, or transformed beyond recognition? It still remains true that the suggestion (made by Edouard Des Places) to speak of Greek religions goes a bit too far.[47] Some Greek gods invited men to strive for oneness with the divine while others maintained an impassable barrier between those who are ever young and the mortals. But all these gods spoke Greek, belonged to the same family, and were quite distinct from those foreign gods that by the Hellenistic era had acquired sanctuaries in Greek cities. The Greeks, for all the political disunity, never doubted that they were one people and Herodotus significantly includes religion in his statement of Greek unity, which is 'of a common stock and speech, common shrines and customs.'[48]

Committed as we are to the view that there was, in the end, but one religion in Greece, we must try to outline, as a conclusion, its major characteristics.

Among the common features of the whole Greek religious world, we should mention first its capacity to enhance the human striving for intelligibility. Nilsson writes that Greek myths, unlike folk tales, have purged themselves of the magical element. The human shape of the gods tames the mysteriousness of the power.[49] There is some rationalism in these formulations but most will agree that, from Homer on, at least the myths and gods of Greece provide men with images of themselves that enable them to fathom their own fate and their own behaviour. Greek religion, like all religion, testifies, at times with dreadful vigour, to the power of irrationality, but even then it tends to enhance the measure of understanding granted to human beings. The tragic insight into fate and freedom grows out of a religious festival, the theatre, that keeps deriving its theme from the lore of myth long after its archaic religious roots in ritual have dried up. Cosmogonic myths elicit a whole series of broodings over the nature of the universe in the context of which science and philosophical speculation alike arise. Myths of the beginning provide a grasp of the nature of man and the pathos of his becoming. Few people sustain as long a reflection on the world order as the Greeks, stimulated alike by their myths and their probing intellect. The Greek mind finds itself at home soon in both *mythos* and *logos*: each without the other is either blind or empty, writes Jaeger.[50]

A second feature in the Greek religious culture is the concern to sense the delicate conditions that foster and maintain friendship between the gods and men. 'Heaven and earth and gods and men are held together by communion in friendship, by orderliness, temperance and justice.'[51] Some groups have transformed this sense of friendship into the affirmation that gods and men are of the same race. Most emphasize the prudence and restraint that are demanded of the human partners if they are to avoid the hybris that ruins the relationship. Hence the preoccupation with boundaries. In either case the gods never overpower: only those who have become mad are destroyed. The gods offer signs: their signs are always negligible. Divine intervention – unlike that of fate – is always resistible. Athena seizing the lock of Achilles' hair stops him in his tracks as he draws his sword upon Agamemnon: she gains for Achilles a moment for thought and recognition, but she does not stay his arm, nor does she issue an order. At the end of the *Oresteia* Athena casts a decisive vote for forgiveness, but she does not thereby achieve a decisive reversal: the hundred-man jury is exactly tied. Gods are always less dramatic than men. Divine power tips the scales in cases where a hint of power suffices. Greek gods are subtle. Human beings must be prudent, sensitive, shrewd. Plato visualizes the gods as making their order-creating power felt by initiating a rhythm: 'they move us and lead our hands, knitting us together with songs and in dances.'[52]

Finally the dominant mood of Greek piety is that of the festival, one of celebration. Greek religiosity is a special kind of vision, argues Karl Kerenyi: it holds onto 'the visionary knowledge attained by festive man.' *Theoria* is the highest joy; it provides the divine feeling of being the joyful spectator who beholds what there is, all that there is, and what there really is.[53] Finley Hooper stresses that the statue of Athena in the Parthenon is not worshipped; it is the focus of human self-expression and celebration.[54] In his funeral speech Pericles refers to the religious culture of Athens once, stating that it provides 'all kinds of recreation for our spirits' through its contests and sacrifices.[55] The sentiment is echoed by Plato: 'the gods in pity for the human race thus born to misery, have ordained the feasts of thanksgiving from their troubles; and they have granted them as companions in their feasts the Muses and Apollo the master of music, and Dionysus that they may at least set right again the modes of discipline by associating in their feasts with gods.'[56] A conservative like the Old Oligarch will see the festivals as decorous social enjoyment. The mysteries will make them more orgiastic. In all cases the feeling is that, while toil is the necessary lot of man, it is not the absolute lot and does not have the last word. The gods have given us festivals where the soul is refreshed and tastes the joy which in the end will be the lot of the righteous. The founding of such festivals is the clearest manifestation of divine benevolence.

An intelligible order, a delicate friendship, and festivals which attune man to the divine world, these are the generalizations we are prepared to venture about Greek religious culture. What did Plato find in it? To answer this question we shall turn to texts where Plato speaks his mind about the quality of the religious life he finds in his city.

3 The expressions of opinion

Two kinds of texts express Plato's relationship to the Greek religious tradition. We find in the dialogues opinions about aspects of Greek religious life and thought. We also find passages in which a speaker, most often Socrates, takes over some aspect of the tradition and expounds views which transmit the substance of some strain or other in the Greek religious culture. In the first case Plato stands on the outside so to speak, weighing the value of some religious beliefs and observances. The second case is much more complex and we shall review the relevant texts in the next three chapters as we examine the content of Plato's philosophizing on religion. For the time being let us merely state that in this second type of text Plato is apparently writing from within a religious perspective of some sort.

Clearly Plato has ambivalent opinions about the state of religious affairs which prevails on the scene in which Greek life is played out and in the context of which individuals must grow into wisdom. His basic stance as philosopher challenges the authority of the poets. One does not arrive at truth by consulting authorities.[57] Plato also repeatedly expresses his contempt for some of the ceremonies of Greek religion, including those commonly considered most sacred by the Athenians, namely the Eleusinian mysteries. The sacrifice of a pig is referred to most slightingly.[58] The mysteries to him are a vulgar and cheap salvation that excuses the self from the need for real self-purification.[59] Downright moral revulsion is Plato's attitude in such cases. The Laws forbids private cults, which open the gates to morally disordered superstition.[60]

In other cases Plato's mood is quizzical. He expresses condescending amusement with humourous, but not sarcastic, emphasis upon the most literalistic interpretations of the hope for immortality. Socrates in the Apology discusses the prospect of his death and states that he would not mind having a chat with Orpheus, Hesiod, Ajax, or Homer.[61] In the Phaedo Socrates is not prepared to assert positively that such key doctrines as immortality are true.[62]

Plato also often blames the poets and other authoritative spokesmen of the tradition for transmitting only imperfect copies of the truth and not being conveyors of actual knowledge.[63] It is allowed that they may occasionally say the truth but it is emphasized that, when they do, they cannot give an 'account' of it; they do not have a grasp of the rational principles that are necessary if the truth is to be truly established and properly understood. Poets, diviners, and soothsayers say many fine things but do not understand the meaning of them.[64] The *Statesman* finds that priests and soothsayers have no worthwhile contribution to make to the task of scientific government: they are supposed to be interpreters of the gods to men but their science is a menial one. The priests who know how to give the gods the gifts that please them and how to ask them for good things are masters only of the art proper to servants. They may have great importance in the eyes of a society but they are far removed from the truly royal art, which is that of knowledge.[65] Strategists, orators, and judges share in that art and they have contributions directed by intelligence or mind to make to the task of government. Religious officials, however, belong in the kitchen of the household. The myth of *Phaedrus* confirms this low rank. Depending upon the quality of the vision of reality it has gained before birth, a soul may be reborn in one of the following nine ranks: a philosopher, a man of musical nature, a lawful king or warlike ruler, a politician, a man of business or financier, a hard-working gymnast or one concerned with the cure of the body, a prophet or someone who conducts mystic rites, a poet or some other imitative artist, a craftsman or a husbandman, a sophist or demagogue, a tyrant.[66] The point is clear: the tribe of religious specialists is far removed from the aristocratic world of those who know.

In a whole series of texts, however, Plato upholds the authority of some features of the Greek religious tradition. There is evidence that the Academy functioned as a sort of religious community.[67] Plato is also very firm in affirming the existence of the gods and linking atheism with immorality. That the famous stories one hears from one's youth become objects of scepticism for many is a grave concern to him. He is vexed and indignant with the men who by their disbelief have put upon him the burden of having to prove these things.[68] Then Plato also at times affirms the wisdom of some of the religious specialists found in the Greek world. Some say things that are true and beautiful. Priests are found who can give a reasoned account of things they are concerned with.[69] Diotima is very much part of such clergy as Greece has; she procured delay in the advent of a plague by bidding the Athenians to offer sacrifices. Socrates refers to her in the *Symposium*: she initiated him to revelations.[70]

Even more than that, Plato affirms the greatness of Socrates by including him among inspired religious figures. In the dialogues Socrates prays twelve times.[71] He has an 'internal oracle' or prophetic monitor, and thus claims to share in the very divinatory experiences that Euthyphro claims to be an expert in. 'I am a *mantis*,' a seer, or a prophet-diviner, he states in *Phaedrus*. In the *Apology* he takes leave of those who have condemned him by uttering a prophecy: one does not escape blame by suppressing one's critics but by making oneself as good as possible.[72] Socrates also very specifically identifies himself with one institution of Greek religion: he has his mission through oracles from the god; and the very oracle at Delphi has informed Chaerephon, a man who never has hesitated to ask a bold question, that Socrates is the wisest man.[73] (One may note here that, if we believe W. Jaeger, the young Aristotle gave Socrates an important place in the history of Greek religion; the dialogue *De philosophia* emphasizes the link between the Delphic 'know thyself' and the new Socratic search for knowledge; Socrates is thus seen as 'the restorer of the ethical principle of Apolline religion.'[74])

Finally, we find that in the *Laws* Plato affirms, most systematically and on practical grounds, that ancient customs (including the religious ones, and perhaps especially those) ought to be kept with great care. In this work, which offers us his last wisdom, Plato grants to the sacred laws laid down in ancient times an authority that he is far from granting in the rest of his philosophy to the sacred books of the past. The philosopher does not acknowledge the authority of Homer but his legislator most emphatically acknowledges that of Lycurgus:[75] 'No man of sense, whether he be framing a new state or reforming an old one that has been corrupted, will attempt to alter the advice from Delphi or Dodona or Ammon, or that of ancient sayings, whatever form they take.'[76] Here again religion as a matter of orthopraxy is taken with the utmost seriousness.

Traces in Plato of a global appraisal of the realities or trappings of religious life are one thing. Expressions of opinion, or implicit attitudes towards the sort of language that is acknowledged as specifically religious, are another, even more complex. Consciousness of the nature of language has manifested itself, we have seen, through a distinction between *mythos* and *logos*. To discover Plato's sense of this distinction, however, is no easy task and it is made more delicate yet by the fact that texts can be adduced from the Platonic corpus in which this type of 'speech-event' that gets called *mythos* in one case is labelled *logos* in another, and vice versa.[77] Clearly the two words must be translated differently depending on context and we shall have to use the Greek words frequently in our text. Generally speaking, the dominant hue that colours the distinction in Plato's writings is that stemming from the two manners of speech identified by Détienne to which we have referred above.[78] *Mythos* is the type of speech that has the prestige (or liabilities) of traditional, authoritative, religiously legitimated speaking. *Logos* is the type of speech that enjoys the dynamic power of deliberative, searching, argumentative speaking, and it has the features proper to the dialogue in which minds test each other's knowledge (and each other's claim to wisdom).

By Plato's time some doctrinaire people were enshrining myths in the sense of traditional stories referring to the gods (or to men in their relationship to the gods) as the depository of all truths. Other doctrinaires saw in such myths nothing but fables that hamper one's grasp of the truth. Plato's own evaluation ranges along this broad spectrum. In the *Republic* Socrates refers to *mythos* as a device employed in the upbringing of young children and adds that 'the fable is, taken as a whole, false' (literally 'a lie'). He nevertheless promptly qualifies that: 'there is truth in it also.'[79] A stronger note of respect is voiced in the exchange precipitated by Phaedrus: reaching the place where Boreas is said to have carried off Oreithyia, the young man asks Socrates whether he believes this tale to be true. The answer is carefully articulated: 'If I disbelieved, as the wise men do, I should not be extraordinary; then I might give a rational explanation' (that is a blast of north wind pushed the poor girl down a cliff). The explanations are 'very pretty in general' and 'the inventions' of 'clever and laborious' men. Socrates, however, has no time for such inquiries. His priorities are different: 'I am not yet able, as the Delphic inscription has it, to know myself, so it seems to me ridiculous, when I do not yet know that, to investigate irrelevant things. And so I dismiss these matters and accepting the customary belief about them ... I investigate not these myths, but myself, to know whether I am a monster, more complicated and more furious than Typhon or a gentler and simpler creature, to whom a divine and quiet lot is given by nature.'[80] By the time Socrates is finished, it is clear that his allusion to the wiser men is ironic, and he puts the finishing touch on his irony by using the mythical figure of Typhon to give expression to his own dilemma about himself. The same kind of attitude (with typically different word usage) is expressed at the end of *Gorgias* as Socrates introduces the concluding myth: 'Give ear then, as they say, to a right fine story (*logos*) which you will regard as a fable (*mythos*), I fancy, but I as an actual account (*logos*); for what I am about to tell you, I mean to offer as the truth.'[81]

In a third group of texts, found predominantly in the *Laws*, Plato exhibits an earnest and religious respect for myths as authoritative stories or likely accounts that enable society to grasp solid truths. With these texts the semantic situation becomes stabilized and *mythos* is used consistently to refer to such myths.[82]

The survey of these trickier texts confirms our general conclusion on the wide spectrum of usage found in Plato. *Mythos* can be the speech which is above all suspicious or even marked with the stamp of untruth, but it can also be the sort of speech that deserves the utmost religious respect. The dialogues after all are intended to reflect a situation of conflict: it is to be expected that different speakers will use the same words to mean different things and that the literary Socrates will express a sense of the awkwardness of words in the matters that lie so close to the centre of his purpose. These semantic muddles confirm the picture of ambivalence and confusion. Plato is of many minds on the subject of 'religious' realities and he cannot see them as a simple, single-textured affair of clearly ascertainable worth.

4 From opinions to doctrines: the trajectory of a philosophy of religion

Plato may be said to have begun his philosophy of religion with the portrayal of the encounter between Socrates and Euthyphro. Where he ends is clear for all to see. The *Laws*, his last work, contains a full statement of religious belief and a developed theology. Having looked at all facets of Greek religion, and endowed with the knowledge proper to a philosopher, Plato works out a religious legislation for a reformed Greek city. There he very clearly puts an end to all the ambiguities found in his works and affirms himself almost unqualifiedly a lover of the gods and a proponent of a religious restoration. Religion is presented in the *Laws* as an invaluable means which enables us to remain in touch with the gods. For the good man to make sacrifices to the gods and to remain in touch with them with prayers, thanks, offerings, and worship is the best path towards blessedness. The law of the city is entrusted with the task of protecting this bond between the citizens and their gods. Finally, in a statement which was to echo throughout the Hellenistic era, Plato affirms that there is a kinship between men and the gods and that this family relationship is what accounts for the propensity in the whole human race to worship God.[83] This passage will be quoted again and again by all those who wish to argue for the natural religiousness of man.

Some have seen in these affirmations the position of an older and sadder Plato, even of a reactionary Plato. The *Laws*, it is implied, abandons the standpoint of free intellectual inquiry into religious matters exhibited for instance in *Euthyphro*. It is, however, misleading to transform the obvious difference between the early dialogue and the *Laws* into a change of mind. The encounter between Socrates and Euthyphro after all is only an initial encounter and has obtained only negative results. At the end the reader, thanks to Socrates, knows that Euthyphro does not know what piety is. But the reader has not learned in what piety truly consists. *Euthyphro* opens the path which philosophy of religion has to take and creates a style of thought on the subject. But the philosopher does not only begin; he goes on. Sooner or later Socrates – and all philosophers – must make good his opening claim: if he can expose ignorance, he must also venture to show forth knowledge.

While much of a philosopher's knowledge will expose the shiftiness of words in times of crisis, sooner or later the philosopher must stop merely speaking about speech, his own or that of others, and venture to speak also of those things that speech is purporting to speak about. Philosophy of religion begins in an act of distancing between philosophy and religion, but when all methodological preliminaries are done, the philosopher must turn towards that problematic object, namely towards the reality to which religion presumes to testify. So Plato decided that 'Socrates' must attempt to develop a doctrine of virtue. He even went further and developed a set of religious doctrines. He took so seriously the philosopher's duty to perform that he did not even rest content with the vision of truth or the utterance of sound doctrine; he proposed steps towards a society where truth would be secure.

The *Laws* rises to a large challenge. The reading of it suggests that Plato has arrived at an almost encyclopaedic knowledge of religious practice. (The text is a most important source for the historians.) More importantly, a sifting occurs in Plato's mind. Choices are made, a politically restorative action is outlined, and a presumably healthy religious system worked out. While we have difficulty discerning in Greece 'a religion' in our ordinary sense of the word, such is not the case with the *Laws*.

In Book 10, in a passage with an unusual didactic, even doctrinaire, character, Plato stresses that the religious life of his city rests on three dogmas: the gods exist; they are careful; they are wholly incapable of being seduced to transgress justice.[84] This shorter catechism is first adumbrated in Book 2 of the *Republic*; it is presented there as congruent with the faith that justice in all cases is best since it affirms that justice is the concern of the highest authorities in the world.[85] In Book 10 of the *Laws*, however, the three affirmations become the climax of a fully marshalled argument – Plato's most complete theological argument and exposition, as a matter of fact. Furthermore, Plato makes of these statements dogmas, namely something wholly unprecedented in Greek religion: his laws prescribe not what should be done but what should be affirmed or believed. The legislation of Plato's second-best city will contain a prelude that will argue for the truth of these propositions. The legislation will also formulate the penalties for those who commit impiety by not adhering to these three fundamental propositions. Plato's defence is that only criminal minds and characters dangerous to the city will find these propositions offensive. Plato's religion is not one that is perfectly at home in the diseased city. It interferes with traditional practice and seeks to change the minds of human beings with the help of the law and its penalties.

Such a move towards publicly upheld doctrines is, in Plato's eyes, a necessity intrinsic to the philosopher's mission. The philosopher's vocation arises at a time when the city is being destroyed by a crisis: perverted traditional doctrines pit themselves against perverse modern ones. The philosopher transcends this conflict of opinions. His claim, however, must still be made against those perverse innovative doctrines that claim that everyone who pretends to speak the truth is merely furthering his own interests. The philosopher must refute the nihilists. The threefold creed aims at just this purpose. We have reasons to conjecture that the clever nihilists had articulated their own air-tight creed: the gods do not exist; and if they exist they do not care; and if they care you can bribe them.[86] So the philosopher must teach positive doctrines. True opinion may no longer defend itself. Wicked men and their verbal insinuations must be warded off.

The shortcomings of any civil coercion in religious matters (obvious to any post-Enlightenment man) should not obscure the real merit of what Plato has achieved by formulating his three doctrinal propositions. That the gods exist, that they are concerned with the fate of mankind, that they cannot be bribed are important theological statements which provide us with a reasonably complete theology. These three dogmas also intelligently sum up the key issues at stake in Greek religious culture. They identify three areas of thought and feeling where the inherited conglomerate have fallen into confusion. They identify precisely the issues adumbrated by the debate on the morality of the gods. Plato is quite credible when he affirms that the chaos of opinions on these three propositions is related to the moral breakdown prevalent in Athens. This theology also shows the mark of the philosopher's striving after the knowledge of forms. With this threefold affirmation theology is taken out of the world of opinions – stories told by poets and more or less wise men, traditions handed down from obscure sources – to the world of knowledge. The knowledge that the three affirmations express is that 'the divine' is good. and something like that for Plato is the ultimate result of the contemplation of the form of the Good as the supreme authority. There is thus perfect continuity between the problems raised at the beginning and the solutions offered at the end. The doctrinaire incoherences of Euthyphro illustrate the cost inherent in any doctrinal vacuum. Doctrinal matters are serious. Euthyphro's commitment to the goodness and non-arbitrariness of the gods gives the philosopher some grounds of hope about religious people and gives direction to his inquiry.[87]

Finally this theology establishes an order which is of moral significance. This is of course implicit in the affirmation of the divine as good. But it must be emphasized since misunderstandings are numerous. G.M.A. Grube has summarized the three dogmas in the following manner: there is order and purpose in the universe; the divine forces are at work throughout the whole world and in every part; and the universal purpose is inexorable.[88] Such formulation paints the power of the divine with the colours of fatalistic and mechanical determinism. That we cannot bribe the gods is not in our mind a despairing message about their unyielding power. It is the affirmation of hope in the power of goodness in spite of our experience of a world where human beings can be bought and sold. Grube's formulation leaves no room for human moral aspiration and endeavour. Plato's threefold dogma is rather a support to men who strive after justice and seek to establish it even in the diseased city. The good can be known by men and it can rule the world if only men attune themselves to it. The gods exist, they are careful, and they cannot be bribed. What this means to us men disturbed by the corruption of our city is that the world is such that we can overcome this pervading decay. There is an order conducive to the human good. The mind has an ecstatic capacity and can become open to knowledge of this order. The process requires finally moral purification; there are no short-cuts.

Under these three headings we can proceed in chapters 6, 7, and 8 to examine the content, namely the positive results of Plato's philosophy of religion. (Chapter 9 will then examine the grounds for the very significant shift in tone in the *Laws*: it is not trivial that we find doctrinaire passages in this work and a novel, systematic praise of piety.) We shall, however, examine the three dogmas in an order different from that established by the older Plato in his catechism. In keeping with the young Plato, who was brought to life as a philosopher thanks to his meeting with Socrates, we shall start with the necessary moral discipline on the part of the self that sets out on the search for the truth. We shall go on with the affirmation of the divine order, and look finally at that most complex question, the affirmation of divine care.

To sum up, Plato began as a philosopher of religion when he sensed the issues involved in the encounter between Socrates and Euthyphro and his like. The two talk but do not understand each other and inevitably break off their conversation. This crisis in communication is to Plato a facet of a larger crisis in speech and in the city. Words have lost the power they apparently once had to mediate our understanding of the truth. The philosopher cannot help but suspect that in most, if not all, cases words have either become the instruments whereby the strong and clever acquire or maintain their power over the weak, or are merely the noise made by the ignorant. Through the art of dialectic Plato believes that we can bring men back to the path along which talking communicates genuine meaning and insight into the truth. Part of this talking will bear on the talking proper to religious people of various hues and practices. And there, too, insight will emerge so that, while he remains aware of the precariousness of his own language, Plato will teach what the gods and the universe are like and what religious customs ought to be. In this final result the knowledgeable ignorance of Socrates and the ignorant assurance of Euthyphro have fused into a working knowledge that is aware of its limits. The doctrines of the philosopher, thus, cannot be compared to those that crowd Euthyphro's mind: they have assimilated the demand for rational justification. The next three chapters aim at outlining the middle part of Plato's trajectory and retracing his steps towards these doctrines he has affirmed in matters of religion and of which he has stated that they ought to be believed.[89]

6

The necessary conversion of the self

Mores and morality among the Greeks

Commentators at the turn of this century were fond of repeating that the Greeks were 'deficient' when it came to a sense of morality, especially personal morality (they were usually measured against Kantians or idealized Christians).[1] Recent analyses have been more historically sensitive. They have been aware of the difference between common morality (everyday attitude) and the moral philosophy put forward by the philosophers.[2] They have also attempted a genetic approach, seeking to account for the history of Greek moral attitudes and conceptualizations.

The impact of the Homeric world is here particularly overwhelming. A.W. Adkins in his *Merit and Responsibility* has ably brought to light both the original constellation of aristocratic values and its enduring influences. Three Greek adverbs can attribute moral value to behaviour. An action can be done skilfully and get happy results, *eu*; it can be done handsomely and get applause, *kalôs*; finally it can also be done justly, *dikaiôs*. The Homeric hero embodies all human excellence but excels primarily at the first two virtues. He does things successfully and with style. Society makes strong demands on him: he must be brave, he must lead, and he cannot fail. As long as he succeeds, he has merit. And as long as society is pleased with him, the hero can press his advantage to get everything he wants. When Agamennon wants Briseis, the claims of justice do not carry much weight. Society needs aristocratic warriors; their reputations give the heroes all the moral worth they need. Merit was thus the most consistent source of moral commendation among Greeks. The gods in Homer share in this ethos.

Against such virtues of the strong, the weak invoke the third value, justice, and insist that Zeus requires it. Atavistic respect for boundaries comes to the fore. Hesiod, Xenophanes, and Solon express the thought that restraint is a highly moral trait and that cities need justice more than heroes. Apollinian religion is prepared to find guilt even in powerful families and teaches a prudence that has more than social shrewdness as its base. New taboos enter into it, but also refined moral sensitivity, and a new civic order slowly emerges. Clearly the emergence of new concerns effects the breakdown of the old aristocratic society. Adkins argues that the spread of the notion of pollution is born of despair; as the old order crumbles, life becomes harder and narrower, and calamities occur which the social order – or what remains of it – cannot cure.[3] People find refuge in Apollinian legalism, in M. Nilsson's phrase.[4]

What emerges in this context is perhaps best labelled a *law* conception of ethics. 'The central virtue is justice, prescribed by a law or some other norm (*nomos*) concerned with all the community to which it applies, and fixing what the good of the community requires from each of its members.'[5] Most people encounter this norm in traditional maxims. Hesiod is full of them. Here, on a page opened at random: 'Do not get base gain; base gain is as bad as ruin.' 'Be friends with the friendly, and visit him who visits you.'[6] Anecdotes and moralistic stories also abound to give striking force to the prudential warnings. The call to prudence either remains general and vague or lists masses of accidental details, with dire warnings for those who neglect the significant one.[7] The religious basis of much of this legalism becomes apparent in the case of those folk maxims which bear on offences against Zeus: the rights of strangers (hospitality), the claims of suppliants, and the duties towards the dead are featured as being particularly sacred. The maxims cover areas where the laws of the city tend to fail; they cover 'intercity' cases dependent upon an underlying Greek cultural unity. The maxims show also the pervasive presence of a practical mentality. *Hora telos* is perhaps the most famous brief one (with *meden agan*, 'nothing too much,' and *gnothi seauton*, 'know thyself'); it means 'consider the end,' 'think of the consequences.'[8] This law conception of ethics receives theoretical expression in the works of Protagoras. The great speech Plato puts on his lips argues that one can make men into good citizens – virtue is teachable. Men originally were naked, unshod, unbedded, unarmed; Prometheus gave them wisdom in the arts together with fire; worshipping gods and articulating speech, men have acquired civic art. Zeus sees to it that right and respect are spread equally among all. Everyone then has a sense of justice and can advise on this virtue. The city punishes wrongdoing: 'The city compels them to learn the laws and to live according to them as after a pattern, that their conduct may not be swayed by their own light fancies.' My own instruction, Protagoras concludes modestly, is merely an addition to the education that Athens already gives her citizens.[9] Meletes, Socrates' adversary in court, has no doubt on what can instruct the youth: 'the laws,' he promptly answers.[10] The *Republic* offers a brief compendium of such commonly inculcated virtues: respect of property, of oaths, of marriage, of parents, and due service of the gods. All human beings have such principles ruling them, it is argued.[11]

But the same period which has grown to appreciate the civilizing ethics of the *polis* also begins to see the very city as a product of human skills. From Homer to Sophocles poets have pictured the gods as artisans, makers of human fate, devisers of good things for human beings. But soon this very technique starts being vested in men.[12] Intelligent men are conceived to be those who control their lives and make what they want of them. Legends arise that see in the artisan the source of all the skills that make life good. The Prometheus theme expands. Gorgias praises Palamedes as a skilled, resourceful doer. Cities themselves are seen as the results of human design. Hippodamus of Miletus, the first city-planner, is highly conscious of what planning can achieve when new cities are founded.[13] Politics themselves are seen as *technè*. In this context the very laws and moral notions which are supposed to bind moral men are perceived by some as strings that may be pulled. Moral notions prevalent in an audience can be played upon by a clever speaker. Man the artisan sees them as tools that he can learn to manipulate in order to do with other human beings as he sees fit. The very sensitivity of the Greeks to the phenomenon of language confirms this disposition to see how moral persuasion *works*. One can henceforth see social and moral evidences as some sort of machinery with which a few can move the many.

The very practice of democracy in the fifth century seems to have been attended by an erosion of the old civic virtues of Solon and the underlying moral consensus. With the proliferation of citizens' debates in the Assembly and the spread of Sophistic education, doing the expedient thing (*to sympheron*) seems more and more to be the only sound moral thing for normal men. In his *Popular Ethics in Ancient Greece* Lionel Pearson has shown how the contrast between the 'just' and the 'expedient' becomes a commonplace in the fifth century. 'Pragmatic' morality remains on the defensive, but Pearson adds that it is equally commonly recognized that a man would be a fool not to choose expediency.[14] Some fifth-century democrats thus update for their purposes the selfish common sense of the Homeric hero. Man must exhibit social shrewdness, keep an eye on his limitations, act according to his portion, and not go beyond his due. There are some rules to be observed in this difficult world if one's honour and good reputation are to be kept. But, in the end, what each pursues – in so far as he can – is his own well-being.

The crafty moral prudence usually practised by the Homeric hero (and which gives a veneer of restraint to his virtues, such as they are) quickly erodes in fifth-century conditions. War, we hear Thucydides say, is a violent teacher. Greeks prey upon Greeks, Athenians upon Athenians. Loyalties do not last long in times of crisis and a stable system of adhering to rules, of making and returning favours, breaks down. Self-interest becomes not only more brutal but more naked as well. Impudent hybris becomes common. Division in the *polis* means the loss of the basis for a civilizing experience; men are then left alone with their potential savagery. In the Melian debate the Athenians feel no qualms about stating that a ruthless massacre will be the normal and expedient course if the Melians resist.

Adkins thus stresses that the moral crisis in the fifth century is no mere lapse in morals and erosion of social restraint. The crisis has a theoretical dimension. Teachers have appeared who seek to demonstrate that 'doing the expedient,' whatever it is, is the path to happiness. *Arete* (virtue) recovers its older Homeric associations to mean the ability to wrest out of public opinion eager (or grudging) admiration for one's swift pursuit of one's own interest. To be *agathos* is, under all circumstances, to work for the prosperity of oneself, one's family, and one's friends. Selfishness is the normal root of all behaviour. To be considered just is an important ingredient in the equation for social prosperity and personal happiness, but, significantly, the appearance is all that the equation requires. The 'immoralists and the power-politicians,' concludes Adkins, have built a strong moral theory in which they have 'plausibly preempted the most valued terms.'[15] Their views quickly spread: they have obviously shed a light on human behaviour that makes sense to most fifth-century Athenians.

The point here is that the glorification of force always or nearly always present as a theme in Greek literature acquires a new social respectability under fifth-century conditions. Pindar's verses speaking of Hercules stealing cattle on the orders of Zeus become famous as an indication of how things get done. Herodotus takes knowledge of them for granted. Callicles in *Gorgias* quotes them to effect.[16] Plain greed in fifth-century conditions acquires a new halo: selfish men have learned to talk with brilliance and force. Their very verbal facility seems to transmute the rawness of their nature.

Socrates and Plato blame these new developments on the Sophists. All Sophists, they argue, either teach that the force of individualistic self-interest (doing as one likes and getting what one wants) is to be reckoned with, or openly profess that nothing but the greater force of somebody else's individualistic self-interest can check it. Today much is made of the contrast between the first and the second generation of Sophists. The former admitted that each pursues his own pleasure but seemed to believe that all this can be done in a civilized manner. This would be the position of Protagoras. These Sophists contented themselves with teaching the individual how to excel in the pursuit of a socially acceptable individual success; they quietly catered to self-interest and aggrandized its skills. But, Plato argues, these teachers feed the monster that knows no other law but that which it formulates for itself as it fancies it at a given time. E. Barker has put it this way: there was iconoclasm in the first Sophists and their opinions were destructive of many institutions and beliefs. And even if they did not themselves release forces that dissolved traditional social cohesion, the rich were eager to learn for their own ends and quickly came to know no other law but the pleasure to do as they liked.[17] The question is delicate. I want to do justice to Protagoras and his like. The misuse of their teachings need not be their fault. But I must add that their very account of the origin of cities, born of weak helpless men protecting self-interest, opened the door to those who professed to be stronger than the rest and saw in morality the reflexes of sheep.

Plato's own view is clear enough: Callicles is the final product of the Sophists' teaching. For him the strong always will get the better of the weak. Social existence does not change that. Words are neither the truth nor even ways of saying what is commonly accepted. They are means of achieving an end, something social beings use to do things with. One calls the action of an enemy unjust when one wants to stir up feeling against him.[18] Such use of words of course entails duplicity. If convinced, the listeners will assume that the action is in fact unjust and that the wise speaker who has just persuaded them of that sincerely believes it to be so. The speaker, on this theory of language, cannot reveal that his use of the words is merely calculated to manipulate.

As he surveys the mores of his day and the moral notions his contemporaries use to appraise themselves, Plato sees the need for a vast reconstruction. The *Republic* has Adeimantus present the current state of affairs: 'Fathers, when they address exhortations to their sons, and all those who have others in their charge, urge the necessity of being just, not by praising justice itself, but the good repute with mankind that accrues from it.' They allow that injustice is pleasant. They also believe that by means of sacrifices and incantations one can get the gods to purify one from one's misdeeds.[19] The law conception of morality has been content with showing that justice is good for society. Plato undertakes to show that justice is a virtue of interest to the individual and thus undercuts the whole tradition and its implication that the appearance of virtue is all that is necessary since it is all that society requires. But how can being just be desirable when everyone knows that it is always difficult and often disadvantageous, whereas being successful never fails to be agreeable? Plato nevertheless tries to alter the bent of Greek moral representations.

Plato thus undertakes a reconstruction of social virtue. A restatement of old-fashioned justice is the main part of his strategy. But his response to the realities of power politics also includes a yearning for purity and for a personal morality. His reorientation of moral representations clearly also owes something to the tradition of the mysteries. 'The soul must learn to fast from evil,'[20] pronounced Empedocles. Since the sixth century many voices repeat that the soul, to be good, must be weaned from impure attachments. The origin of the sense of guilt among the Greeks is also to be traced to the period following the breakdown of the old aristocratic society. A famous passage in E.R. Dodds's *The Greeks and the Irrational* portrays particularly eloquently the shift away from the moral atmosphere proper to the Homeric age. We can witness the rise of a dark sense of human insecurity and divine hostility. To account for the change Dodds points to social disorder and a prolonged experience of human injustice which gives rise to a deep longing for justice. The fear of hybris teaches man to suspect guilty self-assertion behind any triumph or success. The gods are jealous of such successes and punish the pride that accompanies them. The discontinuity between the two ages is not complete, Dodds carefully points out, but it is there. Greece has shifted from a shame to a guilt culture.[21]

So, along with the turn to Apollinian legalism, there is also a turn to what we might call mysticism.[22] From the sixth century on we see new institutions in Greek religion responding to the individual's sense of guilt, unworthiness, and lostness. The purification rites of the sanctuaries of Delphi and Eleusis in particular offer a way out: a ceremony, a vision, a teaching, a community where the person can learn to fast from evil, overcome its soiling inheritance, and join the religious company of the blessed. Many have been tempted to see nothing but pathological superstition in these phenomena. Karl Kerenyi has tried to correct this view in his study of Eleusis. What, he asks, has made the drama shown at Eleusis so moving? The vision gained there, he concludes, is liberating: birth in death is possible; our lot in this world is not the final one.[23] The sixth century witnesses also the rise of Orphicism. This first 'book' religion to take root in Greece makes powerful new contributions to religious speculation. A mythology appears that reinforces one's conviction of belonging to a sect of the pure.[24]

Clearly, to some in the generation of Plato the metaphor of purity expressed a genuine moral yearning and these people sensed in the Eleusinian mysteries and Orphic literature a message of release, an ethical tone that made a promise heard nowhere else in Greek religion. P. Ricoeur goes even further; according to him the vision of the pure and the impure in the religious world was the context of meaning in which philosophy grew to its specific awareness of the human problems and in the midst of which it had to chart its path. It is in this religious world that fear, shame, and restraint acquired their specifically moral quality and developed features that differentiated them from prudent fear of social consequences.[25] It nevertheless seems hasty to affirm as some have done that Plato was initiated at the sanctuary of Demeter. All we can document is that high-minded Athenians in the fourth century were attracted by Eleusis and that the sanctuary had a definite impact on the history of Greek moral thought. When Plato repeats that many are the thyrsus-bearers but few the mystics,[26] he denounces a magical interest in mysteries and their rites but he also echoes the requirements of the more demanding of these mysteries in their finer periods. A hunger for purity and moral reform, love of justice, restraint in one's dealing with one's fellow-men, these were undoubtedly part of the message associated with Eleusis. Book 10 of the *Laws* closes with a condemnation of those who presume to do sacrifices to any god while in a state of impurity.[27] The *Republic* affirms that the good man is beloved by the gods and the bad man hated by them.[28] Plato here echoes the affirmations which the mysteries made in moral rather than superstitious terms. Men must be pure if they are to approach the gods and be worthy of such approach. Goodness is a quality of the person quite distinct from the social status conferred on him by his contemporaries. Homer did not see the point at all; the fifth century has a painful awareness of it. Greek religion grew to affirm the distinctiveness of this quality of goodness. Plato is able to take hold of the whole issue. The virtue of friendship was traditionally linked with bravery – aristocrats take it for granted that friendship flowers among warriors. Plato links it to justice.[29] Citizens are friends. But for citizens to be friends they must have a shared orientation towards the good,[30] a fellow feeling rather like the one that came to expression in the cults.

Plato, writes Iris Murdoch, has made 'one of the earliest European attempts to define the good man as opposed to the hero' (and attached importance to his dignity).[31] The attempt to define was necessary, we can add, because the mores of the Greek people had not received a firm theoretical underpinning. The moral wisdom of ordinary people was 'a jumble of moral maxims, threats and bribes, which are the accompaniment of conventional education from childhood upwards.'[32] As such, ordinary Greeks did not differ from ordinary people everywhere. Their society, however, differed from ours in that our society finds in its midst ethicists or moral theoreticians who claim to have the grasp of some basic principle on which morality can be built as a coherent, ultimately satisfying system. No such theoretician had emerged in Greece in Plato's time. Nietzsche was quite right to suggest that Greek civilization never became stable enough to give rise to a wisdom that could establish ethical norms.[33] David Grene has added that personal ethics in Greece never found an authoritative basis that could distinguish them sharply from the ethics of power politics.[34] The continued hold exercised upon Greek minds by the Homeric aristocratic and heroic models in times when such types had no positive utility is indication enough of this state of affairs. It took a Plato to analyse the whole history of mores and moral notions and seek some firm basis for the understanding and orienting of the whole. I should add, however, that the very absence of a firm theoretical basis enables Greek society to give expression to a very wide range of moral perceptions and analyses. There is no doctrine filtering what people dare to say about what makes them and others act. Plato's privilege then is to develop theoretical moral interests in the midst of a particularly transparent society.

2 The concern with the soul

The image of Socrates is the fulcrum on which Plato rests his effort to reorient the whole Greek moral outlook. Socrates had the courage to say that no one was wise or knew what virtue was. Such a statement, however, did not place him in the camp of the lucid cynics who cultivated self-interest or self-indulgence. For Socrates also had the courage to say no when he found himself pushed to do something he did not think was right. 'Do not ... men of Athens, demand of me that I act before you in a way which I consider neither honourable nor right nor pious.' It all happened as if he found somewhere the 'authoritative basis' for the personal ethics of which Grene has been speaking. At any rate, Socrates spoke of the soul in a novel and serious way: the tending of his own soul was his ultimate concern and it seemed obvious to him that man should suffer all rather than endanger his own soul.[35]

Plato ensures the preservation of the record of this extraordinary man (*daimonion*, 'divine man').[36] He gives us the *Apology* where we see Socrates take his stand, making his grounds as explicit as he can. Plato also gives us, in the *Symposium*, a long speech of praise uttered by Alcibiades. Through his words – and them alone – Socrates exercises a spell on his listeners. But this spell is of a transitory and moral sort: 'he compels me to admit that, sorely deficient as I am, I neglect myself while I attend to the affairs of Athens ... he brings home to me that I cannot discover the duty of doing what he bids men.'[37] Like a sculptured Silenus, and unlike most men, Socrates is ugly outside and beautiful inside. The same note of amazing reversal is sounded when, in conclusion, Alcibiades narrates how he one night offered himself for Socrates' gratification. The conventions of the day called for the older man to approach the younger, beautiful one with kind words and an invitation;[38] this time the custom is reversed – and the result is unusual abstinence.

The *Phaedo* is Plato's most systematic attempt to say what makes Socrates into Socrates. It elaborates on the vocation of the philosopher, develops the notion of soul, and shows Socrates reconciled to the prospect of his death (the dialogue tells how Socrates spent his last day in jail). The message is clear: man must learn to sort out his soul from his body. The ascent of the soul requires a wrenching from daily concerns. Slaves to our appetites, we ordinarily have no leisure for philosophy. The origin of ever-renewed, distracting desires is placed squarely in the body. The soul therefore must liberate itself from the fetters of the body. Here Plato echoes a 'mystical' saying: 'it cannot be that the impure attain the pure.'[39] Such purification is a clear separation; it does not consist in giving up some pleasures for the sake of gaining others. Virtue is not the result of such prudent weighing of hopes and fears.

It is something entirely different. It is a wisdom which is above worrying over and measuring pleasures and pains. A virtue that ponders what is the higher pleasure 'is really slavish and has nothing healthy or true in it; but truth is in fact a purification from all these things and self-restraint and justice and wisdom itself are a kind of purification.'[40]

The source of these views is made explicit. 'I fancy that those men who established the mysteries were not unenlightened, but in reality had a hidden meaning when they said long ago that whoever goes uninitiated and unsanctified to the other world will lie in the mire, but he who arrives there initiated and purified will dwell with the gods. For as they say in the mysteries, "the thyrsus-bearers are many, but the mystics few", and these mystics are, I believe, those who have been true philosophers.'[41]

The view according to which philosophy is a weaning from all worldly concerns is made radical when Socrates states that 'those who pursue philosophy aright study nothing but dying and being dead.' Death as separation of soul from body puts the finishing touch upon the human process of purification. When it exists by itself the soul suffers no hindrance in its search for wisdom. Thus Socrates, who has spent all his life trying to acquire virtue and wisdom, is of good cheer about his soul and departs to the other world without fear.[42]

So the firm morality of the philosopher enables Socrates to die serenely confident that he has lived in conformity with a universal moral law that will still apply after his death. The portrayal of his last moments has always moved readers. The metaphysics of *Phaedo* have not fared so well. 'In regard to the soul men are very prone to disbelief,' noted Socrates. Philosophers who label themselves opponents of Plato's dualism have found in *Phaedo* the best illustration of what they dislike. To them one should respond first that the notion of 'separating' the soul is always spoken of in relative terms.[43] And, then, he who would rather die than accept moral surrender is involved in some act of wrenching; he is striving to free himself from (relative) unreality. We should not hide what Plato has said frankly: moral courage includes breaking our link to the world as we know it, and risking being broken in the process.[44]

In any case, Plato also portrays Socrates with things other than death on his mind and strong enough to resist injustice and the propagators of it in this world. In *Gorgias* we see Socrates pursuing his war against desire by alluding to the view of the Pythogoreans according to which the part of our soul (note: soul) that has desires is like a leaky jar; we cannot ever fill it because it is insatiable.[45] In the *Republic* we see him teach that what is required is nothing less than a complete shifting or conversion (*periagoge*) of the soul, 'which does not look where it should.'[46] The philosopher has adorned his soul with 'self-restraint and justice and courage and truth' and these qualities bear fruit in society. Socrates can resist the teachers of immorality, as is shown by his encounters with *Polus* and Callicles in *Gorgias*, or with Thrasymachus in the *Republic*.

The *Laws* makes perfectly explicit the link between the wisdom proper to the philosopher and the source of justice in society. 'There is an evil, great above all others, which most men have, implanted in their souls, and which each one of them excuses in himself and makes no effort to avoid. It is the evil indicated in the saying that every man is by nature a lover of self, and that it is right that he should be such. But the truth is that the cause of all sins in every case lies in the person's excessive love of self. For the lover is blind in his view of the object loved, so that he is a bad judge of things just and good and noble, in that he deems himself bound always to value what is his own more than what is true; for the man who is to attain the title of "great" must be devoted neither to himself nor to his own belongings, to things just, whether they happen to be actions of his own or rather those of another man.'[47]

The man who has reached purity is finally able to give justice its due. Plato's reconstruction of 'personal' morality here again arrives at the commendation of justice as the highest virtue. As Adkins says, doing things justly becomes the highest standard, more important than doing them handsomely in the eyes of men. An implication of this argument is that Plato's moral reorientation leads to a commendation of the co-operative values over the competitive ones. The ideal statesman weaves together the gentle and the spirited, the conservative and the bold, restraint and courage, the kind-hearted virtues and the tough-minded ones.[48] To give up the traditional models of aristocratic education is not to give up heroic virtues, but it is a redefinition of heroism. 'We can philosophize without mollification of the mind ... we do not think there is an incompatibility between words and deeds,' announced Pericles.[49] Until Plato showed Socrates at work, no one had clearly shown how the word of a good man is a strong deed.

In the end the good man knows that he cannot purchase virtue by making compromises with his fellow-men. There is thus a total seriousness to the morality Plato instils. The soul is immortal and its fate at death depends on what it has done during life. And man must act at any given time on such best insights as he has at the time. The soul 'cannot escape from evil or be saved in any other way than by becoming as good and wise as possible. For the soul takes with it to the other world nothing but its education (*paideia*) and nurture.'[50] Men come to a day of judgment: the measure is just but inflexible. We are then left alone with what we have made of ourselves, and this will be our help or our hindrance in a moral universe where no short-cuts are to be found. The gods, whatever they are, cannot be bribed. There is, there must be, a moral coherence. Note that the Socratic practice forces us into that too. Dialogue requires of the participants some coherent linking of their beliefs; it also requires the giving of some account of one's practice. The coherence of one's words with one's deeds is put to the test.

3 The rejection of tyranny

Plato portrays Socrates as the man who chose death rather than moral surrender. Plato's account of decay in the *polis* can also lead to the portrayal of Socrates as the sort of man who makes tyranny impossible.

Fifth-century Greece is fascinated by the problem of tyranny, as an illustration of the power of desire and the desire of power. Euripides defines the phenomenon: 'A city has no greater enemy than a tyrant, under whom in the first place there are no common laws, but one man rules, having taken the law in his own possession.'[51] Xenophon writes a dialogue on it: *Hiero*. The first part rehearses all the commonplaces on the unhappiness of the tyrant: unlike the private citizen, he has no friends, knows no rest, and always fears for his life.[52] To others the tyrant is the very picture of successful individual greed. Plato transmits in the opening pages of the *Republic* the story of Gyges: thanks to a ring that makes him invisible, the young shepherd can get all the good things he wants with impunity. He becomes a tyrant. The basic accumption of the tale is that anyone who could would act like him.[53] The successful tyrant is man completely unveiled. Another voice stresses that no one can become a tyrant unless a city somehow welcomes tyranny. The Anonymous Iamblichi teaches that it is not the strength of the tyrant that brings him his power but the folly of the citizens themselves.[54]

Plato hated tyranny. He felt it was vulgar and saw it was unjust. More: he showed how it was the last stage in the process of dissolution of civil life. He looked for its broad social causes, believing that societies die largely of internal causes. 'Do you seriously think that a monarchy is ever overthrown, or for that matter any political system brought down, by any forces except those which it harbours in itself?'[55] And he argued that division of opinion among the ruling class is the originating cause of civil decay.[56]

Plato sees also the link with Athens's imperialism; the ruthless invididual is but an imperialist writ small. The *Laws* puts it in a nutshell: liberty in Athens has become 'audacious to excess.' The Athenians have lost the old virtue of *aidôs*.[57] Other Greeks label Athens a tyrant city: it becomes fearful to all others because its character has become uncontrolled and its desires unlimited. It pursues empire compulsively and lacks the conception of an aim that can tell it that it has won the war.[58] This tyrannical ethos has an impact upon the individual character of the citizens: there is no telling what the greed of some will try to perpetrate on the somnolences of others. People become irritated; their opinions fluctuate quickly.

Interested demagogues promptly suggest foreign adventures which may at least enable the multitude to find again a common interest. The citizens of the *polis* are conscious of belonging to a community: this means that none can view the city merely in instrumental terms.[59] But in decaying Athens all other feelings yield to the quick moves of restless desire. Nothing, no feeling of friendship, no rule of justice, sustains order in the city. 'The steadfast can manipulate the greed and lust of others, the feeble is devoured by his own.'[60]

Plato's reflections on the moral forces underlying political behaviour come clearly into focus in the passages in Book 10 of the *Republic* on the tyrannical man. This man is portrayed as the complete, helpless prey of desire, 'always driven and drawn,' least able to do what he wishes.[61] Most men of tyrannical temper remain in private station. Greedy and avid of spirit, they can be played upon by demagogues; thus they are the easy prey of some other man of tyrannical temper who manages to become an actual tyrant. But this man too is only embarking upon further misery: he becomes locked up in a sort of prison-house 'filled with multitudinous and manifold terrors and appetites.'[62] In the decaying *polis* the people are led by their appetites and unrestrained by any sense of measure. They fall victim to a similarly debased man, who keeps his own desires hidden, becomes a tyrant, enjoys the bitter fruits of power in a diseased city. Feeding each other's desires, tyrant and people conspire against justice. In the end they conspire against their own happiness since neither achieves what he wants, even though both are determined to do as they please.[63] We find again the now familiar reversal: tyrants are not masters of all things and free to follow their desires; they are victims of their desires. They think they are about to become gods but they are not even human beings.[64] They are quite simply mad. Far from having a single will, or a single purpose, tyrannical men have several conflicting wills and move incoherently.[65] A tyrant city is also the constant prey of internal conflict.

The city may still pass laws, but it is not living under law. Written laws are modified at the whim of the moment by those who are in a position to modify them. And no unwritten laws remain as hidden but real bonds among men.[66] Men are no longer associated with each other by friendship. Reason and the sense of shame are gone. The *polis* and its usages are for many, then and now, the main source of any sense of morality. The breakdown of the city entails the collapse of morality. Who then can teach Athens? The philosopher Socrates offers his services at this point too. The descent into tyrannical temper is what he most firmly resists.

4 Philosophy as moral therapy

Religious purification rituals spoke of a translation of the self from a world of mud to one of light. Plato dismissed such views: it takes more than leaping with the

Corybants to become pure. He borrowed the language of the mysteries but transformed its import. Recasting the whole meaning of purification, he made it more decisively moral by making it more social.

The whole world of thought elicited by the symbols of cleanliness and purity acquires henceforth a personal dimension: purification is an educational process. The prisoners in the cave find it painful to turn their head to the true source of life and their eyes ache at the radiance. Conversion will be a slow, progressive affair. Such caution shows how hard it is for men to change; it is also rooted in suspicion of emotional religious outbursts. But above all the caution is a token of moral earnestness. Purification of the self, if it is to be thorough, will have to be a struggle of the self against the self.

Plans for political transformation may also make of social regeneration a sort of magical translation: good rules replace bad ones. Plato's early political experience has quickly disenchanted him from such simple views of political reform. Do we know what good rulers are? Are we anywhere near finding such men in our society? Are we even trying to train such men? The *Republic* outlines what a good city would be but admits that there is only one way to bring it into being: have genuine philosophers become masters of the state.[67] This solution merely introduces a new problem: would genuine philosophers want to be its masters? Could they? Would the machinery of the state and public opinion accept – even as an experiment – the rule of philosophers? Here, too, regeneration will be a long struggle if it is to be thorough. The struggle of some against others will be added to the struggle of self against self.

Robert E. Cushman's *Therapeia* has presented Plato's philosophy as a method of education, as a gentle, steady effort to lead men out of the chaos of human existence.[68] To philosophize is to bring to consciousness the petty objectives which dictate our behaviour in our unexamined course of life and discover the new values that dawn before the eyes of those who examine what they do and think. All the symbols of the conversion-oriented cults are relevant to describe the shift. One goes from a cage to the light of the sun; one learns to see with the eyes of the soul; the soul sprouts wings; the man who is wide awake to the realities of the diseased city wakes up to see another reality; the soul becomes liberated from the fetters of the body; man learns to feed and feast upon a different nurture.

But this whole tradition is modified by Plato, who adds to it a unique delicacy of pedagogical feeling. The soul is converted step by step in free exchange and open discourse. The means for therapy is the word.[69] The soul thus converts itself freely. It learns, slowly, of itself, to see the light. Learning, in the eyes of Plato, is a continuous process 'with several stages between (apparent) blank ignorance and knowledge.' This, adds W.K.C. Guthrie, contrasts with the views of the Sophists who keep using crude either/or questions.[70]

The fine hand of Socrates and his method of discussion is of course visible in this view of the learning process. Dialectic exchange makes sure that the soul assents to nothing but what it wants to assent to. And it weeds out misunderstanding, self-serving incoherence, motivated miscommunication, all those words we use to deceive ourselves and others. (There is nothing men like better than what justifies their injustice.) Platonic rhetoric is fair and open; it eschews the conditioning that plays upon prejudices. Social planning for the new city will require a measure of conditioning that plays upon habit, but here too leaders must be gentle as well as brave. Nothing can really bond a society except mutual concord and ties of friendship.[71] Gentle persuasion is an art. 'On this very thing, then, there might be an art, an art of the speediest and most efficient shifting of the soul; not an art of producing vision in it, but on the assumption that it possesses vision but does not rightly direct it and does not look where it should, an art of bringing this about.'[72]

Such an art is encouraged by propaedeutic studies which give a sense of measure: arithmetic, astronomy, music. But it rests above all on the power of the dialectic, which confutes erroneous and contradictory presuppositions, examines hypotheses, and refers them to a higher principle. What is good, and it alone, must remain the object of discourse. The good has basic appeal. It has a unique peculiarity: 'when it comes to the good, nobody is content with the possession of the appearance' (unlike justice as commonly viewed, we might add) 'but all men seek the reality.'[73] Steady, dialectical conversation remains the best means for leading the soul to the vision of the highest good. Always solicited by the Good, the mind wants to be one with it and only needs to have the obstacles removed by the intervention of the philosophic friend.

The dialectic process is not infallible. Success is not guaranteed. It remains always at the mercy of the pupils' willingness to learn. Plato was robustly confident that the human mind could not long sustain a contradiction and was bound therefore to discard the inferior hypothesis. However, he also knew that people like Euthyphro can withdraw from the dialectical process and go no farther on the road of knowledge. Alcibiades was a yet more recalcitrant figure.

Cushman's opening contention is that Plato's philosophy 'represents the supreme and most influential attainment of classical Greek thought respecting the way of human salvation.' That a salvation is needed is an assumption Plato shares with the mystery religions. What the philosopher does, however, is give an anatomy of the distorted soul and show the consequences in social and political life. His therapy, while stemming from the traditions demanding high moral purity, transforms this notion of purity by making it identical to the philosopher's free and loving assent to that which is true and good.

With the Platonic corpus virtue acquires a singleness of intention, a purity of heart, that seems to have been unknown in Greece before. The traditionally good man had a variety of skills; with moderation and discernment he knew when to exercise which. Like a cat, he always lands on his feet, at the end. There is continuity among Greeks in favour of a balanced outlook: greedy joy but also sober restraint; dashes of boldness but also avoidance of hybris. The knowledge of pleasure and of sorrow is part of the whole. Aristotle, pursuing the effort stated by rhetoricians such as Isocrates, restated, and renewed, the outlook that shuns excess above all: virtues are a mean between extremes, extremes of sensualism and of asceticism, for instance. Plato has started moving on a different track. The good man is no longer the one involved in a balancing act. Plato despairs of such acts of measure in the corrupt society. He yearns for something more absolute and invites us to rise to a higher virtue: the assent to that which is absolutely good.

5 *Gorgias*: the story of moral resistance

Before moving on to our next chapter we must take one more step to secure our results in this one. We have claimed to find in Plato the 'trajectory' of a philosophy of religion. The point of the metaphor is that philosophizing in Plato is a progress, and a progress recorded in a special form, the dialogue. This chapter has given us an overview of Plato's sense of a basic moral economy which cannot be escaped by the desirous self. This sense of morality can be expressed, even summarized, in doctrinal terms. Most of the time, however, Plato exhibits it in dramatic dialogues. My purpose here is to gather the results first by normal means of a prose summary and then by indicating something of the movement of thought in *Gorgias*, the dialogue that A.E. Taylor has called 'a prime favourite with all lovers of great ethical literature.'[74]

The prose summary goes something like this. Plato has injected a new note in the history of Greek morals by affirming that justice is the highest good of soul and society alike and is thus the standard that measures all other moral virtues. He thus accepts the notion that ultimately all men yearn after the highest good, that is happiness, rather than merely the good things of life. He keeps a eudaimonistic premise – all Greeks desire to live well. Plato, however, argues that an action can be good for us only if it is done justly, because what is really good for us is only that which is good for our soul, namely the part of us that has a destiny which transcends our earthly life and is inscribed within a universal moral economy. The working out of this universal law contrasts with the events in this transitory life in that all souls in the end get their just deserts. And at any point in our lives we can, through moral seriousness, be already attuned to this enduring law.

Plato does not attack the Greek fondness for pride; all Greeks want to be acknowledged. He does show, however, that there is no pride without self-respect and no self-respect without justice. To achieve this he must argue that the commonly cherished values of success lead to chaos and misery while tending the soul and resisting tyrannical desire will lead man to the kind of good conscience Socrates had. They will also put him on the path of an unceasing pursuit of the good, a quest that is steady, wise, and happy (unlike the restless pursuits of the rewards available in the corrupt city). They ensure justice, that is good order in the city and the ultimate well-being of the soul. Plato lays the basis for the inner-directed pride of the wise Stoic who expects little but folly from his fellow-men. Plato's just man no longer expects to cut a handsome figure among his contemporaries, but he does expect to be happy, happy in the end and happy now with an interior happiness.

Plato stresses that this universal moral economy knows of no exception: the gods cannot be bribed. Here Plato makes a polemical point: he attacks all the charlatans, 'travelling priests and diviners' and other purveyors of cathartic rituals.[75] But the denial hides a positive affirmation. The gods cannot be 'won over when bribed by offerings and prayers' because they rule mankind wisely, justly, and 'are wholly incapable of being seduced to transgress justice.'[76] The Birds had shown two comic Athenians who talked the birds into trying to become the rulers of the universe: the submission of the gods to this ambitious enterprise was obtained by depriving them of their food, that is of the sacrifices which men send to them. Less comic is the superstition of those who try to buy the gods over to their side. (Remember how Socrates exposed a mercenary side in Euthyphro's piety.) Plato very visibly turns his back on all theologies that include the gods in a social world men can manipulate. The universe is not a huge market-place where men barter for such advantage as can be won by flattering the mighty, outwitting the stupid, and exploiting the weak. Plato thus upholds an ostensibly theological view: the gods exercise a wise rule and nothing human beings can do will cause them to swerve from the good path their wisdom has appointed. They cannot be fooled; no game can be played with them. Immune to arbitrariness, they cannot be tyrants.

So much for the moral doctrine and its theological catechetical correlate.

The moral resistance of the good man can also be made visible in the story of Socrates' encounter with bearers of different types of immorality. The Gorgias does not give us the whole story: only political morality is discussed at any length and religious themes appear only at the very end, although decisively then. But the part of the story it gives us is very illuminating because it shows the moral strength of Socrates under trial.[77]

A few years after the death of Pericles, the great Gorgias is in Athens. All praise his art, but Socrates, not surprisingly, wants to know in what exactly it consists. Gorgias, a perfect gentleman, accepts Socrates' questions: he is a rhetorician and rhetoric is the art of speech. Not just any speech, he adds, but speech that deals with 'the greatest of human affairs, and the best' (451d). Socrates equally politely finds such laudatory definition incomplete: what is really the good of man? Freedom, answers Gorgias, namely the ability to have one's way and impose one's will on one's fellow-citizens. The rhetorician points out that persuasive eloquence is the skill that one most needs in a city like Athens. Under further probing Gorgias allows that such persuasive speech bears on matters of right and wrong and can persuade without producing real knowledge and without having real expertise: 'there is no need to know the truth of the actual matters, but one merely needs to have discovered some device of persuasion' (459c). As a matter of fact, with a happy naïveté Gorgias announces that 'before a multitude' 'there is no subject in which the rhetorician could not speak more persuasively than a member of any profession' (including the experts on the matter at hand) (466c). Gorgias in the course of the presentation of his art says that of course the rhetorician 'must use his rhetoric fairly' (457b). He is a sincerely moral man, and would not want to do any wrong. He sees himself teaching an art that helps young men succeed: if such young men abuse this art, the fault is theirs.

So far Socrates has elicited a self-portrait from the master of rhetoric. The atmosphere of the conversation has been one of courtesy: the appearances are of a conversation between two gentlemen who quietly share views and are entirely confident of the other's common sense. Socrates of course has no such confidence but at first he keeps this well hidden from Gorgias. A decisive turn occurs when Socrates points out a contradiction: rhetoric claims to deal with the just and the unjust; thus he understands rhetoric, claims to have some wisdom on the subject, and yet he has just heard that a rhetorician might make an unjust use of his rhetoric (461a). Polus here steps in, and with this second conversationalist the dialogue acquires a new tone. Polus begins by accusing Socrates of bad taste: of course Gorgias will have to say that the rhetorician knows what is just and teaches only that. Polus adds to the conversation a note of straightforwardness: what he frankly says is that human beings cannot be expected always to be frank. A gentleman of good upbringing like Gorgias does not make such blunt admissions. But Polus knows no such modesty: his morality lies in the frank and, as we would say, value-free consideration of the problems. Socrates welcomes this new partner and Gorgias, while still present, remains silent.

So the battleground has shifted, and the tone becomes more blunt. Polus defines rhetoric as an empirical knack, the knack of giving pleasure through words (462c). Socrates' dialectic becomes much more pressing. The art of the rhetorician, he suggests, seems to be a kind of tending, but being without knowledge (as already allowed by Gorgias), it must be a counterfeit art; medicine tends the body well by keeping it healthy, but pastry cooks tend it poorly by giving what will please the palate. Polus balks before the conclusion. The rhetorician does not have a parasitic existence; the orator is the most powerful person in the community. Socrates does not deny this but turns the conversation to the nature of his power. The tyrant does as he pleases but what is the ulterior end of his acts? He tries to secure his own happiness, but, if he reaps evil consequences, of what good is his power to do as he pleases? He should not properly be called powerful.

Polus here bluntly makes a personal attack on Socrates: of course Socrates envies a man who can imprison or kill anyone he pleases. Socrates accepts the challenge: if that is his only choice, he would rather suffer the crime than commit it (469c). Polus is now sure he can pour ridicule on Socrates: he gives the example of an unsavory tyrant, Archelaus; of course everyone envies his ability to cultivate vile pleasures and get away with it. We now know what sort of man Polus is: he envies the tyrant and only his lack of energy keeps him in the camp of those who live relatively ordered lives and are only modestly greedy. Socrates meanwhile holds Polus to his commitment to orderly discussion. Polus makes a distinction between what is 'good' and what is 'noble' – what is noble is a fine thing, but no one is expected to adhere to it if it is unpleasant as well. Close logic demonstrates that Polus cannot defend his distinction. Socrates apparently emerges victorious: to be wicked is not more powerful than to be destitute, but it is much more evil and harmful. So Socrates makes a further point: a competent judge can administer a medicine to the soul, a punishment that will cure it of its wickedness. An unpunished evil-doer is thus more miserable than a punished one.

Faults can be found with Socrates' argument, which is almost purely verbal about the ugly and the evil, the noble and the good. But Polus is no match for Socrates when it comes to logic. Here again the dialogue takes a new turn with the intervention of a fourth character. The contradiction between the morality of Socrates and that which it must resist has gone as far as it can with a man like Polus. It takes a stronger character for the drama to unfold further. Callicles steps in: he is an aspiring politician, a man of action. He has a passionate intensity which makes him a match for Socrates. After his intellectual dialogue with a snobbish, ambitious little man Socrates finds himself involved in 'a direct and absolute conflict between two competing theories of life.'[78] With Callicles the whole debate becomes much more realistic. Callicles is not one to chop logic; he begins with an appeal to facts: if what Socrates says is true, 'must not the life of us human beings have been turned upside down?' (481c). In fact, by nature, suffering wrong is evil. It is only man-made convention that claims that doing wrong is more evil. Such convention is an invention of the weak, who, though the majority, have no other way to defend themselves. But the strong are not stopped by such talk. A man 'of sufficient force' bursts all bonds (484a).

In his speech Callicles has high standards of courtesy: he can afford it; he knows that the trial of strength between his view of life and that of Socrates will not be settled by words and arguments such as are exchanged among intellectuals. In the real world power will go to the stronger. So he warns Socrates not to waste his time with philosophy any longer; it will ruin his life (484c). How will he be able to defend himself if somebody should drag him to prison? (486ab). Is this kind advice, dire warning, or plain threat?

Socrates here again accepts the challenge. The dialogue continues; words are still honoured, but there is a passionate existence on each side. Callicles does not have a consistent definition of the 'superior' man to whom all power belongs 'naturally.' Furthermore unbounded passion is not the sort of thing that can ever be satisfied. Finally the identification Callicles makes between good and pleasure does not hold. Callicles, in the end, must allow that some pleasures are 'better' than others (and must agree that he is not saying thereby that they are more pleasurable). Callicles tries to expand on this notion of there being something that is 'good' for man. Great statesmen like Pericles did improve the Athenians by being hard on them. Socrates leaps to the opportunity: clearly 'correction is better for the soul than uncorrected licence' (505b). Callicles unwittingly accepts the very proposition that earlier excited his contempt. From then on Callicles makes no effort to argue and Socrates goes on alone – and one doubts whether anybody really listens. To commit wrong is the worst evil. To have to submit to it is an evil too, but a lesser one. To avoid this latter evil one usually must make oneself the friend of the ruler or rulers and this may mean sinking to their level. Rhetoric is indeed a useful skill: it can enable one to save one's life through plausible speech. But it is a menial skill and offers no wisdom on the art of living well. Callicles keeps nodding, but clearly he is not convinced. While he has the floor, Socrates cleans up – and develops another point: none of the Athenian statesman has made the citizen better. Socrates, in turth, is the only real statesman Athens has known, for his speeches are aimed 'at what is best instead of what is most pleasant' (521d).

Thus ends the long dialogue on rhetoric or the art of speech. In the course of it the false pretentions of rhetoric have been exposed; more importantly, Socrates has made the claim to possess the only moral art of speech. Set against the standards of his morality, the urbanity of Gorgias, the bluntness of Polus, and the realism of Callicles are all exposed for what they are, varieties of an untrue speech that does not improve men and cannot avoid self-contradiction. but if Socrates unveils false claims, he cannot make his own claim good. His speech has not convinced the interlocutors who have been exposed to it so closely and at such length. Speech communicates only the difference between their respective positions and the fact that his partners do not have genuine respect for truth. But the speech does not mediate truth. The dialogue ends almost tragically with the two forces merely in the presence of each other in a polarized conflict.

Almost, but not quite. Because in the peroration Plato has Socrates telling a tale, a myth. (This is the first time Plato has recourse to such a device in the dialogues, and this particular tale is full of Orphic imagery.) In this manner of speech the absence of participation by the listeners is no longer a jarring note. 'To arrive in the nether world having one's soul full fraught with a heap of misdeeds is the uttermost of all evils,' as the tale (which Socrates says is to him an actual account, *logos*) undertakes to show (522e).

What man does at any point in his life matters forever. Every man who has lived a just and holy life departs after his decease to the Isle of the Blest, while those who have lived unjustly go to Tartarus, 'a dungeon of requital and penance.' Human judges pronounce the sentences. In the past they used to make mistakes. Zeus decided that such errors arose because men were tried in their clothing; such relics of successful appearance confused the judges. Souls, Zeus ruled, are henceforth to be judged naked, 'to the end that the judgment may be just.' 'All the natural gifts of the soul, and the experiences added to it as result of its various pursuits,' become manifest. Those who have achieved 'power' on earth have then no unfair advantage. All that is visible at the time of judgment is whether the soul is curable or not. So Socrates repeats his moral faith: 'doing wrong is to be more carefully shunned than suffering it; above all things a man should study not to seem but to be good, both in private and in public' (527b). And punishment is a remedy to be welcomed by souls that have committed evil, because, if curable, they are thereby restored to the moral order from which derives their health. The wise soul therefore lives in the presence of judgment (and, if need be, punishment) here and now.

7

There is an intelligible order conducive to the human good

We have seen Socrates embodying one conviction: there are no moral short-cuts. The moral economy in the world being what it is, the only wise and safe thing for a man to do is to remain true to such moral insights as he can gain. The course of justice cannot be deflected. Last-minute *ad hoc* action is futile.

These affirmations are powerful: they convey a sense of the need for moral coherence. They do not, however, set forth the nature of this moral order that the individual is supposed to be lucid about. They merely echo an old, terse affirmation found in the only extant fragment from Anaximander: 'Genesis and destruction among existing things happen according to necessity, for they pay penalty and retribution to each other for their injustice according to the assessment of Time.'[1] Of this immanent justice we only know *that* it is; we do not know *what* it is.

Plato firmly asserts that the gods exist; this is the thrust of his second dogma in the *Laws*.[2] He thereby, I contend, affirms that the over-all order is intelligible: to attune oneself to it is not just a matter of moral discipline but also one of intelligence. He thereby also commits himself to a large endeavour: he must unveil the principle of this order, show its nature, set forth its ultimate, overall purpose. To affirm that the gods exist is to affirm that the moral economy is intelligent,[3] and that the use of intelligence can bring us into accord with this order.

Working in the context of fifth-century Greece, Plato gives himself a further task. His moral argument must be accompanied by a reorientation in one's habitual portrayal of the gods. If the thrust of the theological discourse is to converge with that of the moral discourse, the theological discourse must be reviewed. Hence the plan of this chapter. We shall first examine how Plato intervenes in the ongoing Greek tradition of talking about the gods. We shall then examine the argument he mounts to show the intelligibility of the moral order. Finally we shall bring out the implications concerning the nature of human virtue.

I Power and order in Greek religion

Many of the epithets found in the Greek religious vocabulary refer to experiences of power and link such power to problems of cosmic order and disorder. Such, of course, is the case in most cultures. The experience of the sacred, in so far as one can speak of it in general terms, is the experience of a power which welcomes the self into, or submits it to, an all-encompassing order, an order that may be protective or threatening (or a bit of both) but is in any case supreme. *Hieros* refers to the self-authenticating power of something or someone who affirms himself brilliantly and with finality. Something is *hieros* if it does the ordering. *Hosios* refers to the power of religious and moral authenticity that belongs to whatever is in its place or plays its role in the divinely sanctioned and ultimate order.[4] Something is *hosios* if it is properly ordered.

What is characteristic of the universe of traditional Greek religion is that it senses power in two different places. It is aware of two different and contending orders. There is first Fate, a dark, unknown, but ultimately limiting factor. All things are in its unyielding power. What is uses its power for, however, is hard to grasp; possibly it cannot even be grasped at all. (If blind, fate pursues no purpose.) In mythology Clotho, Lachesis, and Atropos, whom Plato calls the daughters of Necessity, take their decisions about the fates of men without having to account for them.[5] But distinct from that of Fate, there is also the power of the Olympians. They live lives, have desires and purposes. Eternally young and extremely powerful, they ignore human restraints. But since they are part of a society, at least among themselves, the power of the gods has similarities with that of men. The gods at least, unlike Fate, understand the purposes of men: they have desires and experience frustrations and their lives set a context of meaning for the human ones. Their will, however, is not omnipotent. Their power is limited by the decrees of Fate.

No supreme power arbitrates between the order established by the gods and that established by Fate (the latter being perhaps only improperly called an order). There is no need: Fate always has the last word. Furthermore, the purposes of the gods adhere only to an uncertain order. Each god is given to fits of fancy and wilfulness. The gods bicker. Zeus tries to maintain some rule over his household, but his own temper and lusts severely limit his capacity to lead in a reasonable and orderly manner.[6]

Often morally blind, and limited in any case, such order as the gods create is always precarious, likely to be shattered by divine passion or overruled by decree of Fate. Greek religion often joins to the sense of the omnipresence of the divine a feeling about this presence being intermittent. Men thus must learn to fend for themselves. There is a tragic perception behind this self-reliance. 'It is part of the terror of the *Iliad* that it shows us a world in which human action is conditioned by powers and purposes even less serious and less moral than our own.'[7] Thus the moral authority of the order stemming from the gods is always open to doubt. Adeimantus launches the inquiry of the *Republic* with the question: do the gods really give blessings to pious men? Are the gods good and powerful enough to uphold the moral order?[8] The poets so affirm, at least at times. The young men who sit at the feet of Socrates will readily grant that some men are pious, good, and just, and thus their lives uphold a moral order that, should it be upheld by all, would bring fulfilment to all. What the young men are not sure of, what they even positively doubt, is that the gods uphold this moral order and distribute blessings according to merit.

The importance of Adeimantus's question is amply documented in the religious history of Greece. *The Clouds* of Aristophanes offers us an alternative between the rule of Zeus or that of Vortex. Impious men claim that Vortex is king, that Zeus is a fable, and they find in that excuses for adultery and perjury. Strepsides, however, believes in the role of Zeus: after all there is rain and there is still honour among men. This text witnesses also the the ability of the Olympians to remain, in spite of all, identified with the side of decency. Many elements in the Olympian tradition have been tempering the irrationality characteristic of these gods and the ultimate insignificance of their power before that of Fate. For instance, from Homer on, Olympian religion conspicuously contends against wild magic. Greek gods have most of the vices of the aristocratic Greeks, but they do not prepare philtres, eat children, or cause the dead to walk. Homeric religion, for all its faults, seems to have purged Greece of an underworld of destructive magic and superstition. The elimination of it is relatively successful in the myths and the folk tales.[9] The *Iliad* affirms that the existence of a single paramount authority is to the good; it then shows Zeus at one end of a golden rope successfully resisting the pull of all the other gods and goddesses at the other end; this being established, Zeus lifts his scale to decide the lot of the Greeks and that of the Trojans. Classic images of impartiality are launched in such passages.[10] A moral authority is for once firmly in charge and it is not swayed by a temporary coalition of squabbling gods pursuing partisan interests. The *Odyssey* goes even further in its presentation of morally credible gods. The providence of Zeus is shown to be moral, profoundly wise, and just. Hesiod and Xenophanes are the next witnesses to the tendency to improve the moral authority of the Olympian gods and disassociate them from the competitive and aggressive virtues of feudal lords. It is as if the Olympians are good enough to be reformable.

And yet they were never entirely reformed. The most powerful attempt to restore confidence in divine justice came from Orphism and what are called the mystery religions. Through these cults men were put in touch with a divine power that did not fail, did not fail above all those upright men who, at the mercy of a cruel fate or a difficult society, put their trust in them. Such 'minority' religions coped in a way that was not entirely public with the most obvious shortcomings of the public cults. They inserted sensitive and hurt consciences into a divine fellowship. These gods were a shelter for the delicate conscience and assured that, if not in this world, then in the next, all would be well with those who do good.

U. Wilamowitz-Moellendorf has stated that to a Greek 'god' is primarily a predicative notion.[11] Similarly, in one sense the gods were always powers rather than people, and commentators are right to emphasize that with the Greeks polytheism was not quantitative. In spite of all the weaknesses of an anthropomorphic portrayal of the divine, the divine *as predicate* seemed to have kept in the eyes of all Greeks a genuine authority. To acknowledge the divine in something or someone remained always a fresh religious experience. 'Of course the gods exist,' wrote Sextus Empiricus with significant naïveté, 'else how could we worship them?'[12] The religious experience kept the power to testify to the presence (or passage) of the divine, contact with which or contemplation of which obviously was the highest blessing a man could enjoy. Thus, in spite of all the shortcomings of the representations of the gods, the dignity of worship was not entirely eroded, this highest blessing was again and again tasted, and the divine kept its position of supreme value. From this perspective the Olympian gods were not always divine enough. Their vagaries, as told in the collections of myths, profoundly influential though they were on the self-images of men, never became the one and only expression of the divine. The touch of the divine in the cult continued to be sensed as something that is not found wanting. So the divine as predicate thus remained undoubtedly worthy of the object of the highest search or the supreme desire. Consider the example of Epicurus: his criticism of the Olympians and of Plato is thorough and radical, but divine happiness remains his object. The Greek gods, adds Walter Otto, need no authoritative revelation. They do not need to speak of themselves, commend themselves, or make promises to elicit the loyalty of a group of faithful. They never want a dogma over themselves.[13] Affirm this of the divine – Otto has always remained blind to the weaknesses of the Olympians – and you can catch a glimpse of the obvious excellence of the divine in Greek eyes. No revelation is needed. Present, the divine is wholly present; its meaning is entirely revealed in its manifest being.

Important though this experience of the divine was in the cult, the whole of religion was not coherently organized around such experience, far from it. As C.H.A. Festugière puts it: 'religion addressed itself to gods who were beautiful, happy and good, but could not co-ordinate these three qualities.'[14] Hence the constant attraction of mystery cults. Hence also the constant (even growing) hold exercised upon thinking minds by the idea of an unbending Fate. Plato faces squarely these unresolved conflicts. First he confronts directly the traditional theology expressed by the poets. Then his philosophical theology will seek to co-ordinate all the divine qualities and find ways of protecting both the supreme authority of the gods and the substance of human freedom.

2 From Homer's gods to the god without envy

Like all Greeks, Plato saw in the poets the actual schoolmasters of grown men. They are 'our fathers, as it were, and conductors in wisdom.'[15] In the course of the fifth century the authority of the poets, associated with old-fashioned ways, fell into discredit, particularly, as we have seen, in Sophistic circles.

Some responded to these developments by making a dogma out of the authority of the poets. By the time of Plato a group of intellectuals known as the Homeridae advanced most extraordinary claims about the *Iliad* and the *Odyssey*: all wisdom, all science, all subsequent speculation were authoritatively expressed in the Homeric poems, repositories of all knowledge that was to come subsequently to expression. The heady wine of allegorical exegesis was first tasted by the adherents of this school.[16] They wished to find an uncontestable, native, and omniscient authority. Thanks to the resources of allegory, they could clear Homer of all the unworthy representations of the divine that had been increasingly blamed on him and credit him with all kinds of subsequent scientific developments.

Plato is quick to discard this way of coping with the problem. The early dialogue *Ion* somewhat brutally exposes the emptiness of the claims made by those who find all wisdom in Homer. One adherent of this school, the rhapsode Ion of Ephesus, appears there and gets trapped into making the claim that his expertise in Homer makes him 'the best general in Greece.' Ion, who claims to be an 'interpreter of interpreters' (the poets being interpreters of the gods), shows himself completely ignorant.[17] He does not know how he knows (by art or by divine dispensation) and his pretention to be an expert on any subject handled by Homer simply because he has studied Homer is quickly challenged by Socrates.

Plato goes further. He makes a frontal attack on the values of Homer as found in his poetry in a way that probably has no precedent. Werner Jaeger, who is prone to overemphasize the unity and continuity of the Greek experience, allows that Plato's confrontation with Homer is 'a turning point in the history of Greek paideia.'[18] A whole tradition of aristocratic excellence is denounced. On very principled grounds the authority of the philosopher is exalted above that of this poet.

But Homer is not the only suspect. All poets, we hear in Book 2 of the *Republic*, must attribute to God his true quality. God is good and can do no evil. So we must suppress Hesiod's tale about the plots, violence, and revenge committed by

Ouranos, Kronos, and Zeus. And a youth must not be permitted to hear Aeschylus state that a god implants a destructive curse on a man whose house he wishes to destroy. Plato expresses shocked disgust at the immoralities attributed to the gods in the mythology and on this matter his position is not original. Euripides, to cite only one example, put on the stage a pious young man, Ion, who is deeply disturbed when he meets Creusa, who has been seduced and raped by Apollo. More significant in Plato is his rejection of fatal, relentless curses and his awareness of the use to which poets are put by men even worse than they. The Sophists in particular, cultured beings that they were, had an impressive array of poetic citations for all occasions. Callicles, for instance, cites Pindar to suit his own purpose.[19] Plato's conclusion is thus very firm: we must not accept from Homer or any other poet the folly of such errors as this about the gods:

> Two urns stand on the floor of the palace of Zeus and are filled with
> Dooms he allots, one of blessings, the other of gifts that are evil.

One must speak of the gods worthily and the most important thing to remember is that 'God is not the cause of all things, but only of the good.'[20]

In Book 10 of the *Republic* the attack on Homer is renewed and the inescapable conclusion formulated: wide though the reverence for Homer is, 'we must not honour a man above truth.'[21] His poetic creations are much removed from reality, 'and easy to produce without knowledge of the truth.'[22] Since he has only the art of imitation but not real knowledge, he cannot educate men.[23]

The thrust of the second attack differs from the first. Homer is not only the exponent of a false theology; he also typifies the dangers of all representative poetry: he weaves together representations of things he knows nothing about or does not know at first hand. He spreads stories, which being attractive or morally self-serving, receive wide circulation among men not concerned to test the truth of what they hear. In the end these stories are, to use Iris Murdoch's phrase, 'easy visions of self-protective, self-promoting fantasy.'[24] Whether promoters of immorality or of self-indulgent daydreams, the poets lack knowledge, the one word Plato consistently uses to express the edge philosophers have over other man.[25]

The authority of Homer was of course likely to be deepest in religious affairs. But as pedagogue of the educated Greeks he had also communicated to them an image of man: victim of a melancholy fate, constantly involved in conflicts stemming from rivalry, always called upon to learn restraint and resignation, yet nevertheless full of zest, with a keen taste for what life has to offer and an aristocratic joy in the brutalities of the contests. A.W.H. Adkins argues that Plato has tried to break with such a contest-ridden view of mankind and consciously seeks for the sources that may strengthen the co-operative rather than the competitive excellence of men. He has, I think, proved his point. Nevertheless Plato does not base his major attack on Homer on the trivial ground that he portrays greedy, lewd, and intemperant gods, or on the ground that he has too aggressive a notion of virtue. Homer is blamed, in the end, for coping poetically with a human condition that he perceives as ultimately meaningless. The *Iliad* as a story of toil and turmoil 'comes to a conclusion,' writes J. Redfield, 'not because the action imitated reaches a resolution but because the poet has conferred on the event, in the manner of his telling it, a form and an ending.'[26] The action reaches completion, or repose, on the aesthetic level: 'what is incomprehensible in experience becomes patterned and even beautiful in the imitation of experience.' Poetry 'recovers for man a tragic meaning in the experience of meaninglessness.'[27] By affirming that the gods exist and that order is intelligible Plato states his confidence that the human mind can understand the course of human affairs. What is apparently meaningless can be, with mental application, penetrated into. We need not rely on the fictions invented by the poets and their aesthetic comforts. Homer's songs are unnecessary to those who know.

What is wrong about Homer's notion of God is therefore not just, or even primarily, a matter of morals. It is mainly a matter of metaphysics. Plato is confident that the mind can know what is and find pattern in experience itself, not just in the artistic imitation of life. This point, however, may well be lost on many. What most see in the attack on Homer is an attempt to displace some stories about the gods by other, better, worthier stories. And this effort has not been lost on the many. Plato conspicuously breaks from what is the common public set of transmitted teachings concerning the divine. And from this blow, the Homeridae notwithstanding, Homer as a religious authority seems never to have fully recovered.

The theological shift brought about by Plato is best shown by the affirmation that 'the god is without envy.'[28] The point cuts decisively against all the moral pettiness of the Greek pantheon.

It seems to be from the Orphics that Plato drew the themes that enabled him to leave this Homeric mainstream tradition on the notion of God. There is a germ of divinity in us and any injustice stifles and repels the divine in us.[29] Members of the Orphic movement also distinguished themselves from other Greeks by claiming to have a hope. That Socrates has a good hope is repeatedly stated by Plato. More than that, Socrates embodies before our very eyes the religious assurance of the man who is of good hope: 'I am going to the gods who are good masters ... I not only do not grieve, but I have great hopes that there is something in store for the dead, and it has been said of old, something better for the good than for the wicked.'[30] That gods are good, that pious men are good and just and will ultimately fare well even though they suffer now because of their virtues, this is a typically Orphic cluster of beliefs. Immortality with them ceased to be what it was with Homer, an attractive vital prospect tantalizingly held before men who fear a life of diminished sensation. It is made into a moral motive: the soul abhors impurity, suffers from committing injustice, and such law is the one that prevails in the end.

That Plato has been brushed by the Orphics, however, should not lead us to attribute to him a sectarian kind of identity in these matters. Socrates in the *Phaedo* states that he does not ask us to believe in every detail the myth of the destiny, punishment, and purification of the soul. The affirmation is not literalistic but it is no less firm for that: 'This or something like this is true.' Souls are immortal; we ought to do our best to acquire virtue and wisdom in life; the prize is fair and the hope great. 'The venture is well worthwhile.'[31]

There is good evidence of the intermingling and weaving together of strains in Greek religion on precisely this point. Plato restates the hope of the Orphics as the heritage of all good men. But when he states that injustice lets the Titanic element of our soul take over from the divine one, the language he uses is Olympian (Hesiodic Olympian) as well as Orphic.[32] Cephalus, who in the *Republic* goes to the public sacrifice and embodies mainstream traditional city piety, affirms the sweet and goodly hope that accompanies those who have done no wrong; Pindar is quoted to this effect. In such a passage the better hope of the Orphic initiates and that of the righteous citizen are inextricably intertwined to affirm that the good man has nothing to fear.[33] Plato is deeply concerned here: all the great eschatological myths emphasize that there is nothing unjust in the workings of time. 'God is blameless,' affirms the myth at the end of the *Republic*. The last line of the whole work is that we who pursue righteousness can be confident that both in this sojourn and in other journeys 'we shall fare well.'[34] The complete implication of the position is presented in *Phaedo*: 'if death were an escape from everything, it would be a boon to the wicked.'[35] The divine affirmation of righteousness knows no loophole: the just are upheld and the wicked are punished, that is purged by a healing god (no vindictiveness there) until they are set right.

3 The form of the Good: argument and tentative analogies

Socrates seems to have started his philosophical course with a robust confidence in the possibility of understanding, of rationally penetrating into all that is. In an autobiographical statement in *Phaedo* he reveals with what pleasure he heard of the proposition of Anaxagoras that 'it is the mind (*nous*) that arranges and causes all things.' The prospect opened before him of an account of the world that would 'explain what is best for each and what is good for all in common.' In fact, Socrates was disappointed. In their speculations Anaxagoras and his followers 'give no thought to the good, which must embrace and hold together all things.' Once frustrated, Socrates set the problem aside to turn to his other man-centred inquiries.[36] But Plato did not leave the problem alone, and the *Republic* took up the task so inadequately carried out by Anaxagoras. To conceive of the form of the Good 'as being the cause of knowledge and truth in so far as known' is presented as the goal of the philosopher's education that is described with such care.[37]

The *Republic* does not hit upon such an idea of the Good intuitively; it gets there by means of a carefully constructed argument. While contemporary philosophers can rightly point to somewhat 'vague standards of proof,'[38] it remains clear that the assembling derives overall strength from its vastness. The *Republic* both builds on previous results in Plato's philosophizing and abandons lines of argument that, Socratic though they were, proved inadequate. In the end the most severe critic allows that Plato's arguments should not be attacked for failing to prove what they did not set out to prove, and that the 'damaging objections rest on principles which themselves require further examination and defense.'[39]

Here then is the argument.

What is justice? A typical Socratic inquiry is formulated at the start. But by the time Plato writes the *Republic* this familiar question has a new, fuller ring (much of Plato's previous work is absorbed in this dialogue). Justice has emerged as the pre-eminent virtue: whoever is just, one must now assume, has found the complete art of living well. And a vast contention has arisen over precisely this virtue among the learned and articulate. Some go on assuming that being just, or treating others correctly, is in the interest of the agent as well as of those acted upon; others have affirmed that justice is the name for what the powerful are allowed to do. Finally, and most importantly, while assuming that justice is a virtue, Plato abandons now the Socratic craft analogy which dominated his inquiry up to and including *Gorgias*. Having a virtue is no longer taken to mean having a skill somewhat like that of an artisan who knows well how to do a particular thing. It is, of course, still assumed that justice is a virtue because it benefits the agent, but Plato departs from the notion that it is a knack that obtains some non-disputed, obviously desirable objective.[40] The inquiry then takes a new turn and asks: 'is there a kind of good which we would choose to possess, not from desire for its after effects, but welcoming it for its own sake?'[41]

What then is 'the good'? becomes the subsidiary question. The point of turning to this epithet, the most traditional and the most threadbare in all the moral vocabulary, is that it places us finally on the most solid ground. The inquiry renounces at once all discussion of appearances.[42] Plato points out that many people are corrupt enough to rest content with the appearance of justice or honour, but 'when it comes to the good, nobody is content with the possession of the appearance but all men seek the reality.' Men are 'baffled' about the good and 'unable to comprehend its nature adequately or to attain to any stable belief about it,' but every soul pursues it and 'for its own sake does all that it does, with an intuition of its reality.[43]

To lead us towards an answer Plato takes a detour: let us imagine a good city, or a city where life is good. By getting us to examine the good city Plato moves to an area where common sense based on ordinary language can bring about agreement: what a good city is like will not be the cause of much dispute. Which one of its virtues shall be recognized as justice? A city will be deemed good if its fellowship provides for human needs in a stable, enduring way. It is not divided. It is not easily destroyed.[44] The key to such order (peace and durability) is to be found in the appropriate division of labour. There is nothing more chaotic – and more likely to erupt suddenly into violence – than a society where everybody claims all the time to be able to do everything. As Wilfrid Sellars puts it, Plato gives us at this point the 'principles in accordance with which the city must be governed if it is to be an enduring and autonomous embodiment of the various forms of excellence of which men, individually and collectively, are (at least in approximation) capable.'[45] That each does that for which he is naturally suited is not just the key to stable overall order; it is the key to individual happiness. When everyone does the task for which his nature fits him, we have a situation where each 'fulfilling his own function is not many men but one.'[46] Each recognizing his difference lives in the sort of inequality that produces political unity, social friendship, and equality of satisfaction.

It is easy for Plato to point out that such a city requires wisdom, bravery, and moderation in its citizens. Justice in this city will lie in the proper ordering of the whole. In each individual justice will consist in an order too: an order in which the brave, the wise, and the moderate parts of the soul are properly performing their own tasks.[47]

A crucial point in the overall argument is that some people – called guardians – are naturally suited to preside over the destinies of this city. 'Naturally suited' means that such human beings can be entrusted with power for they will use it only for the good of the whole (without such guardians the city is doomed to conflicts of power, division, and the quick falling away of all from the good life). The problem lies in recognizing and training individuals endowed with such natures. They must have inner stability, be self-organized and autonomous, and desire knowledge more than anything else. The plans for their education are therefore crucial to Plato's whole undertaking. Thanks to the fruit of a good education building upon a sound nature, these guardians come to understand the nature of the good, and thus the whole structure of appropriate benefits for all is secure. They rise to a grasp of the form of the good. They see that the good may be known, is at the summit of the hierarchy of all that is, and is the ultimate purpose of all men.[48] Plato gropes at this point,[49] using analogies (the sun, the cave, the divided line) in an attempt to help us.[50]

The argument of the *Republic* becomes more expository (or returns to more traditional forms of expression) as it is rounded off by a description of the decay (through greed and overindulgence) that awaits both cities and individuals when defective notions of the good become objects of belief. The case then is allowed to rest: only the lives of just men and women are accompanied by rewards. What has been achieved, need I point out, is a redefinition of rewards. Justice is no longer outward behaviour as it was with the Sophists (who spread the notion that it was just that with the traditionalists). It is an inner health of the good soul that is in harmony with all that is good.[51]

One consequence Plato draws from his affirmation about the form of the Good is epistemological. What is and all that is can be thought about and known. The morally earnest dialectical exchange with fellow human beings can extend the understanding of the world. More and more general hypotheses can be formulated. Provided that men have a genuine passion for the truthful quality of speech, they will rise to truths that are independent of human opinion, and ultimately to a good truth that is totally free from the intellectual, emotional ploys which clever men devise to advance the strategies of their desires. The parable of the cave speaks of an ascent from a false light to the light of the sun. This philosophical dialectical path begins as one searches for forms, for the true meaning of words, and ends with the form of the good, the ultimate form which is the ground of possibility of all that truly is, that is of all that is truly intelligible. In the structure of reality there is a measure, a ground, a formula which accounts for intrinsic intelligibility.[52] The good is also supreme in the world of fact in addition to being the supreme value for man. The real is not only an ineluctable actuality: it also shows good faith: it can be related to in good terms. Alexander Mourelatos, commenting on the famous identification made by Parmenides between mind and being, says that the universe is conceived of in moral terms; the compulsion of constraint-fate-justice is one of gentle persuasion; mind is related to what is in some sort of promissory or contractual relation.[53] The good person is not a helpless alien in the universe, even though he may be an alien in his own city. The universe is under the same sovereignty as he.

One consequence of this metaphysical affirmation is specifically moral – it is significant that the search for knowledge comes to rest in the form of the *Good*. The true doctrine of virtue can be secured, dialectically, once the good man discovers that there is a good we welcome for its own sake and choose to possess, not because we desire its after-effects, but because it is the source of our joy and well-being and needs no utilitarian plea. Such good is transcendent; it is good for us, not because of what it does to us, what appearances it wins for us, what rewards it delivers, but because of what it is. It takes, of course, a conversion to see this Good. 'Goodness is connected with the attempt to see the unself, to see and to respond to the real world in the light of a virtuous consciousness ... "good is a transcendent reality" means that virtue is the attempt to pierce the veil of selfish consciousness and join the world as it really is.'[54]

Hence the new definition of justice: an order in the soul which creates an order in the city and which reflects an order of being. Justice is ontonomic; it regulates itself on reality. Hence also the realism exhibited from the beginning in the Socratic search for definition. To know piety is not simply to know what men mean, or what a whole religious tradition means. It is to know a form, something that is and makes a difference both in our moral struggles and in the course of the universe as a whole. The gods love what is pious because it is pious. That which is is superior to that which is willed, even if willed by such prestigious beings as the gods. What the gods are submitted to, however, is no longer a fate. It is the Good, and this good articulates a hierarchy of values which sheds the true light on every aspect of our quest for the best over the worst. As one commentator puts it, even if Euthyphro's ethics are authoritarian, his metaethics cannot be. The gods are his models; he does what they say without looking into his reasons for doing so. But the gods have reasons for loving what is pious. A philosopher of course, unlike Euthyphro, is not content with such blind following; he will look into these reasons. But he shares Euthyphro's assumptions that the gods know what they are doing as they love what is pious.[55]

4 An austere love of the Good

Most of the religious conservatives contemporary with Socrates and Plato would agree that piety leads to a morally dignified and good life. Isocrates is a particularly good example. To him piety is associated with *aidôs*, restraint, dignity. He too reproaches the Athenians for having lost their virtue; they go through periods of impious neglect of the sacred rites and then through shameless fits of ostentatious, magnificent festivals which are more public entertainment than religious ceremonies.[56] *Aidôs*, writes Werner Jaeger, is 'an honourable feeling of holy shame.' It is 'a complicated spiritual inhibition, induced by many different social, moral and aesthetic motives.'[57] Greek and Roman religious history are full of conservative evocation of the orderly moral restraint characteristic of a more pious age and echoed in the quality of older pious souls.

It would be a mistake, however, to paint Plato's conception of moral virtue in such colours. Plato's trajectory leads to a reconstruction. The dialectic achieves an intellectual cleansing. The soul goes through a moral regeneration. Knowledge leads to a new order in the person's desires, and that order is not one dictated by tradition but that established by the form of the Good and grasped by a new metaphysical insight. Here again Isocrates is a good contrast. As a traditionalist he wants an education for the whole city; he rejects Plato's philosophical basis since the Platonic *paideia* is not directly accessible to all.[58] With Plato the proposition that virtue is knowledge acquires a new character by being integrated into a metaphysic and a cosmology. Virtue is a conformity between the mind and the order of being, and this conformity is achieved by knowledge. Those people are virtuous who, above all things, love knowing.

Such weighty affirmations can be shown to lie along lines opened up by Socrates. The *Republic* builds on the Socratic method of *elenchos* (that is demonstrating that the speaker becomes involved in incoherence as he pursues his assertions.) In this work Socrates forces his partners to confront their beliefs about virtues with their beliefs about the good. That people do not share the same view about what, in the end, is good and desirable signals a new problem which the historical Socrates does not seem to have noticed, but the method of philosophizing remains the same.[59] Socrates embarks on serious talk with anyone he has found, because he believes that anyone has, at the outset, a noble incentive for inquiry. The mind does not inquire unless it believes there is something to inquire into, some way to inquire into it, and some good to be derived from the inquiry. Some tacitly or openly acnkowledged good proposes any inquiry and promotes it at every one of its numerous turns. As a general rule, we might say that a ruling preference of the mind propels every intellectual inquiry.[60] But Plato find out that minds have different ruling preferences. His task, thus, is to show the ultimate moral and ontological ramifications of such ruling preferences. Gorgias, Polus, Callicles, and Socrates are not the same sort of beings. They are moved by different loves, see the world differently. Plato's contribution consists in tracing out which one of the available ruling preferences has the larger interpretative power, namely what ruling preferences or ontological judgments lead men farthest into, or to the end of, the inquiry into the meaning of life.[61] The best ruling preference of course is, with Plato as with Socrates, the desire to know the truth and enjoy what is good. Intellectual inquiry based on this desire leads Plato dialectically to the ultimate hypothesis, that of the form of the Good. The mind that desires good and understanding arrives in the end at the insight that reality is good, or that the good is real.

Obviously the meaning of knowledge has shifted. Knowledge was linked to the capacity to reason, to deduce, to formulate more encompassing hypotheses. But at some point the mind has made a leap; a move is made to the all-encompassing hypothesis. Moreover the hypotheses cease to be just entertained; the object of the hypothesis becomes seen (just as we have said earlier, one *sees* the point of there being forms). The form is no longer conceived of as a possibility but is actually grasped. That there is goodness and not just thought about goodness at some point is seen and known. Knowledge has become reverent contemplation, a contemplation that establishes an existential level at which the human being, converted, reoriented, becomes incapable of wrongdoing.

Theoria (contemplation) before Plato could mean at least three things: with Herodotus it meant sightseeing, observation, inquiry; at Eleusis it meant mystic vision granted at the climax of a rite; in Athens it meant attendance at a festival (watching the parade or being in it). The *Republic* begins with an inquisitive search for knowledge (justice), rises to a visionary knowledge (the Good), and descends again into an inquisition (the causes of decay). Salvation of the soul lies in continuous inquiry but such inquiry, at times, leaps into vision.[62]

Those who are disturbed by the mystical flavour entering into the Platonic redefinition of knowledge might look at the pages in J.S. Mill on the exaltation of knowledge in Plato. That to do right is good is for Plato a matter of knowledge.[63] The name 'knowledge' is reserved for this insight. The word 'knowledge' applies only analogically to such science as we have upon observation of the relations availing in our changing world. Under this view of knowledge one can defend the proposition that no one desires evil knowing it to be evil. To know is to know what the mind is for. And who will deny that it is for the attainment of such good life as is, in fact, possible?

There is something thoroughly rational, we might add, in this affirmation of the unimpeachable sovereignty of the good and in the reduction of knowledge to this insight. Plato's theism, writes Ian Crombie, is a belief in the 'cosmic efficacy of reason.' The mind is independent of the physical world, and of social conditioning we might add. It can rule the world (and not be ruled by it) and establish justice in the city.[64] Man can grow to master injustice so that all beings can proceed in an orderly manner to their own completion. There is a law for the establishment of such justice and this law is something (some) human beings can know, not a convention fostered by a group of men eager to dominate others.

Philosophical love of the good is accompanied by a feeling of mental ease: it stems from intellectual confidence. The joy is, however, austere. Trained to a life-style that clings only to cognitive rewards, the philosophers who rule in the well-ordered city have given up all the rewards usually associated with the possession of power. They are abstemious in their personal tastes and socially self-effacing. One part of their soul has been nurtured, that which has affinity to reality and is strengthened by extra-psychic reality.[65] But they have repressed other parts of the soul: all those parts that demand goods such as are enjoyable only if they are mine alone, and all those desires that are potent because biologically urgent.[66]

To become virtuous, in the full sense of the word, thus seems beyond the scope of many human beings. Plato draws a very sharp contrast between the sense of reality proper to the philosopher and that dominant among other mortals. For those who know and understand it is obvious that the philosopher is concerned about what really matters. But to others the philosopher is a man whose mind is absent, and who lacks the skill that ensures success in this world. No longer absorbed in the concerns of the diseased city, the philosopher, like the initiate, is quite prepared to be an object of derision. *Phaedrus* warns: 'Since he separates himself and turns his attention toward the divine the philosopher is rebuked by the vulgar, who consider him mad and do not know that he is inspired.'[67]

All these themes are brought together in the contrast drawn in the *Theaetetus* between the philosophers and the men of affairs. Philosophers appear ridiculous when they enter courts of law as speakers: they are not masters of the speech that persuades, prevails, and serves the ends of one's will. The men of affairs are skilled at the legal contests that are played in courts; they are tense and shrewd: 'They know how to wheedle their master with words, and gain his favour by acts.' True, their souls become small and warped and accustomed to deceit. Thales, Plato goes on, fell into a pit while studying the stars and the Thracian maid laughed at him: 'The same jest applies to all who pass their lives in philosophy.' They are the laughing-stock of the multitude. The philosopher is awkward. He does not know how to pack his bedding, much less how to put the proper sweetening into a sauce, or make a fawning speech. He does not cultivate any of the excellencies which gentlemen and men of affairs learn in order to be either admired or feared as the occasion requires. The philosopher refuses the name of virtue to these social skills. Is the virtuous only that which enables us to become perfectly righteous and therefore like God? 'We ought to try to escape from earth to the dwelling of the gods as quickly as we can; and to escape is to become like God, so far as this is possible; and to become like God is to become righteous and holy and wise.' The choice before men is between two patterns: the divine and the godless. Cleverness in the practice of injustice offers rewards now but makes men conform to the second pattern and condemns them to remain for ever evil men associated with evil. The sharpness of the difference between the two patterns is such that the clever man cannot see the wise and just as anything else but fools.[68]

The righteous man suffers in the corrupt city. Yet his lot is not the worse fate. Absorbed in the city and reaping its corrupt rewards, the unrighteous undergo a worse punishment: not listening to the testimony of the wise, they progressively become deaf, incapable of understanding, and entrapped in their own ignorance.[69] (This passage is very useful to interpret the body / soul dualism found in *Phaedo*: corruption, or entrapment in the body, means loss of intellectual abilities.) This worsening of their condition causes a practically inevitable increase in the political tension: the more the philosophers are needed, the less likely are they to be called upon.

At this point we cannot say what is likely to happen. The philosophers know that they should reorder the world more justly. To contemplation they ought to add action, when the opportunity arises. Philosophers have leisure to think; they must also keep an eye on the times, in order to act when the opportunity permits. The commitment to the priority of the soul, to the supreme excellence of contemplation, the haste to 'escape from earth to the dwellings of the gods,' these are not with Plato signs of moral and political *laisser-faire*. Such commitment to the 'spiritual' side of life did subsequently become a sign of a surrender, a token of a despair that lost hope of any straightening out of the conditions of the city. Plato perhaps lays the basis for that temptation on his successors, some of whom observed that Plato, in his turn, had failed, just as Socrates before him. For some two failures in a row have a very despairing impact. But Plato, for all his talk of escape, has not given up yet, as is proved by his labours in writing not only the *Republic* but the *Laws* as well.

5 The *Republic*: the arresting of disorder and the rooting of order

It can be said that Plato never tried to improve on the *Republic* and its sweeping argument; his subsequent works focus on related but specific issues. The *Republic* therefore keeps a climactic position in the corpus. We find in it an extraordinary marshalling of argument, artistry, and learning. To use one of its key metaphors, the ascent out of the cave is its topic and it urges us to that ascent by inviting us to a sort of austere mystical submission to the Good that is seen as the only source of the justice that will bring happiness to the individual and welfare to the city. There is an existential seriousness to this statement which, at the limit, may seem to render somewhat trivial the learned discussion concerning the role of the form of the Good in the elaboration of subsequent philosophical theism. So this chapter will conclude with an attempt to portray something of the movement of thought, and of people, in the *Republic*.

Socrates and his companions return to Athens. They went down to the Peiraeus to attend a religious festival; they said their prayers and saw the spectacle. (The whole dialogue repeats the rhythm of speaking and seeing.) The focused quest for an understanding of justice begins with their meeting with Cephalus: he is an upright man of business, of modest means. Old and pious, he enjoys a very temperate life and it is obvious that he has a good conscience; he has no fear of 'having cheated or deceived anyone even unintentionally or of being in debt to some god in sacrifice or to some man for money' (331a–b). Cephalus, however, cannot articulate a theory of justice. He believes in justice, piety, and the usefulness of money. His son Polemarchus undertakes to provide a sharper view: justice consists in helping one's friends and harming one's enemies. Polemarchus, however, quickly reaches the end of his wits: he cannot at all cope with such questions as who are one's real rather than supposed friends and genuine rather than apparent enemies. Thrasymachus, a Sophist of the realist school, steps into the vacuum. He has a definition (and is confident it will resist all assaults): justice is the interest of the stronger. In the course of the discussion Thrasymachus must allow that his 'superior' man must have more than brute force at his disposal; he must also be able to persuade the rest of mankind that he has the interests of all at heart. Modified, the thesis still stands: if practised 'on a sufficiently large scale,' injustice will prosper, will win all advantages for the unjust man, and will gain for itself the appearance of justice (344c). Socrates here moves in with his refutation: the unjust man cannot be happy; injustice spreads hatred whereever it goes; no action in common is possible where injustice reigns (351d). Socrates makes it apparent that Thrasymachus's position is, in essence, conspiratorial. It commits a twofold contradiction which it seeks to mask but which Socrates unveils. 1 / People are prepared to give some of their time to listen to Thrasymachus because they have an interest in justice (an intellectual and moral interest). What Thrasymachus teaches, however, under the guise of a discourse on justice is the art of acquiring and maintaining power to exploit others and get more than one's fair share of the good things life has to offer. But, while that is a fascinating lecture, it is not what his listeners were interested in in the first place – to follow Thrasymachus means to reorient one's initial ruling preference. 2 / The view of Thrasymachus cannot itself as a public position: taught to all, it would bring about a state of war of all against all. But wolves don't want to live in a society of wolves; they want to keep some lambs around. So the 'realist' view can be taught only to the few. No one could possibly wish to have a society where all are raised by such Sophists. In this sort of philosophizing, language, which is the common property of all, has become a means employed by the few to further their plots against the many.

People who talk about justice have a good will: they want to wrestle with a high-minded question, nobly, with their minds. They will listen to a Thrasymachus only as long as they are fooled by him, or only when Thrasymachus has converted them to his Sophistic, that is nihilistic, premise. In the *Republic* Socrates manages to defeat Thrasymachus: he shows that Thrasymachus's position inevitably entails nihilism and is a denial of the point of a discourse about justice. The opening pages of the *Republic* are thus a hinge: the act of resistance of the soul has begun to be successful. The school of disorder has been defeated in its principle: Thrasymachus yields the floor. Note that Thrasymachus, unlike Callicles, does not keep on talking and threaten Socrates. Let us give him his due: he is a decent man and an intellectual; he knows when he is refuted. The two 'neutral' listeners, Glaucon and Adeimantus, turn to Socrates to be taught about justice. And they ae teachable. Socrates has won a battle. It is clear that common sense is on his side: who will deny that people, if they are prepared to talk about justice, are in search of something fair to all? In contrast to Socrates' common sense, Thrasymachus has just been advocating an attractive theoretical construct that sheds some light on some things, and has therefore an undeniable power of explanation, but has nothing to do with what people mean by justice.

Glaucon and Adeimantus are so genuinely interested in justice that their first act is to restate, as fairly as they can, the position just defeated. Glaucon introduces the story of the ring that enables Gyges to become invisible: once invisible and assured of impunity, any man would kill, rob, and sleep with whom he pleases and thus 'conduct himself among mankind as the equal of a god' (360c). So Glaucon grants that there is a common morality that curbs human behaviour, but it is born of fear and prudent social interest. Adeimentus reinforces the thesis by showing how little evidence there is of the gods rewarding justice. So the problem is stated: the decision is between two kinds of life, assuming each to be brought to its own perfection (360e). Let us assume that the unjust man has managed to seem just; and let us assume that the just man does not appear to be just and is therefore reviled and crucified. Can Socrates show the intrinsic superiority of justice, leaving aside all the rewards and honours that may attend it? Is there a good that man in his soul welcomes for its own sake, no matter what social benefits may or may not come with it?

Socrates accepts the challenge and begins a long lecture. He will make a detour through societies to see there writ large what appears only writ small in the case of the individual (369a). The expository part of the dialogue can be quickly summarized. Socrates shows how societies have evolved from primitive simplicity to their present state which we call developed and which he calls luxurious. He turns to the question of 'what kind of natures are suited for the guardianship of such a state' (374e). A special kind of education is obviously necessary for the guardians: of the three elements present in the human soul, in them reason will be most developed. The other two classes will perform their functions best by developing, and reaping the rewards of, the pugnacious and the commercial spirits. In all three groups the individual will practise temperance by being content with the peculiarities of the style of life towards which his nature has inclined him. Justice then appears as a quality of the whole, consisting in the fair differentiation of tasks. It is an order, in the society and in the individual. Each will be just, if he fulfils his proper function (441e).

At this point Socrates receives a fresh challenge: can this policy ever come to existence? (471c). The challenge is flung at him partly indirectly: some details in the scheme for the education of the guardians run against common sense; how is one to take seriously, for real life, a plan that assumes that women are equal to men and that wives and children will be held in common? Socrates accepts the challenge, in general as well as on the points of detail: the ideal can become real. But he defines the precise circumstances: 'Unless the philosophers become kings, or ... our rulers take to the pursuit of philosophy seriously ... there can be no cessation of troubles' (473d). So Socrates embarks on what is practically another lecture: the education of the guardians outlined earlier turns out to have been a provisional account. What the philosophers see and must keep seeing is that the difference between good and evil is not a matter of opinion or convention. 'In constant companionship with the divine order of the world, the philosopher reproduces that order in his soul and, so far as man may, becomes godlike' (500d). His eyes are not fixed downward on the affairs of men. He is trained to attain the Good as the highest object of knowledge. The Good is hard to talk about: the sun is what most closely resembles it; what the sun is to vision, the Good is to intelligence. The parable of the cave elaborates on that.

Having thus gained an intuition of the Good and, equally important, a sense of the movement towards it, Socrates returns to political matters. Access to power in society is safe only in the hands of those who love the Good, and only such people should be asked to rule (521b). Socrates develops further the education required to train such philosophers (mathematics, music, and dialectic). A description of the fall from an ideal state then demonstrates his complete grasp of the dynamics of social and individual life.

All the necessary developments have taken place. Socrates can sum up his case: the unjust man is under the despotism of a master passion and is the unhappiest man. The philosopher has experienced the pleasantness of pleasure and of honour: his preference for intellectual satisfaction is a knowing one. 'The good and just man is so far superior to the bad and unjust in point of pleasure, there is no saying by how much his life will surpass the other's in grace, nobility and virtue' (588a). That much is settled. Glaucon and Adeimantus are satisfied. Socrates admits, however, that one can doubt whether his commonwealth will ever exist on earth (592b–c).

After an interlude on poetry Socrates turns to the question of immortality. The matter of external rewards for justice can now be raised safely. The whole case so far has been proved without the slightest whiff of mercenary considerations. The soul is immortal, and no evil, however foul, ever destroys it, while only justice preserves its health. In this life the just man has the hope of faring well in the hereafter. This leads to the great myth of Er (which borrows many features from Orphic and other mysteries.)[70] Each soul arrives in the afterworld bearing all the marks gained during a lifetime. Its nature is thus fully apparent and fair judgment can be pronounced. The righteous souls go to the right to a kind of festival while the unrighteous go to the left to pay the penalty. After a period of time all souls are invited to pick patterns of life that will determine the character of their next life on earth. A lottery sets the order in which they will draw their patterns. Even he who comes last still has a variety of patterns to choose from. Necessity limits the choices but the choices remain free. In particular, no soul, however evil, remains necessarily fixed on an evil course. It has had an opportunity for reflection and purification during its period of punishment and it too has its moment of choice; the lot it gets is the one it chose: 'The blame is his who chooses: god is blameless' (617e).

Choices, of course, are made on the basis of what the souls have learned during their past lives and during the period of festival or punishment. Many souls make unwise choices. They do not know how to make a reasoned choice. They cannot distinguish between the life that is good and that which is bad. They do not observe the unpleasant ramifications of a life-style that has some pleasant features that capture their attention.

Note the thorough reconciliation of divine decree and human freedom in this myth. The cosmological framework of human destiny is profoundly humanistic: the ultimate moral law ensures that human beings have and keep having an opportunity to learn. While it is upheld in the universe, justice can be achieved only by a freely choosing soul.

8

The divine pull

I Divine care is all-pervading

Different desires stir different people, affirms the *Republic*, thereby breaking with the earlier Socratic (and general Greek) assumption that all people simply want to be happy. How much can be done to orient people who are victims of their lower appetites towards the really good end? The guardians, we hear, are noble by nature and by training. Something, apparently, can be done to improve human beings, but there are limits. Is the moral range of each individual set once and for all?

Plato's third and final dogma is meant to direct us towards the answer. 'The gods care for small things no less than for things superlatively great.'[1] All human beings can rely on their supportive care. Everything in the world is under their tendance (note the echoing of Socrates' own injunction to care about the soul: the vocabulary is the same). Care, the *Laws* elaborates, is the activity of the good owner of a large estate. The gods devise the proper place and function of each part of the whole. Each part thereby achieves fulfilment and the excellence of the whole is maintained. The 'victory of Goodness is the whole and the defeat of evil' is achieved 'most completely, easily and well.'[2] The reference to the overcoming of evil is characteristically qualified. Plato's gods are not lazy but they do not save. All that Plato affirms is that human beings are in need of amelioration and that gods are concerned to heal them.

The divine cure operates through one decree, which is enforced in a daily manner: 'As thou becomest worse, thou goest to the company of worse souls, and as thou becomest better, to the better souls; alike in life and in every shape of death, thou both doeth and sufferest what is befitting that like should be toward like.' Penalty and rewards are always exactly meted out: 'If a man learns not this, he can never see an outline of the truth,' and will never understand in what happiness consists.[3] We might also add that the divine rule, addressed to human beings, is a rule and help in which persuasion and education rather than plain tending play the larger role. In other words, the rule of the gods over men ought to include communication with them rather than mere steering.

This, however, is a consequence that we are prompt to draw. Plato did not draw it so clearly. He faithfully reflected thereby the realities of the Greek tradition which never crystallized its understanding of the movement of the divine towards men in a dominant metaphor. The traditional Greek world is open to the prospect of a very wide variety of forms of divine presence. It is acknowledged that the gods manifested their presence in the past by meeting with men and women, founding families, cities, sanctuaries, festivals. Their presence is reactivated in the life of such institutions. On-going divine influence also comes through special types of individuals, inspired poets, seers, diviners, wise men. Plato does not systematize an understanding of the divine-human intercourse. In particular, and somewhat disturbingly in our eyes, he does not at all draw on metaphors derived from inter-human encounters to describe the type of influence the gods exercise over men. The reason for this is easy to discern: Greek mythology is full of gods dealing with humans in an uncaring way. As A.H. Armstrong puts it: 'If we find Greek philosophical theology chilly, we should remember that the alternative to that chilliness was the heat of Zeus' embraces and Hera's tempers.'[4] So the note of impersonality present in the image of tendance will have to stand.[5]

There is little intimacy in that divine presence. The myth of *Phaedo* nicely gives us the picture. It portrays the men in the upper earth as having real intercourse with the gods. For those in the lower earth, however, such intercourse is available only in temples where the gods dwell, through speech, prophecies, and vision.[6] Such presence is much attenuated. Socrates confesses in jail that in the absence of a divine word he shall have to take whatever human doctrine is best.[7] But all the emphasis on divine remoteness and habitual silence does not deny the divine presence. Let us therefore examine in as positive a perspective as possible what Plato has to say on the modes of this presence.

2 The enthusiastic strain: divination and Dionysiac orgia

Comely rituals, presided over by priests (often elected ones), represent the basic religious form mediating the sense of divine presence in the Greek city. Festivals with parades, music, dances bring human beings together in a happy rhythm that renews the measure that the gods have imparted to the city. And so do the daily sacrifices; no domestic animal is ever butchered without ritual and no meat (except that of the hunt) is eaten that is not consecrated by the ritual of sacrifice. But the history of Greek religion, we have seen, is also the history of the failure of this public form of religious life to achieve anything like a monopoly.

Divination covers a lot of phenomena that purport to offer more, a better sign of the divine, a clearer indication of the will of the gods. The notion that some individuals have special gifts that enable them to discern the will of the gods is an important feature of the Greek religious world from the sixth century on. (There is only one example of ecstatic prophecy in Homer.[8]) E. Des Places correctly points out that the *mantis*, the diviner or ecstatic prophet, appears a good deal more frequently than the priest.[9] The *mantis* guides decisions, gives people revelations about their fate and their wisest next step. H.W. Parke has argued that ecstatic prophecy is typicaly associated with Apollo. It is unsound, he adds, to link it exclusively with Dionysus; the phenomenon is more widespread than that. In the absence of sacred books or an organized clergy with steady opportunities for teaching and other modes of influence, the role of these diviners may be hard for us to visualize. The difficulty is compounded when we realize that such diviners are entirely self-appointed. At most, each diviner is initiated and legitimated by another diviner who took him on as an apprentice. Their role nevertheless remains crucial because they have the accepted methods for ascertaining the will of the gods. Such methods are, broadly speaking, of two kinds.

The first method is called by Cicero technical.[10] It uses crafts. The cautious observation of birds, of the entrails of sacrificed animals (especially livers), of lots drawn, and of a variety of natural phenomena such as fire, water, mirrors, trees enables the diviner to draw conclusions concerning the states of the god's mind. The second kind of divination, called by Cicero intuitive or natural, does not rely upon learned recipes. The diviner is rather 'inspired' by the god and receives his message directly. Dreams are a much favoured divine means of communication, and so are the trancelike states of male or female diviners.

A certain number of great rural sanctuaries emerged where methods of divination became well established, enjoying a traditional reputation and available as a matter of routine. Delphi and Dodona are the most famous of these. We, of course, have more information about such sanctuaries than about the itinerant diviners; the durable vitality of the sanctuaries is well attested. When they came under Epicurean and Christian attack, Stoic intellectuals commonly came to their rescue. It was repeatedly stated that the gods concerning themselves with men were too good not to make available to mankind a gift as precious as divination. *Manteia*, the art of divination, captured the curiosity of intellectuals in the Hellenistic era. We have quite a few treatises, including a famous one by Plutarch, seeking to understand this phenomenon.

The forms of divination prevalent in the sixth and fifth centuries seek to penetrate by insight into what happens (or will happen) rather than what is. The background is a well-attested insecurity about the nature of the divine and the quality of its intentions. The revealing word is often couched in a riddle and is thus in need of interpretation. 'The god who has an oracle at Delphi neither reveals nor hides his meaning, but shows it by a sign,' runs a statement of Heraclitus.[11] The Pythia at Delphi is accompanied by a *prophetes*, an interpreter who decodes the revelation. In a democratic context the message is debated in an assembly meeting. Herodotus narrates how the Athenians met to discuss what the god could have meant when he said that 'the wooden wall' would save them. Themistocles disagreed with the professional interpreters: the Athenians should prepare to meet their enemies at sea, in their wooden ships. Athens agreed and was saved. Herodotus also tells stories of individuals who failed to read the message correctly: their pride, or some other moral shortcoming, blinded them. Croesus, about to go to war, was cheered by the oracle announcing that a great empire was about to be destroyed; he did not realize that his own was meant.[12] Divine messages, helpful as they are, do not short-circuit the normal processes of human deliberation and decision-making. Oracles give one something to think about; they do not close the question.

Since the sixth century Greeks have also been fascinated by more extraordinary types of divination. In such cases the diviner seemed to be 'beside himself,' 'possessed by the god.' It was commonly thought that the soul in such states is let loose from the body, so to speak, or gets out of normally confining circumstances to discern things which are commonly hidden or rise to a truth, access to which is ordinarily denied to average mortals.

Such ecstatic notions reappear in the more philosophical figures who show continuity with the whole tribe of diviners. We should mention in this connection that most intriguing man Empedocles. This colourful character advertises his gifts, especially the capacity to heal and to prophesy. Not surprisingly, numerous legends circulated about this great wonder-worker. His view of man attributes to each individual a *daimon*, which enters from outside and remains attached to the body. But *daimon* is the name Empedocles also gives to love and to strife, the two great cosmic principles, the contest of which brings everything into existence. The inference must be drawn that something in man belongs to a realm of being entirely different from the everyday world, and man's contact with this world cannot be altogether lost. That only like can know like becomes the basic principle of Empedocles' research and speculations into medicine, the elements, and the gods.[13]

Further removed from the magician and closer to the philosopher as we know him we find Parmenides, who opens his book with the account of a 'travel toward truth that takes the form of ecstatic experience.' 'The mares that carry me as far as my heart ever aspires sped me on, when they had brought and set me on the farfamed road of the god [that is the sun], which bears the man of knowledge over all cities. On that road was I borne, driven on both sides by the two whirling wheels, as the daughters of the Sun, having left the house of Night, hastened to being me to the light, throwing back the veils from their heads with their hands.' At the end of a voyage a goddess welcomes the young man and introduces him to the knowledge of the 'unshaken heart of well-rounded truth.' The insight into the identity of being and intelligibility comes at the end of a visionary utterance one does not usually associate with philosophy. W.K.C. Guthrie argues that this insight rests on a genuine experience.[14]

The Greeks also began to associate poetic inspiration with such ecstatic type of experiences. From the time of Homer poetry was associated with the Muses, but we have to wait until Democritus to find an author who claims that poetic inspiration implies a loss of self or a trancelike state. One of Plato's dialogues, *Ion*, echoes the new theory: the poet is not moved by an art in himself but by a divine power, which draws him like a magnet. Like Corybantic worshippers (that is the priests of Cybele) or the bacchants, lyric poets compose while their souls are frantic.[15]

Obviously, then, Herodotus does not give us the whole story of Greek divination. One aspect of it is frenzied, and involves an abnormal experience, a getting oneself outside oneself. Scholars today associate this notion of the soul possessing powers which remain normally hidden with the shamanistic culture pattern. Shamans are individuals whose souls can travel to the world of spirits and then return, with revelations. Only their souls fly; their bodies – mere outer shells – remain bound to the ground. The knowledge shamans attain is superior. Greece in ita archaic period was probably full of shamans; we find in the historic era many modified shamans and other remnants of the whole pattern.[16] These remnants provided Plato with representations to portray the proper identity of the soul, its unique powers, and its ability to leave behind lower realms of knowledge and rise to a higher one.[17]

The whole cultural pattern contains, I must add, a fateful assumption, the body-soul dualism. Can it be that the soul can do its most proper work only when it is disembodied? Can it find an activity worthy of its own powers only outside the world?[18] The questions are huge. Pictures of the human condition take shape which assume that living is at its best when the bonds that tie us to incarnate and social existence are severed.

The bonds that tie individuals to the social order are even more violently torn away in those aspects of Greek religious life that can be properly labelled orgiastic. Dionysiac orgies are the ones we know most about. Maddened by Dionysus, women leave their homes clad in fawnskins, carrying and wearing emblems of the god. They dance away to the hills, frantic, following a young man with long hair, lost in bliss, roused by the tympanum and the flute. In this state women become maenads; wine, in all likelihood, enhances their trance and males seem to be around in the woods to provide sexual release. The wild enthusiasm thus restores the bliss of primitive savagery. Women also hurl themselves upon animals, tear them to pieces, and eat raw meat.[19] The city's usages are left behind, both those of the conjugal bed and those of the sacrificial altar and family table. All boundaries are broken in a collective emotion which breaks the principle of individuation and the restraints which have shaped the self. We can see the power of female visions of a world free of demanding men, free, that is, of fathers, husbands, and sons, asocial, apolitical.[20] Euripides sees the full sweetness inherent in such 'return to nature.' Their babies hunger at home, but, rapturous in the hills, the bacchants give the breast to wild animals.

Let us not underestimate the attractiveness of such experiences of mystical possession, transgressing all barriers, all limits. And let us not attribute it to females only. Cybele, the Great Mother, also has her male Corybants, leaping, entranced. Clearly a deep human desire finds some fulfilment in these orgiastic forms of religious behaviour. Return to a golden age, unbroken unity with animal life, release from all social obligations and, above all, possession: these are the gifts that are sought after. In the orgia man does not choose a god to honour; he is chosen by a god. And possession is not the relatively tame intrusion of a demon that can be exorcised; neither is it the passing trance that leaves a revelation behind; it is properly, fully, mystical, a surrender to and loss in the sacred.[21]

Philosophical minds traditionally recoil before the mere sight of such excesses. 'Night-ramblers, magicians, Bacchants, Maenads, Mystics: the rites accepted by mankind in the Mysteries are an unholy performance': so says Heraclitus.[22] We see Plato echo such sentiments.[23] As cultural heirs of two of the most moral and rational of all religious traditions (that is Judaism and Christianity), most of us hardly think of including such orgiastic excesses within the purview of a philosophy of religion. We prefer our religion mainstream and would rather not look at the Christian gore that surfaces in Spanish mysticism or Texas fundamentalism. But the fact must be squarely faced: in Greece, like everywhere else, orgiastic religious experiences were enjoyable and were actively sought. Can one have an unmediated, uninterpreted experience? The question may remain unanswered, although I incline to the negative; but it is clear that experiences deemed ineffable were and still are enjoyed and that the value of such experiences lies in the fact that they give man 'all he wants' before any attempt is made to articulate their meaning in words.

The sensual gratifications that are part of the experience should not hide their full human significance. The desire is not that of the simple sensualist who, like Gyges, wants to enjoy all the good things of life and live like a god among humans. Neither is it that of power-hungry men like Callicles. The mystical eros entails a note of protest against unjust practices and corrupting social relations; it entails a rejection of dominant languages, rules, and ideologies. It attains an experiencing that has fullness and roundness to it; it is for the whole human being; it makes no sense to ask whether it satisfies the body or the soul. The contemporary philosopher David Hall therefore seems to me to have expressed well the cultural basis of the urge towards mysticism: there is an eros in us that wants completeness of understanding. Such completeness ordinarily eludes us. In the extraordinary mystical experience, however, verbally clear and partial understanding yields before an experiencing that finally delivers an experience of completeness.[24] Our recent, moderate religious outlooks claim that religion is mainly a matter of justified belief. Let us, however, heed Jane Harrison's warning: our theologians expounding their beliefs get it all wrong, but powerful, overwhelming religious experiences are an abiding reality, and they help people live.[25] Human beings crave a transcending of their finitude. We want to experience wholeness and unity instead of being separate individuals sustained and held by a network of relations and obligations. We crave liberation from our acculturated ways.[26] Religious attitudes that are *hosion* show deference to all proper obligations of finite beings. But, beyond all cultural constraints, beyond all moral imperatives, we can experience – and want to experience – the sacred itself, that which is holy, *hieros*, for the holy 'serves as the ultimate ground for the erotic drive toward the intuition of the totality.'[27] Parmenides, before announcing what the goddess has told him, says that the mares conveyed him 'as far as [my] desire reached' or 'as far as my heart could desire.'[28] Once we admit that the philosopher is a creature of desire, albeit noble, reoriented, higher desire, we cannot but look at all alleged fulfilment of grandiose desire.

At any rate, the enduring tension between the comely and the orgiastic strains in Greek religion inescapably forced itself upon the minds of Plato's contemporaries. Euripides' *Bacchae*, the most poignant document Greek religion has given us, shows the tragic, insoluble conflict between the public religion of Thebes and the religion of the bacchants following Dionysus. The conflict between the king and the god, the well-meaning Pentheus and the irresistible Dionysus, is sharp: Euripides knows that an *agon* makes for good drama. The clash, however, is not contrived; something in the body social is being reflected. On the dramatic anvil something deep and pervasive is being brought to consciousness and thematized. To the somewhat dated grandeur of Pentheus, who battles the 'new disease' and 'pernicious rites,' is contrasted the holy rapture that puts an end to cares. As G.S. Kirk puts it, Dionysus 'inspires the Chorus to some of the most moving devotional poetry that has survived from the ancient world, and some of the most inconsistent and self-deluding claptrap in all the history of religions.'[29] Euripides paints a specific historical situation: both types of religion cannot survive in the city. Plato, we shall see, must have come to a somewhat similar diagnosis. *Phaedrus* is the dialogue where we find him least ill at ease with the language of enthusiasm and possession, with the notion of the soul being open to beneficial, or pernicious, influences. To this dialogue we must now turn.

3 The human soul is intelligently open

In the central part of *Phaedrus* Socrates makes a long speech in which he gives an exposition of 'the nature of soul, divine and human, its experiences and its activities.'[30] It begins with a firm assertion: soul is self-moving and immortal.[31] 'What manner of thing it is' would be a long tale to tell. Socrates cannot tell this tale; he can only say what it resembles.[32] The gist of his doctrine is that in humans souls are unwell but open to healing influences.[33] Such influences come from above but man must intelligently respond to them.

But first we must hear about the complex nature of the soul. The soul is tripartite; it can be compared to a chariot pulled by two horses and steered by a charioteer. All three parts are winged and thus rise to the higher heavens where the gods dwell. The souls of humans manage, like the gods, to rise to the summit and look upon the regions beyond the heavens. Toiling upward, crowded, trampling upon each other, they gain only fleeting and partial vision of the Plains of Truth. Many have their wings hurt. They fall, become embodied, and come 'to be burdened with a load of forgetfulness and wrongdoing.'[34] But lamed and darkened though they are, they keep a recollection of what they have seen.

What Plato has affirmed at this point is that the realm of being is an order. It is one, but not in the manner of Parmenides who saw an undifferentiated unity. It partakes of the many, but not in the manner of Heraclitus and his ceaseless flux. A recollection of this perfect order is hidden in every human soul. And this recollection is reawakened by desire when desire is kindled by beauty.

What Plato is also affirming at this point is that the soul is both active and passive. The soul is self-moving (self-steering in the comparison). Its actions are self-originating. But it is distracted, moved, or lured by desires. It is acted upon. How can it place itself in the economy of the world so that the beneficial influences will be strongest? How can it be moved by others to such a desirable position?

Here Plato moves onto the battlefield where all human struggles are waged. Without the sensible world and the desires it occasions the desire of beauty would never stir human beings. And without such aesthetic eros the passionate desire for truth would never arise in human beings. But given the pull from the objects of desire in the world, can human desire ever be converted into a desire of truth?[35] How can human desire be educated?

We have seen that, unlike Socrates, Plato comes to admit that among human beings desire cannot ever receive a univocal definition.[36] Every desire can accidentally lead to another, can suddenly prevail over others. The human heart contends with an indefinite multiplicity: whether frustrated or fulfilled, every single desire risks being only the transitory expression of an indefinite unrest. Are we to conclude that desire, whatever it is, is insatiable?[37] Not quite, says Plato. In the untiring search for worthy objects of desire man discovers that some objects are inadequate to the aspiration (and some particularly so). At this point knowledge alters action by altering desires. Deliberation ceases to be simple choice of means but becomes thinking on the best conception of the end. A rational deliberation fully aware of the nature of one's affections moves from awareness of one's desires to an altered conception of the final good.[38] The human soul is open to new desires and it can, in time, act on its desires intelligently. There can be, therefore, an ascent of desire.

Now it is time for us to pause. This is what Plato says, but what is he doing? He assumes that his readers are in state of desirous ignorance. There is in them an affective side, which should be distrusted but can be appealed to. The language of Socrates is rich in affective tones and overtones; it is meant to move souls. This speech is not in the form of a logical argument but in the form of a tale that makes a comparison. A wealth of poetic images is being poured out before us.[39] The images are drawn, as one might expect, from the most symbolically rich strains of the religious and literary tradition. Two such clusters of images will reward closer examination. Socrates says that there is a divine sort of madness that comes to our salvation. He also says that the feelings of love (*eros*) for another human being are the best and highest form of this madness. Each point shall be examined in turn.

4 Divine madness

In one passage of *Phaedrus* Plato takes a reasoned look at a whole array of religious phenomena which can be called enthusiastic. Socrates here examines what he calls 'divine madness.'[40] He is introducing the speech that will turn into an affirmation of the immortality of the soul and the narration of the tale showing its nature. His point at this early stage is that love is a kind of divine madness, the fourth one we hear about; this leads us to an examination of the first three.

Madness, insanity, was regarded by the Greeks with a mixture of horror and awe. In front of the mentally afflicted the Greeks felt that they were in the presence of a superhuman power, to be feared or respected. So stones were thrown at them, or great respect paid.[41] Divine madness, however, is not an affliction: it involves a suspension of our normal faculties, a rapture away from our state of woe, weakness, or ignorance. That the madness is called divine would mean to all Greeks that is is overpowering. To Plato it will also mean that it is beneficial. Madness is 'a divine release from customary habits,' an earthquake which releases the self from an enslavement created by the routine of life in this world and this city.[42] To acknowledge the existence of madness of this sort is to accept the hypothesis of a superior goodness impinging upon our lives. The divine influence coming through madness is a kind of liberating suffering, a nudge, a blow, which shakes the soul out of a confining state and sends it to a new level where it may start on a new path. 'The greatest of blessings come to us through madness, when it is sent as a gift of gods.' Such a view of divine madness is confirmed by the verbal similarity Plato discerns between *mania* (madness) and *mantike* (art of divination).[43]

The first of the four kinds of madness is *prophetic madness* (Delphi, Dodona), which is a kind of trance in which the normal movements of the soul are suspended and the will of the gods is communicated. Many splendid benefits are thus conferred upon Greece both in private and in public affairs. Then there is *telestic* or *corybantic madness*. Through purifications and sacred rites people in need find 'a way of release.' Those possessed of this madness are liberated from their ills, from an ancient curse, for instance. Plato alludes to the cathartic, Dionysiac type of ritualized frenzy. (In *Crito* Socrates makes a similar allusion and compares the authoritative voice of the laws to Cybele's irresistible flute).[44] This madness which comes from the gods is superior to sanity which is of human origin.[45] The third type is *poetic madness*. It comes upon the gentle and pure soul, inspiring it to song and other poetry 'that educate later generations.' (Plato always speaks well of poetic inspiration when its origin is divine; the *Laws* call the poetic tribe divinely inspired in its chanting.[46])

In this passage on divine madness Plato, I propose, faces the whole Dionysiac tradition and tries to cleanse it. Commentators have long sensed that the power of Dionysus among the Greeks was linked to ambivalence about his meaning. They have also striven to grasp the root of this ambivalence. Harrison is most helpful: she contrasts the eikonic and aneikonic religion: 'Eikonism takes the vague, unknown, fearful thing, and tries to picture it, picture it as known, as distinct, definite – something a man can think about and understand; something that will think about and understand him; something as far rationalized as man himself.' 'Aneikonism does not make its gods, it finds them – finds them in the life of Nature outside man, or in the psychological experience, the hope, the fear, the hate, the love, within him ... Its feet are in the deep sea-wells and in the primeeval slime, its head is swathed in mists and mysticism ... Aneikonism is always imaginatively more awful than eikonism.' Apollo, Athena, and even Zeus are of course eikonic, while Dionysus, the lovely human youth with curled hair who in a moment is a wild bull and a burning flame, is aneikonic.[47] Walter Otto sees in Dionysus's use of the mask one of the most important modes of the god's epiphany.[48] As Park McGinty puts it, 'having a front but no back, the mask was perfectly suited to express the god's nearness which was also paradoxically also a remoteness. As a god of the mask, Dionysus was a god of encounter, yet for the votary there was really nothing which transcended the moment of confrontation with the mask.'[49]

But do we find in Socrates the sort of cant that indiscriminately praises madness and all suspensions of ordinary judgment? Some authors have concluded that Plato cannot take divine orgiastic possession (*enthousiasmos*) very seriously.[50] *Ekstasis*, in a precise, quasitechnical sense of mystical union, is shown by E.R. Dodds to be found in Plotinus, but not before. It seems therefore very imprudent to use the term to describe Plato's position.[51] Most of the time Plato thinks that truth dawns but progressively on man and most of the time he adds that such dawning requires intellectual discernment and moral effort. What there is in divine madness that Plato approves of can, I think, best be understood in the light of what he has to say about drunkenness and music, two external influences that heighten consciousness rather than suspend it. In the *Laws* modest, restrained drunkenness is praised: it relaxes the weight of customary opinion and the awe one feels for accepted ideas and thus enables one to think fresher thoughts; the drunkenness being modest, such thoughts are worth remembering.[52] Music is another type of beneficial influence on the soul. Music, the Pythagoreans say, reorders the soul, good music, that is. (The soul is pushed into disorder by the noises of the chaotic city and its ill-conceived tunes.) In music bad influences are stilled and the divine one presented.[53]

Finally, and most decisively, we should stress that Plato keeps his warmest praise for the fourth, the most personal, the only sociable madness. *Erotic madness* is 'the best of all forms of divine possession.'[54] It is accessible to all. Initiation into it is not restricted. And, most importantly, this kind of madness, aroused by another human being, leads to a blossoming of the *logos* in close persistent dialogue.[55] The lover seeks to *talk* with the beloved. This madness alone is truly dialectical. Words and feelings become intimately intertwined. Here again we must recognize the fine hand of Socrates. The highest form of madness is that which most intimately involves – rather than suspends – the talkative soul. After Socrates, Plato no longer can see the soul in magical terms: it is too closely associated with the conscious powers of man. The knowledge of which the soul is capable is never merely that of mystical vision: it is also such rational knowledge as proceeds from the ability to invite, talk, explain, persuade, and be persuaded.

To sum up: in his doctrine of divine madness Plato offered a systematic theory of all the experiences in which the Greeks confessed that the gods made a morally decisive impact on man. He encountered but shunted aside the notion of gods being present only in both wild noise and silence. He could not accept as divine an experience in which nothing is offered except the experience itself. Religious experiencing gives a nudge or a jolt; it also gives something to talk about, to interpret. That the gods are careful means that they are gentle, never more brutal than we can stand. Plato never used religious experience to appeal to the unsayable or to suggest that the last word in knowledge is to be found above language.[56] But he was aware that there are experiences that make us talk in novel ways, with a powerful impact that apparently leaves us helpless at first. And he considered erotic love to be the most moving example of that. There madness and dialectic work together to civilize;[57] there divine madness keeps uncivilized madness at bay.

5 That bone of contention: love

In erotic madness the issue of the education of desire receives a clear focus: where do erotic sentiments come from and where do they lead? The appetitive man may well wish to stick to elementary genital pleasures; erotic sentiments, however, intertwine them with the most complex, cruel, and passionate dramas in the life of the self.

'First there comes upon him a shuddering ...' Thus begins Plato's description of the desire aroused by 'a godlike face or bodily form that truly expresses beauty.'[58] There is much psychological penetration here. High claims are also made for the process of falling in love: the soul has found 'the only physician for her grievous suffering.'[59] Such a passage deserves to be placed in its full historical context.

A history of love and affection among the Greeks has not been written. Some bench-marks can be quickly indicated. The warriors in the *Iliad* hold on to their women greedily. 'The girl I will not give back,' proclaims Achilles in the opening scene.[60] Book 6 shows a different kind of warrior society: Hector is sad at seeing the impending fall of Troy, while his wife is saddened by the impending death of her husband.[61] In the *Odyssey* we find the full development of what has begun in Hector's household. Family affection and the charms of sexual love are a constant theme and they are carefully elaborated. Ulysses wants to get home to his wife and happily shares affection with attractive women on the way. Loved by his wife, he is a success with other women, and a good father too.[62] The women are not just attractions praised from the man's point of view. Calypso raises her voice in the first recorded protest against double standards: 'you gods cannot bear to let a goddess sleep with a man ... easy livers yourselves.'[63]

Such Homeric heights in human sensitivity seem to have been quickly lost. What is called the love poetry of Archilochus, the first non-aristocratic lyrical poet, is brash masculine vaunting and crude bitching. Whether pleased or angry with women, his amorous sentiments do not seem to rise much above the quest for instinctual gratification. As for the other non-aristocratic poet, Simonides, he is famous for his long tirade against women.

Hesiod formulates at some length and with much mythical underpinning the key tenets of Greek misogyny. Women are lazy and sensual, a honeyed trap that adds immeasurably to men's woes. Hesiod's view of women is part of a vast mythology giving the genesis of man's current miserable estate: in the golden age Earth gave abundant food, sufficient for the nutrition of all, and human beings were born out of her. Now one must work, kill domestic animals to feed, and marry women to obtain sons.[64] This misogyny reflects, of course, a specific social situation (and one that was to prove quite durable). Struggling middle-class households find survival difficult in the early world of the *polis*: nuclear family and hard work within this unity are a necessity of life. In the fierce competition of the city the household has to be economically productive; the woman's rule here is crucial and integral. She also has to produce legitimate heirs. But her rights in either her husband's family or the state are minimal. 'Woman's enforced participation in a society in which she had no concrete stake posed a problem.'[65]

It takes an aristocratic woman to reintroduce loving subjectivity into the talk about the sexes (and probably between them). Sappho unfolds a vision of love that includes delicacy and refinement. P. Friedrich has recently argued that Sappho was not interested only in relationships between women. Her wedding hymns reflect a 'passionate conjugal sexuality.' Love-making becomes praised as a civilized art calling upon kind persuasion and devoid of rapacity. The impact of religious ritual verse linked to Aphrodite is evident in Sappho's poetry.[66] Socrates pays homage to her in the opening conversation of *Phaedrus*.[67]

In the fifth century the theatre emerges in Athens as the great educator in expression and the refinement of personal sentiments. Those who watch the plays broaden their psychological range. They see Clytemnestra a strong woman, Medea a woman scorned and dangerous, Alcestis a self-sacrificing wife. Different facets of the same mythical character are explored. Aeschylus, Sophocles, and Euripides all have a different Electra. True, the theatre begins by marshalling all the resources of myth and poetic eloquence to secure the subordination of women in the civil order. The *Oresteia* is engaged in placing 'the polis at the centre of its vision and endowing it with the creative power to coordinate human, natural and divine forces.' 'If Aeschylus is concerned with world building, the cornerstone of his architecture is the control of woman, the social and cultural prerequisite for the construction of civilization.'[68] There shall be male supremacy in all things, announces Athena; woman keeps only the right to give herself in marriage.[69]

Nevertheless women remain a very strong presence on the stage. Clearly even within this mythical and legal framework women will still make their voice heard. The comedies of Aristophanes should be proof enough of that; the tragedies of Euripides show how far the process went. A new valuation of women emerges. The old misogyny of Hesiod no longer expresses actual perceptions and experiences. Sexual feelings are displayed in all their subjectivity. Eros is personalized. At the same time its overpowering aspect becomes more awesome. *Lysistrata* shows the comedy of it, *Hippolytus* the tragedy. Phaedra, 'taken over' by Aphrodite, is not a woman lost, deprived of her normal judgment, inhuman in her enthusiasm; there is a self in her, attacked but fighting. The psychology of eros is described as human psychology.

> Love distills desire upon the eyes,
> love brings bewitching grace into
> the heart of those he would destroy.[70]

Clearly what has been called the fifth-century enlightenment rises to a fairer understanding and expression of the range of feelings men and women can have for each other.[71]

The feelings and the desire described in *Phaedrus* are, as we very well know, those of homosexual love. The history of Greek homosexuality is an even more obscure affair, with a fair amount of sectarian hypothesizing. It is worth recalling that there is no overt homosexuality in Homer, none whatsoever in Archilochus. A fair amount of it appears in the early fifth century, and speeches in Plato convey the well-known idealization of it: male lovers of males are the most noble of all lovers. The theatre, however, a great shaper of popular attitudes, makes no move towards the idealization of homosexual love and Aristophanes heaps ridicule on it. I am inclined to think that, although Plato's description of erotic sentiment draws upon a broad cultural background that is in the majority heterosexual, the metaphysical significance that he attributes to it in the theory of soul and beauty undoubtedly reflects the attitudes of a more rarefied intellectual and homosexual group.[72] In any case some of the language of homosexual attachment is fed back into heterosexual and marital love.[73] It is also clear that Plato is quite conscious that he is offering a new interpretation of love. The description of falling in love concludes: 'this is the experience (*pathos*) that men term love.' Having established what common experience he is talking about, he adds that it is a mystery, a rite, and proceeds to elucidate 'the cause and the nature of the lover's experience.'[74]

This, then, is what he says. Once desire is aroused, the charioteer must contend against conflicting desires on the part of the two horses. The black, greedy one wants to leap upon the beloved. He can be controlled only with whip and goad. The white horse remembers the form of Beauty and sees it enthroned by the side of Temperance. If the charioteer manages to control the black horse, the whole soul, pulled by the white one, 'follows after the beloved with reverence and awe' and is guided into the ordered rule of the philosophic life, with self-mastery and inward peace. When death comes, the two souls ascend to the uninterrupted contemplation of the truth.[75] Erotic madness thus teaches moderation; while the soul gains a friend with whom to talk, it is above all empowered to fulfil its proper function: to fly to the contemplation of the things above. This is why this madness alone is the ally of the philosopher.

Two points need to be noted here. First, in erotic passion human beings renew their love of talk and learn again to talk joyfully, expansively, generously. Romance wants to move towards that moment where talk slows down and a silent eros gathers momentum. But, in the process of getting there, people flower in talk and take pleasure in talking, even if they talk vaguely. The rigours of Socratic conversation demand clear, coherent, logical sentences. This kind of conversation confines human beings to attentiveness to real facts. It leads to precise affirmations, solid accounts, durable definitions, accepted verities. In erotic conversation the language of order yields before the language of pleasure. And, Plato's point seems to be, this language is needed if we are to renew our aspiration to that which is really desirable. The versatility of desire must be allowed expression if humans wish to avoid submission to habits and received, unarguable verities. In *Gorgias* Plato criticizes the Sophists in the name of truth; in *Phaedrus* he instils suspicion for truths that stand in the way of that which is desirable.[76]

Secondly, the fourth madness is the best because it reawakens a memory, which is *knowledge*. When the souls feasted their eyes upon the Plains of Truth, 'pure was the light that shone around us, and pure were we.'[77] The praise of eros is 'in fact an encomium of memory as the essential requirement of the human condition.'[78] Love offers a ladder that enables us to reascend to that remembered state of knowing. The great tale blends the Orphic doctrine of the immortal soul and the Olympian vision of the enduring beauty of deathless gods to give shape to the doctrine of loving and reverent contemplation as man's chief end.

There is thus a similarity in outcome between the pursuits of lovers moved by a desire for union and the apparently more purely dialectical pursuits of philosophers who work towards understanding of the truth. Behind all our words, and lending dynamism and significance to them, there is an eros, a desire for such a communion. We do not talk or argue for the sheer pleasure of it; we are after something that is not verbal. A unitive vision of the forms is the culmination of a philosopher's desire to know the truth.

What surprises us is the ease with which Plato moves from the story of human sexual desires to the healing of the individual soul thanks to a metaphysical vision of cosmic order. Plato can do it because he gives to eros a quality which we moderns are bound to label impersonal. Eros is prompted by the desire of Beauty itself. Shall we say that cosmic love, like divine tendance, has somewhat the flavour of grease in the cosmic machinery?

But let us give Plato his due. *Phaedrus* begins with a speech that praises the advantages of a hedonistic calculation among sexual partners who are not troubled by love. Against such impersonal, selfish, prudent management of the affairs of one's body, Socrates invites Phaedrus to a love that is a subjective, personal involvement. The fact that a horse can learn moderation and reverence invites us also to think of the soul as being able to attend kindly to the other. Socrates speaks of the pursuer offering services and the pursued returning kind disposition.[79] We should firmly resist, therefore, cthose accounts of Platonic eros that attribute to it a spiritual selfishness (I want to see the forms) that is an idealistic version of plain rapacity (I want my pleasure). As desirous human beings become better, more attentive to reality, they come to be capable of an overflowing kind of goodness. They can thus better transcend their self-interest in concrete circumstances. As N.P. White puts it, 'To apprehend the Good fully along with a situation in which it might be exemplified *simply is* to have a desire overwhelming all others to see that instantiation take place.'[80] On this view we can understand why the *Republic* insists that good men feel the joys and sorrows of all as their own.[81] Whether lover or legislator, a just man tries to embody in the world what he admires or to facilitate the embodiment of it.[82] Starting with a situation of amorous desires, Plato locates the education of desire right in the most enduringly troubled area in the life of the self.[83] Desirous selves for Plato acknowledge each other and have no quick access to impersonal serenity.

We can see now that there is even a subtle point to the specifically homosexual nature of the desire Plato talks about. Beyond feeling embarrassed, troubled, or excited, the philosopher should note that this very fact signals the potential for injustice in quiet talk among males. *Phaedrus* does not present Socrates as someone who would make a pass at the younger man. Athenian convention would not hesitate to attribute the motive to him, although most would find Phaedrus a bit old for that role. I deem it a noteworthy fact that Socrates is not such a man. Alcibiades in the *Symposium* also narrates an incident of amazing non-action. The point is that a philosophically erotic discussion between two individuals on love, 'that much disputed thing,'[84] can easily turn into an effort by the leader to get the other to grant him his sexual desire. An interaction launched by a common desire for truth can insensibly, and in an injust manner, veer towards an exploitation of the weak by the strong, since the desires of the strong can easily wear a mask as they approach the other. The intellectual dispute about love (harmful or good?) can hide another more real dispute: is one of the discussants trying to satisfy his desire? is the leader up to something harmful to the other or is he up to something beneficial?

As two human beings talk, there is thus more than one bone of contention among them. Plato, resolutely setting aside all talk of ambivalence on the part of the gods who can both please and kill, who both shout and remain silent, stumbles onto the ambivalences of humans who do speak. As Jacques Derrida has pointed out, the metaphor of the drug (*pharmakon*) reappears in key places in the dialogues. The drug can heal people or surrender them to the power of another. Eros is called a drugger in the *Symposium*. Socrates is also painted as drugging his listeners, bewitching them, numbing them.[85] The last section of *Phaedrus* asks whether speaking with a view to persuade is not administering a drug about which one does not know whether it will heal or hurt. The understanding of desire and eros opens an abyss before our feet: is the dialectic striving for definition of disputed terms as innocent as it first appears? Is person-to-person talk, like public speaking before crowds, the continuation of exploitation by other means? Is there a desire for power hidden behind Socrates' attempt to persuade his young listeners that only noble desires must be acted upon and that they only can be genuinely satisfied?[86] Is some mad trance sought after behind the veneer of civilized speech?

6 Desire, rhetoric, and the art of writing

Now that the erotic overtones of face-to-face conversation have been brought out into the open, we may well wonder about the sharp condemnation pronounced by Plato on the undercurrents of public speaking in democracies. Can it be that Plato overemphasized the contrast between the worldly greedy Sophists and pure Socrates who did not make political speeches and did not seduce young men?

Rhetoric, in any case, survived Plato's attacks upon it. It went on making claims to moral worth. Isocrates in his fourth-century rehabilitation of rhetoric strove for a universally valid education that avoided moral nihilism without undertaking the Platonic search for absolutes.[87] Rhetoric for Aristotle is to teach as well as to please. This path was a noble one, renewing itself right until the end of antiquity, and many learned through it how to appreciate the best that has been said and done. Rhetoric taught men both the value of persuasion through speech and the valid modes of bringing it about. It is thus unfair to link rhetoric with the dogmatic materialism that reduces all to power relationships. A modern representative of that tradition does link the discovery of rhetorical fields as the environment proper to human life to a serious metaphysical question: 'Who or what made the universe such that it can be apprehended only in a shared language of values?'[88]

In response to this Plato would say that Isocrates is indeed a better man than, say, Gorgias.[89] But he would still maintain his basic point: the knack for knowing how to feel one's way in the dark is a precious thing for those who are prepared to remain in the dark, and even more precious for those who want to prey upon others. The Sophists who develop 'nominal' definitions merely present a shadow-play of words[90] (the allusion to the cave is unmistakeable: a philosopher will want to come to the light). They exercise power over others but they remain captive to the powerlessness of disordered lives. Those who strive to keep peace in the cave are also doomed to frustration: theirs will be no peace at all. To each group alike one can throw the taunt of Shestov (another absolutist): 'What can one say of the labyrinth, except that it is a labyrinth?'[91] Socrates is a literary phenomenon: a man who has no views on others, who talks only to heal, pleases only to teach.

The last part of *Phaedrus* accordingly argues that a philosophy that wishes to teach must itself develop a rhetoric. This rhetoric will be subordinate to philosophy, and thus will be quite different from the rhetoric that is its rival. So the early diagnosis (as found in *Protagoras*, for instance) stands: people who base themselves on poets, laws, traditions, common sense, and civil conventions merely rearrange the opinions of the many; they do not strive after the truth. A sense of shared pleasure, even a sense of equity are the obvious moral virtues that are imparted in this way. But we do not learn thereby the true sense of justice.

The manner of teaching others that Plato commends is based upon a truly philosophical view of language. And this view assimilates the old rhetorical insight, namely that the self has to be moved, the affections trained. *Phaedrus* shows that rich and crucial words, like madness, experience (*pathos*), and love, are in fact uttered by ambivalent speakers, have ambiguous meanings, correspond to more than one form. Just as Plato has early given up the notion that answers can be provided by solemn, oracular, obscure utterances, he must now give up the notion that exact, definitive, fool-proof definitions are the goal of inquiry.[92] (This ideal of perfect language toyed with in *Cratylus* is thus killed before it is even born, if we assume that *Cratylus* is written after *Phaedrus*, that is.) In particular Plato gives up the conceptual atomism (one word, and one only, for everything) that has characterized much older philosophical inquiries.

The argument is launched in this way. What is the method of writing well?[93] The speaker must know the truth about his subject.[94] This is hardly news. We must also remember that Socrates proceeds on the further assumption that he also knows the nature of soul.[95] He understands what sort of beings, that is erotic ones, his listeners are. He knows that he himself is an erotic being. Socrates knows the nature of the two horses in his listeners and in himself and senses the probable source of his words and their probable impact on others. Is intimate talk in fact a conspiring between the black horses of each partner, or is it an appeal from one's white horse to the other's white one? Here lies the significance of the famous method of division. If we are to talk about love, let us try to become conscious of what sort of love we are talking about. Let us make a division between ignoble and noble love. Further divisions are necessary. By going left at every turn one will in the end find 'one particular part bearing the name of "sinister" love, on which one will properly pour abuse.' This is the sort of love that exactly suits the nature of the black horse. By making turns to the right-hand side one will find the divine love, 'source of the greatest goods that can befall us.'[96] To put it briefly, distinctions and further distinctions help the soul discover in itself both the madness of desire that leads to destruction and the divine madness that leads to health. It helps the soul to sort out its preferences and give sovereignty to the preference for the good.

This is what is said to take place in the proper Socratic manner of speaking (Socrates uses his previous speeches as examples of the process). Speaking is not a fight with words but truly an education of desire. What then of writing? Socrates here tells an Egyptian story. Theuth introduced his invention of writing by claiming that it 'will make the people of Egypt wiser and improve their memories'; to this the king replied: 'If men learn this, it will implant forgetfulness in their souls; they will cease to exercise memory because they rely on that which is written, calling things to remembrance no longer from within themselves, but by means of external marks.'[97]

There is much to make us pause here. Is Plato voicing the traditional aristocratic dislike of written law and the preference for oral wisdom preserved in leading families?[98] 'Written words,' explains Iris Murdoch, 'are the helpless victims of men's ill will, and encourage inferior exposition at second hand. Writing can easily become a kind of lying, something frivolously pursued for its own sake, in fact an art form.'[99] But is this Plato's last word?

Fully sensing the irony of such views located in what is perhaps Plato's most artful dialogue, Ronna Burger proposes a key: the king who condemns writing is a god who ignores the limitations of the human condition. Human beings are not prompt at finding the good remembrance 'within themselves.' The Platonic defence of the art of writing is in fact expressed through the Socratic condemnation of its dangers.[100] The one who writes very well draws on the one who has never written a word to condemn written works which are not aware of their own lack of clarity and firmness. The drug of writing is necessary, since human memories are in poor health, but this drug must be administered wisely. The written word can be life-giving if it is in a context that invites recognition of its complexity. A written dialogue cannot be a replacement for living thought but it can invite it. Writing, like eros, cultivates reminders of the truth. A dramatic written dialogue moves; it never achieves perfect fixity. It is an appropriate medium to get the self-moving yet passive soul moving in the right direction.[101]

The dialogues, demonstrating the wrestling between minds, not only show the rise of the truth and its victory over untruth, but shows it in such a manner that the contest of truth with untruth remains part of the record. The victory of truth is thereby protected. We see people reoriented as well as truths uttered. But the true words are not left at the end of a dialogue like a doctrine that can be twisted or misunderstood; we see how people arrived at them. Plato's dialogues thus achieve the objective he has formulated in *Phaedrus*, 'an intelligent word graven in the soul of the learner, which can defend itself, and knows with whom to speak and with whom to be silent.'[102]

Plato therefore has no real nostalgia for the world of priestly hieroglyphics. He fully appreciates the gains that Greeks have made with the invention of the alphabet and the ensuing democratization of literacy. 'If the alphabet serves as a fitting image for the interwoven logos of dialectic writing, the hieroglyph as a single symbol carrying an ambiguous range of meanings is an image for the myth or monologic speech which must be subject to interpretation.'[103]

The dialogues transmit to us powerful drugs inherited from the mythic past. They offer interpretation where interpretation is demanded. They do it within an anthropological context where each noble human being can in turn be interpreter to the other. And 'noble' here refers not to something ascribed by a myth but to ability in *logos*. As the *Alcibiades* puts it, there is only one antidote to the poisons human beings secrete for each other: to submit oneself to mutual test in dialogue, to know oneself by listening to the language of the other.[104] Thus philosophy can be said to bring even more strength to the healing thrust towards democracy started by public, deliberative speaking. A manner of speaking may be found that moves us erotic beings towards understanding the truth.

7 *Phaedrus*: the divine pull at work

Plato believes that the soul's path to goodness is eased by the presence of a cosmic pull that keeps the soul open to transcendent realities and helps it on its way towards them. But how is one to teach about transcendence or the soul's openness? Language is human; it starts with opinion and reflects human ignorance as much as human knowledge. Yet *Phaedrus* was written: the dialogue moves us and opens us to movement and to influences from the divine pull.

The dialogue begins with Socrates meeting Phaedrus, an agreeable youngish man (not so young, however, that one cannot expect him by now to be more than just agreeable.) Phaedrus had spent the morning listening to Lysias, who has made a brilliant speech arguing that an adolescent would grant his favours to the one who is not in love with him rather than to the lover. Socrates is very keen to hear the speech. With a scroll in his hand Phaedrus can draw the philosopher anywhere, so powerful is his drug. So the two walk into the country to find a quiet place under a tree where Phaedrus is to retell what Lysias has said. There is amiable small talk and erotic banter on the way. The altar of Boreas leads Phaedrus to ask: 'do you believe that story to be true?' In answer Socrates comments on the uselessness of 'scientific' explanations of myths. Since Socrates find the countryside lovely, Phaedrus asks him why he is spending all his time in the city: 'the trees won't teach me anything, and the people in the city do' (230d). Socrates remains true to his moral character, yet the whole pastoral setting gives a unique quality to the dialogue: the atmosphere is relaxed, Socrates lyrical and expansive; words flow easily. The dialogue does not take place in the public scene; it has a private quality peculiar to it and it may be called pastoral.

Thus the two sit down and Phaedrus repeats Lysias's speech. Against the accepted view that sexual games between older men and younger ones are ennobling if there is between them a romantic attachment, Lysias argues that the wise adolescent should keep a cold eye on his self-interest and look at the problem with a calculating reason. The older lover is swollen with passion, afflicted with a disease, insane, and has no control of his feelings; only harm can come from him; whereas the suitor who is what A.E. Taylor calls a 'businesslike sensualist' will offer advantages to the young man who is willing to play games with him.[105] The praise of the non-passionate lover mirrors Lysias's own activity as a speech-writer; for a fee he too will, dispassionately, write the effective speech that his customer needs.[106]

Socrates declares himself quite impressed with the argument. Phaedrus agrees: the speech could not be better. This of course is a challenge to Socrates, who quibbles about the form of it. Therefore Phaedrus asks him to try to do better. Socrates enters into the game and proceeds with a speech arguing the same view. There is a delicate ambiguity in Socrates' behaviour at this point. His speech begins with a formal, even grandiloquent, invocation of the Muses. So Socrates offers the appearance of turning to an exalted style, to the style appropriate to more serious utterances. However, Socrates keeps his head wrapped up while he speaks (and masks this act of shame under a pretence). He also significantly, if in a minor way, alters the nature of the speech: his speech is uttered, he says, by a genuinely passionate lover who believes that he will more surely win the young man if he pretends to be a non-lover who argues the merits of a calculating relationship. The appearance of seriousness in Socrates' speech is confirmed by its initial, ponderous point: one must at the outset agree on a definition of love (237d). There are two kinds of desires: one is for plain pleasure, the other for 'what is best,' a more complex good which involves an element of judgment, or opinion. Love is a desire of the first kind that is so strong that it can overrule the other kind of desire. So the suitor who is a passionate lover will make the other a slave to his physical desires, and will do all he can to keep his beloved in a dependant, subservient position. His love is that of the wolf for the lamb. The interests of the young man are therefore safer with a non-lover. Note the subtle shift in meaning in an apparently similar argument: the young man for Lysias is to have more fun and profit with a non-lover; for Socrates what the young man must seek to protect while he is involved is the capacity for independent judgment, the ability to cultivate his soul (241c).

Phaedrus notices that the speech stops early; a positive case for associating with the non-lover is not really made. Socrates thinks he has said enough and announces that he will cross the stream 'before you put some further compulsion in me.' At this point his demon, or divine sign, checks him 'as if he had committed some sin against a deity.' Socrates is a seer and is sometimes brought back to his senses by such signs: 'how prophetic is the soul,' he exclaims. We now hear that he has been distressed all along by the rules of the conversational game started by Phaedrus. The speech he has heard about and the one he has made, he declares, are dreadful, foolish, impious. They have a refreshing simplicity but are erroneous. Socrates has had a good time listening to and comparing the music of these words, but he has been 'buying honour among men by sinning against the gods.' Love is a god or something divine, and the speeches sin against it by treating it as a dangerous disease (242c–e). So Socrates must purify himself, atone, by a recantation. The two speeches have assumed that what passes for love among vulgar people, namely what we call sex, is all there is to love. But there is also a generous love.

Socrates therefore embarks on a new long speech, his second, and the third in the dialogue. It begins by rehabilitating madness and saying that the greatest blessings come through a sort of madness that can properly be called divine. There are four kinds of madness. The first three are well known: the prophetic, the cathartic, and the poetic. The fourth is erotic madness. To understand madness one must understand the soul, how it acts and is acted upon. Therefore Socrates unfolds his doctrine of the soul: the source and beginning of motion, the soul is immortal, destined to regain the vision of truth. Erotic madness is a gift of the gods 'fraught with the highest bliss.' It has nothing to do with those prosaic useful activities that are to mutual advantage. So 'let us not be disturbed by an argument that seeks to scare us into preferring the friendship of the sane to that of the passionate' (245b).

To go further in the understanding of the soul one must have recourse to images. The soul is like a pair of winged horses led by a charioteer. One horse is noble and is guided by words, the other is unruly and troublesome. Being winged, the soul ascends to the realm of the divine and can take a place in a procession of the gods. As the procession moves on, it rises to the Plain of Truth, where the soul beholds absolute justice, temperance, and knowledge. The gods have a steady vision of these eternal realities; the human soul is handicapped by the unruly horse and has at best but an intermittent view. Depending on how much they have seen – and how much they forget – the souls are then incarnated in a whole range of creatures. Only those who have seen the truth become human and only the philosophers among them have wings. And when these humans feel love, the recollection of the perfection they have seen is aroused; beauty alone has the privilege of causing the wings of the incarnate soul to grow again. If the unruly horse is checked, the love that is in the soul will be honourable, temperate, and modest and will lead those who share it to an ordered life. Genuine love is a bridge between madness and order, madness being a necessary transition from disorder to order. So Socrates can return to the original question: the affection of the non-lover is 'alloyed with mortal prudence' and follows 'parsimonious rules of conduct.' There is no friendship among calculating men; their so-called affection begets narrowness in the afflicted souls and prolongs their wanderings on earth (256e). This love is a mere prolongation of didsorder. So the good life is only for those who turn to love of wisdom and 'live for love, in singleness of purpose and with the aid of philosophical discourse' (257b).

The dialogue might well stop here. The truth has been spoken, the unwise speeches displaced. What is perhaps Plato's most moving myth has been unfurled; in such dialogues as *Gorgias*, *Phaedo*, and the *Republic* the myth has the last word. But speaking truly is not enough among philosophers; that true speech must be protected by knowledge of what constitutes its truths. The praise of the open soul must be followed by an attempt to keep the soul open, in so far as this is possible.

A possible next step is the competitive one: ask Lysias to make a better, more philosophic speech. But Socrates prefers to remain on the private level: let the two of them go on discussing what is the method of writing well (258d). True, the heat of the afternoon lulls many into sleep, but this is no time for mental indolence. The examples of the cicadas who sing continually should spur the two of them on: let them talk and not sleep at noontime.

Therefore the two will not be lazy and will demonstrate the stamina of philosophy: from here on they philosophize, moving from the mere dramatic juxtaposition of three types of speech to the general question of good (or bad) speaking and writing (259e). Socrates develops a familiar contrast between rhetoric and philosophy. This enables him to outline principles of style for a true rhetoric which is based upon philosophical knowledge. The speaker should know the truth about his subject and not just master the knack of bewitching through language. A good discourse will have a definite structure, reflecting sound knowledge: 'Knowledge of soul is the necessary, even if unattainable, condition for an art of persuasion.'[107] The method of division is introduced. There are two kinds of love, two kinds of madnesses. The speaker can either remain immersed in the left-handed one, destroying himself and his listeners alike in the endless pursuit of insatiable desires; or he can turn to the right, grow in knowledge of the subject, and disseminate his knowledge. Socrates, thus equipped, is confident that he can judge all writings and all poets. The good rhetorician like the physician must have a scientific knowledge of the larger whole – the body, the world. Plato is obviously impressed by Hippocrates: medicine with him has moved from a knack to a science. Like the physician the rhetorician must also know the art of diagnosis: which medicine to give to whom and when and in what doses. Only thus can the power of speech be a guide to the soul. This leads to a discussion of the limited advantages of writing. Wisdom seems stored in a book, but the book does not answer questions and can fall into the hands of the unintelligent. It cannot defend itself and thus often does little but spread pseudo-knowledge. Nevertheless it is possible to write in such a manner that the piece does not give the impression of 'containing important truth of permanent validity' but presents itself as a 'mere dream image' (277d). This sort of writing is good because it can recall the word of knowledge engraved in the soul through dialectical discussion which alone remains both firm and live.

Many readers have found *Phaedrus* to be the most powerful of Plato's dialogues. Its power comes from shifting emotional vibrations, subtlety of structure and texture, and consummate artistry. Platonic scholarship is full of learned debates about its key subject-matter. The openness of the soul is attested to in at least three ways: Socrates is stopped in his tracks and jolted into genuine inspiration; a moral argument unfolds, with warmth, for the superiority of generous love over constricting love; and the soul's highest capacity, language itself, becomes self-critical. Every trick of language is used and, in time, becomes self-conscious. The self-consciousness, however, is not deadening, since it is there only for those who have ears to hear; language therefore keeps its proper power. There is some truth in E. Voegelin's view that *Phaedrus* is a manifesto which announces the emigration of the spirit from the *polis*.[108] In the dialogue truthful speech prepares for itself a refuge in the community of the philosophers. *Phaedrus* has not done much to maintain the political zeal of philosophers but it does provide them with a sense of their unique identity. *Phaedrus* gives us a special Platonic facet, which has an esoteric, erotic tinge. It is a piece of writing from which many may profit to some degree; a few, however, will feel that there is here something irresistibly precious which is meant for them alone.

9

The goodness of pious ways

I Rearticulation and translation

Chapters 6, 7, and 8 have shown Plato drawing a threefold lesson: we must be morally serious and account to each other verbally for our behaviour; we must strive together to discover the intelligibility of everything in the world and put it into words; and we must be ready to let experience challenge our entrenched formulations. We have just presented these lessons as three imperatives to mental activity and alertness. They can also be stated as three grounds for measured optimism. 1 / There is a moral economy, or order; moral rules exist; the good life can be attained, arranged in time, by human beings; they can work for it methodically, in the context of a stable coherent whole. 2 / The moral order is intelligible; exertions of intelligence help attain the good life. 3 / When minds fail or get entrapped in habit, a cosmic dynamism, a zeal in living, helps us look for new answers. They can also be stated as a threefold lesson on happiness. 1 / A wise man examines his life, his appetites, to strive towards that which is good for him. 2 / A wise man discovers that desire for truth and deference to reality can become a person's dominant love and that this love, when dominating, is the source of the only abiding satisfaction. 3 / A wise man also discovers that the eros in him that teaches him the vanity of appetitive rewards and the desirability of truth also serves to dissolve cramped beliefs that prevent him from seeing the whole.

This summary gives us in a nutshell what we might call Plato's philosophic faith, his sense of what philosophy is all about and what mental activity it can achieve. It gives both imperatives to mental activity and commendation of these powerful life experiences that disrupt mental activity and displace mental habits. The summary also gives us a rearticulation of the meaning of the Greek religious tradition. Plato's threefold affirmations are drawn from the presentation of the human condition that he has discerned in his religious environment. 'He has discerned': the qualification is crucial. The firmness of the moral economy, its intelligibility, and the presence of healing influences are affirmations that Plato *believes* he has found in Greek religion. These affirmations are the result of a rearticulation; but he has found something like them, already articulated. We have stressed – appropriately, I think – the philosophical commitment that comes to expression in *Gorgias*, the *Republic*, and *Phaedrus*, but we should not forget that it is the three dogmas of the *Laws* that put us on the scent of the threefold affirmation: the gods exist, they cannot be bribed, and they tend things wisely. We ought to be morally serious; the universe and the gods who rule it are morally serious and we can see that such is the case; and the gods try to help even those human beings who are neither morally serious nor intellectually penetrating.

What we must now see clearly is that Plato has both a practice of philosophy and a theological teaching. This practice of philosophy brings him to the articulation of a properly philosophical, individual eros towards the good life. But this philosophical truth is to be put to work in society: it has to touch the lives of those who are not philosophers. The process of rearticulation passes over into that of translation.[1] Truth is to be put to work, to meet important human needs, to re-educate not the desires of the philosopher but those of all human beings in their corporate existence. And this is to be done by means of a theology publicly taught.

Our exposition of the threefold result in chapters 6–8 has left the question about the gods somewhat in the dark. We have alluded to what Plato said about the gods but the question of goodness for man has been our sole guiding thread. Now we must focus on what exactly Plato says concerning the divine. And we must realize that Plato does this as part of a programme of translation of his philosophy for public purposes. Having philosophized, the philosopher emerges on the public scene with an attempt at 'solution.' He has a refined sense of morality, an insight into the decay of the city, a vision of truth, a purified desire, and a sense of what human beings really want. He also has insight into the nature of language, its potential and its traps. So he comes to offer some happiness to the distraught, chaotic city. His means are a theology: a set of stories, a set of beliefs, and a set of laws.

2 Theology and the problem of beliefs

In order to function partly on shared consensus and not entirely on terror and imposed conformity a society needs a minimum number of common beliefs. There is no community of shared intention without the sharing of some beliefs deemed plausible. These statements are banal, but they hide some complex issues. 'Something that is believed by nobody is not a belief.' How can one get people to believe *en masse*, especially when one realizes that belief is not an action, the performance of which can be verified? Furthermore, there is the well-known heterogeneity between the social and the individual. Individuals rarely do exactly what 'society' expects them to do. In the end belief is neither social conformity nor logical assent, neither act of the will nor simple feeling. It is an 'unanalyzable private state of mind,' and the only evidence of it is the custom individuals have of making statements of belief[2] and their achievement of a routine consensus. Once it is granted that individuals cannot play-act belief, how can the social reformer seek to displace and replace beliefs?

Plato analyses correct belief or right opinion (*orthe doxa*) in the last pages of *Meno*. We learn there that such opinion 'is as good a guide to rightness of action as knowledge.' It differs from knowledge in being unstable. The individual does not know why his belief is correct. A believing individual has been persuaded; he has not learned. And the process of transmission of correct belief to others is a very hit-and-miss affair: the man of correct belief does not know how to educate or persuade others.[3] Nevertheless a process of transmission can occur: wise tradition imparts beliefs, the practical value of which is not affected if those who transmit and receive them do not fully understand what they adhere to.

The process of translation brings to light Plato's practical (in contrast to theoretical) side. 'While Plato thought that a correct moral theory made moral behaviour certain, he came to realize that moral behaviour does not necessarily imply the understanding of a correct moral theory, but merely the acceptance of a system of guidance.'[4] The three dogmas are offered in the *Laws* as the capstones of such a system of guidance. Plato is proposing a city where the general atmosphere (anonymous, pervasive influences) will tend to make correct belief secure and will be an easier terrain for the acquisition and cultivation of virtue. The edifice of correct belief hangs together thanks to one solid capstone: the doctrine of God. Plato claims that this doctrine is ancient. 'God, as the ancient doctrine tells us, holds the beginning, the end and the middle of all things in his hands, and leads them according to their nature and for the best.'[5] Today's commentator must stress that, ancient though the general idea may be, its architectonic character is very much Plato's achievement.

Werner Jaeger has found an apt formula to convey the shift in theological imagination brought about by Plato: God has become a teacher of the whole world.[6] Instead of the overarching dominance of Fate, under the rule of which a pantheon of gods agitate themselves with varying degrees of moral worth and various degrees of actual success, Plato affirms the dominance of a good god.

To Plato this theological doctrine is true. Its truth guarantees the legitimacy of other beliefs, of which all that can be said is that they are useful. Such further beliefs must be consonant with the belief in the good God. But they will not be true. Not even necessarily plausible. Plato realizes that it is not difficult to habituate people to believe. People who believe that Cadmus sowed teeth into the ground from which grew heavily armed men will believe anything.[7] It is relatively hard to make oneself believe, but it is easy to manipulate the beliefs of others.

We, of course, balk before such a prospect of manipulation. But let us consider the unusual task Plato assigns himself. He examines the problems of a legislator who, endowed with philosophical virtue, and sure of the existence of a good god, wishes to set up a system of guidance, specifically a system of laws, that will bring about a state of affairs in a new city where the best will voluntarily accept to rule and where the rest will voluntarily accept their rule.[8] What is the overall system of religious belief that should be fostered in such a city? What dynamics of the collective modification of desire in the face of reality should be installed among its citizens? 'Installed' is, of course, a term crying for clarification. Plato, like everyone else, knows of only two ways to bring about the reorientation of beliefs: speech and force (*logos* and *bia*). 'Forcing people into better customs' requires more than just speaking, yet Plato recoils before violence.[9] What precise instrumentalities are then included in the art of the statesman, which is that of weaving together the gentle and the strong?

We shall have to return to this particular problem. Let us note now that modern commentators have attempted to resolve the tension in Plato by a developmental account. They speak of an increasing pessimism and a corresponding willingness to do what is good for people no matter what they think.[10] This issue is brought to a head by drawing a contrast between the last work, the *Laws*, and the *Republic*. In the *Laws* there is undoubtedly a heavy didacticism; much doctrine is being taught in it by the Athenian Stranger. This sort of content has appeared in the *Republic*, where Socrates has given long lectures to his little audience, but the thrust of the *Laws* remains distinctive: the doctrines are encyclopaedic and are to be taught to all and embodied in laws. There is also in the *Laws* a patent religious conservatism.[11] Religious festivals are praised for the joy and order they being to the city: 'Let us observe this further rule, – and of rules it is the noblest and truest, – that to engage in sacrifice and communion with the gods continually, by prayers and offerings and devotions of every kind, is a thing most whole and good and helpful towards the happy life, and superlatively fitting also, for the good man.'[12] This commendation of piety should not be seen as evidence of a growing Platonic pessimism and increasing desire to manipulate the masses; it is, rather, part of an increasing attention to the mechanisms of social cohesion. And the older Plato sees the cohesion of the city as one to which all must contribute. Jon Moline has noted that in the *Laws* Plato assigns to the masses 'a larger share of power than he did in the *Republic*.'[13] All can participate in governance since all have a divine principle indwelling in themselves. Friendliness in the city is thus under constant repair thanks to all, and not just maintained from above by perfect rules.

There is also a difference in tone. The *Laws* does not exhibit the bold unrestraint of the *Republic* that lets intelligence have its way. (Socrates in the *Republic* commends equality of the sexes!) The *Laws* is the result of a conversation among old men, that very embodiment of seasoned common sense. What the *Laws* recommends thus seems possible. The *Republic* has described the pattern of a city as being 'laid up in heaven for him who wishes to contemplate it and so beholding to constitute himself its citizen.'[14] How problematic is its implementation is pointed out by Socrates himself when he tells his parable of the ship. In an unruly ship sailors wrangle over control of the helm; none knows the art of navigation, and they are all sure that one cannot learn it at school in any case. They overpower the ship's master, take command of the ship, and appoint as pilot a man who knows nothing of navigation but excels at befriending the sailors. There is on the ship an expert who knows how to read the weather and the stars but is not interested in the art of seizing power, yet how likely is it that the services of this navigator will be sought by the unruly crowd?[15] The problem of actual implementation is thus noted but hardly dealt with. What we then hear in the *Laws* is what laws and doctrines should be taught to everybody. It all happens as if Plato, far from becoming bitter, has simply turned to the problem of implementation among the many only after writing the *Republic*. According to our view, then, the *Laws* differs because it takes up a new, more practical problem, and because Plato is confident that he has finally arrived at an answer.

This could also account for the more worldly tone of the *Laws*. Justice in the *Republic* is essentially transsocial, writes Leo Strauss.[16] Everlasting beatitude is the great business of life. 'The social institutions which fit (man) to attain it are the right institutions or education; all others are wrong.'[17] There is in the *Laws* something like a narrowing of the imagination on the earthly merits proper to the best and most feasible city that wise Greeks can establish at this time. But it is still implied that in such a city there will be something good that will be good for its own sake.

I have no difficulty, therefore, in accepting Thomas Pangle's view according to which the *Laws* gives us an opportunity to learn what Socrates, according to Plato forty years later, would have said to his accusers had he learned how to address assembled citizens.[18] The *Apology* has challenged the city on three grounds: it has a ramshackle system of education that contains absurdities; it punishes rather than educates the criminal; and its theology is so confused that one cannot tell who is pious and who is not. The *Laws* addresses itself to these three issues in a practical spirit.

To offer good laws means to mix reason with non-reason, true doctrine with useful belief. Reason, Plato writes in a telling metaphor, is but a soft gold cord; it is resisted by other cords of strong iron. So the frail cord is to have help from the hard iron cords that can work towards the good.[19] Desire of truth prevails by manipulating, ordering other desires. The pull from noble desires that remain ignorant of the truth can cancel out the pull from ignoble ones. Human beings will always live in some social context; the point of the *Laws* is to devise a context that will habituate them to good habits and sound beliefs. Bearings in reality are learned socially. The best possible city inculcates daily bearings in reality that, in the end, place man in the cosmos as it truly is.[20] The sound social environment is thus to rest on true metaphysics. Thus Plato's first task is to learn to speak of the universe to the many properly and persuasively. But before hearing about the universe, we must hear about what speaks to the many, namely myth.

3 Myths, stories, and history among the Greeks

Should one try to say at the outset what a myth is? What can one say beside the fact that it is language? 'A cognitive structure analogous to language,' writes John Peradotto; that is all he is prepared to venture.[21] I shall be bold: maybe what is particular about myth is that belief comes to expression in this cognitive structure, and that this structure invites belief, suspends disbelief. Let us imagine that the psyche is a web of beliefs; at any given point in its life it has experiences of coming to believe and it moves itself, copes with its life, through acts of believing.[22] Myths are stories that can give enduring embodiment to and keep inviting such experiences and acts. Myth, writes C.H. Whitman, 'is both a commentary and the story it expounds; narrative and interpretation is one.'[23] This view accounts for the sort of well-protected roundness of some myths: questioning minds find it difficult to get leverage on them and break them up into what is said and what is meant. And it accounts for the enduring meaning of myths: they carry significance beyond the original circumstances of their telling.

But enough with preliminary definitional remarks. Here again our approach should be historical. Let us recall that what we can see in Greek history is a group of people moving progressively from an almost exclusively oral culture to a rich written literature blossoming into numerous genres. We can observe shifts in the use of language, shifts in the nature of the things told, shifts in the use and nature of myth. As J.P. Vernant puts it, the Greek world offers a strong invitation to test, over centuries of rich texts, the general theories of myth that modern anthropologists and philosophers have spun out.[24]

Numerous contemporary accounts begin with some statement about archaic or pristine myth. This 'stage' is unfortunately undocumented. G.S. Kirk has shown in *The Nature of Greek Myths* that speculation, not inquiry, dominates in current accounts of 'the early mythical mind in Greece.'[25] He has also shown that these accounts are really imports from theories of myth developed somewhere else and are rather monolithic. So let us adhere to the rule according to which the historian knows only what he is told. The first texts where we can clearly see Greek myths are the works of Hesiod. Myths there are special stories that tell things about the universe, about the gods, about heroes and men of old (and of now). The voice of the poet is discernible at the outset; but he raises his to ask the Muses to tell the story: 'Muses of Pieira who give glory through song, come hither, tell of Zeus your father and chant his praise.'[26]

Can we say that myths already are some sort of literature, namely interpretative stories put forward by an author who is visible enough so that his readers can suspend belief in his story and ask why the author speaks thus? A peculiarity of Greek history is that something like this state of affairs seems to have been arrived at at particularly early times, certainly well back in the prehistoric period. M.P. Nilsson has emphasized that myths in Greece were rarely used as ritual texts (and we have extremely meagre remains of such use) and were thus not used in a context where precise repetition would be expected. Very early, then, what we must call individual artistic creativity felt free to reshape the myths.[27] Very early we also see the myths quite consciously manipulated for political ends; Peisistratus can easily be caught doing this in Athens towards the end of the sixth century.[28]

A further stage is made apparent by the writings of Parmenides. He uses old myths and symbols to say something properly philosophical about mind and being. We have now an individual voice that transmutes older themes for the expression of new cognitive activities. With Parmenides these new affirmations remain the possession of an educated few. This is not the case with the tragedies of Aeschylus: again the myths provide the matrix of meaning. An individual poet uses archaic symbolic materials to make a new point presented publicly on the stage. They are thus 'transformed deliberately in order to fit the exigencies of differentiated, personal experiences.'[29] The *Oresteia*, however, was not received by its audience in the manner in which our public (or fragments of a public) receive the work of our artists. Aeschylus is to the Greeks of his day Moses descending from Sinai and speaking to the assembled people. His art 'aims at collecting within its scope no less than totality' and his utterance is met with collective belief.[30] The way of persuasion and the soundness of Athenian institutions are perceived, gratefully received, and celebrated as being in tune with the entire universe. Whatever may be its process of genesis in the mind of the individual writer, myth is here, again, integrative.

But this grandest of all speech-events does not interrupt human speaking, probing, disbelieving. The tragic theatre shows us two further types of restatement of myth. Sophocles focuses on the great trials of an individual of transcendent stature (rather than on the universe and society as a whole). All that myth can do – and that, need I add, is still a great deal – is point the way to personal maturity, serve the ends of the process of self-knowledge. Next comes Euripides. His views of the gods, his sense of the power of religious feeling have long been puzzles, and so of course has been his use of myth. Cedric Whitman, however, has recently broken through, it seems to me, to a satisfactory understanding: 'Myth is there in abundance ... Euripides is learned in the tradition ... but there is no mythic artifice in the large sense to enclose this multiplicity, no intuition of a grand design, even if limited to the understanding of one person, as in Sophocles.' 'His mind swept over the kaleidoscope of mythology, choosing the little coloured pieces for scrutiny, not estimating the total pattern in the tube but finding, quite honestly, that it is all done with mirrors; the pieces however were real and he viewed them with the eye of a collector.'[31] There is always irony in Euripides: we never hear the myth spoken out of the belly of the universe (or rent heavens): we always hear the poet saying: I am making this sort of character make this sort of mythical utterance. This irony of course tends to dissolve myth qua interpretation. But we still see myth at work on individuals: Euripides' Electra is a victim of myths, not redeemed by any. Hence the psychological nature of his dramas: deeds arise out of the anger of individuals; mythical fragments are bits of language that suffering, angry, evil, pained individuals hurl at each other.[32]

What appears as anger in Euripides is well known to Plato's readers: it is desire run mad in the diseased city. Euripides finds myths hopelessly fragmented because during the course of the fifth century Greeks have attempted to tell of human interaction within a new framework: instead of traditional stories they have tried out scenarios of simple appetite. What happens among humans is a clash of conflicting desires. Until they die – that's the only story.

But is it a story? The basic feature of every story is to have a beginning, a middle, and an end. The fundamental achievement of any story is to come up with, or work towards, an end that counts as an end, namely gives some sense of completion or completeness. 'Following a story is a teleologically guided form of attention.'[33] A myth gives every moment of history the feeling of belonging, belonging to a whole that makes sense (becomes meaningfully completed). Now scenarios of appetite tell a drama that knows no ending except that brought about by the extinction of desire in death. Can this drama still be a story? A sense of an ending is, of course, achieved when I get what I want, but what competitive desire is ever satiated for long? The problems of historiography confirm the diagnosis about the two types of contending stories. Thucydides writes of historical passions: in real life only death quenches them. And he, the writer, the survivor, turns to tragedy with all its mythical sources to round out his story: his story is one of hybris and self-destruction.[34]

The fifth-century yoking of the concepts of *technè* and *tychè* is a further illustration of this search for a framework appropriate for the telling of human stories. *Technè* is human planning, skilful contrivance, energetic pursuit, action, effort, devising art.[35] *Tychè* is luck, what happens. The king in *Oedipus Rex* and Athens in her own self-image have *technè* at its best. They plan, but they meet their limits in sheer *tychè*, simple happenstance. To this duality of concepts is frequently added a third one: *theia moira*, 'divine occurrence.' Mythical stories see the divine occurrence as meaningful. The gods bring wisdom or destruction depending on the use men make of their *technè*. But the Sophists tend to assimilate divine interventions to other bits of luck; *technè* and *tychè* remain the only components of the human lot.[36]

History-writing then emerges as a new narrative mode. It carries with itself a new sense of historicity: men are transformed in time by their own actions upon themselves and upon each other. Men are what they (that is their appetites and skills) and luck make them. It takes, of course, self-conscious political conflict (public talk in assemblies and observed war) to gain this sense of historicity.[37] What should men henceforth do with themselves? The question, however, is seen in a context where appetite is available as an omnipotent interpretative key: historical passions spend themselves aimlessly on the stage of history. What Euripides shows from the side of fragmented mythical utterance, Thucydides shows from the side of scientific observation of human behaviour. What story can we tell about human beings? What beliefs can be shared? What political hopes can be entertained? As the balance sheet is drawn up about a war, one notices that something can be learned from it only if the separate memories of the survivors can become *shared* memories. And to have shared memories one needs a story that has the power to encompass and resolve the whole, namely a story with mythical qualities. Without such a story there is no moral community and no meaningful cultural context in which human devising can be jointly framed – and desires restrained.

In this general context of the state of the narrative art in the fifth century we can proceed to examine Plato and *his* stories. With him, too, just as with Euripides and Thucydides, politics, philosophy of history, love of truth, restructuring of shared beliefs, all hinge on the art of telling an appropriate story. Plato, rather like Euripides, inserts myths; imaginative plays are part of his literary dramas. He borrows mythical themes and one suspects he also rewrites some (but the artist covers his tracks well: we often cannot tell which is which.) He ventures further: he has Socrates tell grand myths at the end of some of the dialogues. Clearly a bid is made to recapture some sort of architectonic role for stories. (What else can have an architectonic role?)

Looking at things more closely, we can find in Plato three kinds of occasions for myth. In the first the myth is a useful device that makes a point; the story is used. *Protagoras* draws upon one myth to tell the origin of society. Socrates uses Typhon to state his question about man. This place of myth is marginal; it is an expository device. In a second kind of occasion the myth has penetrated more deeply in Plato's thinking: when Socrates narrates in the *Symposium* the myth told by Diotima, the whole discussion is raised to a new level; previous erroneous accounts are displaced. The myth here is a privileged vehicle for a major reorienting of attention. The situation is somewhat similar with the three eschatological myths of *Phaedo*, *Gorgias*, and the *Republic*: the understanding of what Socrates soberly believes about the soul's destiny is made 'secure' by these myths even though precautions are ordinarily taken to say that the myths are only an approximate statement. Finally in a third occasion the myth fills the entire work, so to speak. The myth has moved into the centre of the dialogue and all its meaning is the meaning the myth carries. This is the case with the myth of the soul in *Phaedrus*, and the myths of the creation and history of the world in *Timaeus* and the *Statesman*. In such cases what Plato has to say either will be grasped through the myth or will not be grasped at all.[38]

The third occasion is of course the most intriguing. W. Hirsch in his work *Platon's Weg zum Mythos* argues that we can see here a specifically Platonic reason for speaking mythically, a reason that comes to light very clearly at the beginning of *Timaeus*. What the speaker wishes to say on this occasion is the history of life; he wants to show the state exhibiting its qualities in a struggle. Socrates does not feel up to the task. His inability, however, does not particularly bother him: he feels that the poets are not any better at it than he is; those of the present as well as those of the past have been wide of the mark in saying what men are likely to do.[39] So Timaeus, encouraged, undertakes the task of narrating the history of life. Note that this rationale for mythical discourse sheds light retroactively on the myth in *Phaedrus*. There too what is involved is unveiling the nature of the life of the soul and narrating the history of its dealings with the cosmos.[40]

Hirsch thus argues that myth arises inevitably in Plato out of the need to talk about what is alive. Soul and world are alive: they move in time and have a history. What happens to them, or what they do, cannot be grasped through a form. The philosopher, however, needs to understand them. The *logos* and the search for definition, the manners of speech with which the philosopher is familiar, are of little help here. The dialectic communicates no meaning relevant to our temporality. As temporal beings, what interests us is not *what* the soul is, but *how* it is. Myth is the speaking of one's whence and one's whereto. It gives the aetiology of being human. It also shows forth what is at stake in a human lifetime: what a man does now matters for ever; to grasp the wholeness of a life, it is necessary to transcend the limits of birth and death; we live in a cosmos that mirrors a good and divine economy. Myth is indispensable in providing living human beings with reality bearings in a changing cosmos and a conflictual social world.

For Plato myth is clearly far more than a device useful to writers and orators, to be valued or scorned according to the results one tends to obtain through it. In the case of myth, too, language is never to Plato merely an instrument. There is no genuine speaking without reverence, not for one's words, but for the care that went into uttering them and for what one speaks of. The *logos* is at the disposal of man, but being is the measure of *logos*. A poet can write myths, but he always finds some there first.

Such masterful mythical speaking seems to me to be very much Plato's achievement. Socrates hardly speaks in *Timaeus* and the *Statesman*; the myths are told by others. And the great myth of the soul narrated in *Phaedrus* is told by Socrates inspired. In the *Laws* Socrates is entirely absent. Plato's own artistry has forged a language to speak philosophically about what changes. Some historians have argued that the historical Socrates did not speak ill of myths but did not tell any. This judgment may be a bit radical, but it does strike me as probably right, on the whole. The Plato who writes the myths of the *Statesman* and *Timaeus* clearly feels that he has forged a language, and while his imagination had been set on its course by the historical Socrates, the art it creates is different from the art of this teacher. There is wisdom in E. Voegelin's suggestion that the older Plato thought he had managed to recapture some of Solon's qualities. There seems to be an autobiographical echo in the statement Critias, in *Timaeus*, puts on the lips of an old man: 'if only Solon had not taken up poetry as a by-play but had worked hard at it like others, and if he had completed the story he brought here from Egypt, instead of being forced to lay it aside owing to the seditions and all other evils he found here on his return, – why then, I say, neither Hesiod nor Homer nor any poet would ever have proved more famous than he.'[41] Is it possible that Plato chose to let the seditions run their course and worked at poetry for the sake of a more durable gift to posterity?

One last warning. Myth for Plato does not symbolize ultimate reality (Plato's grasp of ultimate reality is not that of any putative archaic myth-maker). Myth symbolizes the movement between the place where we are, where we start, and ultimate reality. Myth is the language of the journey out of the cave, and the language that accounts for the creation of a world in which caves happen. Only *logos* bridges the gap intellectually, scientifically, between the world of opinion and the good. *Mythos* sets changing man in motion towards the good or towards good work in the world.

4 The stories of worlds and of societies

The great eschatological myths (those found in *Gorgias* and the *Republic*) speak of the moral order in the universe and of the destiny of the soul in a moving way: they enact a divine sort of pull on the soul. They confirm the invitation to philosophize. They keep the soul open, in movement towards the truth. I suspect that they are myths that Plato found or rewrote. The great cosmic myths are the ones we need to examine now. Like the eschatological myths, they are stories that are somehow both lawful and agreeable. Their happy relaxed talk is legitimate and serious (a story is a teleological guidance of the imagination). 'For the sake of recreation,' a man may lay aside 'arguments concerning eternal realities' and consider 'probable accounts of becoming,' thereby gaining 'a pleasure not to be repented of.'[42]

The cosmological myths have also, I believe, a public didactic value. They are information for the many, cast in an easy and memorable form. They open a path, a legitimate path, towards shared belief. Here, we see Plato trying to do his inculcating, or rather we see Plato letting his stories do the inculcating. The cosmic myths reopen a path between citizens and the good life (for once talk is not a source of division and oppression). This is of course a very sizeable claim. Let me add that I suspect these cosmic myths may well be myths that Plato wrote.

The rationale for such narratives is easy to discern. Cosmogonies and genealogies are perhaps the most impressive pieces of religious literature the Greeks received from their past. What sort of good and what sort of evil existed in the past, how the present dispensation has come into being, what blend of good and evil can now be expected, all these kept being stated by myths that conveyed at the same time what we would call a philosophy of history and a view of the universe. See Hesiod's *Theogony*: 'tell how at the first gods and earth came to be.'[43]

Contending against these richest layers of Greek myth, the Ionian philosophers advanced 'materialistic' speculation. Thanks to the transitional notion of elements, these 'scientists' developed a cosmology that tended to displace cosmogony. They spoke of the world in immanently developmental terms, without having recourse, as Hesiod did, to some drama among gods or some birth out of chaos. The notion of the eternity of matter gained ground. Plato wishes to contend against these cosmologies (that have the prestige of recent science on their side) because he wants to safeguard a cosmological context adequate to the nature and destiny of the soul as he understands it. The soul in the Socratic sense of the human self knows of a serious moral struggle. Plato like Socrates wishes to reaffirm what the tradition, speaking through Pindar, had promised: 'The happiness of the blessed is no fugitive.'[44] Unlike Socrates, Plato extends this affirmation into a cosmological polemic that creates a world where the soul's access to goodness remains safe under the new conditions of knowledge.[45]

The new worlds created after the *Republic* are devised to make secure the ontological realism of the epistemology and ethics found there. The notion of the Good provides the link. If goodness is ontologically supreme, traces of this supremacy may be expected in the world as it is. Plato's constructive energies in his mature and later years are absorbed by this task: to find and exhibit such traces. It is his mission to leave no stone unturned to 'defend' everything that is 'the offspring of mind,' namely every wise arrangement that results from the work of mind.[46] In all things we ought to seek the divine cause, 'for the sake of gaining a life of blessedness.'[47] *Timaeus* makes both the metaphysics and the ethics secure by narrating the process of creation.

An eternal god, the demiurge (namely the artificer), is the 'Maker and Father of the Universe.' With his eyes fixed upon an eternal model, he assembles a world soul from which depends all motion in the universe. 'The god constructed soul to be older than body and prior in birth and excellence, since she was to be the mistress and ruler and it the ruled.'[48] G. Vlastos stresses how intellectually brilliant was Plato's invention of the demiurge: a divine role is maintained and shown to be at the root of goodness in the world. 'If you cannot expunge the supernatural, you can rationalize it, turning it paradoxically into the very source of the natural order, restricting its operation to a single primordial act which ensures that the physical world would not be chaos but cosmos forever after.'[49] W.K.C. Guthrie stresses the metaphysical breakthrough: the reality of the world contains both something unmoved and something moved, or motion has a place in the real world.[50] The *Laws* confirms and elaborates the point: the self-moving motion is the most ancient of all. The benevolent world soul in this work has to contend with an evil soul which is the cause of disorderly motion, but the benevolent soul has clearly the upper hand, as is shown by the steady regularity of the heavenly movements. The *Laws* also finds a place for the Olympian gods. Below the creator-demiurge, below the world soul, are various divine beings – assimilated to heavenly bodies – presiding over different aspects of life.[51]

The point of these cosmologies is clear. The world is permeated by the divine; the divine has ceased to be a supernatural source of irrational movements and has become the very fount of order. *Tychè*, the old word for chance, shifts its meaning. It is not blind chance, but providential dispensation. And this dispensation rules over the 'physical' and historical or social worlds alike.

How the reality bearings established by a sound cosmology merge into those established by a well-ordered society is shown by the *Statesman*. The discussion is launched by a normal attempt at a definition of the statesman. Following all the rules of division, the Eleatic Stranger defines the statesman as a shepherd of gregarious animals. The result is hardly impressive; the difference between the statesman and all other people who take care of men such as bakers and physicians has not come out. There is at this point a 'story' the Stranger feels it is his duty to insert into the discussion.[52] The myth is nothing less than a history of the cosmos.

The universe at first rotated in a motion caused by God. 'During a certain period God himself went with the universe as guide in its revolving course, but at another epoch ... he let it go.' The universe is a living creature endowed with intelligence; it is self-moving; when 'let go,' it keeps its circular motion – that much perfection it is capable of – but its own self-caused motion is in the opposite direction. The current, ongoing history of societies reflects such a continuing alteration between the divinely caused motion and the self-caused motion. When God rules and supervises, no creature is wild, there is no war and no strife. God himself shepherds men. Having all 'leisure and the ability to converse not only with human beings but also with animals,' men make full use of their opportunities with a view to philosophy. At the next stage 'the helmsman of the universe dropped the tiller and withdrew to his place of outlook, and fate and innate desire made the earth turn backwards.' At this point the gods, who shared in the whole task of supervising and guiding, 'let go the parts of the world which were under their care.' A great earthquake followed from this reversal of the cosmic movement. The Eleatic Stranger inserts here a further pronouncement: all the cosmogonic tales and stories that we have have their source in this catastrophic occurrence. Some of the narrations 'have been lost, and others are told in fragmentary and disconnected fashion.'[53]

Returning to the narrative, we hear that conditions stabilized after a while. 'The world went on in its own accustomed course in orderly fashion, exercising care and rule over itself, and well within itself, and remembering and practising the teachings of the Creator and Father to the extent of its power, at first more accurately and at last more carelessly.' The descent into chaos is slow but cannot be arrested. When separated from its pilot, the world 'always got on most excellently after it was let go, but as time went on and it grew forgetful, the ancient condition of disorder prevailed more and more, and towards the end of the time reached its height.' At all times men 'follow and imitate the universe.' When both are left to themselves, humans are ravaged by fierce beasts and become fierce themselves. And so the universe and societies come to be in danger of destruction. But at one point, seeing the extent of their trouble and fearing that the whole might sink in the boundless sea of diversity, God 'took again his place as its helmsman, reversed whatever had become unsound and unsettled in the previous period, when the world was left to itself, and set the world in order.'[54]

Once the story is told, the error committed in the initial discussion can be discerned: the definition of the statesman has not considered what time we live in. Our political philosophy has to contend with the problems of a world turning the wrong way about, or gone mad we might say. In such an era human beings are no longer docile sheep. They 'take care of themselves'; they are free we would say. They no longer simply accept the rule of a 'natural' shepherd. The statesman's rule will be either forced on the 'flock' or accepted voluntarily.[55] Clearly the science of the statesman must be accompanied by the art of coping with resistance. To build or maintain a society means the binding and intertwining of men good and bad.[56] So, the Stranger says, there are two sciences: one measures exact numbers; the other seeks a right mean and has a sense of the appropriate, the reasonable. Clearly historic statesmen must also master the second science. A true statesman has two methods of action: he can try to persuade or he can send in the military and try to win on the battlefield. His highest ability is to decide when persuasion and when force shall be adopted. His virtue weaves the hard and the soft, the tough and the gentle. And none of that weaving is ever enduring.

The myth that is introduced ostensibly for relaxation and with the hope of somehow breaking the deadlock turns out to reorient the whole thinking of the philosopher. He who confines his attention to the permanent and unchanging (the former, logical method of division) 'misses a great deal, and cannot arrive at an integrated picture of the world.'[57] The philosopher must also sense what process of change his world is caught up in. The statesman today cannot be like the philosopher of the *Republic*, nurtured on mathematics. He must have a sense of history. Sometimes the universe aids the good life; sometimes it is inimical to it. It is not enough to look at the 'pattern in heaven.'[58] Rulers now cannot be modelled on the divine ruler of the golden age who conversed with gods and was an authoritative shepherd of men. The age of priest-kings is gone. The power of the ruler cannot be sacred, of supernatural origin, legitimated by tradition;[59] it must be an art dealing with men as they are. Plato has broken through to what we would call the political realism born of the practice of democracy.

The problem of the resistance, or of the limit, that the idea encounters in the world of change clearly preoccupied Plato. In *Timaeus* the demiurge finds a pre-existent material that was in a state of discordant and disorderly motion.[60] His whole work consists in bending as much as possible this ever recalcitrant matter to the purposes of soul. A degree of success is achieved and the world acquires an orderly motion: time, a movable image of eternity, is born. The same inner tension is found in men: disorderly motives, the sensations, submit them to the irrational, but the soul, a divine part, has the power to take away this chaos to some extent. The narration of the myth introduces a summary statement of what we might call the cosmic equation: the cosmos is generated as a compound from the combination of Necessity and Reason. The whole history of everything that changes is a matter of Necessity resisting or yielding to the intelligent persuasion of Reason.[61] Necessity, then, is to some extent persuadable. The sovereignty of the Good extends that far.

With his stories Plato has managed to make a relatively hopeful statement about the sources of evil, cosmic and social.[62] Two realities coexist in history: one is permeated by mind, the other antagonistic to it. We have travelled a long way from *Gorgias* where the adversary, so to speak, was 'merely' the entrenched hostility of the Athenians to Socrates. We have also moved beyond *Phaedrus* where evil is present only through the image of the bad horse and where its full entrenched weight is ignored by the simple expedient of going to the country. We have come close to the *Laws* and its cosmic 'evil soul,' which, though powerful, remains subordinate. Now Plato has tried to give the opposite principle a straight look and has conceived of it, through a myth, in terms that account both for the material base of life and the obstreperous nature of men when in groups. All this goes back to a fundamental metaphysical condition: the world is made of a contention between the Divine and the Necessary. Everything that happens is the result of a contest between the static perfection of the forms and the limiting factor of a mess of disorderly motion. The divine achievement is an achievement in time: order through orderly motion.

Having grasped what happens in our changing world, Plato can be clear-headed about what is the way up and what the way down and speak of their difference. The way up is followed in the practice of a certain kind of science: the science that aims at the good, pure, and simple. Human excellence on this path is a simple-mindedness in the pursuit of purity and of truth; the practice of dialectic leads there. The way down does not have the simplicity of a process that has a single goal: another kind of science, somewhat like the art of translation, must be learned, the one that knows how best to deal with the recalcitrant and how best to handle the ambiguous (and any best is always an uncertain thing). Human excellence on the downward path is more manifold: *metis* enters into it, ruse perhaps, but above all *doigté* and finesse, that is discernment and good judgment.[63]

Let us note finally that Plato, who has broken so decisively from tradition on the subject of the representation of the gods, seems in his great cosmological productions to express the very substance of Greek religion. The myth of *Timaeus* may well be one of Plato's greatest inventions. It nevertheless remains in tune with something deeply entrenched in the religious tradition.

In the epilogue to his commentary on *Timaeus* F.A. Cornford writes: 'Necessity must be recognized as standing for a factor in the existing world never completely subdued by reason ... There is at all times some chaos within the cosmos.' He adds that this view of the world seems profoundly Greek: the gods are never omnipotent. And the fate that thwarts them is dark and unthinking. Aeschylus tries to resolve the conflict between the two: 'It is no accident that the greatest work of Aeschylus, the *Oresteia*, culminates in the reconciliation of Zeus and Destiny; and that reconciliation is effected by divine Reason, in the person of Athena, persuading the daughters of Necessity to cooperate in her beneficient purposes.'[64] Necessity must be recognized as standing for one factor in the existing world never completely subdued by Reason. The Homeric gods are not omnipotent, Zeus is not one with Fate, wisdom and justice in human society are ineluctably fragile. No triumph of mind, of order, of justice, is ever final. 'There is at all times some chaos within the cosmos.' Yet there is hope only in the attempt to persuade that limiting factor.[65]

Daily intelligence operates also within the perspectives of this deep mental structure. Thucydides is at the most pessimistic end of the spectrum: any order is precarious; at best, the mind painfully achieves some light by striving against the dark limit.[66] His history echoes the *Iliad* and its story of war that ends with a burial. The older Plato seems to me to be more hopeful: his stories do not end with death and the ritual of mourning; they end with a divine restoration of goodness. By this point Plato has created, literally, a world which he means to be taken by all to be a declaration of what the real world is like. (He had previously treated a literary world of intellectual exchange – Socrates and his fellow-conversationalists – that presented itself to philosophers as the really important world.) Within the context of this world, he thinks, the human pursuit of goodness can be confident. Then, as his last work, he has written the *Laws*, where he gives practical advice on running a city: he means, I think, to testify to the permanence of ordinary, everyday, worldly goodness.

5 Plato: theist and founder of religion?

Plato, I have said before, equips his reorganized city with a theology, a set of stories, a set of beliefs, and a set of laws. And we have seen that a doctrine about a good, powerful, and benevolent god ranks highest on the list of correct beliefs. We should, however, heed a warning issued by W. Jaeger: he writes that 'the intense concentration of the spirit on the problem of God' which characterizes most philosophy of religion is in fact an innovation of Aristotle, who placed *theologia* at the very centre of philosophy.[67] *Theologia* appears in Plato only fleetingly to describe the mythological discourse about the Olympian gods.[68] Still Plato does talk a great deal about the gods, the god, and the divine; he does it in various places and in varied modes. In *Timaeus* we hear that the demiurge is an ever-existing god; he reasons about constructing the cosmos, a god too, but one 'which was one day to be existent.'[69] There is also the world soul; it too is spoken of as a god both in *Timaeus* and in the *Laws*. In the *Laws* there is the supreme god we have already referred to. There are further 'the gods' (that is the Olympians). Finally the human soul is in some sense divine. Thales' statement about the world being full of gods comes readily to mind. We, coming after Aristotle, can find in Plato a complete theology, attribute to it an architectonic role, and make Plato a theist. But we should recall that no such theology is found until the late dialogues. At the apex of the *Republic* we find the form of the Good.

Let us first examine the texts where Plato comes closest to being a theist in our sense of the world, namely the great theological passages of Books 10 and 12 of the *Laws*.

Book 10 takes on the matter of the existence of the gods. The order of the universe and the consent of all peoples are brought forward as evidence of the existence of the gods.[70] But there is unbelief, and Plato tries to analyse the roots of it. Modern Sophists tear into such evidence; the stars, they say, 'are simply earth and stone' and there is nothing divine about their movement. Here Plato pauses to contain his anger. Two views are presented, so an argument must be made. But how can he, the Socratic, that is the pious philosopher, make his defence before a court that includes impious men? Plato is vexed and indignant to have to convince, to have to argue, to see so great a truth at the apparent mercy of a court of opinion.[71] He nevertheless proceeds with the task. The gods exist by nature and not by art. They are part of the world that is, not part of the world created by human convention. The proof of this is found in a demonstration of the source of movement. Souls moves bodies. That which comes into being is secondary to that which is really existent. The motion that is able to move itself is prior to caused motion and causes such other motions. A thing that is moved by another cannot be the first of the things that cause change. Soul is of all things the oldest and controls all. And a benevolent world-soul moving according to Reason or Mind is the supreme soul of all.

Plato in these pages has invented the first form of the arguments phrased by Aristotle and taken over by Aquinas. It is awkward, however, that his proof aims at proving the existence of the gods while the preamble to the *Laws* speaks of one supreme god or God. It is also awkward that the proof ends by affirming the primacy of a benevolent soul, apparently taking for granted that such proof will count as proof for the existence of the gods. Guthrie speaks of the 'curious incompleteness' of this theology.[72]

Book 12 returns to the matter to lay down a law: no one is to become a guardian of the laws unless he has laboured long to grasp every proof that exists concerning the gods. Now 'there are two things that lead to belief concerning the gods.' One is the ever-moving soul that provides all things with 'an ever-flowing fount of being.' The other is 'the orderly motion of stars and of the other things of which intelligence [*Nous*] is master.' No one is of so atheistic a cast of mind that upon studying these things he does not come to 'an experience' that leads to the opposite of atheism.[73]

We must note the tone of these pages. The *Laws* devises a civil religion; the theological passages have a moralizing, thumotic character (*thumos* is something like righteous anger). The proofs are more rhetorical than dialectical. Plato speaks passionately, knows it, and says it; that is not the way he usually talks.

Let us now look at the passage in *Philebus* with which R. Hackforth begins his discussion of Plato's theism. In a section that is neither overwhelmingly mythical nor rhetorical in nature we read that Intelligence (*Nous*) is 'the King of Heaven and Earth,' the cause of all becoming in which 'unlimited things are bound fast by the limit.'[74] We recognize here the supreme principle of Anaxagoras, to whom Socrates had referred in *Phaedo*. This principle, absent from the *Republic* with its focus on ideas and its ascent to the form of the Good as unhypothesized beginning, now returns with full force in the ontology of *Philebus*. It is also present in the cosmological construction of *Timaeus*. The demiurge occupies the front of the stage but we are told that he puts all things together for the best, using *Nous* as his model.[75] Hackforth therefore concludes that Plato meets the minimum requirements traditionally laid down by philosophers for being a theist because of what he says of *Nous*. Only *Nous* has 'independent, not derivative existence.' And only *Nous* is the 'source, or cause, of all in the Universe that is good, orderly and rational.' The soul then, whether world soul or human soul, is a subordinate principle of movement that enables intelligence to penetrate the world of motion. Hackforth adds, entirely correctly I think, that, since the *Laws* is a practical work, it does not have to give a complete metaphysical position.[76]

One problem still remains. The architectonic role given to *Nous* after *Philebus* and *Timaeus* is not found in the *Republic*. Hackforth acknowledges this and ends his article with the statement that he does not 'try to fit Plato's theology into his metaphysical system.' The form of the Good emerges at the end of a dialectical ascent. Its role is that of a principle of knowledge; it secures the possibility of absolute moral virtues. But it does not ground any ontology or provide the basis for any cosmological statements. Here I accept part of the argument put forward by H.F. Cherniss that Plato's dialogues up to and including the *Republic* establish that 'a consistent and practical ethical theory depends upon an adequate epistemology.' To be virtuous we need to know what piety, courage, justice, and so on are. There must be forms. The nature of the mental processes also can be explained only by the hypothesis of forms. Real definitions must be possible. But what hypothesis will account for the world, that is the physical world, with its processes, namely its orderly and disorderly movements? 'It is, then, necessary that the study of ontology be undertaken independently of the requirements of ethics and epistemology to discover what hypothesis will explain the data of physical phenomenon as such.'[77] And this study of ontology arrives at *Nous*, king of heaven and earth, guarantee that human virtue is possible in the world. So to arrive at a complete story of the making of heaven and earth one invents a demiurge, an eternal god who shapes immortal gods using *Nous* as a model.[78]

Plato chose to handle epistemological and cosmological problems in different literary forms. This makes perfect reconciliation of doctrinal content impossible.[79] We must be content with a sense of duality when it comes to the architectonic principle in Plato or the Platonic bases for philosophical theology. On the one hand epistemological and moral interests dominate in the *Republic*; we arrive at the sovereignty of the Good and the invitation to orient one's own mental life towards it. On the other hand social and civil interests come to the fore in the *Laws* and we get the public affirmation of a cosmic order (ontologically constructed on the basis of *Nous* in *Philebus* and *Timaeus*). This order is based on a good world soul and leads to the invitation to order one's corporate life accordingly. The first orientation arrives at the intuitive vision of a static form of the Good, the second at the mythical account of a dynamic excellence at work in the world. In the former orientation the thinker remains in what Edward Lee calls in a felicitous phrase 'the threshold perspective.' 'Here all concern is with the contrast drawn between what precedes or leads up to the achievement of noetic activity and that activity itself.' The latter orientation reflects the 'dwellers' perspective.' 'The dwellers' concern is not that of laying-hold-upon, but keeping-hold-of (occupying, or indwelling, as in a homeland).'[80] In the first perspective what matters is a clear, single, firm, stable truth; in the second a multiplicity of relativities properly ordered and understood. The philosopher wants to stay on the threshold; the citizen wants to dwell.

These two perspectives led historically into two pieties. The more mystical searchers for intelligibility (and some Christian Platonists) have been prompt in identifying God with the form of the Good. Stoics (and other Christian Platonists) have not hesitated to identify the world soul with God and have thus leaned towards dynamic pantheism. We may call Plato a monotheist on account of his views of the form of the Good and of *Nous*. We may call him a cosmic pantheist on account of his view of the world soul (but then we should recall that his orderly cosmos, which he calls divine, should not be called God if we want to save this word for what is truly ultimate).[81]

Interpretative rigour forces us to make distinctions and observe the author solving different problems in different texts, with each text having its own coherence.[82] But casual readers, that is innocent readers who believe what they read, ordinarily find in Plato a coherent religious message. There is God (and / or the gods), there is the world, and there is a self-orienting human soul open to healing divine influences but responsible for its fate. And Plato would, I think, be pleased if he were to find out that he has been commonly read in this way.

I find encouragement for this view in a meticulous study of the exact usage to which the adjective *theios*, 'divine,' is put in the dialogues. In the early dialogues *theios* is used in the ordinary Greek senses: religious and hyperbolic. Superior excellence is denoted. Then in *Ion* and *Meno* wise and inspired men earn the epithet. From *Phaedo* to *Phaedrus* the world of forms is linked with the divine (in *Phaedrus* the gods are most divine, because they have viewed the forms longest).

From *Timaeus* to the *Laws* whatever has been permeated by the *Nous* is divine. Thus Plato starts from a traditional base and broadens the sense of the word. There is no strictly philosophical doctrine of the divine. Plato thinks of ultimate reality 'in intellectualist, not theological terms.' The adjective *theios* is used literally, to confer on philosophic realities 'the prestige of a normal human being associated with the divine.' Plato thereby manages to attach to his forms and his ontology part of the ambiant religious fervour.[83] Here again we find evidence that the epithet 'divine' is what remains strong throughout Greek history; and perhaps this gives us grounds to venture that the noun *ho theos*, ordinarily translated 'the god' or 'God,' that is associated either with polytheism or with Aristotle and the New Testament, should be translated 'the divine.'

Plato's constant thrust towards an affirmation of the unity, the comeliness, the orderliness, and the benevolence of the divine comes to a climax in a famous passage of the *Laws* that marks an obvious contrast with the famous statement of Protagoras about man: 'God [the sentence has invited a capital from all translators] is the measure of all things.'[84] Cumulatively all these affirmations have had enormous historical results and enhanced the authority of the divine.

The doctrine of natural law should be mentioned first. Natural law states that there is a moral dimension of the universe that is teleologically organized towards the good, or towards what is best. In such a universe the basic good for each entity is to exist in a condition of active realization. 'Natural law is a universal pattern of action, applicable to all men everywhere, required by human nature itself for its completion.'[85] Values, then, are not the result of individual preference or social consensus. They are what enhances the process of individual teleological development and what enables the entity to contribute to the perfection of the whole. Through this law and the values it creates God does indeed become 'the measure of all things.' There will be justice in the city if every man 'follows in the steps of the god.'[86]

This invitation to the imitation of God is the second momentous consequence. The good man becomes 'like God.'[87] Traditionally it is *hybris* to imitate the gods – and their behaviour is not that morally uplifting. Of course the two reasons coalesce into one, the gods being sheer power.

The goodness of the pious man takes on a new meaning after the dialogues. The good man is more than a demure, devout, cautious, conservative person integrating himself respectfully and obediently in the traditional order of the city as founded by the gods and transmitted by the ways of the fathers. His filial piety is directed to the divine itself, not to the ancestors. And having kinship with the gods, destined to return to a fellowship with them, the human being actively begins to resemble them in this life. He shares actively in the divine activity that slows down chaos and builds order. The active achievement of justice is what man learns once he is measured by God.

That Plato dares to offer imitation of God or assimilation to the deity as the imperative stemming from the highest morality indicates how completely confident he is that he has thoroughly reoriented images of the divine. He fully knows that the behaviour of the Homeric gods has been used as excuses by all kinds of immoralists. He is also aware that the experience of orgiastic communion with the divine in the more rapturous mystery cults has few moral after-effects or has effects that can hardly be commended, since the emotional intensity and speechless self-assurance of the initiate often lead the devout to neglect natural bonds or moral obligations. But in the dialogues there is no doubt that assimilation to the divine will be a schooling in moral measure.[88]

The third momentous consequence of the dialogues is the portrayal of goodness as an outgoing, active sort of benevolence. In the Hellenistic era, with the teachings of Epicurus and the Cynics, the good man tended to see himself as someone who withdrew from the common corruptions of the city, remained untouched by the turmoil, and cultivated a divine sort of indifference. And the divine tended to be seen as impassive, unmoved, blissful, beyond the reach of chaos. (Aristotle, for example, denied that God had any moral role in the universe.[89]) Plato's good man is aloof. He has been weaned from ordinary satisfactions. But he works, he rules, he builds, he steers – just like the gods, who 'know what is needful' and are no more neglectful then good physicians, pilots, or statesmen,[90] who are always actively involved in the slow shaping of the good in the human souls. Neo-Platonists have tried to reverse the tendency begun by Aristotle and attributed to Plato a conception of God's goodness as 'overflowing.' John Rist has shown that their judgment was sensible. To Plato the gods are demiurgic, that is creators of beauty and order.[91]

6 The *Laws*: building order in fourth-century Greece

The *Statesman* arrives at the definition of the good ruler needed by our unruly times: he knows when to use force and when to use persuasion. The *Statesman* also allows that we are not likely even to find such a ruler and put him in charge. Instead of the rule of one wise man we should rather prepare for some more or less successful imitations of that, and our best hope lies in a form of government based on sound written laws.[92] Decent magistrates will then be able to do some good and poor ones will not be able to do much harm. This is perfectly right and good as a practical choice.[93]

The twelve books of the *Laws* are precisely such an undertaking. One might properly call them Plato's testament and his politically realistic contribution to the welfare of all Greeks. When he wrote the *Laws*, probably between 360 and his death in 348, it was apparent to all that the old city-states had had their day. Sparta had followed Athens into a decline. The only signs of fresh political energy were the founding of new cities. Experts were called in as advisers in the task. The *Laws* is thus very relevant to actual historical circumstances and has nothing utopian about it.[94] The sober realization that he lives in an age of cosmic decay and social decadence has made Plato a morally realistic politician. But Plato does not accept historical mortality. His realism is not that of the nihilist. It is that of the moralist who seeks to repair the fabric of his society. In the terms of the myth Plato has tried to slow down, arrest, or reverse the movement into greater disorder. And the *Laws* does it by proposing a package of legislation, which includes educational and religious legislation, that will maintain the health of the city. These laws are to be examined on their own merit, so to speak, by ordinary fourth-century Greeks who have the welfare of their city at heart but do not necessarily understand what Socrates has communicated. The laws are to be evaluated for their ability to bring ordinary happiness to all: 'We are speaking to men, not gods, and the most natural concerns of human kind are pleasures, pains and desires' (732e).

Three old gentlemen, an unnamed Athenian Stranger, Megillus the Spartan, and Kleinias the Cretan (note the pan-Greek emphasis), talk on their way to the cave where Zeus was supposed to have been born. The Athenian Stranger little by little wins the friendship of the other two (who already know each other) and his ideas progressively gain the centre of the stage. As T. Pangle puts it, the opening books show 'how a philosopher might win the confidence of powerful old political leaders and guide them towards a revolutionary refounding.' The work thus shows how the man of reason 'can work with and within the pious traditionalism that dominates most political life.'[95] One should add that the Athenian Stranger never claims to be a philosopher: he presents himself as another wise old man. The Spartan Megillus is asked to describe the virtues of the institutions of his city: they promote efficiency in warfare is the proud answer. The Athenian demurs: the important victory is that over oneself. Institutions should aim at peace and harmony among the citizens. The fact that Spartans prohibit drinking parties while Athenians believe in the merits of them (if moderate) is a significant difference: Athenian conviviality puts every man's self-restraint to the test, and, on the whole, the citizens emerge victorious and thus worthy of their softer institutions. Megillus is quick to point out the excesses of Dionysiac festivals. But the Athenian holds his ground. The lengthy talk on drunkenness ends up suspending somewhat the ordinary rigidities of the old traditionalists: they become (in deed) open to a moderate degree of experimentation; they also become (in word) ready to discuss institutions that condition men's souls.[96] Music, gymnastics, and poetry are thus introduced as pleasant habits that can be cultivated to set the moral tone of a city. The wise regulation of them enables each child to become a civilized individual. A survey of the political history of mankind shows the importance of a proper equilibrium between imposed order and individual impulse. Persia had too much of the first; Athens, in its democratic days, allowed too much of the latter.

At the beginning of Book 4 we learn that Kleinias the Cretan is actually acting as an adviser in the founding of a new city. The conversation has now a clear focus, and the Athenian, who seems to have won the respect of the other two in the course of the preliminary remarks (where he is indeed a model of good manners), proceeds to give a lesson in constitution-making.[97] The new city is to have a small but varied territory, remote from the sea. Its spirit shall not be commercialized. Artisans shall be few, traders fewer yet. There shall be no professional soldiers. Basically the city will be made up of arms-bearing small landholders. The sovereign shall be impersonal law. Law is the divine influence that teaches moderation to all men and lets them be measured by God (that statement falls neatly at the hour of noon.) All citizens of the new city are to be addressed in this way: 'The god, just as the ancient saying has it, holding the beginning and the end and the middle of all the beings, completes his straight course by revolving, according to nature. Following him always is Justice, avenger of those who forsake the divine law. He who is going to become happy follows Her, in humility and orderliness. But anyone who is puffed up with boastfulness, or who feels exalted because of riches or honours or good bodily form accompanied by youth and mindlessness, anyone whose soul burns with insolence and hence regards himself as needing neither ruler nor any leader but rather considers himself capable of leading others, is left behind, abandoned by the god. Once left behind, he takes up with others like himself and leaps around overturning everything; to many, he seems to be somebody, but after no long while he undergoes the blameless vengeance of Justice, bringing complete ruin to himself and his household and city as well.'[98]

Then comes the praise of pious ways which we have already cited.[99] The contrast is fully drawn between the diseased city, full of petulance, insolence, and self-serving but self-destructive pride (in the excessively democratic Athens the crowds at the theatre are noisy and dogs become short-tempered), and the pious city, where *aidôs* is queen and where a friendship is maintained among all. *Aidôs* causes men 'to live as willing slaves of existing laws.'[100] The root of *aidôs* is, in this case, respect for the unchanging law and the divine justice it upholds. And this *aidôs* is manifested by deference to the 'superiors,' from gods and heroes to parents (dead or alive), and by proper respect paid to ourselves and all our fellow-men. This completes the description of the moral tone of the city that is 'free, prudent and a friend to itself.'[101]

In this city all laws will be prefaced by 'preambles' explaining their purpose and eliciting voluntary approval. The laws of the city do not forget that they are written for men, not gods: they make concessions to the human desire for a pleasant existence; life under the law is argued for as being the most pleasant. But human beings are treated as reasonable. The laws are not laconic, declaratory; the preambles are not terse. Plato's civil religion is thus very different from that of Jean-Jacques Rousseau, who stipulates that 'the dogmas of civil religion must be simple, few in number, expressed with precision, without explanation of commentary.'[102] Plato is willing to explain, to leave room for some discussion, and thus to run the risk of disorder that such discussion entails.

Specific laws are introduced. A modest measure of private property is assured to all; steps are taken to ensure that none grows too rich. A complex balloting system effectively reduces the risk of any demagogue being elected; only those respected are likely to win. The city will have a scheme for universal education – commentators ordinarily feel that the psychological base given to education here is far superior to that of the *Republic*. Since departures from the established regimen never fail to precipitate numerous other unthought of changes, the festivals of the city will not be the object of needless innovation. Generally speaking, Delphi is Plato's favourite source for proper religious traditions.[103] But reasoned change even here is introduced: women, for instance, should not stay at home; they are to share in public meals and public rites. All in the city suffer from the disorderliness in women's affairs; the remedy is that 'every practice be shared in common by women as well as men.' This must be done, even though women will resist being dragged into the light.[104] The association of young people and of the sexes will be free and relaxed. Plato does not seem to fear a dangerous degree of sexual disorder (but he bans homosexual attachments). A criminal jurisprudence is proposed which does away with the distinction between voluntary and involuntary acts and introduces the classical one between acts that cause a detriment and those that infringe a right.

Finally the religious creed is introduced, with punishment for heretics, including death for the infectious and incurable. The last book introduces a 'Nocturnal Council.' This group of senior magistrates meets before dawn to deal with a few very special questions: they receive reports from the citizens who have been allowed to travel abroad and play a role in the proceedings against heresy. Taylor calls them the 'brain' of the whole system. They pursue studies that greatly resemble those necessary for the training of the guardians in the *Republic*. They are in fact the only self-correcting mechanism in the city that thas an unchanging constitution. They exercise the necessary vigilance against any signs of decay setting in. Through them the city has a means to protect itself against the devilishly unpredictable onslaughts of chaos.

We obviously do not find in the *Laws* a dramatic movement comparable to that in *Gorgias*, *Phaedrus*, and the *Republic*. Three elderly gentlemen walk, slowly presumably, towards their settled destination. The resistance to disorder, the discovery of the root of all order, the presence of the divine pull are pointed at in dramatic dialogues. The building of a stable social order is told in another genre: the style must be prudent, moderate, slow.

Yet there is tension in the *Laws*. The last three books try to make some room for the claim of philosophy. Is the work going to tell us at the end that philosophers alone know the truth after beginning with a masked philosopher who, never ironic, never oversubtle, is just another civil old man? It is understood that philosophy cannot be made a part of civic education: schools will teach music, poetry, and civil religion. It is also understood that virtues are to serve the city. Yet one senses that virtues transcend the city which they serve. The happiness of the city is the ultimate goal of the laws but one never learns that it is the ultimate goal of human beings. Marriage is in the interest of the city but the duty of raising children has a suprapolitical basis: 'leaving behind children of children, whom one leaves as one's successors in serving the god.'[105] The piety of the city is thus not allowed ever to obscure another piety, that of human beings. Even as he answers the questions of politics, Plato avers that politics cannot provide what is good for the soul. The *Laws* puts forward a concept of god that does not simply mirror the political virtues. As Pangle puts it, the city is to have a mixture of openness and closedness to the truth:[106] closedness for the stability without which there is no order and happiness and to ensure that no experimentation is allowed to wreck the city; openness to allow reform, change, and above all the cultivation of philosophic virtue on the part of those who can venture along this path.

The possibility of philosophic life is thus ever present as a subtheme in this public political work. The reality of philosophic reflection, however, is subordinated to the demands of public morality. In some sense philosophy surrenders its autonomy. An Athenian with the opportunity to shape the life of the many through influence on two old powerful politicians whom he has never met before will not speak in the same way as Socrates alone with Phaedrus in the woods. Joseph Moreau adds that, beside this subordination, the *Laws* accepts an eclipse of the intelligible. God becomes proved in arguments that are put forward with some rhetorical heat. Myths, images that were helps, become truths in themselves, even realities. Cosmic order, instead of being a way that the intelligence has of picturing the organization of matter, becomes an establishment doctrine. The Hellenistic age will show what damages to the life of the mind can be done by official philosophies.[107] I must allow that Plato took these risks. He took others when he wrote *Phaedrus*. The reader of the *Laws*, however, is gripped by political matters, not entrapped. The philosopher persuades the legislators and the legislators strive to persuade the people. Their commitment reflects that of Plato: the *Laws* proposes a path towards implementation that owes nothing to the crafts of a social engineer. The power thrusting towards implementation is that of words. Plato, I submit, is offering his own work as the exact answer to the quest which Dionysos (in the role of the average Athenian) announced to Aeschylus and Euripides towards the end of *The Frogs*:

DIONYSOS Well, now listen, you two. I came down here for a poet.
EURIPIDES What do you want a poet for?
DIONYSOS To save the city, of course.[108]

10

Conclusion

I A philosophy: practice, doctrine, and topics

What we have found in Plato is a philosophy. Philosophizing begins in the free discussion of opinions. In the end it produces reasoned doctrines. The philosophy itself is to be found not in the final doctrine, any more than in the initial querying of opinions, but in the trajectory. Philosophy is a quality of intellectual life. This quality is present whenever the individual acts on the beliefs 1 / that he can organize his mental activities towards an end, specifically towards the end of knowledge; 2 / that having knowledge means striving to put the truth into words; and 3 / that finding true accounts or speaking correctly helps achieve the good life both individually and corporately. The philosopher believes that benefits for our lives are derived from disciplined, verbalized mental activity or that such a mental activity enables us to become aware of the power that we each have on ourselves and on others. It is being taken for granted that, once we are aware of it, we shall use this power to better ends instead of repeating unhappy unconscious scenarios. Briefly put, philosophers believe in the power of fresh thought for future good. In *Phaedo* Socrates alludes to a sort of psychotherapy by verbal means: we are both patients and physicians; we struggle for health by addressing tales to our own psyche.[1] Plato became a philosopher because existing accounts were inadequate, conventional nomenclature was misleading. The existence of forms made it possible to revise usage and progress towards a better understanding. As Jon Moline puts it, Plato needed the forms to articulate the requirements of a disciplined discussion.[2] But real definitions or accurate propositions do not meet all human requirements. A disciplined common life needs shared stories. The conventional stories were also inadequate and had to be replaced. The criticism of stories was based on a better understanding of the nature and ongoing activity of the divine.

As a critic of stories the philosopher must learn to become at ease with the criticism of religious culture. And thus he completes his task. He educates our minds and our desire. Unlike the Sophists, he does not accept the theatre of our appearances the better to act upon existing desires. Unlike Parmenides, he does not leave the theatre to reach beyond. He strives to force moments of truth in the play.

Philosophy as the search for words and philosophy of religion as the education of desire never overcome the condition of being an ongoing practice. For instance, they must ever be prepared to start all over. Socrates at the end of *Phaedo* gives one last piece of advice: his listeners ought to re-examine his argument.[3] As the philosopher arrives at the end, he does not invite others to build upon the affirmation he has reached: those who will go on living must be prepared to start their thinking all over again. Plato philosophized in the pursuit of definitions and then came to see that definitions are not enough. So he gave up this view of precise language and he started to look for vaster stories. Definitions began to be tentative. Definitions even began to behave like poetic symbols: a little mirror which captures some light. And Plato turned the mirrors around; the life of intelligence did not come to rest. The attack on poetry and the move beyond definitional language should be seen as two sides of the same coin. Poetry embodies the language habits of the group. Definitions embody the findings of knowledgeable experts. To attack poetry is to attack error as it exists in society generally, to show the inadequacies of the quick, customary, unexamined response to words. Reasoned analysis is called for. But reasoned analysis is not allowed to come to rest in any 'scientific results' that satisfy the experts who worked together on some problem.[4]

Conversational dramas with participants shuttling between *mythos* and *logos* enable Plato to weave the truest possible statement. The 'false' story is cast in the light of an (inadequate) image of the truth. The 'true' propositional utterance is unveiled as a tool in the hands of ignorant men. And there are pauses. What we call a pregnant silence, that pause in the conversation where some yet unspecified meaning seems to descend speechlessly among the participants, is said by the Greeks to be the moment when Hermes is passing.[5] Meaning in the dialogues becomes unveiled when people start talking again, or make a move. But Plato has an ear for transitions, passages, glimpses of the naked molusc that leaves its outgrown shell to ensconce itself in a new one. The invitation to the practice of philosophy is both a summons to keep talking as accurately as possible and a call to a vague mythic adventure. Writing literary dialogues, Plato keeps creating space for shifts between concepts and metaphors, metaphors and concepts. Metaphorical language reorients the inquiry, gives it new dynamism. Demand for clarification probes into – and shatters – metaphors. Dead ends are discerned and fresh starts allowed at every turn. Dialogues are utterances contrived by authors who want to set interpretation in motion and refuse to present themselves as replacement for living thought.

Some account for the work of philosophers being unceasing by noting that language, they are inclined to think, is forever inadequate; they envisage a sort of ontological insufficiency – words never measure up to reality. Others account for it in a more heraclitean manner: words fail because they do not keep up; realities are forever shifting. These points of view are distinct and each is true. How can human beings define the good? and how can they tell the true story of what is going on in their midst? While we talk painstakingly and clearly, there is always something going on in the darkness. We enjoy talking and striving to understand; yet we have other desires. And these, of necessity, do their work non-verbally. Desire wants to reach out to, touch, its object and fuse with it. The constant distancing brought about by language is the enemy of its goal. And yet only distance creates space for the games that bring desire to consciousness, educate it, and lead it to attend to realities. For what more urgently calls for clarification than the blind endeavours of our desiring selves? Hence the need for the oblique techniques (in any case, anatomy makes it impossible both to speak and eat – or kiss – at the same time), such as are familiar to lovers who tease (and spies who misdirect the attention of others). So quick, nimble minds project the beacon clearly to the left, or right, of what they want to look at, to allow for the sudden sideways foray into what wants to remain hidden. Thus we achieve clarities – surrounded by opacities.

Human beings overcome the insufficiences of language by non-linguistic behaviour. Philosophers qua philosophers give up words linguistically. Socrates has refined the art of irony for precisely this purpose.[6] In Fowler's famous definition: 'Irony is a form of utterance that postulates a double audience, consisting of one party that hearing shall hear and shall not understand, and another party that, when more is meant than meets the ear, is aware both of that more and of the outsiders' incomprehension.'[7] Socrates finds some utterance static, stable, placed on the table and likely to stay there; he even at times helps in nailing it down. And with an ironic comment he puts it all in motion again. The meaning becomes fluid, slippery again; our minds have to stay mobile. He creates a double audience within the listener himself; he thought he understood it, now he does not understand, is pained at his own ignorance, and anticipates a fresh insight. Irony causes pain and it is fun. It shoots arrows of seriousness where there had been only play (fun play or pompous play) and it reintroduces play where grave minds thought they had reached something definitely serious.[8] There is a link between irony and eros. Irony deflates, pricks our words like inflated balloons, and excites a desire for a better apprehension of the truth. It rejects dogmatisms, but without the tired scepticism of the nihilists, and while advertising the experience of eros; current failure to achieve the goal does not diminish the desire to seek it.[9]

So the philosophical intelligence must keep moving, weave patiently diverse material, embark upon studied detours, find the zigzag that will be the straightest possible route because the direct one is blocked. Philosophizing takes time. Lawyers, doctors, and all practical men must be quick on their feet and work within strict time constraints.[10] A philosopher betrays his presence by asking for more time. More time to begin at the beginning, to return to the beginning. How can the measureless be limited by measure except in an unending task? How can the changeable be expressed once and for all? No complete rounded truth can ever be reached – how then can one reasonably hope for a society where truth will be secure? Any insight can be confounded at any time. Defence may have to be undertaken at any point – on a long perimeter.

Plato, writes François Châtelet, does not have a philosophy to defend. He has to fight for philosophy.[11] Hence his artistry, and hence also his abiding pedagogical gifts. 'Plato composed his writing in such a way as to prevent in all times their use as authoritative texts. His dialogues supply us not so much with an answer to the riddle of being as with a most articulate "imitation" of that riddle. His teaching therefore can never become the subject of indoctrination. In the last analysis, says Leo Strauss, his writings cannot be used for any other purpose than for philosophizing.'[12]

But let us not turn Platonism 'into an empty philosophizing.'[13] Philosophizing, we must repeat, equips man with a few doctrines. We have seen Plato provide us with doctrines that are cosmological, theological-moral-political, or religious. Such doctrines can be learned by non-philosophers. This, however, does not make them any less part of the philosopher's *métier*.

So let us take for granted that Plato can always stand at a distance from all beliefs and ironically create distance from his own words, asking ourselves what affirmation, what doctrinal philosophy, we can attribute to him as seriously meant. I believe that two main views contend here for our allegiance. Plato can be seen as a political philosopher or as a religious philosopher.[14]

Leo Strauss, for instance, sees Plato as the fountainhead of a tradition of political philosophy in which 'men make it their explicit goal to acquire knowledge of the good life and of the good society.'[15] Philosophizing begins with awareness of a social crisis that is detrimental to man and concerns itself with the question of the best political order and its instauration. On this view, the political problem provides the architectonic structure for Plato's philosophy and is the source of its unity. Religious Platonists, however, have argued that Plato's philosophy is more appropriately labelled a religious philosophy. I now use the word in its ordinary modern meaning: I call 'religious' any interest in an ultimate reality and in imaginative symbols that mediate a sense of that reality. Numerous Platonists have tended to identify the philosophical act with the religious act. There is truth in that. Philosophizing for Plato is born out of man's unease in the world and in the city: the unease is so radical that no remedy is expected that could cure the city fully enough to make it the exclusive theatre of man's destiny; a human interest is nurtured in something that is beyond the world. On this view, what provides the unity in Plato's philosophy is its grasp of a light that is not of this world and the architectonic structure then comes from the religious concern.

I see little interest in trying to settle whether Plato's philosophy has ultimately a political or a religious focus. the problem itself arises largely because of modern meanings attached to the adjectives 'political' (power brokerage) and 'religious' (private and otherworldly). I find it more useful to remain with Plato's refusal to bifurcate in any definite way the realm of religion from that of politics. To do that I propose that we ponder what I consider the basic doctrine emerging from his philosophical trajectory. Virtuousness includes piety, or piety is a virtue.

As we know, Plato has argued that virtue is not an affair of muscular strength, velocity, and skill; it is not a matter of ease with words or social *savoir-faire*; it is rather a strength of the soul: the well-tended soul has acquired strengths, and these are the virtues. The virtuous man rules his own life and keeps all its movements in order. The virtuous man get his bearings from the form of the Good or from the divine. As E. Voegelin puts it, 'the search for the true *arete* ends with the discovery that the *Aretai* are habituations of the soul which attune the life of man to transcendent reality.'[16]

Virtue is what human beings learn in their lifetime in so far as their learning is intelligent. Modern men might prefer to call virtue a maturity, since they tend to assume that men ordinarily do not acquire strengths beyond some point in their twenties. Virtue establishes a harmony between reason and habit. It is a correct training in regard to pleasures and pains.[17]

Since they are to educate habits, virtues must be attuned to the historic fears and hopes of the society which they serve while transcending it.[18] Piety is a virtue that is warned about the sweeping impact of current fears and hopes. The pious man is strong. Piety, to Plato, never yields to mere power. And there is no virtue without piety in precisely this sense, as a loyalty that does not let itself be shaken by the current power of appearances. It is impious 'to stand idly by when justice is reviled' or to 'buy honour among men by sinning against the gods.'[19]

The range of human habits, however, is very wide and different contexts and needs call for different habits. Piety therefore is one virtue among many.[20] As a form piety cannot be reduced to anything else.

Plato is committed both to the differentiation and to the unity of virtues. Here we should make a distinction, between person-virtue and action-virtue. As they examine each virtue, the dialogues, the early ones especially, tend to focus our attention on action-virtue. What are the features exhibited by pious, courageous, or wise actions? Plato also says that whoever is just must be wise too, and temperant and pious and courageous. Virtuous action need not display all five virtues; some circumstances call for one rather than the other. The virtuous man, however, must be the possessor of all virtues: he cannot have one without the other four.[21] While not always involved in pious action, he is at all times a pious person, disposed to act on his ultimate loyalty. Man is to remain true in changing circumstances, and different occasions call for different virtues.

The stress upon the unity of the virtues is to be expected when one remembers that virtues educate habits by harmonizing them with reason. They co-inhere in the character of the man who is attuned by reason. The man of many virtues is, simply, the good man. The use of this adjective completes Plato's removal of the virtues from the world of pragmatic skills and success-oriented behaviour to give to the virtuous a self-authenticating quality that is complete in itself, regardless of its social or personal usefulness. '*Arete* is a kind of health, beauty and well- being of the soul,' says the *Republic*.[22] This virtue makes possible a good life in the city now and assures that we shall also fare well when we are no longer held by the city.

So much for Plato's doctrine as a philosopher. As a philosopher of religion he also has topics that he examines. He is pious and he examines piety as one topic among others. This self-consciousness is to be expected. Philosophy always also talks about its own talking as it talks about whatever it is talking about. Religious practice has become a part of the life of the city about which all questions can be asked: should it be maintained or abolished? reformed or transformed? So a specialized branch of philosophy emerges in Plato: philosophy of religion, which aims at asking all the questions worth asking about that men think they are doing – or think is happening to them – as they are being religious. An awareness of the peculiarities of religious language is part of the achievement, and so of course is a search for the meaning of that language. What do religious men do with language? What place belongs to that peculiar language in the total scene of human discourse?

In his philosophy of religion Plato asks many questions because he has seen the medley of doings characteristic of desirous, changeable historical human beings. To look at religion is to look at varieties and actualities. His philosophy of religion embarks upon a path demanded by historical religious realities. These realities group themselves under a variety of topics that reflects the range proper to Greek religious life. Plato talks about tendance of the soul, vision of true being, love of beauty, benevolent divine activity, and cosmic soul. Under these topics the dynamics of Greek religion are discerned; its pedagogical and moral import are weighed. Plato, we have said, has rearticulated and translated.[23] He has both restated in a new way and moved into an altogether different language. His philosophy of religion, as a specialized branch of philosophy, tends to branch out into two sorts of results.[24] Some results can enter into Plato's own philosophy: they can provide real symbolic content for what Plato has to say about the career and hope of the soul. In this sense Plato's philosophy of religion is religious and Plato the philosopher is an heir of Greek religion. But some results of Plato's philosophy of religion can also enter into a fresh plan of social action. They provide an understanding of individual and social dynamics which is essential to a renewed search for the just order. In this sense there is a secularizing thrust in Plato's philosophy of religion. Man's problems with himself and with his fellows on this earth figure among the interests which the philosophy of religion serves. The work of the demiurge thus serves also as a good metaphor for Plato's labours as a philosopher of religion. He has his eyes on the divine model: he is a philosopher who has risen above shadowboxing with opinions. But being a philosopher of something, he has to contend against a limit and bring about an opus. The Greek historical religion is a definite religious context with a certain past and a definite (that is limited) potential. Like an artisan or, better, like a physician, the philosopher of religion has to try to bring out all the good that is to be found in the nature of this religion.

2 A transposition of Greek religion

Plato's philosophy of religion strives to interpret the fears and hopes expressed in the Greek religious practice of his day and tries to set in motion a healing process. The medical metaphor is not necessarily in favour today. The modern hermeneutical school, however, is very much involved in the reading of the total religious experience of any culture at any point of time. That there is a commonality of approach can be quickly verified.[25]

There are, writes Thomas W. Ogletree, 'four basic types of interpretative activity ... application, suspicion, retrieval and hospitality.'[26] Plato can be seen to be involved in all four. Initially Plato, like everybody else, works 'quite naturally and appropriately with the "meanings" at hand, the socially shared stock of knowledge.' He repeats, for instance, that people lack *aidôs*. In the hermeneutics of suspicion the conventions are taken to be surface symptoms hiding some deeper dynamics which the interpreter claims to unveil. Thus Plato tells us about the noble and the ignoble horses and the charioteer to show what is really going on in human association. The hermeneutics of retrieval manages to recast the tradition into something deeper, richer, than what is commonly received: 'Rather than foreclosing the future, tradition provides the basis upon which an imaginative production of future alternatives becomes possible.' Thus Plato returns to Crete and praises Delphi. Finally a hermeneutics of hospitality exhibits 'a readiness to welcome strange and unfamiliar meanings into our own awareness, perhaps to be shaken by them, but in no case to be left unchanged.' The perspectives of 'others,' of previously unnoticed, unheard others, are allowed to correct the defects in our perspective. Thus Plato has Socrates refer to the wisdom handed down by Diotima in the midst of an all-male banquet.[27]

One word appropriately describes the nature of the whole process: Plato, we can say, has achieved a transposition of the Greek religious tradition.

A. Diès proposed the notion of transposition in 1913 and showed that it provides a convergent series of keys to interpret what Plato does with what he has found on the Athenian scene. Plato transposes rhetoric, that is he criticizes the existing one but he uses rhetoric (in *Phaedrus*, for instance) in a way that transforms the whole tradition and raises it to a new level. Thereby he turns something that has become profoundly immoral into something enduringly noble. He likewise transposes eroticism; he exposes the passion and criticizes the pursuit of pleasure, but he also reorients the emotion and gives eros a dignity it never had before. The same situation holds with Orphic beliefs about the soul and its fate: he takes a conception still half wrapped in magical notions and transposes it to make it into the principle of a moral and spiritual self.[28] In 1935 A.J. Festugière in his great book on contemplation in Plato put the metaphor of transposition to further use. Greek science and Greek religion alike were groping towards a grasp of truth as it is. Both in their diverse ways wanted the self to acknowledge that which ought to be acknowledged. Each wanted the self to leave its cares aside to see that which is at the source of all order. In his doctrine of *theoria*, a rational contemplation of the truth which is also a religious contemplation of the good, Plato transposed both scientific knowledge and traditional religion, and in the process made a grander claim for the knowledge to which man can rise.[29]

The metaphor alludes to a simple musical operation: a tune familiar in one key is rewritten or replayed in a different key. The tune is recognizable; but its character, its tone, its impact are entirely changed. Often the listener is familiar with the older version as he hears the new one. The sense of change, of novelty, of agreeable unfamiliarity is part of the experience. Transposition is thus a subtle and living process which involves a creative breakthrough. Applying the musical metaphor to Plato's handling of Greek religion will convey, I submit, a sense of what Plato really did with the Greek religious culture. He listened to existing tunes and sang a new one. His hermeneutical activity depended on a text and handed over a new text.[30]

The notion of transposition disposes of the easy alternative between conservation and innovation. In Plato (and, I believe, in Socrates before him) we observe an assessment of a broken-down tradition and a clear departure from many aspects of it. Plato is anti-Homeric as well as anti-Sophistic. In some sense Plato did not find a religious tradition worth keeping. He had to discriminate among what he found. He even felt that he had to reconstitute a version of the wise tradition. Plato was thus involved in a creative philosophical effort. He thought it was innovative and would contribute to the improvement of the religious life as well as to the raising of the level of all life. Religious traditionalists and Socratic philosophy shared a moral concern for the quality of social life and for the statement – or restatement – of the norm that would maintain its order and its health. But to carry out this task Plato had to penetrate into the nature of religion and see through it. He had to reinterpret ancient wisdom as well as depart from the contemporary version.

The notion of transposition also accounts for the paradoxes which we encounter in Socrates and meet again in Plato: a very religious man undermines the religion of his city or an apologist of religion turns out to be very emancipated from dominant beliefs. The transposer has achieved complete mastery in what he keeps and what he does not. And he keeps what he keeps on his own new terms. Plato thus allows that the religious festivals of the city and the mysteries begin the work of attuning men to the invisible good by presenting to them visible gods. But he adds that such contemplation remains imperfect. The visible gods are impure mirrors, or gods that condone and even elicit a degree of impurity in men's love. So the worship that has begun in Greek religious life can be completed only in a reformed religious life in which some features have been altered. Plato, for instance, changes the definition of the gods by saying that they are those souls that have a permanent vision of the forms. He thereby puts the gods under the sway of truth as contemplated by the philosopher.

The transposing arrives at something tangible: a transposed religion, we may say. But that which is transposed always carries with it the flavour of its transposing. Plato gives us reshaped myths, but he tells them in a literary context in which we hear also the speakers of the myths. He uses the language of the mysteries, but always with a safeguard indicating that he means something other than the ordinary meaning.[31] Plato's religious man is not Romano Guardini's (or Euthyphro's) mythical man getting his bearings from decisive fixed figures telling the truth about the world.[32] The age of the uncritical copying of models at hand is over.

It may be useful to draw here a comparison with Aeschylus. he too achieves a transposition, from the religion of the clan to that of the city. Orestes as the one who commits matricide cannot hope ever again to experience fraternity in the company of his blood brothers, sons of the murdered murderous woman. If he is ever again to find brothers, he must look elsewhere. The city offers him such a haven. Citizens are not family, yet they can be fraternal. Civil association provides a new and better framework for common living: it dares to welcome one who has killed his mother and receives from Athena divine warrant for its new way of doing things. With Plato we find the same sort of social and religious intelligence transmuting an old and inadequate myth. Fraternity is to transcend the limits of the *polis*: consider the Athenian, the Spartan, and the Cretan in the *Laws*. And since two women were accepted as pupils in the Academy, I shall even venture to say that sorority ceases to be entirely repressed. Plato however, unlike Aeschylus, does not restate a myth in a near cultic act. His act is literary. He leaves written dialogues, texts.

The notion of transposition also enables us to dispose of some erroneous interpretations of Plato's undertaking in the *Laws*. Some have concluded that Plato's religious interests there were exclusively politicically motivated: he wanted to restore the oligarchic form of government and, in order to do so, he strove to reimpose the mass of traditional cults that had become discredited by science and democracy. Plato, according to this view, would be a reactionary manipulator of religion for class interests.[33] Others saw in Plato a peace-loving conservative who wanted to stabilize the shaken-up Greek religious culture: to put an end to the debates on religious practice and ideas was a *sine qua non*.[34] Finally others have proposed to see in Plato a moderately rational reformer of the Greek religious tradition: his interest according to this view was primarily in soundness of doctrine. Since the religious tradition is out of step with the truth, it ought to be straightened out on the basis of philosophical principles.[35]

Such views fail to recognize the radical nature of what happened when Plato wrote the *Laws*. He wrote a political and pious work portraying three elderly gentlemen discussing the legislation desirable for a city that is about to be founded and agreeing on a basic package. The text is meaningful and can, of course, be discussed as such. But the absence of Socrates should not be lost on us. In writing and publishing this treatise Plato did a meaningful action: he chose to move from dialectical inquiry and testing towards dialogic consensus. After portraying Socratic practice in action, he portrayed statesmanlike practice under the conditions of fourth-century Greece. While being political, he constructs a city that leaves room for non-political virtues. The philosopher thereby attends to non-philosophical matters that are necessary to human beings but without disavowing philosophy.[36] Transposition produces a new tune but its sound does not drown out the transposing process. The new tune founds a society where practically all human beings will spend their lives at a desirable level of existence. What occasions the transposition, however, is the philosophical awareness of ordinarily insoluble conflicts among human beings on the question of what is good for man.

The writing of the *Laws* was Plato's last meaningful action. Before that he had founded the Academy and written all the other dialogues.[37] The metaphor of transposition invites us to think of the latter as records of a process of transposing and the former as the product of a transposition. Plato as a philosopher has founded a private community and left literary pieces portraying individuals debating ideas in free exchange. These texts institutionalize a certain practice: the desirable practice of intellectual life. They embody the pleasure human beings find at being with each other in a small group of those who feel they know. The text of the *Laws* seeks to institutionalize common public practice: the pleasure human beings have at being in a society where all are (more or less) friends. These two types of texts provide us with two types of piety: there is the piety of the cognoscenti and there is public piety.

Both types of piety are equally the result of Plato's philosophy.[38] They will be looked at more closely in our next section. But, as results of meaningful action, as notions found in written texts, they are each at some point removed from the original (oral) practice that gave birth to them. The 'final' doctrines are stated in such a way that they do not lose the glow of intelligence that burned so brightly at earlier stages of the trajectory.

The Socratic practice of philosophy is thus the pivotal point on which turns the whole transposition of Greek religion achieved by Plato's philosophy of religion. As disciple of Socrates Plato can be both outside and inside the religious tradition. Not entirely inside, he can philosophize over it; not entirely outside, he does not merely philosophize about it but philosophizes in it and from it as well. With the Greeks the borderline between inside and outside is of course a highly fluctuating one. The priests never excommunicated anyone and never formulated tests to separate insiders from outsiders (Plato's situation is therefore more like that of twentieth-century Christians than that of their fathers in the nineteenth century, let alone the sixteenth). The position of Plato is unstable: can one both consciously wish to change something as complex as a religious tradition and yet remain schooled by it? People will speak on 'changing the letter while keeping the spirit,' hilding to the essential while modifying the rest, but scholars of religion have found it notoriously difficult to separate the kernels from the husks. Being both outside and inside is an expression with an apparently plain meaning; concretely, in the actual hermeneutical process, it will be difficult to know which foot is inside and which one outside, and what is the exact nature of the ground on which each foot rests – especially when the feet keep moving. The notion of transposition does not remove any of these rich ambiguities.

3 Public piety

The piety that is taught in and embodied in the *Laws* and that I shall call public piety is based on the feelings of *aidôs*. The ancients were better than we are, and nearer to the gods. They believed in a deep, moral coherence holding all things together. 'Wise men tell us that heaven and earth and gods and men are held together by communion and friendship, by orderliness and temperance and justice, and that is the reason, my friend, why they call the whole of this world by the name of order, not of disorder or dissoluteness.'[39] The ancients did not transgress the norms of this coherence. Their customs were good. We should keep them. Public piety is thus a respect for the tradition of the fathers; their customs go back to an age in which, as Plato repeatedly states, men were mindful of their duties to the gods and observant of decencies among men. And Plato and his contemporaries met enough empty-headed twenty-year olds and greedy forty-year olds to find confirmation of their belief that in the days of Pericles, or rather of Marathon, or, better still, of Solon, men were wiser and mores healthier. Public piety is thus also a memory, an ongoing presence of the character strengths of men whose desires were curbed or tamed by the god-given laws of the city and their sense of appropriateness and decorum.

But Plato, like Sophocles, Thucydides, Euripides, and Isocrates, is also involved in something like trying to draw a lesson from recent Athenian history. The city has gone through catastrophies, which must be understood. What fall has occurred between them and the older past must be discerned. That violence does not work is the lesson drawn by Thucydides. Athens offered a better, more civilized social order while Sparta sought to perpetuate an older one. But Athens was cruelly defeated. Sparta, incidentally, always conservative, urged restraint on their victorious allies: they remembered the victors of Marathon. Athens lost because she wanted to carry her mission brutally and at once.[40] Sophocles shows the roots of disaster in *hybris*. Men must keep a measure, a pious and moral measure, or the gods will bring about the self-destruction of the proud. In *Oedipus Rex* we see a man moving towards a genuine piety. Oedipus at the beginning of the play is 'formally pious in action and speech but betraying in one phrase after another a confidence in man's worth as equal to that of the gods.' At the end of the play, chastened and rid of *hybris*, he achieves a new greatness; he knows that the greatness of man is subordinate to that of the gods.[41] Aristotle proclaimed, rather harshly, that 'poetry is something more philosophic and of graver import than history.'[42] This was overlooking the fusion that occurred in the fifth century between poetry and history. The writing of what happened was seen by Herodotus and Thucydides as a statement of the virtues that can help man, if they but learn, to ward off chaos. In this way history came to deal with universals, not just singulars.

So piety is made of restraint, and Plato's generation has seen, more radically than any earlier one, how indispensable this restraint is socially. Socrates' own piety consists in heeding the voice of his demon, and that voice, characteristically, gives only negative warnings; the mere absence of it on the day of his trial confirms to him that he is on the right course in his speech to his judges. The presence of piety makes the other virtues more secure because the brutal innovation in the handling of one's fellow-man in the angry and desperate times of crises is not resorted to. Socrates, for instance, did not go along with the collective trial for the ten generals who were entitled by law to an individual trial. [43]

Plato does not, of course, merely commend or uphold public piety. He provides an account, as complete as he can, of why it is desirable.

The first part of the account links the phenomenon of piety to the whole story of the cosmos. The myths of the *Statesman* and of *Timaeus* invite us to think of public piety as a phenomenon present during the period of cosmic decay: it is a series of memories which remind men of the order that used to prevail when the world was guided by God. Such memories are gifts which the gods leave behind as they abandon the world: 'such needful information and instruction' are kept in old traditions which give a shape to human life as we know it (all the historical knowledge men have, according to Plato, are records of an age of decay). Men must take care of themselves; their shepherd is no longer with them – and they would not in any case accept the rule of a literal shepherd – but they do keep a memory of what the order once was. Religion is thus made of remnants, records of a lost truth, which are handed down in a fragmentary and garbled manner. [44] This religion is itself victim of the law of decay and sinks in disorder. History is seen by Plato not as a cumulative process of experience but as a 'length of time' with successive catastrophic destructions that cause loss of records (with occasionally 'a remnant of unlettered mountaineers' keeping a memory of what had gone on before). [45]

We can thus say of public piety (or of religion in general) what *Timaeus* says of the universe. It too is 'a mixed result of the combination of Necessity and Reason. Reason overruled Necessity by persuading her to guide the greatest part of the things that become toward what is best.' [46] Under the skill of the demiurge emerges an ordered world, teleologically organized to guide all things towards the blessedness and peace of which each is capable. In the social world public piety is a relic of such divine guidance.

Public piety being an unstable, impermanent combination, it matters much to know in what sort of equilibrium this phenomenon currently finds itself. So the second part of Plato's account is a story of recent social dynamism. I discern in particular two specific time-bound diagnoses: one bears on what religion was in a recent, better past, the other on what can best be expected of religion now.

In the recent past public piety has achieved a ceremonial equilibrium between law and pleasure. The democratic symposium is an image of that happy state of affairs. Wine and friendship expand the souls and refresh the bodies. The democratic symposium keeps, however, the measure established by civil talk. No one interrupts, no one engages in private conversation, no one suspends talk to surrender to less subtle pleasures. A heightened pleasure is shared and no law is broken.[47] As the *Symposium* will show, our coarser age sees this order disrupted and the banquet degenerates. Music is another example of the festive equilibrium that pleases body and soul by imparting a measure to both, and a measure which is, of course, not resented by either.

The gods still help men by means of music and festivals.[48] But such rhythms are now attenuated and no longer sway the whole city. In this context a different religious force manifests itself. It is the pervasive force of shame, and of its antidote, the ritual affirmation of legitimacy. Models of behaviour are given that shelter the self from having to feel ashamed. Marcel Détienne has shown that the four major forms of protest against the city and its public religion either transgress food taboos or harden them into strict and complete abstinence. Pythagorism and Orphism renounce the eating of meat and require vegetarianism; the Dionysiac enthusiasms and the Cynic protests encourage the eating of meat raw. All derive their meaning from the rejection of the sacrificial system that allows the killing of innocent domestic animals but surrounds this awesome deed with ritual gestures (sacrificial killing and roasting and cooking).[49] The *Laws* rejects the two primitive uncivilized extremes of vegetarianism and cannibalism.[50] It is also notorious for the support it brings to the systems of taboos. Total innocence or unrestrained violence are not existential possibilities in our age that lies between the golden age and chaotic animality. A similar structure manifests itself around the phenomenon of sex. The four kinds of protesters here too embark on two opposed courses that diverge from a mean: some extol (and practise) total chastity; others indulge in (ecstatic or routine) indiscriminate mating. The city demands legitimate marriage. The work of procreation is required of all and the disruptive pleasures of sex are confined to privacy, both legitimated and controlled in the conjugal bed. The institution of the pious family forces men out of the innocence that ignores women, and out of the innocence that ignores the erratic and uncanny forces of sexual pleasure. But barely out of innocence, men see their sexual desires repressed by monogamy, even though private pleasures remain.[51] Whether in relation to food or sex, religion elicits feelings of shame and provides antidotes to their potential paralysing results. It helps men move from madness to measure.

At this point Plato's account of the desirability of public piety moves into its third part, something we should label today an anthropology that considers human beings as acculturated beings. In the make-up of each man there is *thumos*, that is heart, temper, spirit, a sense of honour. Every human being is a social being: he wants to be well thought of and is readily brave in the pursuit of this end. This courage, it must be stressed, is quick, spontaneous, ingrained, so to speak. Thumotic man takes pride in seeing things well done. His anger flares up at the sight of wrongdoers and he bravely sets out to straighten things out. Cowardice is opposed to *thumos*. Thumotic man is full of stories, passionately held to, about who is right and who is wrong. *Thumos* takes pride in the standards (whatever they are) that men have set for themselves. Artificial though they be, these standards of civilization are felt by thumotic man as second nature, fruit of his experience of life, wedded to his affectivity. Demosthenes proclaims that 'all men have shrines to justice, order and respect [*dike, eunomia,* and *aidôs*], some the fairest and holiest, in the very heart and nature of each man, others built for the common worship of all.'[52] That man has *thumos* means that these shrines are there inside him, and always will be. Man, if he is noble, will always rush to the rescue of what, to him, is required by his notion of justice, order, and respect. Religious passion is self-love transmuted into self-esteem, self-righteousness.[53]

In a decent city good laws will then commend, instil, the proper pleasures of pride and anger. The citizen will have his thumotic passion properly aroused. A civil religion is based on such passions and, if decent, will instil a piety made of deference, restraint, and moderation.[54]

There is a contradiction inherent in public piety. It tries to harness immoderate forces in the service of moderation, and is thereby liable to the charge of being two-faced. Public piety is lived as habitual, unthinking, even blind devotion. There enter into it elements of blind fear. Strauss argues that piety is necessary because there must be some sacred, unwritten laws, almost taboos, that will contradict the strongest desires in corrupt souls.[55] Plato's account of the desirability of public piety becomes a normative theory of culture and civilization. Through art human beings create a way of life that can *coercively* claim to be the only way good for human nature. The law in any society, whatever it may be, always has an initial credibility as it claims that it delivers a common good.[56] Quite naturally the Greeks thought that the laws (customs) they had superimposed upon nature were fair and good.[57] It is good then to have social norms that make the promise of delivering a common good, and that elicit blind *aidôs*. It is good that thumotic man unthinkingly accepts the promise and acts on it. Tradition persuades without even pressing its claim to know. (And Plato has never claimed that daily life will ever be guided by knowledge alone.[58]) How fully Plato is prepared to articulate the promise can be seen in the *Laws*: *aidôs* is indispensable to a society that wishes to protect liberty, equality, and concord. W.K.C. Guthrie pointedly stresses that these ideals of the model society of the conservatives are those of the French Revolution![59] The desirability of the promised end should not mask the nature of the means. Public piety is necessary but inauthentic management of human desires. It focuses attention on the dangers of moral discord: it demands conformity as insurance, shelter against the dangers. By stating the norms it provides human beings with a certain sort of necessary quietness, but it does not reason out the intrinsic necessity of its own set of norms.[60] As a matter of fact, it masks its own exercise of power, and aspires to being acknowledged as plain, natural, or reasonable. Hear the address to the new colonists in the *Laws*: 'If we live in accordance with these rules, each of us will get the reward we deserve from the gods and such beings as are superior to ourselves, and live in a spirit of cheerful confidence for most of the years of our lives.' The duties of piety being thus outlined, the speech moves on to list the duties to one's equals (or inferiors), children, relatives, friends, and fellow-citizens.[61]

The propaganda for tradition is not morally irresponsible. Plato is willing to say that what is not true can help firm up opinion. A due weight of respect for the rules that customarily order our relationship to the authorities helps men to curb the wild beast in themselves and submit themselves to the authority of reason. In this sense Plato believes that submission to the traditional law is an attitudinal preparation for obedience to the natural law. Piety, when public, is the virtue of a self that is concerned with attuning itself to what is noble and gets its sense of what is noble, somewhat darkly, from habit and tradition. This is, it seems to me, the answer Plato comes up with after he looks into the dark hole created by Athenian moral breakdown and tries to figure out what sort of society there can be that can provide a man with all the education of which he is capable.

To sum up, under conditions in Greece in the early fourth century the public piety of religion is a cultural force that can, through shame, foster among most men as they now are moderate behaviour that has a degree of conformity with the measure of reason. Decaying though it may be, religion is a cultural force contending against worse forms of decay. Religion enhances the credibility of stories, of myths that stabilize patterns of expectation. Knowing what mixture of good and evil can normally be expected in this world, religious men and woman will resist the play of historical passions. They will not be like putty in the hands of demagogues who know how to stir their greed and their fears. Religion thus is an ally against the forces of tyranny.[62] Eteocles in Euripides' *Phoenician Women* identifies very well what exactly religion is up against:

If one must do a wrong, it's best to do it
For the sake of power, otherwise let's have religious virtue.[63]

In the fourth century civil passions are the most powerful excuse for setting aside morality. Conservative myths are a healthy influence in such a society.

The philosopher seeking allies for reason in the forces of *thumos* has acquired the art of looking at 'objects' reflected in symbolic stories as well as those reflected in reasoned argument. The problem of implementation has opened the philosopher's eye to the role of such stories: he has also learned to discriminate between the good and the bad ones.[64] The problem of implementation, I might add, has also brought Plato to a point where the philosophy of religion demands a philosophy of history and becomes wedded to a political philosophy. In the current decay of the city men have memories and anticipations. They also need a pragmatic art.

Aristotle, we may add, refused to call *aidôs* a virtue even though he allowed that the man of *aidôs* is much to be praised.[65] *Aidôs* is a feeling – a passion, the Greeks would say – and as such not trustworthy, although healthy as far as it goes. After all, *aidôs* was the most pervasive ethical emotion in the *Iliad*, and we know it was not enough.[66] *Dike* must be added to *aidôs* if we are to have friendly ties among men. And *dike* is emphatically not satisfied by traditional goings on. Here Plato shifts to what we shall call the piety of the cognoscenti. The actual piety of the citizen must yield to the search for the piety appropriate to man. Persuasion henceforth shall be deemed to require knowledge. The concerns of *thumos* must yield to those of reason.

4 The piety of the cognoscenti

Much prudent wisdom, of the somewhat pusillanimous, constricted kind, can be derived from Plato's version of public piety, and much moral exhortation. Public piety, thanks to a deep social and individual chemistry, achieves a restraining and rerouting of desire. We may need to believe that *thumos* is ordinarily noble and certainly was so in the past. But in the corrupt society *thumos* is yoked to the service of greed. Self-righteous anger glorifies the errands of selfish desire.[67] Public piety, to be sure, denounces these extreme, restless forms of self-assertion; thus it helps men see through the magic fostered by the vigorous individuals who use social conventions to their own purposes. The remembered virtues of another age, even the magic of the past, liberate us from contemporary trickery. But public piety contains within itself the seeds of another kind of delusion.

Public piety exerts a constant sort of verbal pressure. It cajoles, or forces, people to work at living a communitarian existence. Public piety lives in human hearts thanks to the unexamined grip of some myths. Symbols from the past are reborn in the present to do hidden work; they satisfy man's will to live in an ordered community that has continuity with its past and is full of customs shared by all. Public piety also utters pieties that settle opinion. Hence a compactness in discourse, a finality of utterance, a rigidity of doctrine. The Platonic corpus that has begun by placing man's best hopes on disciplined public discussion ends up by seeing a sort of tyranny in public moral discourse. So public piety is not enough to foster the power of disciplined thought over life. Where will human beings find the creative piety that will overcome the current protective rigidities? Where can we find the human beings who know more?

Plato's answer is simple and has abiding power. Some human beings should be allowed or encouraged to start afresh. They should take time to apply their minds as much as possible to the practice of philosophy. In the *Republic* Plato begins by removing gifted children from the normal educational influence of the city they are to serve. Just as the *polis* has broken from the nurture provided by the family, Plato breaks from that provided by the *polis*. In real life he starts the Academy, a school for philosophically inclined adults. He also writes dialogues showing adults spending their time in philosophical discussion. The impact of all this is clear: reason, and only reason, can now work at the transmutation of desire. No city can be safely left with either fluctuating or entrenched opinions. There must be in its midst some who know, and who constantly work at knowing. The point can also be made more modestly: there should be some who take time to know more.

These people I shall call the *cognoscenti*. They know or they claim to know; in any case, they strive to make their particular claim as persuasive as possible. The many think what they think because they think it; to put it plainly, they do not think. Those touched by public piety think what they think because they think they should think it; and when the piety is sound, they have a good case for establishing that they should think it. Those who know go through an even more rigorous thought process: they think what they think because they must, because they think it is true.

Somewhat removed from the common stream of society, the cognoscenti are always critical of, and ironic about, its shared beliefs. They discern false certainties and exercise the right to challenge them. They are confident about the correctness of their own insight. They have risen to a superior point of view. Their piety starts with unbelief about common pieties. It gives up cherished common loyalties to save its care and love for something that transcends all societies: the divine in itself. The piety of the cognoscenti is not the fondness one may have for one god or other, or even for a whole family of them; its object is the divine in general, indeterminate, abstract. It is *to theion*, not *theos tis* (the divine, not some god).[68]

Guardini has very properly portrayed this attitude: 'Piety means above all things an effort to apprehend the divine. It means not sticking fast in traditional ideas, but inquiring after the essence, and thinking this essence as purely and worthily as the best powers of the mind are able. In this process contradictions of tradition and environment may appear; the divine may raise itself to heights far above the familiar, natural ideas, and thus there may occur a kind of religious emptying-out of immediate existence. But all this must be endured for truth's sake, for the truth of the divine itself.' Guardini emphasizes the social and moral implications of this piety and correctly articulates the peculiarily Socratic experience and its rising, universal scope: 'This piety is put to the proof as soon as the divine commission comes into conflict with the demands of one's environment and has to be carried out with loss and danger ... This experience too is primarily a biographical peculiarity of Socrates; behind it however, lies something deeper and more universal, is that watchfulness for the numinous command which is evinced not by rational considerations but only by its specifically religious validity.'[69]

While they keep a critical distance from other peoples' myths, the cognoscenti are overtaken by a myth of their own. They tend to believe in their superiority. Speaking of the philosophers, Plato says that on account of their adherence to the divine they become, so far as one possibly can, 'of a like character.'[70]

Plato clothes the philosophers in all the qualities that have been perceived in traditional religious figures. We have seen in *Phaedo* the claim that they are the true mystics.[71] *Phaedrus* echoes it: the philosopher is the perfect initiate; his mind, and his alone, has wings. Keeping the memory of the realities the soul once held, the philosopher has communion with 'those things the communion with which causes God to be divine.' 'A man who employs such memories rightly is always being initiated into perfect mysteries and he alone becomes truly perfect.'[72] In the *Symposium* Socrates says that Diotima has introduced him to rites and 'revelations' and he uses the very word used at Eleusis.[73] The *Sophist* repeats that the philosopher is divine.[74] The entire practice of philosophy is sustained by a religious story. The souls of the just and the unjust are ultimately, after death, dealt with justly, without reference to their reputation on earth. Justice finds support elsewhere than in human wills and social traditions. Human hope is not tied to the fate of societies. Human beings are not caught in a cycle of decay: they direct their own lives, and their souls, which are at times at sea about everything, can also be firmly grounded in the truth. This grounding, affirm the cognoscenti, occurs in an act of attention. Human beings are capable of attending to God, God being, as Iris Murdoch puts it, 'a single perfect transcendent non-representable and necessarily real object of attention.' The moral implication of such understanding of God is that fantasy, 'the proliferation of blinding self-centered aims and images,' is counteracted by 'attention to reality inspired by, consisting of, love.'[75]

Plato casts the piety of the cognoscenti in an austere light. Union with God means the dissolution of all other ties. The philosopher's life (as Plato sees it) cannot be separated from the sense that the truth is not here, but rather elsewhere, that there is the superior and the inferior, the true and the apparent. And as S. Pétrement puts it in her study of Plato's dualism, 'the rule of the superior on the inferior can be achieved only if the superior is separated from the inferior.'[76] *Phaedo* invites the philosopher to a complete tearing of the fabric that weaves body and soul together. Narrating with emotional intensity Socrates' last moments, Plato affirms without qualification that philosophy is a training for death and as such is impatient to be rid of the body. The *Republic* lacks the extreme flavour of *Phaedo* but it does assume the split between those who prefer to cultivate the pleasures of necessity (wealth and honour) and those who scorn them because they taste the delight of knowing the truth.[77] The piety of the cognoscenti has a grasp of the eternal rather than of the cherished continuities of society and history. It weans man from his wants; at the limit it invites him to give up the will to live.[78]

The philosopher is removed from the pleasures of necessity, but he does enjoy the pleasures of the intellectual life. 'He lives in the delight of knowing the truth and the reality' and 'is always occupied with that, while he learns.'[79] The cognoscenti are austere individuals who, in principle, pursue rigorously all the demands of truth that press themselves upon their own minds: they spurn consensus, but they enjoy each other's company and mutual esteem. The society of those who know has fluid borders and few dogmas. But those who know recognize each other and know how to keep out those who do not belong. So irony should also be turned on the ironists. There is self-indulgence in the society of the cognoscenti, and they flaunt it at times. Private pleasures are not enough for them. They like to poke fun at the solemnities of others – and hide their own cozy cliquishness. Their banter is an ingredient essential to the freedom of thought. But thought must also be responsible. Plato the philosopher also wrote the *Laws*. The philosopher in him endorses both the three serious old men who think about founding a city and the playful young men who enjoy discussing any topic with Socrates, while the city goes on its meandering way.

To sum up, the demands of public piety should be honoured, while the claims of the piety of the cognoscenti are pressed. The result is conflict. The city ruled by custom has something intrinsically tyrannical and this comes to the fore when the society defends custom thumotically. Athens did not tolerate the individual who strove to educate his fellow-men to a new level of existence. 'I believe that no greater good came to pass in the city than my service to the god,'[80] Socrates declared in vain at his trial. Plato, however, remembered. To him the public piety that permeates the city must provide room, a path for the philosophic pursuit of virtue.

In the end public piety, even that of the *Laws*, transmutes desire only imperfectly. Through the growth of common *thumos* it tames individual greed; it does not defeat it. And *thumos* is, by nature, unstable. Common *thumos* can prove powerless as the city disintegrates into civil war; or it proves effective only in the stirring up of war against another city. *Thumos* never engages the whole soul; only eros does. Public piety does not rise to an erotically ordered hierarchy of desires. For instance, it keeps suggesting that being virtuous is in the end both right and pleasant. Its loves do not serve a dominant, ultimate act of loving attention. The transmutation of desires stops short of that point. The rational desire of the good is not allowed to emerge: public, historical passions remain to block it.[81] Public piety remains morally imperfect because it is not cognitively rigorous enough. It hands down as desirable beliefs, beliefs of which all one can say is that many believe them to be desirable. Rigorous testing of beliefs is desirable.

The whole intellectual process which man enters into when his mind submits itself to the dialectical method brings about reorientation of his loves as well as a growth in insight. To grow in virtue is not to grow more efficient in practice.[82] Loves that use our rational capacities to manipulate the appearances for the largest measure of private advantage must yield to pure, uncalculating love. Let me not, however, in my writing now, so praise the piety of those who know that I eclipse the piety shared by those who do not: *both* are virtues. The life of the philosopher is a struggle against delusion, outside and inside. Plato writes philosophical dramas, dialogues. The victory for wisdom is not achieved yet, even among philosophers, and can be shown only in the making.

5 The philosopher caught between mysticism and politics

Piety, a virtue and a necessary part of the goodness of the good man, enables man to grow akin to the divine and co-operate in the struggle of the divine against necessity. This co-operation is carried on at two levels. The first kind of piety is a demure respect for the religious tradition as a body of symbols and customs which can resist the disordered energy of selfish wills and thus serve as a brake on the necessary. A second kind of piety wrenches itself free of such necessary pieties to rise mystically to the level of contemplation of the divine.

Now is the time for the interpreter to take a position at some distance from this twofold presentation of piety. A distinction has been suggested between mythical and mystical piety. What is the meaning and import of such a distinction?[83]

The root of the tension between mysticism and religion is to be found in the tension between the social dimension of life and its demands and the human ability to transcend the social (and be unsocial and antisocial). Public piety is profoundly social; it is penetrated by an *aidôs* that internalizes the demands of a social order requiring restraint. Public piety maintains and repairs social barriers. Civilization graces – and organizes – the satisfaction of instincts with ritual. Mystical piety is born in the vacuum created by the collapse of the homogeneity of the social world. But in the world where some rise to the height of a piety that is attuned to a good god above society, some, released from the bonds of public piety, fall into permanently disordered antisocial lives or into grey, dull lives with periodic orgiastic release.

It is as if people hunger for non-verbal experiences that will release them from the pressure of the expected, correct verbal utterance. In pious cities people are expected always to say the proper thing; their gift of speech is controlled: hence the permanence of a longing for a release from the requirements of speech. I suggest that mystical experience is to be understood as providing just such release. Mythical utterance tries to convey how things, in general, are. Thanks to mystical experience the self can reject the finality of this utterance and know that things are different, better. We have seen how in Greece, at the fringes of urban life, religious orgia provide some with an opportunity to break social barriers and lift norms and taboos to give the absolutistic rewards associated with the surrender to lawless behaviour. Plato does not condone such excesses, nor is he very impressed with the quieter sects that practise celibate abolition of sexuality or strict ideological vegetarianism.[84] He stays firmly within the cultural mainstram upheld by the city's sacrificial system. But Plato is enough of a mystic to desire an openness of the self to that which is beyond, above, what society legitimates. The *Republic* and *Phaedrus* commend contemplation and divine madness. Even the restrained *Laws* commends mild drunkenness as an inducement to fresh thoughts. Thus Plato wants the release from words to be restrained by some conventions. In answer he creates the philosophical dialogue, where every utterance is open to question, where everything, for a while, is open to debate. And at times, in this discussion, speech points beyond itself, as in irony, for instance. We shall develop this point further in our next section on language. For now we must focus on Plato's sense of the political responsibility of the philosophical writer. He knows the tension between mythical public piety and the sense of piety proper to those who know. What does the philosopher do in such circumstances: think some more? or make a clear, public utterance on policy?

We have seen that Plato makes explicit a tension between the theoretical and the practical life. Against traditionalists, pragmatists, and busybodies Plato presses the claims of the theoretical life. In politics he will tell them that what the city needs is not the strong man but the philosopher king, the scientific ruler who contemplates the truth, has a mystical love of justice, and hungers no more. But against the strong men who claim to reorganize the city Plato hastens to plead for the old decencies; he then supports the authority of traditional laws and presses the claims of the inherited practical common sense.[85] Mythical religion becomes promptly rehabilitated. Plato can never take his stand on the theoretical life alone. He knows that there is in the theoretical life a fulfilling quality that easily keeps one aloof from practical issues. He also knows that there is in the practical life an absorbing care that tends to make one unfit for the theoretical life. Furthermore the practical life is hard in itself: it intrinsically resists the influence of goodness. Circumstances do not always lend themselves to the embodiment of wisdom. Yet Plato's message is clear: when the conditions are appropriate, no philosopher will fail to play an active role. 'The possibility that the philosopher's "theoretical life" may at any moment change into the "practical" gives it a wonderful tension and excitement entirely absent from "pure science".'[86]

Polar tensions create a rich balance which elicit much thinking but they also create ambiguities. To suggest that only specific circumstances will enable the philosopher to judge whether or not to insert himself into the affairs of his contemporaries is an invitation to flexible good sense. But it does not say why the philosopher should act. What reasons does he have to descend from what is clearly the superior life? What motivations should habitually prompt him? Love as a motive is never clearly urged, let alone acknowledged. The texts rather suggest that *noblesse oblige* or some sort of higher pride is the motive of the wise men's descent.

Very perplexing too is Plato's uneasy balance between force and persuasion as the means proper to the life of action. Normally one expects the philosopher to act in a manner that prolongs the cosmic motion of loving persuasion. Consider the following quotations from *Gorgias*, the *Symposium*, and *Timaeus*. 'Wise men tell us that persuasion holds together the order of the universe.'[87] 'Love is a carrier between and interpreter between men and gods and binds the whole together.'[88] The universe came into order 'through necessity yielding to intelligent persuasion.'[89] But other passages show the philosopher ready to use what we must call force. Plato has foresworn any thought of brusque seizure of power by philosophers for good ends, but, once in power, his philosophers have a hand strong as well as delicate. There is no room for brutal rashness, but there is ruse, manipulation, and in the end trials for harmful teachers and the possibility of the death penalty. Plato's legislators or his guardians run the city and work on a realm fundamentally opposed to the pure inwardness of the Socratic dialectic.[90] The law, announces the *Republic*, harmonizes and adapts 'the citizens to one another by persuasion and compulsion.'[91] The whole of the *Laws* aims at securing that seeming contradiction: a mild rule, a persuasive coercion. But it does allow that the law *is* heterogeneous: it persuades and it uses force and there is no middle ground between the two.

That the motivation for 'returning to the cave' remains obscure and that Plato, for all his commitment to reason and persuasion, does hold onto the sword as the *ultima ratio philosophorum* have led many moderns to write of the 'downward' movement of the philosophers in depressing terms. We often respond so fully to Plato's invitation to intellectual contemplation and to the separation of the pure from the impure that the road to action seems a path of foul compromises or at best a perilous duty. And there are insinuations that the philosophers who return to the cave are 'really' power-hungry, like everyone else. But I do not think that Plato is at all apologetic about the need for action after contemplation, any more than he is apologetic about man leading a social life. In one sense the problem of the return to the cave arises from a misuse of the metaphor. Embodied, the philosopher never leaves the cave; or he leaves it only metaphorically.[92] Furthermore, taking care of what is soulless is a permanent, essential function of soul.[93] In *Phaedrus* the soul's condition is defined by its crucial, pivotal location: the charioteer feeds on ideas and guides the horses. The figure of the demiurge in *Timaeus* reinforces the model by giving it a truly cosmic scale. As an artisan the demiurge copes with a material problem, and Plato constantly emphasizes the perfection he achieves rather than his need to compromise. We do not read that he sees that the work of his hands is good, but we are told that the created world is 'a perceptible God, most great and good and fair and perfect.'[94] The story of the demiurge blending the necessary and the divine has been called the myth of the mayonnaise: the point, appropriately, is the perfection of the new stuff created of incompatible elements.

The soul guiding the horses after having contemplated the truth, the demiurge keeping an eye on the truth and installing and repairing a cosmic order, these are myths. As such they provide the philosopher with a self-image and enhance his motivation as he pits himself against chaotic desire in himself and unruly chaos in society. Identifying with the soul and the demiurge, the philosopher knows himself well enough not to be paralysed by self-doubt over the origin of his ordering efforts, but he keeps the prudence of one trained in reverence, reticence, and aware of the limits against which he must contend. Plato, who is famous for his praise of mathematical intelligence, also brings about an unprecedented rehabilitation of the practical intelligence, the intelligence of the artisan, a lowly being in all hierarchies. Science and *technè* are *not* completely separated in Plato; the physician is also a model of the scientist. Plato above all believes in the need of *metis*: the intelligence appropriate to man is not only that of the geometer and his straight lines but also that which is quick, flexible, as mobile and hefty as life, which is crafty, and can master deception without being caught up in it.[95]

All this is true. And yet ... The goodness of the created world is upheld in a myth, and here I think it appropriate to say, *only* in a myth. And the dynamics proper to the way downward arise only because Plato, rightly or wrongly, has identified the political problem in dualistic terms: philosophers ponder the problem of rule in a society which includes non-philosophers (even has a majority of them). Socrates was a free wise man; he chose those with whom he was going to speak (except on the day of his trial ...). Plato accepts the problem of a sovereign who tries to love and serve all his subjects and tries to create a bond among all men of a society (whether or not they have philosophic affinities for each other).[96] The *Republic* has refuted the view according to which no one is willingly just, but Plato goes on, nevertheless, to develop a political philosophy on the premise that we are in a society where some, possibly many, are 'just' only unwillingly. Plato's attractiveness may be related to the fact that he does not suffer any illusion about the prompt spread of the voluntary co-operative principle, but can we accept his enshrining of the problem of force as an essential, perennial problem of politics? Force, if necessary, but not necessarily force, answers Plato in the *Statesman*: the royal ruler knows when to use persuasion and when to use force. As John Gould puts it, 'Plato's acceptance of the conditions of human life implies, to some degree at least, abandonment of his scheme of values.'[97] What guides this compromise and what establishes the proper degree is never stated. But can one define in advance the criteria for compromise? So we must remain with an affirmation of the heterogeneity between the two invitations: the soul must ascend and must descend. The way up and the way down are not the same. The duties of the way up are not those of the way down. The former demand full light; the latter maintain the city in a twilight state which assures the welfare of the many and enables a few to rise to the contemplative life.

This kind of society, born of compromise with 'necessities,' has many features which we must label 'inauthentic.' Leo Strauss formulates the limitations in this way: 'the good city is not possible without a fundamental falsehood. It cannot exist in the element of truth, of nature. A noble lie is necessary to blur the distinction between nature and convention.' These limitations are inescapable. 'The city constructed in accordance with the highest need of man is not possible. Plato lets us see the essential limits – the nature of the city.'[98] Voegelin points out the positive side of the life of uneasy compromise: 'The order of the psyche is not absorbed in its entirety by the order of the polis.'[99] Paradoxically, we might add, it is in the city that uses coercion that the individual has a life of his own. In the perfectly integrated society, without resistance and without jails, the individual is lost. As long as one believes that the person has a vocation to a life that transcends the political common good, one must rejoice in the obdurate imperfections of the political.[100]

In the end it is as if Plato can never decide whether he is a mystic or an ardent, although conservative, reformer. He wants to escape the bad *polis* and its illusions. The problem of the realization of the good *polis* also taxes him. He is not a pure mystic because he is concerned about bringing it about for all, and soon. As he works on the conditions for this realization, he gives offence to purists: they find him too prompt to compromise. Why should one be concerned about a religion which strives to 'manage' inauthentically, when one has the key to a piety that liberates from inauthenticity?

As far as I am concerned, Plato is a great philosopher because he ventures, openly, into the management of the inauthentic. He tries to find a *modus vivendi* between philosophy and public religion. Philosophy and private mysticism can easily coexist in the same individual. There is perhaps even an affinity between the two. The example of Wittgenstein should be enough to cause us to ponder these points (that of Heidegger should also be adduced). But I find it difficult to envisage a philosophy of mysticism. There is a shortage of ascertainable facts and of meanings to be examined. And should the philosopher take lightly the threat of silence? Wittgenstein has warned that very little is achieved when philosophical problems are solved and he affirms that 'what we cannot speak about, we must pass over in silence.'[101] Plato wants philosophy to move into ever new territory. When he cannot speak about something, it means that the time has come to find yet another way of speaking. Offering us a philosophy of religion, Plato moves into territory where there is no threat of having nothing to say: there are always myths to be examined, policies to be weighed. He enters into the twilight territory where being and non-being are in contact and contention. There is so much to be seen, understood, talked about. Philosophy, then, is in no danger of stopping. Our common life never ceases to produce religious phenomena that can be brought to the level of common consciousness and can become objects of a common or even public discussion. Discussion of mystical experience, whether in the first or in the third person, gives us little to talk about. Plato can inaugurate a philosophy of religion that has so much to say because, caught between mysticism and politics, he has turned with eager curiosity to the historical, the mythical, the social. I do not hesitate to recognize in that move the mark of a concern for his fellow human beings, even for the non-philosophers among them. There is to me a deep ring of truth in R.C. Zaehner's pronouncement on the mystic: 'he has had a vision in which all things cohere and conspire towards the good, in which everything falls into its due place – except our fellow men.'[102] The obdurate, cursed, individuality of our fellow human beings must remain in the field of vision of the philosopher. Much is said in Platonic scholarship about the city refusing to be ruled by philosophy. Something should also be said about the shortcomings of the philosopher. Why should he accept political responsibility when he still has some way to go towards perfection in authenticity? Who is he to think he can intervene more wisely than others in the world of the inauthentic?

The point, according to Plato, is that the philosopher should not, if he can help, break any of his bonds with his fellow human beings. The interpreter today can attribute optimism to Plato. The cosmology is profoundly optimistic: the entire cosmos is ruled by soul; all souls have a common father; there is a kinship between men, the whole universe, and the wise and just god. There is generosity, even in the *Laws*: 'We must take our chance with the crowd.'[103] The pole of the divine is a strong luminous presence among men. But the dark pole of necessity is still there. Men are stupid, blind, inattentive. The law cannot ever control chaos completely. So we may come to the pessimistic view: the persecution of the righteous seems the only thing certain in this world.

We should not forget, however, that pessimism and optimism are views of the mind. A dialectical philosopher weighs such views, pits one against the other, but never comes to rest on either. And as public man, teacher, and writer, Plato seems to have been guided by what we might call a practical wisdom. Is it pessimistic or optimistic to affirm that 'it is better for everyone to be governed by the divine and the intelligent, preferably indwelling and his own, but in default of that imposed from without'?[104] Such practical wisdom eschews plain certainties. Plato's message will never be single but always ambiguously polar: either contemplate the truth or obey your betters. The presence of such an alternative is inherent in man's mixed condition. While embodied, some souls will learn and some won't. Either know or take counsel from those who do, says Xenophon's Socrates.[105] This practical wisdom does not seem unique to Plato's generation. The *Nicomachean Ethics* quotes Hesiod once: 'that man is altogether best who considers all things himself and marks what will be better afterwards, and at the end; and he, again, is good who listens to a good adviser; but whoever neither thinks for himself nor keeps in mind what another tells him, he is an unprofitable man.'[106]

Plato knows he has two kinds of publics. In the *Apology* we see Socrates testifying to a pure and most austere piety, and expressing it in public before his many judges. In *Crito* we see Socrates in private arguing philosophically on behalf of the laws of the city and the public pieties. The *Republic* envisions a city ruled by a few pure, virtuous people, The *Laws* a city with widespread, common, ordinary virtues. The philosopher remains sensitive to the call of mysticism and to the demands of politics. This kind of literary activity on Plato's part gives us the clue to a vexing question: why no dialogue about piety, 'solving' what *Euthyphro* has left unsolved? Because it would not be politically responsible. A manifesto for public piety would be reactionary and is out of the question. But an open philosophical attack on it would play into the hands of the barrier-breaking Sophists and their political pupils. The wisest thing to do about public piety is to leave it alone and trust that it will go on having some influence in the city. Let us not forget that public piety is a living historical whole: one cannot systematize it any more than one can redesign the horse. A dialogue on scientific piety, however, would tend to dissolve public religion further. Any radical, innovative manifesto for the piety of the cognoscenti would play into the hands of thoughtless men who like to get drunk on language. One also wonders whether such a dialogue would not depart from the principle laid down in *Letter VII*; the best, the highest secret cannot be responsibly, fairly, written down.[107] So Plato's ultimate message on piety is to be gathered from all the creative tensions in his works. He introduces a new piety in the history of religion but he achieves this precisely because he does not speak that much and that clearly about it. It all happens as if piety were too important to him to be defined. Only the commentator who comes twenty-three centuries later is academic enough to think that more good than harm can come from defining both public piety and the piety of the cognoscenti.

6 The languages of a philosopher of religion

We have seen that Plato has invented a literary genre, that of the philosophical dialogue, which portrays intellectual conflicts and yet transcends them thanks to an art of discourse, cultivated among polite intellectuals. In this new, distinctive milieu talk becomes relaxed. Instead of having to conform to opinion in all their public utterances people can, for once, talk as if their ideas have no consequences and are not liable to be disapproved of. It is as if the net of language that is usually woven so tightly around human beings becomes loose. Fresh demands reappear however. People are expected to be reasonable, that is to be coherent (have all their utterances free of mutually contradictory features), to agree to have their incoherencies pointed out, and to be willing to listen to each other's stories (provided they get reasonably quickly to the end). In other words, relaxed though the surroundings may be, people must still adhere to the rules of *logos* and *mythos*.

Philosophical practice requires the exercise of the unique power of the *logos*. Dialectical rigours ask the individual human being to give an account, in words, of his behaviour, of his beliefs, of his quest for what is good. Philosophy demands lucidity about oneself, attention to particulars, precision in expression, coherence. Thus the individual is invited to weave a tight net of language around himself. *Logos* abhors ambiguity. Mythical language has contrasting but equally unique abilities. It can tell in significant terms the story of something alive, such as the soul or the cosmos. It can tell a story in pleasant, probable, loose, living terms. There is something accusatory about the rigours of the dialectic, and something charming about the lilt of stories. Note, however, that Socrates, who cross-examines, is never an ardent, thumotic prosecutor; always kind, he asks his questions only of willing partners; and for him being refuted is not being defeated but being purified.[108]

The problem of a philosophy of religion is to achieve a proper integration of mythical language into philosophical discourse, to make it fully self-sconscious, and thus to establish limits to the claims that *mythos* and *logos* have over each other.

Let us note that the challenge is first literary. The conventions of polite exchange can accommodate the most radical moral confrontations. There is no precedent, however, for the integration of mythical discourse into such social situations. How can oracular utterance, inspired speaking, recourse to myth be inserted as authoritative speaking within the conventions of polite conversation? The inadequacies of a Euthyphro are significant: in the context of the dialogues with Socrates he simply does not have the words to make his behaviour intelligible. Should the limitations of a Euthyphro be deemed too obvious, consider the examples of Glaucon and Adeimantus in the *Republic*: all the arguments they have assimilated buttress a position opposite to that which they hold: they must dumbly ask Socrates to show them in words what they do believe is true. Obviously *logos* and the conventions of probing verbal exchanges have been much 'secularized' or, better, have become a fit vehicle unfit for the expression of any serious dedication of the self, except that to its own interests, as it sees them. Religious convictions, so to speak, come close to being shut up within the selves that have them. The heterogeneity of *mythos* and *logos* is such that giving a free rein to each within a single literary piece presents problems that may well be insurmountable. How can *logos* be itself if it cannot dissect *mythos*, and how can *mythos* be itself without casting aspersions on *logos* and its playful erosion of the weight which traditionalists place on their words? Here again the dialogue as drama provides the answer: in a complex social situation different types of speech find their appropriate place: *logos* and *mythos* in the end do find their specific voices.[109]

Plato, I have suggested, writes dialogues because he has to. The speech of a philosopher must be more than a doctrine that can be assimilated or a witness to the life of an individual subjectivity; it must also be 'an intelligent word graven in the soul of the learner, which can defend itself.'[110] To do justice to Plato as a *philosopher* of religion, we must do more than convey the doctrinal truth, the *logos alethes*, that he arrives at; we must also become conscious of his way of saying it. What then is his specific way? We may start with the question on which interpreters have most frequently stumbled: which myths are to be taken with a grain of salt and which ones are to be heard with utmost seriousness?

The answer to the question lies in realizing that Plato wants us to ask the question. In fifth-century Athens there is no traditional monopolistic hold on the utterance of truth. The tension between *logos* and *mythos* in the dialogues is there to instil in us a sense of the limitations of all language. Consider how often a myth is introduced with warnings about the inadequacy of the language. Why introduce a poor way of saying things except to correct a poorer way yet? With the myth the distortion at least is open and explicit – and questions can be raised about the language that is not aware of its shortcomings.

In the shift between *logos* and *mythos* there is quick movement. Intelligence gifted with *metis* must have subtlety, ruse even, to run fast and catch its prey. There is room for dull plodding in the pursuit of truth in the world as it is. The quick movement enables each language to test the limits of the other. *Mythos* tries to invade the territory claimed by *logos* as its own, only to be invaded in its turn. Who can utter truth with precision? with clarity? The boundaries intrinsic to each manner of speech are not clearly set; the mutual pushing transgresses what boundaries seem established. Language then breaks out of its routines – and remains alive. The weaving together of *logos* and *mythos* even allows for some dramatic reversals. In the cave there are misleading appearances. Some influences (from public speakers and poets, for instance) that seem beneficial are, in fact, harmful. Dionysus unbinds, makes free, loosens, but his emancipated orgiasts are in fact enslaved to a destructive frenzy. Truthful talk must cut through illusions, and what better way is there than leading us into some minor illusion and then pulling the rug out from under our feet, the better to open our eyes so to speak. *Mythos* and *logos* together teach discernment; each language manages to uncover something that remains hidden behind the other manner of speaking. P. Friedländer is most insightful when he indicates the kinship between myth and irony.[111] Philosophy begins in irony, in a detachment from detachment; the philosopher knows that words are inadequate yet has found a way to use words to go beyond words. Mythical discourse is the voice of the mature ironist. It always suggests that the world can be looked at in another way. Most moderns dislike the reticence of this ironist. We are sure that more would be said if more were to be said. Plato knows that, once the distance has been seen between words and things, irony and myth acquire a privileged place among the skills proper to those who are free from *hybris*. *Logos* has begun the emancipation from dead copies of a lost truth; *mythos* continues it.

The philosopher of religion can do his work only thanks to the weaving together of both *mythos* and *logos*. As philosopher *logos* is his native art: looking at religion he looks at *mythos* and appropriates, after transposing it, what *mythos* has to convey, thereby protecting the truth of *logos* by showing its limitations. Modern readers will hardly need to be reminded that philosophy rests upon the prosaic examination of meanings and all the arts of *logos* and of the ongoing exchange. They may need, however, to be reminded of the merits proper to *mythos*. Plato's balancing act between the two is not a peculiar historical position, a transition, say, between a primitive and a more rational age; rather it exhibits a permanent tension in civilized discourse.

Thanks to the dynamic tension, *logos* can remain itself and not become doctrinaire. The philosopher is master of his own *logos* (and responsible for it) but he finds that his *logos* is dependent on a *mythos* that is not his own. Whenever *logos* is not simple expression of desire (or modulation on the theme 'I want'), it is comment, critical most of the time, but comment within a received framework of meaning. *Logos*, the *proprium* of the philosopher, arises along a horizon of which it cannot give a complete account. As W. Hirsch puts it, 'logos is true to its own nature when it denies to itself the capacity to speak of its own rise.'[112] One can see a parallel between the condition of the philosopher of religion and the tragic condition made manifest in the great tragedies: the hero is master of his own action, but he finds that the meaning of it can be discerned only by acknowledging the presence of divine powers. Plato and his reader alike begin with a word that does not entirely come from the free human subjectivity and its intention to speak; it does not even come ultimately from shared intersubjectivity. It is received from the widest horizon.[113]

By leaving *mythos* and *logos* true to their own dynamics and by offering a constant weaving of the two Plato avoids the dead-end characteristic of those religious philosophies in which *mythos* and *logos* are allegedly fused in some doctrine or where some claims are made for the 'philosophical' truth of some theological statement.[114] Plato works within a philosophical tradition that has elaborated its *logos* by a rejection of *mythos*; he can also feel the claims of a religious tradition that speaks the language of *mythos* and eschews the easy evidences of *logos*. Plato re-establishes a link between the two streams but does not merge them. The life of the mind simply acquires the art of living in the movement between the two. The language of the philosopher, even of the philosopher of religion, has given up the yearning for oracular, sacred utterance. The body of the world and the cloth of language still do not fit exactly. But there is a life to the language that emulates that of the divine animal. Language is freed from any doctrinaire attempt to freeze it in any set of rules. *Mythos* remains a discourse along with that of *logos*.

Thanks to this permanent tension, *mythos* keeps its liveliness and inventiveness. No single overarching myth is allowed to do its rationalizing, encompassing work unchallenged. New stories, highly imaged language keep suggesting that there is more said elsewhere. Myths in a piece of writing interrupt the lulling, persuading power of closely reasoned prose that operates so effectively within a hidden framework of meaning. Myths are, within writing, a safeguard against the perils of writing. At best, one stops reading and lays the book aise to start thinking. Plato 'eschews converting reflections into doctrines,' writes R. Weingartner.[115] This restraint has something to do with the ongoing living presence of mythical discourse. We do not witness in Plato that dreary decaying of philosophy into doctrinaire metaphysics that occurs so often in the hands of 'religious' or 'secular' philosophers who try to hard to protect their 'rational' doctrines.[116] The recourse to mythical discourse serves to check the confidence one has in the common outcome of logical discourse.

Finally, and perhaps most importantly, *mythos* is necessary to reawaken in the soul the forces of eros. We have seen how in dialogue *logos* allies itself with *thumos*: the interlocutor cannot lose face by becoming incoherent; he must push on talking in good faith and consistently.[117] But the alliance between *logos* and *thumos* is fraught with danger. We have just said that in post-traditional societies *logos*, left to itself, can degenerate into self-assured, rigid, humourless doctrines. It can also degenerate into the heated decayed rhetoric practised by the power-hungry who play upon the thumotic passions of the many; there *logos* had become the language of evil persuasion. The evil persuasion of *logos* is inherent in all public language upholding buttressing order. All architects of consensus, praiseworthy beings though they are, are unwilling accomplices of some form of oppression. The clarities offered always mask the repression of some: there are, always, victims of consensus.[118] Thus every definite utterance about the Good must be negated. Because every such utterance is also social fact. Social order is loyal to power, to those in power. Eros is more egalitarian. (Sex, I should recall, is the most democratic pleasure.) Stories always awaken individual interests. By its very nature mythical discourse interrupts the powerful flow of persuasiveness aimed at the listener. The listening soul gains breathing space, so to speak, to be itself again. For once, something is left unsaid. Besides the speech that persuades, teaches Aristotle, there is also the poetic speech, which makes men whole by representing (imitating) the truth, by showing the truth rather than by teaching the truth about it. Aristotle's poetry does not argue, and on this point is is a recognizable descendent of Plato's *mythos*.[119] While images interrupt the persuasive process that aims at agreement on a point, they establish contact – and very persuasively – with the inner, secret desire for a fuller life. Even those of us with a strict sense of reality still have a little confined world of fantasies where the desire for greater happiness is rampant. There is no love of life, I think, without these happy fantasies. Myth re-establishes contact with that secret yearning. It creates some legitimate space for an individual's love of life and of the world.[120] The vague, loose, imaginative quality of myth and the playful shifts to it are thus antidotes to the hardened and frequently despairing or cynical obscurities created by clear routinized prose.

To let images stir that inner eros is of course dangerous.[121] Using the concepts of an anthropologist we can say that mythical discourse introduces liminality into human discussion.[122] Human beings on thresholds are neither here nor there; the boundaries of the ego seem about to be dissolved. By showing characters caught up in aesthetic visions and released from the pressures of consensus Plato introduces threshold language in the texture of his discourse. This manner of writing, as always, endangers existing structures. Everything shown at the borders of an existing ordered world carries the threat of disorder as well as the promise of a better order. Every individual in process of change risks disintegration as well as maturing. Pentheus finds Dionysus suspect – yet Dionysus attracts others. To let *logos* and *mythos* interact is to risk the sort of drama exhibited in the *Bacchae*. Eros is a welcome ally against the constrictions of a *thumos* that has become a selfish passion. But eros in its search for new authority may also fail to transmute desire and abandon itself to yet more unreliable authorities. *Logos* is always prudent rationality; it usually knows very well how to circumscribe the risks inherent in *mythos* stirring erotic fantasy. Today many have come to believe that poetry is 'only' an aesthetic enjoyment. Myths, many say, have become mere literature.[123] Plato knows better: myths have the power to orient an action-determined imagination. To tell stories has a powerful thrust, and must be done with care.

At this point Plato would say, I believe, that to stir eros is a *kalos kindunos*, a noble risk. For the prize is fair and the hope great (these are Socrates' terms about belief in immortality).[124] There is for him a divine madness. I would hasten to add that the risk is controlled. First of all, the only myths that let the periphery enter into the centre are myths that narrate a destiny of the soul that stresses its teachability and a destiny of the world that emphasizes the power of mind over it. An eros stirred by these images is not about to be blinded into tearing apart the flesh of its own son. Furthermore, all myths appear within the civilized conventions of polite dialogue. The literary reality embodies Plato's beliefs about what myths are allowed to become central. The play of myth is always controlled and kept within secure limits: Jacques Derrida writes that with Plato the game is always contained within the boundaries (*garde-fous*) of ethics and politics.[125] We must recall that Plato has consciously chosen to be an author, and a somewhat elusive one; he appears twice at the fringe of his dialogues and does not write a single preface. For him publishing is not a philosophical act but a moral and political one.

To sum up, no sequence of *logos* and no myth is ever allowed to entrap the mind in a false certainty. What we find in Plato is a balanced movement. *Logos* is lucid, as far as it goes, perfectly, but it can never say things fully. Ever since Heraclitus, philosophers have feared that their speech may well have to be unending if it is to try to say it at all.[126] In contrast *mythos* has a nice roundness and seems to hit the nail on the head, but it remains partly obscure and does not offer an exact meaning. On the things that matter most to them men can achieve a measure of understanding only by a discourse that achieves some sort of balance between *logos* and *mythos*.[127] No single language is entirely adequate. But *logos* and *mythos* together enable man to move towards measure. As literary dramatist Plato achieves a balance between reality and illusion, rationality and irrationality, tradition and innovation. This balancing act, says B. Simon, is that of sanity itself.[128] There is in Plato a great confidence in the powers of language, limited though each of the modes may be. He has the artistry to call on yet further powers – this he must do if he is to persuade – and the control never to let any further power become tyrannical. Plato has no patience for the oracular authority of the old magicians (the *goes*) and does not yet share the Hellenistic awe before the divine sage (the *magos*). Yet he never lets his language sink into the dull plains of prose that bewitch no one, except the dull. He is prepared to let language, for a while, go on a holiday. For Wittgenstein 'philosophical problems arise when language goes on holiday.'[129] 'The results of philosophy,' he adds, 'are the uncovering of one or another piece of plain nonsense and of bumps that the understanding has got by running its head up against the limits of language.'[130] Plato's erotic philosopher keeps running against the limits of language. And to Plato the limits, while there, are sometimes somewhat soft, and certainly hardly ever in a precisely predictable location. The natural skills of language are beautifully used in Plato; they are also carefully protected. He never interferes with them in the name of some unnecessarily crude theory of what language can do. Paradoxically his *logos* as philosopher of religion remains firm because it remains fluid.

Philosophy of religion may well be Plato's greatest achievement because it shows the full range of his battle. Philosophy, writes Wittgenstein, 'is a battle against the bewichment of our intelligence by means of language.'[131] The whole man, Plato would add, is the victim when there are such bewitchments. A bewitched mind cannot pay 'attention to reality inspired by, consisting of, love.' And then the process of the transmutation of desire is blocked. Plato battles against bewitchment on specific fronts as his philosophy becomes philosophy of religion. He battles against the bewitchment still caused by the slow, solemn power of decaying myth. *Logos* does the work here. He also battles against the quick, lusty errands of desire. Historically Plato's philosophizing is located between the mellow voice of conservative piety and the strong, novel historical passions. I am prepared to say that philosophy of religion still has a job to do against the bewitchment of our intelligence by means of conservative pieties and progressive passions, immobile dogmas and ever renewed historical appetites.

There is one final warning. The philosopher of religion talks about his own talking. He thus can see how the transmutation of desire is done, how the powers of language are stretched. but being absorbed in the looking means interrupting the process. The natural powers of language are expressed when they are expressed, not when they are looked at. We must therefore return to one dialogue of Plato's, not to observe how it is done, but to see what is shown.

7 The *Symposium*: the philosopher of religion at work

Again we should try to let Plato himself make the demonstration. The *Symposium* is our best opportunity to see him philosophizing about religion. First of all, the dialogue exhibits the full variety of levels of speech to which Plato has recourse. Secondly, by focusing on the topic of love, the dialogue turns to the areas of concern which are those of religion, both in its traditional public and in its philosophical personal form: love is the link between men and gods; it is the source of the yearning for perfection and immortality; and it is the source of all genuine solidarity and spiritual relationship among men. No one denies that a religion of cosmic love is among Plato's legacies to the Hellenistic era. That the *Symposium* is the dialogue which is most relevant to our understanding of Plato's philosophizing on religion is to me so obvious that I must express surprise at not seeing the point made more often. This is probably because, in keeping with the conventions of his day and his class, Plato's discussion of love draws at first all its illustrations from paederastic or homosexual love; this has often shocked or embarrassed readers, and the impression has grown that the dialogue focuses its understanding of love on a rather 'special' topic. But it is easy to get two things clear: every single speaker directly handles the world of myth, and from Phaedrus to Socrates all try to find in myths of love the key to an understanding of the human condition. None of the other dialogues as a matter of fact is so rich in myths, and Hirsch appropriately calls the *Symposium* 'a pyramid of myths.'[132]

Plato the poet stages for us a meeting between Apollodorus and his friend in which the former is asked to narrate, yet once again, the events that occurred and speeches that were spoken at a banquet many years ago. The scene promptly shifts from this 'real' dialogue to the narration by Apollodorus of a series of exchanges (chat, fast dialogue, and longish speeches) at a banquet in which he was not a participant but of which he has heard from a witness, Aristodemus. Apollodorus has had occasion to polish his account by telling and retelling it; more important, he has had occasion to check some details with Socrates, who also was a participant. The impression should nevertheless stand that we hear of the banquet through many and somewhat unreliable filters. Chronological distance is patent; around 385 Plato writes about a conversation that is supposed to have occurred around 400, and that conversation narrates what is supposed to have happened at a banquet in 416. The reader cannot escape a sense of temporal remoteness and doubtful or incomplete transmission. Apollodorus was not there in 416. Aristodemus, his main witness, fell asleep and did not hear the end; he is also a notorious atheist. Furthermore three of the participants, Phaedrus, Eryximachus, and Alcibiades, were, at a date following that of the banquet, associated in the desecration of the Hermae, the most scandalous impiety that their generation had known. The discussion of 'religion' proceeds in, to say the least, ambiguous circumstances. S. Rosen says that this overall context 'moderates the religious aspects of the speeches.'[133] To this I might add that the discussions at the banquet at first occur, naturally, in the state of mild drunkenness which is commended in the *Laws*. The discipline of the *logos* is relaxed; mania can seep through and bolder thoughts be expressed. The discussion of religion, therefore, takes place in an atmosphere that we might call 'demonic,' clearly in an ambiguous, troubling one that is, in some regards, inauspicious. Can it be that Plato wants to convey that in religion we do not see the ascent of the soul to the Good; we hear of it at some remove; and when we are told, whatever we do see is through murky waters? In religion we never hear the voice of God pure and unsullied.

And then the banquet itself has inauspicious beginnings. Invited to it, Socrates dresses up, that is he takes a bath and puts on sandals. But arriving at the house, he stops in his tracks and stands in the hall, caught up in solitary thought. In vain the host begs him to come in. This unusual guest is no slave to polite conventions (Socrates after all was claimed by the Cynics as their model). Has his demon stopped him? What distant drummer is he listening to? Does he have doubts about the company he is about to keep?

Socrates finally joins the other guests; the meal proceeds. With the food out of the way and the drinking about to begin, it is decided to embark on a series of 'speeches in praise of love.'[134] The participants are invited to find their religious voice, their own tone of expansive conviction. We do not expect exercises in analysis. It is agreed that each will speak in turn. The point is made that, 'whereas other gods have poems and hymns made in their honour, the ancient and mighty god, love, has never had a single encomiast among all the poets who are so many.' And yet in time even the utility of salt has been made the subject of some discourse.[135] The dialogue, quite boldly, presumes to add another piece to the religious literature of Greece. A daring poet, we are to understand, has finally arisen who will praise love and will try to hymn it worthily. But this poet is also a philosopher; his praise will not be a straightforward hymn. A complex piece showing the meanderings of men as they try to praise love is the only way to offer praise suitable to the great god in an age where men are victims of numerous errors, have lost touch with the gods, and need to be awakened and shrewdly led to the truth. The new songs Plato consciously injects into the tradition of religious hymnary will thus be presented in a new way.

In the first part of the dialogue we hear four speeches which turn out to be four types of 'modern' fifth-century 'theologies' or religious philosophies. The first speaker, Phaedrus, culls from the pre-Olympian mythology a variety of 'evidences' about love. He is something of a literalist (and on this point reminds me of Euthyphro) and assembles texts that praise this most wonderful god. At no point is he aware of other ways of looking at his subject, or that the lore about Eros is an ambivalent one. His evidences support a very simple doctrine: love is the cause of all of our highest blessings. Lovers are inspired to zeal and courage and thus can do what is noble. Love provides us with all virtue and happiness.

The simplicity of Phaedrus is brought to light by the next speaker, Pausanias, who refuses to praise love in such an indiscriminate manner. He notes that there is a heavenly Aphrodite and a common one. His whole approach is reminiscent of the allegorists and other moralists who discriminate in the tradition by considering the wholesomeness of its influences. (Pausanias is somewhat naïve on another point, however: the noble and the ignoble are to him unambiguous concepts.) Thus Pausanias has no praise for the vulgar love practised by the meaner sort of men, who love women as well as boys, who are focused on the body rather than the soul, and who care not 'if the manner be noble or not.'[136] Noble love has a passion only for bright boys: it brings about a strong friendship and noble attachment, and those who find the aspect of gratification disgraceful understand nothing of it. What Pausanias offers, thus, is praise of the higher paederasty, in which an older and wiser man and a youth mutually improve each other and are fired to feel a zealous concern for their own virtue. This love is thus precious for both public and private life. In contrast with Pausanias, what Phaedrus had to say appears singularly utilitarian and uncouth: love is good because useful. With Pausanias the manner and the intent matter. Pausanias, however, who makes such strong claims for the moral superiority of his own 'refined' cultural tastes, cannot find a basis for standards of goodness except in the manners of his own 'educated' class.

The third speaker, Eryximachus, a physician, reflects the speculative cosmologies that flourished in Ionian circles. Myths, there, have been reinterpreted and have become scientific explanations of sorts. To Eryximachus love is an affection found universally, a life force or universal fluid, one might say. All arts, from medicine to divination, strive to separate fair love from foul and 'convert one into the other.'[137] The physician, a sort of technical demiurge, serves as the model for all human actions. All natures have their own tendencies; their loves are to be properly nursed, curbed or strengthened, so that peace, happiness, and friendship are made to reign everywhere. Love properly tended is the purveyor of communion and friendship between gods and men and among men themselves.

These 'scientific' pieties are succeeded by 'another vein of discourse,' offered by Aristophanes.[138] Aristophanes is downright funny. And his comic relief is welcome. For one thing, after all this talk of souls communing, the body reasserts its rights. Aristophanes has missed his turn in the speaking because of hiccups. And, when he speaks, he calls a spade a spade. His account of the three kinds of original round human beings, male-male, female-female, male-female, of their split in half and subsequent attempts to reunite, never eschews anatomical details and manages to introduce the idea that procreative heterosexual coupling is quite natural, at least for some.[139] One should note also that in this fourth speech the handling of religious myths has lost the appearance of seriousness. At this stage in the development of religious philosophy myths can become completely aestheticized; they are amusing stories, which, when cleverly told, charm, entertain, and make witty points. We should of course ask ourselves whether there is not more seriousness in Aristophanes' jollity than in all the ponderousness of the three previous speakers; his intervention after all has a very demystifying impact.

These four speeches are enough to establish an atmosphere. There is a variety of religious philosophies. Numerous different religious doctrines have arisen now that *logos* has become distinct from myth. All these religious philosophies try in different ways to find a human way of speaking about divine things, or of telling the truth about a god like love. And these philosophies all have their say in an atmosphere of relaxed pluralism: everyone declares himself quite pleased with everybody else's speech, and the search for the best speech is a gentlemen's pastime. That all the speeches share in the same refined ethos (with the hint of an exception for Aristophanes) should not, however, obscure their profound incompatibilities: doctrines buttressed by texts serving as proofs and scientific speculations do not mix in religious philosophy.

At this point in the banquet an interlude introduces one of those shiftings of gears that raise the participants to a new hypothesis and higher level. Agathon, the next speaker, is self-conscious about his speaking: 'let me say first how I ought to speak, and then speak.' Philosophy, as we define it, seems to come to maturity only in this speech. Along with the art of speaking about one's own speaking as well as about the thing one speaks on comes the genuine turn to 'reality' or the objective correlate. Agathon makes this point emphatically: 'the previous speakers, instead of praising the god love and unfolding his nature, appear to have congratulated mankind on the benefits which he confers upon them. But I would rather praise the god first and then speak of his gifts.'[140] The rule of love, we then hear, is but recent among the gods. Love is the youngest of all the gods and remains ever young. Always delicate, he finds his abode in soft and tender things. After such praise of the god comes the recounting of his benefits. Love is alien to all violence and never gives injury. He wins all men's willing service: a poet himself, his skill is to enable all men to poetize, that is to teach, to create. Love gives men a creative excellence. So Agathon concludes by inviting all to follow in love's footsteps, 'sweetly singing in his honour and joining in that sweet strain with which love charms the souls of gods and men alike.'[141] Tumultuous applause greets this speech. The bloom of successful early maturity (Agathon is approximately thirty) is clearly visible: he is the happy host; he is the beloved of Pausanias; and his first tragedy has just been a success.

But Plato does not let this well-received speech of Agathon's stand as the final word, far from it. Socrates' turn comes next, and he begins, as usual, by asking questions. In the manner of the earliest dialogues, Agathon is forced to start from the beginning. First of all, he is made to see the relational nature of love – which is always love of something (this point had been forcibly made by Aristophanes but was wasted on Agathon). Then Agathon is driven to the conclusion that love desires that which he has not already (200e). Love desires beauty – and is not beautiful. He knows want (this casts doubt on his divinity). Agathon's words were beautiful enough, but at the end of the exchange he must confess that he knew not what he was talking about (201b). The whole lovely cumulative edifice of speeches has collapsed. Men's elegant babble has not brought them near the truth. Philosophy shatters any easy sense of unity between men, their beliefs, their speeches, and the divine; a conversion and an ascent must occur. Men start their serious speaking only when they examine their differences. The *logos* is at first dialogue. The philosopher is fully conscious of the fact that the *logos* of men occurs in a social context and is not at all the kind of speaking that the mythical mind used to hear in myths. From this perspective all five of the previous speeches, for all their sophisticated 'secular' outlook, are but attempts to prolong mythical thought in an age of reason: the myths are rationalized in some manner or other, but in their expansive mood the gulf between human speaking and divine reality is somehow papered over. The philosophical dialogue cannot escape the conclusion that love and speaking on love alike both start in lack or want, lack of the beautiful, lack of a grasp of the truth, lack of an adequate language, lack of the good. Only Socrates is fully conscious of this human starting-point of all speaking. Pausanias spoke of his desire to attain virtue, but since he does not know what virtue is, his admission of want hides *hybris*. Agathon does not at all realize that human speaking about love has to start with the real sense of an absence.

The state of want being perceived, Socrates returns to the conventions of the banquet and proceeds, in his turn, to give his speech. We are, however, no longer treated to the exhibition of another type of religious doctrine. The decisive philosophical turn has occurred; the soul has realized that what it yearns for is absent. Men have started their ascent; perhaps they now have a chance of not misinterpreting what Socrates has to say. His speech is a narration of how he himself has been instructed on love by a wise priestess named Diotima.[142] Love, she says, is a *daimon* (not a god), the son of Poverty and Resourcefulness. Diotima proceeds then to set in clear light the exact object of love's desire: behind everyone's desire for good things and happiness lies the fact that all (note the emphasis that all are lovers) mortal natures desire immortality. Mortal natures, however, can succeed in only one way: by generation. And 'leaving behind a new creature in place of the old' is achieved first of all by having children, and then also by 'impregnating souls,' namely by communicating virtue. Human beings who have been so far tutored in the lore of love can advance (and only the philosophers do so) to the grasp of a higher mystery. They may rise to a wondrous vision: 'beauty absolute, separate, simple and everlasting' is the final object of all who delight in beautiful things. They may rise to the contemplation of essential beauty. Love is the best helper our human nature can find towards this ascent.[143]

Let us now pause to reflect on the contrast between the speech of Socrates-Diotima and the previous ones.[144] Some ironies should not be lost on us. That the religious truth comes to this audience from the lips of a woman is itself an irony. That the apparently most sophisticated case for the paederastic view of love is made by Agathon is another; as every reader of Plato's dialogue knows, when he was older, Agathon was ridiculed as an effeminate, as Aristophanes did on the stage five years after the alleged date of the banquet (Agathon is no Doric youth learning manly arts in the company of the older Pausanias). Then there is a major doctrinal contrast: to Diotima love is not a god but a self-movement that is interior to the soul and present in all souls. Furthermore, in human beings love must obey the rules of human nature. One of them is that immortality is to be achieved only through paternity or maternity and moral influence on other human beings. The other is that, if we want to be 'creative' and transmit spiritual things, we better tend first to the demanding business of procreation and nurturing of children. Note that from this perspective the reproach of self-centered utilitarianism can be made against the view of love held by all speakers and not just by Phaedrus: whether crude or refined, all hold a calculative view of human reason aiming at securing one's worldly ease; all consider love a good investment from the point of view of the individual.

Finally, says Diotima, love is a demon. (Although not divine, we would say love is religious.) The demonic realm, or the spiritual, is between the divine and the mortal: 'God with man does not mingle: but the spiritual is the means of all society and converse of men with gods and of gods with men.'[145] Love happens, grows or dies, in history. Myths are the appropriate ways of speaking of it. As a religious reality love is a bridge between men and gods. Men are submitted to the law of becoming and must die. But in love men are religious; through love, through the procreation and nurture of their own, through the cultivation of moral and political virtue, they can achieve a measure of immortality. The experience of love places mortal men on a bridge between themselves and the gods, a bridge which may be wide and strong, or weak and narrow, depending on the state of health of mankind at a given point in its becoming. That spiritual bond, historical though it is, has a nature, and men flout this nature only to their detriment. Specifically, lovers must learn to care for what they love as well as care about it.

What Plato has just accomplished is a redefinition of eros. What initially has been conceived of as a desire, a desire to own, has in the end turned out to be an aspiration. Desires can be satisfied. An aspiration is capable of transcending the satisfactions awarded by obtained objects. An aspiration sees the inadequacy of these much desired objects and renews the impetus of desire towards new areas. If eros is still to be labelled a desire, let it be a desire for all really good things, a desire for happiness, and thus an educable desire. By redefining eros and making it an aspiration Plato makes it a movement of the soul that is capable of educating and orienting the desirous part of the soul and directing it to ever worthier objects. How thorough is the redefinition of eros can also be shown by the shift from the hunger for possession to the desire to beget. Lovers are viewed as people who move from the wish to acquire to the wish to bring forth.

From this perspective Agathon's speech, which had the appearance of being the best, is by far the worst. His adherence to the formal rules of philosophy has made his speech an apparent progress in the dialogue, but it is in fact a regress. Its tone of seriousness, its elevation of feeling, and its philosophical intensity are dangerous and mask a moral shortcoming: caught up in his cult of youth, infatuated with artistic creativity, Agathon celebrates creativity for its own sake; of all things, this poet has the self-serving impudence to claim that homosexuals are the most creative! Callicles has given us the brutal, power-crazed version of the world upside down, Agathon the sophisticated, cultured version. His is the version of an intelligentsia of weak men who are inebriated with their verbal facility and cultural poise: they find their spiritual 'activity' much superior to the productive and generative activities of common householders. But those who praise 'spiritual' genesis over generation, and at the cost of generation, have reached social sterility. They have also lost touch with that which is.[146] The first five speeches marvellously excite yearnings and elicit associations in a way that rarely fails to draw out the reader's sense of his own eros. But only the touch of Socrates awakens us from the dream of desire so well fostered by imaged language. He reorients us towards the dream of the desirable. All objects of the dreams of desire are inadequate save that which is desirable. Diotima is the educator of desire.

But let us return to the dialogue. Even Socrates' doctrine (which is the true doctrine and stands a chance of being properly received by the soul) is not the last word. His inspired speech gives way to an ambiguous human scene. Drunken revellers led by Alcibiades knock on the door and are asked in. We have left the sublime; the scene is decidedly human again. This has the immediate effect of relieving the moral tension. Without such an interruption the serious, and I mean *serious* this time, existential clash between Socrates and Agathon and his like was bound to break into the open. The first speakers have an erroneous view of love; they are caught up in illusions. But as the most ordinary experience of love shows, a lived, felt illusion becomes the truth to the experiencer.[147] Deriding Socrates or labelling Agathon as the victim of an illusion and as a morally sordid lover would have been a grave breach of the conventions of hospitality and bibulous commensality. And yet such jarring notes are bound to occur when the religious truth has been spoken in the world of erroneous religious opinions.[148] So we are spared that unpleasantness by the arrival of the revellers, and an unexpected speech is made by one of them, one by the way who is well in his cups. Bibulousness, moderate at first, held before us the promise of a heightened 'inspired' speech that would raise mankind to a new level and enhance its ordered life. And bibulousness did open up the depths of the souls so that the conflict between the sort of desire embodied in Agathon and that in Socrates became visible. But from this point on, drunkenness disrupts the sympotic order. The banquet as a social form henceforth disintegrates.[149]

Informed of the topic under discussion and invited to take a turn and speak, Alcibiades chooses not to praise a god but to praise Socrates. (The reasons he gives are part of conventional small talk; the fact, to my mind, is that he is not a man to speak of divine things and is in no condition to do so; we do not remain at the height reached by Socrates but Plato does not let us fall too low. Alcibiades, like Aristophanes, is graced by a certain charm based on honesty.) Socrates is compared to a Silenus (we again hear of a fascinating appearance that may mislead.) Beautiful virtues hide behind an ugly exterior. Like a flute-playing satyr, Socrates bewitches all those who come near him, but when he has drawn them to himself, all he does is philosophize; he does not *use* his prey, but talks with it. Alcibiades also praises Socrates' endurance (especially his endurance of cold, a quality much admired by Dorians), his martial courage, and his self-control. Note the irony: this most drunken speech ends up with a praise of restraint and temperance. There is also a contrast: Alcibiades' speech is far from self-serving; it is rather self-deprecating. In all other cases save Socrates, the loosening of the tongues only allowed the speakers to make thorough fools of themselves. There are thus many redeeming features in the speech of Alcibiades, the young man who came to a bad end. He does not attempt the inspired level of Socrates (whom he did not hear in any case). He launches a new genre: the praise of the philosopher. And his praise has a quality of moral honesty: he knows that philosophy is not for him, or rather that his preferences take him elsewhere. His speech is also quite worldly. But for all his low style he cannot avoid all mythical expression: he describes Socrates as a *daimôn* (all subsequent presentations of Socrates as a mythical figure are rooted in this speech and its great metaphors). Being no philosopher, Alcibiades cannot rise to an appreciation of the demonic or religious as such, but he is human enough to acknowledge the power of the religious reality that has touched him. Note also that his speech thereby accepts the rule laid down by Socrates in his absence: a speech on love is to praise a demon, not a god.

Through this speech of Alcibiades Plato maintains a subtle architectonic structure. He, as philosopher of religion, has taken us all the way to a potentially conflictual expression of his religious philosophy; he now takes us back to an affirmation, not of some pseudo-religiousness, but of philosophical commitment. What Alcibiades remembers best is that Socrates does not get caught up in the fascination of love but wants to *talk* all the time. The dialogue does not sustain Socratic heights throughout, but when its intense vision of truth relaxes, it comes to rest in praise of dialogue. Thus is affirmed a twofold Platonic heritage: as religious and philosophical poet Plato has founded the interiorized religion of cosmic love that the Hellenistic age learned from the speech of Diotima-Socrates (a religion to which, we must add, only a philosopher could arrive, as the *Symposium* shows, even though non-philosophers can assimilate it). As philosopher, however, Plato's major contribution is a philosophy of religion, the enduring message of which is the method rather than the doctrine. So Alcibiades brings us down to anecdotes, daily details that show the master of irony at work in conversation. Alcibiades is drunk, but he testifies to the value of the most sober, uninspired speech. The *Symposium* that has begun with grand mythical world-views finishes with a rather common, cool description of the sober and austere habits of a man who does not act on illusions.

When Alcibiades is finished, more revellers come in. There is no order left (*kosmos*) and all 'are forced to drink a vast amount of wine.' The reader is taken away from a process that now leads nowhere. Some of the guests leave. Aristodemus, our narrator's source, falls asleep; he wakes up at dawn, only to see that Socrates and the dramatists Aristophanes and Agathon are still talking, with Socrates driving them to the conclusion that the same man can have the knowledge to write both comedy and tragedy – and driving them to sleep as well. Philosophy does not stop until there is only one left to philosophize. With the last lines Socrates takes on mythical proportions in the eyes of the reader as well as those of Alcibiades. The two dramatists fall asleep at dawn; Socrates leaves the house, goes to a gymnasium, washes up, and spends a usual day. This man does not need to rest; this man, we sense, will never die.

11

Un-Platonic postscript

I The end of tragedy?

The *Symposium* ends by telling us that Socrates, Aristophanes, and Agathon spent the rest of the night discussing tragedy and comedy, with the philosopher arguing before the comic poet and the tragic poet that the same man can have the knowledge required for writing both sorts of plays. Plato is so skilled at writing philosophy in a manner that requires philosophical interpretative activities on the part of his readers that he even leaves us an unrecorded conversation to comment upon.

Clearly the interpreter is now on his own. The Platonic dialogues show us the birth of philosophy (we have had occasion to stress the vigorous pedagogical power of the foundational discourse). The account of the origins of philosophy, however, should not be allowed to exercise a numbing power. Thus I shall venture to take on the problem that is left unsolved: in what way can philosophy articulate the conflict between the tragic vision and the comic one and thereby rise above both?

Jean-Yves Chateau has argued that historically tragedy and comedy together made philosophy possible.[1] A conflict existed between the two highest forms of public speaking. Tragic plays make human beings conscious of their condition and of the dimensions of powerlessness implicit in it: tragedies elicit wonder, awe, fear, even a sense of scandal. They hit us with a strong sense of our limitations; they feed a hunger for understanding. There is so much for us to think about, and what we have to think about gives us so much to think. And yet human beings seem to think so rarely – and then so poorly: they keep coming up against walls they have failed to see. And in their passionate and blind pursuits they kill and get killed. No justice seems possible among them, except the divine sort of justice that keeps punishing those who prove themselves unable to learn. There is nevertheless a redeeming feature in the tragic religious awe: insight into our initial inability to learn and our subsequent opportunity to learn through suffering brings some relief.

Comedy has a counter-message. Living human beings eat, drink, carouse, and make love (heterosexually): the repetitious pursuit of simple pleasures, then, puts grander problems in perspective. Of course human beings do not learn: but all can laugh at the silliness of others and occasionally at their own. And laughter brings relief and occasionally some cure. In any case, no one gets killed for ignoring his or her limits; the consequences of stupidity turn out to be lots of ridicule or a few blows. Comedy shows that the ideas we have in our heads are more foolish than the performances of our bodies. Above all it becomes clear that human beings should not take themselves too seriously. Getting the audience to laugh at the sight of a (fake, oversized) erect phallus is both crude and easy; it is also profoundly meaningful because it conveys a sense of insolence and a boldness that undercut the self's absorption in the tragic articulation of his problems. If tragedy articulates the seriousness of life, comedy by having fun casts a cooling glance on the games we play and restores a grasp of some of the simplicities of life. Comedy enhances the power to think objectively (if not passionately) about our problems. The tragic hunger for justice and understanding together with the witty levity and ironic resources of comedy jointly give birth to philosophy. The works of Aeschylus embody the magic of language that ventures to cast its light into the darkest unknown. The works of Aristophanes give us the antidote: we see actors speaking crudely, ignorant of the contradiction between their works and their deeds, and we see that human living goes on in spite of the contradiction.

There is an apparently deep and insoluble conflict between the two paths open to the endeavours of human intelligence. The tragic course follows the direction originally given by the *Iliad*: human discourse comes to rest only in the becalmed narrating of a funeral. An absolute limit is what human beings keep coming up against. Social passions, eros and *thumos* together, are irrepressible. And they make for disaster. Agamemnon and Achilles, who suffer from no shortage of women, fight over Briseis to save face. Social desire flowers in ambition, rivalry, hybris, war. All social efforts are tragic because a hidden scenario overrules that of calculating individual or corporate desire and controls the sequence of events. Angry men lose control, come to nought, literally, before the will of the gods and death. The city, where we act out our lives motivated by *thumos* and eros, is a Mycenaean prison: it has massive stone walls that have not built and we come out of it only in death.[2]

Comedy unfailingly shows how intelligence survives. Through luck and pluck Odysseus stays alive while all his companions get killed. And the *Odyssey* ends with him getting home and climbing into bed with Penelope. Little dignity (or none) is seen in suffering, unless the sufferer learns from it how to become happy again. Social passions are exposed as silly. What is really irrepressible is ordinary desire (the erect phallus again). Why make fools of ourselves in tiresome social rivalry when simple pleasures remain available? Aristophanes punctures all socially acquired dignity by drawing attention to the simple biological limit below – male politicians are ridiculous: this is proved by their wives who refuse to sleep with them until they make peace. The city where we act out our lives motivated by *thumos* and eros is as flimsy as a leaky peasant hut. Its demands are a comic sham and the body reminds us that we ought to ignore them. We are not inevitably crushed by our limits; we can be sustained within them.

The theatre, tragic or comic, shows what is beyond language, in language. Dionysus the uneikonic negates our images. The unimaged, unimaginable, is allowed to impinge upon our structured consciousness, tragically or comically. The theatre rearticulates the power of the inarticulate. Oedipus is tragically shattered: in his suffering he maintains his passion for self-recognition; he rises to a pure disinterested knowledge of being and of his relationship to it. His peace, such as it is, comes from words of insight into himself. The male politicians fall apart, comically. On the comic stage no one ever sees clearly into himself: but some see clearly what others are up to (and if we are prepared to see others as mirroring ourselves, we can learn indirectly something about the limits of our insights into ourselves). The sufferings of the tragic hero are relieved by language and the katharsis of insight. In comedies the boy who loves girl does not seek verbal comforts to relieve his suffering. Katharsis comes only when he gets girl. And so to bed. Euphoria. End of story. In both cases the theatre suspends socially entrenched reality, moves out of a dead hypothesis, resymbolizes social existence, restates reality. Human intelligence progresses thereby; it learns how to live with those things it cannot change, or it learns to change those things it can change.[3]

Socrates, we have said, believes a man can be knowing enough to write both tragedies and comedies. Philosophy claims to rise about the division of genre and show everything that is beyond language in language. The fragmented truths of tragedy and of comedy are restored to wholeness. In the juxtaposition of comedy and tragedy as genres we do not know whether what we have in fact are two different perceptions of our encounter with our limits or two different types of encounter. Philosophy tries to say the whole truth within a single genre. It tries to encompass the lessons of both. 'Philosophy endangers manliness; but it is the only source of true human courage, without whose protective influence manliness collapses into tragedy,' writes Thomas Pangle.[4] Tragedies indeed show men and women caught up in a vision of 'virile,' self-assertive heroism that leads to aristocratic chain murders. Philosophy, I should like to add, also endangers sensuousness, but it is the only source of true human tenderness; without its protective influence sensuousness collapses into the repetitive dramas of sensuality.[5] Comedies show men and women caught in irrepressible sensual drives that lead to rustic drunken stupors: this can't be all there is to life. Philosophy opens a common path to men and women; it gives women access to a dignity that does not ape the antics of aristocratic warriors and men access to a kindness that is not the episodic one encouraged by sex. The hard and the soft virtues cease to be gender-specific. Instead of men and women murdering each other on the stage or getting together for sex, philosophy sees them associated in all human ventures. Between men and women, too, philosophy wants justice and not just tragic justice or comic justice.[6]

'Platonism,' writes George Grant, 'is the first rationalism. Its identification of rationality, virtue and happiness was a prodigious affirmation of optimism.'[7] Philosophy itself, it seems to me, is wedded to the notion that the values of rationalism are cosmically sustained. There can be justice in this world. Intelligence can work towards it. Intelligence is not doomed to travel only the roads of tragic maturing or of comic relief. It can see reality whole; it can attune the whole human being to it. It can show the way to a piety that is not gender-specific and help realize justice now. Plato's work is that of a poet: the dialogues are a sort of *poiesis* that is a mimetic representation of life. But they invite to a *praxis*: to political activity that acts with attention to the reality seen. Virtuous action is to be rational (perfectly lucid in relation to the facts of the case) and to eventuate in common happiness. What is this if not overcoming tragedy?

2 Plato's obvious failure

Plato's promise was not kept; his work did not heal his city during its crisis. His answers apparently were not good enough or not presented persuasively enough. His philosophy of religion is in this sense – and that is a sense that concerned him – a failure. Numerous aspects of his proposed revitalization of Greek life were extremely influential,[8] but everyone now knows that the political decay of the Greek city-states was not arrested. In 338 Philip crushed the Greek armies at Chaeronea and Macedonian power became firmly established. Under Alexander and under the Romans Athens was nothing more than a small university town. Its institutions kept functioning but dealt only with local issues. Political life, as deliberation over public ends, was over. As V. Ehrenberg puts it, the political animal became an economical animal.[9] The symposium among citizens became an orgy among consumers.[10]

That Plato's energies and insights could not cure the disease he apparently diagnosed so well clearly disturbs us. Many moderns conclude that his reconstruction should be set aside on the simple grounds that it did not work. Three questions at least should temper our haste to consider the case closed: how long a period of time should a plan be given before it is definitely found wanting in the eyes of 'history'? How accurate anyhow is our own diagnosis of the failure (was it caused by flaws in the plan itself, or did the plan encounter an unusual amount of human cussedness)? And how conclusive, in any case, are the experiences of history? Such queries force us pause before we decide that the subsequent course of history comes down decisively against Plato.

One question, at least, should be faced squarely: could the philosophy that overcame tragedy fall itself victim to a historical tragedy? Was Plato's rationality in the long run doomed just as the rationality of the King of Thebes was in the short run? Yes, answers François Chatelet; the Platonic corpus offers a tragic philosophy of history.[11] Everything comes to an end. Plato himself knew it. The binding and intertwining of men good and bad cannot ever be lasting.[12] Yet Plato, I think, wanted to do better than Socrates. He tried to be politically more successful. He failed. But his trying should be an invitation for us to try better in our turn.

In a vague way the very passage of time between Plato and us, the mere opportunity to analyse his failure, will convince most of us that we have the opportunity to learn something he did not know. (The frequently inarticulate confidence that with the mere passage of time mankind comes to know more is a characteristic feature of moderns.)

Let the issue therefore be this: Plato's failure may well have been inevitable – and for any one of a variety of reasons. But let these reasons be specified and carefully examined. Otherwise, to deem Plato's failure inevitable may well mask a way of surrendering ourselves today to apparent necessities and failing to follow Plato in the effort of thought.

The sense that something must have gone wrong either in the conceptualization or the presentation of the Platonic plan and that we should be able to discern what is was may be overconfident but that much confidence in the power of retrospective human thinking I am prepared to make my own. The demands of our common life today require that this effort of thought be pursued. My conclusions shall, therefore, be un-Platonic in two senses. I known an outcome that Plato could not know. And unlike him, I shall seriously explore the notion that, now that new stories have been told, intervening events should decisively count against his philosophical doctrines.[13] I today differ from him in thinking both that we – on some point or other that is to be articulated carefully – either know better or know different than he did, and that this has a decisive importance for our own historical future. My task thus is to examine critically some of the articulated standpoints that try to make good the modern claim to greater insight.

3 The analysis of a social scientist

The American sociologist Alvin W. Gouldner wrote his book *Enter Plato* to show the Greek origins of social theory.[14] Plato's analyses, he tells us, are among the earliest secular diagnoses; they offer the first self-conscious set of remedies devised for the human condition as a socially organized one. Plato thus embarks upon a gret innovation: critical reflection on human relations. The Greek culture, adds Gouldner, is characterized by the contest system. Envy is highly developed, sensitivity to opinion high, pessimism rampant. The goods men compete for are scarce and uncertain. Any contest must have a loser as well as a winner. Friendships are strained. Few close relationships validate the self. There is an endemic crisis of intimacy. For the most part the lives of Greek men are outward and activist. This develops rationalism: the constant search for better ways to achieve one's objectives accompanied by a lucidity about the impermanence of the self's hold upon what it cherishes.

This contest system tends to undermine the traditional proprieties of interpersonal relations. By the end of the fifth century the undermining has brought about a crisis. Social cohesion has vanished and with it order and any justification the society might have for its claim of ensuring justice among all. Plato, argues Gouldner, develops his therapeutics in these critical circumstances; he bases them on an appeal to reason and he seeks to celebrate both Socrates' loyalty to conscience and his loyalty to the city. He invites the Greeks to an inner-directed existence (to the cultivation of the goods of the soul which are not those one can grab from another man) and marshals a case for believing that the cultivation of such virtues will ensure social order and personal fulfilment.

With the benefit of current social theory Gouldner can unveil hidden assumptions and identify lacunae in Plato's argument.[15] Plato, he tells us, remains something of a tribalist. He sees the horror of civil war but is blind to the evil for foreign wars which remain for him a normal part of life. His reading of poverty is also too simple: he sees in it something that disrupts social solidarity, not a deprivation of human beings. His answer accordingly is to restrain desire, not to increase productivity. In any case he is convinced that there is something insatiable about the body and any attempt to cater to it leads one only into a downward spiral. Plato moreover does not question slavery and does not see it as incompatible with his goal of social justice. Finally, he never suggests that the strife he dislikes so much is caused by a lack of love; it is as if for Plato the emotion of love is too closely linked to bodily needs.[16] He therefore calls men not to love of one another but rather to love of wisdom and of the forms. Plato's overall diagnosis is characteristically and fundamentally ahistorical, concludes Gouldner: he focuses on universal and invariant sources of social ills; he sees all problems originating in bodily desires; he thinks that such problems cannot be remedied but only held at bay. Gouldner shrewdly points out that, unlike piecemeal criticism, there is radicalness in such ahistorical criticism, but there is also pessimism: problems are seen as eternally recurrent.

Gouldner proceeds with a criticism of Plato's therapeutics. Plato offers a 'model-guided strategy of change.' The design proposed is conceived once and for all. While the appeal to reason is coupled with a strategy for change based on consensus, Plato nevertheless infuses reason with an authoritarian bent.[17] The features of such authoritarian power are precisely delineated: reason insists on a hierarchical status for itself which vilifies and renders worthless all other faculties (non-authoritarian reason seeks to co-operate with rather than dominate the lawful dispositions in phenomena). The roots of such authoritarianism are to be found in the slavery society: reason is not meant to be used by and for all men. Reason sees itself in a world drifting to disorder and constantly threatened by restless and chaotic forces. Such a metaphysical picture reflects the social situation: it is the vision proper to a privileged man in a society that exploits slaves.[18] Plato thus seems doomed to produce a social theory suffused with a tragic outlook. His theory of forms invites a radical criticism of society, but at the same time Plato assumes that the society is unchangeable in some structural essentials. Plato is a reformist and yet he does not believe in a history oriented towards an end. For the future he sees only an endless pouring of materials into the ageless mould of the forms and the endless corruption of the casting.

Such a reading certainly sheds light on Plato's effort. One might accept it in order to argue that Plato's reconstruction failed because he was, in spite of all, too bound to a particular group to lead the way to a social order suitable for all, or for most; tolerance of slavery would, in this case, be the major warping factor. A dualistic division between the above and the below keeps reappearing in his work as a deep thought pattern. The description of the earth and the heavens given in *Phaedo* places mud and rot down below and pure jewels up above.[19]

Such contrasts are deeply embedded in Greek myth and literature. Marcel Détienne in *Les Jardins d'Adonis* has unveiled a whole classificatory system of vegetables and minerals that places the wet, dark, and rotting things in the lower world and the dry, luminous, and incorruptible ones in the upper world.[20] Plato the poet cannot help acknowledge the beauty of the sensuous world. But the thinker in him always wants to raise the sights of the writer. A. Kojève has a very nice formula: the world in which Plato lived seemed to him less ugly than it theoretically should have been.[21]

A social label has been given to this sort of classificatory division: social conservatism. A good society is made up of a self-renewing rural aristocracy and of rustics who know their place and acknowledge their betters. There may be thick stupidity (at both ends) in that world but there is discipline. And as Kleon put it to the Assembly (according to Thucydides), 'stupidity coupled with discipline is more useful than cleverness coupled with licence.'[22] Kleon was quite clear and Hobbes translated him tersely: 'a city with the worse laws, if immoveable, is better than one with good, when they be not binding.' There are clever people in cities, they keep arguing with each other, but not one ever obeys. Better a society with dull clods below and conservative heroes above than one where iron and gold are constantly mixed, with the purer metal for ever unable to rise to the top. There are traces of such an aristocratic outlook in Plato: his moral strength is tinged with a touch of contempt for the morally incompetent crowds.[23]

But Plato, I should like to argue, is not a class-bound reactionary. Gouldner reads him wrong on at least one point: *philia* among the citizens is one of the major goals of the *Laws*. Furthermore there is not a trace of ruralism in the dialogues. As a matter of fact they can be most credibly presented as a spirited defence of the urban form of life Plato's civilization has adopted. As Gerry S. Clegg put it, Plato has tried 'to justify in terms of its own philosophical heritage an urban and scientifically oriented society that had developed doubts about some of its most distinctive values.' His Socrates is a city-loving sage, who inquires constantly, accepts that right opinion is the best we can attain in empirical matters, and accepts 'the essential rectitude of the city-state as man's proper interim home.'[24] His achievement is that he has refuted those aspects of the philosophical tradition that tend to undermine the urban civilization (the mysticism of Parmenides and the nihilism of some Sophists) and gathered those features which support the sort of intellectual efforts that are pursued in cities. Clegg adds that Plato never questions one feature of this tradition: the notion that only the unmoving is intelligible; his efforts therefore result in a dualistic system, laden with paradox.[25] Thus on this issue we are back to the world of purity above and rottenness below. Yet at the top of his city we do not find aristocratic warriors but a meritocracy of scientists. Plato, one might suggest, appears to be metaphysically traditional but morally and politically progressive.

Philosophy, we have said, is born at a time when tragedy and comedy have articulated, separately, the whole range of potential human interaction. The intent to control human interaction can henceforth take shape and be in its turn articulated. Plato does it, we should acknowledge, with a heavy and pervasive dependence on the (aristocratic) tragic metaphors. That which controls is always embattled – and heroically takes on the burdens of battle: to be at least true to itself. Reason perceives itself as independence from dominant lies. The rational ruler has to contend against persistent, possibly invincible ignorance. Ignoble desires are to be represented from above, weeded out in constant effort. But with many the effort is doomed; the repression may well be too costly. Let them wallow in their mire – that's what they enjoy. Desire can be educated in some, and only partially repressed in others. As Gouldner puts it, Plato in the end is constrained to limit the reliance he places on reason; he must in turn 'strengthen coercive mechanisms to control those whose consent to the new order is not voluntary' (and, in the case of slaves, could not possibly be). 'In the end, therefore, the appeal to reason comes to be seen as less secure in its results than the manipulation of costs and rewards.'[26] Severe words.

The ambiguities of the aristocratic (or meritocratic) temper in politics, even in progressive politics, are deep and their sources enduring. Too much blame, it seems clear to me, should not be laid at Plato's own personal door in this respect. But one aspect of this heritage, being more doctrinal in nature and very influential in the whole subsequent metaphysical tradition, should be honestly evaluated.

I refer to Plato's handling of the body-soul distinction. Plato's view of the body is a common source of unease, or should be. The doctrine of the *Phaedo* – we are better off when we shed the body, its needs and wants – comes immediately to mind but similar estimates keep reappearing. Slaves, for instance, are not amenable to the rule of reason; banausic citizens (that is sedentary workers who lack the self-control of farmers and sailors) are to be manipulated because in them the passions of the body are not checked by a kingly ruler in the individuals themselves. Plato is prone to see in the soul a being unfairly thrown into the body as into an alien and hostile environment. The hostility between the two is not merely endemic; it is natural, essential. Religious sources for this view are found among Plato's antecedents. We have seen that shamans and Orphics, unlike Homer, made of the soul a separate principle. The permanence of this hostility is attested to by even the more measured Aristotle. The soul, says he, can rule the body only despotically, not by persuasion. There can be no friendship between the two, just as there cannot be between master and slave.[27] Plato, argued D. Grene, experiences 'an impersonal hatred of the body which can only be alleviated by the assurance of a design which overrules the material.'[28] 'Overrules' is the important word: the rule is by force. The material always resists and always foments disorder. There is in Plato, beside his commitment to persuasion (the divine does persuade), a sense of the limits of persuasion and a willingness to overstep these limits through despotic force. The rule of the soul over the body, of Gods over men, or rulers over the city gains an impersonal quality. The kingly ruler is either powerless (and withdraws, biding his time) or powerful (and takes on the traits of a fatal ruler). At worst one suspects that persuasion is only a front; at best it is a preferred solution which is, tragically, occasionally set aside. The idea of tendance, frequently used to express the rule of the Gods, expresses well this impersonal quality. The ruler always is, and feels, so uninvolved. I realize that this point is made here in anthropomorphic terms; I shall return to this problem later.

This vision of the limits of persuasion is mythically underpinned by the metaphysics of the divine and the necessary. There is in Plato a cramped and compulsive quality to the authority of reason: the limits that persuasion senses produce anxiety, defensiveness. Plato has a passion for establishing an order. He never sees the comedies such passions create. He is also totally unwilling to risk that order in an act of love. E. Voegelin has noted the appearance in Plato of a split among human beings: some rise to become semidivine souls, others remain mired beasts.[29] The attitude to the body is indeed the key to an emerging generic difference. We have consistently presented the divine moral norm as one that establishes the difference between predators on the social body and contemplators. It is also true that Plato presents this duality as one between sensual and spiritual beings. There is something uneasy in the human awareness of our embodied existence. But the Platonic quality of contempt for our physical selves and their activities offends. I am not suggesting as an alternative a wisely eudaemonistic management of the body as 'all there is' and even less am I proposing a lyrical extolling of the physical joys. (Incidentally, Plato, always many-faceted, is enough a Greek to have a taste, even a lust, for sensual ecstasies and knows that their fragility and transitoriness in no way kill their attractiveness.) What I am asking for is an estimate that avoids the systematic vilification of the body and the pseudo-intellectual pleasure derived from stressing that the world of the senses is a world of decay, because it is a world of corruption. Can we today do better on this point?

4 Is metaphysical thinking relative?

It is commonly said that Christians introduced into the pagan world of late antiquity a new way of expressing human embodied existence. The point can easily be underlined by contrasting Plato's body-soul anthropology with that of Augustine and that of Aquinas.

With Augustine a bold – although chastened – autobiographical I steps onto the stage. He speaks of himself with the help of verbs. This man knows that he exists, has an immediate feeling of his dynamic life, pays attention to it, aspires to a fuller life, but finds obstacles in himself.[30] We hardly hear about body and soul. The new autobiographical I sidesteps the whole problem. A new philosophical anthropology is in the making: *to be* acquires an active quality. The nature of the self is expressed by verbs: *esse, nosse, velle,* 'to be,' 'to know,' 'to will.'[31] But this active being is sick: even the Homeric heroic principle of success against odds through bold action does not hold forth any promise of happiness. The abyss of an incurable restlessness is opened before us. And Plato and his disciples have nothing of any value to say here.[32]

Consider also the way in which eight centuries later a very sober mind, Aquinas, handles the body-soul distinction in his so-called treatise of man; namely in questions 75 to 83 of the first part of the *Summa theologiae*. Aquinas emphasizes there the absolute unity of man. He takes over Aristotle's definition of the soul, 'the actuation of a physical organic body with power to live.'[33] The soul is the form of the body and the body its matter. Man is the essential unity of both. As one commentator puts it, these sections did much 'to confirm Christians in the realisation that ensoulment (active) and embodiment (passive) are the same process looked at from different angles.'[34] In an earlier treatment Aquinas had roundly dismissed Plato's views: Plato was wrong to affirm that there are multiple souls in the body; he erred in picturing the soul in the body as a sailor in the ship. Such a Platonic conception of the union of both, as mover and moved, or representations of the soul as using the body makes the union of both merely accidental. In fact, man is one, both body nd soul, by his very nature.[35] That the soul cannot leave the body at will is given as a decisive argument. It was so already in Aristotle, who clearly had no leanings towards the shamanistic cultural pattern. Aquinas even goes so far as to affirm that it is against nature for the soul to be without the body (which leaves him in a nice quandary when it comes to understanding death).

That we have to wait until Christian thinkers to find such reasoned and decisive breaks from Plato on the body-soul question has suggested to many that fundamental shifts in human self-images occur but slowly and only as part of a vaster set of cultural changes which rework the context in which all human self-perceptions proceed. The doctrines of Augustine and of Aquinas are related to a new story of the world and of man. The two Christian philosophers operate with different 'absolute presuppositions.' Such shifts in perspectives, it is added, occur as part of the process whereby civilizations succeed each other. Aquinas's handling of the notion of human person clearly rests upon centuries of Christian theological, christological, and anthropological debates. These in turn were provoked by a new voice (that of the Gospels), a new type of religious faith, the faith in Jesus, that led to the doctrine of the Incarnation, God becoming man, that is like us in all things (save sin) that we might be reconciled with him.

The claim that the rise of 'a new religion' brings such a shift in human perspectives that it relativizes all the previous results of metaphysical thinking and ushers in a new kind of thought (which perhaps will also become obsolete in its turn) cannot remain unchallenged, but it will have to be examined later. For the time being, let us examine what is being claimed about the two different kinds of perspectives.

Among the numerous attempts to summarize the shift in the world-views brought about by the spread of Christianity, we can select that put forward by H.A. Armstrong and R.A. Markus in their *Christian Faith and Greek Philosophy*. With the Greeks, they write, the world is assumed to be eternal. The Christian affirms that God only is eternal and that the world is created. For one the expression of God is found in eternal (static) ideas, for the other in an action, issuing from grace; thus the Trinity becomes the normal expression of the divine. Furthermore, divine action breaks into the world of time. The world for the Greek is either evil or divine; the Christian accounts for its ambiguity by saying it was created good but is fallen on account of the sin of the creatures. For the Greeks man has a fixed nature. For the Christian he has an open and unfinished nature; love in human beings is both a natural inclination and a self-imposed inclination or a deliberate choice. Love inclines man to seek what he was made to seek and what he makes himself seek; the good action is thus not a simple expression of rationality but also a fruit of love.[36]

That the Christians have a 'new' understanding of love is very well known. It is commonly highlighted by their frequent use of a new word, *agape* (ordinarily translated as 'love' or 'charity'), which occurs alongside the classically used *eros* (love-desire) and *philia* (love-friendship). What I want to emphasize is that the Christians also had a new practice of love. And this can be shown, I think, by referring to changes in marriage practices and in the sacrificial system.

Marriage in the ancient city was a family affair. The bride entered into the husband's family. Kinship ties were strong and durable. In contrast, the Christian message asked individuals to leave father and mother and the Christian community upheld a view of marriage based on individual choice (and presumably inclination) and not on family policies and alliances. Everywhere in the West Christianity, in the end, won out in this matter. Marriage became a sacrament, that is God and his church do it, and the church asked the individuals, not their kin, to say yes.[37]

The sacrificial system was also entirely shattered. That the meat bought at the butcher was previously sacrificed to the gods is a matter of indifference to Paul. Sacrifice occurred once and for all on Golgotha in Christ's oblation. 'God designed him to be the means of expiating sin by this sacrificial death' (Romans 3:25). The sacrifice is offered to a father, by an obedient son; it is voluntary self-immolation. René Girard has stressed how this unique deed puts an end to the chain of mimetic violence: societies no longer need acts of violence against a scapegoat to guarantee their internal order.[38] This deed, however, is the single source of a series of subsidiary acts of sacrifice. Some are liturgical: the priest offers the host as sacrifice in each mass. Some are internalized as spiritual and moral deeds: 'Therefore, my brothers,' writes Paul, 'I implore you by God's mercy to offer your very selves to him: a living sacrifice, dedicated and fit for his acceptance, the worship offered by mind and heart' (Romans 12:1). As Manuel de Diéguez points out, the human lamb displaces the animal slaughtered on the altar, and now even the poorest are rich enough to offer a sacrifice to God: they have their obedient hearts and their bodies.[39]

It is obvious that there is a deep egalitarian thrust in the Christian movement. Faith, the highest state which human beings are capable of actualizing, is perceived as being within the reach of all, whatever their mental capacity or social position. As a matter of fact, it was assumed at first that faith prospered most among the humble. The practice of philosophy is no longer the highest potentiality of man. Faith, God-given faith, is the summit. Soon, however, faith was to welcome even philosophy, as a help towards understanding.

It is easy to see that Plato's metaphysics of the divine and the necessary, of persuasion and its limit, is set aside in the new doctrine of God and of man. But such a recasting is not just a shift in the conceptualization dominant in a literate élite. The whole cultural context for human self-awareness is being changed – and this affects everybody. This may be emphasized by taking a look at the contrast between the Greek and the Christian concepts of time.[40] Clearly the Christians have been marked by Jewish eschatology and have a different sense of history.[41] To the Greeks time is but a transitory life-form, that of the world produced by God. (Space, however, is enduring.) Time destroys; in time one forgets. Time is thus assessed as something inferior, with a touch of evil. It is a medium of absence, temporary absence presumably. To the Hebrews, and to most Christians after them time is qualitative. Important events occur in it. It is assessed as time of opportunity. Trial, maturing, inventing, meeting, each occurs in time. Love is practised in time. As such, time is a medium of presence. Augustine brings this new view of time to conscious clarity. Time is a distance, perhaps to be viewed somewhat like an empty space, a delay, an expectation, in which a personal work can occur. Far from a loss of eternity, what occurs in time is memory, spiritual life, and the presencing of eternity.[42] When Plato calls time a movable image of eternity, he is speaking of starry time, not of the sublunar time we live in. Our time is to him a medium of change, of genesis and decay.[43] The Christian has a more positive experience of time: eternity can be in it. (The Word was made flesh. The couple gives birth to a soul; they do not just fashion a body into which some pre-existent soul is lodged.)

It is even possible to trace such a different conception of time to a shift in the cultural conditions under which something as biologically basic as our five senses are experienced and assessed. It is well known that the Greeks are fundamentally visual people. 'Vision is the cause of the greatest benefits to us,' writes Plato.[44] Thinking henceforth consists in noticing and paying heed to form, objectivity, and immutability. The Hebrews, however, get their decisive impressions from what they hear. God cannot be seen but is heard. This is not the basis for a more 'spiritual,' less 'sensual,' approach to God; it is a different sensual basis for dominant patterns of thinking. What we hear is constantly changing, has a dynamic and qualitative nature, and calls for responsive involvement.[45] Thinking is perceived as arising along a horizon primarily made of human interaction, not within a cosmic scenery. Truth is a matter not of something being unveiled but of someone being faithful. The Greeks focus their mind on the world, and then seek to live in accordance with what they have found out. Christians are preoccupied with life rather than with things, and the primary source for their thinking is a history.[46]

This did not happen, 'it always is,' affirmed the emperior Julian. He thought he was placing himself upon the most solid ground; the Christians were not impressed.

It is, therefore, not enough to say that Plato erred in his ethics and his politics. He had the ethics and the politics that his world-view called for and that his metaphysics deserved. To do better than he in ethics and politics requires an alternative metaphysics, and that in turn requires a different story, a different understanding of the environment for man's existence in the world. The implantation of the new story requires a conversion, a deep and massive historical revolution that affects even the way in which we use the input of our senses.

Plato then, we could perhaps credibly suggest, failed because he did not or could not find such a new world-view or story.

This affirmation is quite momentous. It differs from the social scientific analysis on one important point. Gouldner tends to suggest that Plato could have held the conglomerate together, could have reformed Greek religion and brought health back to his divided city, if he had but overcome a class or nationalistic narrowness in his personal vision and 'risen' to some higher standpoint.[47] Most commentators on the relativity of metaphysical thinking, however, would rally round the affirmation just ventured; they tend to hold that such relativity is complete, fatal.[48] Marxists, for instance, argue that Plato, while separated from his class, remained so locked within its assumptions that no group in his society could hear his call to a new life. No class could wed its interest to the interests of Plato's city.[49] His failure was therefore inevitable. According to another view, equally deterministic, there were in Greek society forces that inevitably led to disintegration and no individual in that society – not even a philosopher of Plato's stature, hard though this may be to admit – could marshal influences that could stop such decay. Civilizations, it is argued, decline; the process cannot be arrested by the forces of a mind. A healthier society, it is thus suggested, has necessarily to be built anew, by others, on different principles. All such views have one common thrust; there was nothing that Plato, good metaphysician though he was, could do about it at this point in history. The different welter of images brought about by the Christian faith was to be the basis of further development. A restoration of, or move forward towards, reason depended on ultimately irrational historical forces.

This conclusion is not without some credibility. There are grounds for believing that it is in their religious imaginations and religious lives that human beings first overcome the dead weight of outworn assumptions. Numerous contemporary accounts stress that Jesus did not bring new doctrines but new stories, and add that the Christian movement brought about a restructuring of the imagination. The human imagination may indeed be viewed as the instrument of historic change. That Plato had to devise means of coercion means that he failed to create the new powerful myth that would elicit the voluntary moves towards a new restructured order. The Christians did have such new myths. Through their story of Fall and Redemption they offered a new interpretation of the human predicament and released new energies for living it together. They were specifically aware of the human ability to rewrite history, something the Greeks denied; what they meant, of course, was the ability to discern new features of one's past and thus open new possibilities for the future.[50] That Plato failed was thus not just bad luck (*tuchè*), or proof of poor planning (*technè*). It was fate (*theia moira*). It was historically inevitable.

Such a view, however, demands further thought. I have referred to historical inevitability, irrational historical forces, the rise of a new world religion, sweeping historical revolutions. All this (credible enough) talk of a different metaphysical basis made available by a great historic change implies a philosophy of history. What this philosophy of history is must be enucleated and clearly stated. From the point of view of historically victorious Christianity the matter is simple. Plato erred because he did not receive from God the revelation which has been vouchsafed to Christians. Like Dante guided by Beatrice, the Christians have received further light from God. Beatrice is not a better philosopher than Virgil; she is a God-given addition. Plato, like Virgil, went as far as humans can go on their own. Christians go further, by grace. But Christians never merely claimed to have found a Saviour who opens to them the door to paradise; they also believed that they understood life before death better than the pagans. They pave the way, thus, for philosophers who argue that the Christian reorientation of the imagination – whether a divine gift or not – is a step forward, which leads in turn to a better grasp of human living. This in turn paves the way for the notion that such progressive historical force is now spent, and that a new key for good living together should now be found. The philosophy of history that starts with the notion of a God-given progress ends up with tyrannical relativism. Human beings are entrapped in their historical age, toys of the historical forces of the hour. Time is history, that is a succession of blinding and chaotic forces that provide a fateful frame which rigidly limits the scope of our strivings.[51] Changes of religion are irrational changes that provide a better, more workable frame – for a while.

I, for one, am all in favour of beginning every inquiry as though everything were relative. Greek and Christian metaphysics alike must be related to the conditions of the societies and ages in which they arose and flowered. But I cannot let the matter rest there. Which one pays closer attention to reality? Or which one should we heed now? In our next section we shall examine a philosophical case on behalf of the better standpoint made available through Christianity. This will be examined carefully, especially since it allows for an enduring significance for the Plato beyond whom the Christians have moved.

Before doing that, however, I want to conclude this section by offering some resistance to the tendency towards polarization that is inherent in typological contrasts.

Plato keeps correcting himself: in spite of all temptations, he did not become a gnostic. His dualism is real but it did not crystallize into the doctrine of total alienation of the soul in the sublunar world. Plato believed in cosmic religion, namely in the amenability of the world to the power of the design. Platonists, along with Stoics, maintained the faith in such cosmic religion and consistently resisted the threat of gnosticism.

Furthermore, Plato, who developed the distinction, did not accept the divorce between theory and practice or between action and contemplation. (Surprisingly enough, Aristotle did separate them more radically.) Everything in Plato repeats that the philosopher needs to return to the cave. Plato's mysticism is an alternative to politics, but terrestrial politics remains with him both a constant concern and a duty. There is more here than the ambivalence of one who both loves and despises the world of the senses. There is genuine care for and watching over the material conditions of men's terrestrial lives.[52]

Most importantly, it must also be added that the Academy, unlike the Sicilian venture, was a lasting achievement. The school trained Aristotle, philosophy there came of age, acquired an institution, became a cumulative tradition, an ongoing wisdom, that acquired its classics and ceased to be a mere clash of ideas among creative seers, itinerant thinkers, and clever rhetoricians. And we are still heirs of its method. As Voegelin puts it, 'the order represented by Callicles has gone down in ignominy, the order represented by Plato has survived Athens and is still one of the most important ingredients in the order of the soul of those men who have not renounced the traditions of western civilisation.'[53]

5 The argument of a Christian philosopher

None of us today can be a Platonist. Every philosophy belongs to its own time and is restricted by the limitations thereof. It is impossible for us to go back to Plato, for reason now makes higher demands on us. We must stand above him and acquaint ourselves with the needs of thoughtful minds in our own time or, rather, we must ourselves experience those needs.

Such are the words of Hegel.[54] In keeping with the method of his entire history of philosophy, Hegel tried to evaluate philosophically the value and place of the

Platonic corpus as a philosophy of the past. This was done in full awareness of Plato's stature: we do not find 'opinions' in his works but rather philosophy itself. Philosophy became self-conscious in Plato. (Hegel himself owed his philosophical vocation to a steady reading of the dialogues.[55]) Plato showed that philosophy is work: some passages in *Phaedo* are sublime and fondly remembered but there is also strenuous dialectic in it. Unlike the Romantics, who flit above the blossoms, the philosopher must wrestle with the thorns and thistles of speculative dialectic.[56] Philosophy is to become a science and bring to consciousness the spiritual element which belongs to thought. Plato saw that all reality is thought.[57]

Platonic principles, adds Hegel, are fundamentally sound. His statement that God is devoid of envy was a great thought and a most significant departure from the common attitude of the ancients who saw the divine as Nemesis, *Dike*, as fate and jealousy. Such archaic conceptions of the divine were not moral: the punishment of Nemesis is only the humiliation of what oversteps limits; such petty gods do not suffer what is excellent or elevated to exist.[58]

Having said this, Hegel examines the shortcomings in Plato's philosophy. The dialogue form contains very heterogeneous elements. The discourse is not systematic, the progress in thought neither steady nor orderly. Characters always make what appear to be arbitrary interventions in the conversations, and the dialogues thus always give the impression that the matter might have turned differently. Plato furthermore speaks of god in the ordinary manner common to his time. He also speaks of the idea of the Good or of the absolute reality of things. But the two manners of speaking of God remain separated; he has not fully thought out these matters. Pictorial expressions and philosophical notions are not reconciled. The very recourse to myth is a proof of his weakness.[59] His notion of contemplation is defective: 'this contemplative life seems aimless, for the reason that all its interests have disappeared.' We moderns rather have something concrete before us and desire to reduce it to a settled order. To us freedom is not just a thought.[60]

The root of the matter, continues Hegel, seems to lie in something that appears most clearly in the *Republic*, a work which has as its essential purpose 'the suppression of the principle of individuality.' (Here, of course, Hegel continues in the vein of the anthropology initiated with Augustine's autobiography; he clearly sidesteps the body-soul dichotomy.) Plato, thinks Hegel, cannot conceive a divine and moral order that includes and produces free, subjective individualities. 'The want of subjectivity is really the want of the Greek moral idea.' The idea of Plato emerges only in an abstract form that cannot tolerate concrete, realized, individual life.[61] Here Plato is fully a child of his times. The established morality, such as it is, is maintained as divine. The Greek individual does not, and cannot, say 'I will.' He does not dare attribute to himself the power of ultimate decision, and he is accustomed to rely on a higher insurmountable authority to make decisions for him. So army generals consult oracles and democracies fill some offices by drawing lots rather than by suffrage.[62]

We today know how different Plato was from established morality; we must still agree, however, that the difference did not include what Hegel calls the principle of individuality, or of subjective freedom.[63] After all, Socrates listened dutifully to the laws of Athens when they told him that they brought him into the world, nurtured him, and gave him a share of all the good things. Socrates consented to see himself as bound by contract to these laws, as their child and slave. To escape would be to proclaim oneself a destroyer of laws and that simply on account of 'desiring life with shameless greed.'[64] Socrates, in the end, submitted to the extent of drinking voluntarily the hemlock, dying without apparent violence and without anyone in the city incurring pollution.[65]

The new principle of individuality, Hegel affirms, has come to light and realization with Christianity. He is most emphatic: with Christianity the true religion has come into the world, and supplies principles which solve matters for which the Greeks could not find an answer.[66] The new religion has made the intelligible world of philosophy the world of common consciousness. Hegel quotes Tertullian to the effect that even children have now a knowledge of God which the wisest men of antiquity alone attained to.[67] This intelligible world has remained hidden to the consciousness even of philosophers until it is brought to light before all in what Hegel calls the idea of Christianity.

To describe this idea Hegel first emphasizes that in Christianity the idea is known 'in its necessity.' The Necessity known by the Greeks was a blind necessity, without wisdom and devoid of purpose or content. This Necessity is the fundamental determination of Greek religion: all is under its sway. With Christianity God is spirit and thought. He has an intelligent will. It becomes apparent that true necessity is an idea, with a concrete content. It develops meaningfully. Everything that happens is the result of this necessity. Everything real is rational. The task of philosophy is to discern the necessary unfolding of what in the idea is at first implicit and unconscious and becomes with time free and fully self-conscious. The divine and the necessary no longer contend. Necessity is divine and rules all 'wisely.' ('Contingency must vanish on the appearance of philosophy.'[68]) Hegel can thus be reconciled to the failure of Plato: it is part of the laws of spiritual development that a philosophy should arise on an incomplete principle and give way – necessarily – in time to a more advanced principle.[69]

This view of necessary development is of course in sharp contrast with Plato's views. Everything generated for Plato is 'for the sake of being.'[70] Copies have their end in the eternal model. With Hegel being itself gets dynamically involved in generation, in positing its negation, for the sake of arriving in the end at free self-possession. Thereby the very Platonic dualism between tradition (the best in the world of change) and metaphysics (true contemplation of the abiding) is overcome. The will of God pursues its idea through development. Traditions or civilizations have a dialectical life according to a metaphysical idea; each stage necessarily gives way to a higher one and metaphysics cannot be grasped apart from such ongoing life of the traditions. A dynamic reason, not a decaying nature, brings about the death of civilizations and makes room thereby for a new civilization closer to the idea.

The different understanding of necessity represents the new idea on the objective side so to speak. On the subjective side Christianity introduces also a decisively new and higher principle, the absence of which accounts for another set of dead-ends among the Greeks. Christianity finds the spirit an actual spirit, immediately present in the world here and now; Christianity affirms the absolute worth of the individual. The principle of absolute subjective freedom is understood in all its ramifications: the individual is not constantly asked to conform or to develop himself according to a pre-existing pattern. The individual's aims, inclinations, and interests attain to an absolute independence. 'The arbitrary choice of the individual, the outward expression of the individual, is necessary.'[71] The Greek moral idea could not cope with this kind of subjectivity. Plato (linking it to bodily desires) ignored it or disparaged it. The subjective freedom entered the Greek world as a destructive reality that undermined the life of the Greek state.[72] This new impulse, however, is obeying a higher, wiser necessity. Self-conscious individuals arise, who, in a consciousness of duty, are actively, dynamically involved in the process whereby the universal spirit realizes itself in history (or whereby the principle of Christianity becomes the principles of the world). In this way is achieved a genuine conversion of the finite.

Hegel thus claims that Christianity affirms both the fullness of the idea and the full energy of free subjectivity. Hegel caps this twofold affirmation with the affirmation of their ultimate unity. God and human beings freely realize themselves. The divine nature and the human nature are revealed as one. With Christianity, on Hegel's view, man comes to grasp genuinely the rule of Providence. Providence, unlike Fate, accomplishes the perfect assumption of individual striving in the unfolding odyssey of the divine spirit on its way to self-realization. The dominance of Fate brought to Greek religion a certain melancholy; the Greeks knew sadness because of the limits that they necessarily encounter. The moderns, however, know *Verdruss*: contrariety. Their free will, determined by duty, encounters obstacles which are not merely disappointing but create an inner unrest because the will now fully knows what ought to be.[73] In the end, however, providential reconciliation does take place: contingent events are not in the power of fate but in the hands of Providence. The consolation that occurs is not the Greek consolation which consists of resignation but a full consolation in which the previous negation turns into an affirmation.[74] As one commentator puts it, Greek serenity is based on renunciation but the Christian on union with God. The Christian's peace with reality is not submissive but voluntary: freedom has penetrated the reality.[75] On freedom, evil, and providence Plato could find no answer. For all his efforts reason had to admit defeat.[76] In the new religion man achieves essential freedom, and, although he commits evil (rooted in freedom), the Spirit, providentially, overcomes even that, the most radical of all oppositions. God is known as reconciling the world to himself.

The new principle differs from the Platonic one in that it brings all under the sovereignty of reason – and of reason alone. The goal of philosophy is thereby reached in that 'the universal is comprehended as the all-embracing existence, or the existent is laid hold of in a universal form.'[77] The mind of man encounters no irreducible obstacle in its effort to know. The idea no longer has to contend with an alien limit. The spirit realizes itself in the world and ultimately overcomes everything that opposes it (posited by itself in the first place). The historical character of man is affirmed, his free self-realization vindicated and providentially taken up into ultimate reality. Hegel achieves all this because he finds in the new religion a better theology. God here is a dynamic absolute: creating a world *ex nihilo*, he reconciles all the opposing freedoms. All opposition is God's own dialectical work; it is never what it is in Plato, namely something for always already found there.

The contrast between Plato and the philosophers of the subsequent era clearly comes to a head in matters theological. For the Platonic contest between the divine and the necessary is being substituted, in a vast and clear sweep, the drama of the relationship between God and man, or, as Hegel would also put it, the dialectic between infinite and finite spirit. God has become a sovereign agent, whereas the classical God, as brought to full expression in Aristotle's metaphysics, moves all things by the desire they have of him. Man has also become an agent who transcends nature. St Leo struck a deep new chord when he announced in a sermon that 'what everyone of the faithful has in his own soul is more than what he admires in the sky.'[78] There is a genuine drama in the course of life of such 'souls.' Plato, like Hegel, is interested in a world of action and politics. Unlike Hegel, however, he finds no appropriate religious symbols to legitimate such interests. His gods never create or restore. All his religious perspectives seem to impose a dualism on him. The divine is impassive, motionless; movement is a characteristic of the troubled human world.

One does not need to be a Hegelian in the full sense of the word to grant him that the new principles of Christian theology instilled in the minds of men (or released in them) enormous energies for pressing on towards a closer intellectual penetration into the individual striving inherent in the human condition. C.N. Cochrane argues for the superiority of the new principle mainly by showing how it rejects the classically understood notion of nature. To see the Trinity rather than nature as fundamental principle provides a better basis for understanding both man's personality and the world.[79] Voegelin, who is not suspected of Hegelianism, argues that Plato's philosophizing remains bound by the compactness of the Greek soul: everything remains within a cosmic rhythm of order and disorder. The myth of nature dominates all, the world is aging, and only one kind of ascent to God is possible under these conditions.[80] So let me urge generosity in our estimate of Hegel's achievement. On three points, I think, a decisive contribution should be acknowledged. First his ontology of the Absolute as Spirit should be said at least to give much food for thought. Secondly his discussion of Christianity as a world-historical phenomenon opens the prospects of grasping the essence of Christianity; moreover it offers a meaningful account of this essence: in the religion of the Incarnation and of love the finite spirit is offered a full reconciliation with God. Finally he seems to have offered also an account of the historical peculiarities of the western Christian world, and in particular of what appeared in 1800 to be its unique world-historical dynamism. One can thus praise Hegel for having done justice both to philosophical truth and to historical truth. It is thus not surprising that his system provides also a history of philosophy and a philosophy of history that has no precedents in scope or insight.

Numerous questions, however, arise about the metaphysics that Hegel has structured thanks to his reconstitution of the interaction throughout history between the human subject and the divine Subject. A first question can be articulated by drawing the contrast between the social scientist (Gouldner), the dialectical materialistic (the Marxists), and the absolute idealist. I appreciate Gouldner's cultivation of the sense of a bond between Plato and us. he shows that Plato has strong ties to his own day and age, just as we do. He assumes that we know better than he on some points, but he does not let this confidence grow into the hybris that believes we have nothing further to learn from him.[81] The Marxists sever the bond: Plato ran on what we know know is a dead-end road. We study him only because there are lessons to be learned from our surveying of past errors. Hegel thinks both that Plato is *dépassé* and that there is still something positive to learn from him once he is properly interpreted. The cost of this solution is a sizeable hermneutical claim, namely that we can do Plato the honour of understanding him better than he understood himself. But is not this hommage rather an insult?

A second question can be brought to light by examining what happens in the Hegelian system to the old Platonic contrast between action and contemplation. Hegel, at first sight, finds irrelevant any Platonic duality between action and contemplation. He has numerous Christian antecedents here.[82] Augustine, for instance, has begun with the classical notion of action as a sign of fallenness or of temporal existence (man fell when he became eager to experience the power of his own activity). From such an unpromising basis, however, Augustine begins the rehabilitation of action. Charity constrains him to admit that being useful to the other is often a Christian injunction, but he goes further. Charitable action can also aid the neighbour to fulfil his own desire for contemplative bliss. Augustine thus remains with the philosophical justification of the contemplative life but his sense of community leads him to cease seeing in action merely a rival of contemplation. Action undertaken by love is a step in the soul's return to eternity.[83] Aquinas is much further removed from the classical view and does not make a fundamental motif of the distinction between the active and contemplative lives. As a Dominican and as a teacher he is confident that he has achieved a synthesis of the two. With Hegel action clearly no longer needs any rehabilitating. To him assertion in action is natural to personality. 'This is the absolute right of personal existence – to find *itself* – satisfied in its activity and labour.'[84] As a modern philosopher puts it, 'the essence of man is no longer specific but individual, and his perfection is no longer to be substance of a form but to be subject of an activity.'[85] The truly ethical man is politically involved: he acts with his fellow-citizens on the stage of history. He can believe that there is reason in history: self-conscious willing is not abandoned to mere chance but manifests itself in the light of the rational idea.[86]

This claim is enormous and gives us much to think about. C. Taylor writes, with a slight smile, that Hegel holds forth a uniquely beautiful promise: the ideals of radical freedom and integral expression can be united.[87] Perfect action! A perfect community of united and mutually transparent free men can be brought to life. Men can thus feel at home in the world. Stanley Rosen sternly notes that this assimilation of theory into practice opens a threatening prospect, 'the rendering absolute of practice.'[88]

Yet it is clear that such promises and prospects are not really Hegel's last word. Hegel, we have said, claims to know the end towards which the divine-human interaction is moving. Subjects must keep striving towards it. Yet, while commending purposeful action, Hegel in his writing commends a self-image of the philosopher as someone who has seen all and contemplates the whole. Hegel knows the place of everything in the universal order. Thereby, he also tells us, philosophers know rest, are dispassionate. They contrast with passionate historical actors. The whole life of heroes is labour and trouble, that is passion hardly lit by the quiet light of contemplation.[89] Philosophy to Hegel is not really heroic; it is the only fully conscious form of spiritual self-possession. It is basically contemplative. Knowing thus is still remembering – just as it was in Plato. There is of course a difference from Plato. To Plato remembrance meant 'that the psyche must venture beyond history, while Hegel demanded that it encompass the totality of history.'[90] But what we find is a contemplation of the whole that never again issues an invitation to descend towards the past.

That one can find in Hegel a hommage to Plato that may be insulting and an apparent overcoming of the tension between action and contemplation that may be in fact a hardening of it should at least indicate that there are serious problems behind his achievement. The radical question might well be raised: can one really ever claim to have surveyed the whole and thus truly to have reconstituted the complete dynamics of the interaction between human subjects and the divine Subject?

6 Another philosophical argument

To criticize Hegel is a notoriously difficult task (unless one starts with hostility). He seems to earn the sympathy of anyone who makes the honest attempt to understand him. The more one pursues the effort, the more attractive the rewards. At the very least one keeps finding he has finely balanced answers to the numerous problems he has perceived. In the end I have ventured an act of free subjectivity and cast suspicion on the very core of his doctrine.[91]

This, of course, may have been too peremptory. But consider how endless would be any debate between Hegel and Plato. Clearly Hegel is right in saying that in Greece only a few were free and that Plato had no sense of the need to overcome that ... Clearly, however, Plato keeps addressing us, when he says, for instance, that truth is a hard beast to catch in the nets of our language ... And so on, and so on. In the end, any discourse that would go on and on ... on the one hand ... and on the other, putting together little bits of Plato with little bits of Hegel, would be boring. And one would lose in the process the power proper to either philosophy.[92] One would end up with doctrines, sound ones probably, but it would not be philosophy. After all children outgrow the teeter-totter; it goes nowhere. Shall we, then, like the push-me-pull-you, keep our gaze steadily fixed on both?

In order to break the deadlock I propose to look at yet another philosopher, this time a twentieth-century existentialist.[93] Lev Shestov (1866–1938) does not start from the confidence that modern western Christians can do better than Plato.[94] Rather than seeing in western thought a development that takes up in a Christian context the achievements of Greek philosophy, he sees in it a constant struggle between Christian or biblical views and the rationality fostered by the Greeks and subsequent philosophers. What has Athens to do with Jerusalem? Tertullian asked at the dawn of the Christian era. Why keep trying to reconcile Jerusalem with Athens? asks Shestov nineteen centuries later. Why in particular surrender Jerusalem to the judgment of Athens?[95]

Shestov begins his argument with the description of the Greek philosophical discovery of Necessity (*Ananke*). Necessity does not let itself be persuaded, affirms Aristotle. The truth, adds the Stagirite, constrains us necessarily.[96] As Shestov sees it, the stage is clearly set for the whole subsequent course of philosophy. Philosophy surrenders to Necessity, accepts it, resigns itself to it, and deludes itself into thinking that this truth does not coerce but persuade. Plato allows that the gods themselves do not fight Necessity. God himself has to share his power with Necessity and, in the very act of creation, accepts a compromise which introduces imperfection and evil in the world. Divine power is thus in the condition of having to struggle constantly and always improve on what it has done. As Euthyphro points out, even the Gods do not choose: they too must obey. What is pious is there for them to acknowledge, to accept.[97] Men, of course, can do no other. Philosophy goes even further: it makes this surrender lovable. It manages to hide any questions concerning woes that may arise from it. It invents katharsis, that is separation of the soul from the body. We have no mastery over body and world; let us learn to live without either; we do not belong down here.[98]

In fully conscious revolt against an entire philosophical tradition Shestov affirms that the truth which coerces but cannot persuade is not really the truth. Why should philosophy take pride in yielding to Necessity? Should philosophy not be the ultimate struggle of the human spirit rather than an intrigued look backward on what necessarily is or necessarily happens? Why enthrone logic above God and glory in that? Why affirm with satisfaction that even God cannot undo the evil done? Is it not rather more philosophical to affirm that the death of Socrates at the hands of his fellow-citizens is not forever an eternal truth but that the day may come when it will be true to say that this horror did not occur and is not. Original sin for Shestov lies in the knowledge of what necessarily is and in the assent to it.[99]

What Shestov calls the philosophy that struggles (rather an anti-philosophy since its effort runs against the grain of the philosophical tradition so exalted by practically all philosophers) has for him a biblical basis: Abraham, unlike Socrates, did not surrender to Necessity (Shestov reads Abraham in Kierkegaard's manner; he has faith that God will save the Son whom he orders to be killed). To Shestov philosophy ought to be like faith; that is, it should be a venture forward, a struggle, not a knowledge or a look backward. Faith is bold, full of will; it issues commands; it is not a rational acceptance of things as they are. It leads man out of the confines of ordinary thought and his constant effort to drive everything miraculous out of life.[100]

Shestov's rejection of the 'lessons of reason' owes a great deal to Dostoyevsky's *Notes from Underground*. There reasonable men have been scolded for their total absence of rebelliousness. 'Confronted with the impossible they subside at once. The impossible means the stone wall! ... a wall, you see, is a wall.'[101] Entrenched common sense, what everybody 'knows,' is the enemy for Dostoyevsky. He, says Shestov, conquers the self-evident. He writes the genuine critique of reason (and without technical language!).[102] Shestov's ultimate source, however, is the Bible.[103] 'Holy Scripture,' he writes, 'provoked through its profound disagreement with the spirit of Greek philosophy the most surprising reactions among those who were destined to experience the supreme anxieties of human existence.'[104] Biblical philosophy teaches that trust in reason is the biggest sin.[105] The Bible does not have in Shestov's eyes any dogmatic authority. By being there and saying what it says, it stirs the imagination and opens prospects. It brings the mind to a point of total bafflement, where the choice is between living in faith, that is in total darkness, or giving up life itself.[106]

Such passionate attacks on reason and all its works are undoubtedly trying to the patience of many a reader. Shestov, however, redeems his repetitiveness; he has a very lively sense of the violence that ideas do to people. Put this way the idea is trite, yet Shestov earns sympathy for his endemic suspicion of dominant conceptualization. The certainties of some individual minds have very frequently become cruel tyranny exercised upon other minds: '"Scratch" any European, even if he be a positivist or a materialist, and you will quickly discover a medieval Catholic who holds frantically to his exclusive and inalienable right to open for himself and his neighbour the gates of the Kingdom of heaven.'[107] 'At the risk of appearing paradoxical, I venture to assert that ideas have been invented only for the purpose of giving the right to mutilate people.' Grouped together, clerics undertake to build the Tower of Babel, not with bricks, but with human souls.[108] 'Life's horrors are less frightening than the ideas imagined by reason and moral conscience.'[109] Matter is quite docile before the efforts of man: ideas never yield. We must do battle with them to overcome the falsehood of the world.[110] Truth and humanity are at stake: for the creators of rationalism 'created their reason in the image of a sword.'[111]

Shestov aims at a major reversal. Instead of going on with all philosophers and weighing the problem of knowledge (what we do know? how do we know?), he asks us to consider that knowledge may be a problem.[112] Philosophy is bewitched by self-evident truths.[113] And this spell ruins the value of knowledge. Human beings, after all, are fallen. The thirst for knowledge, which Aristotle saw as the fundamental aspiration of all human beings, has now deviated from its goal. It was true originally, but now we are close to the state of affairs described by Henri Bergson: we think only in order to act.[114] And we act to control, in particular to dominate other human beings. Our submission to reason is a play of power. Shestov refers to Seneca: if you want all to submit to you, submit yourself to reason.[115] Thus Shestov unveils the mechanisms of the unreasonable mind; it claims to have entirely submitted to reason.

Shestov believes that the art of searching for truth is best placed in the hands of adventurers.[116] He himself practises what he preaches. His manner of writing is aggressively anti-rational. One should not sacrifice thinking to logical development. His paragraphs are coherent enough: but what he is best at is writing series of thoughts (one or three pages long) which are devoid of any exterior connection.[117] He sides with Pascal against Descartes: 'If life is filled with complications, philosophy cannot and must not aspire at any cost to "clarity and distinctness". If there are contradictions in life, philosophy must live from these contradictions.'[118]

Hegel saw his completely conceptualized system as a clear advance over Plato's collected dialogues. Shestov brings us back to philosophizing in ordinary but occasionally elusive language. To him, of course, Hegel is offensive for more than his literary style. The worst thing Hegel does is, under allegedly Christian principles, to give Necessity a throne more exalted than ever. Following Kant and Spinoza, who in their own time did their best to protect themselves from any biblical contagion,[119] Hegel keeps exalting knowledge and its superior dictates. The tree of science bears a fruit good to eat, and man must eat it. Most cunningly, while Hegel sides with the serpent and against God, he manages to cite the Bible as if it approved him.[120] Hegel thus manages to bring Christianity under the sway of *Ananke* and its eternal truths. A decisive part of this process occurs when he praises knowledge above faith and makes faith into a popular surrogate for knowledge.[121]

In contrast with Hegel's monstrous achievement, Plato looks good in the eyes of Shestov. Plato cannot accept the execution of Socrates; he cannot surrender to it as to something inevitable. He affirms as a principle that everything is to be dared.[122] Plato wants to escape the iron laws of Necessity; he does not accept the conventional sources of truth; he wrestles with the difficult and with the insoluble problems.[123] Plato sees his whole philosophy as an attempt to escape the cave where shadows pretend to reality, where truths tyrannize the soul and petrify it. He repeats that truth is ineffable. In the end, however, he let Necessity have the final sway and allows that conflicts among truths are to be settled by force.[124] One might add that the dialogue, at least for a while, makes the interplay of power visible along with the exchange of words. Thus Shestov, who is no easy prey of other-worldliness, ends with what amounts to a counsel of despair: let us accept the intelligible world of Plato 'even though it does not appear to us as the only real world or, rather, precisely because it does not appear to us as the only real world. It is beautiful, but there are many other beautiful things on earth – where nothing is known of the struggles for existence, where there is no fear and therefore no *logos*, where men sing and do not demonstrate, where they cannot even understand why proofs were invented.'[125]

Shestov's case has force. It rests on a particular conception of the human will and on a biblically inspired distinction between faith and reason. With faith Shestov associates will, that is movement, hope, and even passion, while reason is for him a passive knowledge that surrenders to what has been or apparently must be. We can see that Plato is constrained by the obvious limits in his grasp of the nature of the will. The cosmos being what it is, the will for him has nothing to do except choose sides in the pre-existent, eternally rehearsed struggle of the divine against the necessary. Therefore Shestov has little trouble in affirming that Plato, while sound in parts, does not go far enough in affirming the revolt of the will against Necessity. But can Shestov's case also be sustained against Hegel? Hegel is so sure of having overcome what he thinks is the Platonic dualism between contemplation and action, he is so confident of having affirmed the rights and energies of the freely striving subject, that he even acknowledges the positive necessity of the labour of the negative. Knowledge to him is no static contemplation but a dynamic dialectic process. What is wrong, we want to know, with placing this kind of knowledge above faith? Yet, in the end, the repose of resigned acceptance is probably valued by Hegel even more highly than the struggle of the will. In characteristically misleading Christian terminology Hegel states that philosophy 'unites the Sunday of life when man in humility renounces himself, and the working day when he stands up independently, is master of himself and considers his own interest.'[126]

Should we affirm a human freedom (or for that matter a divine one) other than that found in Hegel? Or should we rather affirm human freedom in a different manner? Shestov answers yes on both counts. He derives from the Bible a picture of a divine and human interaction that is not constrained by any Necessity. A free god creates free human beings *and blesses them.*[127] The category of Necessity is simply not in order. Everything is possible. There is no Platonic contention of the divine with the necessary. There is no Hegelian affirmation of the divine as necessary. The picture of free interaction between God and human beings is of course a mobile, even an unstable, picture. (We can understand why human beings would want some stable necessities restored.) Is everything possible at every point in time? Chaos, writes Shestov, is unlimited possibility, absolute freedom. No order limits the possibilities of life.[128] Shestov, it seems to me, here misreads his Bible. God has replaced chaos by an order that he deems good. This order of divine creation is there as a call to *human* freedom (not a constraining force, as the story in the Garden of Eden shows). I, therefore, cannot accept Shestov's notion of freedom since I see in it only sheer purposeless negativity. Hegel is right to think long and hard on the goal of human freedom. But the presence of this order does not invite freedom to surrender. Shestov on this point has sound instincts. Biblical images invite the self to an existence in boldness and in faith which is not to be constrained by crude beliefs about what is possible and impossible. The bounds of the possible and of the impossible are not fixed by reason.[129] We do not know them and have to live in ignorance on this point.

Thus I shall part company with the irrationalism of Shestov.[130] Freedom is not to be defined purely irrationally; it is to be seen as open to reason (close attention, of course, has to be paid to the notion of reason). But the extent of our rational knowledge is never such as to foreclose the scope of freedom. Freedom is to be affirmed arationally. Therefore we must affirm human freedom in a manner different from Hegel. The point of the biblical picture of divine-human interaction is that freedoms interact as persons. They are open to each other; freedom is called to a certain quality of interaction; and there is nothing necessary, mechanical, or organic about this interaction.

At this point I can conclude, then, that Plato's error lies in thinking that there is reason in getting human beings to think of the divine always in impersonal terms. Like all Greeks, he speaks of the tending exercised by gods over men but this care is singularly devoid of concern and affection. There is something sterile about the supreme goodness: vast and generous though it is, it is without any will to relate. All such features are to the Greeks philosophically unacceptable anthropomorphic expressions implying that the divine can suffer frustration in a personal way. The craftsman works with unvarying skill and design, but he cannot be said to love his creatures whom he strives to perfect (this would, it seems, imply a want on his part). Whether man achieves his goal or not is a matter of indifference to the Greek philosophical God. There is nothing in the Greek tradition like the arresting image of the shepherd rescuing the lost sheep.[131] This and the drama of the God who suffers in circumstances clearly indicating that he does so out of love for man bring us to an entirely different world of thought and create new reality in the relations between God and man.

Human freedom in Plato is thus always asked to insert itself impersonally in an impersonal order. For Plato, writes Kojève, human beings are either stones that crumble in pieces or ore drawn by a magnet.[132] The question of the individuality of the soul cannot arise in Plato: what the soul remembers is a passive contemplation of an impersonal order. Man, writes W. Hirsch, does not have a soul, but his soul has him.[133] The dominance of circular metaphors always invites the self to a perfection that is the closest thing to solitary immobility that motion can achieve.[134]

The trouble with Hegel is that he thinks there is reason in telling human beings that nothing can resist the effort of their reason to know. As the cap-stone of his system he arrives at a Providence that makes no surprises. The Aristotelian idea of Necessity is refurbished in the neo-Platonic manner to give it the qualities of infinite, overflowing, and impersonal dynamism. A Christian flavour is even given to it by speaking of the subject being Spirit and unfolding itself in time. But in the end we still hear that in the world and in history there is a logic that we can know and to which we ought gladly to surrender. The arationality of our will is but a moment – to be overcome – in the relentless unfolding of reason. Hegel thus places his Christians in a world which knows nothing of the freshness of will inherent in brave ignorance and nothing of the hope in divine grace.

7 What philosophy of religion today?

Plato, Hegel, and Shestov wrote at different points in time. Can we also see them as located at different places in space? Instead of seeing them in a historical sequence, can we see them as three contemporary texts? Can we think of them as three boundary-stones that delimit the field in which philosophy of religion is to be found now? Their work would then bring some definition to our striving. Their irreconcilable differences would map our task. And their stature would invite to humility: we would be looking for a philosophy of religion (even though the title could capitalize on the ease with which the English language drops articles).[135]

Let us try. And then we shall begin to see. We shall see that by religion we should mean all that Plato, Hegel, and Shestov mean by it. Our use of the word shall not be cramped by local usage or the merits of some (hidden) theory. We shall also see the same thing about philosophy: whatever the practice of it may be, it is broad and complex enough to encompass the work of these three people. So to do philosophy of religion today shall mean, at least for me, to see Plato, Hegel, and Shestov simultaneously. All of them are texts. All of them challenge our current conceptualizations. (We should thus not challenge them on grounds that they are a Greek aristocrat or a nineteenth-century German.[136])

I shall admit, at the outset, that I find myself most at ease in Plato's corner. To the question 'can reason understand religion?' I cannot answer with Hegel's unqualified yes or with Shestov's resounding no! What I hear in Plato is a cautious: let us see ... I find in the dialogues an endeavour to philosophize, an attempt to place before the reader something to decide about – has he or has he not understood religion? But then it is also clear that I cannot remain entirely with Plato. Let us say that, after Plato, Hegel, and Shestov, we should venture a better attention to reality.

To start with, let us ask: what is the point of trying to philosophize about religion?

In contrast with the aims of science we shall not try to move from uncertainty to certainty. Neither shall we aim at achieving a move from uncertainty to practical decision.[137] In keeping with the classical tradition in philosophy, the point, I think, is to grow in wisdom. Uncertainty is not to be abolished, but to be more wisely lived with. There is here no intent to scorn the achievement of science or the dignity of sound decision. The point of *this* piece of writing, however, is growth in wisdom, progress in the education of desire. Desire educated is desire socially alive, erotically committed to the continuation and enhancement of corporate life. It is also desire individually alive, autonomous, orienting itself among the realities of life. The education of desire is neither the extinction nor the manipulation of it, neither the curbing of it in suffering nor the expansion of it in happiness. It brings an art of dealing, of coping.

I shall add, however, that wisdom, as I understand it, bears its practical fruits indirectly – wisdom, *tout court*, is not practical wisdom. For a philosopher thinking about human living in general has priority over thinking about the cosmos and the things (alive and otherwise) in it. The philosopher allows, of course, that practical questions cannot ever be far from human concern. But I find it necessary to repeat here that wisdom is not the art to succeed; it is not power. Philosophers to date are not kings (but they should never forget that they, in fact, live under the rule of some sovereignty; it would be a poor wisdom indeed that pays no attention to this reality). Philosophy was born in fourth-century Greece at a time when the ideal of good rule by wise human beings could arise in human minds. It was also at a time when conditions did not lend themselves to the easy establishment of such a rule. I do not see any grounds to think that our predicament has significantly changed on these points.

How philosophy today can strive to understand religion will be looked at in three sections.

1 / First we shall examine the notion of reason. Plato, Hegel, and Shestov sharply differ in their sense of what it is that a philosopher labours at. They also differ in their philosophical style. I refer here specifically to their practice of writing. Mindful of these historic precedents, what sense should we shape today of the endeavour (or endeavours) of reason?

2 / Next we shall look – not too surprisingly – at religion. We shall look at *a* religion, the Christian one. I am aware that numerous philosophies undertake to examine religion in general. W.C. Smith has marshalled imposing evidence to argue that the disparate enterprises of Christian theology, Islamic theology, and so on should begin to yield to a world theology that examines the meaning of human, generic faith.[138] It is clear that the time is past when we can visualize the world's great religions as somewhat like separately built, independently steered boats sailing the great unknown ocean (with only one in secure possession of a true compass and accurate map of the whole). Such a view of the world's religions has been dominant in the West, and it has transformed the keys that could open mysteries into swords that slaughtered those who saw the mysteries differently. Such a view is, I hope, on the way out.[139] It nevertheless remains true that, to most of us Westerners, Christianity is still in some deep cultural sense our own religion. This, of course, is true of historic Christianity (including, for instance, its disastrous self-image) and not of some ideal Christianity. The very need to

understand *our* present as rooted in *our* past would warrant such apparent narrowing of historical vision.[140]

There is a further reason. Modern western man is post-Enlightenment man. One feature of the Enlightenment is that philosophers at that period cease seeing religion as something complex and within themselves and begin to see it as something possibly complex but certainly largely or totally outside themselves (on the stage of history, for instance). They proceed to seek the foundations of religion elsewhere than in themselves. Some find these foundations to be solid, others find them weak, but the search frequently becomes a potentially technical specialized question; it has ceased being a personal foundational one. And the Enlightenment, as Hegel shows, proceeds to judge truth by the criterion of utility. Religious life, I believe, summons in us or awakens in us something interior and something hidden behind the selves that are so deft at being utilitarian. It is not easy for post-Enlightenment human beings to recover this depth. The way to a reawakened sense of religion as something both complex and within us must be through a search for our own, real historical selves. We Westerners cannot arrive at our real selves by sentimental dreams or mystical evasions. We must understand our past and own up to it. We cannot give ourselves a pure future or another past. This spells out, I think, a most urgent task for those of us who are Christians, even if only culturally: examining squarely our Christian identity as rooted in our Christian past.

3 / Finally I shall raise the matter of hope. What hope for the human race?[141] To my mind hope, in the end, is the choicest fruit of wisdom and understanding. I do not see the future as a harbour that lies there waiting to welcome the boat; we build it as we sail towards it. Let me quote Simone Weil: 'The future brings us nothing, gives us nothing; it is we who in order to build it have to give it everything, our very life. But to be able to give, one has to possess; and we possess no other life, no other living sap than the treasures stored up from the past and digested, assimilated, and created afresh by us. Of all the human's soul's needs, none is more vital than this one of the past.'[142] In other words, true authority, the authority that can augment our being, can only be taught. It cannot be thought up.

8 The endeavours of reason

Those of us who had our initiation into philosophy in the 1950s and early 1960s will probably agree that the philosophical task we have taken on lies in the broadening of traditional rationalism.[143] How can reason explore that which has been deemed irrational and integrate it within an expanded vision, asks Maurice Merleau-Ponty?[144] Reason, it seems, no longer centres itself upon itself and seems to move towards that which it is not (its own autonomy is now secure). But, one may ask, is it to extend its empire, reduce the other to the same, and rise to a single vision? Or is reason about to lose its identity, become other with the other, convert so to speak to what it is not?[145] The stakes are high.

Such broadening moves seem to take place now along two axes.[146] Reason requires that the real should be seen rationally and that human beings be reasonable. Right away a disjunction appears between rationality and reasonableness. Rationality yields to evidence; reasonableness lets itself be persuaded by human beings. Rationality seeks to discern the laws of facts, even the very language of the universe; reasonableness listens to what human beings now have to say. Institutions make one reasonable; only thinking makes one rational. Each axis of endeavour opens before reason a long and exciting course of learning. But each casts also a suspicion upon the dispositions of the other. Get along with human beings, yes, but at the cost of truth? Follow the evidence wherever it leads, yes, but at what costs to human beings?

Fortunately contact occasionally occurs between the two axes and man is thereby spared what is perhaps most ridiculous about him, namely the one-sided pursuit of a single objective. Plato has written an anecdote that puts it all before us: 'Take the case of Thales. While he was studying the stars and looking upwards, he fell into a pit, and a neat, witty Thracian servant girl jeered at him, they say, because he was so eager to know the stars in the sky that he could not see what was there before him at his very feet.'[147] (The girl, of course, is tactful: she does not add that he is also incapable of seeing *who* is there before him.) Absorption in the endeavour of rationality brings a loss of the other. What more stunning, stinging form can the other human being take for an aging astronomer than that of a young woman who is not interested in mathematics? Reasonableness can make its demands felt. However, Socrates in *Crito* (or in the *Apology*) does not want to be reasonable. What men have to say as they seek to persuade him is irrelevant to his endeavour. He wants to be rational in a coherent way; he has to be true to himself and to the evidence he sees. The dialogues have the singular merit of showing a group of human beings reasoning: reason is at work, honouring both a reasonableness that is immanent within the group and a transcending presence that has to be individually, rationally, and systematically acknowledged. There seem to be two brains in human beings: while one chases after something, the other observes what meanings the former invests in or derives from the chase. As the meaning is observed, it is relativized. There is more to life than following the evidence. But there is also more to it than Thracian maids.

Reasonableness alone falls under the tyranny of common sense. Common sense is a sixth sense that fits the data of our five senses into a common world and puts upon this world the seal of reality. If our five senses agree on it, and if other human beings agree on it, obviously it is there as something to be contended with, and, adds common sense, that is all there is to it. Rationality demands, however, that the human being wrench himself from this common world, overcome the deep sensation of reality that suffuses it, in order to *think*. Thinking is an ability to consider the coherence of the whole, elicited by wonder before the whole. Thinking tries to pay attention to the unity behind all facts and events. Thinking is thus inherently outside the world of common sense; the thinking ego is homeless, writes Hannah Arendt.[148] The reasonable ego is a victim of the tyranny of appearances. What is commonly seen is limited to what is commonly deemed relevant; it becomes a confining world of possible, admissible experience. Thinking opens the horizon. Common sense is anxious to learn to handle all there is to know within its limited frame of experience. Thinking suspends the desire for that immediately useful knowledge to wonder about the unity of the whole, the frame itself, and what lies beyond it.[149]

The thinking ego committed to rationality, however, frequently becomes entrapped within its own thought-out conception of coherent rationality. The process can be caught, neatly visible, on a page of Descartes. The philosopher has just formulated his rule VIII, according to which the mind should stop at the point where intuitions cease to be clear and not waste time trying to go further. He then argues that the original blacksmith who used two rough stones as anvil and hammer did not proceed right away with the production of useful objects for sale but turned rather to the production of more precise tools, such as better metal anvils and hammers, and pliers as well.[150] This argument is a most revealing bit of mental stupidity. Anybody will grant that the clear notion of an adequate anvil is not arrived at at first try but can be hammered out only through practice, and practice at making the sort of daily objects one wants ultimately to produce. A vague intuition of an anvil is a small step forward, subject to checking at the hands of practical experience; the search for the ideal anvil is not much helped by the theories of rationalist blacksmiths who know the difference between a vague and a clear intuition. Rationalists are unfortunately given to restrictive theories of coherent rationality (and prompt and scornful surrender to irrationality of everything that cannot measure up to their criteria). For instance, many in the western world have become committed to a view of rationality (which some do not hesitate to call scornfully a myth of rationality) that shows interest only in unveiling the laws governing the behaviour of things and offers success in controlling them as the reward for commitment to such view. This view of rationality is so sure that the behaviour of matter is intelligible, that the world reveals its truth to the scientific mind, that it never pauses to examine the subjective motivation of the human beings who accept this view and is completely blind to the will to power that lurks behind this form of the desire to know the world.[151] Reasonableness, of course, always has an eye for one's own motives as well as those of others. The management of things must replace the government of men, quietly announces the Utopian Henri de Saint-Simon. He believes he is thereby putting an end to the oppression of man by man; who does not see today that this plan opens the road to the most totalitarian oppression?

The diverging merits of reasonableness and rationality call our attention to the perils inherent in the tyranny of appearances and the tyranny of any (intellectual) seeing through of appearances. Reason therefore must always live in agonistic tension with the distortions of reason.[152] There is a distortion in the reasonableness that speaks on behalf of a common-sense solution to all human differences; such appeal is intellectually slothful and remains within the confines of a common-sense world – which is always largely the world of the current equilibrium between the powerful and the weak. And there is a distortion in the rationality that rejects such a common-sense world and becomes totally committed to some articulated theory. Minds then become caught in a debate between those who accept the appearances and those who reject them. Meanwhile the appearances are not improved.[153]

Appearances should be improved – because something lurks behind our practice of reasonableness and our talk of rationality, namely the practice of control over human beings. The common-sense world has an ethos of control of appearances, which is itself largely controlled by the powerful ones. The rationality it acknowledges is the cramped, scientific one (know things to master them). It tends to be blind to the control human beings exercise over each other. The rejection of this common-sense world and its pseudorationality usually finds its dynamic power among those who have to suffer from it; their rationality takes shape in some presumably emancipatory doctrine which claims to see behind the appearances and which, in its turn, seeks to achieve control over men.

This brings us to the problem of ideology. A dilemma lies between apparently reasonable men who dislike ideology and believe that the *status quo* in human associations and interactions can improve itself on its own momentum and apparently rational men who denounce the entrenched injustices in the *status quo* and find in some ideology the key to the transformation of human relations. It is easy to point out that no ideology is as innocent as it makes itself out to be. It too is a thought that does service to social power (a minority social power that strives to be on the ascendancy). Furthermore ideologies protest too much; they spend most of their time seeking to prove their innocence. Ideology enrols subjects in a project, teaches them to repeat the acquired world-view, and does it all merely by talking. There is, of course, much legerdemain in this explanatory and hortatory talking, but the new magic does wonders because it resists the old dominant magic.[154] It is a closed world-view but it wants to obtain quick results in an unjust world, and that seems enough to overlook this.

Contemporary scenarios of conflict between peace-minded reasonableness and militant rationality present society and history as a stage for constant warfare. The will to control is rampant on both sides. Appearances are managed in the name of reasonableness and their management denounced in the name of rationality, but both activities mask a hidden agenda of control over human beings. Separate reasonableness and separate rationality claim to see the totality of human affairs, claim to have encompassed the total universe of possible meaning. Nothing opaque is allowed to remain in the world. Everything is interpreted out of its condition of being something open to interpretation. Nothing new is expected. The best that can take place is contained within the thought-out totality. War is the cipher for human existence encompassed within totality. The one who believes he can think the whole strives to place the other in his place in the whole. Thus human beings meet each other in their strength; some win, some lose.[155]

Hope for breaking the deadlock lies, I think, in a hermeneutical activity that is aware of its historical condition. Reason is historical and embodied.[156] It is subject now to the demands of both rationality and reasonableness. Reasonableness rejects quite rightly philosophies of history; teleologies are suspect; behind anyone who claims to know the end of man lies someone determined to force human beings to turn freely towards it. Ideologies with their demand for rationality (as they see it) reject the piecemeal handling of snippets of history that reasonable people undertake; management of means, they say, leads to technocratic tyranny unless ends are clarified – this too is right. Reasonableness is too prone to think it is bearer of ahistorical ideals. Ideologies for their part are too prone to think that the thinker has seen the end of history and can proceed to organize the last hours – or years – accordingly. A hermeneutical activity knows that it is located somewhere in history between an undiscernible beginning and an unknown end. It challenges distortions that mask the human exercise of power and violence. It gets its bearings from a scrutiny of the symbolic interaction between human beings. It searches the records of intersubjective failures – or of achievements in fellowship. What it observes, above all, is how human beings, and groups, negotiate their relationships. Appearances are accepted, with a view towards their improvement.

The conflictual scenarios perceived by reasonable or rational human beings tend to see human activity as a mechanical or organic sort of interaction. Symbolic interaction in fact is more diplomatic, more commercial, and more political. It is a negotiation. One talks with a hidden agenda. But the hidden intent remains short of destructive. Ulysses wants to win, but by talking. The intent to control imposes some limits upon itself. Is there need to stress the dignity of negotiation? To negotiate a boat through reefs – or a canoe through rapids – is not just occasionally useful; it generally enhances self-confidence. It can be a dominant metaphor for the intelligent art of living. Merchants and diplomats have a thing or two to teach intellectuals. The historian of Renaissance diplomacy Garrett Mattingly has shown that Machiavelli and many writers after him exaggerate both the power of the pen and that of the sword; in contrast Renaissance diplomats know well the limits of each and are given neither to idealism nor to inverted idealism. They know that temporal power is only temporal power. Their realism knows the limits of all attempts to ground the use of temporal power on some transtemporal formula.[157] The Bible shows us human beings negotiating with God himself. Abraham does it on behalf of others, on behalf of the righteous few who may be in Sodom and Gomorrah: 'wilt thou let the righteous perish?' (Genesis 18:16–33). Job does it on his own behalf, as he seeks to wrestle an answer out of God: 'Why is light given to him that is in misery?' (Job 3:20). The face-to-face interaction inherent in negotiation wrenches human beings out of totality, to place them in the realm of infinity. Something can happen. Something does happen. The presence of the other opens possibilities.

The hermeneutic of negotiation has much to learn from prephilosophical expressions of human wisdom, especially from comedy and tragedy. I have argued that in the days of Socrates comedy and tragedy had reached such heights in the public articulation of the recurring crises of common life, that they had so successfully fathomed what is pleasant and unpleasant about human interaction (and had become so conscious of what is depressing and heartening about being aware of it all) that philosophy could appear as an attempt to understand the whole – and an intent to bring it all under control. In their separate ways comedy and tragedy still recall us to a freshness of vision, to insights that unmask the fragility of our attempts at wise control and bring us anew a sense of what human beings actually do in the course of their negotiating. They keep immersing us in a real world of living symbols that give us much to think and of living symbolic interactions that leave much to be desired. Religious discourse will also receive a privileged attention in this hermeneutic: its constant feature is the calling up of a divine presence, namely a presence which cannot be in any way controlled, cannot be entirely anticipated.

The philosophical enterprise is thus closely wedded to a particular attention to dialogic language. Negotiation is the highest achievement of discourse. Human beings who negotiate learn as they do so. As Merleau-Ponty puts it, they are firmly immersed in something that remains inaccessible to our psychological and historical science and to our dogmatic metaphysics, namely the spontaneous activity that actually teaches. It is by talking that one learns to understand.[158] Emmanuel Lévinas writes that we should not think of reason as creating the relationship between me and the other, but rather that the rapport between me and the other (in so far as it is the open copresence that allows for pluralism) creates reason.[159]

The phenomenology of language seeks to protect this art of learning by seeing how it happens and by holding at bay accounts of the process that arrest or handicap it. Philosophical endeavour is thus often involved 'only' in being a corrective. Theories of language have been known to settle for what Antoine Vergote has called linguistic idealism: words are meanings experienced and created by living speakers: their origin is entirely in the subjects that utter, or share, them. Or they have committed themselves to mystical realism: words utter the innocent fullness of things themselves; the mouths that convey them are mere vehicles of what they have heard or seen.[160] In fact words are always anchored both in people and in things. Where can we see this better than in negotiation, where people verbally struggle over things? And the process breaks down if one side denies either the presence of its desires or the relevance of the facts. In negotiation neither the appearances nor the rejection of them can remain tyrannical. Language is the promise of reason.[161]

Should I add that, in addition to learning to see what language achieves, philosophers should also learn to write. How else can their writings embody reasonableness as well as rationality? Hegel has wisely pointed out that philosophy cannot be enthusiastic; it cannot be like a gunshot that does all it does at the outset, in one blow, and thus 'begins immediately with absolute knowledge.'[162] It takes time and work, as the philosopher finds out as he seeks to write. Bergson has added one more ground for modesty: writing on and on, the philosopher believes he is making his work more complete; he is in fact correcting himself.[163] Truth is truth only on condition that it is being honoured in a statement, in a paragraph; but each one of these is partial and provisional ...

Philosophers are usually what Kant has called, with a touch of irony, professional thinkers. Their trade has consisted for at least the last two centuries in providing us with fully articulate accounts of rationality. They have not until recently focused with equal zeal and learning on the features of reasonableness.[164] (And they have not stood out among human beings for their reasonableness.) There are grounds to quote the Talmud here, and its famous warning against speculative ardour: 'It were better for the man never to be born who thinks about four matters: What is above and what is below, what was before and what will be afterward.'[165] Putting it positively, what we should think about is what is here and now; it is our neighbour and the problems we have with each other. Reasonableness knows how to attend to that. Reasonableness attends to immediate ends, and considers practicable, humane, mutually acceptable means. Rationality attends to ultimate ends, and postpones consideration of means. Reasonableness alone can let the means become ends, and freedom evaporates under a daily practice of tyranny. But rationality alone can let its thought-ends (merely intended or achieved in fact?) justify the means and open the way for a tyranny of political terror. These problems have been particularly poignant since the days of Hegel:

one feature of the modern world is that universal values have become systems of coercion[166] – consider the hopes that were once placed in rational bureaucracy, in science and technology. Reasonableness keeps an ear for what is desired by human beings as they are. As such it has a moral sense of acceptable means that is precious. But reason, individual reason, ideal reason, can help us only because it deliberates about ends *and* about means, about means *and* about ends. To lose the *and* is to expose ourselves to an absolutism resting on absolute ends – or on absolute means.

9 The religion of will (a hypothesis on Christianity)

My task in this section is to give an account of Christianity in a way that will show what correctives philosophy can bring today to a set of historical religious realities. Let me restate that Christianity is singled out for historical reasons: this religion has been dominant in the history most readers call their own; I also have in mind a task to be assigned now to Christians. To say that reason brings correctives may offend some Christians. I can only ask them to read on. We may yet agree on the correctives, no matter our differences as to their source. I am clearly concerned to avoid the easy contrasts that make philosophy rich in questions and religion more or less rich in answers. Christianity, as I see it, has been full of probing questions and the philosophical tradition has not been void of affirmation.[167] And if one thing is to be learned from the nineteen centuries of exchange between the Christian and the philosophical traditions, it is that each has been prompt in seeing problems where the other saw solutions.

I propose to unfold my hypothesis concerning the correction of Christianity by calling it the religion of the will.[168] In the ancient world Greeks and Romans joined the church in a voluntary act. Conversion is still part of the tradition, at least in the vocabulary. Furthermore, the notion of the will draws attention to the peculiar historical destiny of Christians. It may help discern the historical shape of their common past. The essence and manifestations of Christianity as a historical religion may perhaps be brought out in their unity and variety under this heading.

There is, however, a preliminary question. What is the will?

Should we not begin here by saying that we know very well what it is, provided nobody asks us?[169] And should we not add that definitions of it do not help? As Leslie Farber points out, 'the subject of will has never suffered abstraction gladly.'[170] We can understand the will, I shall say, only by seeing it, or feeling it working, working – or not working – in concrete situations. Merleau-Ponty helps philosophers look for it when he writes: 'At the origins, consciousness is not a "I think that" but a "I can".'[171] In the end also the will is a feeling that I can.

Along the way the will is aware of itself as having specific choices. Consider

Bassanio in *The Merchant of Venice*: the suitor faces three caskets and will win Portia's hand if he opens the one that contains her portrait. The three boxes are made of lead, silver, and gold, thus laden with natural symbols. They also have a man-made inscription, dictating three scenarios of choices. 'Who chooseth me' either 'must give and hazard all he hath' or 'shall get as much as he deserves' or 'shall gain what many men desire.' Such exteriorization of interior choice at specific moments I shall call figures of will. The figures tell of events in which the will is decentred, is involved in something else, and is experiencing the story of a concrete choice. Figures of will, like the caskets, bear a message: the will feels it knows what it is about to do; but the figures are also opaque, the outcome remains hidden. Interpretation is potentially unceasing, prospective before the will acts and the hand opens the lid, retrospective afterward.[172]

Shakespeare's scene shows what happens at some important junctures: Bassanio meets forced options; different figures of the will are dictated to him and his choice is limited to those offered. But the requirements of action occasionally leave some respite; human beings then imagine new figures of the will. These, of course, are the ones that come closest to their desire. The will knows what it wants; rationality indicates what must be, reasonableness what can be. Imagination charts a path from here to there, working out an itinerary through obstacles that are presumably realistically evaluated. The will, in anticipation, can travel the road towards the desired end. Such figures of will negotiate a course of action for an educated and dynamic desire that is conscious of the facts at hand. I may perhaps borrow a metaphor from Schopenhauer. Our consciousness is like a sphere: it is 'brighter and more distinct the further it extends towards without, so that its greatest clearness lies in sense perception, which already half belongs to things outside us, – and, on the other hand, grows dimmer as we go in, and leads, if followed to its inmost recesses, to a darkness in which all knowledge ceases.'[173] At the centre of the sphere is the will.

Tyrannical wills attempt to force their way through obstacles; they cloud the surface of the sphere the better to blind themselves to real obscurities and difficulties. 'I will, I know, it must be' is the formula of desire gone mad.[174] 'By the simple exercise of our will we can exert a power for good practically unbounded' writes Conrad's Kurtz as he outlines his plan for a benevolent transformation of Africa. *Heart of Darkness* shows that a will's eloquence is not enough. Kurtz did not know himself; he lacked restraint; 'he was hollow at the core.'[175] The darkness and wilderness devoured him. Or consider the complex stories of *Les Liaisons dangereuses*. In this prerevolutionary aristocratic milieu human beings are cut off from the ordinary demands of life and have little to do but talk to each other and about their common acquaintances who are absent. Two protagonists pursue an intrigue: they see themselves as intelligent schemers, adept at getting pleasures. And the pleasure they need right away is that of revenge. So they cause painful events to happen in some people's lives simply by making these people believe things. The edifice of their lies creates decisive realities: thus they manipulate the feelings of others and bend them to their will. They coerce, but never through force, only through verbal persuasion. They seduce; they cause others to seduce and be seduced. They ruin reputations and safeguard their own. They break hearts – and they have none. Their schemes give them what is to them the only valuable enhanced feeling of life: the sense of a successful will, the sense of exercising power over others as an end in itself (it is amusing and it gives one prestige). The bodies of others are just a field on which to win the battles that offer the keenest mental pleasures. What the book presents, writes Malraux, is a mythology of the will.[176] Mythology here is to be taken in an adverse sense: a web of illusions. These experts who play on others to impose a fate on them become themselves victims of perfectly ordinary fates. The less skilled of the two becomes victim of the righteous anger of others and, ironically, the cleverer of the two, the more self-conscious one, the one who had claimed to have made herself, becomes victim of her own body, which she had used but ignored. The completely masterful will is only an illusion that the inexperience of the weak makes possible for the strong. Human beings cannot be just planners, whether high-minded missionaries of progress or petty domestic schemers. Human beings should endeavour not to repeat Adam's error, who, caught up by his fancy, had to admit (too late), in Milton's words, 'My will concurred not to my being.'[177]

Which will, however, can always rest content with dictated figures which declare what is and invite submission to what the world and society say must be? Is not every will always alert, always seeking to negotiate new scenarios for becoming? Is not our greatest achievement as human beings the discovery that, thanks to imagination and perseverance, a new path has been found so that the desire of our heart and the realistic judgment of our intellect can meet for once, so that happy acts of will can show themselves on the public scene?

Figures of will therefore are, at their best, dynamic socialized expressions of desire. Although born of limitations, they are not instruments of coercion. They reflect the freedom we have in our inner space to dream that things might be better and the chances we have to embody our intent. They provide human beings with achievements in meant co-operation. They can become the minimal shared stories that give joint paths to our wills. Anxiety is the price we pay when we do not know how to imagine and negotiate suitable figures of will. 'Anxiety is that range of distress which attends willing what cannot be willed.'[178] Acts of will, then, are sterile; they do not move along appropriate figures of will, and they fail, again and again. 'In isolation from such powers as intellect and imagination, the will can only will; reflection about its own adversities being beyond its capacity.'[179] It becomes rigid and lives blindly.

The notion of figures of will, crucial as it is to the task of self-knowledge, is also indispensable to those who wish to penetrate into the intricacies of social interaction. Such figures enable people to see what is at stake for themselves, for their own freedom, among the fluidities of social interaction. What we ordinarily call social situations are such situations as are observed by an exterior observer. Persons then become seen as things moved by impersonal forces. But sociological observation should give way to a fuller hermeneutics of the social interaction that asks what kinds of stories the selves believe they enact.[180] What does each will find in a shared transaction? What symbolic actions embody figures of will? Figures of will, I must repeat, are movable types. They are part of a process that composes, decomposes, or recomposes reality. But something positive must always be said about figures of will: they hold the freedom of the self during the process; they maintain a sense of the trustworthiness of the world (shifty though it may be) and of the freedom of the self to commit itself to action.

Let us return to the Christian tradition as a cultural tradition. My hypothesis proposes to see it as a religious tradition that enables selves to try on models of will and see what wills they have. It also proposes that Christianity can be understood by reviewing what it has done to human wills in the past. What sort of education has it in fact conveyed to those human beings it has seen as beings endowed with a will?

The exposition of my hypothesis will fall under three headings: 1 / Christianity's discovery of the will, or its historic way of addressing man qua will; 2 / its attempt to improve the will, or educate it; 3 / the reappropriation of the Christian tradition that I should like to propose now.

1 / To speak of Christianity as a religion that addresses the will sharpens the contrast with the Greek world. The will, writes Bruno Snell, 'is a notion foreign to the Greeks.' This view is too extreme.[181] The Greeks see choices, and strive to actualize some rather than the others. It is true that they have no specialized vocabulary of the will and make no earnest attempt to distinguish it as a specific ingredient.[182] Michael J. O'Brien speaks of haziness at the boundary-lines between psychic functions.[183] Aristotle, however, comes up with an analysis which singles out the will for a limited but decisive role. The basic scenario he discerns behind action is the classic Greek one: reason is in conflict with desire and inclination. Action should execute the commands of reason and should itself be reasonable (that is exhibit practical intelligence). The conflict between reason and desire is not a crude clash of forces. Each produces in the mind preferred choices; what actually clashes is these possible intentions. When we weigh these intentions, what we deliberate about is only which possible choice best marshals the means of achieving our end. For Aristotle we do not deliberate about or choose our ends: they are inherent in human nature. But we have warring inclinations about the means towards them.[184] At this point *proairesis*, the philosophical

birth-place of a notion of will, comes into its own. It is an arbiter between several possible sets of means. And it chooses.[185] What the Greeks arrive at, then, is a sense of there being in fact, for us, a limited range of free choices available. They are not clear about the limits of the range. What they are missing in comparison with us is the sense of the will being our mental organ for the future, the mental endowment we have for beginning something new.[186] One could also express it by saying that the Greeks do not believe it is wise (or possible) to commit ourselves to a particular long-range effort in regard to the future.

This view can be confirmed by looking at the peculiar anxiety Greeks feel about the future. It does seem that, unlike many of us, they do not feel they have an organ for coping with it. They always want to know how things will end. It seems that ignorance on this point is very hard for them to bear. Hesiod, we remember, sees the wise man as one who knows the end of things. Herodotus reveals much about himself when he has a Persian grandee state that, 'of all the sorrows which afflict mankind, the bitterest in this, that one should have consciousness of much but control over nothing.' Solon's warning not to count a man happy until he has spent his last hour is a most frequently cited saying.[187]

The Greeks, as a consequence, view hope in a rather peculiar manner. *Elpis* is commonly translated 'hope' but at times it means merely the power to anticipate the future in one's imagination; it thus can mean fear as well. Man has two foolish councillors, pleasure and pain, we hear in the *Laws*. Each has its own *elpis*, or expectation, or apprehension.[188] Desire and hope, writes Thucydides, jointly produce the intoxication that causes the greatest calamities.[189] Desire conspires with hope to delude the self about the possible impending disaster and imagine only the best, which is what one wants. 'Hope and danger are twins among mankind, spirits of evil both,' says Theognis. We read in Simonides that 'hope and alluring temptation feed us all, straining after the unattainable.' Desire and hope, adds F.M. Cornford, are also viewed as angry ghosts and counted among the avenging spirits.[190] Hope is, to most of us, a blessing rather than a woe, and most of us believe we can trim our hopes to a reasonable level. To the Greeks hope is always a temptation that the wise resist, a deep delusion, conceived in lust by greed upon the unpredictability of the future. It is as if the Greeks do not trust in their ability to form realistic, reasonable anticipations of the future. The man who has *elpis* only believes he can see; in fact he is as blind as the one who has no thought about the future.[191]

All this is changed among the Greeks and the Romans who become Christians. They convert, that is join the church in a voluntary act and believe they have a transformative experience of eternal significance. They feel that in an act they have achieved – or undergone – an immediate response and unity with the will of God. and they see this event as an event of faith or of conscience that cannot be invalidated.[192] Furthermore their Scriptures keep addressing them as beings who can and must form volitions.[193] The Bible (Hebrew and Greek) has God addressing human beings, calling them with a promise: 'I am the Lord your God' (Exodus 20:2). This address creates the human being as subject: the subject is acknowledged by the Creator, invited to listen, to obey, to respond, and be true to his or her word. Separation is not the breaking of a whole but the constitution of a self capable of independent relations. The human being is also summoned to answer for his or her action before an Other who searches the loins and the heart.[194] The divine promise ('I have come down to deliver them out of the land of the Egyptians, and to bring them up out of that land to a good and broad land': Exodus 3:8) can be responded to only in a trusting, voluntary action that has classically received the name of faith.

We can thus accept Arendt's view: the faculty of the will 'was discovered as a result of experiences about which we hear next to nothing before the first century of the Christian era.'[195] The faculty so discovered has a measure of consciouness of itself: because human beings do not know, they have to will. Willing moves into an area, the future, where there are no certainties. The human being, as he wills, moves into this area with personal seriousness, with all his or her character and strength.

There is something else that is novel about the New Testament: the power to form volitions heightens its self-consciousness to the point where we observe a self-objectivation of the will. The crucial text is chapter 7 of Paul's letter to the Romans. As analysed by Hans Jonas, this document reveals the abyss of the will. In it Paul no longer simply says 'I will.' He antecedently says 'I will that I will' and that leads to the inevitable ensnarement of the will in itself. Do I really will to will? Or do I merely think I will? Why can't I simply will? Why can't I do the good I will (or naïvely believe I will)? Why do I do the evil I don't will (or naïvely believe I don't will)? Why does every act of volition leave something to be desired so that it is immediately countered by an opposing act? The requirement of a holy will heightens the despair: certitude about having an unholy will becomes irresistible since willing, aware of its ambiguity, has lost any possible purity. Any satisfactory performance of the will, any itinerary through a figure of the will, becomes ruined by self-enjoying observation – and self-commendation. Even merciless self-criticism can become in its turn enjoyable. In the abyss of the will freedom becomes endlessly reflective and powerlessness is its inevitable fate.[196]

Jonas remarks that this self-objectivation of the will arises mainly thanks to the 'side-glance of comparison with others' (thus recalling Jean-Jacques Rousseau's distinction between honest self-love and corrupt love of self that wishes to be something in the eyes of others). Self-consciousness of will and self-objectivation of will lead to social and cultural determination of desire. Desire seeks to realize itself by playing out scenarios on a stage crowded with symbols. We want our figures of will to compare favourably with those of others. René Girard has put it in a poignant phrase: desire has given itself a triangular structure, has become mimetic. I want to have what he has; I want to be what he is. What he gets is, thanks to symbols that swim in my head, promoted by me to unique attractiveness (the child is sure that the ice cream cone the other child has is bigger or better).[197]

The scenario is thus set for the inner conflicts within western human beings and the outer conflicts among them. The Christian religion, however, did not begin as powerless diagnosis of an insoluble deadlock. The will that hinders itself and cannot be helped by friendly advice is coming to expression in the context of the confession of a cure. Thanks to God's mercy and fellowship with the risen Christ the will is healed. The philosopher may well wish to suspend judgment on both the nature of the disease and the merits of the cure but there is something for him to observe in the fact that the war between will and counterwill is overcome in the experience of a community. Ignatius of Antioch succinctly gives the formula for this community: 'Faith the beginning; and love the end.'[198] The community begins in mutual trust and leads to mutual enjoyment. The point here is that the will healed is not again what it was before its disease. It has experienced within itself a symbolic structuring of its relationship with others and with itself such that it rejects outright the alimentary view of desire. What man wants is not consumption of objects but a mode of interaction with persons, not a state of self-enjoyment but a state of mutual enjoyment.

The shift can be observed quickly. There is plainly a visible contrast between Plato's mysticism and the mysticism of the Christian Platonist Gregory of Nyssa, the founder of Christian mystical theology, the theology that came to a particular blossoming in the Eastern Church. In Platonic mysticism desire comes to rest through fruition: its object may be impersonal. In Christian mysticism the soul never rests filled with any acquired possession but is always dilated, expanded further through its meeting with God. The object of the mystical search must be personal and is not such as can be possessed in a final manner. The activity of human love, unlike all others, never ceases and its enjoyment never produces satiety.[199]

Augustine brings out the full potential inherent in such destiny of the will. First of all he roundly affirms that there is no cause of the will independent of the willing subject. Then he straightforwardly lets the individual stand or fall with his will. What are we except wills? (Augustine illustrates the human predicament from the feelings and behaviour of children: they do not have the fullness of reason but they have the fullness of will).[200] Will focuses our attention and thereby unites all our faculties. The basic undeniable facts about these beings endowed with will are that they love their own existence and that they are invited to do something. Every human being is a new beginning, created by God that a beginning might be. Arendt nicely adds that, while the Greeks have taught us to call human beings mortals, we could have learned from Augustine to call them natals.[201]

To this Augustine adds that we have the wills we have. And the bodies we have. And that to will and to be able is not the same. And even that there is 'nothing prodigious in partly to will and partly not to will.' And, even further, that two wills contend in man, an old one, carnal, and a new one, spiritual.[202] The self is diseased; no good will emerges out of it ready to respond to and accept the divine good will. Salvation comes only through a great storm, a loss of control, an experience of surrender. God converts the self to himself.[203] It must also be seen that in this experience of surrender the Christian will merges with the Christian practice of sacrifice. The will gives up the goods achieved by relative control to surrender to a greater good. There is a painful loss but there is the gain. Self-sacrifice become a fundamental theme among figures of the will (self-sacrifice even unto death). Self-sacrifice is the most poignant of all boundary situations: in it an old self is destructured and a new one is presumably restructured. Augustine speaks of the disease and cure of his will with a candour that is still amazing (he is still unique among theologians for the anchorage he gives to his words in his own body). And he has come out of his experience with a sophisticated doctrine of love.

Love, Augustine affirms, always settles the actions of ambivalent or undecided wills. Hence the phrase: my weight is my love.[204] The orientation of our will, in the end, depends on the story of our loves. The story unfolds – we seek, find, lose, and reorder our loves – as we become aware of the economy of wills in which we are placed: beside our will there is the will of God – who loves us – and there are the wills of our fellow-men. Man is not primarily a mind opposed to nature but a will relating to other wills.[205] There are basically two patterns of relation. Either the will loves self even to the contempt of God. Such wills together found the city of man. They experience conflict and only such collaboration as is found in the short-lived conspiracies of a few. These wills have power: power to wage war. The deadlocked, 'powerless' person will never for long stay content with powerlessness. His loves make him act, but if the person acts on love of self, even to the contempt of God, his apparently powerful act only entrenches his powerlessness since it perpetuates conflict. His love of self leads only to a hateful life and a hate-filled city. Or the will responds to the love of God and acts on its love of God even to the contempt (or sacrifice) of self. God has founded a city for such wills: it is the City of God where human beings enjoy God and enjoy one another in God.[206] The story of our loves can educate our wills to the enjoyment of this overall economy. Self is fulfilled in the city of God – and miserable in the city of men.

Sociability, implies Augustine, is intrinsically ennobling. 'All love implies necessarily an element of goodwill toward those who are loved.'[207] And God, Augustine believes, keeps recalling the self to himself through the economy of its intimate and social loves. Augustine's argument is that our loves can in time educate our will (unless our will remains entrapped in the treadmill of actualizing the anxious power of solitary powerlessness, and it takes only the fiat of the will to reactualize this sort of existence). The important breakthrough is that the pattern of mutuality is seen to exist both between man and man and between God and man. Augustine brings to the West the Christian mysticism we have encountered in Gregory of Nyssa and discerns it sosial ramifications. He thereby lays the intellectual basis for the view of social life as a co-operative exchange among all wills that becomes realized in the medieval cities of northern Europe: no family is allowed to build a castle inside the city walls; existing ones are torn down – and every man's home is proclaimed his castle. A social order is sought where all wills are safe and none threatening.

Eight hundred years later Duns Scotus is still true to such insights about the nature of the will.[208] By their will human beings can transcend everything created. Will can resist both desire and reason. Will can find a perverse pleasure in affirming itself in defiance of everything. Man can hate God and find satisfaction in such hatred. Divided wills are 'redeemed' by activity. Buridan's ass, hesitating between two equidistant haystacks, at some point stops choosing and starts eating. Sheer activity begins the transformation of willing into loving. Loving activity, at its best, is purified of need/desire. Love is the actuality of an exercise that has an end in itself. It knows an active (but not restless) peace, 'the serenity of a self-contained, self-fulfilling, everlasting movement.'[209] Duns Scotus is also very clear on the fact that human processes are contingent as they occur. Arendt stresses that with Scotus contingency for the first time loses its derogatory associations: 'contingency is a positive mode of being, just as necessity is another mode.'[210] Everything that is past is absolutely necessary; it has *become* a framework of necessary conditions. The past is beyond the reach of the will *now*; but the future is not.

Hegel, therefore, can be credited with drawing the correct conclusion about a whole cultural development as he writes that Christians have 'realized an ever-present sense that they are not and cannot be slaves ... This will to liberty is no longer an *impulse* which demands its satisfaction, but the permanent character – the spiritual consciousness grown into a non-impulsive nature.'[211] Plato believes that there can be too much freedom (he identifies freedom with impulsiveness). To Hegel and Shestov there cannot (they would, however, disagree on the meaning of freedom). Socrates was prepared to curb his impulses even to the point of accepting death (and others to the point of accepting slavery); he drank the drug (*pharmakon*) handed to him by the civic official. He did not call it a poison and did not find the very substance of his life outraged by this invitation.[212] Hegel quite rightly draws the conclusion that social conflicts in the Christian world arise over the matter of recognition. Each free human being wants to have his right to freedom recognized, to have the meaning of his strivings acknowledged and his achievements endorsed.[213]

Such a view of freedom as permanent character opens the prospect of a metaphysics that cannot ever complete the circle, cannot ever find an all-encompassing meaning, cannot ever affirm an overall structure, cannot ever acknowledge some experience of being that should be obeyed. Some Christians quite squarely accept these implications. 'The historical (i.e. contingent) irruption of the divine word is a scandalous riddle for the metaphysical mind and the desire of mystics, which are both fascinated by the One-All.' In their nostalgia human beings yearn for some sort of fusion: A God who speaks to some at some point of time demands that all such yearnings be renounced as illusion.[214] Human beings who respond to God must now give up the God of metaphysical speculation and of mystical desires. There is no necessity in the relationship between God and his creatures. Hegel is wrong. But the divine word does more than issue a challenge to human freedom. Here Shestov is wrong. The contingent encounter opens a dialogue, an interaction, that has a character. Will in human beings is not a defiant fiat: when human beings form figures of will, they integrate bodily spontaneity (something involuntary) and they venture to deem something possible in the world. It is not mere wish but real work. There are conditions for the will's free work in the world and with other human wills.[215] Merleau-Ponty has pointed out that, while being and freedom are sharply distinct, they cannot be antithetical if there is to be any historical work done.[216] To act is to work at not being what one now is, but it is not simply flinging a rejection into the dark. It is a project which entails a judgment about compossible ends. These conditions must be attended to by historical acts of attention to reality. But such acts cannot be systematized into a coherent single view of a historical or ahistorical while. This is the case because the acts of attention to reality are not some listening to being but acts of attention to historical realities and to the reality of persons.

Lévinas is the shrewdest analyst of the sort of attention that human beings have for each other. Present in the face, the otherness of the other is a non-threatening otherness: it exhibits a mastery that does not conquer but teaches. We can thus have for the other a sort of desire that is not fulfilled or extinguished by any pleasure. People in love desire each other, not some universal. The other does not limit any freedom: in infinity there is always enough room; in totality there never is. But to stand before the other is to allow that my freedom can be judged.[217]

If this view is sound, then Christianity as a religion that addresses the will must contend now as ever against the ontotheological ambitions of many of its theologians. Plato's *Republic* made a thought experiment that offered the idea of the Good as an all-encompassing sovereignty that had to be attended to. This was hardened by Aristotle's systematic metaphysical theology. Christian theologians then used it, modified it to suit their views, but remained with the idea of a system that could achieve the metaphysical equivalent of parliamentary closure and provide a definite framework for all judgments of reality. What has recently been called the death of God may be only the disappearance of the cap-stone that closed the vault we so much like to feel above our heads and the definitive discrediting of all ontotheology.[218]

What Christians understand by faith carries the idea that man is essentially unfinished – faith responds to a promise – and that man does not yet *know* how he will be finished. It is acceptance of novelty. It is also acceptance of life in an open universe. And this acceptance is secure enough to be quite conscious as itself as faith. We can now understand why the Greeks, who undoubtedly had beliefs and hopes and courage as well, cannot be said to have had faith. There was no self-consciousness prepared to commit itself to its beliefs.

2 / We can now move to the second of the two questions I formulated at the outset. In addition to seeing humans as being endowed with wills the Christian tradition also attempts to bring education to these wills. If the Greek religious tradition can be said to teach religion to the mind by teaching it reverent contemplation, the Christian tradition teaches religion to the will by teaching charity to its loves.

Through its Scriptures, its liturgy, devotional literature, sermons, and individual spiritual guidance the Christian tradition gave Westerners a side range of possible figures of will. This religious tradition had begun by telling new stories and writing a new kind of text. Mark's record of the conversation between Peter the fisherman and an anonymous servant girl and of Peter's subsequent tears had more significance than the histories of all the Herodians. Paul revealed something of his hidden self-consciousness and inner conflicts to his parishioners.[219] Augustine wrote of a family crisis at the beginning of his adolescence: he got an involuntary erection at the baths; his father noticed it and, overjoyed, went to tell the mother; she was not amused and did not hide her distress.[220] Pope Gregory, pondering Luke's account of the journey to Emmaus, found in it the major features of common religious experience. He spoke of Christian longing as 'supernal desire,' meaning thereby a desire that finds no durable satisfaction this side of the heavenly home. Christian living was thus defined as a pilgrimage during which sojourners experience both a fullness and an emptiness, both a presence and an absence. Such theological themes kept reappearing in the medieval tradition of letters of friendship and in countless popular pilgrim plays. Throughout his life, it was thought, man 'ambivalently meets in another man the deity he so ardently desires.'[221] Thus there was a pattern in Christian texts: whether learned or popular, they revealed how individuals contended with their daily fears and hopes, their joys and longings. They proposed figures of will: Christians could then experiment with those that fitted their experience best. The range of available figures was bounded by two heresies: the Pelagian one that taught that all depended on the will, and the quietist one that recommended extinction of the will. In between, the repertory was vast: the living will, ever desirous, could always test the extent of its power and the dimensions of its powerlessness. But it could never rest content with a sapiential self-image as a prudent one who is strong because never attempting the impossible. Desire is ever keen to remain desirous, even if it is only to dream the impossible ... So new strategies of will are always needed by a will that is committed to an active life within limits. The Christian tradition can teach much to such wills.

My purpose now is to render this potential as explicit as possible. But before honouring the religious intelligence found in the Christian tradition I should like to be clear, briefly and polemically clear, about some peculiarly Christian forms of religious stupidity. First, Christianity has managed to instil much self-hatred in many of its adherents. I refer to figures of the will telling stories of self-sacrifice. From very early times martyrdom was actively sought and the bones of martyrs treasured as the most precious relics. From very early times an ascetic streak in Christianity commended *contemptus mundi* and practised bodily mortifications, which it deemed legitimate because of their punitive and redemptive effects. A celibate streak strove for totalitarian control of the body and what it called its sinful lusts. Pelagius is sure pure chastity is within the reach of all. Before the Fall, believes Gregory of Nyssa, human beings were neither male nor female. Augustine disagrees: human beings were male and female then, but they had perfect control over their bodies; they were never unwillingly sleepy, and coitus was a cool deliberate activity undertaken for procreative purposes only, since it was not attended by any special pleasure. Over and against these views one recalls that one must hold on to a holistic view of the self, that bodies are the best pictures of minds, and that sexual self-expression is one among the many articulations of human freedom.[222]

Secondly, Christianity, since Constantine and Nicea, has occasionally pursued particularly vigorous and insidious attempts at totalitarian political and / or social control by requiring adhesion to a creed. I find it significant that the elaboration of the public orthodox creeds introduced the most learned metaphysical concepts into the formulation of the faith. What epistemological pride and what lust for power presided over the whole enterprise can be captured in the formula of (Pope) Gregory the Great: 'What do they not see, who see Him who sees all things?'[223] This striving for creedal control has produced among some and occasionally many

Christians a particularly ardent hatred for the institutions and dogmas of their church. Christianity has elicited among some of its adherents an anticlericalism and militant atheism that has few matches in the history of religion. This I tend to relate to the fact that Christian élites rarely remained with Plato's condescending tolerance for silly fools below. The fools below were too frequently viewed as dangerous devils who had to be saved against their will – or repressed at all costs. The ascetic and the political-totalitarian distortions of Christianity share in the same obsessive practices of a perfectionist or tyrannical will. The will is committed to a project, deemed perfect, and pursues it rigidly, single-handedly. The will always wants to be in charge, alone. The Calvinistic pursuit of productive work is a third historic form of this distortion. In all such actions the self is filled with assurance that its action is perfectly sound and thus embodies an absolute belief. Wills are set on their course and cannot be educated.[224]

The most important thing to say about the education of the will is that the human being addressed by the other human being discovers in himself the arousal of a desire which is not a need. Like oysters we have our needs. But unlike them we handle matter; and we can speak and listen. Consider the work of our hands. We handle food, clay, wood. It resists us, yet we shape it, clean it, make it into something good, useful, beautiful. We decentre ourselves, to dream about the enjoyable reality our wills are about to create. We share with others the work of our hands and discuss its qualities. Consider also erotic experience. One of our strongest needs comes to expression in this desire. And this desire takes shape, as Jacques Lacan has written, in the open space where the request gets torn off from the need.[225]

We ask the other before acting on our need or act on our need by asking the other. Thus we both desire and desire to be desired. We live our biology by giving and receiving calls. And we are open even to the extent of seeing the point of an answer that is not exactly the answer to the question we had formulated. We can even enjoy seeing our questions reformulated and our desires reoriented. (In contrast, our needs cannot be redefined; only diet according to formula satisfies them.) In our human desires we are open to a transcendent, free other. We want to become absorbed in doing things with the other. Our creativity thus becomes cocreativity. The God of Christian religion is likewise an irreducible other: non-threatening, but unwilling to be a plug to our holes. Lévinas makes the point by saying that two things together make a totality (which can be added up and summed up). The I and the other do not make a totality but an infinity.[226] Their interaction creates a world of symbols, to articulate what they say and what they are up to. And this world created by the interaction cannot ever be closed. Much can happen in it; what cannot happen is satiety and the fulfilment of the wish of absolute consciousness. No one can speak of the I and the other from one point of view and see the totality of it. One cannot find perfect transparency; the symbols are never perfectly adequate. And one does not find self-sufficiency; only the other can elicit symbols of interaction.[227]

Instead of finding its expression in the definiteness of needs requiring fulfilment, the will can be transmuted to the point of finding its expression in vagueness and good will. It knows its figures must alter. It can grow to a sort of lack of affective focus. The imprecision is important. Human relations, writes Paul Valéry, are based on ciphers: 'To decipher them is to quarrel. A cipher says without saying; mutual opinions are kept suspended, *reversible*. Ciphers allow interaction without decisive and definitive judgments which are true only at a given point of time.'[228] In this very vagueness indefinite good will blossoms. Juxtaposed human beings do not fit (and never will make a totality) yet are tolerant of each other. No mechanical or organic causality presides over this state of good will. No struggle for recognition either; it is more like a state of availability for mutual amusement. no sovereign good is envisaged to preside over the common endeavour. Wills seek their interaction rather than their fulfilment.

Human beings in face-to-face relationships both see and hear each other. What they hear and say is, however, the privileged road to their education.[229] Totalities can be gathered and seen in space. Space is the medium of absolute identity. There can be more or less of it, but it remains always equal to itself. To see the loved one appeases desire. Yet the human being can look back and seek to reduce me to the status of an object. But then I can also close my eyes and cease to see. Visual sensual inputs encourage the illusion of control of others – or the illusion of independence from them. Sound inputs have a different impact: I cannot close my ears; I have less freedom for selective attention. And the spoken order knows the limits of its power. To be heard one must gain attention. The loved one heard gives something new. The other seen is potentially threatening: it can rob me of myself, make of me a needy lover or a tortured self. The other heard invites to a listening that is a non-alienating obedience. Subjects remain subjects in the relation. Speculative ontology is built on the desire to see and unfurls a mentally visible world of words. The Bible speaks of a God who speaks and develops the desire to listen. Truth is not an object in space out there, quietly basking even when I do not look at it; it is an event that occurs when human beings speak and listen, when stories get shared. And what is spoken and heard in the medium of time cannot be brought to a totality. Human stories are never rounded. Eschatology, the uniquely biblical religious form, does not say how history will be closed. It rejects every attempt to see it – and make it – whole.[230]

In the event of listening the willing self is decentred. This decentring keeps us within the human pale, puts us in motion among humans; it lets compassion and justice dawn on us. It is the foundational experience of morality.[231] Achilles is angry when decentred; his will becomes restless. Ulysses, however, becomes interested. Of course we want that what we love be the good, and that what we say be the truth. But Ulysses can become unglued; his desires and his ideas do not stick to him. Perhaps there is yet another facet to the good or to the truth. The blblical decentring is even more radical. Abraham sets out to travel to a goal he has not seen, accepting a promise from a god who will accompany him on an adventure without return. In biblical terms the fellow human being is not primarily one who helps me return home – or prevents me from doing so. The widow and the orphan meet me as the weak others who have nothing that fits my needs. But they meet me, low though they are, with a height that makes a demand because they are from God. Seeing this, the will has learned faith and charity. It breathes in a world of symbols where the needs of the other have as much weight as my own. It accepts giving up the desired possession of objects it saw.

To charitable selves 'I love you' means 'I want you to be' (it does not mean 'I want to have you' or 'I want to rule you'). Selves, then, are not just recognized for what they do or claim to be; they become valued for what they are. This highest potential of the will, however, can be actualized only in a given historical context of symbolically lived human interaction. At its best this interaction is a story of cocreativity: each self is artistically involved in shaping the material of its own life and of those that surround it.[232] Furthermore a world of symbols can elicit the potential for generosity and mercy only if it is genuinely lived in by actual selves, only if it concretely mediates real life to human beings and does not simply hover above them as an ideal or confront them as a norm. The philosopher, therefore, cannot just ahistorically affirm the need for such symbolic mediation: he must see the real historical world of lived symbols and seek to understand them in their distinct singularities.[233]

Literature, of course, is our best source for catching actual wills at the business of inventing figures and interacting.[234] Shakespeare's *Antony and Cleopatra* shows us two people losing their grip on world power – and meeting their ruin in self-inflicted death. But the play is not tragic in the sense that the heroes are not the pathetic playthings of a ruinous passion. These aging lovers no longer have the illusions and delusions of youth. They are mature wills; their character keeps fluidity; their action is willed and intelligent – and their language remains full of bounce. Their interaction remains vital to the end; they create – and recreate – a world of symbols that enables them to remain themselves under the circumstances. Rarely has the liveliness of the will – and the power of speech – been so beautifully exhibited. Style enables this imperial man and this royal woman on their downward path to defeat the inherent tendency towards dissolution of the frail sphere for interaction that is mediated by language. *The School for Wives* of Molière tells another story. Although in a very different historical context, it is again a lesson on the power of the will that is brought home. Arnolphe is the archetypal domestic tyrant: he wants to have Agnes as a wife entirely in his power and devises everything to this end. Agnes nevertheless discovers she has a will – and sees that men play a game in which they tend to give her only the role of the prize. Such an involuntary role she quietly rejects. When confronted with her voluntary resistance, Arnolphe wishes to strike her, but this he cannot do. Anger at her resistance to his will is high, but the will to strike her cannot emerge. He is a civilized tyrant. He has internalized a strong code of manners. He is deadlocked: he has lost fluidity of character; he cannot reach his desire – and cannot express his pain. There, for a fleeting moment, he is tragic. Agnes has no acquired character yet: she is at that happy stage where 'no' is all it takes to express one's freedom. The will of one is paralysed, that of the other is at the moment of birth.

The human beings who wrote and watched these plays have travelled a long way since the days when tragedies and comedies were performed in Athens. The characteristic new feature, I think, is the presentation of the individual will as intrinsically social and open to intelligent interpersonal negotiations. In the grand noble play the heroes are not really tragic: they are destroyed, but not by each other. In the funny bourgeois play the individuals are not purely comic: their wills are linked to minds. The gap between the tragic and the comic genre has been narrowed. Tragedy is mellowed and comedy refined.

These two examples also bring to light what is probably the major problem in the modern hermeneutics of the will. The interaction of Antony and Cleopatra encompasses the public as well as the private stage. While there is a whole civilization behind Arnolphe's practice of authority, no kingdom has its fate depend on the outcome of his story with Agnes.[235] We have trouble enough today repairing the intermediaries between human beings in face-to-face interaction and weaving the necessary mediations between initial intention and communicative outcome. Frequently we have no hope of seeing such mediations repaired at the level of a society. We suffer at the social level from a serious crisis of intermediaries.[236]

The same road in the end opens the way to fuller potentialities in the privately symbolized interaction and in the publically symbolized one.[237] Inherited symbols must be hermeneutically reappropriated, remembered, but not for their own sake – creatively remembered, one might say. Remembered with a view to reopening paths of dialogue between human beings, to repairing communicative symbolic mediations, giving shape again to a free style of existence among freedoms. The work of artists is of major help here. Modern literature, from Shakespeare to Kafka, can be shown to ponder the nature of the will and of its power. Corrupt at the outset? Corrupted by its exercise of power? Corrupted by society? Redeemed by grace? Healed partially? By loyalty to social arrangements? Capable of lending some virtue to social arrangements? Capable of some step that will be the essence of innocence? Capable of bringing into existence a society where all will be fair?[238] Artists give concrete answers to these questions in their work. And theologian Gibson Winter can write a book showing that what people do in real life is best compared to the artistic process.[239] In his turn, Girard shows how artists manage to criticize what people do. The novelist, in particular, achieves a truth by denouncing the romantic lie. The illusions of Don Quixote's life are undermined by putting Sancho Panza next to him.[240]

We have seen that autobiographical details previously deemed trivial became religious literature and forged the self-consciousness of a religious tradition and a civilization. After such origins it is not surprising that literature *tout court*, the theatre, the novel, have in their turn also undertaken to educate our wills towards an active self-knowledge and dynamic love.

3 / A few suggestions are in order concerning the sort of hermeneutical reappropriation of the Christian tradition that I would like to venture now. The first step, of course, consists in replacing Christian symbols in their cultural, social, and biographical contexts (and thus overcoming the theological and ecclesiastical bent of histories of Christianity). One can then hope to discern again there the power proper to religious language which is that of redescribing the human existence in the context of worldly reality in such a way as to reawaken unexpected and unformulated possibilities rooted in the goodness of our birth, namely in the goodness of God and the potential goodness of human beings. The future can be opened to us, the eschatological message heard, provided we accept going through an archaeological moment and acknowledge that our imagination, once awakened, is caught between the utopian follies of pulsating need and the slavery of accepted truths. But the imagination must be aroused; our past must be overcome. The God of religion cannot be the God of the wars of religion.[241] The wars of religion were deep, massive cultural facts; they were not just pursued by a religious and political élite. To overcome this heritage does not mean simply to think more purely of God, but rather to bring a more human solution to the socioeconomic and cultural systems of relation betwen human beings of different convictions. In one word, although a hackneyed one, overcoming this heritage means striving to overcome alienation.[242]

The objective may also be expressed – perhaps more usefully – by saying that we should aim for a Christian religion without ideology and without neurosis. A symbolic system is ideological in so far as it brings integration to the group at the cost of systematic distortion. Ideology gives idolatrous worship to some ideas that seem intensely needed and thereby hide something. What is commonly hidden is the oppressive exercise of authority within the group and the exploitative violence done to those outside. Oppression is, of course, all the more rigidly maintained among human beings when the dominant thought system denies that the phenomenon exists. Moderns have been fascinated by Hegel's account of the relationship between master and slave: an immanent account of the process of human domination holds the promise, so it is thought, of an immanent process of liberation from all exploitative relationships. As J.B. Metz points out, theology, if it is to have any confidence in its task, must be able to describe and call upon a praxis where Christians manage to modify oppressive social conditions.[243]

But communication can also be neurotically distorted. (There are, of course, links between neurosis best exhibited in face-to-face interaction and the ideology that seizes groups, but I have not seen any adequate theoretical account of the relationship.) A neurosis is a bent taken in a person's character unknown to himself or herself; it issues forth in behaviour that mystifies the person. The psyche is formed at the junction between the physical organism (its needs and impulses) and the cultural world of symbols. The person is always involved in working out an equilibrium between the two. Solutions are pathological if they are entrenched, if they acquire the automaticity of repetitions. Conflicts then are deadlocked and lead always either to the self-mutilation inherent in obsessive guilt or to the social disruption involved in hysteria. What is lost in this pathology is the attention to reality that gives new experiences and offers new solutions to the will.

Ideology and neurosis freeze linguistic behaviour. Speaking as a psychologist, Vergote writes that the speaking power of language occurs when the instinctual life is structured by the laws of discourse, or when imaginative desire enters into our talking. The play of language can be destroyed, or the self be absent from it, and then language becomes a symptom rather than the cure.[244] A similar analysis can be offered at the level of large groups. There public language must structure the desires of groups and embody them, keeping open the negotiation with other publicly constituted groups.

There is no such thing as common life without ideology or neurosis. The best that can be done is to relativize the ideologies and the neuroses: keep individuals and groups in touch with each other. The best way to keep alert to the dangers of ideology and neurosis may well be to keep in mind what Walter Benjamin has so aptly called dangerous memories: namely remembrance of the dead, those who suffered and were defeated.[245] (Ideologies and neuroses have the obsessive outlook of those determined to be winners.) Most dangerous are the memories of the evils we have committed or the costs we did not or could not correct.[246] Although committed to the urban life-style, Plato remembers that his city killed Socrates. In contrast, philosophy of history since Hegel offers a repulsive spectacle: excuses (evils for a greater good) or self-exculpation. The attempt to think teleologically of the historical whole may attribute guilt to others but never to the writer and his spiritual fathers. Augustine in contrast knew that the unveiling of the course of one's life, confession, included confessions of guilt before God and human beings.[247] He was not so neurotic as to have covered up all his dangerous memories.

Twentieth-century Christians are easily caught between religious institutions that are not all that manifestly redemptive or publicly relevant and a religious mysticism that is so confined to the optimization of personal interests that it does not bear many social and political fruits. Both the institutions and the mysticism lack imagination; both fail to convey the hope that liberates the will from figures of powerlessness and despair. A recovery of the speaking power of religious language will renew the contact with the original power of hope. Religious language has great decentring power: it liberates from rigid projects and desired desires (object-centred desires) to articulate the grander desire of life which may be called *desiring desire*, the will to find a human dwelling where one can live with oneself, with others, and with the entire cosmos. Such desire is an always necessary utopia; it encourages us to think, and imagine, beyond ideology and neurosis. With religious language this utopia ceases to be speechless; it receives a shape. 'A religion,' writes T. Patrick Burke, 'is the expression of a desire to hope, given form by the experience of a concrete threat to hope.' He adds that, in Christianity as in the other Semitic religions, the threat is 'the sheer nastiness, the hardheartedness of human beings toward each other.'[248]

One should see clearly the connection between renewed hope and the problems of the will. The Christian tradition has spent centuries modulating its exhortations to the conscious will. Like the existentialists after it, it has exhorted Christians to powerful resolve (unlike the existentialists, it holds out the promise of success since God is presumed to help those who pray). But, as the cost of that effort, it largely ignores that preconscious realm of experience 'in which will is joined to all appropriate human capacities – mental and physical, intellectual and emotional – to form a seamless whole enclosing me that pushes me in a particular direction at the same time that the direction in the world enlists my will and the faculties wedded to it.[249] The peculiar rapport with the body that the Christian tradition has tended to inculcate has, of course, much to do with this. And with this ignorance Christians have too often fallen into the pattern of 'the will trying to do the work of the imagination' (Yeats's diagnosis).[250] All too rare have been the occasions where warm, imaginative Christian discourse lets a fresh imagination rise and give body to hope.

All shaping of human hopes can, of course, in time, be disproved by facts. But, being commonly perceived, this shaping helps wills work together and overcome some of the present threats and disprove some of the currently established facts. Speechless utopia is irrational. But life without utopia is unreasonable. Moved by desiring desire, the will ceases to be paralysed or rigidly committed to a single project.

There is an initial similarity between such a view of desire transmuted by imagination and will into charity and Plato's view of the measuring of men by God and the overcoming of greedy desire. But, when considered concretely, in terms of the self-understanding of actual human beings, the two paths travel into different worlds. The visual experience dominates the Platonic transformation of loves, not the auditory one with its invitation to mutuality. Plato can see no surrender of love except to objects of contemplation or in bestial frenzy. He cannot articulate the legitimacy of the yielding of a human will to another will, the very root of the process of human companionship. He cannot show how our wills are remoulded as we live responsively with other human beings. Plato remains bound within the simple archetypal grasp of the will found in Homer: a heroic power that wrests happiness in difficult conditions and even against insuperable odds. Plato, of course, rejects this course for the moral man; but the alternative he sees is a mere negation of the Greek lust for acquiring and defending one's acquisitions of the good things that life has to offer. For the technical rational will that knows how to get and keep things Plato substitutes the contemplative rationality of the will that knows the abiding truth and loves nothing else. But both wills have something equally impersonal and ignore the fluctuation of the real interrelationships between persons. They are both abstractions from the fullness of a personal life (a fullness Plato consistently seems to fear and suspect).[251]

So we may conclude. That the Christian tradition has historically addressed the will and that it still has the potential to educate it even in this post-Christian world makes one point inescapable. Philosophy of religion should today not merely speak of educating desire but also of educating the will and analysing its figures. Will as conscious purpose has redrawn the map of the passions with which the Greeks were familiar. Often praised for their endurance, Christian wills have been known to be blind to real desires, unaware of the limitations of the willing self, obstinate and merciless.[252] The will to will has even been extolled. Plato was right: there are ultimate, desirable (vague) ends, but he erred in not seeing that they can be reached only if all subjects are free and freely striving towards them. Will is an original beginning in every one of us, a brave initiative, a constancy in care, a firmness in good intention, a strength in adversity, a willingness to learn new figures, even a taste for challenging all the forces and voices that say: it cannot be.

Plato's therapy is, therefore, unsound for us. Our own inner lives are so differentiated that Plato's call to imitation of the divine life is bound to be an enslavement. Hegel's more dynamic, more individualized, more historicized answer, asking the individual to devote his free energies to the promotion of the universal in his day and age, has greater merits; but against Hegel, one must repeat, in the light of Shestov, that his reconciliation of necessity and freedom in the concept of Providence is legerdemain. Providence must remain a matter of faith, not of knowledge, of a faith which is a movement forward in trust and love, and which transforms man even though it is devoid of knowledge. The Christian philosophy of Augustine is here better than Hegel; Augustine departs from Aristotle and the Greeks not because he *knows* better, but because, through his faith in Christ, he trusts that the higher wisdom has been communicated to him. That the divine will is also grace is equally an affirmation of faith, and such affirmation would always have to maintain against Hegel that the meaning of history is not entirely found in the order immanent within history. Furthermore, Hegel's invitation to accept the order of history has also come to taste of enslavement to many moderns. And once individual freedoms have become suspicious – and Shestov well illustrates to what extent that has occurred since Kierkegaard and Nietzsche started the philosophy of anti-philosophy – therapists must be able to do more than merely insinuate suspicions about suspicion. An ordered symbolic world must be found to become the context of orderly and oriented human growth. Freedoms dread order, even the order that upholds their freedom. There is little point in repeating that individuals are brutish and miserable without participation in a meaningful whole. Victimized by the oppression of historical wholes, they have come to decide that, misery for misery, that of alienation is preferable. Whatever skills the hands of the therapists in Plato and Hegel may have had in their time, they certainly are not sufficient now, and it seems that the pedagogue must seek ever more subtle methods to undertake an education that addresses itself to freedoms where they are and as they are.

10 The matter of hope

The objection might well be expressed at this stage that my view of unfinished reason and unfinished man, of reason as corrective and the Christian tradition as corrigible, betrays a pre-arranged harmony. Is my view of the task of philosophy in fact one that is coloured by my Christian belonging? And is my view of Christianity coloured by my philosophical temper? A philosophy of religion that offers a dialogue between a Christian philosophy and a philosophical Christianity may well be branded as a muted dialogue, backsliding from the universality and impartiality usually associated with philosophy. In addition to responding that the historically alert thinker cannot present himself as someone able to rise above his whole history as well as above the totality of the history of others, I should like to argue in this final section that such a view has the merit of really leaving room for hope.

An utterance of hope is really alive, that is neither ideological nor neurotic, only, I think, if it is openly and deeply rooted in biological, biographical, and religiocultural soil. We must therefore be careful to express hope only in such a way as to leave room for the birth, rebirth, and growth of actual hope. This is the time to gather some previous results. We have spoken of the incompleteness inherent in any Platonic dialogue, and of the tragic and comic voices always audible behind this greatest of all philosophical voices. We have spoken of a permanent disjunction between the endeavours of reason, between rationality and reasonableness. We have also spoken of the permanently unfinished processes of negotiation and love between wills. Writing on hope must embody in its very texture and voice the local but open nature of all our unfinished endeavours (be they in life or in art), and therefore it must always start where we are born and raised and go on from there while keeping in touch with our origins. Doctrinaire hope is destroyed hope. There is about living hope always something personal and unspoken.

The crisis about hope is a deep one in our society. Our recent views of history have oscillated between elated inebriation and painful, guilt-ridden hangovers. Confidence has been placed in abstractions: the state, religion, education. Many of our intellectual leaders have thought that they could survey the totality of history, see it for instance as a teleologically arranged process of growth towards freedom and happiness. But most keys to the meaning of the whole, most institutions forged to deliver progress, turn out to provide journeys into terror. The view of the totality, instead of increasing confidence in man-made progress, has sharpened fears about man-made totalitarian control. But how can we give up totality, the dream of a complete grasp of the whole, without falling into hermetic fragmentation? By developing a view of reason as self-correcting corrective and, I suggest, by seeing how our oldest, most weighty cultural tradition, namely Christianity, can be seen to be corrigible. Under such conditions hope can be legitimate, and hope can perhaps be expressed in personally vibrant terms.

The matter of hope is thus the last test that is to be put to the philosophies of Plato, Hegel, and Shestov. We saw their trajectories arriving at doctrines. To what hope do they arrive?

Plato is intensely aware of the problematic nature of hope. His best regime (that outlined in the *Republic*) is presented as being impossible to achieve. Pessimism? Perhaps. But it also means that judgments of desirability are not to be limited by our views on attainability. Plato knows that it is unreasonable to demand in advance whether the philosopher will be successful in his reasoning with the tyrant.[253] He may be executed; he may succeed partially; he may succeed in a big way for a while. Plato believes in the reformability of the world and of existing states. In fact, he adds, it takes lots of work and good luck to boot.[254] As the myth of the *Statesman* makes clear, the history we live does not depend entirely on us: we may strive while the world is on a swing towards chaos; we cannot arrest such motion, although we can slow it down or alleviate the sufferings of humans caught up in it. The gist of it all is that we are not allowed to trust in the future or despair of it. This, I believe, is what it takes for hope to arise as a possibility. We may hope, we need hope, but we have no guarantees to underpin the peculiar hopes we form and act on at a given time. Hope is accompanied by very sober views about historical prospects.

Hegel for his part finds it contradictory to deem an ideal unrealizable. Everything that can be thought (provided one adheres to rational rules of thought) is or will be real. Trust in the lucidity of the subject and in its ability to relate to the future is so complete that hope seems neither possible nor necessary. Here readings of Hegel differ. The guarantee that the teleologically striving subject will reach its end may mean that rationality is omnipotent and will achieve freedom for all in history; it can guarantee moral control on history. Or it can ensure that, having surveyed the whole, the subject may not rest in its perfect rationality and abide by itself without going anywhere; it then guarantees peace no matter what history.[255]

Shestov sees that the speculative achievement of Hegel is the ruin of hope and of freedom. It is not true that everything including the future reveals itself to patient inquiry. It is not true that God must reveal himself to us if we are willing to be serious with him.[256] The reality of contingency is affirmed again and room is found for the will. But the intersubjective dialogue among wills is not pursued. The existentialist self is taken to the point when Agnes finds it in herself to say NO – and left there.

In the end Hegel assimilates all intersubjective discourse, retrieves all acts of hermeneutical penetration, to reach a complete *logos* that finishes its tour of reality. Shestov reaffirms the right to subjective utterance but only opens the work of *logos* among historical subjects. Plato's unique strength is that he pursues such work, takes it a long way without finishing it. He opens a course for hope by inviting us to place our confidence in a discourse that goes beyond the start – without reaching the end.

The dialogues, may I repeat, place philosophical discourse in a historical situation. They reveal that language is not forever equivocal. Progress, communication occur. But language cannot ever become univocal: misunderstandings are always possible. Thoughts cannot ever come to rest in a perfectly balanced, securely firm utterance. Unbalanced and unbalancing utterances keep reappearing. Plato is notorious for having spawned many heresies among Christians. Aristotle, so successful at finding one distinct meaning – and only one meaning – for each word, never aroused the imagination of Christians with dangerous pagan thoughts and was welcomed by strict, limiting, systematizing orthodox minds.[257] But it is precisely this danger of Plato that keeps us mentally alive and reminds us that our world and our history give us much to think and leave much to be desired.

Plato has a fluid sense of reality. *Mythos* and *logos* alternate, without either language displacing the other. The gaping lack of certainty opens a space: for freedom, for time, for dialogue, for continued discourse. Plato errs in affirming that only God, not man, is ever to be taken seriously.[258] But he is right when he shows us that man's language is never to be taken with serious finality. The appearances in our society cannot be real, but neither can our verbal piercing of these appearances. In the cave what the Sophists are up to cannot be seen because there is too much darkness. The light of pellucid utterances is equally deceptive. The philosopher, we hear in the *Sophist*, is also hard to see, 'on account of the brilliant light of the place.' Our intelligence does its real work when it discerns and acts upon lighter shades of grey. Reality is not real. The world we are really in is made up of shades of difference, among which we must navigate, not of yes-and-no dichotomies we can settle once and for all. The *Sophist* demonstrates that an idea can be defined only by what it is not, and therefore that it consists of the difference between it and other ideas. *Parmenides* faces the issue head-on: even the difference between being and non-being is only a relative difference; there is a sense in which non-being exists. Parmenides, the founder of ontology, has to be abandoned; there are different levels of being, and they entertain complex relations with each other. If there is one clear result of Plato's *Parmenides*, it is that we cannot encompass (reduce to any wholeness) the relations between what we see and what we think, although we can understand some of them in some respect. Reality cannot be encompassed in our judgments but we can pay attention to it and judge some realities. Let us learn, therefore, to judge relative differences. Let us strive to improve appearances.[259]

The sense of the relative worth of one's insights and utterances can be constantly renewed only if we keep the sense of the absolute as something confronting us. Irony is close to but distinct from scepticism. E.N. Tigerstedt has a beautiful description of Plato's ironic surrender of all claims to absolute wisdom to those who believe they have received a divine visitation. We, unlike you, says his Plato, do not believe to be inspired. You utter the thoughts of the god, but do not know what he says. Therefore, 'do not try to understand yourself, still less to explain to others, the fine things you have been saying for that is not in your power. Leave it to us who are not possessed by the god and have only human wisdom, which is but a poor thing, such as it is, whereas you have a nobler gift, divine madness.'[260] The same can be said to those philosophers who are conceptually systematic. He who proves too much proves nothing. He who places himself fully in the sun's light ceases to be visible to us who have only human wisdom.

Tigerstedt's point, of course, is that the source of such irony is religious. Socratic irony leaves room for the admission that being a wise man among fools still makes me a fool if measured by divine measures. The Platoic dialogues are ironic because they leave room for yet a further thought qualifying that where the conversation has temporarily come to rest. True philosophical discourse leaves room, leaves silence, leaves a void at the end of its utterance.[261] No philosophical conclusion is allowed to fill the gap.[262] Neither should any religious dogma. This suspension of discourse leaves an openness, which is the openness to the emergence of new possibilities. The philosopher never knows in advance where the wall will sound hollow. Philosophy, writes Merleau-Ponty, cannot anticipate what it is going to find; it cannot ever rise to a unity inside being with some already constituted philosophy presumed to rest there. Philosophy is always the language of someone who belongs to the world and cannot rise above it to survey it all. The daily, concrete, naïve intercourse with the world, he adds, reveals that the visible and the invisible are but two sides of the same coin: visible things have an invisible lining so to speak, the meaning of which adheres to them as we perceive them; invisible truth, ideas conveyed in utterances are really another experience of what we see as visible.[263] Language is therefore unfinished, as is our experience of the world. The most apt metaphors carry us to the brink of a revelation they withhold. But each time a new meaning is allowed to dawn, the spell created by the circle of our previous utterances is gone, and conformation is born that there is hope for us. Each time language becomes freer, real prospects are opened.[264] Shared, ongoing language gives a body to hope, overcomes the split between the visible and the invisible, and redeems the matter of which hope is made. Shared, unfinished language weaves links between private dreams and a personal will publicly joining reality.

The *Republic* opens with an unpremeditated meeting between Socrates and his friends. The friends have to beg the philosopher to explain himself; he refuses to set himself up as a teacher. Philosophy is unplanned, incomplete, and the philosopher is ignorant. But thanks to his lacks, silence can move into speech and speech into silence, the visible can leave room for the invisible and the invisible for the visible. His lacks create a space that gives us room to move out of our entrapment in silence or in talk, out of our captivity among things or among our ideas of things. Thus truth can arise in the shuttle of discourse instead of being masked by the illusions of stupidity or the illusions of pseudoknowledge. Philosophy, being everywhere and nowhere, gives to every exchanged conversation the opportunity to make room for such an unveiling of truth.

Thus a philosophy of a religion makes, it seems to me, a nobler promise than the philosophy of the religion. The mind should not visualize itself running around the earth, circling it high above historical realities. Far wiser it is to dig within one's own historical location, confident that we will all meet at the centre in the end. And, while we dig, the unfinished nature of our philosophical *logos* is an invitation to engage in dialogue with those whose digging starts elsewhere.[265] Horizons are open and fuse in moments of communication – as this postscript illustrates, for it is un-Platonic but could not have been written without Plato. Giving body to philosophy in his dialogues, the pupil of Socrates has given us an ear for philosophical questioning, philosophical argument, and philosophical finding, thereby giving us an ear for the frail truth accessible to us. The verbal means used to approach the truth are not allowed to obscure it.[266]

Philosophy as practised by Plato keeps the ability to arouse in us the desire to pay attention to reality and thus keeps giving a living body to human hope. I know of yet another manner of speaking which gives an even more personal shape to this body. In the parables as practised by Jesus, a human being steps into the silence to *offer*, to give a meaning that brings hope. Parables are sharply contrasted with myths (Plato knew only the latter, of course). Myth gives one a final word about reality; it provides structures of expectations and thus a frame of security. (We have seen that Plato qualifies the 'final': myths are words that will do for now.) The parables of Jesus overturn one's structures of expectations and threaten the security of one's man-made world. 'Parabolic religion continually subverts final words about "reality" and thereby introduces the possibility of transcendence.'[267] The parables, writes John D. Crossan, tell of the Kingdom's advent as 'that which undermines world so that we can experience God as distinct from world.' 'The only absolute we keep glimpsing is the Kingdom snapping our absolutes like dried twigs.'[268] The biblical thrust against idolatry extends to the disruption of idolatrous language. Uneikonic religion dissolves our victimizing absolutes. But the speaker in parables does not wear a mask – and does not oscillate between silence and shouts. He makes a parabolic utterance. His personal presence affirms that upon this insecurity the action and life which the Kingdom demands can be built. Wise and prudent readiness are impossible.[269] But the speaker of parables, the fellow human being, abides. The attention to reality is accompanied by the mutual presence of human beings with each other. And the parables of Jesus invite us to trust in God (distinct from world) as well as in each other. In the dark light of parabolic speaking God is doing some serious playing with human beings: he has faith in us and in the future we can – in the newness of God-given opportunity – bring to each other.[270] Transcendence – that which cannot ever be surveyed in an all-encompassing look – comes then to us with the richest gift. To the natural grace of the real world that ever again relieves us of boredom is added the divine grace that offers to redeem us from our misery.

Notes

Full bibliographic information for works cited in the notes in abbreviated form may be found in the Bibliography: on the Greeks, pp 373–8, and on Plato, pp 378–82.

INTRODUCTION

1 Geddes McGregor, *Introduction to Religious Philosophy* (Boston: Houghton Mifflin 1959), is a good example of the first kind. Anthony Flew and Alasdair MacIntyre, eds, *New Essays on Philosophical Theology* (London: SCM Press 1955), contains the most important arguments on the unverifiability of religious propositions.

2 See Richard R. Niebuhr, *Experiental Religion* (New York: Harper and Row 1972), ch 2.

3 See Wilfred Cantwell Smith, *Belief and History* (Charlottesville: University Press of Virginia 1977). Ch 1; 'The Meaning of Religious Statements,' shows what harm this focusing on beliefs has done to the efforts to understand religion.

4 Rodney Needham, *Belief, Language and Experience* (Chicago: University of Chicago Press 1972).

5 The terms are borrowed from Ninian Smart, *The Philosophy of Religion*, 2nd ed (New York: Oxford University Press 1979), p 72.

6 T. Patrick Burke, *The Reluctant Vision: An Essay in the Philosophy of Religion* (Philadelphia: Fortress Press 1974), p 4. See also his follow-up in *The Fragile Universe: An Essay in the Philosophy of Religions* (London: Macmillan 1979).

7 Smart, *The Philosophy of Religion*, pp 87–9, 139–160.

8 A.N. Whitehead, *Process and Reality: An Essay in Cosmology* (New York: Harper and Row 1960), p 23.

9 Susan Sontag, 'Piety without Content,' in *Against Interpretation and Other Essays* (New York: Dell 1969), p 254.

10 Smart, *The Philosophy of Religion*, p 4; Burke, *The Reluctant Vision*, p 7.

11 I must be fair. How much can one give of it in 190 or 136 pages? And both stress that there is much to be learned yet by looking at the facts. 'The full richness of religious phenomena is only slowly becoming available through the comparative study of religion, anthropology and the history of religion – themselves rather latter-day disciplines': Smart, *The Philosophy of Religion*, p 186.

12 See the analysis by Francis E. Sparshott in 'The Central Problem of Philosophy,' *Looking for Philosophy* (Montreal: McGill-Queen's University Press 1972), p 103: 'There fall within the purview of certain philosophical disciplines (aesthetics, philosophy of religion, ethics, metaphysics) experiences or objects of experience of which the following seem true: a philosophy which ignores them or prescinds from them is condemned to aridity or triviality, and may quite fairly be accused of evading the most important issues in its field; but a philosophy which treats of them either falls into an uninstructive and merely tiresome rhetoric, or makes statements which, though they may be true, so fail to be adequate to their subject-matter that unless one reads them with a vivid sense of the kind of experience to which they refer one cannot make sense of them at all, and which on the other hand cannot be properly integrated with the more pedestrian and systematic parts of one's discourse. And this quandary arises, not through anyone's negligence, but through the very nature of the experiences in question. How is the philosopher to cope with it?'

13 'Those first philosophers who absolutely made philosophy because it was absolutely unexistent – or, strictly speaking, got it under way, for they did not succeed in making it – are the true professors of philosophy to whom we must hark back across all the din set up by all subsequent professors of philosophy': José Ortega y Gasset, *Concord and Liberty* (New York: Norton 1963), p 111.
See also Drew A. Hyland, *The Origins of Philosophy: Its Rise in Myth and the Pre-Socratics* (New York: Putnam's 1973), pp 16–17.

14 Jacob Burckhardt has remarked that history is the one field of study in which one cannot begin at the beginning: quoted in Finley, *The World of Odysseus*, p 16.

15 A discussion of the evidence for the appearance of the concept in fifth-century Greece can be found in Michel Despland, *La Religion en Occident: Evolution des idées et du vécu* (Montréal: Fides 1979), pp 9–22.

16 There are three ways of 'frisking' a philosophy, writes O.K. Bouwsma: 'You may try to misunderstand it, which in philosophy requires almost no effort at all'; you may try to refute it, or to understand it. See *Philosophical Essays* (Lincoln: University of Nebraska Press 1969), p 75.

17 For an attack on this view, see Arthur Schopenhauer, 'On Man's Need of Metaphysics,' ch xvii from Supplements to the first book of *The World as Will and Idea* in *The Will to Live: Selected Writings of A. Schopenhauer*, ed R. Taylor (New York: F. Ungar 1967), p 10.

CHAPTER I

1 This is the first time in Greek literature that we hear of such officials. Plato keeps their function in the legislation of the *Laws* (759d).
2 Burnet, *Plato's Euthyphro, Apology of Socrates and Crito*, p 25.
3 *Euthyphro* 4d.
4 Other reasons have been advanced to explain the date 399 for a suit in Athens over a homicide in Naxos. In particular one can speculate that Euthyphro's father did not lose his holdings in 404 and that the trial in 399 is over a very recent affair. But the case then would have merely another set of legal complexities: why is an Athenian court concerned in a crime that has occurred in foreign territory?
5 Euthyphro's case could also be technically based on the fact that the second dead man is his day labourer and that this poor man has no one but Euthyphro to champion him. (Plutarch uses the same Greek word to designate the Roman *cliens*, and it is well known that Roman employers could sue and were morally expected to sue on behalf of their protégés.) Euthyphro's case could also be based on a fear of pollution felt by the father himself. On this view, however, the father should have co-operated with the whole purifying process.
6 Our reconstruction of the sequence of events from the first homicide to the appearance before the king follows largely the commentary of Burnet.
7 Attempts have been made to catch the flavour proper to *hosios*, one of the numerous adjectives used to designate what we call sacred, holy, saintly, pure, pious, consecrated, etc. The peculiar meaning of *hosios* arises from a contrast with *hieros*. In the ritual (sacrificial) slaughter of animals some meat is 'given' to the gods and burnt; this meat is *hieros*, set apart, dedicated to the gods, sacred; the remaining meat is made available for human consumption; it is *hosios*, pure, liberated for human, profane use. *Hierai hemerai* are sacred days, festival days, holidays; *hosiai hemerai* are non-holidays, days available for ordinary activities. *Hieros* money is money that belongs to the gods and cannot be spent. The temple is *hieros*, site of sacred activity; the city is *hosion*, site of profane-pious activity. *Hosios*, then, is what gods approve of for men, a quality peculiar to human beings whose behaviour is 'in order,' consonant with divine requirements. It must be translated as 'pious,' not as 'holy.' See Pangle, *The Laws of Plato*, pp 518–19, n 7.
According to Des Places, the man is *hosios* who has fulfilled all his obligations to the gods, does not owe them anything any more, and is thus 'free' of them. 'Thus in contrast, a man who is *hieros* could be either a priest, especially consecrated, or someone under a curse from the gods.' The emphasis on *hosios* is moral and the reference is quite free from the magical or ritualistic notions of purity. Rudhart contrasts *hosiotes* with *eusebeia*. *Hosiotes* is religiously and morally sound behav-

iour that is in keeping with, or that harmonizes with, an objective order. *Eusebeia* is religious behaviour that precedes from good interior dispositions. See Des Places, *La Religion grecque*, p 337; Rudhart *Notions fondamentales de la pensée religieuse et actes constitutifs du culte dans la Grèce antique*, p 15.

8 See Panagiotou, 'Plato's Euthyphro and the Attic Code on Homicide,' pp 419-37.

9 On the whole matter of pollution full discussions are found in Adkins, *Merit and Responsibility*, ch 5; Dodds, *The Greeks and the Irrational*, ch 2; and Lloyd-Jones, *The Justice of Zeus*, ch 3.

10 *Works and Days*, vv 249-51; see also Gernet, *Recherches sur le développement de la pensée juridique et morale en Grèce*.

11 Yet breakdowns still occurred. Demosthenes tells of a case where apparently no one could be found who could possibly prosecute murderers; see 117, para 55.

12 Vernant, *Mythe et tragédie*, p 31.

13 *Agamemnon*, pp 773-81.

14 *Euthyphro* 12d, 4d.

15 *Laws* 864d-e.

16 *Euthyphro* 4d-e.

17 Morrow, *Plato's Cretan City*, ch 6.

18 Karl Popper introduces another of his characteristic anachronisms when he assumes that the historical Socrates took for granted the right of the day labourer to due process and humane treatment. He does grant that the Socrates of *Euthyphro* backs up the ancestral notions about the sacredness of the father but he traces this to Plato's distortion of the Socratic record to serve his reactionary ends: *The Open Society and Its Enemies* (London: Routledge & Kegan Paul 1966), I, 191-2, 608.

19 If homicide law in general is not characterized by clarity of principle, laws specifically covering the murder of slaves are more unsatisfactory yet. We have seen that in Attic law a slave owner can execute the murderer of one of his slaves, if the murderer is caught in the act. Such an owner incurs no penalty if he kills a slave of his own, presumably in anger or in punishment. Plato is exercised by this problem and proposes some modifications to the legislation: a man who accidentally kills his own slave must undergo ritual purification; if he kills the slave of another, he either voluntarily makes restitution of the value of the slave or runs the risk of being sued for twice the value, and he must also be purified (*Laws* 865c-d). Although comparisons have been made about the degree of protection afforded to slaves by Attic practice by the Platonic proposals, these are inconclusive, since the relatively few cases covered by Plato do not overlap with those about which we know Athenian practice. After a thorough survey of the evidence Levinson remarks that, whichever set of laws is given most benefit of the doubt, will appear the superior one in the comparison: *In Defense of Plato*, appendix 3. In both Athenian law and Plato the

notion that slave blood is also human has hardly been translated into suitable legal and procedural protection.

20 Quoted in Dodds, *The Greeks and the Irrational*, p 207.
21 *Euthyphro* 5d.
22 Nilsson, *Greek Folk-Religion*, p 137.
23 Nettleship, *Lectures on the Republic of Plato*, pp 16, 17.
24 *Euthyphro* 5. In what way does he differ from Antigone? Is he not rejecting what is to him a human law, in the name of a divine one?
25 *Euthyphro* 3b.
26 *Alcibiades* 116e.
27 *Meno* 80a–b.
28 *Euthyphro* 11b.
29 *Euthyphro* 5d.
30 *Euthyphro* 6c.
31 *Euthyphro* 6e.
32 *Euthyphro* 9d.
33 *Euthyphro* 10a–11b.
34 *Euthyphro* 12e.
35 Chateau, *Euthyphron de Platon*, p 124.
36 *Euthyphro* 13d–14b.
37 *Euthyphro* 14c–15b.
38 *Euthyphro* 15b–16a.
39 *The Clouds*; see also Guthrie, *History of Greek Philosophy*, vol III, sect 12.
40 *Republic* 378a–b.
41 Guardini, *The Death of Socrates*, pp 10–12.
42 See Grube, *Plato's Thought*, pp 185–203, 30–1.

CHAPTER 2

1 *Euthyphro* 3c–e.
2 *Apology* 24b. See Burnet, *Plato's Euthyphro, Apology of Socrates and Crito*, pp 102–5. See also Reverdin, *La Religion de la cité platonicienne*, pp 208–17.
3 Randall, *Plato: The Dramatist of the Life of Reason*, p 85.
4 Burnet, *Plato's Euthyphro, Apology of Socrates and Crito*, p 104. See the discussion in Beckman, *The Religious Dimension of Socrates' Thought*, pp 54–60.
5 Lysias, *Against Andocides* 8; see also 13. It is accepted that Lysias is not the author of this speech. Some have argued that it is pronounced by Meletus himself, who, it is known, did speak at this other trial for impiety. See Burnet's commentary on *Euthyphro* 2b–c.

6 *Euthyphro* 5a–b.

7 Jaeger, *Paideia*, I, xiii.

8 Havelock, *Preface to Plato*. Havelock also demonstrates that Plato's attack on Homer is an attempt to change the most basic mental habits and attitudes.

9 Vernant, *Mythe et société en Grèce ancienne*, p 95. Vernant locates the rise of this pattern of a circle with the speaker in the middle to the warrior groups who deliberate on what is to be done next.

10 De Romilly, *Magic and Rhetoric in Ancient Greece*, p 37. See also Kennedy, *The Art of Persuasion in Greece*, chs 1–3.

11 *Fifth Nemean Ode*, lines 1–2.

12 See Svenbro, *La Parole et le marbre*, pp 156–7.

13 *Poetics* 1450b.

14 'It did these two things through the twin devices of the "actor" and the chorus. Through the actor who *was* the hero standing before him, and the chorus who was 'like himself', the ordinary Athenian was enabled to feel, to sympathize, with the hero in a new direct way': Else, *The Origin and Early Form of Greek Tragedy*, p 76.

15 *Poetics* 1448b.

16 Here again the Greeks do not completely understand what they are going through. They can all along affirm that the oldest laws are bound to be the best and yet be quite conscious of the good process set in motion once all the laws become written. See the whole praise of common law by Theseus in Euripides' *Suppliant Women*: 'when laws are written down, both rich and poor possess their equal right' (lines 429ff) See also De Romilly, *La Loi dans la pensée grecque*, pp 9–24.

17 De Romilly, *Magic and Rhetoric in Ancient Greece*, p 6.

18 *Aidôs* and *nemesis*. The old virtues that are missing are primarily a feeling of awe that restrains and the quick flare of righteous indignation at the sight of wickedness: Hesiod *Works and Days*, line 200.

19 Xenophon, *Memorabilia*, 1.6.b.

20 *Gorgias* 456e.

21 *Republic* 493.

22 Thucydides, *Peloponnesian War*, 3.82.4. *Republic* 560d echoes this passage.

23 *Euthyphro* 6a, 8be.

24 *Euthyphro*, 11b–d.

25 *Euthyphro*, 8c.

26 *Theaetetus* 172b.

27 *Phaedrus* 261d–e.

28 *Phaedrus*, 275d–e.

29 *Phaedo* 99e. Guthrie's translation, *History of Greek Philosophy*, IV, 334, 352, n 1.

30 The literature on Socrates is enormous. An older classic is Taylor, *Socrates* (1933).

A more recent treatment, with full bibliography, is found in Guthrie, *History of Greek Philosophy*, vol III.
31 Nettleship, *Lectures on the Republic of Plato*, p 15. Nettleship refers to Aristotle's *Nicomachean Ethics*, 6.11.6, for a statement that we should attend to the undemonstrated experience of old men, because experience has given them the eye to see rightly.
32 *Memorabilia*, 1.3.1.
33 *Apology* 33c.
34 *Apology* 37e.
35 A good account of the complex issues related to this famous sign is found in Friedländer, *Plato*, pp 32–6.
36 *Phaedo* 60e, 85b.
37 *Meno* 86b–c.
38 *Apology* 30d.
39 *Phaedo* 62b, 63c.
40 *Apology* 32d, 35c.
41 *Phaedo* 58e, 59a.
42 *Apology* 41d.
43 N. Söderblom, *The Living God* (London: Oxford University Press 1933), p 256.
44 *Euthyphro* 11c–d.
45 See Tuckey, *Plato's Charmides*.
46 *Lysis* 222e. See Gadamer, *Dialogue and Dialectic*, p 20.
47 *Euthyphro* 5d; *Republic* 334c. See also *Theaetetus* 175c.
48 This point can be further elaborated by drawing the contrast between Socrates and Euthyphro on their respective need for certainty. Euthyphro has a mind that wishes to work in a straightforward manner, without detours (*euthus* means 'straightforward'). He wants quick certainties and believes he can reach them. It is always the fault of others if there is mental confusion: 'my statements would sit quiet if it depended on me' (11d). Yet the cost of his haste and directness is that he stumbles, incoherently, from one assured doctrine to another. That Socrates is striving for certainty is apparent mainly from the fact that he shatters false certainties. Instead of dogmatic zest, he seems to be driven by critical zeal. He knows that the best way to stick to a point involves a detour rather than the quick, straight dash. One might also say that Socrates is too much a man of faith to accumulate hasty beliefs, that he is too philosophical to place too much faith in words. He is subtle. I thus cannot accept the arguments of Détienne and Vernant in *Les Ruses de l'intelligence* that Plato strives to discredit all the ways of oblique intelligence. On the matter of 'detour' in Plato see R. Schaerer, *Philosophie et fiction* (Lausanne: L'Age d'homme 1978), ch 4.

49 *Euthyphro* 3d–e. See Chateau, *Euthyphron de Platon*, pp 50–1.
50 Burnet, commentary on *Phaedo*, p lx.
51 Friedländer, *Plato*, p 153.
52 Vellacott, *Ironic Drama: A Study of Euripides' Method and Meaning*, p 177. Vellacott's point is that Euripides shares in these gifts.
53 *Euthyphro* 14b–c.
54 See Grube, *Plato's Thought*, p 122.
55 For the vocabulary of activity see Simon, *Mind and Madness in Ancient Greece*, p 162.
56 Taylor, *Socrates*, p 134.
57 *Charmides* 156b and ff.
58 Rist, *Eros and Psyche*, p 138.
59 Xenophon, *Memorabilia*, 2.6.39.
60 See Teloh, *The Development of Plato's Metaphysics*, p 26.
61 See Adkins, *Merit and Responsibility*, ch 12. The challenge of the fifth-century moralist is to show that virtue and enjoyment of good things are possible only thanks to the cultivation of justice and show this in a cultural context where many assume that the power to get the good things and keep them is all it takes to be able to enjoy them.
62 *Laches* 184e.
63 *Gorgias* 464d–e.
64 *Republic* 345c–346e.
65 Thucydides, *Peloponnesian War*, 6.39–40.
66 See Gould, *The Development of Plato's Ethics*, ch 2.
67 For Socrates, unlike Plato, desire for drink is desire for good drink. See Penner, 'Thought and Desire in Plato,' pp 96–118.
68 See Versényi, *Holiness and Justice*, p 135.
69 *Theaetetus* 175c.
70 *Euthyphro* 13e.
71 Gould, *The Development of Plato's Ethics*, p 26. See also the discussion of virtue in Teloh, *The Development of Plato's Metaphysics*, p 34: a virtue is a psychic state or power which 'motivates or causes behaviour, and provides a reason for that behaviour.' On this view Euthyphro cannot tell what piety is, because he does not ask himself in what condition his psyche should be (ibid, pp 46, 60).
72 *Gorgias* 527b.
73 Goldschmidt, *Questions platoniciennes*, p 61.
74 Snell, *The Discovery of the Mind*, p 81; see also p 187.
75 *Gorgias* 527b.
76 Vernant, *Mythe et société en Grèce ancienne*, p 99.

CHAPTER 3

1 As Diès puts it, the picture of Socrates at work easily turns into a symbol, and the symbol very naturally becomes expressive of doctrines; see *Autour de Platon*, I, 175.

2 Chateau notes that the *Euthyphro* has a place in the history of the philosophy of religion. Before our eyes religion in this dialogue takes shape as a philosophical problem just as philosophy becomes aware of its own problems. 'Religion is made into the object of a discourse which is distinct from religious discourse.' The same standpoint of critical exteriority reappears in Spinoza. In AD 1665, however, religious language has assimilated large doses of philosophical language, whereas in 399 BC religious discourse is poetical and mythological (doctrinal nevertheless, we would want to add): *Euthyphron de Platon* pp 190–2.

3 See some of the documentation I have put forward in *La Religion en Occident* (Montréal: Fides 1979), ch 1.

4 On this movement see Jaeger, *The Theology of the Early Greek Philosophers*.

5 On this movement see the chapter on 'Rationalist Theories of Religion' in Guthrie, *History of Greek Philosophy*, vol III.

6 *Phaedrus* 242b–e.

7 See, for instance, P. Ricoeur, *Finitude et culpabilité* (Paris: Aubier 1960), II, 104–8. See also *Nicomachean Ethics*, 1109b 30, 1135a 3.

8 *Apology* 34e.

9 *Euthyphro* 8c–d, 13a.

10 *Iliad*, 23.536.

11 Adkins, *Merit and Responsibility*, p 56.

12 *Euthyphro* 7e–8e.

13 Xenophon, *Apology*, sect 3.

14 Xenophon, *Apology*, sect 4.

15 Xenophon, *Memorabilia*, bks 3, 7, 6.

16 See *The Wasps*. Plato seems to have considered Aristophanes a good critic of Athens; he is said to have advised the reading of Aristophanes' comedies to the tyrant of Syracuse. What does Plato make of the portrayal of Socrates in *The Clouds*?

17 *Phaedrus* 272d–e.

18 *Theaetetus* 172c–173a. See Levinson, *In Defence of Plato*, p 555.

19 *Letter* VII 325d.

20 *Republic* 405b–c.

21 *Republic* 561c–e. Nettleship, *Lectures on the Republic of Plato*, p 111.

22 *Peloponnesian War*, 3.81–3. Fifth-century analyses of moral decay almost inevitably take the form of an indictment of democracy. See de Romilly, *Problèmes de la démocratie grecque*.

23 This paragraph rests on the argument brilliantly marshalled by Cogan in *The Human Thing: The Speeches and Principles of Thucydides' History*.

24 *Peloponnesian War*, 6.24.

25 Ibid, 2.65 (Hobbes's translation). Commentators point to this passage as one of the very few where Thucydides expresses his own judgment.

26 *Eumenides*, lines 824–36, 968–75. See the debate in Euripides, *Suppliant Women*, lines 417–22: 'The people is no right judge of arguments.'

27 *Peloponnesian War*, 5.82–116. Thus as a social critic Thucydides goes much farther than Aristophanes who was something of a conservative idyllist, prompt to think that ordinary peasants, if let alone, will certainly know how to live well.

28 Ibid, 6.18.

29 Ibid, 3.40.

30 Ibid, 3.84.

31 *Ajax*, line 1073.

32 See Knox, *Oedipus at Thebes*. What the Athenians would praise as the king's swift and apparently intelligent decisiveness is called *polypragmosune* by Plato; to him it is a fault. See *Republic* 434b, 444b. As Moline defines it, *polypragmosune* is the disposition to try to cope with everything without expert help, despite one's inability to do so.

33 *Republic* 357b.

34 Goldschmidt, *Les Dialogues de Platon*, p 338.

35 Grene, *Man in His Pride*, p 139.

36 For a definition of 'practice' see Alasdair MacIntyre, *After Virtue* (Notre Dame, Ind: Notre Dame University Press 1981), p 175: 'By a "practice" I am going to mean any coherent and complex form of socially established cooperative human activity through which goods internal to that form of activity are realized in the course of trying to achieve those standards of excellence which are appropriate to, and partially definitive of, that form of activity, with the results that human powers to achieve excellence, and human conceptions of the ends and goods involved, are systematically extended.'

37 *Republic* 539b.

38 *Meno* 83d.

39 *Crito* 49a–d; see also *Republic* 346a.

40 *Protagoras* 347c–348a.

41 *Phaedrus* 258d–e.

42 *Euthyphro* 9c.

43 *Gorgias* 474b; see also 475d–476a.

44 *Theaetetus* 171d. The phrase 'individual level of existence' is borrowed from Voegelin, *Plato*, p 26.

45 Goldschmidt, *Les Dialogues de Platon*, pp 33–4.

46 *Protagoras* 336b–c.
47 *Protagoras* 334d.
48 *Protagoras* 338a.
49 *Gorgias* 491b–e.
50 *Phaedrus* 272c.
51 *Euthyphro* 8c.
52 Adkins, *Merit and Responsibility*, p 292. See chs 12 and 13.
53 *Meno* 75d.
54 *Euthyphro* 15b–c.
55 *Euthyphro* 11e.
56 Socratic cross-examination brings out this admission of what the person believes to be good, just as a trial brings out the jurors' notion of what is good. As Irwin puts it, Socrates assumes that an interlocutor forced to decide on his views 'will prefer his choices to converge on a final good, though they need not have previously converged on it': *Plato's Moral Theory*, p 95.
57 Hackforth, *Phaedrus*, pp 53, 82.
58 *Gorgias* 464–5.
59 See the article 'La Transposition platonicienne,' in Diès, *Autour de Platon*, II, 537–603.
60 *Phaedrus* 243c, 266a, 266e.
61 One may further note that, while all truth is supposed to be uttered by the inter-locutor, it is very much Socrates who leads the game. The introduction of the superior hypothesis is only his most conspicuous way of doing it. He gives decisive orientations by the kind of questions he asks. For instance, he injects a teleological note into the assumption that he and Euthyphro seem to share by asking what kind of product service of a god aims at? That religious behaviour aims at something may be true, but it certainly is a notion that Socrates, in these circumstances, has introduced surreptitiously. One may even ask whether such an introduction is a trap: is he steering Euthyphro towards a clearer confession of a mercenary kind of piety that aims at pleasing the gods because it fears what they may do to one's health and safety? As an observer sympathetic to both Euthyphro and Socrates, I must remark that the previous turn of their conversation (especially Euthyphro's granting that the gods love the holy because it is holy) would equally have warranted an entirely different question such as, for instance, 'why is it that the gods deserve to be served?' Such a question might even better have helped Euthyphro to rise to the heights he is capable of and would have kept him away from a search for the worldly results of pious behaviour. Can it be said that Socrates is perhaps more interested in exposing Euthyphro than in getting the truth out of him?

Furthermore, philosophy decisively leads the game in that it keeps the record. A philosopher, a disciple of Socrates, has written the account of the encounter. A version of the dialogue written by Euthyphro, or by a disciple of his, would have looked quite different; the impression given of why the conversation ends would certainly not have been the same.

62 For a most rigorous analysis of the dialectical practice exhibited by Socrates in the early dialogues see ch 2 in Moline, *Plato's Theory of Understanding*; pp 39–41 on the constraints placed on answers and questions are brilliant and concise.

63 Xenophon, *Apology*, sect 5, 6.

64 Xenophon, *Banquet*, 8.20.

65 Taylor, *Socrates*, pp 102, 118.

66 Goldschmidt, *Questions platoniciennes*, p 57.

67 Hegel, *Lectures on the History of Philosophy* (London: Routledge & Kegan Paul 1955), vol I. See also J. Glenn Grey, *Hegel and Greek Thought* (New York: Harper & Row 1968), p 62.

68 See Gould, *The Development of Plato's Ethics*, p xii.

69 *De officiis*, 2.25.

70 Friedländer, *Plato*, III, 440.

71 *Apology* 31e–32a. See also Goldschmidt, *Questions platoniciennes*, p 57.

72 *Meno* 92e.

73 Thucydides, *Peloponnesian War*, 6.39.

74 *Apology* 22d.

75 *Republic* 365b–c; *Phaedrus* 247–8.

76 Crombie, *Plato: The Midwife's Apprentice*, pp 172–3.

77 On the practices in the Academy see Albert William Levi, *Philosophy as Social Expression* (Chicago: University of Chicago Press 1974), pp 72–83.

78 See Voegelin, *Plato*, pp 5, 68: 'We are not concerned with "a platonic philosophy" or "doctrine" but with Plato's resistance to the disorder of the surrounding society and his effort to restore the order of hellenic civilization through love of wisdom.'

79 Xenophon, *Apology*, sect 6, 7.

80 *Apology* 31d.

81 *Republic* 496c–e.

82 See Friedländer, *Plato*, p 172.

83 Jaspers, 'Plato,' in *Plato and Augustine*, pp 58–9. The perils of one-sided enlightenment are well expressed by Murray's 'First comes inspiration and the exultation of the breaking of false barriers; at the end comes the mere flabbiness of having no barriers left to break and no talent except for breaking them': *Aeschylus*, p 79 (quoted in Voegelin, *Plato*, p 190).

84 Wilamowitz-Moellendorf, *Der Glaube der Hellenen*, I, 224.

85 Plato offers 'an interpretation of the nature of Greek ethical life.' Hegel praises Plato for having sought 'to master the corruptive invader.' Not content with providing an 'empty ideal,' Plato strove to apprehend 'the present and the actual': preface to *Philosophy of Right* (New York: Oxford University Press 1971).

86 *Meno* 81c.

87 Guthrie, *Orpheus and Greek Religion*, p 238.

88 Woodcock, *The Greeks in India*, pp 149–63; Jaeger, *Aristotle*, p 131.

89 See Burkert, *Love and Science in Ancient Pythagoreanism*, p 298. I thus do not entirely agree with Dodds, *The Greeks and the Irrational*, p 209.

90 Schuhl, *La Fabulation platonicienne*, pp 45–51. Skemp has made a similar demonstration with the myth of the *Statesman*; see his *Plato's Statesman*, pp 82–111.

91 See Chateau, *Euthyphron de Platon*, pp 133–4.

CHAPTER 4

1 *Euthyphro* 5d.

2 *Euthyphro* 6d.

3 There has been a series of attempts recently to assess the philosophical import of *Euthyphro*. Most brilliant and sound is that of Allen, *Plato's Euthyphro and the Earliest Theory of Forms*; I am very much indebted to his analysis. Equally sound is Chateau, *Euthyphron de Platon*. Least impressive is Meyer, *Plato's Euthyphro: An Example of Philosophical Analysis*; Meyer argues that Socrates wishes to show that Euthyphro's attempts to define 'pious' are unsuccessful because they fail to accord with the customary use of the term. Allen disposes rather well of views of this kind in pp 115–18 of his book. Several articles have attempted to unveil 'fallacies' in Socrates' reasoning; Anderson, 'Socratic Reasoning in the *Euthyphro*,' reviews them and challenges them. He also supplies a more plausible interpretation of Socrates' arguments. He defends the view that Socrates in the dialogue gives Euthyphro a lesson in good definition. See also Sharvy, '*Euthyphro*, 9d–11b: Analysis and Definition in Plato and Others'; and Paxton, 'Plato's *Euthyphro*, 10a–11b.'

4 Hesiod, *Works and Days*, lines 226, 217, 218. See Snell, *The Discovery of the Mind*, p 229.

5 *Euthyphro* 2c.

6 *Euthyphro* 12e.

7 *Euthyphro* 13b.

8 Allen has translated all the words of the *hosion* family by 'holiness,' 'holy,' etc. So does Lamb in the Loeb translation. I have decided to depart from this usage and use the term 'piety.' This has also meant rejecting Burnet's suggestion that the enquiry about *to hosion* asks 'what is the religious?' (*Plato's Euthyphro, Apology of Socrates and Crito*, p 4). This has to be done once it seems right to emphasize that the enquiry in *Euthyphro* is about the religiously correct course of action. Euthyphro is not a saffron-clad holy man who lives in a cave. To say that he is a pious man better describes him. Finally, after Otto's book *The Idea of the Holy*, the 'holy' has come to mean a quality in beings, events, encountered by us. The 'holy' directs us to think

about something found outside of man. *To hosion* does occasionally have this meaning but not in *Euthyphro*, and, in any case, the more common Greek term to designate this powerful object or realm of being which elicits awe is the 'divine' (*to theion*) or the 'sacred' (*to hieron*). The terminology of sacrifice settles the matter decisively in my mind. Some meat is consecrated to the use of the gods (*hieros*) and some is consecrated to the use of men (*hosios*); the former is burnt on the altar, the latter eaten at tables. See Kahn, *Hermès passe ou les ambiguités de la communication*, p 43. *Euthyphro* is inquiring about a religion which is moralized and anthropocentric. The religious man we hear about is not the bearer of some sacred effulgence but the human being who does the ultimately appropriate thing.

9 *Meno* 100b. Socrates, says Aristotle, has fixed thought on definitions (*Metaphysics* 987b). His word (*horismos*), probably never used by Socrates, also means that which sets a boundary.

10 *Phaedrus* shows well the importance of definition. The first debate about love is trivial and useless because the participants have not examined the love about which they claim to have such certainties.

11 *Euthyphro* 5d.

12 *Hippias Major* 287e.

13 *Euthyphro* 6e.

14 See Allen, *Plato's Euthyphro*, pp 69–79.

15 In 'Plato's Earlier Theory of Forms' Rist is critical of Allen's conclusions. Socrates is not, he thinks, after definitions; he is rather after 'markers' so that 'the holy and the unholy shall be recognized and separated from one another.' See p 343.

16 *Euthyphro* 12d.

17 Chateau, *Euthyphron de Platon*, p 101. He refers to the passages in *Meno* (80d–86c) where Socrates argues that to know is to reminisce.

18 Allen, *Plato's Euthyphro*, pp 82, 113, 25.

19 *Sophist* 247a–b.

20 *Theaetetus* 171d–172a.

21 *Phaedrus* 275b–c.

22 *Phaedrus* 270e.

23 *Republic* 476c.

24 Havelock, *A Preface to Plato*, p 228. White, *Plato on Knowledge and Reality*, p xi; see also pp 15, 19.

25 *Peloponnesian War*, 6.2.1.

26 See the excellent book by Moline, *Plato's Theory of Understanding*. For Plato, to have knowledge is to speak well and not to be refuted, and such a condition is the result of what we should call understanding. A person who understands gives an account about something and cannot be swayed by purely rhetorical means.

27 Friedländer, *Plato*, II, 85.

28 It is commonly allowed that Plato wavers in his account of what counts for knowledge. The discursive account of forms states that, thanks to the forms and

knowledge of them, people can give a secure account. The visual account of forms makes them separate entities (it accepts the assumption of Parmenides that every thought must have an object). See a convincing argument against the unitarian thesis, namely against the view that Plato holds only one view of forms, in Teloh, *The Development of Plato's Metaphysics*.

29 Quoted in Gadamer, *Dialogue and Dialectic*, p 96.

30 Klein, *Plato's Trilogy*, p 3. The trouble with 'idea' is that people may think they have ideas without words. (Berkeley thought he had in his head 'bare notions,' 'naked undisguised ideas,' separated from 'all that dress and encumbrance of words.')

31 That here is the hub of the new situation confronting Plato has been argued by Allen, *Plato's Euthyphro*, pp 157–64.

32 *Statesman* 266d.

33 Fragment 16, quoted in Jaeger, *Paideia*, p 171.

34 *Phaedrus* 242e (Jowett translation).

35 *Gorgias* 485d.

36 *Republic* 358d.

37 This means, as Goldschmidt points out, that definitions have no worth in themselves, only 'through the soul of their fathers:' *Les Dialogues de Platon*, p 88). Only a man committed to the reality of piety and justice can come up with the real definition of them.

38 Crombie, *Plato: the Midwife's Apprentice*, pp 56–7.

39 Findlay, *Plato and Platonism*, p 21.

40 Clémence Ramnoux, 'Hegel et le commencement de la philosophie,' in Jacques d'Hondt, ed, *Hegel et la pensée grecque* (Paris: PUF 1974).

41 *Republic* 538c–e.

42 *Meno* 97d–98a. See Moreau, *Le Sens du Platonisme*, pp 25, 27.

43 *Phaedrus* 268a–b, 272a.

44 S.C. Humphreys, ' "Transcendence" and intellectual roles,' in *Wisdom, Revelation and Doubt: Perspectives in the First Millenium B.C.*, *Daedalus*, Spring 1972, p 92.

45 *Theaetetus* 175c.

46 This description of the alternative has its source in Richard Rorty, *Philosophy and the Mirror of Nature*, 2nd ed (Princeton: Princeton University Press 1980). Did Plato wish to institutionalize his vocabulary and build for eternity? or was he reactive? Rorty allows that we still don't know; see p 369. The alternative, of course, is implicit in the phrase 'looking at objects as reflected in reasoned argument.'

47 F. Nietzsche, *The Will to Power*, no. 432 (New York: Random House 1968), p 237. It must be allowed that it is the breakdown of the *polis* that moved the Greeks to political theory. Note that Nietzsche credits this decay to the joint effort of the philosophers and the mob: both through dialectics negate all achievements; see *The Will of Power*, no. 427, p 231.

48 See Simon, *Mind and Madness in Ancient Greece*, pp 174, 181.

49 See Clegg, *The Structure of Plato's Philosophy*, p 26.

50 Festugière, *Contemplation et vie contemplative*.

51 On mind as the eye of the soul see *Republic* 533d; *Symposium* 219a; *Theaetetus* 164a; *Sophist* 254a.

52 *Theaetetus* 175c.

53 *Iliad*, 9.443.

54 See J. Pieper, 'The Philosophical Act,' in *Leisure the Basis of Culture* (London: Faber and Faber 1962).

55 See *Ion* 532d. Svenbro shows that Plato's notion of the private man harks back to the ideal of self-sufficiency promoted by Hesiod, 'the poet of the small land-owning class': *La Parole et le Marbre*, pp 210–2.

56 *Iliad*, 19.76–7; *Odyssey*, 20.37.

57 A little pamphlet from the American School of Classical Studies at Athens, *Socrates in the Agora*, gives an excellent portrait of Socrates by discussing the manifold archaeological evidence of his locales. See also the chapter on the *agora* in Wycherley, *How the Greeks Built Cities*.

58 Herodotus, 1.153.

59 *Politics*, 7.11.2.

60 Gadamer, *Dialogue and Dialectic*, p 2.

61 *Iliad*, 9.307–13.

62 *Theogony*, lines 81–97.

63 On the power of musical spells and incantations see Moutsopoulos, *La Musique dans l'oeuvre de Platon*, pp 13–22.

64 *Agamemnon*, lines 385–8.

65 *Theogony*, line 27.

66 Ramnoux, *Etudes présocratiques*, p 252.

67 Parmenides, fragments 342, 344, 347, in Kirk and Raven, *The Pre-Socratic Philosophers*, pp 266–73.

68 Détienne, *Les Maîtres de vérité*, p 132.

69 Fragments 197–8, in Kirk and Raven, *The Pre-Socratic Philosophers*, pp 187–8.

70 Ramnoux, *Héraclite ou l'Homme entre les choses et les mots*, pp 22, 177, 341; *Etudes présocratiques*, p 63.

71 *Metaphysics* 1010a, lines 10–15.

72 Ramnoux, *Etudes présocratiques*, pp 178, 183.

73 Redfield, *Nature and Culture in the Iliad*, p 48. See also the discussion in ch 6 of Harriot, *Poetry and Criticism before Plato*.

74 Guthrie, *History of Greek Philosophy*, III, 51; see also p 193.

75 De Romilly, *Magic and Rhetoric in Ancient Greece*, p 16.

76 The whole of the *Gorgias* harps upon the difference between rhetoric and medicine. Both use drugs (*pharmakon*). But doctors adhere to an accepted ethic: they use drugs to make people well and people know the difference between sickness and health.

However no such common moral framework exists to guide the rhetoricians in their prescriptions. Plato also makes the point by saying that only doctors have a science.

77 Murray, *The Rise of the Greek Epic*, p 94.

78 Heraclitus, fragment 60, in Burnet, *Early Greek Philosophy*, p 137. See also Ramnoux, *Héraclite ou l'Homme entre les choses et les mots*.

79 Parain, *Essai sur le Logos platonicien*, pp 48, 65, 72.

80 Kojève, *Essai d'une histoire raisonnée de la philosophie paienne*, I, 29–30.

81 See Havelock, *Preface to Plato* and *The Greek Concept of Justice*; and Simon, *Mind and Madness in Ancient Greece*, pp 82–8, 180–2.

82 The pioneering work on the importance of the literary form is Schaerer, *La Question platonicienne* (1938). Goldschmidt has analysed the dramatic structure of all dialogues in *Les Dialogues de Platon*. For a brief discussion see O'Brien, *The Socratic Paradoxes*, pp 6–11.

83 Gadamer, '*Logos* and *Ergon* in Plato's *Lysis*,' in *Dialogue and Dialectic*.

84 Phaedo 89c–90e.

85 *Cratylus* 388b, 386d.

86 *Cratylus* 440a.

87 Our interpretation closely follows that of Weingartner in *The Unity of the Platonic Dialogue*.

88 See Versényi, *Holiness and Justice*, p 129. The dialogue does not give reflections; it moves us to reflect.

89 *Symposium* 194b.

90 *Republic* 476c.

91 See Havelock, *A Preface to Plato*, p 209.

92 Shorey, 'Plato's Ethics,' II, 17.

93 Gouldner, *Enter Plato*, p 262.

94 Détienne, *Les Maîtres de vérité*, p 143.

95 *Gorgias* 511a; *Sophist* 232a–233c. Plato also portrays Protagoras as someone who chooses what styles of speech (*mythos* or *logos*) to use with a view to pleasure and effect. About to launch into his demonstration that virtue is teachable, Protagoras asks his listeners whether he should put his explanation 'in the form of a story, or give it as a reasoned argument' (Guthrie's translation; Lamb has 'in the form of a fable, or a regular exposition'; and Jowett, 'in an apologue or myth, or shall I argue out the question'): *Protagoras* 320c.

96 *Parmenides* 135b. See Sinaiko, *Love, Knowledge and Discourse in Plato*, p 276.

97 *Phaedrus* 271c. 'Wrong words are not only undesirable in themselves, but they infect the soul with evil' (*Phaedo* 115e).

CHAPTER 5

1 Jaeger, *Paideia*, II, 69.

2 Gernet, *Recherches sur le développement de la pensée juridique et morale en Grèce*,

p 435. Gernet adds that increased social complexity gives rise to this sort of state. Students of baroque Europe never fail to observe a similar systematization of beliefs.

3 *Phaedo* 107d.

4 *Euthyphro* 302c.

5 *Laws* 887d–e.

6 *Hippolytus*, line 189 (translation by Dodds, 'Euripides the Irrationalist,' in *The Ancient Concept of Progress and other Essays on Greek Literature and Belief*.

7 *Laws* 885. See also *Republic* 588d–667a.

8 *Phaedo* 7c. See also *Meno* 81a–b: 'poets and priests have said the soul is immortal.'

9 Guthrie, *Orpheus and Greek Religion*, p 157. Guthrie refers particularly to the Orphic teaching.

10 *Laws* 738c.

11 *Republic* 378a.

12 Murray, *Greek Studies*.

13 Nilsson, *History of Greek Religion*, p 77. It is, of course, not always easy to see the grass and appreciate its diversity, yet it must be done. Nilsson 'consistently felt that studying the masterpieces entailed starting at the wrong end of Greek culture and ignoring the roots from which the later products had grown and which made their meaning intelligible': McGinty, *Interpretation and Dionysos*, p 107. The works of Guthrie are particularly helpful here. He can both celebrate Greek intellectual development and at the same time uphold the dignity of Greek religious life and the legitimacy of its religious thought; see ch 6 of *Interpretation and Dionysos*.

14 Dodds, 'The Religion of the Ordinary Man in Classical Greece,' in *The Ancient Concept of Progress and Other Essays*, p 142.

15 The modern historian, writes Vernant, must build afresh the interpretative framework he is to use in his studies of Greek religion; frames found useful in the study of Christians or primitives will not do (*Religion grecque, religions antiques*).

16 The later Cycladic is also called Minoan and flowered in Crete.

17 Nilsson, relying too heavily on Homeric evidence, seems to have made Mycenaean religion too northern and thus sharpened the contrast between Crete and Mycenae. Archaeological evidence indicates deep similarities. See Demargne, *The Birth of Greek Art*, p 267.

18 See the chapter on 'The Matrilineal World' in Butterworth, *Some Traces of the pre-Olympian World in Greek Literature and Myth*.

19 Beye, *Ancient Greek Literature and Society*, p 4. Aristotle says that the antithetical style is pleasing because contraries are easily understood: *Rhetoric* 1410–20.

20 Dietrich has argued against such a view in *The Origins of Greek Religion*. The rise of the city can, in his eyes, entirely account for the tension between the chthonic and the Olympian elements. See also Hooper, *Greek Realities*, p 71.

21 Gernet, *Anthropologie de la Grèce antique*, pp 16–19.

22 See Whitman, *Homer and the Heroic Tradition*, pp 296–7.
23 'I am planning for you just as I would do for my own self ... I have no spirit of iron inside my heart, rather it is compassionate' (*Odyssey*, 5.188–91). 'It is not right to plan harm for each other' (16.423). 'It is an unholy thing to glory over slain men' (22.408–13).
24 Pettazoni, *La Religion dans la Grèce antique*, p 30.
25 Vernant et al, *Divination et rationalité*, p 13.
26 Vernant, *Mythe et société en Grèce ancienne*, p 119.
27 Guthrie, *The Greeks and Their Gods*, pp 113–16.
28 Sabbatuci, *Essai sur le mysticisme grec*.
29 Détienne, *Les Jardins d'Adonis*.
30 *Odyssey*, 8.301ff.
31 Voegelin, *The Order of the Polis*.
32 Murray, *Five Stages of Greek Religion*, pp 58–65.
33 Sabbatuci, *Essai sur le mysticisme grec*, pp 67–73.
34 Vernant, *Religion grecque, religions antiques*, stresses the originality of this sacrificial practice: unlike the Vedic practice, it does not repeat an original foundational divine activity but a deal struck by heroic initiative.
35 Otto, *The Homeric Gods*, pp 170, 240–1.
36 Vernant, *Mythe et tragédie*, p 33.
37 Whitman, *Homer and the Heroic Tradition*, pp 248, 233.
38 Snell, *The Discovery of the Mind*, pp 22, 25.
39 Hegel, *Leçons sur le philosophie de la religion*, II 12, 143.
40 Levy, *The Gate of Horn*.
41 H. Nohl, ed, *Theologische Jugendschriften* (Tübingen: J.C.B. Mohr 1907), pp 28–9.
42 *Laches* 198e; *Charmides* 173c.
43 Beye, *Ancient Greek Literature and Society*, p 3. 'Perhaps' is unnecessary prudence.
44 Cornford, *Principium sapientiae*, p 144.
45 Nilsson, *A History of Greek Religion*, p 263.
46 Cornford, *From Religion to Philosophy*, pp 110–23.
47 Des Places, *La Religion grecque*, p 9.
48 Herodotus, 8.144.
49 Nilsson, *History of Greek Religion*, pp 52, 156.
50 Jaeger, *Paideia*, I, 156.
51 *Gorgias* 508a.
52 *Laws* 653e–654a.
53 K. Kerenyi, *The Religion of the Greeks and Romans*.
54 Hooper, *Greek Realities*, p 113.
55 Thucydides, *Peloponnesian War*, 2.38.
56 *Laws* 653d.

57 *Protagoras* 347d–348a.

58 *Republic* 378a.

59 *Republic* 364–6. See also *Republic* 560e; *Euthydemus* 277e; *Gorgias* 497c; *Theaetetus* 155e–156c; *Symposium* 218b. See also Grube, *Plato's Thought*, p 153.

60 Morrow, *Plato's Cretan City*, p 152.

61 *Apology* 41a.

62 *Phaedo* 63b.

63 Grube, *Plato's Thought*, p 203.

64 *Apology* 22b–c.

65 *Statesman* 290c–d.

66 *Phaedrus*, 248c–d.

67 Guthrie, *History of Greek Philosophy*, III, 19–21.

68 *Laws* 887c–d.

69 *Meno* 81a–b.

70 *Symposium* 201d, 209e.

71 These 'literary' prayers are identified and discussed in Jackson, 'The Prayers of Socrates,' pp 14–37. The author argues that Plato would not have written prayers incongruous with Socrates' character.

72 *Apology* 40a; *Phaedrus* 242c; *Apology* 39d.

73 *Apology* 20e–29a, 33c.

74 Jaeger, *Aristotle: Fundamentals of the History of His Development*, p 130.

75 Goldschmidt, 'La religion platonicienne,' *Platonisme et pensée contemporaine*, p 106.

76 *Laws* 738c; *Phaedrus* 275b–c.

77 This has been pointed out by Hirsch in his great study *Plato's Weg zum Mythos*, p 220, referring to *Phaedrus* 237a. Hirsch correctly emphasizes also that the whole range of meanings for *logos* found in a dictionary can be found in the dialogues (p 78).

78 See above pp 72–3.

79 *Republic* 377a.

80 *Phaedrus* 229c–230a.

81 *Gorgias* 253a.

82 *Laws* 712a, 752a, 927a.

83 *Laws* 716d, 921c, 889d.

84 *Laws* 907b.

85 *Republic* 365d–366.

86 This creed is modelled on a fragment in which Gorgias sets out to prove that nothing exists; and that if it exists, it is incomprehensible to man; and if it is comprehensible to anyone, it is not communicable to anyone. For a discussion of the fragment see Guthrie, *History of Greek Philosophy*, III, 193.

87 See the two articles by MacKinnon and Meynell on 'The Euthyphro Dilemma.'
88 Grube, *Plato's Thought*, p 178.
89 My approach is thus partly chronological. The next three chapters will, among other matters, look successively at *Gorgias*, *Republic*, and *Phaedrus* and will thus follow Plato's own sequence. My exposition, however, will also focus on the three dogmas and thus will entail systematic features. My contention is that as Plato's thought is developing in the years between *Gorgias* and *Phaedrus* it is laying the basis for an ultimately coherent whole.

CHAPTER 6

1 'There seems to be comparatively little moral substance in the early Greek calls to virtue,' writes Snell in 1948 in *The Discovery of the Mind*, p 178.
2 'It often happens that if I try to do as I wish I necessarily frustrate what someone else wishes. By the "morality" of a culture I mean the principles, criteria, and values which underlie its responses to this familiar experience. By "moral philosophy" or "ethics" I mean rational, systematic thinking about the relationship between morality and reason': Dover, *Greek Popular Morality in the Time of Plato and Aristotle*, p 1.
3 Adkins, *Merit and Responsibility*, pp 94–7.
4 Nilsson, *History of Greek Religion*, pp 181, 194.
5 Irwin, *Plato's Moral Theory*, p 17.
6 *Works and Days*, pp 352, 353.
7 As an example of the general call, see the famous lines of *Works and Days*: 'The man is altogether best who considers all things himself and marks what will be better afterwards and at the end; and he, again, is good who listens to a good adviser; but whoever neither thinks for himself nor keeps in mind what another tells him, he is an unprofitable man' (lines 295–7).
8 See Snell, *The Discovery of the Mind*, p 157.
9 *Protagoras* 320c–328d.
10 *Apology* 24e.
11 *Republic* 442–443b.
12 See O'Brien, *The Socratic Paradoxes and the Greek Mind* p 59.
13 See Wycherley, *How the Greeks Built Cities*, p 17.
14 Pearson, *Popular Ethics in Ancient Greece*, ch 1.
15 Adkins, *Merit and Responsibility*, p 233.
16 De Romilly, *La Loi dans la pensée grecque*, pp 53–4. *Gorgias* 484b.
17 Barker, *Greek Political Theory*, pp 86, 88.
18 *Gorgias* 483c–d.
19 *Republic* 362e–364c.
20 Guthrie, *History of Greek Philosophy*, II, 256.

21 Dodds, *The Greeks and the Irrational*, pp 28–50. For a critique of Dodds see Lloyd-Jones, *The Justice of Zeus*.

22 Nilsson, *History of Greek Religion*, ch 6.

23 Kerenyi, *Eleusis: Archetypical Image of Mother and Daughter*.

24 See Guthrie, *Orpheus and Greek Religion*.

25 P. Ricoeur, *La Symbolique du mal* (Paris: Aubier 1960), pp 39–50.

26 *Phaedo* 69c.

27 *Laws* 910d; see also 716c and ff.

28 *Republic*, 612–13.

29 Hutter, *Politics as Friendship*, p 95.

30 Gadamer, *Dialogue and Dialectics*, p 79.

31 Murdoch, *The Fire and the Sun*, p 74.

32 Gould, *The Development of Plato's Ethics*, p 54.

33 See Ramnoux, *Etudes présocratiques*, p 149.

34 Grene, *Man in His Pride*, p 32.

35 *Apology* 35c, 29e.

36 *Symposium* 219c.

37 *Symposium* 216a.

38 *Symposium* 218c, 219d.

39 *Phaedo* 67b.

40 *Phaedo* 69b. Findlay finds in Plato a 'Great Inversion of the common ontology'; reality resides not in concrete instances but in abstracted generic realities to which he gives the name of ideas or forms: *Plato and Platonism*, pp 9–10, 21–3. A similar inversion is taking place in ethics: what is real virtue is not the acquired ability to exercise this or that power to achieve this or that pleasure but the very ability to have power over oneself.

41 *Phaedo* 69c–d.

42 *Phaedo* 64a–65c, 114b–d.

43 Beckman, *The Religious Dimension of Socrates' Thought*, p 25.

44 *Phaedo* 114.

45 *Gorgias* 493d–e.

46 *Republic* 518d.

47 *Laws* 731d–732a.

48 *Statesman* 310d–311c.

49 *Peloponnesian War*, 2.40.

50 *Phaedo* 107d.

51 *Suppliant Women*, lines 492ff.

52 See the discussion by Strauss, *On Tyranny*. This book is most noteworthy, since it shows that the first thing to be aware of as one studies a philosophical dialogue is that

the writer has chosen to put it as a dialogue. It also argues that society will always try to tyrannize thought and that 'Socrates' rhetoric is the classic means for ever again frustrating these attempts' (p 26).

53 *Republic* 359d–360d.
54 'Only a city that has already lost its respect for law and order can fall into its clutches': Guthrie, *History of Greek Philosophy*, III, 73.
55 *Laws* 863e.
56 *Republic* 545d.
57 *Laws* 698b, 701b–e.
58 Cogan, *The Human Thing*, pp 34, 112.
59 These are Hegel's terms. See S. Avineri, *Hegel's Theory of the Modern State* (Cambridge: Cambridge University Press 1972), p 84.
60 T.S. Eliot, *Murder in the Cathedral*.
61 *Republic* 577d.
62 *Republic* 579b.
63 See *Gorgias* 467b.
64 *Republic* 568d.
65 See Simon, *Mind and Madness in Ancient Greece*, p 169.
66 For Plato on unwritten laws see *Laws* 793a. On the moral, religious, and occasional aristocratic connotations of unwritten laws in the fifth century see de Romilly, *La Loi dans la pensée grecque*, pp 26–49.
67 *Republic* 540d.
68 Cushman, *Therapeia*.
69 See ch 3 in Lain Entralgo, *The Therapy of the Word in Classical Antiquity*; and ch 9 in Simon, *Mind and Madness in Ancient Greece*.
70 Guthrie, *History of Greek Philosophy*, IV, 257.
71 *Statesman* 311c.
72 *Republic* 518d. Cushman in *Therapeia* rightly asks whether the range of dialectic is wide and powerful enough to be an instrument of social salvation (p 301).
73 *Republic* 505d.
74 Taylor, *Plato, the Man and His Work*, p 103.
75 *Republic* 364b–365a; *Laws* 909b. We very much agree with this point of Dodds's interpretation of Plato on religion: it implies a 'drastic interference with traditional belief and practise.'
76 *Laws* 885b–907b.
77 Read for its logical arguments, *Gorgias* is the last of the Socratic dialogues. For instance it still depends on the acceptability of the view that compares virtue to a craft. Read for its human drama, *Gorgias* is the first great Platonic existential statement. What Socrates does is more important than the logic he mouths. The dialogue

concludes with the utterance of a myth. It also gives Socrates mythical proportions as the speaker who slays tyranny.

78 Taylor, *Plato, the Man and His Work*, p 122. See also Voegelin, *Plato*, p 31: 'Callicles will have to refute not Socrates but his love.'

CHAPTER 7

1 Kirk and Raven, *The Presocratic Philosophers*, p 117.
2 Too sharp a division should not be drawn between the first dogma (the gods cannot be bribed, or appeased by sacrifices) and the second (they exist.) Jointly they affirm that our individual pursuit of the good takes place within a firm overall context: goodness *is*, it is not a projection of the fancies of a desirous self; it can be approached only along a path that is coherent with its nature. The gods love what is pious because it is pious. Euthyphro at that point adumbrates the root of theistic affirmation and Plato, thanks to Socrates, draws the full moral consequence. As Meynell puts it, at the end of his discussion of the issue in 'The Euthyphro Dilemma': 'To believe in God is to believe in a universal context in which men will not ultimately get away either with the moral renunciation of refusing to pursue the good, or with the self deception which consists in declining to advert to it' (p 231). It remains true, nevertheless, that Plato distinguishes between the two dogmas. Euthyphro can rise to the sense that the gods cannot be persuaded by our evasive tactics (to this extent he can be true to such insights as he has). But he never comes close to an articulation of who the gods are.
3 Committing himself to a full argument about the nature of the moral order, Plato clearly undertakes to know more than Socrates ever claimed. To frame the dogma by reference to the existence of the gods undertakes to show intelligibility, not blind Fate, to be supreme.
4 Rudhart, *Notions fondamentales de la pensée religieuse et actes constitutifs du culte dans la Grèce classique*, p 63.
5 Plato does limit the power of the Fates. In the *Republic* (617c) men take lots from their laps. The Fates narrow the range of choice, but do not determine it.
6 Remember Zeus scattering good and evil lots as fancy strikes him: *Iliad*, 24.527 and ff.
7 Redfield, *Nature and Culture in the Iliad*, p 131.
8 *Republic* 363a–b.
9 Nilsson, *History of Greek Religion*, pp 49, 52, 72, 57, 98, 156.
10 *Iliad*, 2.204–6; 8.19–27, 68–72.
11 Wilamowitz-Moellendorf, *Der Glaube der Hellenen*, p 9.
12 Sextus Empiricus, *Against the Dogmatists*, 3.123.
13 Otto, *Theophania*, p 29.

14 Festugière, *Contemplation et vie contemplative*, p 6.

15 *Lysis* 214a.

16 See Buffière, *Les Mythes d'Homère et la pensée grecque*.

17 *Ion* 541b, 535a.

18 Jaeger, *Paideia*, II, 360.

19 *Gorgias* 484b–c.

20 *Republic* 377e, 380.

21 *Republic* 595c.

22 *Republic* 599a. Plato adds a criticism of those who claim that Homer knew all knowledge: for instance, no war was led by his counsel.

23 *Republic* 600c.

24 Murdoch, *The Fire and the Sun*, p 79.

25 Note that in the *Laws* Homer is considered a reliable source on the early constitution of the Greeks (680b–681b).

26 Redfield, *Nature and Culture in the Iliad*, p 219.

27 Ibid, p 223.

28 *Timaeus* 29e.

29 Guthrie, *Orpheus and Greek Religion*, p 156. Guthrie adds that Orphism failed because it was too sophisticated, too doctrinal for the masses. And its doctrine was couched in terms too mythological to capture the minds of the emerging rational philosophers. Plato's merit, of course, was to reconcile *mythos* with *logos*.

30 *Apology* 41c; *Phaedo* 63c. See also *Phaedo* 114d; *Republic* 331a.

31 *Phaedo* 114c–d. In *Phaedrus* (229c–d) Socrates gives a complementary warning against the simplicity of mind of the true unbelievers who put a literalistic faith in their clever rationalistic explanations of the myths.

32 *Laws* 701c.

33 *Republic* 331.

34 *Republic* 621.

35 *Phaedo* 107d.

36 *Phaedo*, 97b–99c.

37 *Republic* 508e.

38 Irwin, *Plato's Moral Theory*, p 189.

39 Ibid, pp 189, 12.

40 Ibid, pp 131, 177–8.

41 *Republic* 375b.

42 *Republic* 360e–361d.

43 *Republic* 505d–e.

44 Aeschylus, Euripides, Thucydides have analysed the disorder caused by disunity. The call to unity has become a commonplace. See the third part of de Romilly, *Problèmes de la démocratie grecque*.

45 Sellars, 'Reason and the Art of Living in Plato,' p 353. One might point out that as an activist political philosopher Plato is still pursuing the mastery of a craft. The task of ordering a city rests in the end on a 'complex system of recipes for crafting a world.' But craft is not everything to the human beings in this world. The world 'includes not only instrumentalities but satisfying lives' (p 376).

46 *Republic* 423d.

47 *Republic* 441c–442d.

48 Joseph puts it this way: 'At least it must be shown, on the one hand, that only the good is completely intelligible and therefore knowledge in the full sense can have no other object; and on the other hand, that only the good can be the object of rational purpose – i.e. of purpose in which there is no self-contradiction – and therefore purposive activity in the full sense can have no other object': *Knowledge and the Good in Plato's Republic*, p 12.

49 Joseph is here also a good guide: 'what is most real is object of thought and not of sight. Visible things may be put together for us by another, and given us to see. But the object of thought can be 'seen' only by thinking it oneself. Only the process of reaching it can present it to us reached': *Knowledge and the Good in Plato's Republic*, p 2.

50 *Republic* 613c–614a.

51 Guthrie, *History of Greek Philosophy*, IV, 475, 538.

52 The education of the guardians is calculated to cultivate obedience to measure or to enhance the sense that measure has an objective basis.
The discipline necessary to approach the Good is mathematics; it cultivates the best powers of the soul and prepares us to see what is best in the realm of being. A sense of musical harmony is equally essential. The physical and moral climate surrounding the young is the object of much attention so that 'they may drink in good from every quarter, whence, like a breeze bearing health from happy regions, some influence from noble works constantly falls upon eye and ear from childhood upward, and imperceptibly draws them into sympathy and harmony with the beauty of reason, whose impress they take': *Republic* 401c (Cornford's translation). Beautiful orderly motion is the link between the austere authority of goodness and the diversities of life.

53 Mourelatos, *The Route of Parmenides*.

54 Iris Murdoch, 'The Sovereignty of Good over Other Concepts,' in *The Sovereignty of Good* (London: Routledge and Kegan Paul 1970), p 93. All three essays in this volume are an excellent restatement of Platonic morality. See p 92: 'One might say that true morality is a sort of unesoteric mysticism, having its source in an austere and unconsoled love of the Good.'

55 Cohen, 'Socrates on the Definition of Piety: *Euthyphro*, 10a–116,' p 159.

56 Isocrates, *To Nicocles*, sect 7, 8.

57 Jaeger, *Paideia*, III, 117–22.

58 Ibid, III, 150.

59 Irwin, *Plato's Moral Theory*, pp 222, 158–9.

60 As Irwin puts it, 'an interlocutor forced by the elenchos to decide will prefer his choices to converge on a final good, though they need not have previously converged on it': *Plato's Moral Theory*, p 95.

61 Cushman, *Therapeia*, p 21.

62 Scolnicov, 'Reason and Passion in the Platonic Soul.'

63 J.S. Mill, on Plato, in Gross, ed, *Great Thinkers on Plato*, p 184.

64 Crombie, *Plato: The Midwife's Apprentice*, pp 27–8.

65 Moline, *Plato's Theory of Understanding*, pp 78, 51.

66 Plato sees that desire for drink is desire *simpliciter*; he would not accept the Socratic argument that it must be desire for good drink. See Penner, 'Thought and Desire in Plato.' Hence Plato's pessimism about those human beings whose loves are poorly oriented.

67 *Phaedrus* 249d.

68 *Theaetetus* 172–176d.

69 *Theaetetus* 177a–c.

70 See Cornford's translation of the *Republic*, p 349.

CHAPTER 8

1 *Laws* 900c.

2 *Laws* 904b.

3 *Laws* 905c.

4 Armstrong, 'Platonic Eros and Christian Agape,' p 110.

5 Adkins quite rightly notes that the words which denote the relationship between man and God 'play only an inconspicuous part in the ethical writings of Plato and Aristotle': *Merit and Responsibility*, p 132.

6 *Phaedo* 111b–c.

7 *Phaedo* 85c–d. See also *Republic* 368a, 492a.

8 *Odyssey*, 20.351ff. Plato refers to it in *Ion* 539a. This is the only example acknowledged by Parke, *Greek Oracles*, p 15. Flacelière also refers to the less fully described instances found in *Iliad*, 7.44–5; *Odyssey*, 11.96, 15.172–3: *Devins et oracles grecs*, p 34.

9 Des Places, *La Religion grecque*, p 145.

10 Cicero, *De divinatione*, bases his distinction on that found in *Phaedrus* 244c–d.

11 Burnet, *Early Greek Philosophy*, p 133.

12 *Histories*, 7.140–5; 1.53.

13 Guthrie, *History of Greek Philosophy*, II, 122–265.

14 Ibid, II, 12.

15 *Ion* 533d–534a.

16 Dodds, *The Greeks and the Irrational*, pp 210, 217–18.

17 Ibid, ch 5. See also Burkert, *Love and Science in Ancient Pythagoreanism*.

18 Rohde attributed such views to Plato: *Psyche*, II, 465.

19 See pp 145–54 in Guthrie, *The Greeks and Their Gods*. See also Détienne, *Dionysos mis à mort*, pp 77, 149, 153.

20 Greek males, I should hasten to add, also have their phantasms. The mythology shows numerous traces of their wish to get rid of the other sex. The first human beings were born of the earth, without sexual reproduction. In Hesiod's *Theogony*, argues Loraux, women are seen as a subsequently crafted artefact, which is contrived to trap men and which severs the simple unity men have with themselves and with the gods; see *Les Enfants d'Athéna*, pp 22, 65, 81–3, 117. Misogynous hunters also abound: at the borders of civilized life, far from cities, fields, women, and domestic animals, these marginal young men prolong their adolescence, have sex, if any, with each other, and roam alone, naked in the night, hunting or fighting enemies at the borders; see Vidal-Naquet, *Le Chasseur noir*, p 172.

21 Sabbatucci, *Essai sur le mysticisme grec*, pp 52–4.

22 Fragment 14, in Freeman, *Ancilla to the Pre-Socratic Philosophers*, p 25.

23 See above, p 98.

24 David L. Hall, *Eros and Irony: A Prelude to Philosophical Anarchism* (Albany: State University of New York Press 1982), pp 35, 43, 50, 76, 170, 204.

25 See McGinty, *Interpretation and Dionysos*, pp 73–6.

26 Sabbatucci argues that the mystical experience is the experience of an absolute and dissolves all relative relations; instead of relating to it, the self is immersed in otherness. See his *Essai sur le mysticisme grec*, pp 32–3, 120. One should recall here the theses of Georges Bataille: individuals desire to overcome their separateness and experiences of discontinuity: they want fusion, unbroken continuity, with something other than their separate selves. In fusion isolated individuals enjoy losing themselves. In eroticism, religions, and sexual orgasms they experience such a return to continuity. Death is the permanent end of discontinuity. See his *L'Erotisme* (Paris: Editions de Minuit, n.d.).

27 Hall, *Eros and Irony*, p 211.

28 Fragment 1, translations by Freeman and by Kirk and Raven.

29 *Bacchae* (translation by Kirk), p 18.

30 *Phaedrus* 245c.

31 The immortality of the soul is argued about in *Phaedo*. But even there what matters are the brave and hopeful affirmations made by Socrates on the last day of his life. See Gadamer, 'The Proofs of Immortality in Plato's Phaedo,' in *Dialogue and Dialectic*.

32 *Phaedrus* 246a.

33 'The unrest in a man's psyche may be luminous enough to understand itself as caused by ignorance concerning the ground and meaning of existence.' Reason is 'existential philia'; it is 'the openness of existence raised to consciousness.' See Voegelin, 'Reason: The Classic Experience.'

34 *Phaedrus* 248c.

35 Chanteur, *Platon, le désir et la cité*, pp 178, 181.

36 Kant has said the same of happiness.

37 Machiavelli and Hobbes take it for granted.

38 Irwin, *Plato's Moral Theory*, pp 170-1, 253.

39 The philosopher knows what each part of the soul is inclined to. Its stories, like charms, promise each part what it loves. See Moline, 'The Achievement of Psychic Harmony' in *Plato's Theory of Understanding*, pp 62-71.

40 *Phaedrus* 244e-245c.

41 Dodds, *The Greeks and the Irrational*, p 68.

42 *Phaedrus* 265a.

43 *Phaedrus* 244a-c, 245c, 249d-e.

44 *Crito* 54d. Another allusion to corybantic rites has been taken by some to indicate that Socrates had been initiated into them. See *Euthyphro* 277d; and Dodds, *The Greeks and the Irrational*, pp 99, 104n.

45 On this subject see the two articles by Linforth, 'The Corybantic Rites in Plato' and 'Telestic Madness in Plato.'

46 *Laws* 682a. These lines on divine madness are the farthest Plato has ever gone in the rehabilitation of enthusiastic phenomena. The Platonic corpus also teems with warnings against too positive an appraisal of them. In the discussion of divination in *Timaeus* Plato emphasizes that 'prophets [i.e. interpreters] are necessary to pass judgment upon divination' (71e). 'It belongs to a man when in his right mind to recollect and ponder the things spoken in dream or waking vision by the divining and inspired nature' (72c).
The *Laws* discuss corybantism and the raptures of the Bacchants as a disease born of fear: a quiet lulling motion is the better way to restore a sound state of mind (*Laws* 790d, 791b). Begging priests and soothsayers are pointed to in the *Republic* as sources of a common mercenary notion of virtue (364c).
Most crucial is the vigorous and repeated rejection of the common Greek idea according to which offended, jealous, or vindictive deities curse men and women by afflicting them with a destructive madness. Mythology is full of tales of gods punishing men – with or without just causes – by making them insane. Euripides frequently echoes these tales; the tragedies of *Medea*, *Herakles*, *Hippolytus*, and of course the *Bacchae* readily come to mind. To Plato madness from the gods is always a blessing.

47 Harrison, 'Alpha and Omega,' in *Alpha and Omega*, pp 202-5.

48 Otto, *Dionysos, Myth and Cult*, pp 86–91.

49 McGinty, *Interpretation and Dionysos*, p 171.

50 Dodds, *The Greeks and the Irrational*, p 117.

51 See Dodds, *Pagan and Christian in an Age of Anxiety*, pp 70–2. See also Solmsen, *Plato: Theology*, p 125. Misleading, then, is the whole argument in Pieper's *Enthusiasm and Divine Madness.*

52 Strauss, *The Argument and the Action of Plato's Laws*, pp 20–1. See Book I of the *Laws.*

53 *Timaeus* 47d–e, 90c–d.

54 *Phaedrus* 249e.

55 I do not entirely agree with the passage in the article by Verdenius that takes the view that madness does not make a moral demand or persuade the self: 'A Muse who condescends to so completely taking possession of her servant should be expected in some way to guarantee a correct understanding of her revelations': 'Plato's Doctrine of Artistic Imitation,' II, 263. The issue is sharply put. The Greeks do believe in Muses who do not worry about what their servants understand. The Christian God, in principle, always guarantees proper understanding. Plato's divine influences are halfway in between.

56 See Joly, *Le Renversement platonicien*, esp p 107.

57 Friedländer, *Plato*, III, 515, n 41. See also vol I, ch I.

58 *Phaedrus* 251a.

59 *Phaedrus* 252b.

60 *Iliad*, 1.29.

61 *Iliad*, 6.390–502.

62 See chs 2 and 3 in Stanford, *The Ulysses Theme*.

63 *Odyssey*, 5.119–20. Samuel Butler cites this passage as evidence that the *Odyssey* was written by a woman.

64 See the discussion of *Works and Days* and *Theogony* in Détienne and Vernant, 'A la table des hommes,' in *La Cuisine du sacrifice en pays grec*.

65 Arthur, 'Early Greece: the Origins of the Western Attitude toward Women,' p 25.

66 See ch 5 in Friedrich, *The Meaning of Aphrodite*.

67 *Phaedrus* 235c.

68 From Zeitlin, 'The Dynamics of Misogyny in the *Oresteia*,' pp 149, 150.

69 *Eumenides*, line 737.

70 *Hippolytus*, lines 525–8 (Grene's translation).

71 See Wilkinson, 'Classical Approaches to Women's Liberation.'

72 I do not see any group of ordinary Greeks giving much serious attention to the notion that eros leads one metaphysically farther as long as one does not copulate. See *Phaedrus* 253e–254e.

Dover, *Greek Homosexuality*, has convinced me that the basic facts of Greek homosexuality were as follows. Everyone in fifth-century Athens assumed that men's desires would be aroused by handsome youths and some extolled the affectionate relationship that would ensue if the pursuer persuaded the pursued. While the pursuer would gain genital pleasures, it was assumed that the pursued would find none and would respond with a feeling of esteem and admiration. Moral reprobation was sharp for those youths who granted their favours for money or allowed themselves to suffer anal copulation. It was taken for granted that such erotic relationships did not prevent the men from keeping their taste for women or the youths from soon acquiring it. On the fringes of this phenomenon the historian also observes aggressive men who enjoyed forcing anal penetration upon weaker ones, pathic men who settled for a life-time of passive roles, and some fooling around among youths and some making-do among men deprived of women. Dover is not sure about the theories tracing the ennobling version of the practice to archaic, 'manly,' Dorian military organizations.

73 Flacelière points to Plutarch as the Platonist champion of conjugal love: *Love in Ancient Greece*, pp 184–5. I do not accept his assumption that homosexuals helped civilize heterosexual relationships in Greece.

74 *Phaedrus* 252b–c, 253c.

75 *Phaedrus* 254e, 256a–b.

76 See Benoîst, *Tyrannie du logos*, p 11; and Jambet, *Apologie de Platon*, p 179.

77 *Phaedrus* 250c.

78 Burger, *Plato's Phaedrus*, p 61.

79 *Phaedrus* 255a.

80 White, *A Companion to Plato's Republic*, p 49.

81 *Republic* 462a–d, 520c.

82 See Irwin, *Plato's Moral Theory*, pp 239–43. What Plato does not say is that good people take deep personal satisfaction in lovingly caring for others.

83 Aristotle, writes Gould, does not believe in tapping dark passions to climb to visionary heights: *Platonic Love*, p 145. The charge of impersonality in the theory can, it seems to me, be properly laid at the door of Aristotle.

84 *Phaedrus* 263c.

85 *Symposion* 203d–e, 194e; *Meno* 80a–b. See Derrida, 'La Pharmacie de Platon.'

86 Subsequent history has demonstrated that there can be a powerful *libido dominiendi* among men of pure austere lives who have demonstrably renounced all easy pleasures. Callicles in *Gorgias*, before being refuted by Socrates' demonstrations, has the time to point out that there is a complicity at times between the desire to write and persuade and the practice of political power. Plato, always fair, also lets Gorgias testify to the health and vitality of desire. The desirous man overflows and spends; he is not a leaky barrel that can never be filled. and the filled barrel that experiences no desire is more dead than alive. For this new slant on the metaphor in *Gorgias* 493c–494b see Benoîst, *Tyrannie du logos*, pp 163–6.

87 See Jaeger, *Paideia*, III, 53, 60, 82–196; and Kennedy, *The Art of Persuasion in Greece*, ch 3. In his famous praise of *logos* Isocrates develops a basic theme: 'eloquence is the source of most of our blessings': *Nicocles*, sect 5.

88 Wayne C. Booth, *Modern Dogma and the Rhetoric of Assent* (Chicago: University of Chicago Press 1974), p 136.

89 See Hackforth, commentary on *Phaedrus* 266c–269c, p 143.

90 *Sophist* 254a, 268d.

91 *Potestas clavium*, p 102.

92 See White, *Plato on Knowledge and Reality*, ch 5, pp 117–30.

93 *Phaedrus* 258d.

94 *Phaedrus* 259e.

95 *Phaedrus* 245c.

96 *Phaedrus* 265e–266b.

97 *Phaedrus* 274e, 275a.

98 See de Romilly, *La Loi dans la pensée grecque*, pp 26, 44, 190. See also *Laws* 793a–c.

99 Murdoch, *The Fire and the Sun*, pp 22–3.

100 Burger, *Plato's Phaedrus*, pp 90, 70. Ever moving, the soul is never secure in any of its preferences. Rhetoric keeps alive a sense of the good by imaging greater goods. It is, finally, the 'means by which the impulse of the soul to be ever moving is redeemed': Richard Weaver, *The Ethics of Rhetoric* (South Bend: Gateway 1953), p 25.

101 Ibid, pp 90–109.

102 *Phaedrus* 276a.

103 *Alcibiades* 132b. See Derrida, 'La Pharmacie de Platon,' p 138.

104 Burger, *Plato's Phaedrus*, p 98.

105 Taylor, *Plato, the Man and His Work*, p 302.

106 In his discussion of *Phaedrus* Weaver writes that the eulogy of the non-lover implies praise for the 'neuter form of speech,' 'incapable of inducing bias in the hearer': *The Ethics of Rhetoric*, pp 5, 7. An illusion is entertained, that of value-free talk that conveys information and lets the listener decide coolly. In fact all speech is erotic and seeks to move: it can move towards the good or towards evil. 'Any utterance is a major assumption of responsibility' (p 6).

107 Burger, *Plato's Phaedrus*, p 71.

108 Voegelin, *Plato*, p 139. Yet Burger quite rightly notes the ghostly presence of Lysias, 'haunting the apparently private scene.' 'From beginning to end, this most private erotic conversation is determined by the public nature of the written word': *Plato's Phaedrus*, p 4.

CHAPTER 9

1 The distinction between rearticulation and translation is adapted from McGinty, *Interpretation and Dionysos*, ch 1.

2 This analysis is based on Rodney Needham, *Belief, Language and Experience* (Chicago: University of Chicago Press 1972). It is striking how this anthropologist has arrived independently at conclusions recalling Paul Tillich's famous passages on the intellectualistic, voluntaristic, and emotional distortions of faith in his *Dynamics of Faith* (New York: Harper and Row 1957).

3 *Meno* 97b, 98a, 99b. There is also a discussion of belief in *Timaeus* 37b–c.

4 Rist, *Eros and Psyche*, p 141.

5 *Laws* 715e (translation by Pieper in *Leisure the Basis of Culture*, p 113).

6 Jaeger, *Paideia*, III, 242.

7 *Laws* 664a.

8 *Statesman* 276e.

9 A serious deadlock frequently occurs on this point between Plato and his modern readers. Plato does speak of imposing the good life by ruse or by force. Readers automatically read this to mean imposing the ruler's notion of the good life.

10 For the developmental view see Gould, *The Development of Plato's Ethics*. Vlastos has written a critical review-article under the title 'Socratic Knowledge and Platonic Pessimism,' pp 226–8.

11 We must realize that modern political science ordinarily considers the removal of religious influences one of its preliminary tasks.

12 *Laws* 653d, 716d–e.

13 Moline, *Plato's Theory of Understanding*, pp 49–50.

14 *Republic* 592b.

15 *Republic* 488.

16 Strauss, *The Argument and the Action of Plato's Laws*.

17 Taylor, *Plato*, p 266.

18 Pangle, *The Laws*, p 379.

19 *Laws* 645a.

20 Chanteur, *Platon, le désir et la cité*, pp 241, 257–8.

21 Peradotto, *Classical Mythology*, p 1. To this useful survey of the literature add Burkert, *Structure and History in Greek Mythology and Ritual*.

22 See Teloh, *The Development of Plato's Metaphysics*, p 61.

23 Whitman, *Euripides and the Full Circle of Myth*, p 105. Myths can be very elaborate. One definition of myth, adds Whitman, is that it is 'a complete hypothesis of order' as a recourse for communication (p 137). I do not care to recall how many definitions of myth I have encountered in the course of this study. Let me cite only one, persuasive, but heavy and loaded: 'Myth, both traditional and created, is the narrative form of those particularly archetypal symbols which together make a coherent revelation of what man knows and what he believes': foreword in N. Frye, L.C. Knights, et al, *Myth and Symbol: Critical Approaches and Applications* (Lincoln: University of Nebraska Press 1963), p v.

24 Vernant, 'Religion grecque, religions antiques,' p 29.

25 Kirk, *The Nature of Greek Myths*. See my review of this work in *Studies in Religion/ Sciences Religieuses*. See also Kirk, *Myth: Its Meaning and Functions in Ancient and Other Cultures*; this book is discussed in Peradotto, *Classical Mythology*, pp 57–8.

26 *Works and Days*, lines 1–2.

27 Nilsson, *Cults, Myths, Oracles and Politics in Ancient Greece*, p 11. See also Kirk *The Nature of Greek Myths*, p 287. Claude Lévi-Strauss maintains that a myth is always the transformation of other myths. Right. But I should add the point made by Barthes, that in myth things lose the memory of their fabrication: John Sturrock, 'Roland Barthes,' in John Sturrock ed, *Structuralism and Since: From Lévi-Strauss to Derrida* (Oxford: Oxford University Press 1979). pp 42, 64.

28 Kirk, *The Nature of Greek Myths*, p 152.

29 Voegelin, *Plato*, p 185.

30 Whitman, *Euripides and the Full Cycle of Myth*, p 107.

31 Ibid, p 108.

32 On anger see Vellacott, *Ironic Drama: A Study of Euripides' Method and Meaning*. Whitman also argues that, at least in the three romances he examines closely, some sort of harmonious wholeness gets restored and a semblance of order is captured by characters moving homeward into myth: see *Euripides and the Full Cycle of Myth*, pp 146–8.

33 F. Kermode, *The Genesis of Secrecy* (Cambridge, Mass: Harvard University Press 1978), p 118.

34 See Cornford, *Thucydides Mythistoricus*, p 221. For a similar process in Herodotus see the comprehensive study of Lachenaud, *Mythologie, religion et philosophie de l'histoire dans Hérodote*.

35 The notion of *technè* appears frequently in Plato; it is also an important expression of ambivalence. Plato has a low opinion of technics, that is artisans; the *Laws* especially distrusts them. Plato does not value much those human beings who have useful knacks. But the legislator and the demiurge, those supreme models of human excellence, do what artisans do, although their raw material is human beings, however, rather than clay or iron. The most telling metaphor Plato has for the statesman is that of the weaver. Plato does not seem to be aware of his dichotomy between noble and humble *technè*. See Vidal-Naquet, 'Etude d'une ambiguité: les artisans dans la cité platonicienne,' in *Le Chasseur noir*, pp 289–316. There is also a systematic blurring of the border between art and nature. The legislator has art; his art, however, is such that the city founded by him appears to be grounded in nature.

36 See *Gorgias* 448c.

37 See Chatelet, *La Naissance de l'histoire*, pp 10, 22, 48.
It is significant that the most eloquent attack on myth among the literary-critical analyses of the sixties has argued that the craze for myth represents the fear of history. See Philip Rahu, 'The Myth and the Powerhouse,' in John B. Vickery, ed,

Myth and Literature: Contemporary Theory and Practice (Lincoln: University of Nebraska Press 1965): 'History is that powerhouse of change which destroys custom and tradition in producing the future' (p 111). Rahu adds that the fear of history is at bottom the fear of the hazard of freedom. 'In our time the historical process is marked far more by loss and extremity than growth and mastery, and this fact is interpreted by the spokesmen of traditionalism as completely justifying their position. The mythic principle appeals to them because of its fixity and profoundly conservative implications' (pp 117–18).

I might also refer to the point made by Hannah Arendt: 'The thread of historical continuity was the first substitute for tradition': *Between Past and Future* (New York: Meridian Books 1968), p 28. It takes a story, of course, to have a thread.

38 Our account is indebted to Friedländer, *Plato: An Introduction*, pp 171–210; Friedländer, however, speaks of three levels of myth.

39 *Timaeus* 19d–e.

40 Hirsch stresses the similarity between the myths of the soul and those of the cosmos. One should not, however, forget that the myth of *Phaedrus* belongs to the middle period and has a kinship with the eschatological myths in the other dialogues of the middle period: it also serves as an invitation to the philosopher's calling. The myth of the cosmos belongs to the later period with its doctrinal interests: it is a myth one can easily see taught in the public religion.

41 *Timaeus* 21c–d. See Voegelin, *Plato*, p 179.

42 *Timaeus* 59d.

43 *Theogony*, 5.108. On the whole subject see Guthrie, *In the Beginning: Some Greek Views on the Origins of Life and the Early State of Man*.

44 *Dirges*, line 134.

45 Note that Socrates, while present, plays no decisive role in such dialogues as *Timaeus*, *Critias*, and the *Statesman*; he is absent from the *Laws*.

46 *Laws* 890d.

47 *Timaeus* 68e.

48 *Timaeus* 34c.

49 Vlastos, *Plato's Universe*, p 97. This work is the most useful commentary on *Timaeus*.

50 Guthrie, *History of Greek Philosophy*, v, 141–7. Motion both is and is not. It is identical with itself and is not identical with that which aboundingly is. Parmenides' problem is overcome. See v, 151–4.

51 *Phaedrus* 246e–247a; *Laws* 906a, b.

52 *Statesman*, 268d–e. On this dialogue see Klein, *Plato's Trilogy*; and Gill, 'Plato and Politics: The *Critias* and the Politicians.'

53 *Statesman* 269b.

54 *Statesman* 273d–e.

55 *Statesman*, 276d–e.
56 *Statesman* 390e.
57 Guthrie, *History of Greek Philosophy*, v, 183.
58 *Republic* 529a–b.
59 Skemp, *Plato's Statesman*, p 65.
60 *Timaeus* 28c.
61 *Timaeus* 48a.
62 See the discussion in Guthrie, *History of Greek Philosophy*, v, 92–7; and the article by Cherniss, 'The Sources of Evil According to Plato.'
63 Détienne and Vernant have brought to light in *Les Ruses de l'intelligence* the deep sense that the Greeks have of pragmatic intelligence as a clever art. It is unfortunate that their glimpse at Plato (pp 301–4) overlooks the *Statesman* and identifies too closely his grasp of intelligence with the processes of the exact sciences.
64 Cornford, *Plato's Cosmology*, pp 361–4.
65 This sense of the limiting factor brings to light a point on which the Greeks are profoundly coherent. There is no anti-God in Greece, but there is no creation *ex nihilo*. The divine is always set in a polarity, but the other pole is a sort of dark nothing. 'Greece kept wavering between the temptation of religious dualism and the refusal of it,' writes Ramnoux, *Etudes présocratiques*, p 227.
66 Finley, *Thucydides*, p 314.
67 Jaeger, *Aristotle*, p 56.
68 *Republic* 379a.
69 *Timaeus* 34a. See also *Timaeus* 92c: 'the universe is a perceptible god made in the image of the intelligible.'
70 *Laws* 886a.
71 *Laws* 887c–d.
72 *Laws* 899. Guthrie, *History of Greek Philosophy*, v, 360.
73 *Laws* 966c–e. See the discussion by Jaeger, in *Aristotle*, pp 161–2, who draws the contrast with the famous Kantian passage: 'Two things fill the spirit with ever fresh and increasing wonder and awe, the more often and the more persistently they are reflected upon, the starry heavens above me, and the moral law within me.'
74 *Philebus* 28c, 27d, 30c.
75 *Timaeus* 30a–b.
76 Hackforth also shows that the theological passages in the *Laws* are compatible with what we learn in *Philebus* and *Timaeus*. See 'Plato's Theism,' reprinted in Allen, ed, *Studies in Plato's Metaphysics*. More recently Lee has examined the passages on *Nous* and on rotation in the *Timaeus* and his results tend to confirm the view just reached. Launching what must have been at first an apparently farfetched comparison, which, however, promptly became familiar and entirely 'natural,' Plato compared the activity of intelligence to the motion of a sphere rotating upon itself. 'The model represents a subjectivity entirely absorbed in and subordinated to the

apprehension of its object, wholly reduced to an abstract, pure aboutness ... Plato's model of rotation represents *Nous* as a psychic activity in which an object is apprehended in [a] non-perspective way': Lee, 'Reason and Rotation.' Clearly *Nous* emerges as an ultimate, uncaused, explanatory principle, and is Plato's contribution to the emergence of philosophical theism.

77 Cherniss, 'The Philosophical Economy of the Theory of Ideas,' pp 3, 8, 9.

78 I differ from Cherniss in giving ontological significance to the *Nous* found in *Philebus* and afterwards rather than to the form of the Good found in the *Republic*. On behalf of Cherniss's solution one can point out that the second passage on the idea of the Good makes it the cause of all that is good (*Republic* 517c). My decisive principle is attentiveness to literary form and distrust of overly coherent accounts of Plato's views.

Subsequent debates do point to the existence of a lack of coherence. Platonists have tried hard to ascertain whether the forms are in the intelligence of God or outside. Taking his cue from the pages on *Nous*, Aristotle has said that God has himself as the constant object of his thought. Others have tended to place the ideas outside, noting that the form of the Good is independent of any intelligence contemplating it. See Joseph, *Knowledge and the Good in Plato's Republic*; and Wolfson, 'Extradeical and Intradeical Interpretations of Platonic Ideas,' in *Religious Philosophy*.

79 Plato is like a playwright. Any discussion of Euripides' plays seeking to establish whether the dramatist has changed his mind on the nature of man will either turn to an erudition unaware of its ridicule, or will stall on the realization that the inquiry is getting past, or remaining this side of, the point. See Randall, *Plato: Dramatist of the Life of Reason*. The dialogues are 'pictures of men talking, discussing, arguing, sometimes even thinking'; 'Plato is a philosopher *because* he is a poet' (pp 2–3).

80 Lee, 'Reason and Rotation,' pp 90–2.

81 Dodds, *The Greeks and the Irrational*, arrives at a different view, based on his own theory of what can elicit religious feeling. The form of the Good as an absolute 'is hardly a possible object of worship.' Plato's religious feeling is for the benevolent and mighty demiurge. This highest God of his personal faith could be integrated 'into a world scheme only at the mythical level' (pp 120–1).

82 And let us recall that Plato is mindful of the extraordinary difficulties involved in any attempt to discuss what is most important. In the *Republic*, when Socrates speaks of the form of the Good, Glaucon interjects, dismayed by the hyperboles; to which Socrates replies that the responsibility for strained language lies on the one who has compelled Socrates to utter his thought on the subject (*Republic* 509c). The *Laws* warns more solemnly about the inadequacies of all talk about God: let us not create a darkness at noon and spread obscurity while aiming to shed light. In either case the speaker stands at a limit where the greatest intelligence and virtue are required if his utterances are to be more helpful then deleterious.

83 Van Camp and Canart, *Le Sens du mot theios chez Platon*, pp 409–23.

84 *Laws* 716c.
85 Wild, *Plato's Modern Enemies and the Theory of Natural Law*, p 64.
86 *Laws* 716c.
87 *Phaedo* 79d–81a; *Republic* 501b, 613e; *Theaetetus* 176a–b; *Laws* 716c–717a.
88 Austere love of the Good and cosmic piety are not identical attitudes, but there is a moral convergence between the two. Whether one contemplates the form of the Good or moves in harmony with the world soul, in either case our minds and our lives are shaped by a supreme canon of all goodness, and become liberated from the power of opinion and conventions. Man is to be conceived as a deferrent, responsive being who assimilates himself to the totality of his environment. The wise man knows his position in the economy of things and thus attunes himself to the widest possible context and not to the narrow context of his personal and social surroundings. As Nettleship puts it, he simply reads the world (*Lectures on Plato's Republic*, p 155). And that implies a painful effort. Most men have embodied in the life of their group an order opposed to the divine one. They live the upside-down existence. The making of such inversion begins with the difficulties inherent in embodiment. 'The evil is that the soul of every man, when it is greatly pleased or pained by anything, is compelled to believe that the object which caused the emotion is very distinct and very true; but it is not' (*Phaedo* 83c). In the corrupt city social rewards and punishments gain the prestige of reality. Men live in the dream of their desires and fears. The fabricative tendency of men leads them to honour their own constructions more than the universal order assembled by God. Respect for our subjective acts, our wishes, and the mechanisms we contrive to cope with them is the root of inversion. See Voegelin, *Plato*, p 79; Wild, *Plato's Theory of Man*, p 310.
89 See *Nicomachean Ethics*, 10.8.7: the gods only contemplate; 'all forms of human conduct seem trifling and unworthy of them.'
90 *Laws* 902.
91 Rist, *Eros and Psyche*, pp 33, 159, 161.
92 The *Laws* praises writing: laws written are a stabler bond, and stability in this case is an advantage (Book 10, 981a, and Book 12, 957c–958a). On unwritten customs see Book 7, 793b–c.
93 See *Statesman* 297c–e.
94 See Taylor, *Plato*, pp 463–4; and Morrow, *Plato's Cretan City*.
95 Pangle, *The Laws of Plato*, pp 11, 377.
96 A treatise of the Hippocratic corpus, *On the Winds*, affirms that when drunk 'souls change and with them the thoughts they contain.' Men, forgetting their present woes, accept the hope of future ones.
97 See Strauss, *The Argument and Action of Plato's Laws*. The *Laws* is Plato's only political work; the Athenian Stranger engages in political activity. 'In the *Republic* Socrates founds a city in speech, i.e., not in deed' (p 1).

98 *Laws* 715e–716b (Pangle's translation).
99 See above, p 173.
100 *Laws* 698b, 701b–c.
101 *Laws* 693b.
102 *Laws* 719c–723d. Rousseau, *Social Contract*, IV, 8. See Pangle, 'Politics and Religion in Plato's Laws,' III, 27.
103 'In the field of religion, as in that of morals, the great enemy which had to be fought was antinomian individualism; and he looked to Delphi to organize the defense': Dodds, *The Greeks and the Irrational*, p 222.
104 *Laws* 781. It is understood that private cults would thus lose their appeal with their best clientele.
105 *Laws* 773a–774a.
106 Pangle, *The Laws of Plato*, p 485.
107 Moreau, *L'Ame du monde de Platon aux Stoiciens*, pp 80–2.
108 Aristophanes, *The Frogs*, lines 1420–1.

CHAPTER 10

1 *Phaedo* 114d–e. See Moline, *Plato's Theory of Understanding*, pp 68, 69.
2 Ibid, p 180.
3 *Phaedo* 107b.
4 'Propositions were never central themes of interest in the thought of Plato, and were certainly never conceived of as ideal entities like the Ideas; they only become central topics in the Aristotelian theory of demonstrative science, and were never hypostatized till the nineteenth century': Findlay, *Plato and Platonism*, p 27. Plato is like the Greeks in general, in that knowledge is for him a matter of direct acquaintance, i.e. seeing things. Aristotle begins to be interested in sentences, and takes temporally indefinite sentences (sentences to which we can subscribe on the basis of some features of the occasion on which they are uttered) as paradigm of all informative sentences. See Hintikko, 'Time, Truth and Knowledge in Ancient Greek Philosophy,' pp 1–14.
5 Plutarch, *De garrulitate*, pp 502–3.
6 Hall finds the antecedents for it in Greek comedy. 'The *eiron*, whose mock-humility masked his ambition and cunning, always gained the upper hand at the expense of the *alazon* – a haughty, pretentious pseudosophisticate, whose unjustified sense of self-importance made his fall a source of delight for Greek audiences': *Eros and Irony* p 214.
7 H.W. Fowler, *A Dictionary of Modern English Usage*, 2nd ed (Oxford: Clarendon Press 1965), p 305.
8 See the contrast between *spoude* and *paidia* in *Epistle* VI 323d. See also the discussion in Guthrie, *History of Greek Philosophy*, IV, 62.

9 See Hall, *Eros and Irony*, pp 56–7; the whole book has much to teach on the link between eros and irony. I shall add a further point based on Fowler's double audience. The wink is ironic and singles out an audience of one. Teasing is ironic and tells the other that my words are sharp but I am friendly.

10 *Theaetetus* 172e–177c (see also p 48).

11 Châtelet, *Platon*, p 157.

12 Strauss, 'On a New Interpretation of Plato's Political Philosophy,' p 351.

13 Tigerstedt, *Interpreting Plato*, p 103. Gadamer has admitted that his early work tended to push too much into the background the basic theme of Plato's doctrine: *Dialogue and Dialectic* p 125.

14 Attention can also be paid to Plato's ontology, the reconciliation of Parmenides and Heraclitus with the doctrine of the one and the indefinite dyad. On this see Guthrie, *History of Greek Philosophy*, V, 439–41.

15 Strauss, *What Is Political Philosophy?*, p 10.

16 Voegelin, *The World of the Polis*, p 193.

17 *Laws* 653b. See Strauss, *The Argument and Action of Plato's Laws*, p 22.

18 See ibid, p 38.

19 *Republic* 368c; *Phaedrus* 242d.

20 Plato's lists of virtues vary but five main ones keep reappearing: wisdom, justice, piety, courage, and temperance. Each of the virtues seems at times to claim it alone has the key to human health. Wisdom is most frequently cast in this role (see *Laches*, *Protagoras*, *Meno*). But in the *Republic* justice is the one virtue that must be found if man is to find his true measure, and a grasp of wisdom, courage, and temperance follows from the discovery of justice. In the *Laws* temperance looms largest.

21 This distinction is put forward by Vlastos in 'The Unity of the Virtues in Protagoras,' p 231.

22 *Republic* 444d–e.

23 See above pp 170–1.

24 The sequence should not be made into a strictly temporal one. The hermeneutical task and the doctrinal are in some sense carried out simultaneously. It seems fitting, however, to mention the hermeneutical first.

25 What is at stake here is not the issue of demonstrated or probable historical influences. Did Socrates already know the Pythagoreans? Or did Plato come into contact with this world of thought only during his sojourn in Italy? Can one find signs of a conversion of Plato to Orphism, as Dodds (*The Greeks and the Irrational*, pp 227–8) believes he can discern, at the time of the writing of *Gorgias*? Such questions are of course important, and in the end the total picture of Plato's relationship to Greek religion must be built on the available evidence on a variety of points of detail like this. The details, however, should not mask the larger issue, namely that about the nature of the hermeneutical process, or that of cultural continuity and cultural

innovation in the transmission of thought patterns and religious substance. Traditional interpretations of Plato's relationship to Greek religious life range all the way from strong affirmations of continuity to equally strong affirmations of discontinuity. Des Places, for instance, emphasizes that Plato's philosophy, while being far better than a mere eclecticism, is one that does not repudiate any heritage (*La Religion grecque*, p 246). Jaeger concludes that Plato arranges and systematizes the spiritual inheritance of his nation (*Paideia*, I, x, 85–7). In other formulations, however, Jaeger underlines more the creative aspects of Plato's achievement. Those affirming continuity seem to me to rest their case too exclusively on the *Laws*; they overlook the role of Socratic inquiry and the discomfiture it imposes on Euthyphros. Philosophy in Plato does expose the intellectual barrenness and moral danger of much that passes for religion.

The case for discontinuity has been made most persuasively by Voegelin. He emphasizes that by the time of Plato the myths had become teachers of immorality, part of a warped order in the soul. Plato, he argues, knows there can be no question of really returning to the wisdom of the past. Such wells have gone dry and, in any case, the old order never was perfect since it lies at the basis of the present disorder (*Plato*, pp 131–3; see also p 190 and its paraphrase of *Laws* 886d).

26 Thomas W. Ogletree, 'The Activity of Interpreting in Moral Judgment,' *The Journal of Religious Ethics*, 8:1 (Spring 1980), 16.
27 Ogletree adds that together these hermeneutics move towards a new and common ground which makes fitting action possible (Ibid, p 19).
28 Diès, *Autour de Platon*, II, 400–49.
29 Festugière, *Contemplation et vie contemplative*, pp 75–370.
30 As Levinson has put it, Plato exercises 'the right of conceptual reessentialization.' 'The conventional ideal is deepened and extended by being caught up into a wider pattern of systematic totality': *In Defense of Plato*, pp 417–18. Or, in the words of Morrow, 'the historical facts have gone through the crucible of his daemonic genius, have been refined in the fire of his philosophic criticism, and have taken on some of the glory of that supersensible perfection whose vision was never absent from Plato's imagination': *Plato's Cretan City*, p 592.
31 De Vries sees irony as the major safeguard. In 'Mystery Terminology in Aristophanes and Plato,' pp 7–8, de Vries argues convincingly against Adkins, who sees Plato becoming more and more in favour of initiation to mysteries.
32 See above pp 13–14.
33 See Farrington, *Science and Politics in the Ancient World*.
34 See Dodds, *The Greeks and the Irrational*, ch 7.
35 See Solmsen, *Plato's Theology*; and Morrow, *Plato's Cretan City*.
36 This interpretation of the *Laws* rests on the works of Strauss and Pangle.
37 On the comparison between text and meaningful action as part of the hermeneutical

process see Paul Ricoeur, 'The Model of the Text: Meaningful Action Considered as a Text,' in John B. Thompson, ed and trans, *Hermeneutics and the Human Sciences* (Cambridge: Cambridge University Press 1981), pp 197–221.

38 The great 'fable' of Protagoras on the creation of man and the rise of society gives the necessary headings for these two results of Plato's philosophizing. We hear that men 'as often as they were banded together ... did wrong to one another through the lack of civic art, and thus ... began to be scattered again and to perish. So Zeus, fearing that our race was in danger of utter destruction, sent Hermes to bring respect and right among men, to the end that there be regulation of cities and friendly ties to draw them together' (*Protagoras* 322b–c). 'Respect' and 'right' are *aidôs* and *dike*: unlike special skills, these are distributed to all and all can partake of them. Public piety rests on *aidôs*, which Plato rehabilitates. The piety of the cognoscenti gives full development to the love of justice.

39 *Gorgias* 507e–508a.

40 Finley, *Thucydides*, p 221.

41 Knox, *Oedipus at Thebes*, pp 168, 194–6.

42 *Poetics* 1151b, line 6. See Finley, *Thucydides*, p 325.

43 *Apology* 326c.

44 *Timaeus* 22a–c.

45 *Critias* 109d. See also Jaeger, *Aristotle*, p 137.

46 *Timaeus* 47e–48a, 68e.

47 See Dupont, *Le Plaisir et la loi*, ch 1. The *Laws* takes the view that a civil theology must teach all men that the pleasant and the just, the good and the noble, are the same (663b–c).

48 See *Laws* 652–660a. See also *Republic* 607a.

49 See Détienne, *Dionysos mis à mort*, p 153.

50 *Laws* 782b–c.

51 See Pangle's commentary, *The Laws of Plato*, p 472.

52 *Against Aristogeiton*, 1.35.

53 See Winnington-Ingram, *Euripides and Dionysus*; and Dodds, 'Euripides the Irrationalist,' in *The Ancient Concept of Progress*.

54 Pangle, *The Laws of Plato*, pp 401–2, 456.

55 Strauss, *The Argument and the Action of Plato's Laws*, pp 119, 123. Strauss alludes to the taboos about incest and paederasty.

56 Pangle, 'The Political Psychology of Religion in Plato's *Laws*,' pp 1066, 1068.

57 De Romilly, *La Loi dans la pensée grecque*, p 163. Aristotle squarely affirms that tradition is based on nature. See Verdenius, 'Traditional and Personal Elements in Aristotle's Religion.' 'It is impossible that the views held by many men and men of old should be entirely mistaken' (*Nicomachean Ethics* 1098b, line 27).

58 He even claims the opposite. Goldschmidt, *Platonisme et pensée contemporaine*, pp 264–5.

59 Guthrie, *History of Greek Philosophy*, v, 339–40. Thucydides offers an indirect proof of the merits of *aidôs*. His passionately corrupt city ignores *aidôs*. Men experience only the fear called *deos*, a fear without moral quality, the fear of those who worry only about their own skin. See de Romilly, 'La crainte dans l'oeuvre de Thucydide,' pp 119–27.

60 Mary Douglas has argued that all cultural systems focus attention on some risks and offer protection against – and explanations for – disasters that occur when the protection is incomplete or does not work.

61 *Laws* 716c–718a.

62 This point must be underlined after centuries of Christian civilization during which it has been assumed that truth is all that is required in religious matters, and we have it.

63 *Phoenician Women*, lines 524–5. For the sake of power is, literally, for the sake of tyranny. Religious virtue is *eusebein*.

64 'The significance of religion for morality relates not so much to the *definition* of the good ... as to its implementation': Reynell, 'The Euthyphro Dilemma,' p 232.

65 *Nicomachean Ethics* 1108a, lines 30–5.

66 Redfield, *Nature and Culture in the Iliad*, pp 115, 58.

67 Fifth-century men saw the virus of violence spreading in the social body. The commendation of piety is accompanied by discernment of what René Girard calls the mimetic effects of violence: *La Violence et le Sacré* (Paris: Grasset 1972). In the corrupt society *thumos* loses the quality of noble indignation that punishes offences against the common order. It becomes the poly-destructive and self-destructive anger. Homer has shown us Achilles gripped by this madness (anger is the opening word in the *Iliad*). His passionate inward conceptions of honour have become murderous – and suicidal – absolutes. Irascible Achilles will rather kill and be killed than allow any compromise. See ch 9 in Whitman, *Homer and the Heroic Tradition*. In the fifth century there seem to be no Ulysses left, no epiphanies of Athena to stay the hand of murderous heroes. Thucydides draws our attention to the atrocity of reprisals – which call for more atrocities (*Peloponnesian War*, 3.82–4). The city that could once stop the cycle of blood revenge and lock up the Erinyes is now unleashing all sorts of furies. Anger, says Medea speaking of her own *thumos* aroused by the behaviour of her husband, 'has been the cause of greatest evils to mortals,' and she promptly proves it by killing children (*Medea*, lines 1079–80). If there is one message in the theatre of Euripides, argues Vellacott, it is that the rigidities of anger fill the air so much that pardon has become impossible: *Ironic Drama*, ch 9. In vain the nurse in *Hippolytus* climaxes her view of life with the words 'forgive; we are human'; the 'innocent' young man is much too angry about women (verse 615).

While it is true that there is no moral community among humans without common thresholds of moral indignation, it is also true that individuals, when they see their self-image or self-interest threatened, quickly reach their different thresholds and lash out angrily. When is the point reached where the wars of individual indignation can no longer be stopped by common indignation?

68 Hence the flavour of impersonality characteristic of Hellenistic philosophical piety. Prayer is perceived only in its vulgar forms, an attempt to influence or change the will of the gods. Seneca does not talk with God. 'I do not obey God, I agree with him'; see Epistle 96, sect 2. See also Dihle, *The Theory of Will in Classical Antiquity*, pp 3, 18.

69 Guardini, *The Death of Socrates*, pp 54–5. The rational considerations to be neglected here are, in my opinion, those of moralistic, persuasive reasonableness. The rigour and the coherence demanded of rational philosophy remain pertinent.

70 *Laws* 716c. See also *Letter VII* 343e–344b.

71 *Phaedo* 69d.

72 *Phaedrus* 249c–d.

73 *Symposium* 249c–d.

74 *Sophist* 216b.

75 Murdoch, *The Sovereignty of Good*, pp 55, 67. Will, she adds, is obedience, not revolution (p 40).

76 Pétrement, *Le dualisme chez Platon: Les Gnostiques et les Manichéens*, p 119.

77 There is more than a touch of contempt for the many in the *Republic*. Those who want a minimum of work and a maximum of fun get just that under the rule of their guardians.

78 See the discussion of Plato by John Dunne in *City of the Gods: A Study in Myth and Mortality* (New York: Macmillan 1965), pp 93, 107, 121, 131, 136, 223. Dunne, however, misleads by bringing in the anachronistic notion of utopianism. On utopianism see Voegelin, *Plato*, pp 208–9. Plato does not fall for political black magic, i.e. for the dream of organizing men according to a blueprint instead of forming them in an educational process.

79 *Republic* 581d–e.

80 *Apology* 30a.

81 Rationality to Plato is a separate desire attending some goods and capable of winning the upper hand. There is a contrast here with a view exemplified by Freud in which rationality is not a desire but a sort of technical management that wishes to succeed in the handling of alien desires and is, at best motivated by an anxiety seeking to avoid too painful a failure in the satisfaction of permanent desires. See Gould, *Platonic Love*, pp 69–70. If reason is not a desire, the illusions created by manipulative demagoguery can flourish among the many. What the demagogue promises is all the listeners want – and are capable of wanting.

82 The so-called Socratic dialogues seem to accept the craft analogy, namely virtue is to the whole man somewhat like his craft to the artisan. But Plato quickly saw the limits of the analogy, and saw that progress in morality is affective as well as intellectual. See Gould, *The Development of Plato's Ethics*; and the critical discussion of it in Rist, *Eros and Psyche*, Part II, ch 1. O'Brien returns to the whole problem in *The Socratic Paradoxes and the Greek Mind*, ch 6.

83 Let me say once again that Plato's interpreter has many reasons to underline the continuity between the two kinds of piety. Mythical religion and mysticism do not mix, but they can coexist in a given society, even a given individual. Transposition requires a touch of mysticism free from mythical religion. Transposition arises out of mythical religion and mythical religion remains in the new picture. Let us not forget, in any case, that no man, as long as he is alive in a body, will be a pure mystic. The whole embodied man is religious rather than mystical.

84 Plato remains an élitist, a highly educated man, who has little feel for the desperate behaviours that the dispossessed can turn to. The violent challenge to the sacrificial system remains out of his field of vision. As we shall see, Christian radical sects arose later, where the dispossessed articulated their will not to be oppressed and acquired some political savvy.

85 See Morrow, *Plato's Cretan City*, p 587.

86 Jaeger, *Paideia*, II, 278.

87 *Gorgias* 507d.

88 *Symposium* 202e.

89 *Timaeus* 48a.

90 See Gould, *Platonic Ethics*, p 115.

91 *Republic* 519a.

92 Sinaiko, *Love, Knowledge and Discourse*, pp 183–4.

93 *Phaedrus* 246b.

94 *Timaeus* 92c. See Vlastos, 'Socratic Knowledge and Platonic "Pessimism",' pp 231–2.

95 Joly, *Le Renversement platonicien*: Frontisi-Ducroux, *Dédale: Mythologie de l'artisan en Grèce ancienne*.

96 Strauss, *De la tyrannie*, p 165. See also B. Groethuysen, *Anthropologie philosophique* (Paris: NRF 1952): having contemplated ideas, the philosopher must act as philosopher; having to act on non-philosophers, he cannot act as philosopher (p 33).

97 Gould, *The Development of Plato's Ethics*, pp 223–4. 'Acceptance,' I should stress, cannot be made into a theory; it is an act of suffering. As Moline shows, the theory commends persuasion, at all times; see *Plato's Theory of Understanding*, pp 76–8.

98 Leo Strauss, *The City and Man* (Chicago: Rand McNally 1963), pp 102, 138.

99 Voegelin, *Plato*, p 88.

100 This is one of the themes of Jacques Maritain, *Man and the State* (Chicago: University of Chicago Press 1951), p 149.

101 L. Wittgenstein, *Tractatus Logico-Philosophicus* (London: Routledge and Kegan Paul 1963), pp 5, 151.

102 R.C. Zaehner, *Dialectical Christianity and Christian Materialism* (Oxford: Oxford University Press 1971), p 70.

103 *Laws* 968e.

104 *Republic* 590d.

105 *Memorabilia* 229.

106 *Nicomachean Ethics* 1–4 7, quoting *Works and Days*, lines 295–7.

107 *Epistle* VII 341c–d.

108 I owe this point to Moline, who has pointed out to me that Socrates refuses to fight. 'Gorgias and his pupils use the language of conflict and with Polus and Callicles, discussion is hardly more than a slightly cleaner *agon* than more physical ones' (Moline refers to *Gorgias* 457e, 479b, 505c).

109 In his article 'Philosophy as a Kind of Writing' Richard Rorty contrasts those thinkers for whom philosophy is a rational dialogue of minds with those who periodically attack this consensus and rely on the energies of paradox and style: *New Literary History* (1978), X, 141–60. The Platonic dialogues are, of course, the source of both traditions.

110 *Phaedrus* 276a.

111 Friedländer, *Plato: An Introduction*, p 209.

112 Hirsch, *Platon's Weg Zum Mythos*, p 216.

113 For an account of the Platonic myth, namely that which *he* received, from the widest horizon, I refer the reader to the work of Zaslavsky, *Platonic Myth and Platonic Writing*. That myth is speech about the genesis of knowledge and the genesis of writing. Writing generates immortality, not an individual one, but that of the *logos*. See pp 48, 213.

114 There is here a contrast with Empedocles who, according to Ramnoux, opened the door to all gnostic doctrines by merging the philosophical and the mythical language: *Etudes présocratiques*, p 115; see also pp 213, 260.

115 Weingartner, *The Unity of the Platonic Dialogue*, p 201.

116 'Religious' philosophers try so hard to protect their understanding of the mysterious ground of the *logos* that they distort the light of the *logos* by insisting on their well-meaning dogmas. 'Secular' philosophers have forgotten the ground that is beyond the light of reason and distortions arise from that neglect too.

117 See above pp 45–6, 82.

118 On the exclusion of some from the benefit of any public order see Jambet, *Apologie de Platon*, p 163. A richer world is preferable to a logically coherent one, argues

Hall. We need language that provides significant depth and vagueness to our world so that we shall not be allowed to claim certain knowledge where none exists: *Eros and Irony*, pp 80, 110, 175, 178. 'No single order can define the nature of that which is' (p 136).

119 *Rhetoric* 1.11.23.

120 Speaking of Shakespeare's romances, Northrop Frye writes that they show us a world which is an 'imaginative model of desire': *A Natural Perspective* (New York: Harcourt, Brace and World 1965).

121 'I think it best,' writes Freud, 'to acquit dreams.' He refers to Plato's dictum that 'the virtuous man is content to *dream* what a wicked man really *does*': *The Interpretation of Dreams* (New York: Avon 1965), VII-F, 658. The reference is probably to *Republic* 571c–d.

122 See Victor Turner, *The Ritual Process: Structure and Anti-Structure* (Ithaca: Cornell University Press 1975), ch 3.

123 For the view that literature is displaced mythology see Northrop Frye, 'Myth, Fiction and Displacement,' in *Fables of Identity* (New York: Harcourt, Brace and World 1963). 'When a system of myth loses all connection with belief, it becomes purely literary' (p 32).

124 See *Phaedo* 114c–d.

125 Derrida, 'La Pharmacie de Platon,' p 180. Plato himself refers to myths being a game played with decency and piety (*Phaedrus* 265c).

126 Heraclitus, fragment 45. See Hyland, *The Origins of Philosophy* pp 30, 32, 150.

127 Can one find an echo of this balancing act in this prosaic statement of Aristotle? 'The scanty perceptions to which we can attain of celestial things give us, from their excellence, more delight than all our knowledge of the world in which we live ... On the other hand, in certitude, in completeness, our knowledge of terrestrial things has the advantage' (*De Partibus animalium* 1.5).

128 Simon, *Mind and Madness in Ancient Greece*, pp 147ff.

129 L. Wittgenstein, *Philosophical Investigations* (London: Routledge and Kegan Paul 1963), p 19.

130 Ibid, p 48.

131 Ibid, p 47.

132 Hirsch, *Platon's Weg zum Mythos*, pp 236–7.

133 Rosen, *Plato's Symposium*, pp 7–18. Among the sources for my interpretation I should also list Léon Robin's edition (with preface), *Le Banquet*: and his book *La Théorie platonicienne de l'amour*. Among the articles: Cornford, 'The Doctrine of Eros in Plato's Symposium'; Markus, 'The Dialectic of Eros in Plato's Symposium'; Moravcsik, 'Reason and Eros in the "Ascent" Passage of the Symposium'; and Plochmann, 'Supporting Themes in the Symposium.' There is also a useful psychiatric discussion in Yvon Brès, *La Psychologie de Platon*, pp 233–50.

134 *Symposium* 172a.
135 *Symposium* 177a–b.
136 *Symposium* 180c–d, 181b.
137 *Symposium* 186d.
138 *Symposium* 189c.
139 Obscenity keeps sexuality sane, notes Rosen in *Plato's Symposium*, by curbing its bend towards *hybris*.
140 *Symposium* 194e.
141 *Symposium* 197e.
142 Rosen, *Plato's Symposium*, and Cornford, 'The Doctrine of Eros in Plato's *Symposium*,' believe that Diotima is a fiction invented by Socrates and proof of his delicate courtesy: he can assure Agathon that he too erred on the subject of love until he was straightened out by someone who knew better.
143 *Symposium* 297d, 211b, 212b.
144 My interpretation is indebted to the article by Moore, 'The Relation between Plato's *Symposium* and *Phaedrus*.' I am convinced by his case for the somewhat heterodox view that the *Symposium* was written after *Phaedrus*. He bases his case on the greater maturity of the view of love in the *Symposium* and the better use of the method of collection and division. I am also indebted to Rosen's commentary in *Plato's Symposium*. Called oversubtle, and deservedly, this commentary has the merit of showing that the dialogue contains a statement of the moral natural law and a skilled debunking of the moral claims made by the higher paederasts. (I keep the animus against the moral claims, not against the sexual orientation.) On the mystique of the transmission of manly virtues among the Dorians through phallic penetration see Vanggaard, *Phallos: A Symbol and Its History in the Male World*. On Plato's own handling of the homosexual tradition most helpful is the appendix 'Sex in Platonic Love' in Vlastos's article 'The Individual as Object of Love in Plato.'
145 *Symposium* 202e–203a.
146 Note that according to this view Plato's message is bound to be lost on some. Homosexual sex is banned in the *Laws*. In the *Symposium* Plato is interested in philosophy, and most Athenians interested in philosophy took homosexuality for granted. Rather than condemn their tastes and make a moral issue of them, Plato seems to have tried to educate them out of their ways. At the end of the dialogue the one praised is Socrates, the *pater familias* who has refused to 'gratify' the young man in love with him. And everyone knows that Aristophanes, the first speaker to display a touch of realism, believes in the irrepressible nature of heterosexual desire in normal human beings.
What a permanent hold 'cultural creativity' has acquired over the minds of intellectuals can be hinted at with the help of two references. First, from a good Christian, Petrarch: 'We perpetuate our name through talent and not through

marriage, with books and not with children, with the help of virtue and not with the help of women'; quoted in Jean Delumeau, *La Peur en Occident* (Paris: Fayard 1978), p 314. Secondly, from one of the sources of Nazi ideology, Hans Blüher: the homosexually inclined are the most socially creative, because their eros is not dissipated in the care of children; quoted in George L. Mosse, *The Crisis of German Ideology* (New York: Grosset and Dunlap 1964), p 213. To Socrates the creativity available to human beings lies in begetting and in giving birth. The sophisticated homosexuality can thus be seen as a cipher of all fabricative, non-propagative creativity that seeks to find infinite scope for its pursuit of eternity in technology or aesthetics.

147 Brès, *La Psychologie de Platon*, ably shows that it is in the very nature of love to create real illusions. Moralists rarely capture its essence but commonly unveil its illusions.

148 In *Gorgias*, in the *Republic*, and in the *Laws* such jarring notes between human beings escalate to conflict, to the threat of violence, and to the considered examination of the use of force. It is normal for force to be considered within the horizon of the political; there is no room for it in the field of the religious.

149 Dupont has written a study of the banquet as a literary genre. She argues that at first the banquet offers the promise of a reconciliation between pleasure and law. Body and soul flower, sweetly fragrant, and each speaks in his turn on grave topics of public concern. A freedom is realized that brings happiness to the participants and holds the key to the happiness of the city. But drunken soft talk promptly loses the ability to hold everything and everyone together. At Trimalchio's feast guests and host become obscene, and, while everyone talks of everything, no one listens. Plato's banquet shows an intermediate stage: words mediate understanding but it takes a philosopher, who drinks water, to reorient self-indulgent drunken talk. See *Le Plaisir et la loi*. The banquet, Dupont adds, by separating drinking from eating, makes a distinction between businesslike daily desires (food, women) and elevated, noble desires (wine, love of boys). Presumably, a yet higher stage would be reached as one feeds on one's own breath and plays only with oneself. Eating food, drinking water, rejecting the advances of Alcibiades, Socrates rejects these rarefied aristocratic conventions and their claim to being the civilized ones.

CHAPTER 11

1 Chateau, *Euthyphron de Platon*, pp 182–6.
2 On tragedy see Else, *The Origin and Early Form of Greek Tragedy*, which loosens the ties which anthropologists have seen between the tragedies and Dionysiac rituals and places the tragedies more squarely within the context of the city. See also Little, *Myth and Society in Attic Drama*.

3 The contrast just drawn does not cover very well the tragedies of Euripides. The insight gained by his tragic heroes has lot much of its socially redeeming quality. One certainly does not find in him frequently the grounds for social celebration that were found by the audiences that watched Aeschylus.

4 Pangle, 'Interpretative Essay,' *The Laws of Plato*, pp 487–8.

5 For an elaboration of the distinction between sensuousness and sensuality see ch 2 in Charles Davis, *The Body as Spirit: The Nature of Religious Feeling* (New York: Seabury Press 1976).

6 Common associations between men and women on a broad front of human endeavours are already present in the *Odyssey*. With Aristophanes women regain voice in society, but only through comedy. One should note that some plays of Euripides manage to show men and women being human with each other outside the conventions of comedy. But then Euripides is a contemporary of Socrates. It is the *Republic*, of course, and not the *Laws*, that shows philosophy thinking of human roles in a way that is not gender-specific.

7 George Grant, *Time as History: Massey Lectures 1969* (Toronto: CBC Publication 1969), p 32. He adds: 'The optimism of philosophy destroyed the ecstatic nobility which had been expressed in the tragedies. But now that rationalism has dug its own grave through the truthfulness of science, there is no returning to that earlier height' (p 35).

8 Morrow, in *Plato's Cretan City*, lists all the consulting work done in legal and political matters by Plato and the Academy (pp 8–9).

9 Ehrenberg, *The Greek State*, p 240.

10 Dupont, *Le Plaisir et la loi*.

11 Châtelet, *Platon*, p 236.

12 *Statesman* 309e.

13 I shall not toy with the idea that he may be guilty: I recognize his good faith as he announces that those who contend on the side of divine forces are never guilty if they fail to overcome necessity.

14 Gouldner, *Enter Plato*.
Another social scientist, Yvon Brès, has written an all-encompassing interpretation of Plato's work, this time from the point of view of a scientific psychology. His *La Psychologie de Platon* focuses on Plato's understanding of love and finds in his homosexuality the major warping factor. I have chosen Gouldner as representative social scientist because his argument stands on much firmer ground. We know something of Plato's social biography; we know next to nothing of his psychological story. And a society with slaves is clearly a bad moral offence: it calls for priority attention.

15 Gouldner's work contains some interpretative errors. We shall, however, focus only on his weighty points that deserve a hearing. Unlike the attacks on Plato made in the fifties by people like Crossmann and Popper, Gouldner's book does not assume that

it is easy to do better than Plato. For a rebuttal of these other attacks see Levinson, *In Defense of Plato*.

16 On this point Gouldner should be challenged, as Vlastos does in his article 'The Individual as an Object of Love in Plato,' pp 11–12. Vlastos blames the Jowett translations for attenuating what Plato has to say on bonds of fraternal love.

17 Gouldner further suggests that the tactics of change (free dialectical exchange) and the strategy (imitation of the model) may well turn out to be incompatible. See *Enter Plato*, p 260.

18 Ibid, pp 352–5.

19 *Phaedo* 110a–e.

20 Détienne, *Les Jardins d'Adonis*, p ix.

21 Kojève, *Essai d'une histoire raisonnée de la philosophie païenne*, II, 135.

22 *Peloponnesian War*, 3.37.3f (translation by Dover in *Greek Popular Morality*, p 119).

23 The impact of the heroic temper on Plato is perhaps verified by his reading of Odysseus. The King of Ithaca, when contrasted with Achilles, can be seen as the model of more democratic values. In the myth of Er at the end of the *Republic* Plato presents him as a tired sufferer who wishes the quiet obscure private life. To Plato, it seems, only the aristocratic temper is suited for the public life and the virtues of versatility, adaptability, and diplomacy seem somewhat lost on him (*Republic* 620c–d).

24 Clegg, *The Structure of Plato's Philosophy*.

25 Ibid, pp 192–3.

26 Gouldner, *Enter Plato*, pp 307, 286. Clegg argues that here Plato is conceptually coherent: extra-argumentative persuasion is inevitable among those who lack knowledge and cannot shape argument or respond to it: *The Structure of Plato's Philosophy*, p 183.

27 Aristotle, *Nicomachean Ethics*, 8.11.6.

28 Grene, *Man in His Pride*, p 199.

29 Voegelin, *Plato*, p 141.

30 Groethuysen, *Anthropologie philosophique* (Paris: NRF 1952), pp 103–29.

31 Augustine, *Confessions* 13.11.12.

32 Ibid, 7.9; 10.42.

33 Thomas Aquinas, *Summa theologiae*, I/I, quest. 76, art. 5. Aristotle, *De anima*, 2.1.412, a15–b6.

34 T. Suttor, 'Introduction,' in *Summa theologiae* (London: Blackfriars 1970), vol II.

35 Thomas Aquinas, *Summa contra gentiles*, Book II, pp 57–73.

36 Armstrong and Markus, *Christian Faith and Greek Philosophy*. See also A.H. Armstrong, 'St. Augustine and Christian Platonism' (1967), repr in R.A. Markus, ed, *Augustine: A Collection of Critical Essays* (Garden City, NJ: Doubleday 1972).

37 R. Nisbet, *The Social Philosophers* (New York: Pocket Books 1982), pp 80–2. For

the ramifications of this issue in medieval France see Georges Duby, *Le Chevalier, la femme et le prêtre* (Paris: Hachette 1971).

38 Among the works of René Girard see especially *Des choses cachées depuis la fondation du monde* (Paris: Grasset 1978).

39 See Manuel de Diéguez, *L'Idole monotheiste* (Paris: PUF 1981).

40 This is the time to reject the still commonly drawn contrasts between a presumably cyclical Greek view and the 'linear' Jewish and Christian view. Boman, *Hebrew Thought Compared with Greek*, ch 3, has gathered more than adequate evidence to dismiss such oversimplifications. Where Greeks and Hebrews differ is on the assessment of time. Boman also does justice to the old question about who 'invented' history: his answer is that the Greeks gave us the science of history and the Hebrews a historical religion. See also James T. Barr, *Biblical Words for Time* (London: SCM 1962).

41 On Christian individualism and the importance of the historical existence of each man see Davis, *The Body as Spirit* (n 5 above), pp 73–6.

42 Augustine's view of time is developed in contrast with that of Plotinus. See Jean Guitton, *Le Temps et l'Eternité chez Plotin et Saint Augustin*, in *Oeuvres complètes*, vol IV: *Philosophie* (Desclée de Brouwer 1978), pp 440–1, 460–1.

43 *Timaeus* 37c–e. This is said of cosmic time, an abiding, regular movement. See also his description of the universe as a perceptible God made in the image of the intelligible (*Timaeus* 92c). In contrast, 'hold infinity in the palm of your hand / And eternity in an hour,' writes Blake in *Auguries of Innocence*. See J.L. Vieillard-Baron, *Le Temps, Platon, Hegel, Heidegger* (Paris: Vrin 1978).

44 *Timaeus* 47a–d.

45 Boman, *Hebrew Thought Compared with Greek*, ch 5 and conclusion. For a contemporary philosophical praise of sight see Hans Jonas, 'The Nobility of Sight: A Study in the Phenomenology of the Senses,' in *The Phenomenon of Life: Toward a Philosophical Biology* (New York: Delta 1966).

46 L. Laberthonnière, *Le Réalisme chrétien et l'idéalisme grec* (1904), repr in *Le Réalisme chrétien* (Paris: Seuil 1966), pp 247, 259–60.

47 Gouldner does not articulate his own alternate metaphysical basis. At times it seems to be the liberal egalitarian faith. On occasions he indicates the role of the Christian faith in bringing about different assumptions and remedying Platonic lacunae.

48 After pointing out all the differences Adkins, in *Merit and Responsibility*, concludes that Plato nevertheless remains trapped within the Homeric premises. The group must survive, and its survival depends upon an élite. Plato differs from Homer only in seeing that his days require that the élite should practice the co-operative rather than the competitive excellences (pp 311–12).

49 See Châtelet, *La Naissance de l'histoire* p 219.

50 This 'rewriting' can be bold. In a stunning formula F. Kermode says that the

Christians created a new book, the Old Testament, by simple hermeneutical fiat: *The Genesis of Secrecy* (Cambridge, Mass: Harvard University Press 1978), p 19. Reinterpreting the Hebrew Bible and even giving it a new title does not, however, amount to rewriting it.

51 See Grant, *Time as History* (n 7 above).

52 Rist, *Eros and Psyche*, pp 157, 180.

53 Voegelin, *Plato*, p 39.

54 Hegel, *Lectures on the History of Philosophy* (London: Routledge and Kegan Paul 1965), I, 45–7; II, 10. Since our questions bear on the historic failure of Plato and on the ongoing historical significance of his work, we must turn to Hegel and cannot use Aquinas because he does not treat his difference from Plato historically. Many German contemporaries of Hegel dreamt of going back to Greece. Hegel thinks that the past cannot be ressuscitated and that nostalgia is sterile.

55 Jean-Louis Vieillard-Baron, *Platon et l'Idéalisme allemand (1770–1830)* (Paris: Beauchesne 1979), p 19.

56 Ibid, p 282. Hegel, *Lectures on the History of Philosophy* (n 54 above), II, 55. The thorns and thistles are of course those of Genesis 3:18. The old Hegel stays with Plato. See para 552 of the 1830 *Encyclopaedia*.

57 Hegel, *Lectures on the History of Philosophy* (n 54 above), II, pp 1–2.

58 Ibid, II, 73.

59 Ibid, II, 16–21.

60 Ibid, II, 71.

61 Ibid, II, 113–14; see also I, 48–9.

62 S. Avineri, *Hegel's Theory of the Modern State* (Cambridge: Cambridge University Press 1972), pp 226–7, referring to Hegel, *The Philosophy of History* (New York: Dover 1956), p 254. See also Hegel, *Lectures on the History of Philosophy* (n 54 above), I, 434–5.

63 Ibid, II 98–9.

64 *Crito* 51c, 53e. Hegel, *Lectures on the History of Philosophy* (n 54 above), I, 446–7.

65 To execute Christians the Romans threw them to the lions. They, of course, did not think that the Christians were noble enough to commit suicide. The Christians accepted martyrdom. On the manner of one's exit the misunderstanding was total.

66 *Encyclopaedia of the Philosophical Sciences* para 552, in W. Wallace, trans, *Hegel's Philosophy of Mind* (Oxford: Clarendon Press 1971), p 290.

67 Hegel, *Lectures on the History of Philosophy* (n 54 above), III, p 8.

68 Hegel, *Leçons sur la philosophie de la religion* (Paris: Vrin 1959), II/2, 110–12, 155; see also III, 62.

69 Hegel, *Lectures on the History of Philosophy* (n 54 above), I, 36–7.

70 *Philebus* 54a–c.

71 Hegel, *Lectures on the History of Philosophy* (n 54 above), II, 114–15.

72 Ibid, II, 109, 99.

73 Hegel, *Leçons sur la philosophie de la religion* (n 68 above), II/2, 125.

74 Ibid, II/2, 148, 111.

75 J. Glenn Gray, *Hegel and Greek Thought* (New York: Harper and Row 1968), p 50.

76 Hegel, *Lectures on the History of Philosophy* (n 54 above), I, 48.

77 Ibid, I, 94.

78 St Leo, Seventh sermon 'In nativitate Domini,' cited in Armstrong and Markus, *Christian Faith and Greek Philosophy*, pp 37–8.

79 C.N. Cochrane, *Christianity and Classical Culture* (New York: Oxford University Press 1957), p 362.

80 Voegelin, *Plato*, pp 62, 70, 115–57, 174.

81 There is, of course, a sceptical temper in Gouldner: Plato did not know everything – and neither do we.

82 See Nicholas Lobkowicz, *Theory and Practice: History of a Concept from Hegel to Marx* (Notre Dame, Ind: University of Notre Dame Press 1967); and Terence Ball, ed, *Political Theory and Praxis – New Perspectives* (Minneapolis: University of Minnesota Press 1977).

83 R.J. O'Connell, 'Action and Contemplation,' in R.A. Markus, ed, *Augustine: A Collection of Critical Essays* (n 36 above).

84 Hegel, *The Philosophy of History* (n 62 above), p 22. See also Hegel, *Lectures on the History of Philosophy* (n 54 above), II, 71. *We* are not interested in purposeless contemplation: *we* are freedoms.

85 M.B. Foster, *The Political Philosophies of Plato and Hegel* (Oxford: Clarendon Press 1968), p 59.

86 Hegel, *Reason in History* (New York: Liberal Arts Press 1953), p 12.

87 C. Taylor, *Hegel* (Cambridge: Cambridge University Press 1975), p 33.

88 S. Rosen, *Hegel: An Introduction to the Science of Wisdom* (New Haven: Yale University Press 1974), pp 280–1.

89 Hegel, *Reason in History* (n 86 above), p 41.

90 J. Shklar, *Freedom and Independence: A Study of the Political Ideas of Hegel's 'Phenomenology of Mind'* (Cambridge: Cambridge University Press 1976), p 52.

91 To speak of overcoming Hegel is a commonplace among French philosophers today. Jacques Derrida has come to the conclusion that the debate with him is interminable. To beat the master at his game, he adds, is still a victory for the master of the game. See Vincent Descombes, *Le Même et l'autre: Quarante-cinq ans de philosophie française (1933–1978)* (Paris: Editions de Minuit 1979), p 174.

92 'Perhaps we should understand that the task of the philosophy of history does not at all lie in depicting the 'process of development' of philosophic systems, that such a process can indeed be observed, but that far from initiating us into the holy of holies of philosophers, into their most secret thoughts and experiences, it actually robs us of

the possibility of holding intercourse with the outstanding men of the past': Lev Shestov, 'Children and Step Children of Time,' in *In Job's Balances* (Athens: Ohio University Press 1975), p 257.

93 What I find most offensive in Hegel's treatment of Plato is the condescending praise he heaps on him, coupled with complete blindness on those points where Plato might score against him. Hegel behaves too much like the older brother who wants to be fair to the younger one, but takes for granted that his longer memory automatically makes him smarter. Pierre Macherey has written a book showing that Hegel's feeling of superiority over Spinoza is based on a thorough misreading of his predecessor. It becomes easy for him to reconstitute what Spinoza would say had he lived after Hegel. See *Hegel et Spinoza* (Paris: F. Maspéro 1979). So it is appropriate to introduce here a philosopher who, having come after Hegel, has a memory yet longer than his.

94 'The proud tower of Western culture is now in ruins' Shestov writes in 1918; see 'A Thousand and One Nights,' in *Potestas clavium* (Athens: Ohio State University Press 1969), p 21.

95 Shestov, 'Science and Free Inquiry,' in *In Job's Balances* (n 92 above), pp xlii–xliii.

96 Aristotle says this in his discussion of Parmenides. See L. Chestov [Lev Shestov], *Athènes et Jérusalem* (Paris: Flammarion 1967), p 30.

97 Ibid, pp 58, 255, 118–19.

98 L. Chestov, *Kierkegaard et la Philosophie existentielle* (Paris: Vrin 1948), pp 44–5.

99 Chestov, *Athènes et Jérusalem* (n 96 above), pp 30, 35, 37.

100 Ibid, pp 91, 105. Chestov, *Kierkgaard et la Philosophie existentielle* (n 98 above), pp 353–4.

101 Dostoyevsky, *Notes from Underground*, Part I, no. 3. See Léon Chestov, *La Philosophie de la tragédie* (Paris: Flammarion 1966), p 86.

102 Shestov, *In Job's Balances* (n 92 above), p 21.

103 Shestov was Jewish by birth and upbringing. The books of *Genesis* and *Job* are frequently quoted by him. But so are Paul and the rest of the New Testament. I do not know of any interest on his part in the notion of Jewish philosophy; such notion, I might add, was not in the air when he was writing. He showed much interest in the discussions of Christian philosophy that were so intense in Paris in the thirties. He even undertook to reason with his Christian friend Berdyaev, trying to explain to him that his philosophy was not really Christian. Berdyaev too, argued Shestov, submitted faith to speculation. Shestov also had lengthy polemics against Catholicism, which is 'determined entirely by the goals which Greek thought had set for itself': *Potestas clavium*, p 234.

A good *mise au point* on Jewish and Christian elements in philosophy will be found in Hans Jonas, 'Jewish and Christian Elements in Philosophy: Their Share in the Emergence of the Modern Mind,' in *Philosophical Essays: From Ancient Creed to*

Technological Man (Englewood Cliffs: Prentice Hall 1974). While arguing that Christianity alone or almost alone transmitted the Jewish share to the West, Jonas maintains that Jewish and Christian elements can still be distinguished. By Jewish he means whatever Christianity still has in common with Judaism, i.e. the concept of creation and its rejection of necessity. By Christian he means what Christianity has all to itself, i.e. the concept of Incarnation. Unfortunately he makes no statement on what Judaism has beyond the 'common element.'

104 Shestov, *Potestas clavium* (n 94 above), p 234.
105 Shestov, *In Job's Balances* (n 92 above), p 236. The phrase 'biblical philosophy,' like that of 'biblical religion,' is out of favour now, on account of its ambiguity. Does Shestov speak of the Jewish Bible or of the Christian one? But it is the expression he uses repeatedly.
106 L. Chestov, *Sola fide: Luther et l'Eglise* (Paris: PUF 1957).
107 Shestov, *Potestas clavium* (n 94 above), p 47.
108 Lev Shestov, 'All Things Are Possible,' II, 33, in *All Things Are Possible and Penultimate Words and Essays* (Athens: Ohio University Press 1977), pp 96–7.
109 Chestov, *La Philosophie de la tragédie* (n 101 above), p 87.
110 Shestov, *In Job's Balances* (n 92 above), pp 146–8.
111 Shestov, *Potestas clavium* (n 94 above), p 356.
112 See 'Momento mori,' his long examination of Husserl, in *Potestas clavium*. Reason is sovereign only over ideas, not over human beings; they have free will (p 337).
113 Shestov, *In Job's Balances* (n 92 above), pp 366–7.
114 Ibid, pp 112–13.
115 Ibid, p 260.
116 Chestov, *La Philosophie de la tragédie* (n 101 above), p 216.
117 Ibid, p 190. What he finds most boring in the books he reads is their general idea.
118 Shestov, *Potestas clavium* (n 94 above), p 282.
119 Chestov, *Athènes et Jérusalem* (n 96 above), p 28.
120 Ibid, pp 115–16.
121 Ibid, pp 84–6. A 'smuggler of genius,' he manages to hide contraband most effectively.
122 *Theaetetus* 196d. The same verb (*tolman*) is used by Plotinus to point to the guilty audacity of individual existence. Shestov, *In Job's Balances* (n 92 above), pp 253–4.
123 Chestov, *Athènes et Jérusalem* (n 96 above), pp 56–61.
124 Ibid, pp 73–81. Necessity gains complete sway with Aristotle.
125 Shestov, *Potestas clavium* (n 94 above), p 182.
126 Hegel, *Lectures on the History of Philosophy* (n 54 above), I, 92.
127 Shestov, *In Job's Balances* (n 92 above), p 253. Shestov contrasts this picture of anthropogeny with that found in the fragment of Anaximander, which can be read as saying that all separate existence is sin doomed to punishment.

128 Shestov, *In Job's Balances*, pp 225–6.
129 Shestov, *Potestas clavium* (n 94 above), p 396.
130 The difficulty with Shestov, writes Berdyaev, is that he has no critique of revelation. As he wants to overcome theological rationalism, he overlooks that fanaticism has also been based on revelation and faith. See *Truth and Revelation* (London: Bles 1953), pp 66–7. Where Shestov knocks, says Gabriel Marcel, there is no door; quoted in the preface to *La Philosophie de la tragédie* (n 101 above), p 16.
131 Reacting against oversimplified presentations of the contrast between Greek eros and Christian agape, Rist tries to show that pagan neo-Platonist writers like Plotinus widen eros to include a downward movement, think of love in non-appetitive terms, and clearly give an overflowing quality to divine goodness. Armstrong goes even further, showing that in Plato himself eros has a 'downward movement.' Rist and Armstrong prove their point. It still remains true that in Plato we find nothing more than hints to allow for this development and that, no matter how far the development goes, it never arrives at a God with a personal loving will. Any personalization of the divine, it seems, is liable to return to the immoral anthropomorphism of Olympus. See Rist, *Eros and Psyche*.
132 Kojève, *Essai d'une histoire raisonnée de la philosophie paienne*, II, 118.
133 Hirsch, *Plato's Weg zum Mythos*, p 155.
134 See Ballew, *Straight and Circular: A Study in Greek Philosophy*. Homer and Hesiod associate goodness in human beings with straightness, i.e. with a quality in interaction.
135 Among the contemporary sources that have nurtured my search for a philosophy of religion, I should mention the Rome colloquia held under the leadership of Enrico Castelli, especially those held in 1968, 1973, 1976, and 1977 and published (Paris: Aubier, in those years) under the titles *L'Herméneutique de la liberté religieuse*, *Démythisation et idéologie*, *Herméneutique de la sécularisation*, and *La Philosophie de la religion*. I must also mention the works of Paul Ricoeur. A convenient introduction to them in English is found in Charles E. Reagan and David Stewart, eds, *The Philosophy of Paul Ricoeur: An Anthology of His Work* (Boston: Beacon Press 1978). The references will be found on pp 255–6. On religious language I am most indebted to Antoine Vergote, *Interprétation du langage religieux* (Paris: Seuil 1974).
136 The point can also be made by saying that there is no metalanguage to adjudicate existing languages and that there should be no debased language.
137 Hegel, of course, sees science as the achievement of his philosophy. Shestov invites to decision, like all existentialists (I would want also to argue that his understanding of decision is defective).
138 See W.C. Smith, *Faith and Belief* (Princeton: Princeton University Press 1979).
139 For an excellent treatment of the intrinsic modifiability of any historical religion see

Peter Slater *The Dynamics of Religion* (San Francisco: Harper & Row 1978). Anybody who pays any attention to the argument there cannot ever again think of religions as massive boulders that dot the cultural scenery, immovable, unchanging, until the next glaciation.

140 To be religious, writes W.C. Smith, is 'a creative act, of participation in a community in motion.' See *Towards a World Theology: Faith and the Comparative History of Religion* (Philadelphia: Westminster Press 1981), p 35. Participation in the motions of *our* community is the issue I want to join.

141 For this reason the hermeneutic of religious realities cannot long stay blind to the political realities and the decisions we ought to take about our future. Practical wisdom will not be forgotten.

142 S. Weil, *The Need for Roots: Prelude to a Declaration of Duties toward Mankind* (1943; repr Boston: Beacon Press 1952).

143 In France the traditional rationalism is basically a neo-Kantian criticism. For a survey of the recent course of French philosophy see Descombes, *Le Même et l'autre* (n 91 above).
In the English-speaking world the rationalism is that of logical positivism, subsequently logical analysis. For a powerful overcoming of it see Richard Rorty, *Philosophy and the Mirror of Nature* (Princeton: Princeton University Press 1980).

144 M. Merleau-Ponty, 'L'Existentialisme chez Hegel,' in *Sens et non-sens* (Paris: Nagel 1966), pp 109–10. Merleau-Ponty credits Hegel with the initial effort, subsequently pursued in Marxism, Nietzsche, phenomenology, existentialism, and psychoanalysis.

145 See Descombes, *Le Même et l'autre* (n 91 above), p 25.

146 This section is much indebted to the proceedings of the 1977 Ottawa symposium, *Rationality Today – La Rationalité aujourd'hui*, ed T.F. Geraets (Ottawa; University of Ottawa Press 1979). I must also mention Hannah Arendt's *Thinking*, vol I of *The Life of the Mind* (New York: Harcourt Brace Jovanovich 1978); and Manuel de Diéguez, *Le Mythe rationnel de l'Occident* (Paris: PUF 1980).

147 *Theaetetus* 174a.

148 Arendt, *Thinking* (n 146 above), p 199.

149 What is commonly called thinking in the modern West is the attempt to systematize the world of useful common knowledge, with a view to extending our power to do things. It has lost its connotation of overcoming the limitations of any given horizon for the sake of contemplation of the whole. See H. Arendt, *The Human Condition* (Garden City, NY: Doubleday 1959), pp 262–8.

150 René Descartes, 'Regulae ad directionem ingenii,' in *Oeuvres et Lettres* (Paris: NRF 1953), p 65.

151 De Diéguez opens up an interesting avenue of thought: he states that the rationalist myth, as it accepts the idealist myth of a world that itself speaks, falls into an archaic

sacrificial cast of mind: if the world speaks, it must feed; we must offer it sacrifices. Reason then becomes a master of sacrificial ceremonies. See *Le Mythe rationnel de l'Occident* (n 146 above), pp 68, 78, 99.

152 Plato thought that the enemy of reason was the body and its desires. From Hegel we have learned that reason today first confronts distortions of reason: truth is not a minted coin. Daily coinage must be restruck; fixed thoughts must be made fluid. See 'Preface' to *Phenomenology of the Mind*, in Walter Kaufmann, ed, *Hegel: Texts and Commentary* (Garden City, NY: Doubleday 1966), pp 50, 56.

153 Plato, argues Clegg, sees the damages that result from 'the individious contrast between intelligible, real rest and unintelligible, illusory motion' (a contrast launched by Parmenides.) According to this view all there is for minds to do is escape illusion or manipulate it. But Plato argues that what matters to human beings in the world is that some appearances are better than others, and that appearances ought to be improved. Some motion is teleologically organized, aims at the imitation of the perfection of rest, and some do not. See *The Structure of Plato's Philosophy*, pp 22–34. I do not accept Plato's ontology but I commend him for his acceptance of the urban task: live together in an effort to improve appearances.

154 Olivier Reboul, *Langage et idéologie* (Paris: PUF 1980), shows that ideology has five traits: it is partisan, collective, dissimulating, rational, and at the service of power. It gives a group the possibility of common action, but it resists linguistic competency. Words are always made to do something underhanded. Speaking, when personal and responsible, is not ideological.

155 The *Iliad* sings this encounter of might with might. It shows how might wielded by men rules over them all, losers and winners, and traps them in its fatality. 'Ares is equitable; he kills those who kill.' It shows sorrow over this petrification of human life, over the sight of young men reduced to something 'dearer to vultures than to their wives,' but hardly knows how to overcome this fate. See Simone Weil, 'The Iliad, the Poem of Might,' in *The Simone Weil Reader*, ed George A. Paniclias (New York: David MacKay 1977).

156 The thought of Merleau-Ponty is the best school for those who wish to discover the dignity of embodied, historical reason. For an introduction see Samuel B. Mallin, *Merleau-Ponty's Philosophy* (New Haven; Yale University Press 1979).

157 Garrett Mattingly, *Renaissance Diplomacy* (Boston: Houghton Mifflin, n.d.), pp 40, 118.

158 M. Merleau-Ponty, 'Sur la phénoménologie du langage,' in *Signes* (Paris: NRF 1960), pp 121–2.

159 Emmanuel Lévinas, *Totalité et infini*, 4th ed (The Hague: Nijhoff 1971), p 230.

160 Vergote, *Interprétation du langage religieux* (n 135 above), p 62. 'What makes a "word" is knowledge together with love,' writes Augustine in *On Trinity*, 9.10.15.

161 See Mikel Dufrenne, *Language and Philosophy* (Bloomington: Indiana University

Press 1963), p 84. Dufrenne goes on to show how language tends to become degraded. But he doubts that it can ever be perverted. He cautions against Heidegger: he 'is mistaken in believing that mere talk and chatter are radically unauthentic' (p 99).

162 'Preface' to *Phenomenology* (n 152 above), p 42.
163 Quoted by Jean Wahl in *L'Expérience métaphysique* (Paris: Flammarion 1965).
164 Hannah Arendt wonders whether professional thinkers are congenitally less pleased with freedom than with necessity; she believes that they are more inclined to interpreting the world than changing it. See *Willing*, vol II of *The Life of the Mind* (New York: Harcourt Brace Jovanovitch 1978), pp 33, 195, 198.
165 Chagigah, II, I. Quoted from Arendt, *Willing*, p 72. Plato writes that the philosopher is ridiculed because he never lowers his attention to anything close at hand (*Theaetetus* 173e–174a.)
166 Shestov is the voice to be heard here. Plato and Hegel are confident that rising to the universal will be emancipatory.
167 See Merleau-Ponty, 'Partout et nulle part,' in *Signes* (n 158 above), p 184.
168 Christianity is commonly called the religion of love. Beside being self-serving, this characterization is semantically too vague. This section is much indebted to Arendt, *Willing* (n 164 above). It contains a history of the concept and reflections on the view philosophers have taken of the will.
The works of Emmanuel Lévinas have been decisive in my attempt to overcome the spell of non-Biblical ontology. See *Totalité et infini* (n 159 above), available in English as *Totality and Infinity: An Essay on Exteriority* (Pittsburgh: Duquesne University Press 1969); and *Autrement qu'être ou au-delà de l'essence* (The Hague: Nijhoff 1974).
The contest between Hebraism and Hellenism is the running thread of Jacques Derrida's weighty article 'Violence et métaphysique: Essai sur la pensée d'Emmanuel Lévinas' (1964), in *L'Ecriture et la différence* (Paris: Seuil 1967). See in particular p 138: no totality ever extinguishes desire; infinity summons its freedom. For recent work and bibliography see Marc Faessler, 'L'Intrigue du Tout-Autre: Dieu dans la pensée d'Emmanuel Lévinas,' *Etudes théologiques et religieuses*, 1980, p 4; and Steven G. Smith, *The Argument to the Other: Reason beyond Reason in the Thought of Karl Barth and Emmanuel Lévinas*. (Chico, Calif: Scholars Press 1983).
For the best in the psychological approach see Leslie H. Farber, *The Ways of the Will: Essays toward a Psychology and a Psychopathology of Will* (New York: Harper & Row 1966); and Rollo May, *Love and Will* (New York: Norton 1969). Two works of literary history and criticism have been informative and suggestive: Rebecca West, *The Court and the Castle: Some Treatment of a Recurring Theme* (New Haven: Yale University Press 1957; repr New York: Kraus Reprint 1971); and René

Girard, *Deceit, Desire and the Novel: Self and Other in Literary Structure* (Baltimore: Johns Hopkins University Press 1965).

169 Here I echo what Augustine says on time; see *Confessions*, 11.14.

170 Farber, 'The Two Realms of Will,' in *The Ways of the Will* (n 168 above), p 3. See also 'I understand will to be the category through which we examine that portion of our life which is the mover of our life in a direction or toward an objective in time': in Leslie H. Farber, *Lying, Despair, Jealousy, Envy, Sex, Suicide, Drugs and the Good Life* (New York: Harper & Row 1978), p 4.

171 M. Merleau-Ponty, *Phénoménologie de la perception* (Paris: NRF 1945), p 160. Early in the nineteenth century Maine de Biran stressed that there is in man a power to direct his attention and to will. The 'primitive fact' is not a sensation but a self united to a resistance.

172 Paul Ricoeur has taken great pains to show that interpretation of symbols is always both archaeological and teleological: why did I respond to the symbol the way I did? and what was I after? See his *De l'interprétation: Essai sur Freud* (Paris: Seuil 1965), pp 478–503.

173 'The Will as Thing in Itself,' ch 25 from Supplement to the Second Book of *The World as Will and Idea*, in *The Will to Live: Selected Writings of Arthur Schopenhauer*, ed R. Taylor (New York: Ungar 1967), p 41.

174 Paul Claudel, *Tête d'Or* (Paris: Mercure de France 1959), p 155.

175 Joseph Conrad, *Heart of Darkness*, Penguin ed, pp 72, 83.

176 John Milton, *Paradise Lost*.

177 Choderlos de Laclos, *Les Liaisons dangereuses* (Paris: Gallimard 1972), p 19.

178 Acts of will are thus deep personal involvements of the self with its physical and social environment. They do not issue from some hypothetical watcher in the head examining and deciding what can be done. The relationship between reason and will is personal, or, better, is a personal event. The will moves, driven by eros, and reason also moves, confident that it has perceived reality correctly. An act of will is an act of trust. See the criticisms formulated by Coleridge and Newman against the errors of Locke's psychology in Stephen Prickett, *Romanticism and Religion* (Cambridge: Cambridge University Press 1976), pp 185–9.

179 Farber, *Ways of Will* (n 168 above), pp 42 and 44. On p 44 Farber continues: 'The failure of will which is said to be characteristic of anxiety stems from the deprivation of resources and the withering of the will's goal in the face of the will's demands.'

180 For an account of the hermeneutics of social situations see Paul Ricoeur, *Hermeneutics and the Social Sciences: Essays on Language, Action and Interpretation*, ed and trans John B. Thompson (Cambridge: Cambridge University Press 1981).

181 Snell, *The Discovery of the Mind*, p 182. Snell defines the will as the 'mainspring of action.'

182 See Dover, *Greek Popular Morality in the Time of Plato and Aristotle*, pp 150–1. Dover adds that they may have been wiser than we on this point.

183 O'Brien, *The Socratic Paradoxes and the Greek Mind*, p 53.

184 One might recall here that Kierkegaard has described the pagan self as inscribed within nature, as a point of engagement of cosmic forces. In contrast, the Christian self is spirit. See Louis Mackey, *Kierkegaard: A Kind of Poet* (Philadelphia: University of Pennsylvania Press 1971), p 135. In his analysis of involuntary action in Plato Moline rightly refers to *Republic* 430e–431e: doing evil is involuntary and means being weaker and inferior to oneself; see *Plato's Theory of Understanding*, p 72.

185 Arendt, *Willing* (n 164 above), pp 57–63. See also Reagan and Stewart, *The Philosophy of Paul Ricoeur* (n 135 above), pp 61–3.

186 These are Arendt's definitions; see *Willing* (n 164 above), pp 13, 195.

187 Let me recall that Hegel spotted the Greek anxiety about the future and the essentially passive relationship to it. See above pp 256–9.

188 *Laws* 644c–d.

189 *Peloponnesian War*, 3.45.

190 See Cornford, *Thucydides Mythistoricus*, pp 168, 222, 234.

191 The Greek historians tried to acquire and convey the art of weighing probabilities in human affairs. They managed to mould a long series of events into a plan determined by an art form (Cornford, *Thucydides Mythistoricus*, p 134). Seeing patterns in human events is a step towards seasoned judgment about future prospects. Plato ponders the art of the statesman as a prospective art that strives to give form to the future of a society. Therefore, besides Aristotle and his psychology of choice, we should add the psychology of planning made possible by Thucydides and Plato to the Greek anticipations of our concept of the will. I find it significant that Heidegger, who sees in the will to will the original human sin, has to turn to the pre-Socratics to find the true ontology and the true anthropology. The pre-Socratics honour no concern for the future: they see in it only evil care.

I must add that Plato's planning is always perceived as a threatened art. There are no techniques to ensure implementation. There is always a gap between thought and action – and between action and success.

192 Dihle, *The Theory of Will in Classical Antiquity*, pp 12, 82.

193 Arendt, *Willing* (n 164 above), p 68: 'It was the experience of an imperative demanding voluntary submission that led to the discovery of the Will.' Arendt makes a distinction between the Hebrew Bible, which says 'Thou shalt do,' and the New Testament, which says 'Thou shalt will.' The point is well taken but should not be pushed too far. The Hebrew Bible does say 'Thou shalt love.'

194 See Vergote, 'Mythe, croyance et foi,' in *Interprétation du langage religieux* (n 135 above), esp p 92.

195 Arendt, *Willing* (n 164 above) pp 3, 55.

196 Jonas, 'The Abyss of the Will: Philosophical Meditation on the Seventh Chapter of Paul's Epistle to the Romans,' in *Philosophical Essays* (n 103 above).

197 Plato clearly adumbrates such a notion of desire. Socrates in *Philebus* (35d) concludes an argument by saying that memory leads us towards objects of desire; all the desire is in the soul, not in the body. His memory, however, is not the historical one. While he clearly sees the ravages of mimetic behaviour, in the end he does not overcome it so much as seek to set it aside by returning to the memory of eternity.

198 Letter to the Ephesians 14:1.

199 See Jean Daniélou, *Platonisme et théologie mystique* (Paris: Aubier 1944).

200 In contrast, Descartes sees the fact that 'we were children before we were men' as an accident that tends to cloud our judgment: 'Discours de la Méthode 2,' in *Oeuvres et Lettres*, p 133.

201 Augustine, *The City of God*, 12.20. Arendt, *Willing* (n 164 above), p 108.

202 Augustine, *Confessions*, 8.5.10; 8.9.21.

203 Ibid, 8.12.28–30. In his account of Hellenistic religion, Sabbatuci calls attention to the frequent recourse to the allegory of a ship threatened by storm. Religious people, he adds, move from the primary desire to navigate well towards the new desire to be saved: *Essai sur le mysticisme grec*, p 213.

204 Augustine, *Confessions*, 13.9.10.

205 Hegel is here sounder than Shestov since he places the individual in a large and complex economy while Shestov remains Platonic in locking the will in a struggle against necessity.

206 Augustine, *City of God*, 19.13.

207 Homily on 1 John 4:12–16, in Augustine, *Later Works*, ed John Burnaby (Philadelphia: Westminster Press 1955), p 321. To love someone is to want him / her to be. Augustine is not always clear and sometimes ambivalent on this point. Love of the other creature can be a rival to the love of God. He knows about lust and fears its effects. But he also knows about charity and mutual support. On this point there are no problems in his thought that semantic clarification would not clear up.

208 Aquinas knows that human beings do by their reflexivity impose desires on themselves. But he remains within a broadly intellectualist premise: he is entirely at ease with the notion of knowledge being compelling.

209 Arendt, *Willing* (n 164 above), pp 125–46.

210 Scotus, quoted in Arendt, *Willing*, pp 134–5.

211 *Encyclopaedia*, Part III, para 482, in Wallace, ed, *Hegel's Philosophy of Mind* (n 66 above), p 240.

212 *Phaedo* 117a. Derrida misses this ambiguity in his long article on *pharmakon* in Plato.

213 Plato's Gyges could, thanks to the ring that makes him invisible at will, 'take what he wished' and 'lie with whom he pleased'; the view of happiness presupposed here

today seduces only the adolescent (*Republic* 360b). The invisible Gyges does not enjoy recognition and his unhindered consumption of the good things of life is not for us the picture of a free existence, but rather of empty pleasures devoid of any human quality.

Leo Strauss points out that Hegel's anthropology opens the prospect of human beings knowing no other control except the desire for recognition and living without any interior sense of sacred constraints. To be approved of can then be the only end known to freedoms. And everything not confirmed by social and historical verification becomes confined to the realm of subjective opinion. See *De la tyrannie*, pp 308 and 258. Hegel also shows in the passages on the master-slave dialectic that the struggle for recognition may lead to a regime of terror. Is the will still pure impulse after all? Or can the religion of the will teach religion to the will?

214 Vergote, *Interprétation du language religieux* (n 135 above), pp 158, 183. For a contrasting view see Frederick C. Copleston, *Religion and Philosophy* (Dublin: Gill and Macmillan 1974). Metaphysics as 'the drive to know the totality' and seeking 'conceptual mastery over reality as a whole' (p 43) is presented as expressing 'a genuine religious impulse' (p 2). The case is well put: it is aware of all the suspicions Christian theologians entertain against metaphysical and speculative philosophy.

215 See Reagan and Stewart, *The Philosophy of Paul Ricoeur* (n 135 above), p 67.

216 Descombes, *Le Même et l'autre* (n 91 above), p 71.

217 Lévinas, *Totalité et infini* (n 159 above), pp 146, 154, 192, 171, 280.

218 Heidegger's overcoming of the ontotheological tradition as a result of a return to pre-Socratic ontology offers no answer to my problem since it does not acknowledge the dignity of the will that cares. Lévinas muses over Heidegger's studied ignorance of biblical literature and his turn to a hearing, an obedience without a fellow-man. His sense of existing is deeply pagan. See Faessler, 'L'Intrigue du Tout-Autre: Dieu dans la pensée d'Emmanuel Lévinas' (n 168 above), pp 520–1.

219 For a literary analysis of the passage in Mark see Eric Auerbach, *Mimesis: The Representation of Reality in Western Literature* (Garden City, NY: Doubleday 1957). On Paul see Thomas J. Altizer, 'Paul and the Birth of Self-Consciousness,' *Journal of the American Academy of Religion*, 51:3 (Sept. 1983), 359–70.

220 Augustine, *Confessions*, 2.3, 6.

221 On St Gregory and the subsequent medieval tradition see F.C. Gardiner, *The Pilgrimage of Desire: A Study of Theme and Genre in Medieval Literature* (Leiden: Brill 1971).

222 Instead of educating desire, much of the Christian tradition exhorts wills to alter human desire. Need I say it fails. Have we finished counting the costs of this attempt and this failure?

223 Gregory is quoted by Aquinas in *Quaestiones disputatae de veritate*, 2.2, and by Pieper, 'The Philosophical Act,' in *Leisure the Basis of Culture*, p 76.

224 I find a rich sane streak in Christianity among the writers in whom Auerbach has discerned the Christian realistic style. The story of Christ 'with its ruthless mixture of everyday reality and the highest and the most sublime tragedy ... conquered the classical rule of styles.' See *Mimesis* (n 219 above), p 490. This literature resists the solutions of the problems inherent in the human condition through the picturing of two worlds: artistic mimesis stresses the actuality of events; the whole world context is revealed in individual destiny. See Auerbach's *Dante: Poet of the Secular World* (Chicago: University of Chicago Press 1961), pp 174–9. Christianity thus transforms the interpretation of reality by transforming style. The individual is not identified with the soul; he is 'identical with his unique history and fate'; the person is viewed as 'the sum of all his acts of decision, defined in a final state of universal significance by the will as it reached that state through all of its choices from moment to moment in the course of its temporal existence': J.A. Mazzeo, *Varieties of Interpretation* (Notre Dame, Ind: University of Notre Dame Press 1978), p 35. The second chapter is an excellent introduction to Auerbach.
225 Jean-Michel Palmier, *Lacan* (Paris: Editions universitaires 1969), pp 93–9.
226 See Emmanuel Lévinas, *Ethique et infini* (Paris: Fayard 1982), pp 86–7, on the distinction between need and desire: desire is the presence of the Infinite in a finite act. See also Lévinas, *Totality and Infinity* (n 168 above), pp 23–4: 'Eschatology does not introduce a teleological system into the totality; it does not consist in teaching the orientation of history. Eschatology institutes a relation with being beyond the totality or beyond history, and not with being beyond the past and the present. Not with the void that would surround the totality and where one could, arbitrarily, think what one likes, and thus promote the claims of a subjectivity free as the wind. It is a relationship with a surplus always exterior to the totality, as though the objective totality did not fill out the true measure of being, as though another concept, the concept of infinity, were needed to express this transcendence with regard to totality, non-encompassable within a totality and as primordial as totality.'
227 The threefold characterization of the wish of absolute consciousness is found in Ricoeur; see Reagan and Stewart, *The Philosophy of Paul Ricoeur* (n 135 above), p 9.
228 *Choses tues*, in Paul Valéry, *Oeuvres* (Paris: NRF 1960), II, 491.
229 In the *Symposium* what is seen educates eros.
230 Lévinas, *Totality and Infinity* (n 168 above), p 53: 'Between a philosophy of transcendence that situates elsewhere the true life to which man, escaping from here, would gain access in the privileged moments of liturgical mystical elevation, or in dying – and a philosophy of immanence in which we would truly come into possession of being when every 'other' (cause for War), encompassed by the same, would vanish at the end of history – we propose to describe, within the unfolding of terrestrial existence, of economic existence (as we shall call it), a relationship with

the other that does not result in a divine or human totality, that is not a totalization of a history but the idea of infinity. Such a relationship is metaphysics itself. History would not be the privileged plane where Being disengaged from the particularism of points of view (with which reflection would still be affected) is manifested. If it claims to integrate myself and the other within an impersonal spirit this alleged integration is cruelty and injustice, that is, ignores the Other. History as a relationship between men ignores a position of the I before the other in which the other remains transcendent with respect to me. Though of myself I am not exterior to history, I do find in the Other a point that is absolute with regard to history – not by amalgamating with the Other, but in speaking with him. History is worked over by the ruptures of history, in which a judgment is borne upon it. When man truly approaches the Other he is uprooted from history.'

231 See Thomas J. Ogletree, 'Hospitality to the Stranger: Reflections on the Role of the "Other" in Moral Experience,' in American Society of Christian Ethics 1977, *Selected Papers* (Waterloo: Council on the Study of Religion 1977): 'The commencement of moral consciousness is manifest in ... a readiness to welcome the other, to show hospitality to the stranger' (p 27).

232 For an elaboration of views on human interaction that compare it to the artistic process see Gibson Winter, *Liberating Creation: Foundations of Religious Social Ethics* (New York: Crossroads 1981).

233 We must warn here against what Benjamin Nelson calls 'meta-histories,' namely fundamental stories that claim to lie behind all stories told. Scenarios of desire, be they Platonic or Freudian, cannot be allowed to obstruct the weaving of new symbolic designs. See 'Perspectives on the Therapeutic: A Dialogue between B. Nelson and D. Wrong,' in R. Boyers, ed, *Psychological Man* (New York: Harper & Row 1975), p 143.

234 Philosophy reflects the fundamental subjectivity of language and of human beings. Literature shows it. Literature also has style, namely warns about the existence of a speaker and struggles against any illusion that the words might be the things. For an elaboration of this view see Etienne Barilier, *Le Grand Inquisiteur* (Lausanne: L'Age d'homme 1981).

235 Rebecca West points out that our society, unlike Shakespeare's, no longer has a king as supreme user of power (and symbol of the individual will). Westminster and Whitehall have dispersed and fragmented the national will. See *The Court and the Castle* (n 168 above), pp 148–9, 161–2. On pp 237–9 she quotes Paul Valéry's diagnosis: today 'what calls itself 'the great world' is composed purely of symbolic figures. Nobody can play a part in it unless they represent an abstraction. It is necessary that all social forces should meet one another: that somewhere *money* should be talking to *beauty*; that *politics* should be on good terms with *elegance*; that *literature* and *truth* should come to an agreement and have tea together. As soon as a

new force arises, not much time elapses before its representatives appear in society.' The real complications of human interaction can be studied only on the 'little stage.' The representative of a force can be shown there to have a human body and a soul. There the subtle novelist finds suitable material. See *Oeuvres* (n 228 above), I, 773–4.

236 The weakness – or self-consciousness – of our ritualistic life is one more symptom of it. Faith realizes itself in three works, writes Vergote. Prayer opens the dialogue between man and God; ethical responsibility forces the acknowledgment of every human being as called to such dialogue. Ritual is the most complex because the least voluntary of the works of faith. It involves body, language, community, and cosmos in celebration. It alone keeps awakening the silent potentialities of faith. See *Interprétation du langage religieux* (n 135 above), pp 209–10.

237 I accept Arendt's warning: the intimacy of dialogue cannot become paradigmatic for the political sphere: *Willing* (n 164 above), p 200. But we also have a cultural tradition of political mediations.

238 In the end it seems that the will is at least intrinsically dangerous, the more so with those who do not acknowledge its danger. See West, *The Court and the Castle* (n 168 above); the English edition has a suggestive subtitle: 'A Study of the Interactions of Political and Religious Ideas in Imaginative Literature.'

239 Winter, in *Liberating Creation* (n 232 above), also shows very aptly how modern society, with its technologies and bureaucracies, is wedded to unilinear, monologic visions of power and control and undermines all dialogic power. Liberation has to be viewed as a break from the continuous processes of technology. Against productivism human beings should recall that work is desire integrated into time and that unproductive Dyonisiac excesses give expression to the will to live together. For an exploration of these themes see Michel Maffesoli, *Logique de la domination* (Paris: PUF 1976); and *L'Ombre de Dionysos: Contribution à une sociologie de l'orgie* (Paris: Méridien / Anthropos 1982).

240 See Girard, *Deceit, Desire and the Novel* (n 168 above). For a further illustration of historical hermeneutics of the will through the analysis of literary works see Alain-Gérard Slama, *Les Chasseurs d'absolu: Genèse de la gauche et de la droite* (Paris: Grasset 1980). The author shows the repeated conflict between the right-wing and the left-wing temperament in France from Joseph de Maistre to Jean-Paul Sartre.

241 The point is made with his usual intellectual vigour (and with an unusual poignancy) by Léon Brunschwicg in *De la vraie et fausse conversion* (Paris: PUF 1950), p 120.

242 For a most thoughtful treatment of the range of issues involved in any attempt on the part of religious thinking to liberate itself from alienated thought see Gregory Baum, *Religion and Alienation: A Theological Reading of Sociology* (New York: Paulist Press 1975).

243 J.B. Metz, *La Foi dans l'histoire et la société* (Paris, Cerf, 1979), p. 102.

244 Vergote, *Dette et désir*, pp 33–4.

245 Articles by Walter Benjamin have been translated and collected in *Illuminations*, ed H. Arendt (London: Jonathan Cape 1970); and in *Reflections* (New York: Harcourt Brace Jovanovitch 1978).

246 Morality cannot exist apart from such awareness through memory.

247 Augustine, *Confessions*, 10.2.2.

248 T. Patrick Burke, *The Reluctant Vision: An Essay in the Philosophy of Religion* (Philadelphia: Fortress Piers 1974), pp 69, 21. See also the good discussion on pp 37–53 of how facts confirm or contradict the meaning of religion.

249 Farber, 'The Two Realms of Will,' in *The Ways of the Will* (n 168 above), p 8.

250 Quoted by Farber, ibid, p 3. Farber further defines the issue: 'The problem of the will lies in our recurring temptation to apply [the conscious will] to those portions of life that not only will not comply, but that will become distorted under such coercion. Let me give a few examples: I can will knowledge, but not wisdom; going to bed, but not sleeping; eating, but not hunger; meekness, but not humility; scrupulosity, but not virtue; self-assertion or bravado, but not courage; lust, but not love; commiseration, but not sympathy; congratulations, but not admiration; religiosity, but not faith; reading, but not understanding' (p 15).

251 Individualism is eradicated in the *Republic* and nothing is more typical in this respect than the banning of private shrines; no separate individual cultivation of a relationship with the divine is to be tolerated. The potential intimacy of monogamous marriage is also ruled out for the élite. The demiurge, writes Iris Murdoch, 'wishes us and hopes for our salvation (he admonishes human souls at *Timaeus*, 42d), but we are not necessarily at the centre of his concern. He is probably more interested in the stars': *The Fire and the Sun*, p 51.

252 See Goethe's *Faust*.

253 See Leo Strauss, *De la tyrannie*, p 61.

254 *Epistle* VII 326a.

255 See Macherey, *Hegel et Spinoza* (n 93 above), pp 251–5.

256 Shestov, *Potestas clavium* (n 94 above), p 20.

257 See Régis Jolivet, *Essai sur les rapports entre la pensée grecque et la pensée chrétienne*, 2nd ed (Paris: Vrin 1955), pp 182–91.

258 *Laws* 811c, 803c.

259 *Sophist* 254a.

260 Tigerstedt, *Plato's Idea of Poetical Inspiration*, p 72.

261 *Cratylus* 428d.

262 'As for him who wishes to seize the truth, to grasp it in his crude human hands, to "incarnate" it in order to be able later to show it everywhere and to all – he is condemned to eternal deceptions or even to live in illusions: all incarnated truths were never anything but incarnated illusions': Shestov, *Potestas clavium* (n 94 above), p 236.

263 Paul Ricoeur argues that Kant's criticism of the transcendental illusions is the keeper of hope: in Castelli, ed, *L'Herméneutique de la liberté religieuse* (n 135 above), p 235. The same can be said of the deadlocked series of alternatives found in *Parmenides*.

264 Maurice Merleau-Ponty, *Le Visible et l'invisible* (Paris: NRF 1964), pp 172, 166, 48, 59, 77, 199; Merleau-Ponty, *Signes* (n 158 above), p 161.
Boccacio shows what the artist can do to give body to the hopefulness of well-bred adults: they converse in a garden, isolated from the plague, and their honesty is held within slightly freer boundaries (end of sixth day). Fears and pieties are suspended. One should also keep in mind the point made by Sallie TeSelle: metaphor is grounded in the sensuous stuff of the earth and the body and the familiar: *Speaking in Parables: A Study in Metaphor and Theology* (Philadelphia: Fortress Press 1975), p 61.

265 See the exchange between Paul Ricoeur and Raymundo Pannikar in Castelli, ed, *L'Herméneutique de la liberté religieuse* (n 135 above), pp 247–8.

266 Dorothy Emmet, *The Nature of Metaphysical Thinking* (London: Macmillan 1961), pp 226–7.

267 Plass, 'Philosophical Anonymity and Irony in the Platonic Dialogues.'

268 John Dominic Crossan, *The Dark Interval: Towards a Theology of Story* (Niles, Ill: Argus Communications 1975), pp 101, 128.

269 J.D. Crossan, *In Parables: The Challenge of the Historical Jesus* (New York: Harper 1973), p 82. On recent discussions of the parables see also Mary Ann Tolbert, *Perspectives on the Parables: An Approach to Multiple Interpretations* (Philadelphia: Fortress Press 1979). The author stresses that parables require that the reader participate in the creation of their meaning.

270 Crossan, *In Parables*, p 120. See also his *Finding Is the First Act* (Philadelphia: Fortress Press 1979).

Bibliography

I THE GREEKS

Adkins, A.W.H. *Merit and Responsibility*. Oxford: Clarendon Press 1960
American School of Classical Studies at Athens *Socrates in the Agora*. Princeton, NJ 1979
Anton, John P., and Kustas, George C. *Essays in Ancient Greek Philosophy*. Albany: State University of New York Press 1971
Armstrong, A.H., and Markus, R.A. *Christian Faith and Greek Philosophy*. London: Darton, Longman and Todd 1960
Arthur, Marilyn B. 'Early Greece: The Origins of the Western Attitude toward Women,' *Arethusa*, 6:1 (Spring 1973)
Ballew, Lynne *Straight and Circular: A Study of Imagery in Greek Philosophy*. Assen: Van Gorcum 1979
Barker, Edwin. *Greek Political Theory*. 1918. London: Methuen 1970
Beckman, James *The Religious Dimension of Socrates' Thought*. Waterloo, Ont: Wilfrid Laurier University Press 1979
Beye, C.R. *Ancient Greek Literature and Society*. Garden City, NY: Doubleday 1975·
Boman, Thorleif *Hebrew Thought Compared with Greek*. London: SCM 1960
Buffière, F. *Les Mythes d'Homère et la pensée grecque*. Paris: Belles Lettres 1956
Burkert, Walter *Love and Science in Ancient Pythagoreanism*. Cambridge, Mass: Harvard University Press 1972
– *Structure and History in Greek Mythology and Ritual*. Berkeley: University of California Press 1979
Burnet, John *Early Greek Philosophy*. New York: World Publishing Company 1957
Butterworth, E.A.S. *Some Traces of the Pre-Olympian World in Greek Literature and Myth*. Berlin: Walter de Gruyter 1966
Châtelet, François *La Naissance de l'histoire*. Paris: Editions de Minuit 1962
Cogan, Marc *The Human Thing: The Speeches and Principles of Thucydides' History*. Chicago: University of Chicago Press 1981

Cornford, F.M. *From Religion to Philosophy*. New York: Harper & Row 1957
– *Principium sapientiae*. New York: Harper & Row 1965
– *Thucydides Mythhistoricus*. 1907. Philadelphia: University of Pennsylvania Press 1971
Demargne, Pierre *The Birth of Greek Art*. New York: Golden Press 1964
de Romilly, Jacqueline 'La Crainte dans l'oeuvre de Thucydide,' *Classica et Mediaevalia*, 17 (1956), 119–27
– *La Loi dans la pensée grecque*. Paris: Belles Lettres 1971
– *Magic and Rhetoric in Ancient Greece*. Cambridge, Mass: Harvard University Press 1975
– *Problèmes de la démocratie grecque*. Paris: Hermann 1975
Des Places, Edouard *La Religion grecque*. Paris: Picard 1969
Despland, Michel Review of G.S. Kirk, *The Nature of Greek Myths*, in *Studies in Religion / Sciences Religieuses*, 5:2 (1975), 204
Détienne, Marcel *Dionysos mis à mort*. Paris: NRF 1977
– *Les Jardins d'Adonis: La Mythologie des aromates*. Paris: NRF 1972
– *Les Maîtres de vérité*. Paris: Maspéro 1973
Détienne, M., et Vernant, J.P. *La Cuisine du sacrifice en pays grec*. Paris: NRF 1979
–*Les Ruses de l'intelligence: La Métis des Grecs*. Paris: Flammarion 1974
Dietrich, B.C. *The Origins of Greek Religion*. Berlin: Walter de Gruyter 1974
Dihle, Albrecht *The Theory of Will in Classical Antiquity*. Berkeley: University of California Press 1982
Dodds, E.R. 'Euripides the Irrationalist.' In *The Ancient Concept of Progress and Other Essays on Greek Literature and Belief*. Oxford: Clarendon Press 1973
– *The Greeks and the Irrational*. Berkeley and Los Angeles: University of California Press 1963
– *Pagan and Christian in an Age of Anxiety*. Cambridge: Cambridge University Press 1968
– 'The Religion of the Ordinary Man in Classical Greece.' In *The Ancient Concept of Progress and Other Essays*. Oxford: Clarendon Press 1973
Dover, K.J. *Greek Homosexuality*. New York: Vintage Books 1980
– *Greek Popular Morality in the Time of Plato and Aristotle*. Oxford: Blackwell 1974
Dupont, Florence *Le Plaisir et la loi*. Paris: Maspéro 1977
Ehrenberg, V. *The Greek State*. 1960. New York: Norton 1964
Else, Gerard F. *The Origin and Early Form of Greek Tragedy* New York: Norton 1972
Farrington, B. *Science and Politics in the Ancient World*. 1939. London: Allen and Unwin 1965
Finley, John H. Jr *Thucydides*. Ann Arbor: University of Michigan Press 1967
Finley, M.I. *The World of Odysseus*. New York: Viking Press 1965
Flacelière, Robert *Devins et oracles grecs*.Paris: PUF 1961
– *Love in Ancient Greece*. New York: Crown 1962
Freeman, Kathleen *Ancilla to the Pre-Socratic Philosophers*. Cambridge, Mass: Harvard University Press 1971

375 The Greeks

Friedrich, Paul *The Meaning of Aphrodite*. Chicago: University of Chicago Press 1978

Frontisi-Ducroux, F. *Dédale: Mythologie de l'artisan en Grèce ancienne*. Paris: Maspéro 1975

Gernet, L. *Anthropologie de la Grèce antique*. Paris: Maspéro 1976

– *Recherches sur le développement de la pensée juridique et morale en Grèce*. Paris: Leroux 1917

Grene, D. *Man in His Pride*. Chicago: University of Chicago Press 1950

Guardini, R. *The Death of Socrates*. Cleveland: World Publishing Company / Meridian Books 1969

Guthrie, W.K.C. *The Greeks and Their Gods*. London: Methuen 1968

– *A History of Greek Philosophy*. Volume III: *The Fifth Century Enlightenment*. Cambridge: Cambridge University Press 1969

– *A History of Greek Philosophy*. Volume IV: *Plato: The Man and His Dialogues: Earlier Period*. Cambridge: Cambridge University Press 1975

– *A History of Greek Philosophy*. Volume V: *The Later Plato and the Academy*. Cambridge: Cambridge University Press 1978

– *In the Beginning: Some Greek Views on the Origins of Life and the Early State of Man*. 1957. Ithaca: Cornell University Press 1965

– *Orpheus and Greek Religion*. New York: Norton 1966

Harriot, R. *Poetry and Criticism before Plato*. London: Methuen 1969

Harrison, Jane 'Alpha and Omega.' In *Alpha and Omega*. London: Sidgwick and Jackson 1915. Pp 202–5

Havelock, Eric *The Greek Concept of Justice from Its Shadow in Homer to Its Substance in Plato*. Cambridge, Mass: Harvard University Press 1978

– *Preface to Plato*. Cambridge, Mass: Harvard University Press 1963

Hintikko, Jaako 'Time, Truth and Knowledge in Ancient Greek Philosophy,' *American Philosophical Quarterly*, 4 (1967), 1–14

Hooper, Finley *Greek Realities: Life and Thought in Ancient Greece*. New York: Scribner's 1967

Hutter, Horst *Politics as Friendship*. Waterloo, Ont: Wilfrid Laurier University Press 1978

Hyland, D.H. *The Origins of Philosophy: Its Rise in Myth and the Pre-Socratics*. New York: Putnam's 1973

Jaeger, W. *Aristotle*. New York: Oxford University Press 1962

– *Paideia*. 3 volumes. London: Oxford University Press 1939, 1943, 1944

– *The Theology of the Early Greek Philosophers*. London: Oxford University Press 1967

Kahn, Lawrence *Hermès passe ou les ambiguités de la communication*. Paris: Maspéro 1978

Kennedy, George *The Art of Persuasion in Greece*. Princeton: Princeton University Press 1963

Kerenyi, Karl *Eleusis: Archetypical Image of Mother and Daughter*. London: Routledge and Kegan Paul 1967

– *The Religion of the Greeks and Romans*. London: Thames and Hudson 1962

Kirk, G.S. *The Bacchae: A Translation with Commentary*. Englewood Cliffs, NJ: Prentice Hall 1970

– *Myth: Its Meaning and Functions in Ancient and Other Cultures*. Berkeley: University of California Press 1970

– *The Nature of Greek Myths*. Harmondsworth: Penguin Books 1974

Kirk, G.S., and Raven, J.E. *The Pre-Socratic Philosophers*. Cambridge: Cambridge University Press 1957

Knox, B.M.W. *Oedipus at Thebes*. New York: Norton 1971

Kojève, André *Essai d'une histoire raisonnée de la philosophie paienne*. 3 volumes. Paris: NRF 1968

Lachenaud, Guy *Mythologie, religion et philosophie de l'histoire dans Hérodote*. Paris: H. Champion 1978

Lain Entralgo, Pedro *The Therapy of the Word in Classical Antiquity*. New Haven: Yale University Press 1970

Levy, G. Rachel *The Gate of Horn: A Study of the Religious Conceptions of the Stone Age and Their Influence Upon European Thought*. London: Faber and Faber 1948

Little, Alan M.G. *Myth and Society in Attic Drama*. 1942. New York: Octagon Books 1967

Lloyd-Jones, Hugh *The Justice of Zeus*. Berkeley: University of California Press 1971

Loraux, Nicole *Les Enfants d'Athèna: Idées athéniennes sur la citoyenneté et la division des sexes*. Paris: Maspéro 1981

McGinty, Peter *Interpretation and Dionysos: Method in the Study of a God*. The Hague: Mouton 1978

Mourelatos, Alexander P. *The Route of Parmenides: A Study of Word, Image and Argument in the Fragments*. New Haven: Yale University Press 1970

Murray, Gilbert *Five Stages of Greek Religion*. 1925. New York: Doubleday n.d.

– *Greek Studies*. Oxford: Clarendon Press 1946

– *The Rise of the Greek Epic*. 4th edition. London and New York: Oxford University Press 1967

Nilsson, M.P. *Cults, Myths, Oracles and Politics in Ancient Greece*. 1931. New York: Cooper Square Publishers 1972

– *Greek Folk-Religion*. 1940. New York: Harper 1961

– *The History of Greek Religion*. 1952. New York: Norton 1964

O'Brien, M. *The Socratic Paradoxes and the Greek Mind*. Chapel Hill: University of North Carolina Press 1967

Otto, Walter *Dionysos, Myth and Cult*. Bloomington: Indiana University Press 1965

– *The Homeric Gods*. Boston: Beacon Press 1964

Parke, H.W. *Greek Oracles*. London: Hutchinson University Library 1967

Pearson, Lionel *Popular Ethics in Ancient Greece*. Stanford, Calif: Stanford University Press 1962

Peradotto, John *Classical Mythology: An Annotated Bibliographical Survey.* Urbana, Ill: The American Philological Association 1973

Pettazoni, Rafael *La Religion dans la Grèce antique.* Paris: Payot 1953

Pieper, J. *Enthusiasm and Divine Madness.* New York: Harcourt Brace and World 1964

- 'The Philosophical Act.' In *Leisure the Basis of Culture.* London: Faber and Faber 1952

Ramnoux, Clémence *Etudes présocratiques.* Paris: Klincksieck 1970

- *Héraclite au l'homme entre les choses et les mots.* Paris: Belles Lettres 1968

Redfield, James *Nature and Culture in the Iliad.* Chicago: University of Chicago Press 1975

Rohde, Irvin *Psyche: The Cult of Souls and Belief in Immortality among the Greeks.* New York: Harper and Row 1966

Rudhart, Jean *Notions fondamentales de la pensée religieuse et actes constitutifs du culte dans la Grèce antique.* Genève: Droz 1958

Sabatucci, Dario *Essai sur le mysticisme grec.* Originally published in Italian 1965. French translation Paris: Flammarion 1982

Simon, Bennett *Mind and Madness in Ancient Greece: The Classical Roots of Modern Psychiatry* Ithaca: Cornell University Press 1980

Snell, Bruno *The Discovery of the Mind: The Greek Origins of Thought.* New York: Harper & Row 1960

Stanford, W.B. *The Ulysses Theme: A Study in the Adaptability of a Traditional Hero.* Oxford: Blackwell 1963

Strauss, Leo *The City and Man.* Chicago: Rand McNally 1963

- *De la tyrannie.* Paris: NRF 1954

- *On Tyranny.* 1963. Ithaca: Cornell University Press 1968

- *What Is Political Philosophy?* New York: Free Press 1959

Svenbro, Jesper *La Parole et le Marbre: Aux origines de la poétique grecque.* Lund 1976

Vanggaard, T. *Phallos: A Symbol and Its History in the Male World.* Translated from the Danish by the author. New York: International Universities Press 1972

Vellacott, Philip *Ironic Drama: A Study of Euripides' Method and Meaning.* Cambridge: Cambridge University Press 1975

Verdenius, J. 'Traditional and Personal Elements in Aristotle's Religion,' *Phronesis*, 5:1 (1960)

Vernant, J.P. *Mythe et société en Grèce ancienne.* Paris: Maspéro 1974

- *Mythe et tragédie.* Paris: Maspéro 1972

- *Religion grecque, religions antiques.* Paris: Maspéro 1976

Vernant, J.P., et al *Divination et rationalité.* Paris: Seuil 1974

Vidal-Naquet, Pierre *Le Chasseur noir: Formes de pensée et formes de société dans le monde grec.* Paris: Maspéro 1981

Voegelin, Eric *The World of the Polis.* Baton Rouge: Louisiana State University Press 1957

Weil, Simone 'The Iliad, the Poem of Might.' In *The Simone Weil Reader*. Edited by George A. Paniclias. New York: David McKay 1977

Whitman, Cedric *Euripides and the Full Circle of Myth*. Cambridge, Mass: Harvard University Press 1974

– *Homer and the Heroic Tradition*. New York: Norton 1965

Wilamowitz-Moellendorf, U. *Der Glaube der Hellenen*. 2 volumes. Darmstadt: Wissenschaftliche Buchgesellschaft 1959

Wilkinson, L.P. 'Classical Approaches to Women's Liberation,' *Encounter*, May 1978

Winnington-Ingram, R.P. *Euripides and Dionysius: An Interpretation of the Bacchae*. Cambridge: Cambridge University Press 1946

Woodcock, G. *The Greeks in India*. London: Faber and Faber 1966

Wycherly, R.E. *How the Greeks Built Cities: The Relationship of Architecture and Town Planning to Everyday Life in Ancient Greece*. New York: Norton 1976

Zeitlin, I. 'The Dynamics of Mysogyny in the *Oresteia*,' *Arethusa* 11:1 (Spring and Fall 1978)

2 PLATO

Allen, R.E. *Plato's Euthyphro and the Earliest Theory of Forms*. London: Routledge and Kegan Paul 1970

Allen, R.E., editor *Studies in Plato's Metaphysics*. London: Routledge and Kegan Paul 1965

Anderson, Albert 'Socratic Reasoning in the Euthyphro,' *Review of Metaphysics*, (1969), 461–81

Armstrong, A.H. 'Platonic Eros and Christian Agape,' *Downside Review*, 255 (Spring 1961), 110

Benoist, Jean-Marie *Tyrannie du Logos*. Paris: Editions de Minuit 1975

Brès, Yvon *La Psychologie de Platon*. 2nd edition. Paris: PUF 1973

Burger, R. *Plato's Phaedrus: A Defense of a Philosophical Art of Writing*. University, Ala: University of Alabama Press 1980

Burnet, John *Plato's Euthyphro, Apology of Socrates and Crito*. Oxford: Clarendon Press 1963

Chanteur, Janine *Platon, le désir et la cité*. Paris: Jirey 1980

Chateau, Jean Yves *Euthyphron de Platon: Traduction et commentaire*. Paris: Editions Pédagogie Moderne 1979

Châtelet, François *Platon*. Paris: NRF 1965

Cherniss, H.F. 'The Philosophical Economy of the Theory of Ideas.' In R.E. Allen, editor. *Studies in Plato's Metaphysics*. London: Routledge and Kegan Paul 1965

– 'The Sources of Evil According to Plato.' In G. Vlastos, editor. *Plato: A Collection of Critical Essays*. Volume II. Garden City, NY: Doubleday 1971

Clegg, Jerry S. *The Structure of Plato's Philosophy*. Lewisburg: Bucknell University Press 1977

Cohen, S. Marc 'Socrates on the Definition of Piety: *Euthyphro* 10a–11b.' In G. Vlastos, editor. *The Philosophy of Socrates*. New York: Doubleday 1971

Cornford, F.M. 'The Doctrine of Eros in Plato's Symposium.' In G. Vlastos, editor. *Plato: A Collection of Critical Essays*. Volume II. Garden City, NY: Doubleday 1971

– *Plato's Cosmology: The Timeaeus of Plato, Translated with a running Commentary*. London: Routledge and Kegan Paul 1937

Crombie, I. *Plato, the Midwife's Apprentice*. London: Routledge and Kegan Paul 1964

Cushman, Robert E. *Therapeia: Plato's Conception of Philosophy*. Chapel Hill: University of North Carolina Press 1958

Derrida, Jacques 'La Pharmacie de Platon.' In *La Dissémination*. Paris: Seuil 1972

de Vries, G.J. 'Mystery Terminology in Aristophanes and Plato,' *Mnemosyne*, 26 (1973)

Diès, A. *Autour de Platon*. 2 volumes. Paris: Beauchesne 1927

Festugière, A.J. *Contemplation et vie contemplative selon Platon*. 1935. Paris: Vrin 1967

Findlay, J.N. *Plato and Platonism*. New York: Times Books 1978

Foster, M.B. *The Political Philosophies of Plato and Hegel*. Oxford: Clarendon Press 1968

Friedländer, P. *Plato*. 3 volumes. Princeton: Princeton University Press 1958

– *Plato, an Introduction*. New York: Harper & Row 1964

Gadamer, H.G. *Dialogue and Dialectic: Eight Hermeneutical Studies on Plato*. New Haven: Yale University Press 1980

Gill, Christopher 'Plato and Politics: The *Critias* and the Politicians.' *Phronesis*, 14:2 (1979)

Goldschmidt, Victor *Les Dialogues de Plato: Structure et méthode dialectique*. Paris: PUF 1947

– *Questions platoniciennes*. Paris: Vrin 1970

– 'La Religion Platonicienne.' In *Platonisme et pensée contemporaine*. Paris: Aubier 1970

Gould, John *The Development of Plato's Ethics*. Cambridge: Cambridge University Press 1955

– *Platonic Love*. New York: The Free Press of Glencoe 1963

Gouldner, A.W. *Enter Plato: Classical Greece and the Origins of Social Theory*. New York: Basic Books 1965

Gross, Barry, editor *Great Thinkers on Plato*. New York: Capricorn Books 1969

Grube, G.M.A. *Plato's Thought*. Boston: Beacon Press 1958

Hackforth, R. *Phaedrus*. Cambridge: Cambridge University Press 1972

– 'Plato's Theism.' 1936. Reprinted in R.E. Allen, editor. *Studies in Plato's Metaphysics*. London: Routledge and Kegan Paul 1965

Hirsch, W. *Plato's Weg zum Mythos*. Berlin: Walter de Gruyter 1971

Irwin, Terence *Plato's Moral Theory: The Early and Middle Dialogues*. Oxford: Clarendon Press 1977

Jackson, B. Darrell 'The Prayers of Socrates.' *Phronesis*, 14:1 (1972), 14–37

Jambet, Christian *Apologie de Platon: Essais de métaphysique*. Paris: Grasset 1976

Jaspers, K. 'Plato.' In *Plato and Augustine*. New York: Harcourt, Brace and World 1962

Joly, H. *Le Renversement platonicien: Logos, episteme, polis*. Paris: Vrin 1974

Joseph, H.W.B. *Knowledge and the Good in Plato's Republic*. Oxford: Oxford University Press 1948

Klein, Jacob *Plato's Trilogy*. Chicago: University of Chicago Press 1977

Lee, Edward N. 'Reason and Rotation.' In W.H. Werkmeister, editor. *Facets of Plato's Philosophy*. *Phronesis Supplement* 2. 1976

Levinson, R.B. *In Defense of Plato*. Cambridge, Mass: Harvard University Press 1953

Linforth, Ivan M. 'The Corybantic Rites in Plato'; 'Telestic Madness in Plato.' *University of California Publications in Classical Philosophy*, 13:5 and 6 (1946)

MacKinnon, D.M. 'The Euthyphro Dilemma.' *Aristotelian Society*, supplementary volume 46. London 1972

Markus, R.A. 'The Dialectic of Eros in Plato's Symposium.' In G. Vlastos, editor. *Plato: A Collection of Critical Essays*. Volume II. Garden City, NY: Doubleday 1971.

Meyer, R.S. *Plato's Euthyphro: An Example of Philosophical Analysis*. Communications of the University of South Africa, C. 45, 1963

Meynell, Hugo 'The Euthyphro Dilemma,' *Aristotelian Society*, supplementary volume 46. London 1972

Moline, Jon *Plato's Theory of Understanding*. Madison: University of Wisconsin Press 1981

Moore, J.D. 'The Relation Between Plato's Symposium and Phaedrus.' In J.M.E. Moravcsik, editor. *Patterns in Plato's Thought*. Dordrecht: Reidel 1973

Moravcsik, J.M.E. 'Reason and Eros in the "Ascent" Passage of the Symposium.' In John P. Anton and George C. Kustas. *Essays in Ancient Greek Philosophy*. Albany: State University of New York Press 1971

Moreau, Joseph *L'Ame du monde de Platon aux Stoiciens*. 1939. Hildesheim and New York: G. Olms 1971

– *Le Sens du platonisme*. Paris: Belles Lettres 1967

Morrow, George *Plato's Cretan City*. Princeton: Princeton University Press 1960

Moutsopoulos, E. *La Musique dans l'oeuvre de Platon*. Paris: PUF 1959

Murdoch, Iris *The Fire and the Sun: Why Plato Banished the Artists*. London: Oxford University Press 1977

– 'The Sovereignty of Good over Other Concepts.' In *The Sovereignty of Good*. London: Routledge and Kegan Paul 1970

Nettleship, R.L. *Lectures on the Republic of Plato*. London: Macmillan 1968

Panagiotou, Spiro 'Plato's *Euthyphro* and the Attic Code on Homicide,' *Hermes*, 102 (1974), 419–37

Pangle, Thomas L. *The Laws of Plato*. New York: Basic Books 1980

- 'The Political Psychology of Religion in Plato's Laws,' *American Political Science Review*, 70:4 (1976)
- 'Politics and Religion in Plato's Laws: Some Preliminary Reflections,' *Essays in Arts and Science*, 3 (1974)

Parain, Brice *Essai sur le logos platonicien.* Paris: NRF 1969

Paxton, Thomas D. 'Plato's *Euthyphro* 10a to 11b,' *Phronesis*, 1972, pp 171–90

Penner, Terry 'Thought and Desire in Plato.' In G. Vlastos, editor. *Plato: A Collection of Critical Essays.* Volume II. Garden City, NY: Doubleday 1971

Pétrement, Simone *Le Dualisme chez Platon, les Gnostiques et les Manichéens.* Paris: PUF 1947

Plass, Paul 'Philosophical Anonymity and Irony in the Platonic Dialogues,' *American Journal of Philology*, 84 (1964), 254–78

Plochmann, G.K. 'Supporting Themes in the *Symposium*.' In John P. Anton and George C. Kustas. *Essays in Ancient Greek Philosophy.* Albany: State University of New York Press 1971

Randall, C.J. *Plato: The Dramatist of the Life of Reason.* New York: Columbia University Press 1970

Reverdin, O. *La Religion de la cité platonicienne.* Paris: E. de Boccard 1945

Rist, John *Eros and Psyche: Studies in Plato, Plotinus and Origen.* Toronto: University of Toronto Press 1964
- 'Plato's "Earlier Theory of Forms",' *Phoenix*, 29 (1975), 343

Robin, Léon, translator and editor. *Le Banquet.* Paris: Belles Lettres 1970
- *La Théorie Platonicienne de l'Amour.* Paris: PUF 1964

Rosen, Stanley *Plato's Symposium.* New Haven: Yale University Press 1968

Schaerer, René *La Question platonicienne.* 1938. Paris: Vrin 1969

Schuhl, P.M. *La Fabulation platonicienne.* Paris: Vrin 1968

Sellars, Wilfred 'Reason and the Art of Living in Plato.' In Dale Riepe, editor. *Phenomenology and Natural Existence: Essays in Honour of Marvin Faber.* Albany: State University of New York Press 1973

Sharvy, Richard 'Euthyphro 9d–11b: Analysis and Definition in Plato and Others,' *Nous*, 6 (1972), 119–37

Shorey, Paul 'Plato's Ethics.' In G. Vlastos, editor. *Plato: A Collection of Critical Essays.* Volume II. Garden City, NY: Doubleday 1971

Sinaiko, H.C. *Love, Knowledge and Discourse in Plato: Dialogue and Dialectic in Phaedo, Republic, Parmenides.* Chicago: University of Chicago Press 1965

Skemp, B. *Plato's Statesman.* London: Routledge and Kegan Paul 1952

Solmsen, F. *Plato's Theology.* Ithaca: Cornell University Press 1942

Strauss, Leo *The Argument and the Action of Plato's Laws.* Chicago: University of Chicago Press 1975
- 'On a New Interpretation of Plato's Political Philosophy,' *Social Research*, 13 (1946)

Taylor, A.E. *Plato, the Man and His Work*. 1926. Cleveland: World Publishing Company 1956

– *Socrates: The Man and His Thought*. 1933. Garden City, NY: Doubleday 1953

Teloh, Henry *The Development of Plato's Metaphysics*. University Park: Pennsylvania State University Press 1981

Tigerstedt, E.N. *Interpreting Plato*. Stockholm: Almquist & Wiksell 1977

– *Plato's Idea of Poetical Inspiration*. Helsinki: Helsingtons 1969

Tuckey, T.G. *Plato's Charmides*. Cambridge: Cambridge University Press 1951

Van Camp, John, and Canart, Paul *Le Sens du mot theios chez Platon*. Louvain: Publications Universitaires 1956

Verdenius, W.J. 'Plato's Doctrine of Artistic Imitation.' In G. Vlastos editor. *Plato: A Collection of Critical Essays*. Volume II. Garden City, NY: Doubleday 1971

Versényi, Laszlo *Holiness and Justice: An Interpretation of Plato's Euthyphro*. Washington: University Press of America 1982

Vlastos, George 'The Individual as Object of Love in Plato.' In G. Vlastos. *Platonic Studies*. Princeton: Princeton University Press 1973

– *Plato: A Collection of Critical Essays*. 2 volumes. Garden City, NY: Doubleday 1971

– *Plato's Universe*. Seattle: University of Washington Press 1973

– 'Socratic Knowledge and Platonic "Pessimism",' *Philosophical Review*, 66 (1957), 226–38

– 'The Unity of the Virtues in Protagoras.' In *Platonic Studies*. Princeton: Princeton University Press 1973. Pp 221–69

Voegelin, Eric *Plato*. Baton Rouge: Louisiana State University Press 1966

Weingartner, R. *The Unity of the Platonic Dialogue*. New York: Bobbs Merrill 1973

White, N.P. *A Companion to Plato's Republic*. Indianapolis: Hackett 1979

– *Plato on Knowledge and Reality*. Indianapolis: Hackett 1976

Wild, John *Plato's Modern Enemies and the Theory of Natural Law*. Chicago: University of Chicago Press 1953

– *Plato's Theory of Man: An Introduction to the Realistic Philosophy of Culture*. Cambridge, Mass: Harvard University Press 1948

Wolfson, H. 'Extradeical and Intradeical Interpretations of Platonic Ideas.' In *Religious Philosophy: A Group of Essays*. Cambridge, Mass: Harvard University Press 1961

Zaslavsky, Robert *Platonic Myth and Platonic Writing*. Washington: University Press of America 1981

Index of Themes

This index includes entries for gods and places.

Index of Names

II CONTEMPORARY SCHOLARS CITED

This section of the Index of Names includes references to authors whose works are relevant to the pursuits of the philosophy of religion; bibliographic information on their works is found in the notes. For authors dealing with Plato and the Greeks see the bibliography.